POLICIES TOWARD CHINA

Published volumes in the series,

"The United States and China in World Affairs"

Alexander Eckstein

Communist China's Economic Growth and Foreign Trade:
Implications for U. S. Policy

A. M. Halpern (editor)

Policies toward China: Views from Six Continents

A. T. Steele

The American People and China

POLICIES TOWARD CHINA

Views from Six Continents

Edited by

A. M. HALPERN

A VOLUME IN THE SERIES,
"THE UNITED STATES AND CHINA IN WORLD AFFAIRS"

PUBLISHED FOR THE COUNCIL ON FOREIGN RELATIONS BY

McGRAW-HILL BOOK COMPANY

New York · Toronto · London

100078978X

LC 65024892 T

POLICIES TOWARD CHINA: Views from Six Continents

Copyright © 1965 by Council on Foreign Relations, Inc.

All Rights Reserved. Printed in the United States of America.
This book, or parts thereof, may not be reproduced in any form
without permission of the Proprietor, Council on Foreign Relations,
58 East 68th Street, New York, N.Y. 10021.

Library of Congress Catalog Card Number: 65-24892

First Edition
25622

Foreword

This book is one in a series on The United States and China in World Affairs being published by the Council on Foreign Relations as part of a three-year program, begun in 1962 under a generous grant from the Ford Foundation. This program comprises discussions, studies, and publications arranged by the Council to encourage more active and better informed public consideration of one of the most important areas of foreign policy with which the United States must deal.

The Council's program, which has been guided by a Steering Committee under the chairmanship of Allen W. Dulles, does not aspire to produce a single and simple set of conclusions. The phenomenon of China's role in the world, including the question of Taiwan, is far too complex for that. Each study in this series therefore constitutes a separate and self-contained inquiry written on the responsibility of its author, who has reached his own judgments and conclusions regarding the subject of his investigation and its implications for United States policy. The authors include persons with a variety of backgrounds in Chinese affairs and foreign policy. Some have had long personal experience in China. Others have studied China and Far Eastern problems during recent years or dealt with them as officials and administrators. They represent a variety of viewpoints and have, in each case, been able to consult with a group of individuals invited by the Council on Foreign Relations to meet from time to time with the author in order to give him the benefit of a diversity of qualified views.

The present volume is different from the others in this series in that it is not written by a single author but by several, each contributing a chapter on the policies and attitudes toward China of a country other than the United States. Except for Yugoslavia, the policies of the other Communist countries toward China are not dealt with in this volume, as they have been examined at length elsewhere since the development of sharp cleavages in the Communist world.

In planning this series it was our strong feeling that the relations between the United States and China had to be seen as part of a worldwide problem involving many other nations as well. The issues posed by the division of China and the policies of the Communist government on the mainland have been felt around the world. All countries have been affected by them, and each has had to develop its own policies toward Peking and Taiwan. The United States has found itself frustrated as well as supported by the actions of other governments, each one of which has seen the China problem in light of its own background and interests. American policy toward China can be better understood in this broader perspective and can be developed effectively only if the positions of other countries are taken into account.

This volume was edited by Dr. A. M. Halpern, who has also written the introduction and a concluding chapter which draws together the various threads running through the individual contributions. Taken together, these chapters, written by authors of several nationalities, show how different countries of the world look at the problems posed by the emergence of the mainland of China as an important world power under Communist control. An understanding of these policies should help the United States better to appreciate its own position in relation to China and the significance that the views of other countries have for us.

Dr. Halpern edited this volume while he was a research fellow at the Council on Foreign Relations. He has a long background of scholarly activity in Asian affairs, has taught at the Universities of Chicago, Michigan, and California, and was for many years a staff member of the RAND Corporation, specializing in Far Eastern politics. He has written widely on the international relations of Asia, particularly Chinese foreign policy.

ROBERT BLUM,* Study Director
The United States and China in World Affairs

---

* The work on this volume was substantially completed, and the Foreword written, before Dr. Blum's untimely death. Professor Lucian Pye, Massachusetts Institute of Technology, succeeded Dr. Blum.

Preface

There are several questions that will normally be asked about the policy of any country toward present-day China. Is the content of China policy determined primarily by economic considerations, or by military ones, or by political ones? What groups in a given country have a significant interest in relations with China, and how is this interest related to their other interests? Does the policy rest on a consensus, or is there an opposition view? Is the country satisfied that its present policy meets its needs, or does it expect to have to make some changes in the near future? To many non-Communist countries their relations with the United States are of considerable importance. The analyst will therefore want to examine the effect on other countries of U.S. policies and practices toward China and the attitudes that these countries may hold concerning this aspect of American foreign policy.

This kind of analysis could be made by any competent observer with access to the facts. There are, however, intangible factors which play a part in national decisions and which a foreign observer may find elusive. It is difficult, for example, for a non-Japanese fully to understand the significance to the Japanese of their sense of cultural affinity with China, for a non-Indian to appreciate how the late Prime Minister Nehru's world view affected his perception of the China problem, or for someone who is not French to respond to De Gaulle as a Frenchman does. Judgments of the relevance to policy formation of such intangibles are best made by native observers or by outsiders who, by reason of long residence or study, have achieved a special comprehension of the local atmosphere. In compiling the present volume of studies, we have chosen to take advantage of the insights that result from the observer's feelings of involvement with the issues, at the risk of some possible loss of objectivity.

The contributors to this volume, in the order in which their chapters appear, are:

Richard Harris, Far Eastern Correspondent for *The Times* (London).

François Fejtö, specialist on world Communist affairs for Agence France-Presse and editor of the journal *Arguments*.

Heinrich Bechtoldt, editor of the journal *Aussenpolitik* and professor at the University of Tübingen.

John W. Holmes, director general of the Canadian Institute of International Affairs.

Shigeharu Matsumoto, chairman of the Board of Directors of International House of Japan and well-known political commentator.

Coral Bell, lecturer in government at the University of Sydney.

Vidya Prakash Dutt, professor and head of the Department of East Asian Studies at the Indian School of International Studies.

Khalid B. Sayeed, associate professor of political science at Queens University, Kingston, Ontario.

Arnold C. Brackman, journalist and author.

John H. Badgley, assistant professor of government at Miami University, Ohio.

Michael Leifer, fellow in South East Asian studies at the University of Hull.

George Modelski, professorial fellow in international relations, Australian National University, Canberra.

John C. Campbell, research fellow of the Council on Foreign Relations.

Colin Legum, Commonwealth correspondent of *The Observer* (London).

Malcolm H. Kerr, assistant professor of political science at the University of California (Los Angeles).

José Honório Rodrigues, professor of economic history at the University of the State of Guanabara and formerly director of the Brazilian National Archives.

In accordance with normal procedure of the Council on Foreign Relations, each chapter was submitted for comment to a number of qualified readers. Space does not permit me to list the names of all such individuals, but this omission does not detract from the Council's appreciation of their generous cooperation. We are especially grateful to the following institutions and individuals for organizing group discussions of draft chapters: the Australian branch of the Congress for Cultural Freedom; International House of Japan; the Indian Council of World Affairs and Prof. S. L. Poplai, secretary general of the Council; the Royal Institute of International Affairs and Mr. A. S. W. Olver of Chatham House; the Centre d'Études de Politique Étrangère and M. Jacques Vernant.

Robert Blum gave the volume the benefit of his wisdom and experience through the whole course of its preparation. The intricate task of editing, including preparation of the Appendices, was performed diligently and conscientiously by David E. Albright. Richard Sorich translated Chapter 3 from the German and in other ways gave valuable help in the editing process. Typing and other indispensable clerical duties were performed cheerfully by Miss Lorna Brennan and her staff and by Miss Adrienne M. Sullivan and Mrs. Ruth Pashman. Miss Sally Lydgate provided essential help in the final stages of preparation of the book.

A. M. Halpern

July 1, 1965

Contents

POLICIES TOWARD CHINA

Abbreviations

(used in two or more chapters)

AAPSO—Afro-Asian People's Solidarity Organization
AFP—Agence France-Presse
ANZUS—Australia–New Zealand–United States Security Treaty
CCP—Chinese Communist Party
CCPIT—Chinese Committee for the Promotion of International Trade
CENTO—Central Treaty Organization
CHINCOM—China Committee of COCOM
COCOM—Coordinating Committee of the Consultative Group (NATO)
FLN—(Algerian) National Liberation Front
KMT—Kuomintang
MCP—Malayan Communist Party
NATO—North Atlantic Treaty Organization
NCNA—New China News Agency
OAU—Organization of African Unity
PKI—Indonesian Communist Party
P.R.C.—People's Republic of China
SCMP—Survey of the China Mainland Press
SEATO—Southeast Asia Treaty Organization
UAM—Union of African and Malagasy states
U.A.R.—United Arab Republic
U.N.—United Nations
U.S.—United States
U.S.S.R.—Union of Soviet Socialist Republics

Introduction

BY

A. M. HALPERN

In the two decades since the end of World War II, and especially in the somewhat shorter period since the establishment of the People's Republic of China on October 1, 1949, China has come to mean many things to many people. When the authority of the Kuomintang crumbled on the mainland, and was replaced by the authority of the Chinese Communist party, the form of future relations with China seemed a relatively simple question for other Communist-ruled states which either already existed or came into existence soon thereafter. Except for Yugoslavia, these states functioned within a system into which the P.R.C. could, in principle, be easily fitted. The problems to be faced, if they could be called problems at all, were problems of detail. In the years since then, the system has undergone changes, some brought about by changes in its relationship to the other major existing state system and to the emerging nations, some generated from within. The processes by which the P.R.C. has become a source of conflict in the world Communist movement and a second center of authority in competition with the Soviet Union have been extensively analyzed by a number of writers.

For countries other than those belonging to the Communist bloc, the problems arising from the establishment of the P.R.C. seemed, at least initially, much more complex. With the withdrawal of the Government of the Republic of China (Nationalist) from Nanking to Taipei, the theoretically simple question of whom to treat as China became in actuality a difficult one. This issue can hardly be dismissed as a mere cold war problem. The cold war was not an arbitrary condition willfully imposed on the real world by a few vengeful spirits but a political fact reflecting the anxieties and uncertainties of the postwar years. While many, if not most, states would like to see juridical status correspond to governmental control, in fact this condition has been hard to achieve. Some countries—not only

Britain, but also the Netherlands, Norway, and Israel—found that the P.R.C. did not automatically accept diplomatic relations with all who offered recognition. Other countries deferred action for reasons which might be considered extraneous to the purely legal question. The war in Korea had a significant effect in this connection.

Different countries have found a variety of solutions to the question of recognition as a legal question, inasmuch as the Nationalist government continues to exist and to perform some of the functions proper to a government of China. The problem has not disappeared but has come to have even more of a political tinge than before, as the circumstances surrounding France's recognition of the P.R.C. in January 1964 show. But entirely apart from the legal question, there are certain brute facts to which the China policies of all countries must address themselves. With every passing year it becomes more evident that the government directed by the Chinese Communists does indeed exercise authority in mainland China and disposes of China's resources in the fashion normal to established governments. A few countries are in a position to view these facts with indifference. For several others the situation of China is not one of the most salient aspects of the world. But for many, if not most, existing states, the facts of the Chinese situation require thought and action on several levels. China impinges on their hopes for a satisfactory world order, on the ways they take to secure their own national security, stability, and internal development, and on their foreign trade programs.

The genesis of the present volume is the situation just described. China's role in the world stems from her own resources and ambitions, but a full account of it also requires consideration of the way others respond to her. The P.R.C.'s relations with other Communist countries and with the Communist movement throughout the world constitute a distinctive pattern, which this volume does not examine except insofar as it affects the China policies of non-Communist countries. The present volume presents a survey of the problems of China policy as seen from a number of national standpoints other than those of the Communist countries and the United States. Yugoslavia is included because of its opposition to blocs and its special role among the nonaligned countries.

We have not tried to be exhaustive in our coverage, but we have tried to deal with a representative range of cases. This introduction and the concluding chapter supply some pertinent material for countries like South Korea, Nepal, Israel, and others not treated in separate chapters. Their main purpose is not to summarize the content of the individual chapters, but to direct attention to a few axes of comparison along which the variety of China policies can be ordered.

THE QUESTION OF HISTORICAL CONTINUITY

When a revolutionary social and political change occurs in any country, other countries must inevitably review and perhaps revise their accustomed methods of dealing with it. When the area and population of the site of the revolution are as large as China's, the review must include an appraisal of the impact of the revolutionary change on a number of other situations. In the first few years after the establishment of the People's Republic, the immediate problem —for the European countries in particular—was how to enter China in an equation whose major terms were the United States on one side and the Soviet Union on the other. The answer was not predetermined, nor was it taken for granted that the equation itself was eternal. No matter how revolutionary the change in China, it did not change geography, and one could at least surmise that Chinese national interests in some form would survive. In the first postwar decade the European countries were ill equipped to change the equation or any of its terms. As they withdrew, with good or bad grace, from their colonial possessions, their direct points of geographic contact with China became fewer. They were in any case preoccupied with their own problems of reconstruction.

The possibility of continuity between present-day policy toward China and pre-World War II policy arose effectively only after the reconstruction process was well advanced. Further, it depended on the realization of what many Europeans had looked forward to—the adoption by the P.R.C. itself of a foreign policy clearly distinct from that of the U.S.S.R. The process by which this latter development took place was not what had been envisaged in 1949—in many respects it was the opposite—but the result sufficed to make the question of continuity a relevant one to raise. Obviously some of the basic conditions have changed. Imperialist interests and methods no longer enter into the definition of Europe's role in the world. Yet there is evidently a feeling that some basis remains, in the character of past relations, for the establishment of bilateral relations with China as between equals.

4   POLICIES TOWARD CHINA

In practice, this feeling seems to amount to little more than an expectation that reasonable communication is possible now with people with whom it was possible in the past. In the United States and some other countries, notably some Asian ones, consciousness of ideological differences exercises a dominating influence on orientation toward the P.R.C. and inhibits communications with it. Many non-Communist countries, however, regard ideology as a secondary matter and envisage a relationship to China as still primarily one between nations. But the content of the relationships has changed. Britain, as Richard Harris so aptly puts it, has become aware that its prewar vision of China as a passive "object" of policy, an area of competition with Russia, is obsolete, and must be replaced by a vision of China as a "subject" or originator of policy. The specific decision which this change of vision affects in the near future is whether British disengagement from Asia has or has not arrived at a terminal point in Malaysia. Present French policy toward China is much less a revival of past sympathies than an aspect of the Gaullist dynamic, which directs itself toward the resumption of a major, independent role in the world. China becomes involved partly as it affects French interests in Indochina, partly as it affects the French effort to define similar, and therefore cooperative, roles for the middle powers, including Japan. In West Germany little or nothing of the prewar political vision of Asia seems to survive. In political terms, Asian problems are subordinate to those nearer home. The China question is approached *de novo*.

In Asian countries, the historical perspective is longer, and there is some continuity of problems resulting from the presence in many places of overseas Chinese communities. Both factors are treated in the appropriate chapters below.

The impact of historical perspective on policy is felt most in those old countries (whether or not they are young states) which in centuries past were part of the Chinese imperial domain. In Thailand, what George Modelski calls the "pattern of careful avoidance" persists into the present. It helps to sustain a predisposition to continue along what seems to have been a successful line of action as well as resistance to considering some conceivable alternatives. In Burma, past experience nurtures the expectation that the Chinese will respect Burma's autonomy so long as Burma refrains from unnecessary provocation. Thus history justifies discrepant approaches, which, however, remain effective only to the extent that they prove themselves in their application to current problems. The latter are of very recent origin.

It is implied here that countries like Burma and Thailand look at the China problem in national terms and see it as being not essentially different now than in the past. The present ideology of Communist China does, however, play a role. It is a little easier for the Thai and the Burmese to follow their present China policies because of their perceptions of the difference and the similarity, respectively, between their domestic social goals and those of the P.R.C. In Nepal, whose inclination toward China has several points of similarity to Burma's, satisfaction with the present state of relations with China is somewhat tempered by concern that further intimacy on the cultural level may have some undesired effects on the central objective of preserving Nepal's national independence and cultural integrity. In some South Korean circles, a residual attachment to Confucian ethics helps form the emotional basis for political solidarity with the Nationalist government in Taiwan.

It takes some temerity to argue, in the face of the obvious convictions of many Asians, that the overseas Chinese do not constitute a foreign policy problem. Large numbers of the overseas Chinese retain Chinese citizenship, not solely for lack of a choice or for reasons of practical advantage, but out of pride in their identity. They can at times be used as an instrument of Chinese policy, Communist or Nationalist. Their pride in their Chinese nationality may stimulate them, as it has in some instances in Singapore, to use their influence in favor of pro-Chinese policies. But, as Arnold C. Brackman points out below, Peking treats the overseas Chinese as an expendable resource; there is unavoidably a somewhat contrived air about the Indonesian contention that Malaysia is doomed to become an extension of the P.R.C.; and any country has it in its power to make the problem of citizenship a domestic matter. Whatever the main thrust of China policy may be in countries with an overseas Chinese "problem," there is ground to argue that it is determined by considerations of national security and territorial or political ambition. The overseas Chinese problem is closely entwined with, but not the source of, China policy.

Elsewhere in the neighborhood of China, the discontinuities are more conspicuous than the continuities. The postwar Sino-Japanese relationship is obviously of a wholly different order from the prewar relationship; yet some subtle continuities of attitude can be discerned.

These are treated in detail in Shigeharu Matsumoto's chapter below, and the concluding chapter contains some additional observations. The emergence of the P.R.C. has put China in a place it never before occupied in Australian calculations. India inherited the Tibet problem in a more or less traditional form, but her China policy for a number of years was as much or more dominated by Nehru's feeling of kinship with all anti-colonial forces than it was by geography. In areas more remote from direct contact with China, a similar feeling for the unity of the previously dispossessed has colored policy toward the P.R.C. In these areas, however, there is no history of important relations with China and thus no basis for speaking of a continuation of traditional policy.

ECONOMIC FACTORS

Three things characterize the economic aspect of the China policies of many non-Communist countries: interest, disappointment, and hope for a brighter future. The development of "normal" trade patterns has been hindered on one side by an embargo on trade with China by the United States and other powers (especially in the form defined from 1951 to 1957 by the so-called CHINCOM list) and on the other by the P.R.C.'s preference, up to 1961, for dealing with the Soviet Union and Eastern Europe. It is generally thought that the embargo did not have any significant impact on the P.R.C.'s economic development. The remaining restrictions on trade observed by members of COCOM—for the most part European countries—are not a major factor in holding down volume. In the past few years, since the P.R.C. showed a greater disposition to deal with the West, the main limitation has been the small size of the P.R.C.'s total trade volume.

Mainland China is not an essential supplier to any other country. Potentially it could be a preferred source of iron ore, coking coal, and nonferrous metals to Japan, but in practice it has not been. There have been problems of quality and price, and the unilateral cancellation of trade contracts by the P.R.C. has left substantial doubts in the mind of the Japanese steel industry about reliability. For a certain period some Southeast Asian countries hoped that the P.R.C. would become a useful source of cheap consumers' goods, especially textiles, but since 1959 this hope has not materialized. One cannot conclude, however, that the P.R.C. is wholly negligible as a supplier. In many instances it has been jealous of its good reputation, and individual traders testify that the Chinese made a special effort to fulfill the terms of their contracts. But China's virtues as a supplier are felt more by individuals than by national economies.

As a purchaser, the P.R.C. has at times been much appreciated by some countries. In 1950, a mutually advantageous exchange of rubber for rice was worked out between Ceylon and the P.R.C. Ceylon still values this trade, although the terms are not as advantageous as they were at first and the market for rubber is not as unfavorable as it used to be. Details of advantageous sales of Burmese rice, Pakistani cotton, and Australian and Canadian wheat are covered in the appropriate chapters below. The volume of purchases is not necessarily the only measure of their value. Nepal's sales to China account for a small percentage of total exports, even though made at premium prices. They are deemed important, however, because they correspond to Nepal's wish not to be exclusively dependent on the Indian market—somewhat in the way that 10 years ago some Japanese, and more recently some Brazilians, looked to trade with China as a source of flexibility and a way of lessening dependence on the United States.

In the over-all view, an unusual feature of the P.R.C.'s economic relations with non-Communist countries is the comparative insignificance of its trade with its immediate neighbors. The mainland Chinese market today is much more oriented to distant than to nearby suppliers and more actively interested in the advanced industrial countries than in the underdeveloped. Interest in China trade in the advanced countries needs no explanation. It is found among people who make a living by buying and selling, and it is stimulated by international competition. Up to now its disappointing features have been the natural and artificial limits on its scope and the difficulty of arriving at stable patterns of exchange. The hope for the future persists not only because of the size of the Chinese market but because of the more immediate prospect that after 1965, when the P.R.C. will have liquidated its remaining debt to the Soviet Union and attained some degree of recovery from its economic difficulties of the last several years, its purchasing power will grow.

The expansion of trade with China entails the possibility of political consequences. It will depend in part on the extension of credits, at least in the form of deferred payment agreements, which require government decision. Such decisions in some ways may serve as precedents affecting trade with the Soviet Union and Eastern Europe, the volume of which is much more significant than that of

China trade. There is, besides, the possibility of political pressure arising from expanded trade, especially in countries which do not now recognize the People's Republic. Economic interests played a part, though not a decisive one, in France's recognition of the P.R.C. In Japan some observers believe that the total volume of Sino-Japanese trade may double or treble in the next five years. At some point in this process, the inconvenience of not having formal government channels through which to work—an inconvenience which at present is not serious—will become great enough to generate effective pressure from business circles for "normalization of diplomatic relations." As noted below by Coral M. Bell and John W. Holmes, Australian and Canadian wheat sales to China contain the potentiality of creating a vested interest in diplomatic relations on the part of groups who, though by no means constituting a majority, in some circumstances may have the ability to swing the political balance on matters of China policy.

In underdeveloped countries which have relations with the P.R.C., Chinese economic assistance has a bearing similar to that of trade in the advanced countries. The Chinese aid program is limited in scope. Its record of performance, like that of all aid-giving countries, is mixed, but the degree of appreciation it evokes is high. Its success is due in part to the comparative absence of political strings, in part to the modesty of the program's aims, in part to the diligence and willingness to endure hardships of Chinese personnel. Chinese aid has the psychological effect of the "widow's mite." In some parts of Africa the major Chinese efforts are in agriculture, where they compete only with Israeli activities and complement aid from other sources. The P.R.C. programs enjoy perhaps no greater success than those of Israel or Nationalist China on the same continent. P.R.C. assistance to industrial and infrastructure development in several of the underdeveloped countries of Asia and Africa addresses itself to small enterprises. It is a type of aid which either reduces or diversifies, even to a small degree, dependence on outside sources. Mishaps which occur in these programs, such as the low quality of plywood produced in Cambodia or the abandonment of a cement plant in Nepal (explained by some people as due to a mistaken choice of site by the Chinese experts, by others as due to China's failure to obtain Czech machinery it had counted on), tend to be tolerated more easily than those which occur in more grandiose programs of other donors.

The P.R.C. apparently does not emphasize competition with other donors. The Nepalese were openly told that the total amount of Chinese aid would deliberately be set at a lower level than that to India so that even the appearance of competition would be avoided. Such assistance is appreciated, though not overvalued, by the recipients. It is nowhere indispensable, and nowhere does it create exclusive dependence on China. It is thus in no case the fundamental element in any country's China policy, but in many cases it contributes to the belief that good relations with the P.R.C. are not only possible but distinctly beneficial.

In general summation, interest in trade with China is widespread, and such trade is regarded in many countries as advantageous in several ways. In no case is the economic factor an overriding one in China policy as a whole. Where trade occupies a large place in a country's China policy, it usually does so by default, and it is an indication that China is not of major importance in that country's total foreign policy. By the same token, where China policy is motivated primarily by economic considerations, the variety of political groups interested in China is likely to be small, and China tends not to be a live issue in domestic politics.

SECURITY, STABILITY, WORLD ORDER

The P.R.C., it was clear even before the first Chinese nuclear detonation of October 16, 1964, is a military power of significant size yet not a power which can consider itself secure. It also possesses political resources through which it can affect the internal politics of other countries. It not only has demands to make on how others should treat it, but it has programs which it advocates as desirable for other countries to adopt in pursuing their own affairs. The P.R.C. also claims a legitimate place in the conduct of world affairs, a place which it obviously has not secured.

It is precisely these matters that require of other countries the most accurate policy calculations, yet those that are hardest to make, most likely to be affected by concern for other international relations, and most dependent on the structure of domestic political attitudes. Further, since there is a widespread expectation that all the elements in the calculations are likely to change, policies based on them are of necessity provisional. By way of introduction, I shall briefly sketch the range of variation in policy calculations. More detailed examination of individual cases is contained in the several chapters which follow.

Several of China's nearer neighbors think of themselves as targets of Chinese expansionism through the use of force, direct or indirect. At any given time, few of these countries feel themselves immediately threatened. For those who do feel immediately threatened, the policy problem is simply where they can get help. For others, the question is rather to estimate China's weight in the local balance of power, both at present and in the future. It is this estimate that decides whether a country will depend on its own resources, a bilateral alliance (typically with a country outside the area), or a multilateral alliance.

Others of China's neighbors either believe that they are not threatened by Chinese expansionism or that the threat will not become actual if a proper relationship can be established with the P.R.C. The pattern of Asian power politics enables some countries to promote their own interests by one or another form of cooperation with the P.R.C. Still others accept the prospect of Chinese hegemony in Asia as a virtual certainty and try to adapt themselves to it.

Concern for security is naturally greatest among China's neighbors but is not confined to them alone. Local situations in Africa make it possible for small increments of military capability, such as can be supplied over great distances and at small cost, to have a real impact. The security of Asia and Africa is also not solely the concern of those who live there. Nor, for that matter, is it to be taken for granted in any individual instance that only China is seen as a threat. The Western presence—even in some cases a benign Western interest —can also be viewed as potentially disturbing. Many of these considerations come to bear on the attitudes, favorable and unfavorable, of various countries toward the Chinese Nationalist government and the problem of Taiwan.

China's ability to affect domestic stability is also greatest among her immediate neighbors, though not confined to them. Here much depends on local political conditions. Where there is wide consensus on national values and goals, especially where there is a local Chinese community of some size, and where relations with the West are conducted without undue strain, the tendency to avoid contact with the P.R.C. is strong. In many Afro-Asian countries, however, such a consensus is lacking, or the dominant values are comparatively inhospitable to the West, or an important (though partial) similarity between local values and those of the P.R.C. is sensed. There is thus a mutual attraction between the P.R.C. and some Afro-Asian countries or political movements. The P.R.C. is sensitive to the existence of this mutual attraction and devotes much attention to cultivating it. Where the attraction is between the P.R.C. and incumbent rulers, opposition sometimes arises from local political elements less receptive to the Chinese Communist appeal. Other practical political considerations often prevent official friendliness from becoming one-sided dependence on China and thus reduce the effect on domestic stability. Where the attraction is felt primarily by an opposition group in a country whose official relations with the P.R.C. are not close, China policy may become an important—albeit often symbolic —domestic political issue, and the effect on domestic stability can be serious. Distance is a major factor in this connection. Sympathy for the P.R.C. in Europe and in countries with a strong European tradition is on the whole more sophisticated, more reasoned, and probably more lasting than in many Afro-Asian countries. Its political impact, however, is obviously smaller in Europe than elsewhere.

China's place in the world order is a matter of universal concern. The obvious issue is the question of representation in the United Nations. In many countries, including some which have voted against it, there is much support for acknowledging the P.R.C. as the representative of China. The idea receives support for a variety of reasons. It conforms to a widespread feeling in favor of universality in world organizations. Some advocates believe it would be a just recognition of a valid claim, others that it would correspond to reality. Some argue that it would modify the P.R.C.'s international behavior in desirable ways, others simply that it would provide for an increase in regular communication which could hardly fail to be fruitful. The major obstacles, apart from the specification in the U.N. charter that the China seat is to be held by the Government of the Republic of China, are the moral and political consequences of a sudden change in the status of Taiwan and the importance which many countries attach to supporting the United States. As John W. Holmes notes in the case of Canada, maintenance of American prestige is a national interest of many other countries.

Support for seating the P.R.C. in the United Nations apparently grew, at least in intensity, following the Chinese nuclear detonation of October 1964. This tendency appears to reflect a virtually universal belief, which existed before the detonation, that no ultimately viable solution of the disarmament problem—something which interests everyone—can be reached without the participation of the P.R.C. In 1963, when the P.R.C. denounced the partial nuclear test ban treaty and circulated a note to all governments proposing a world conference on total prohibition of nuclear weapons instead, almost no non-Communist country could fully accept the Chinese position, but many of them (especially Afro-Asians) showed in their replies to the note that they conceded the P.R.C.'s right to a respectful, if not sympathetic, hearing. International response to the October 1964 detonation was much along the same line, and replies to a similar note circulated by the P.R.C. after its second atomic detonation (May 1965) showed an even greater tendency to discuss the issues raised by the P.R.C. as if she were already an established nuclear power with a significant bargaining position. Among Asians, however, there were some definitely negative reactions. There was not the convulsion of popular feeling which many had feared but instead something of an awakening to the substantive implications of nuclear proliferation. In India, and to a lesser degree in Japan, the Chinese detonation quickly brought into focus the issue of independent nuclear capability for themselves. As these observations are written, it is not certain what the decisions will be. Indonesia has given signs of being beguiled by the apparent Chinese gain in prestige. It is evidently tempted to emulate the Chinese example.

It is difficult to see exactly how seating the P.R.C. in the United Nations would contribute significantly to solving the problems which arise in the wake of the Chinese detonation. The P.R.C. seems to prefer, in practice, narrower international forums, preferably Afro-Asian ones. It is in these arenas, including the Geneva conferences on Indochina in 1954 and on Laos in 1961–62, that non-Communist countries have had their concrete experience of dealing with the P.R.C. on matters which affect world order. These experiences, as much as bilateral contacts, provide the best evidence of what the Sino-Soviet rift means for practical dealings with Communist China as a national entity. In the first months of 1965, after Indonesia withdrew from the United Nations, the P.R.C. published a series of violently negative comments covering the whole range of U.N. activities. While the U.N. question remains the single most important symbolic test of attitudes regarding China's place in the world order, there are a number of other routes capable of leading to a resolution of the problem. The analyses of individual national policies in this volume indicate how these other routes have been explored.

Chapter 1

BRITAIN AND CHINA

Coexistence at Low Pressure

BY

RICHARD HARRIS

A 19th-century historian, noting Britain's prominent role in opening up China to Western enterprise or tracing European expansion to its maximum extent, might have expected the British position in China and the interest China aroused at home to be important to this day. The British dominated the foreign communities in the treaty ports, and they were second only to the United States in the number of missionaries they sent to China. Yet the survivors of the China-based merchant and missionary groups are by now few and without much political significance. In the 1920s and 1930s, as the sense of geographical contraction followed the peak of empire, China could quickly recede from the British mind simply because it had never been firmly fixed there. China lay far beyond the limits of a view of the world centered upon Europe. For the British, with three centuries of maritime experience in Asia, China retained a sense of unapproachability; it was a land empire at which the seamen could only nibble.

What sets China off most of all in British consciousness is that it always lay outside the farthest imperial domain. The aim was never to annex it—except in the occasional euphoric fantasy of a Shanghai merchant. "It is well for our countrymen in China," wrote *The Times* in 1875, "to understand once for all that we are not in the

13

mood to undertake the responsibilities of another India." This sharp rejection of imperial endeavor survived the scramble for concessions at the end of the century. Apart from the oddity of Hong Kong—an oddity not least in the fact that it should survive in 1965 as Britain's largest colony—Britain's empire never extended into East Asia.

CHINA AND BRITAIN BEFORE 1949

British interest in China, from the first contacts in the 17th century and the establishment of trading posts in the 18th, to the missions of Macartney in 1793 and Amherst in 1816, had always been founded on the pursuit of trade. Other interests were secondary. The pressures on the British government for action against the government of China—from the Anglo-Chinese war onward—were generated by the merchants. Insofar as the government responded, it did so because the age was one of free trade. But the realization that British interests could be pressed too far on this pretext (something the merchants were very ready to do) also quickly grew. There thus developed a conflict between the government in London and the merchants in China. The officials in London exercised restraint, which aroused the chagrin of the more expansive merchants. In the last resort, the British government of the day invariably found itself sharing the view of Sir Rutherford Alcock, British Minister in the 1860s, that it was difficult to see "to what uses, political, military or commercial any portion of China could be applied by European powers."

The relevance of these facts to Britain's outlook today is that they restricted British involvement in China. Knowledge of the East was confined to those parts of the world where British rule brought the servants of empire out to their years of duty in the tropical heat. Through such men, a knowledge of India or Ceylon or Burma or Malaya was fed back into the educational system of the country, into the channels of government, and into the areas of interest and responsibility of the ruling class. China was never fully part of the British experience in Asia, never known—geographically, ethnographically, or culturally—in the same palpable way as other parts of Asia.

In any case, China lay in what Europe called the Far East. Throughout the 19th century, the popular British view pictured China as a large, walled domain which could only be breached at certain points. From the west and south, where British rule in India and Burma touched on the fringes of a failing Chinese authority, Britain poked and pressed. She was for long uncertain what resistance might be provoked but eventually concluded that the body was moribund. From the east, what used to be called gun-boat diplomacy was exercised to exact rights for British merchants and missionaries. But at no time did the British ruling class ever commit itself to major responsibilities in connection with China. No substantial number of men from its ranks journeyed to China to study its civilization, to understand and administer its people, or to try to spread British political ideas and institutions as they did in South Asia. It is indeed an irony that the one country which followed the Chinese example most closely, when it recast its civil service in the 19th century and set the standards of scholarship and dedication which characterized British imperial power at its best, should never itself have come into contact with the Chinese service. With perhaps the minor exception of the navy, the public services of Victorian England had no continuous apprehension of China's significance.

The role of British individuals in China should not, however, be minimized. Notably in the customs administration, in the salt gabelle, and in the postal service, British civil servants of the same training and quality as those in the British imperial service were employed. But they were employees of the Chinese government and not servants of empire. They had no minister in London to answer for their actions or to advertise their achievements. They had no official channels through which they could make known their views on China.

Thus, an interest in China or an appreciation of its civilization remained exceptional. It was almost something eccentric in a way that a knowledge of India was not. This statement is true despite the powerful lobby of the China merchants, who used such political influence as they could to bring home the vast opportunities for trade which they dreamed existed in China. If the facts of trade had supported them, they might have had more success, but they certainly had little lasting effect on the study and awareness of China in Britain. As the years passed, their contempt for the ailing body of China only grew, but occasionally some among them succumbed to China's lure. Often their hopes of trade were romantically conceived rather than hard-headedly businesslike. As a result, to be dubbed "old China hands" carried the implication of concern with some peripheral mystery with which others could not be bothered.

Nor were the missionaries much better. They at least went into what became known as "the interior" (a revealing picture of the Western outlook). They learned the language and sometimes became sinologists. Until recent years, the few British university posts for the study of China were filled from the ranks of the missionaries. Yet the missionaries, it is important to realize, were more often than not nonconformists. At the peak, about 1925, when British missionaries in China totaled more than 3,000, less than a third of them were Anglicans. Thus they tended to be as much outsiders to the British establishment as the merchants.

Finally, there was the consular service, set up in 1860 to staff the many consular posts which served as the thin substitute for the firm British authority in China that the merchants craved. It, too, was a separate service and was kept somewhat at arm's length from the diplomatic service until the amalgamation in 1942. The consular service produced some scholars—and some engaging eccentrics—but it was too much of a byway in the British public service to do more than add another variety of "old China hands."

The pioneer work in the scholarly discovery of China had its British contribution. Morrison, Legge, and consular officials such as Meadows have left their mark. But late in the 19th century the stream dried up, and the universities took no steps to train their own sinologists. So dry had the stream become in this century that between the First and Second World Wars the chairs of Chinese at Oxford, Cambridge, and London were usually filled from continental Europe or the United States. An almost continuous admiration for Chinese art and literature, it is true, came from men like Laurence Binyon, Lowes Dickinson, and Arthur Waley, but they were identified with the pursuit of the arts or were considered scholars outside the mainstream of public life. Few leading ambassadors or high officials of the Foreign Office had any experience of China. No British ministers in the governments of this century have had any knowledge of the country. As for a knowledge of the Chinese language or Chinese history, that was the province of the Orientalist and not of the educated man in public life.

As the 20th century advanced and China's weakness became ever more apparent, the country sank in British estimation, and it played little part in British political consciousness after the First World War. Thus Churchill could be astonished, on a visit to Washington during the Second World War, at the enormous place China occupied in Roosevelt's mind; to Churchill it was inexplicable.

His attitude was by no means exceptional. It should be emphasized, therefore, that British policy toward China is a much smaller matter in public consciousness than it is in the United States—even now with the growing recognition of China's future importance. This divergence between Britain and the United States, which became apparent in wartime and caused some disagreement about the allotment of manpower and supplies to different theaters of war, contributed greatly to the differing attitudes which emerged when the Communist government was set up in 1949. At that time, Britain's imperial withdrawal had set in. India, Pakistan, Ceylon, and Burma had all become independent. Though the change in Britain's imperial role was being resisted by die-hards, the bulk of British opinion, especially of the younger generation, was sympathetic to Asian countries setting out to rule themselves and to develop their own economic life. In this general postwar attitude toward Asia, China had some share. As the Communist victory loomed up in 1949, therefore, the British did not automatically associate Communist China directly with Stalinist Russia. Readiness to allow China's new government the benefit of the doubt was encouraged by the fact that the Chinese Communists seemed independent, dedicated, and disciplined. Thus, they might require different standards of judgment from those applied to Stalin's Russia. Perhaps this attitude, much modified as it has been by events, still survives as the foundation of the British outlook toward China.

DIPLOMATIC POLICY AND RELATIONS

Britain recognized the People's Government on January 6, 1950, three months after it had been proclaimed in Peking. The prospect of Communist power had been obvious in the spring of 1949. While on a visit of inspection to Hong Kong in June of that year, a British minister said that Britain looked forward to neighborly relations with whatever government the Chinese people might choose. In September, the British Foreign Minister, Ernest Bevin, held talks with Dean Acheson, U.S. Secretary of State, but no agreement over policy toward China could be reached. In October, after a conference of British heads of mission in the Far East had met in Singapore, recognition of the government then newly proclaimed in Peking was urged. The recommendation of the British ambassador in China was supported by the surviving elements of the British business community.

Having experienced the chaos in China after World War II and during the civil war, they felt that nothing could be worse. Some looked favorably on the Communists' efficiency and obvious drive for economic development and thought it would be possible to continue in business; others thought that recognition at least offered some hope of recouping on their investments. Such indications as were made from the Communist side had encouraged them to stay.

But the attitude of the British trading community was by no means the only element in the decision to recognize the new government. Another factor that should not be overlooked was the influence of the developing Commonwealth relationship. India, Pakistan, Ceylon, and Burma had all emerged as independent nations during the last years of the Chinese civil war, and a new British policy toward what is now called the developing world was evolving. The role of these countries in keeping the peace in Asia, a role to which the Labor government then in power in Britain attached much importance, depended upon effective British partnership. The Asian Commonwealth countries led the way in recognizing China and urging its recognition on others. Britain chose to stand with them, even though other Commonwealth members such as Australia and New Zealand were hesitant.

Nor, on the other hand, was the decision to recognize a product of Labor as against Conservative policy. The traditional view, accepted by both parties, was that when a government manifestly controlled a territory, diplomatic relations should be established. In November 1949, when the question of recognition of the new government was discussed in Parliament, Winston Churchill supported recognition on the Conservative behalf.

The British press and public opinion generally approved the decision. Only a few critical comments suggested that a longer delay, so as to act in concert with the United States, would have been preferable. The British government certainly assumed at the time that U.S. recognition would soon follow.

The British decision, however, immediately ran up against difficulties. In acknowledging the British note, Chou En-lai, the Chinese Foreign Minister, asked that a representative should first be sent to Peking to "negotiate" diplomatic relations. Although Britain did not accept the implications of this Chinese request, a mission, headed by the chargé d'affaires, journeyed from Nanking to Peking to make inquiries. According to the Chinese, three matters needed to be settled before an exchange of ambassadors took place. The most important was British support for the seating of the new government in the United Nations. Secondly, there was the Chinese property in Hong Kong, property claimed by the Communist government. Third, there was the British consul on Taiwan, who was accredited to the provincial government and not the Nationalist government. (This last issue was not pressed.) By June 17, exchanges of notes on these matters had reached the point where Britain asked formally whether or not the Chinese were willing to exchange ambassadors. Then the war in Korea broke out, and the British received no reply to their note. In fact, however, Britain did vote for Peking's admission to the U.N. General Assembly in September 1950, before the Chinese intervened in the Korean War. After the Chinese intervention, attitudes naturally changed again.

The arguments for keeping the "negotiating" mission in Peking during the Korean War—even though British troops fighting with the U.N. forces faced Chinese "volunteers" on the other side—outweighed arguments for withdrawal. On the whole, British opinion never thought of operations in Korea as a war against China, nor was China, in a national sense, seen as the villain. British troops, it was felt, were participating in a necessary though distasteful police action. It was only at the end of the war, when evidence about the Chinese treatment of prisoners became public, that the image of China suffered a severe setback in the British mind.

At the end of 1951, a Conservative government succeeded the Labor government, but it adopted the policies of its predecessor. It sought to limit the area of operations in Korea and supported Soviet moves for peace when they were put forward by Yakov Malik. The broad lines of British policy toward China were confirmed in Parliament in February 1952—though by this time all the hopes of the British business community had been disappointed. Most firms had withdrawn. A few had successfully realized their assets, but the majority had found spurious liabilities built up against them by taxes or by excessive demands for severance pay and had gladly forsaken their assets in settlement of their debts.

After the Korean armistice, British relations with China entered a new and optimistic phase. The optimism was prompted by the success of the 1954 Geneva Conference on Indochina and the part Britain played in it. As co-chairman of the conference, Anthony Eden, learning from the Russian Molotov that China was very much her own master (as he recounts in his memoirs), approached Chou En-lai directly. Eden found him at first "rigid and disagreeable." But later, after Eden "twitted" him about not having a representative in London, he agreed that China should send a chargé d'affaires. On September 2, 1954, Peking at last made a formal reply to the British recognition of January 6, 1950. Since 1954, missions headed by chargés d'affaires have been maintained in both capitals, but there has not yet been an exchange of ambassadors. After the 1954 Geneva Conference, China also sent its first official trade mission to Britain. British private travel to China grew to reasonable numbers in the next several years. In July 1956, the *People's Daily* observed that there were "pleasant signs" that Britain was taking the path of peaceful coexistence. One undoubted sign of a changed Chinese attitude was the prompt apology and payment of compensation when the Chinese shot down a British-owned passenger aircraft near the coastline off Hong Kong.

Improved relations with China had not, however, altered Britain's desire to postpone an awkward debate over the Chinese seat in the United Nations. Differences with Dulles over policies in Europe were quite enough to handle. Before any further steps on this matter could be taken, events sharply changed the Chinese attitude. Suez and Hungary brought a shift of feeling in 1956, and in 1957 the "hundred flowers" episode showed something more of the Chinese temper. At the National People's Congress meeting in February 1958, Chou En-lai remarked that if Britain "does not change its double-faced attitude towards China . . . Sino-British relations would inevitably be adversely affected." In March, a Labor member of Parliament asked whether Britain would try to strengthen the United Nations by pressing for the admission of Peking. He was told that such a step might have a contrary effect while current deep divisions lasted. The Chinese finally struck the British off the list of possible coexisters when British troops moved into Jordan in July 1958 at the same time American troops landed in the Lebanon. A Chinese theater troupe touring in Britain closed down at a moment's notice and left a surprised audience with no show. Visas previously granted were not honored, and further applicants were rebuffed. There were demonstrations outside the British embassy in Peking. A coolness developed that has never since been changed on the Chinese side, nor has the freedom of intercourse between the two countries returned to the conditions of the 1954–57 period.

Despite the coolness, British policy remained firm. By the early 1960s, though, the maintenance of a mission in Peking had lost much of its novelty and some of its original promise; the British chargé d'affaires naturally had no access to senior Chinese ministers. Nevertheless, in 1961, again influenced by Commonwealth opinion, Britain once more took up the question of Chinese representation at the United Nations. She now withdrew support from the standard U.S. position which called for the postponement of any discussion of the China issue, and she voted in favor of a Russian motion supporting Peking's admission. In doing so, however, she specifically reserved her position on Taiwan. That reservation affirmed that the Japanese had renounced all claims to the island in the San Francisco peace treaty, but that the treaty had not assigned sovereignty to any other power. In making this reservation, the British added that they did not exclude the possibility that Taiwan might become an independent entity.

British support for Chinese admission to the United Nations on this basis has been maintained since 1961. However, a British suggestion that ambassadors should be exchanged—made on the assumption that the British vote for the Peking government had altered matters—met with no response on the ground that Britain's reservation on Taiwan was unfriendly. In 1964, after French recognition led to the exchange of ambassadors, Britain's Trade Minister, Douglas Jay (Labor party), while on a visit to China, suggested a similar exchange with Britain, but his suggestions were rejected by the Chinese.

Britain's policy of recognition and support for China in the United Nations now seems basic and unlikely to be changed by events —if only because, over 15 years, it has begun to seem normal. Under Conservative governments, there have been few criticisms of the decision made by the Labor government in 1950. Latterly, with China's belligerent attitude toward the world at large, there have been few opportunities for any fresh initiative in Anglo-Chinese relations. Indeed, the advent of a Labor government which publicly supports American policy on Vietnam has brought relations probably to their lowest point.

NON-GOVERNMENTAL RELATIONS

British relations with Communist China since recognition in 1950 may be summarized under several headings:

Delegations and Cultural Relations. A few sympathetic delegations and individual visitors went to China before 1954, but the first important visit was the Labor party delegation in August 1954. This delegation was led by Lord Attlee and accompanied by journalists from the leading newspapers. Visits by journalists were frequent in the next few years, and delegations included intellectuals of no proclaimed political sympathy. A British ballet company toured China in 1958, and individual artists have been occasional visitors. On the Chinese side, a delegation led by Liu Ning-yi came to Britain after recognition in 1950. But its itinerary was carefully arranged by the British Communist party, and its public effect was thus small. At the invitation of the Royal Society, a delegation of the Academia Sinica came in 1961, and the Society returned the visit in 1962. A Chinese theater company was brought to Britain by commercial sponsors in 1956. Some private tourism to selected Chinese centers such as Hangchow, Nanking, and Canton has been permitted.

A private arrangement between Reuters and the New China News Agency has permitted correspondents to be stationed in the two capitals without break since 1955. A few members of Parliament, including the present leader of the Labor party, Harold Wilson, have visited China, but not enough to create any informed opinion about China in the House of Commons.

Trade. Trade with China, through Hong Kong as an entrepôt or through British firms in Shanghai or Tientsin, died away in the first years of the regime—particularly with the imposition of the trade embargo in May 1951 during the Korean War. Since then, with intervals of some difficulty, British businessmen have gone to China on trade visits, and in recent years they have been free to visit the Canton trade fair. The quantity of British trade has never been substantial, though from time to time the old dream of China's potential riches crops up again. The facts show that in the last 10 years neither British imports nor exports have ever exceeded £35 million. The peak year for the combined value of trade was 1960 with nearly £25 million in imports and more than £30 million in exports. This trade constituted less than one per cent of total British trade for 1960. The figures for 1964 may reach this level again, but no substantial increase is expected.

The China Association, the old established body of China merchants which dates from 1889, still exists and acts on behalf of about 190 member companies. There is also a section of the London

Chamber of Commerce devoted to trade with China. The problems which private firms encountered in dealing with Communist China's national trading corporations led in 1955 to the formation of the Sino-British Trade Council, a body with direct contacts with the official Board of Trade. Associated with the council are the Association of British Chambers of Commerce, the China Association, the Federation of British Industries, and the London Chamber of Commerce. This council maintains contact with the China Committee for the Promotion of International Trade in Peking and is responsible for organizing joint efforts such as the exhibition of British industry which was held in Peking in November 1964.

On the Chinese side, there has always been a tendency to deal with firms politically well-disposed toward China. One example would be the so-called "48" group of companies, now sponsored by the British Council for the Promotion of International Trade, which was set up in 1952 after the Moscow economic conference. The Chinese have provided some advantages to firms known to be politically sympathetic and associated with the BCPIT, but their policy has not been consistent in this respect. The British Board of Trade and the Sino-British Trade Council naturally aim to avoid political emphasis in trading matters. Some Communist elements in British commercial circles have supported the Chinese effort to exert political pressure through trade, and that support has not been affected by Sino-Soviet differences. The Chinese, however, have apparently not gained any advantage from this effort.

Trade with China has changed a good deal in other ways. While many of the old companies (Jardine Matheson, Butterfield and Swire, etc.) are still active, most of them have now diversified their interests so that they are no longer devoted solely to this trade.

British businessmen have visited China regularly, though for a time after 1958 visas were not easily available. Since her split with the Soviet Union, however, China has shown an increased desire for contacts. The Chinese maintain a commercial counsellor's office in London which is separate from their diplomatic mission. It has a staff of nearly 20 officials. In 1963, the first trade delegation from China, headed by Lu Hsu-chang, Vice-Minister of Foreign Trade, was received officially in Britain and toured industrial areas.

Friendship Associations. The Britain China Friendship Association was set up, after the Chinese Communists came to power, under the sponsorship of the British Communist party. The BCFA sent delegations to China, brought art exhibitions to Britain, and arranged lectures. However, it has been affected by the Sino-Soviet dispute in which the British Communist party has followed the Soviet line and has attacked China. At the annual meeting of the BCFA in 1964, the control of the British Communist party was asserted, and an attempt to get a pro-Chinese line in the association was voted down. The main organization promoting friendship with China thereby became, paradoxically, hostile to the Chinese position. As a result, a new, and more sympathetic, Society for Anglo-Chinese Understanding was formed under the chairmanship of Dr. Joseph Needham in 1965.

The office of the Chinese chargé d'affaires in London in the past maintained relations with the BCFA and has welcomed the new society, but it has not otherwise been very active in propaganda on behalf of the new China—though literature supporting the Chinese side of the Sino-Soviet dispute is made freely available. Within the small Chinese community in Britain, mostly of Hong Kong origin, propaganda on behalf of the new China has concentrated on workers —seamen, restaurant waiters, etc.—rather than scholars or professional people.

Public Opinion. A noticeable shift in British public opinion toward China—matching China's shift of opinion toward the outside world—grew out of the Great Leap Forward of 1958. Direct Chinese hostility toward Britain—over British intervention in Jordan—might not have been noticed, but the tone and temper of the Leap Forward was. The note of belligerence, the excessive zeal for collectivism, and the boasts about what China could do in a few years now that politics had taken command—all of which followed the repression of 1957—caused many of those who had previously been ready to make allowances for China's difficulty to revise their attitude. This statement applies particularly to the moderate left and especially to a great body of Labor party opinion. The change became more pronounced as the facts of the Sino-Soviet dispute were publicized and as the Indian border conflict led to bloodshed. Above all, left-wing opinion was jarred by the Chinese action against India, for it was among such opinion that Indian neutralism and Prime Minister Nehru's role in Afro-Asian affairs had, up to that point, enjoyed the greatest support. Naturally, the great body of ex-officials of empire found the Chinese action comprehensible only on the assumption that China was an aggressive, insensitive, and expansionist power—

perhaps for nationalist rather than Communist reasons, but none the more worthy for that.

The most prominently expressed opinions in Parliament and the press condemned China for her action. Such condemnation did not reflect all British opinion, though. Paradoxically, some of those on the right who had been hostile to India's pretensions as a neutralist leader now found cause to sympathize with China. And after the Chinese attack in the autumn of 1962, a good many people began to see that China had something of a case, however foolishly she had asserted it. Even in the matter of the Sino-Soviet dispute, the natural British disposition to support an underdog produced much wry sympathy for the Chinese or caused many British to see greater logic in the Chinese arguments. But all these things put together could not restore the generous and hopeful attitude toward China which had existed from 1954 to 1957.

Thus, declining British sympathy for China since 1958 has not been arrested by any steps on the Chinese side. On the contrary, Britain, viewed as an unimportant satellite of the United States, has tended to become less and less important in the Chinese mind. Only recently, with the emergence of General de Gaulle's distinctive policy, have the Chinese begun to consider Western Europe as a potentially separate element in the Western world. Thus far, this attitude has not impinged on British awareness of China or affected China policy in any observable way. It could be a factor in the future.

Despite the change in British opinion in the last two years, British official relations with China have been even less disturbed in this period of doctrinal stress than they were in the earlier years. The residue of the old days has been swept away. Even the British role in China in the century after 1840 has receded from memory, for the Chinese—quite unjustly, of course—treat the United States as the main villain. Only Hong Kong remains as a direct issue. The tacit assumption on both sides—that is, to leave the status quo untouched —was made explicit during the Sino-Soviet exchanges. Taunted by Premier Khrushchev at having done nothing about Hong Kong or Macao, the Chinese replied in March 1963 that these problems "should be settled peacefully through negotiations . . . pending a settlement the status quo should be maintained." [1]

It may be the result of a neglectful sense of superiority on the

---

1. "Comment on the Statement of the Communist Party of the U.S.A.," New China News Agency, March 8, 1963.

Chinese side or of major Chinese concerns elsewhere, but little belligerent current flows through the thin channels that do exist between
London and Peking. That these channels are valuable and should be
maintained is not questioned in British government circles. Britain
has had some knowledge of China, and that knowledge has been continuous because of the mission in Peking. It is a point of contact
that should not be undervalued if at any time there is a major threat
to world peace. That the Chinese also hold such a view we may
deduce, not from their tough ideological statements but from a reference in the military current-affairs journal which is circulated on a
classified basis within China. (A captured series was released in
Washington in 1963.) One commentator poses the question: Which
country might act as a bridge between China and the United States
—Japan? Britain? "We are not opposed to the erection of a
bridge." [2] The structure may not look impressive or seem much
used, but it is there.

ATTITUDES TOWARD TAIWAN

When the British recognized the People's Republic, recognition
was necessarily withdrawn from the Nationalist government then in
Canton. However, the British consulate was not withdrawn from
Taiwan. It was retained there, though accredited to the Taiwan
provincial government, when the Nationalist government formally
established itself in the island. The decision to keep the consulate
there was a *de facto* decision with no bearing on recognition, but
Peking alleged the decision showed an improper partiality to Chiang
Kai-shek. In the tentative negotiations to establish diplomatic rela-
tions during the early part of 1950, however, British retention of the
Taiwan consulate was a relatively minor issue.

The Korean War soon brought Taiwan's status to a head, and
Britain had to decide how far she would go in flouting American
opinion and how far in supporting Peking on the disposition of the
island. When President Truman announced his decision to prevent
any assault on Taiwan from the mainland while hostilities in Korea
were pending, this commitment was not regarded as a British commitment. But it did, nevertheless, sharpen the distinction of attitudes. In November 1950, when fear of the use of atomic weapons

---

2. *Kung Tso Tung Hsun,* no. 17, April 25, 1961, tr. in *China News Analysis*
(Hong Kong), no. 511, April 10, 1964.

sent Attlee hurrying to Washington to talk to President Truman, their communique, while admitting differences over recognition and Chinese representation in the United Nations, stated that the question of Taiwan should be settled by peaceful means "in such a way as to safeguard the interests of the people of Formosa."

Once British opinion admitted these interests, the future of the island tended to be viewed as an international problem. By this time, Chinese intervention in Korea had reconciled British opinion to postponing the issue of Peking's admission to the United Nations and, with it, the contentious issue of whether the Cairo declaration had finally settled the future of Taiwan. At the end of 1951 when the Conservatives came to office, they attempted to make British policy toward China seem closer to that of the United States. Though the basic differences of policy remained, the attempt did bring a slight shift on the Taiwan question. In a speech to a joint session of the U.S. Congress, Churchill affirmed that Taiwan should stay in non-Communist hands.

This position did not in any way imply support for the government of Chiang Kai-shek—still less for his pretensions of overturning the Communist government on the mainland. British support for an independent, non-Communist Taiwan has never attached itself to the Nationalist government as such. But as that support grew, even those who argued that the island was part of China and should rejoin it at some future time tended to insist that unification must be peacefully negotiated and not be achieved by force.

Opinion, therefore, had shifted somewhat by the time the Korean armistice was signed in 1953. Only the British right wing regarded American backing for the island as support for a non-Communist government which was beginning to lose some of the tarnish it had earned in its last years on the mainland. Moderate opinion was veering toward the view that Taiwan should only be disposed of in accordance with the wishes of its inhabitants. Those who preferred this solution interpreted American support for the Taiwan government as essentially support for such self-determination.

The growth of this attitude over the last decade should be distinguished from support for the Nationalist government itself. A few British have visited Taiwan, and they found the Nationalists' performance there better than that on the mainland. But no effective British lobby has backed Nationalist claims. A monthly newsletter is published by the Friends of Free China Association, and literature from Taiwan is distributed. Members of Parliament have visited the island—notably Sir William Teeling (Conservative) in 1957, who was the first visitor after the change in British attitude— but spokesmen for the Nationalist case are few. There has been little news of the island in the British press (though this deficiency applies equally to countries like Korea or the Philippines). A few students from Taiwan have come to study in Britain, and shortly after the mainland sent a Peking opera troupe, Taiwan sent one as well.

At no time have the British seen Taiwan, in contrast with West Germany, as a "free" Western-type government opposing a Communist government in a divided country. Nor do they view it as comparable to the non-Communist halves of divided countries such as Vietnam or Korea, though it has occasionally been presented in this light. Taiwan is simply a special international problem to be solved by negotiations at some future date. That it is a separate matter from the mainland has been more and more accepted since the 1954 and 1958 crises in the straits. In each case, British opinion overwhelmingly favored a Nationalist withdrawal from the offshore islands, for the islands seemed a dangerous cause of war, yet unquestionably a part of the mainland. This insistence on treating the offshore islands as a separate question from Taiwan, and as part of the mainland, has increasingly made Taiwan itself a separate problem.

The problem, however, is thought to be an American problem, almost an American obsession, in which British concern would be useless and otiose. If a common "British" viewpoint were defined, it would probably be that the people of the island should be independent and detached from China. Most accounts of Taiwanese opinion agree that this status is what they want. But to bring it about while the Nationalist government still exists is beyond British power or British interests, and there the matter rests.

The British have never attempted to influence the newly independent members of the Commonwealth to recognize Communist China. Some governments, such as Nigeria, have recognized neither Peking nor Taiwan. Some, such as Cyprus, Sierra Leone, and Jamaica, support the Nationalists. In this sense, therefore, Britain's China policy is independent of any Commonwealth initiative. Canada, Australia, and New Zealand have refused to recognize the Peking government, while India, Pakistan, Burma, and Ceylon all recognized it. The matter has been left for individual decision. At the Commonwealth Prime Ministers Conference in 1961, there was a move to try to coordinate policy at least so far as the U.N. representation problem was concerned. Nothing very much came of it, and the attack on India effectively ended it.

Labor party policy, as stated in a pamphlet published in 1961, favors a neutralized Taiwan under U.N. administration and protection. This policy differs from a "two-China" policy, which assumes that both governments should be seated in the United Nations. The Labor party pamphlet emphasized that neutralization meant the withdrawal of Chiang Kai-shek and the Nationalist government and an eventual referendum on the island: "not two Chinas but China and a freely chosen Formosan Government, if that should be the people's wish." If Peking were to make it worth their while, the pamphlet suggested, the people of Taiwan might opt for Peking.

It will not be until a vote favorable to the seating of the P.R.C. in the United Nations is passed that China policy will necessarily involve further thinking about Taiwan. Such thinking will certainly look to the time when leaders other than the Kuomintang could represent the island. Beyond that fact it is difficult to forecast what government or British public opinion will be, for the issue has had little significance for either in recent years.

BRITISH POLICY AND THE UNITED STATES

It would not be too much of an exaggeration to say that British policy toward China has been most prominently before British public opinion when it differed most markedly from American policy. This observation is less true since the advent of the Kennedy and Johnson administrations and the noticeable increase in British hostility toward and suspicion of China which followed the Indian border trouble of 1962 and the Vietnam crisis. Thus, containment of Chinese power has become a more defined basis of British policy. At least its importance in British eyes is more akin to that attached to it in the United States. The presence of a British mission in Peking serves American interests as a valuable means of contact which the United States cannot contrive. Despite improved understanding of each other's position, and despite the relative harmony between Washington and London officials concerned with the China problem, a basic difference of outlook nevertheless remains.

In the past, the fact that Britain was the only major Western power which had recognized the Peking government proved much more important than the British had foreseen at the time they made their decision. In the first decade after the Communist take-over, Britain to some extent became a mediator or led those who most strongly criticized American policy. That situation was somewhat altered by French recognition. Still, it is not inconceivable that Peking's admission to the United Nations could lead, publicly at least, to a sharp divergence. It seems more likely, though, that a friendly agreement to differ will subsist, for the British now assume that the United States will come round to their point of view before long.

There were differences over China long before the Communists came to power. Roosevelt insisted, against Churchill's skepticism, on including China in the U.N. Security Council as one of the big five powers. During the civil war, there was growing British criticism of American support for the corrupt and failing government of Chiang Kai-shek. This criticism, of course, occurred during 1947 and 1948 when the prospect of a Communist solution to China's appalling chaos was easier to contemplate and understand than it was under cold-war conditions as they had developed a year later. Even then the British tended to believe that the Chinese Communists were likely to be independent of the Russians and thus to behave in somewhat the same way as Tito has done in Yugoslavia—an assumption fulfilled in the Sino-Soviet dispute, though not in the way that was foreseen in 1949.

Yet in 1949 it was probably never thought possible that the division between Britain and the United States over China could become as serious as it did. Though the Bevin-Acheson talks in September 1949 produced no agreement on recognition, there was not then any indication that much more than the question of timing was involved. As a gesture toward the American position, Britain abstained on a Soviet motion to seat the Peking government in the United Nations on the ground that it was too early to take the step, although the vote came a week after Britain's own recognition.

Two months later, Britain began to press the issue, but a series of incidents in China, such as the seizure of American consular property in Peking, had by then begun to delay even further the prospect of American recognition. The North Korean attack across the 38th parallel and U.N. intervention on behalf of the southern government necessarily exposed Anglo-American differences even further, for the differences over the prosecution of the war all related to China. President Truman's decision to neutralize Taiwan was not seriously opposed in Britain, but it was clear that the United States was acting on its own, without British participation. At several points during the prosecution of the Korean War, Britain was reluctant to support American initiatives. When Chinese warnings of intervention were first given, the British military chiefs preferred that the U.N. advance should go no further northward than the narrow point of Korea. When the Chinese did intervene, it was the British who urged that a Chinese delegation should be invited to the United Nations. Among the attempts at mediation were Foreign Secretary Ernest Bevin's message to Chou En-lai on November 22, 1950. It stated that the U.N. forces were not intended to threaten Chinese interests.

British fears, spurred by what was known of General MacArthur's preferences, that atomic bombs might be used in the war finally brought Prime Minister Attlee to Washington. Significantly, the feeling of British differences with the United States, a feeling which these fears had greatly heightened, resulted in a slight British move toward the U.S. position. A joint communique issued after the Truman-Attlee talks stated that Taiwan was an issue to be settled by peaceful means and in accordance with "the interests of the people of Formosa."

Nevertheless, this critical period continued with Britain leading the way in attempts to conciliate China while the United States pressed for firmer measures. The U.N. resolution defining the Chinese as aggressors dramatized the situation, for the British were greatly reluctant to accept this measure even though their support for the U.N. action had been strong. Although Britain participated fully in the operations in Korea, the British mission in Peking remained, and the trade embargo might not have been imposed but for U.S. insistence.

The Korean War provided a good illustration of a basic British attitude toward China. It might be defined as a readiness to look at all newly independent countries in somewhat the same light, regardless of whether they had once been under British rule or not. Conciliation, coupled with firmness where vital interests have been at stake, has been preferred to any attempt to overthrow a regime, however unfavorable it may be. There is a disposition—weakened considerably by recent events—to treat China in this light even though its government is Communist. There is a stoical readiness (if we overlook the Suez aberration) to take some of the post-colonial kicks.

The first Anglo-U.S. differences over Communist China had developed under a Labor government. The Conservative government which came to office in November 1951 was eager to move closer to the United States. After a visit to Washington in January 1952, Churchill and Eden joined in a declaration that Formosa should stay out of Communist hands—a more positive position than that adopted by the previous Labor government. Yet the right-wing Conservative opinion that would have liked tougher policies toward China, even to the extent of withdrawing recognition, was soon shown to be insignificant and unrepresentative. And at the next point of crisis, British opinion was again behind a conciliatory attitude.

This crisis occurred at the Geneva Conference in 1954 when Eden and Dulles differed sharply over the aid that should go to the French forces surrounded at Dien Bien Phu. While this matter did not strictly involve China, it was plainly the attitude toward China which determined the difference. Eden's part in the conference after this difference, and the obvious improvement in relations with the Chinese, only hardened the separation.

It has often been assumed that the Chinese were disposed to exploit differences between British and American policy, but no evidence of such exploitation can be produced. On the contrary, the Chinese tendency has always been to point to the British as really only slightly different. Thus, in March 1953 when Foreign Secretary Eden was visiting the United States, the British were dubbed the lapdogs of the United States. And certainly after 1957, especially while Britain voted with the United States to postpone discussion of the China seat in the United Nations, there was no disposition to think of British policy as of any interest to China. This attitude did not change even after the British voted to seat Peking in 1961, and it seems unlikely to change now that British policy toward Vietnam has aligned the Labor government with the United States. The Chinese now dismiss Britain as a junior partner of the United States which will never take any real initiative that is likely to disturb the U.S. government.

With the development of the Sino-Soviet dispute over the last four years, the scope for Anglo-American differences might seem to have expanded. Here again, Britain has tended to take a quiescent view. She certainly has not thought that exploitation of the dispute is either possible or profitable. But the differences over the dispute—its causes, motives, and outcome—have found as many divided opinions on one side of the Atlantic as the other. The Chinese have at all times maintained that the dispute is an internal matter of the Communist camp—of importance to the revolutionary world of Asia, Africa, and Latin America, but of no concern to the "imperialists." Nor will China become any closer to the West as a result of it.

On the other hand, it is becoming increasingly apparent that the Chinese are looking at their relations with Western Europe in a new light. In part, they feel they must deal directly with an area which no longer falls, as far as they are concerned, within the Russian sphere. This view was given theoretical justification when the *People's Daily* found Western Europe to be a second intermediate zone [3] after the revolutionary intermediate zone of Asia, Africa, and Latin America; that zone was one in which a striving for independence (from the United States) was manifest—in France especially. The implication was that China would look favorably on this striving.

Now that China has exchanged ambassadors with France and trade with Western Europe is expanding, a conscious Chinese presence in Western Europe could influence Chinese policy toward Britain. Thus far, signs of such influence are slender, and Chinese hopes have not been at all quickened by the advent of a Labor government. China may thus remain a cause for irritation, but not for major differences, in relations between Britain and the United States. Nevertheless, to the British public, American attitudes toward China seem the most inexplicable and unsympathetic of all American international attitudes.

BRITAIN, CHINA, AND THE FUTURE

In the half century since China shook off the authority of the Manchu dynasty, the relative status of Britain and China in the world has changed more, perhaps, than that of any other two nations. In the world of 1912, China was becoming weak, divided, and leaderless. Britain stood at the peak of her global power as the British Empire had reached its maximum extension. Today, British responsibilities in the world have receded because of the voluntary relinquishment of imperial rule. Those overseas bases which were the symbol of

---

3. *People's Daily (Jenmin Jihpao)*, January 21, 1964.

British maritime thinking have been cut back. China looks bel-
ligerently out on a world which, if it does not yet admit her to world
power status in any economic or military sense, does not doubt that
that status will be achieved.

Even at its maximum extension, British power never took much
cognizance of China as a prime mover in world affairs. At no time
after the end of the 19th century was there any fear of what China
might do, but only fear of what others might do or acquire in China.
The power most feared in Asia was Russia. Russia as a rival was a
concern of British power; China was only an object of it. Russia
was a threat to Central Asia and the northern fringes of India, to
Manchuria, and possibly even to northern China. To guard against
this threat, Britain signed the Anglo-Japanese alliance in 1902 and
renewed it again after Japan defeated Russia in 1905. For the rest,
the gun-boat diplomacy which had opened up China continued as
nothing more than a minor naval responsibility, and the China station was a pleasant *cul-de-sac* in the career of a naval officer.

Hence the great differences in British and U.S. attitudes toward
China are rooted in the facts of geography. For the British, who
were committed to a maritime outlook during the era of 19th-century
expansion, China meant a country at the very end of the sea roads—
beyond the area of British responsibility and isolated from British
global concerns. After the First World War, the facts of power
began to turn against Britain, and nothing marked the change more
than the Washington Conference of 1921, which ended Britain's
outward preeminence as a naval power. With the substitution at
that conference of a four-power agreement for the Anglo-Japanese
alliance, the real British withdrawal from East Asia began. Her gun-
boats remained to defend the treaty ports. Weihaiwei was not ceded
to China until 1932. But these facts were only part of a time lag.
Britain had withdrawn what power she had had in this area even
before the end of the empire came after the Second World War.

Thus, the British global view after the war, however much it
now recognized the shrinking of British power, had long ago discarded China from its calculations. Therefore, the rise of China as
a world power, in the form of a Communist China, had little impact
in Britain until recently. In terms of air power, as well as sea power,
China still remains beyond the area of significance. China lies at
the far end of the Eurasian land mass—distant by sea and even by
air, beyond the vast zone of the Soviet Union.

We must consider, then, to what extent growing Chinese power has imposed a reappraisal upon Britain despite the facts of geography. In the foregoing sections, it was suggested that China's Communist government grew in power at the same time as the British withdrew from South Asia. There was a tendency in Britain, though only half-defined, to think of China as another of the newly independent, developing countries in Asia along with India, Pakistan, and the rest. It was the biggest and the most extreme in its doctrines, but it belonged basically to the same class in outlook, pretensions, and prospects.

This attitude is being revised as events show it to offer altogether too limited a framework. The force with which the Chinese acted in the border dispute with India and, even more, the relentlessness with which China has pursued her dispute with the Soviet Union, have shown what China's role as a great power might be. Only in the last few years has it seemed necessary to reflect seriously on the part China might choose to play in the world if she does become the leader of a group of revolutionary nations. China could, it is assumed, displace Russia as the leader of a doctrinaire communism, and she might see it as her duty to lead the struggle against the capitalist world with the aim of bringing about its eventual destruction.

Such reflections about China should be considered in any forecast of future British reaction and future British policy toward China, but they should also be balanced against other factors which affect British policy. First, the emergence of China as a power of such dimensions could only affect Britain in steadily more limited areas— in the Middle East (to a minor extent) and (to an even lesser extent) in those substantial areas of Africa where British policy matters or is felt to matter. Britain's defensive role in Southeast Asia is more directly affected. But in a global strategic sense, China simply is not a British problem. Second, and related to the first factor, is Britain's interest in Europe. For the moment, this interest may seem in abeyance, since British entry into the Common Market was set aside and since the Labor party is diffident toward Europe. Most students of British political life would nevertheless regard this issue as a vital one, and the trends in commitment, particularly among the younger generation, point toward a closer association. Third, the British attitude toward revolution combines an acceptance of revolutionary change as a part of the nature of things, skepticism about the source of revolutionary potential, and an expectation that revolutions, in time, evolve. The British tend to see revolutions first as manifestations of trouble in the society in which they occur, and only secondarily as manifestations of outside influences. Just as in the past the British (except for the right-wing fringe) were less disposed than the Americans to see in the Russians the source of all revolutionary movements, so, now, there is less tendency to see China as such a powerful factor because she is a supporter of revolution throughout the world.

In any case, whatever may be the future forecast for China, the evidence does not suggest to the British that China is now or has the immediate prospect of being a world power. After the failure of the Great Leap Forward, there may have been some tendency to downgrade China just as there had before been a tendency to overrate China's progress.

China as a Military Power. The British note that China has not built up, and has apparently not tried to build up, any naval or air striking force; such weapons as she has are defensive. As a military power with vast and almost unlimited manpower, China's strength is much respected. That strength was demonstrated in Korea and has lately been displayed in quite different terrain in the Himalayas. But her power has a limited range. Chinese potential operates on its own periphery and not far beyond.

Undoubtedly Communist China's developing nuclear capability has added to the apprehension about the P.R.C. as a world revolutionary power. Informed opinion varies about the uses to which Chinese nuclear power will be put. British opinion about the influence a nuclear potential would have on China varies. The British, for example, disagree about whether it would be used defensively or offensively, and about whether it would be at the service of Chinese national interests or of world revolutionary interests. They are divided on whether or not China can be brought into some kind of world agreement on the control of nuclear weapons before she acquires a significant stockpile. They do not consider British power directly involved in any nuclear threat China may pose, except for the unlikely case that India may have to be provided with a nuclear "umbrella" in the event of another Chinese attack. It is known that a real nuclear potential does not follow until several years after the first experiments. When China has reached that point, there may be some serious thought given to the matter, but the pragmatic British view tends to concentrate on the obvious dangers of China as a military power on her own borders rather than as a nuclear world power.

China as a Revolutionary Power. The threat of China as a revolutionary leader has obviously struck home in some quarters. In a speech at the United Nations in October 1963, Sir Alex Douglas-Home, the British Prime Minister, spoke of the new prospect of cooperation between the West and the Soviet Union, and he contrasted that prospect with China's attitude—thinking she might inherit the earth from a nuclear holocaust. He also commented adversely on Chou En-lai's statement, after his tour of Africa early in 1964, that the area was ripe for revolution.

At the Commonwealth Conference in June 1965, Mr. Wilson's proposals on Vietnam precluded any direct initiative in regard to China. Yet despite differing attitudes among Commonwealth members, some joint Commonwealth initiative in this area remains a future possibility.

Let us summarize British attitudes thus: there is a wary observation of China's progress toward becoming a world power and of China's role as a revolutionary force, but much skepticism remains as to whether, in either sense, China presents an imminent threat, if a threat at all.

The fact is that the British, through direct experience since 1949, have accumulated knowledge of China which is quite precise on some points. This knowledge shows China to be a far more peaceful power in its actions than many people would assume from its words. Britain, after all, has remained the ruler of Hong Kong through 15 years when China's prime aim has been the restoration of her authority over lost territories. This is not the place to go into all the reasons why Hong Kong has survived, but a few observations are pertinent. From the British point of view, Hong Kong has never been a candidate for self-government or independence as other island colonies have been. In the period immediately after Indian independence in 1947, there was no Chinese government to which the colony could have been returned if such a move had been considered. Since the Chinese Communists came to power, there has been no reason for change. Equally, the Chinese have seen no reason to assert their claim. Indeed, in 1955, they actually approached the British government with a proposal to station a Chinese representative in Hong Kong, and when that proposal was refused, they continued to accept the status quo.

At the local government level, cooperation between Hong Kong and the mainland has been satisfactory. In 1960, Hong Kong's water shortage was relieved by an arrangement to draw water off the Shum-chun Reservoir, and in 1964 a further agreement was reached to take water by canal from the West River to Hong Kong by adding to an existing scheme in Kwangtung Province. From time to time, there have been minor disturbances and protests over such survivals as the walled city of Kowloon, in which China has recently reasserted her traditional residual rights, but the tendency on both sides is to prevent trouble. Coexistence could not have a nearer or more accepted example.

As for British interests, the naval base has been given up in favor of Singapore, and British troops are maintained in Hong Kong for internal security purposes only. Hong Kong is no longer relevant as a base for trade with China, though it has some value as a contact point for other purposes. To the Chinese it may be worth about £100 million (sterling) a year in foreign exchange, and to Britain about £50 million in trade in each direction.

As Britain sees it, Hong Kong lives from year to year with no special expectation about its future. In 1997, of course, the 99-year lease on the New Territories will expire, and the accepted opinion is that Hong Kong could no longer survive as a separate entity when these territories are returned to Chinese control. So Hong Kong's days are numbered; sufficient unto the day is the capital and interest thereof.

British interest in Southeast Asia, though currently affected by the Vietnam crisis, is now really concentrated in the Commonwealth areas of Malaysia. Here there is a surviving British base which may continue for some years yet—if only because Malaysia as a national entity is unstable and threatened directly by Indonesia. This "confrontation," it is true, has the backing of Communists, but there is no sense of direct Chinese action or interest. In day-to-day matters, British policy toward Indonesia, in defense of Malaysia or in retention of the Commonwealth base in Malaya takes no special account of China as a power, but the British are very much aware that China sets the dimensions of policy and is the one significant long-term presence in the area. The Chinese interest in Southeast Asia remains a major factor in British strategic thinking. The presence of Chinese throughout the whole of Southeast Asia provides an added reminder of this interest. For Britain, these overseas Chinese are most important because they are concentrated in Malaya, Singapore, Sarawak, and Sabah. British policy tends to regard them as local inhabitants rather than as potential arms of Peking. Throughout the Malayan emergency—which began before the Communist government came to power in China—the Chinese who played the dominant role appeared to have little connection with the Chinese mainland, and this observation seems even more true of the revolutionary forces that exist today. They may be Communist, and they may be a problem, as they still are in Singapore and in Sarawak. But they are not directly related to China, and they are not viewed as part of a generalized Chinese threat in the area.

As we move further through the arc of South Asia, there is China's threat to India. At the time of the Chinese attack in 1962, there was an incipient disposition to regard this threat as a major one which required full British support for India. Aid was arranged after the event and would certainly be forthcoming should another attack materialize. In general, however, this frontier is not thought to be as dangerous as it seemed at the time of the attack, nor do Chinese intentions seem as threatening. Nevertheless, the British do maintain a general interest and responsibility in the whole South Asian area and necessarily pay attention to Chinese political and strategic thinking.

It was the bitterness of the Sino-Soviet battle that contributed to Chinese action over India, as the Russians have admitted. China has now carried its case against the Russians outside the Communist movement to every possible revolutionary nationalist forum to which it can gain entry. Indonesia has proved a ripe field for this propaganda, and the Chinese have asserted their leadership by opposing an invitation to the Russians to take part in the Afro-Asian conference.

If the Chinese ever get far in exerting leadership in Afro-Asian affairs, their power in Asia might be very great. No country which seriously needs economic or military aid, however, can contemplate so close an attachment to China as will anger the Russians. (The case of Cambodia may possibly be the exception to prove the point.) The British view of China in Asia might thus be that there is a built-in resistance to China throughout South and Southeast Asia but that this resistance is not strong enough to dispense with Western backing. If the non-Communist countries are firm, some sort of peaceful coexistence with China can continue despite Chinese protestations about their sympathy for revolutionary movements and their expectations of change.

CONCLUDING REMARKS

The range of British opinion about China can be seen from an analysis of the views of the various political parties. The Conservatives were in power for 12 years. Their policy can be summed up as one of trade and diplomatic dealings with China. They wish to see China brought into the United Nations, but they would not press the issue so strongly as to cause serious difficulties for the United States. The Liberals share these attitudes. The Labor party is the only party to have published (in February 1961) a detailed analysis of China and the West. Its main points are:

1. That Washington will respect plain speaking from Britain.
2. That China must be thought of as a world power.
3. That, in light of point 2, British relations with China must be conceived as "on a similar level to" those with the U.S.S.R. and United States.
4. That, in light of point 3, China must be seated in the United Nations and brought into any world summit meetings.
5. That no attempt should be made to exploit the Sino-Soviet dispute.

This document, of course, does not bind the Labor party now that it is in office. With French recognition, it is also evident that Britain's position as the leading Western power with diplomatic relations with China has been altered. The views of all political parties as they existed prior to French recognition will to some extent have to be reexamined with this factor in mind.

In general, China is beginning to acquire the image of a world power in British eyes but is still some way from filling it out. There is in Britain, however, no section of the public, no faction in government and public life, no body of active opinion, no sufficient commercial interest to bring any weight to bear upon attitudes and policies toward China. Curiosity about China exists and is growing. There is more academic study of China in Britain; and thanks to the British mission in Peking, a good many of those in the upper ranks of the Foreign Office have had the experience of serving there. But against any potential interest must be set the territorial shrinking of British power and the likelihood of a closer attachment to the European continent. It is not easy, therefore, to forecast China's role in the British imagination and in British global policy. One can only say that Britain is likely to stress mediation, understanding, and co-existence, to keep open diplomatic channels, and to maintain trade relations.

Chapter 2

FRANCE AND CHINA

The Intersection of Two Grand Designs

BY

FRANÇOIS FEJTÖ

On January 27, 1964, after a psychological preparation conducted by the rules of traditional diplomacy, France and Communist China made public their decision to establish diplomatic relations. Three months later, according to schedule, Peking and Paris announced the nomination of their ambassadors.

Few political events of the post-World War II period have caused such lively interest, such impassioned comment as this rapprochement between a member of the Atlantic alliance and a Communist power which considers the leader of that alliance, the United States, its principal enemy. Some persons went so far as to interpret this establishment of relations as a true turning point in world politics, the end of "bipolar" equilibrium and the beginning of a new period designated by the somewhat barbarous term "polycentric."

The two states made contact with each other without regard to the views of the leaders and of the other members of their respective alliance systems. In both cases, it was quite apparently a matter of demonstrating independence. But this demonstration, which for France was coupled with a breach of Atlantic discipline (China's ties with the Soviet Union were already almost completely cut), cannot be isolated from the general context of world developments. The movement of France toward China and of China toward France seems symptomatic. It can be interpreted as a reaction to the undeniable, though precarious, rapprochement between the two main world powers, the United States and the U.S.S.R., both equally interested in maintaining the status quo that resulted from the war. This rapprochement was put into concrete form by the establishment of direct, secret, bilateral contacts between Washington and Moscow and by the conclusion of the nuclear agreement of July 1963.

This rapprochement, this movement which seems to tend toward a sort of global condominium of the two big nuclear powers, has accelerated the disintegration of the Sino-Soviet bloc. There, under the veil of a Marxist monolith, autarkic, nationalistic tendencies have survived and display themselves with as much, if not more, vigor as in the capitalist countries. One of the most important causes of the rebellion of the People's Republic of China against Soviet hegemony lies precisely in the Soviet-American rapprochement. This rebellion has probably helped to decrease Soviet pressure against Europe and to diminish that fear of Soviet invasion which was perhaps the best mortar of the Atlantic alliance.[1] At the same time, the countries of Western Europe—especially, but not only, France—have attained a degree of prosperity which, from the economic point of view, makes them markedly less dependent upon the United States and stimulates them to formulate their individual interests in a less timorous spirit.

In any case, the parallel processes of evolution on both sides of the line of demarcation which still separates the two worlds, Communist and capitalist, are striking.[2] France's action may be the most spectacular, but there are other recalcitrant allies, other "problem children" in the bosom of the Western alliance. The British, too, although they conduct themselves with more respect for forms and perhaps also with more hesitation than the French, have created some knotty problems—for example, in matters of East-West trade and in attitudes toward Cuba. In another part of the world, Pakistan, moved by resentment against India, is binding itself closer and closer to China. In the Communist world, Albania, while remain-

---

1. "There is no longer any danger of war between the U.S.S.R. and the West," stated Sir Alec Douglas-Home on April 6, 1964, at Norwich. It is true that on April 27 General Lemnitzer, supreme commander of NATO forces, emphasized before the House Committee on Foreign Affairs that "the Soviet military menace has not declined."

2. See André Fontaine, "Les Nouvelles convergences," *Le Monde*, March 3/4 and 5, 1964.

ing socialist, defies the U.S.S.R. with as much surliness as Cuba does
the United States. First Poland and more recently Rumania have
shown in the most obvious fashion their refusal to "keep in step,"
which has aroused the United States to modify its attitude toward
them. Profiting by the decline in international tension as well as
by the U.S.S.R.'s annoyance with Chinese "undermining," the East
European satellites behave less and less like satellites—to the point
where one wonders whether some of them still deserve the name.
The era of unconditional obedience seems ended. On both sides,
one detects a current of diversification, fluidity, regrouping. There
are more and more countries "at once aligned and nonaligned." [3]

This current makes itself felt more easily since the two great
powers, who have settled down to a mutual surveillance by which each
prevents the other from swinging the balance its way, tend to neutralize one another. The U.S.S.R. and the United States appear to
the Europeans to be crushed by the weight of their atomic armament
and by the joint responsibility they bear for the survival of our planet.
They do not seem to possess the political or ideological means which
would permit them, in the existing framework, to impose their will
on the malcontents in their own camp or to satisfy the demands of
these malcontents by giving them a share of responsibility. They
do not even seem to be able to dominate, to channel the decolonization process, which is one of the characteristic features of our time
and which proceeds in great confusion. For these reasons, as Walter
Lippmann has recently noted, the United States finds it impossible
in practice to profit from the Sino-Soviet dispute. On the other
hand, the U.S.S.R. is unable to profit from the disagreements between
France and Pakistan on one side and the United States on the other.
Meanwhile, secondary powers, like China, France, England, Rumania, and Yugoslavia, seem to have greater freedom of action and
play a role out of proportion to their real power. Everything happens as if evolution, instead of confirming the trend toward political
integration which logic tells us should be inherent in the course of
history (consider the expansion of international trade), were moving
in the opposite direction—toward the revalidation of national sov-
ereignties which had been thought outmoded. Paradoxically, national
independence appears as a supreme value.

3. The phrase is from a statement by Foreign Minister Ch'en Yi which was
reported in *Le Monde*, May 5, 1964.

By using the antagonism between East and West, between the Atlantic alliance directed by the United States and the Communist alliance managed by the U.S.S.R., the young states of the Third World have for several years past tried to secure for themselves, by virtue of a certain nonalignment, the assistance of the two groups and to strengthen their position of independence. All these countries consider the Franco-Chinese rapprochement as a confirmation of their aims, which consist above all in limiting the fields of influence of the two big powers while playing one off against the other. *The appearance on the scene of two new competitors—China and France —seems to improve the chances of the nonaligned to charge a high price for their neutrality.* China and the U.S.S.R. engage in a veritable auction to secure the favors of the Afro-Asians, who do not hesitate to set a cash price on their support.

These comments suffice to indicate the breadth of the problems posed for the United States and the Soviet Union, and for the world, by the establishment of relations between Gaullist France and Maoist China, both of whom set themselves up as champions of independence. Can one believe not only that this rapprochement reflects a disturbance of the relationships of forces within alliances, but that it *also modifies the fundamental premises of international equilibrium?* Certain declarations from across the Atlantic, some authorized,[4] give reason to think so. It has been judged that France's decision "was unwise" and that, by recognizing China, France and De Gaulle struck a blow at the cohesion of the Atlantic alliance and encouraged Chinese aggressiveness. Others, like former Premier Edgar Faure, on the contrary, have held that revision of the Western attitude toward China was a necessity and that France, by serving as forerunner, performed a definite service to the whole free world, and especially to the United States, which would not be long in following her example.

The debate continues, and this paper does not seek to settle it. My aim is more modest: to clarify the problem. First, I will review the past. This historical analysis appears essential to explain the undeniably favorable response of practically all sectors of French opinion to recognition. It would be mistaken to see this diplomatic action as the expression of the will, the designs, the "grand design" of a sin-

4. For example, President Johnson's interview of March 15, reported in *The New York Times*, March 16, 1964.

gle individual.[5] I will try next to elucidate this design itself (to the extent that it can be grasped), to call to mind the diplomatic, political, economic, and cultural interests whose coincidence seems to have determined, on one side or the other, the decision of January 27. Finally, in conclusion I will try to envisage some of the consequences, immediate and remote, of the new Franco-Chinese relations.

FRANCE AND THE "ETERNAL CHINA"

Eternal China: In his press conference of January 31, 1964, General de Gaulle, in a style that would not have disgraced his friend André Malraux, sketched a gripping picture of it. This picture reflects the image, compounded of admiration and wonder, that more than two centuries of intermittent and contradictory contacts had engraved on the collective memory of the French. "China, a great people, the most numerous on earth; a race in which the capacity for patience, labor, and industry of its individuals has for thousands of years compensated for its collective lack of method and cohesion and has built a very special and very profound civilization. . . ." I wish I could cite *in extenso* this piece of bravura, designed to have a place in future anthologies.

Of course, the same author, in another international context, had used other colors to depict China. At that time (November 10, 1959), China appeared to him as "innumerable, wretched . . . looking about her at the expanses over which she will one day have to spread." Critics[6] have not failed to take malicious note of this shift of focus. And surely the "affinities notoriously existing" between China and France which "have always extended each to the other the most profound sympathy and consideration" would by no means have sufficed to produce, against and despite everybody, the establishment of diplomatic relations. This development stemmed from more immediate and pressing causes.

But the governmental action *did not go against the current*. It was facilitated by a quasi-traditional interest, by a rather favorable

---

5. A poll conducted in early January 1964 by the Institut Français d'Opinion Publique revealed a trend rather favorable to normalization of relations between China and France. Of those questioned, 39 per cent favored official recognition, 26 per cent opposed it, and the remainder did not reply. On the development of commercial relations, 58 per cent were in favor, 17 per cent opposed, 25 per cent made no reply. See *France Soir*, February 21, 1964.

6. See Sirius in *Le Monde*, February 2/3, 1964.

predisposition of the French, especially the French elite, toward China. It may be true that statesmen enjoy using tradition to justify diplomatic moves inspired only by reasons of state, but in the case of France and China the justification does not appear entirely artificial.

As for the distant past, we can distinguish four principal periods in the evolution of relations between China and France:

1. In the 17th and 18th centuries, the French interest was first of all a *religious* one, as illustrated by the activities of the Jesuits. Then there was a certain *intellectual* curiosity and sympathy, of which one finds striking examples in the cases of the physiocrats, Voltaire, and the encyclopedists. An American historian, Lewis Coser, has recently related with humor the vagaries of this "love story of the philosophers with China," which coincided with a rather similar "flirtation" by the same philosophers with the Russian autocracy.[7] Surely this love story was inspired by a rather cursory acquaintance with things Chinese. The attraction of the distant and the exotic, the desire to escape too confining surroundings played the principal role. Fashion also was involved, for in the same period *chinoiseries* took the place of *turqueries* at Versailles. (The return to classical taste later drove them both out.) It is tempting, nevertheless, to compare Voltaire's enthusiasm for this "nation which passes as the most virtuous and orderly in the universe" to the quite similar infatuation of some of our contemporary philosophers—Jean-Paul Sartre and Simone de Beauvoir, for example—who also have gone to the farthest ends of Asia to find their ideal, as De Tocqueville said of the physiocrats. What Voltaire found admirable in the organization of the Chinese Empire was that it was based "on paternal authority." For him and his friends, the China of Confucius and Lao Tzu represented the archetype of a society placed under the paternalistic direction of philosophers, of literate men. And is not present-day China also run by ideologues? Since 1949 it has served as a vast laboratory for utopian-revolutionary intellectuals. Is this not the key to the seductiveness of China for the most idealistic (I would also say the least adapted to neo-capitalistic realities) sector of French society, whose master thinker is Sartre; for the rebels who, disillusioned by an ever more *embourgeoisée* Russia, have set themselves to search for a new myth, a new location for utopia?

2. From 1842 (the end of the Opium War) up to the First World

---

7. *Arguments*, no. 23, 1961.

War, bourgeois, imperialist France took part in the same capacity and in much the same spirit as the other great powers—England, Russia, and the United States—in the "many interventions, expeditions, missions" which, according to the previously cited speech of De Gaulle, "inflicted on China . . . many humiliations and dismemberments." In 1858 the French took a hand in the famous looting of the Summer Palace. As the only Catholic country among the colonizers, France constituted herself the protectress of all the Catholic missionaries, and in this respect there was no loss of continuity between the Second Empire and the anti-clerical Third Republic. France wrung concessions and installed herself in an Indochina torn from Chinese suzerainty. For a long time, she considered as an enemy this country against which, as French Consul Montigny put it in 1899, "one must dare in order to prevail." "China is not, like Turkey, a sick man; it is a cadaver ready for dissection, which submits itself to the knife," wrote another diplomat, Paul Claudel (who nevertheless was responsive to the spell of the Far East) in 1898. France mistreated China, made war on her in 1857–58, in 1860, and in 1900—though in the French view these operations were nothing more than police actions—and carried out a policy of penetration similar to that of Britain, Germany, and Russia and more intransigent, more implacable—in my view—than that of the United States, which vacillated between the older and the more modern forms of imperialism.

Of course, even during this period, currents of interest and sympathy existed. As Roger Lévy has stressed, "a large fund of goodwill was expended." Penetration involved some aspects that were not purely negative, if only because it aroused among the Chinese elite an awareness of the need for profound reforms to enable their country to recover. Chavanne created modern sinology; his disciples, Pelliot, Maspero, and Granet, were, as Jean Escarra said, to carry French sinology to glorious heights.[8] Sylvain Lévi revived Buddhist studies. French schools played their part in the awakening of the Chinese intelligentsia.

But the dominant factors were the commercial interest and, even more, the imperialist, colonizing interest—the desire to share in the plunder.[9] Thus when the *People's Daily*, in its editorial of March 8,

---

8. *La Chine passée et présente* (Paris: Armand Collin, 1949).
9. For fuller information, see Roger Lévy, *La Politique française en Extrême-Orient* (Paris: Paul Hartmann, 1939); Loung Chang, *La Chine a l'aube du*

1963, raised the problem of "unequal treaties" against the Soviet Union, it mentioned France after the United States and Great Britain but before Russia, Germany, and Japan. France, in other words, occupied third place among the imperialists and colonialists who devoted themselves to "unrestrained aggression" against China.

3. After the conquest of Indochina, the major objective of French policy toward China was the preservation of gains. However, the Chinese revolution of 1911 and the proclamation of the Republic aroused some stirrings of conscience in radical, Freemason France, which suddenly remembered its liberal, democratic, fraternal vocation. The names that come to mind are Paul Painlevé, Anatole France, and later Edouard Herriot. From 1911 on, Paul Painlevé demanded that the French government recognize China. In 1912, he brought into being the first interparliamentary group organized by republican China and another nation, founded the Institut des Hautes Études Chinoises at the University of Paris, and initiated an imposing demonstration in honor of the young Chinese Republic, at which Anatole France made a speech. During the war, when China became an ally, a flood of Chinese workers and soldiers came to France under the aegis of Painlevé, who was then Minister of Defense. It was he also who after the war founded the Association Économique Franco-Chinoise, which had a counterpart in China. His active sympathy for this tumultuous country, which he went so far as to call "the mother of democracies," was expressed in a bold prophecy: "The 20th century will be the century of China, as the 19th was that of the unprecedented flowering of America."[10]

Technical, scientific, cultural, and sentimental ties which mitigated the effects of colonialist harshness were then established. In 1919–20, more than 2,000 Chinese students attended French universities.[11] Of these, 1,600 earned their living by manual labor while they were studying. They came to France precisely because living conditions there seemed easier to them. But they were also attracted by their elders, intellectuals and philosophers like Ch'en Tu-hsiu,

XIX-ième siècle (Paris: Nouvelles Editions Latines, 1962); Chang Chung-tao, *Les Traités inégaux de la Chine et l'attitude des puissances* (Paris: Librairie des Sciences Politiques et Sociales, 1929); and the fine anthology of texts illuminating China's past, Roger Pelissier, *La Chine entre en scène* (Paris: Julliard, 1964).

10. *La Mission Painlevé en Chine* (Paris: Editions Politiques de Pékin, 1921).

11. Conrad Brandt, "The French-returned Elite in the Chinese Communist Party," in Edward Szczepanik, ed., *Symposium on Economic and Social Problems of the Far East* (Hong Kong University Press, 1962).

who were settled in France before the First World War and were linked to the mayor of Lyon. Thanks to him a Franco-Chinese institute was founded in that city.[12]

Among the students residing in France on the eve of World War I were several future Communist leaders of the country—Chou En-lai, Ch'en Yi, Li Fu-ch'un (later chairman of the State Planning Commission), Nieh Jung-chen (later chairman of the State Scientific and Technological Commission), and Teng Hsiao-p'ing (later secretary general of the Chinese Communist party, who in 1960 and after was to play such an important role in the development of a policy of independence in regard to the Soviet Union). As Guillaume Georges-Picot, chairman of the Groupe France-Extrême-Orient and a member of the Conseil National du Patronat Français [National Council of French Management] (whose pioneer work in connection with the new rapprochement is well known) has stressed, these former students "seem to have kept good memories of the years spent in France; they would like to see Chinese students take the road to France once again."

France, or rather the French Communists, was the intermediary for the conversion of Chou En-lai and his companions, as well as Ho Chi Minh, to the Communist religion. It is curious to find them remembering their stay in France with seemingly sincere sympathy at the very moment when Russia, in their eyes, appeared faithless to its promises. The fact remains that in 1963 French travelers and emissaries, like Georges-Picot and Edgar Faure, would regard the presence of persons with a certain knowledge of French and of France at the summit of the Chinese hierarchy as a trump card ready at hand.

4. Let us pass rapidly over the period between the two world wars and that of the Second World War, which were dominated by a concern for preserving gains under rather delicate circumstances. In 1938, a French military mission replaced the German military mission in China. China again became an ally. France, in turn, was invaded and defeated. The leader of Free France, according to his *Memoirs*, calculated rather early that, "in the face of the rise of America and Russia, with the rise of China to come. . . ," France, even less than England, "will not quickly regain her former power," [13]

---

12. Ch'en Tu-hsiu, formed by radicalism and inspired by the 18th-century French philosophers, later became secretary-general of the Chinese Communist party.

13. *Mémoires de guerre: Le Salut, 1944–46* (Paris: Plon, 1959), p. 52.

especially in Asia. While Admiral Decoux was exerting himself, well or badly, to maintain French sovereignty over a Japanese-occupied Indochina by means of neutrality, De Gaulle's National Committee considered itself at war with Japan and sent Commandant Escarra as a delegate to Chiang Kai-shek. After the liberation, it named as ambassador Zinovy Pechkoff, whom the Generalissimo assured "that he had no ambitions in Indochina."

The matter, however, was complicated. What a temptation it was for the Chinese Nationalists, after the Japanese surrender on August 15, 1945, to substitute themselves for both the French and the Japanese in Indochina—especially after the Potsdam Conference had directed the British and the Nationalists to disarm Japanese troops in Tonkin, Laos, and Annam.[14]

Under these conditions, the agreement concluded at Chungking on February 28, 1946, in which France, in return for renouncing extraterritorial rights and making economic concessions (retrocession of the Chinese section of the Yunnan railroad and establishment of a free port in Haiphong),[15] obtained the evacuation of Chinese troops and confirmation of its sovereignty in northern Indochina, appears an undeniable diplomatic success. The Chinese press spoke of a "big present" made to France. It seems that Chiang Kai-shek—who had need of his troops in Manchuria to fight the "Reds"—saw the return of France as, after all, a lesser evil than the installation, with Chinese Communist assistance, of the Viet Minh of Ho Chi Minh, whose ties to the Communists of North China were well known. Thereafter, France returned to her "Asiatic vocation," which she had for a period ignored, to serve as shock absorber or buffer between those greater than herself.

Finally, six days after the Chungking agreement, France on March 6, 1946, signed the agreement recognizing Vietnam as a "Free State, with its parliament, army and finances, forming a part of the Indochinese Federation and the French Union."[16] And soon, left alone to face the Viet Minh, France began that tragic hand-to-hand struggle, that war in which there would unavoidably be two losers: the independence and unity of Vietnam and the power of France. But that is another story.

---

14. Lecture by Pierre Colombani, *Les Chinois en Indochine*, p. 12; Roger Lévy, *L'Indochine et ses traités* (Paris: Paul Hartmann, 1947), p. 18.
15. "Le Chemin de fer de Yunan," *Notes et études de la documentation française*, May 31, 1946.
16. Henri Navarre, *Agonie de l'Indochine* (Paris: Plon, 1956).

FRANCE AND THE CHINA OF MAO TSE-TUNG

The history we have sketched in broad outline leads us to the threshold of a new period in Franco-Chinese relations, a period which, beginning in 1949, proceeds through the Geneva Conference of 1954, the accession of De Gaulle in 1958, and the end of the Algerian War in 1962 to recognition.

Relations between France and China at the beginning of this period were marked by the arrival, at the end of 1949, of the victorious troops of Mao Tse-tung at the Tonkinese border. (In the autumn of 1950, the French Army would lose control of the Chinese frontier. This development would in effect decide the outcome of the Indochina War, for it would thereafter be impossible to carry on the war except by internationalizing it. The Viet Minh would become more and more dependent on Chinese aid, and the French on American aid.) [17]   France, however, did not recognize Communist China when Great Britain did in January 1950. Circumstances led in another direction. Then came the outbreak of the Korean War, in which France took part at the side of her allies. Relations were no longer simply a question of recognition. Bridges between the two, though, had not yet been completely burned. French representation followed Chiang Kai-shek in his retreat to Taiwan, but the first counselor of the embassy stayed at Canton, whence he communicated with Paris until the summer of 1950. Another French diplomat stayed in Peking until the middle of 1951. (Nevertheless, French businessmen and bankers packed up, Catholic missions closed their doors, scholarly institutions were seized, and the personnel of the consulates were expelled.) [18]

France resumed contact with the new China at the Geneva Conference of 1954. The interview of Pierre Mendès-France, newly invested as Premier, with Chou En-lai looked like an important event in Franco-Chinese relations. The Geneva agreement can be ex-

---

17. Same, p. 60; Robert Guillain, "L'Aide chinoise au Vietminh," *Le Monde*, March 16, 1954.

18. Serge de Ginsburg, "Les Relations franco-chinoises depuis la Deuxième Guerre Mondiale," Agence France Presse (AFP), January 27, 1964.   On the types of French persons and institutions in China, see also Pierre Frédérix, *Une Porte s'ouvre sur la Chine* (Paris: Hachette, 1955); Robert Guillain, *Six cents millions Chinois sous le drapeau rouge* (Paris: Julliard, 1956); Lucie Faure, *Journal d'un voyage en Chine* (Paris: Julliard, 1958); Dr. André Migot, *Chine sans murailles* (Paris: Arthaud, 1958).

plained by fear—which France shared with England on one side and with China, the U.S.S.R., and Vietnam on the other—of the "Koreanization" of Indochina, of the internationalization of the conflict. As for China, she seized upon the conference to demonstrate her power —the *People's Daily* of February 22, 1954, wrote that "the convening of a five-power meeting at Geneva shows beyond question that the voice of China cannot be ignored"—and the reality of her independence of the Soviet Union. "In our capacity as a great Asian power" were words Chou En-lai used on May 22, 1954, at Geneva. He expressed views not only about Korea and Taiwan but also on the problem of Berlin. On the day after the conference, Chou praised Mendès-France as well as Pham Van Dong, Molotov, and Eden for "the fine spirit of conciliation they have shown." [19] It seems that one objective of Chou's overtures was to dissuade France from subscribing to the Southeast Asia Treaty (SEATO), a treaty toward which Mendès-France had taken a rather reserved attitude. During the exchanges of views which took place, the Chinese never raised the question of recognition. [20]

For domestic as much as for international reasons, the contacts established at Geneva had no sequel. France was barely free of the Indochinese entanglement when she found herself engaged in Algeria in a way that again restricted her field of diplomatic maneuver. Chinese actions only increased the restrictions. After 1958, China, the first Communist country to recognize the People's Revolutionary Government of Algeria, unceasingly and loudly displayed its sympathy for and solidarity with the Algerian people. The FLN (Algerian National Liberation Front) soon became one of the stakes in the fierce struggle for prestige to which Peking and Moscow began to devote themselves in seeking the "leadership role" among the African and Asian peoples.

The French government continued to regard China as an enemy —much more of an enemy than the U.S.S.R., which, to separate Paris from Bonn and Washington (especially after De Gaulle's accession), showed a certain understanding of French policy in Algeria. But behind the facade of hostility, within the scope of France's intended rapprochement with the U.S.S.R., contacts were established which laid the groundwork for the future. "Since Dien Bien Phu and

19. Statement made at Geneva, July 21, 1954, in *Notes et études de la documentation française*, no. 1901, July 31, 1954.
20. Colonel Jacques Guillermaz, personal communication.

Geneva," stated Roger Lévy in 1956, "the People's Republic of China has showered on France invitations and smiles . . . doubtless because she does not want to remain, economically speaking, under the exclusive influence of the U.S.S.R. and the six European satellites." [21] French political circles and the Quai d'Orsay could not but be attentive to the role played by China in Southeast Asia, from which France was not resigned to complete and final ejection.

From 1955 on, many Frenchmen traveled to Peking with the evident aim of putting out feelers, of facilitating normalization. Let us list the most important of them. In September 1955, a senatorial mission headed by Edmond Michelet visited China. In July 1956, Roger Seydoux and Jean Sainteny were guests of the Institute of Foreign Affairs of Peking. In May 1957, Etiemble led a delegation of sinologues to Peking, and at the same time, Edgar and Lucie Faure were received there for the first time with many honors. In 1960, it was the turn of René Capitant (to whom Ch'en Yi related his great pleasure at reading De Gaulle's Memoirs), and in 1961, François Mitterand. By no means to be overlooked are the 1956 and 1957 economic missions led by Henri Rochereau, for these achieved certain results.

Clearly, a special place on the list should be accorded former Premier Edgar Faure, to whom the Chinese were grateful for having received a Chinese youth delegation at the Hôtel Matignon in 1955. (This gesture was perhaps the source of the hospitable reception he enjoyed in Peking.) One has only to leaf through Faure's book on his 1957 trip [22] to see how much acceptance his ideas have gained.

At one point, he raises the question of why he, as Mendès-France's successor as Premier, did not recognize People's China in 1955. He emphasizes that "the question of recognition is surrounded by an international context: the problem of Formosa, the situation in the United Nations, etc." He could also have mentioned Algeria and France's Atlantic obligations. In 1955 the question was not ripe. Nor was it any more ripe in 1957. But Faure was able to discover on the part of Chou En-lai, with whom he had several meetings, some understanding that France could not break with Taiwan as long as People's China set this rupture as a prior condition for any opening of diplomatic relations. Faure explains to his readers that

---

21. "La Plus grande Chine," Revue de la défense nationale, August 1956.
22. Edgar Faure, Le Serpent et la tortue (Paris: Julliard, 1957). English translation, The Serpent and the Tortoise (New York: St. Martin's Press, 1958).

what France "could reasonably do, though not without taking certain risks, [is] to send an ambassador to Peking, while keeping a chargé d'affaires in Formosa, to discuss transitional formulas relating to the United Nations. . . . Well, what we can reasonably do," Faure concluded, "not only does not interest them but also disturbs them. It would be a breach in the system of all-or-nothing which they clearly prefer, since they know that by holding to it they will one day obtain all." (This situation did indeed occur.)

We note further a statement made to Faure by Mao Tse-tung: "France," he said, "can once again play a role of rapprochement, of mediation. . . . France has a glorious history." This theme has recurred often in conversations between Chinese statesmen and French visitors.[23] Other themes have been added: France's interest in not having the modernization of China carried out "not only without us, but against us";[24] Chinese sympathy for French culture; the presumed coincidence of French and Chinese views on the execution of the Geneva provisions and especially on the neutrality of Laos.[25]

But for all these guideposts to lead somewhere, France had to free her hands by settling the Algerian problem and equipping herself with a conception of foreign policy within whose framework the risks of a rapprochement with China would appear acceptable. It was De Gaulle who effected these two conditions. On the other side, China had to display a policy clearly distinct from that of the Soviet Union. Such a policy emerged at the time of the 1962 conference on Laos (where the Chinese made *appels de pied* to the French), and it became even clearer in 1963 (when the last chances of reconciliation between Moscow and Peking disappeared).

CHINA IN THE "GRAND DESIGN" OF DE GAULLE

A digression becomes necessary here, for I must say a few words about the manner in which the political thought of General de Gaulle has colored French policy toward China. The *a posteriori* justifications given by President de Gaulle for normalization—the impossibility of ignoring this people of 700 million, China's effective inde-

23. Lucie Faure, cited, quotes a remark of Chou En-lai's to her husband: "France, you know, has a great role to play. She can be the bridge between the U.S.S.R. and the United States."

24. Edgar Faure, cited, pp. 146, 223, 236; Roger Lévy, "La Plus grande Chine," cited, p. 110; Etiemble, "Pour un avenir franco-chinois," *Le Monde*, January 23, 1958.

25. François Mitterand, *La Chine au défi* (Paris: Julliard, 1961), p. 32.

pendence of the U.S.S.R., the impossibility of doing anything in Asia without the Chinese being aware of it, etc.[26]—coincide with what had been thought and said by political personalities like Faure or Mendès-France, against whom nobody has brought the same accusations of ultranationalism. In fact, most French objections to De Gaulle's policy, if examined closely, were directed at form rather than at content. The same policy, formulated a little less haughtily, with "more modesty," [27] would have appeared less "shocking."

But apart from questions of form, what is truly distinctive about De Gaulle's policy is its systematic, clear-cut character. For him, realism is not simply to act realistically. He is moved by a particular concept of political realities and of values to be realized. Others placed at the head of French governments would have tried to practice a policy of independence—let us say a nationalist policy. With De Gaulle, nationalism takes on a doctrinal, philosophic, absolute quality.

Many people have referred, in connection with the recognition of China, to "the grand design." Everyone speaks of it, though no one can exactly define what it means other than to have France play as important a role as possible. (Some would say an even more important one.) De Gaulle, who likes secrecy, has nevertheless revealed enough of himself, in his Memoirs as well as in his speeches, to enable us to evaluate the "francocentric" character of his thought. His is an ideology that suspects ideologies, that believes, basically, only in ambitions. "What I want to consider," he stated in regard to the Sino-Soviet dispute, "are the profound realities, which are human, national, and therefore international. The banner of ideology in reality covers only ambitions. I am sure this has been so since the world was born." [28]

A suspicious, cynical philosophy—thanks to which De Gaulle was one of the first Western statesmen to perceive, as early as 1954–55, the signs of tension "under the cloak, each day more tattered, of ideological solidarity" between China and the U.S.S.R.

De Gaulle's own ambitions are summarized, it seems to me, in a

---

26. Press conference of January 31, 1964. On Chou En-lai's role at Geneva, see his talks with Georges Bidault and Pierre Mendès-France. Especially on the division of Laos, Cambodia, and Vietnam, see Jean Lacouture and Philippe Devillers, La Fin d'une guerre, Indochine 1954 (Paris: Seuil, 1960), pp. 231–232, 257–259.

27. Editorial, Le Monde, April 30, 1964.

28. Press conference of July 22, 1963.

remark made in 1960 on the subject of the reform of NATO: "Clearly France cannot leave her own destiny and her own life in the hands of others." His initiatives in diplomatic affairs—his overtures to the U.S.S.R. in 1959 and to China in 1964, the treaty with Bonn, the idea of the neutralization of Laos and South Vietnam, the gestures toward Latin America—derive from a *whole* at whose foundation one always discovers the plan for the independence of France, whose symbol is the *force de frappe*. In this plan Paul Reynaud was not in error in uncovering an absence of "sentimental ties" with the "great democracies." [29]

The elements of the *whole* can be modified, for there is in De Gaulle as much pragmatism in details as doctrinairism in general objectives. The notion of "from the Atlantic to the Urals," an appeal to the "Europeanism" of the Russians, can be replaced by the theme of Western solidarity against the subversive action of the Soviets "reinforced by that of Communist China" [30] and then by a global vision of an expanding world with France as one of its centers of radiation. The essential, the invariable, is the will to create "that new situation . . . which is French independence" and to which "it is for . . . our friends and allies . . . to adapt themselves that there may no longer be the shadow of a cloud between them and us." [31]

Theoretically, this national or nationalistic aim is not incompatible with either the American alliance (of which De Gaulle still affirmed in July 1963 that it remained "the fundamental premise of French policy") or the Atlantic pact (which is "an elementary necessity"). A moderate defender of Gaullist policy, Maurice Schumann, emphasized in the Assembly on April 29, 1964, that this policy is only a variant, a particular mode of conducting the dialogue with Washington on "the best way of establishing western solidarity," which should not "be confused with systematic alignment."

In the end, it was into this ever more strained dialogue that the recognition of China, realized in spite of appeals by Washington for Western solidarity, obtruded. A deliberate, limited act of indiscipline, the rapprochement with China must be examined in the light of more general objectives of De Gaulle's foreign policy. These could be defined as:

29. Paul Reynaud, *La Politique étrangère du Gaullisme* (Paris: Julliard, 1964).
30. Press conference of September 5, 1960.
31. Speech at Basse-Terre, *Le Monde*, March 22, 1964.

1. To make the United States take account of the increased weight of France and of her interests and opinions;

2. To draw the attention of other powers, like the U.S.S.R. on one side and Japan on the other, to the position claimed by France in the settlement of problems which are as much European as they are Asian;

3. To confirm the vanguard, or "leadership," role of France in Europe;

4. To prepare new negotiations on Southeast Asia, concerning which De Gaulle in September 1963 again put forward the idea of neutralization;

5. To exploit, in order to reinforce the international position of France, the growth in prestige accorded her in almost all the neutralist countries and the countries of the Third World—from Algeria to Mexico, from Rumania to Cuba—because of the affirmation of French independence of Washington.

The recognition of China could have been conceived as a measure which would contribute to the realization of all these aspects of the *politique de grandeur* and also give French exporters a good position in international competition for the Chinese market, where the economic quasi-rupture between Peking and Moscow has opened new possibilities. One need not go further and attribute to the French government a desire, for example, to adopt the political theses of Peking or to make France "the footstool of China on the international scene" (something that Pompidou took care to deny to the journalists of the Association de Presse France-Japon).[32] The convergences in the interests and "designs" of Paris and Peking are too limited to speak seriously of the establishment of a Paris-Peking axis or of a league of the malcontents in the two blocs.

FRANCE IN THE "GRAND DESIGN" OF MAO TSE-TUNG

The "grand design" of Mao Tse-tung, if one can speak of such a thing, took shape in a national and international context fundamentally different from that of De Gaulle, though there are, as we have already noted, some points of contact. In speaking of China's national objectives, Colonel Jacques Guillermaz, one of the best-informed men on the subject in France, has especially noted "political and ideological expansion in East Asia and future ideological expan-

32. *Le Monde*, April 25, 1964.

sion in the countries of the Third World, as well as the restoration of China to formal ranking among the five great powers, and finally admission of China to the United Nations." [33]

The leaders of Communist China consider the United States, especially since the war in Korea, the principal obstacle to the realization of their objectives (which, it goes without saying, also include the recovery of Taiwan). Thus they have constantly striven to sway the policy of the socialist camp in the direction of maximum intransigence toward the United States. Doubtless it was for this purpose that Mao Tse-tung tried, after the death of Stalin, and with greater emphasis after 1954, to transform the Eastern alliance into a community in which China would have the right of co-decision.[34]

In 1958–59, Peking must have realized the complete emptiness of its attempts to share in the control of the policy of the Communist world and to obtain from the U.S.S.R. that *force de frappe* which Mao, like De Gaulle, regarded as a means of intimidation and *Machtpolitik* and as a symbol of strategic independence. It was no accident that bilateral talks between the Soviet and Chinese parties broke off in July 1963 at the same time that the first Soviet-American nuclear agreement, worked out without the participation and despite the objections of China, was concluded.

Since then, while still enjoying the uninterrupted protection of the Soviet "nuclear umbrella" [35] and regarding the consolidation of the socialist bloc as a basic premise of its policy,[36] China (a country, in Ch'en Yi's words, "at once aligned and nonaligned") has fought on two fronts to breach the political and economic isolation in which the United States was no longer alone in wanting to enclose her.

The necessities of this struggle restored vigor to China's longexisting attempts to exploit the great and small disagreements between the United States and her allies, especially France. "We have no conflicts with France," Mao Tse-tung had told François Mitterand in 1961.[37] On the same occasion, he emphasized that China would not contest the rights granted to France by the Geneva agreements of

---

33. "Hierarchie des objectifs de la politique étrangère chinoise," in *Politique étrangère*, no. 5, 1960.

34. See François Fejtö, *Chine-URSS, la fin d'une hégémonie* (Paris: Plon, 1964).

35. Confirmed by a speech by Gomulka on April 4, 1964, and Khrushchev's message of April 17, 1964.

36. See Chou En-lai's report on the international situation to the National People's Congress, April 1964.

37. Mitterand, cited, p. 30.

1954, and he referred to the coincidence of French and Chinese interests in the matter of the legal status to be given to the Souvanna Phouma government in Laos—a coincidence "somewhat" confirmed by the 1962 conference.[38]

It was not at all surprising that China should have intensified its overtures after the nuclear agreement of July 1963. The article in *Red Flag* of October 23, reproaching the party of Maurice Thorez for having left to De Gaulle the task of raising high the banner of French independence, did not go unnoticed. On November 19, the same journal justified China's efforts to approach the actual or potential rivals of the United States in proclaiming that such a rapprochement, by dividing the enemy camp, would serve the cause of world revolution. On the same day, the New China News Agency commented favorably on French policy, against which "the American government has unleashed a campaign for isolation."

Since then, the Chinese propaganda apparatus has devoted itself to proving that the U.S.S.R. is betraying the revolutionary spirit by approaching the leading imperialist powers, while China remains faithful to Leninism by driving a wedge between the United States and its allies. One certainly cannot accuse Mao Tse-tung of failing to lay his cards on the table. The first commentary from Peking on the establishment of Sino-French relations [39] saluted this event as "a new important success of China's foreign policy," proving the "blind alley" into which America's non-recognition policy had wandered. On March 7 the *People's Daily* analyzed in searching fashion the various aspects of the struggle

> sometimes open, sometimes camouflaged, which pits the United States against her allies, whom she seeks to dominate. . . . As a great power in the capitalist world, France will never let herself be placed under American tutelage. . . . What France wants at present is to get rid of American hegemony and to seize for herself an equal part in the direction of the Western world. Even while working to strengthen her own position to the utmost, France profits from the difficulties of the United States and conducts intense activity in various parts of the world. . . . With this in view, France pays great attention to Asia and particularly to Southeast Asia, where the United States has undergone successive defeats in its policy of aggression and where France has what she calls traditional ties. . . .

38. De Gaulle press conference of January 31, 1964.
39. *People's Daily (Jenmin Jihpao)* editorial, April 29, 1964.

Nevertheless, what emerges from this analysis, which also applies to the divergences between the United States and Great Britain or Germany, is that Peking does not exclude the possibility of "ups and downs," of compromise between the Americans and their rival Western allies. The *People's Daily* recalls that the countries of Western Europe stood by the United States "on problems putting the fundamental interests of the United States at stake." But it is obvious that China intends to draw as much profit as possible from Western divergences. It is also obvious, or at least it should be, that France and the other Western countries will try to draw profit from the schisms and regroupings taking place in the East.

RECOGNITION: THE DIPLOMATIC PREPARATION

The weight of evidence and of reason increasing day by day, the French Republic estimated, for its part, that the time had come to place its relations with the People's Republic of China on a normal, in other words a diplomatic, basis. We have met with an identical intention in Peking, and therefore on this point, former Premier Edgar Faure, requested to make an unofficial sounding on the spot, returned to Paris with positive indications.[40]

The peroration is well known, as are also the events mentioned. We will not take the time to recite them at length. It is enough to recall that when former Premier Faure, before his departure for China, had two interviews with General de Gaulle, the overseas press, followed by the French press, immediately concluded that his trip was of an official, not a private, nature. It was stated in official circles that "if it does not seem that establishment of diplomatic relations is to be expected in the immediate future, it is felt in France (1) that in the existing state of antagonism between Peking and Moscow the West 'should treat both parties in the same manner,' and (2) that the most effective method of regulating the difficulties in South Vietnam and Laos would be to make contact with Peking." [41]

At the same time, the growing interest in China from an economic standpoint was recalled. This interest explained the dispatch of a mission, headed by Georges-Picot, to explore the possibilities of trade.

Doubtless Faure's mission consisted above all in surveying the ground, to determine whether the Chinese leaders still insisted on a

---

40. De Gaulle press conference of January 31, 1964; also *Le Monde*, February 2/3, 1964.
41. AFP commentary for provincial newspapers, October 19, 1963.

break with Taiwan as the precondition for any recognition—a condition that General de Gaulle did not want to accept. To judge by the result, Peking never agreed to consider a solution which could have appeared to be a concession on its part to the "two-China" principle. There could, then, have been no question of recognizing People's China while still maintaining representation with Marshal Chiang Kai-shek. Robert Guillain has said that the primary credit for finding the way out of this impasse, and for persuading the Chinese to take it, belongs to Edgar Faure. Of course, he found it "by going around the obstacle rather than eliminating it." [42] France would recognize China without promising to break, without accepting the precondition. But it was understood that France would recognize only one China and that it would say so audibly. This situation would then drive Taiwan into initiating the break. Chiang Kai-shek was known to be no less hostile to the "two-China" principle than the Peking government.

If such was the calculation, it proved correct. The mission carried out in January by General Pechkoff confirmed that point. What remains uncertain is how Peking would have reacted if, as Dean Rusk is said to have advised,[43] Taiwan had not broken or suspended its relations with France. A statement issued by the Ministry of Foreign Affairs of People's China on January 28, 1964, insisted that "recognition of the new government of a country naturally implies ceasing to recognize the old ruling group overthrown by the people of that country" and that it was "with this understanding [dans cet esprit] [44] that the Government of the People's Republic of China reached agreement with the Government of the French Republic on the establishment of diplomatic relations and the exchange of ambassadors between China and France."

The intransigence of Taiwan, which announced the break on February 10, saved France from interrogation "on the real value of the expression 'absence of prior conditions,' " of which mention had been made.[45] And in his January 31 press conference, General de Gaulle made a farewell gesture of melancholy elegance toward Marshal Chiang Kai-shek by paying homage to his "worth, patriotism, and nobility of spirit."

---

42. Le Monde, January 25, 1964.
43. See Aurore, January 29, 1964.
44. The possible lack of correspondence between the phrases "dans cet esprit" in the French version and "with this understanding" in the English version of the New China News Agency (NCNA) has been noted by several commentators.
45. Le Monde, January 30, 1964.

It has been asked: To what extent were the United States and France's other allies informed and consulted? Toward mid-December 1963, certain American sources spoke of "assurance that France is said to have given to Washington, according to which recognition would not be envisaged in the immediate future." But this statement was not confirmed from the French side.[46] It is known, further, that on the occasion of the NATO ministerial meeting in Paris, the subject was brought up, and it appears that De Gaulle and Dean Rusk discussed it. On January 14, De Gaulle received Ambassador Bohlen at the Elysée Palace. Edgar Faure, in his *Figaro* interview of January 9, indicated that the United States was supposed to have asked France not to carry out its decision before the coming Presidential election—that is, the end of 1964. "This is one of the reasons why I think on the contrary," Faure commented, "that it would be preferable for us to act immediately, before the electoral campaign begins. Thus we would avoid arousing storms in a very sensitive period in the public life of the United States." This idea prevailed likewise in the thinking of De Gaulle.

"As a result of former errors which should not be blamed on the present authorities," Faure also stated, "the Asia policy of the United States today finds itself in an impasse. An innovation on our part would in some ways unblock the problem." This view, it must be stressed, is shared by many spokesmen for French opinion despite the categorical opposition of the United States to a recognition capable of enhancing "Peking's ability to promote its announced goal of imposing communism through any means at hand, including force and violence." [47] Most French experts whom I have interrogated on this point tend to feel that the establishment of ties with China, the recognition of her legitimate national aspirations, would help "defuse" China's most explosive feature, its *national communism.*

Only experiment will show which is the winning bet: the one that is staked on the incurably bellicose fanaticism of Peking or the one that feels, with Edgar Faure, that "the hour for dialogue is here."

RETURN TO THE ASIAN SCENE

General de Gaulle's well-known declaration on the desirability of an independent, reunified, neutral Vietnam, a declaration which aroused some emotion in Washington, was made on August 29, 1963.

---

46. AFP diplomatic commentary, December 18, 1963.
47. *The New York Times,* January 10, 1964, quoting State Department spokesman Richard Phillips.

Then came the disappearance of Diem and France's "rather sullen" recognition of a new government of South Vietnam. Later, Prince Sihanouk's demand for an international conference to guarantee the neutrality of Cambodia found support in Paris, while Washington remained reluctant. Finally, in April 1964, the *coup d'état* in Laos, which in Paris was believed to have been encouraged by Washington, aroused keen anxiety in the French capital.

One could ask, with certain British observers, if it is not dangerous to present a divided front in Asia. But this question can be raised in regard to all aspects of Western policy.

According to a detailed analysis by André Fontaine,[48] De Gaulle's Asian policy includes: first, strengthening of ties with India and Japan; second, encouraging the will to independence of the states of the former French Indochina, where France retains some influence; and third, rapprochement with China, without whose agreement it would be useless to think of achieving stability in Southeast Asia. De Gaulle himself indicated his views in his January 31 press conference by speaking, in vague terms of course, of "a neutrality which, by definition, must be accepted by the States of Southeast Asia, guaranteed on the international level, and which would exclude both armed agitations supported by any one among them in one or another of the States, and the various forms of external intervention."

These last proposals aroused keen interest in Hanoi, where Ho Chi Minh, according to French experts, continues to maneuver against a total takeover by China.[49] But President Johnson stated on February 3 that he did not agree with them. On March 8, in Washington, Dean Rusk expressed the opinion that "talk of neutralization, which implies merely that the United States should withdraw its support of South Vietnam, tends to undermine the morale of South Vietnam." Rusk softened this harsh judgment, however, by adding that he could envisage the neutralization of Vietnam if Hanoi and Peking would leave their neighbors alone.

Then at the SEATO meeting in April 1964, Foreign Minister Couve de Murville set forth quite explicitly the French government's view that in South Vietnam the United States was engaged in a battle which could not be won. Elsewhere Premier Pompidou had said: "There is, of course, the risk that communism will gain the victory

---

48. *Le Monde*, January 21, 1964.
49. See especially the statements made on this subject by Ho Chi Minh to an Australian correspondent and reproduced by NCNA, April 25, 1964.

over neutralism everywhere, but the longer one waits, the better the chances of communism's winning." [50]

The problem has subsequently followed a complex course. Its final solution will depend on the development of the military situation, the ripening of opinion in the interested countries, and other factors (like the Sino-Soviet relationship), whose exact bearing cannot be clearly foreseen as this chapter is being written.

STUDY OF MARKETS

While economic interests doubtless did not play a determinant role in the Franco-Chinese rapprochement, they did contribute to it. Without seeing De Gaulle (as the Marxists do) as the champion of French neo-capitalism, one can admit that he, as well as his Prime Minister, was responsive to the arguments of the Conseil National du Patronat Français, which visited Communist China from September 18 to the end of October 1963. This mission was the sequel to the two Rochereau missions of 1956 and 1957. The members most interested in finding new outlets were the representatives of the mechanical and chemical industries. It concluded that trade could be developed in all sectors, but especially in the areas of supplying capital goods and engineering services.[51] (In this regard, France was preceded by Great Britain and West Germany. French exporters often grumbled about having been left behind by competitors who interpreted the strategic embargoes of NATO less strictly than the French.) An agreement was reached for the organization of a French technical exposition to take place in Peking September 2–25, 1964, under the direction of Jacques Duhamel, deputy from the Jura.

There had already been a Chinese purchasing mission in France from March 1963 on. After its initial efforts, according to information supplied the French parliamentary delegation due to leave for Peking, studies were made in China to see whether the higher prices of French materials were justified by their recognized technical qualities. Among the results already obtained in this area one can cite the signing, in January 1964, of a contract for the Société SPEICIM to sell a factory for the manufacture of industrial alcohol (butanol),

---

50. See "France Presses Her Drive for Neutralized Vietnam," *The New York Times*, February 28, 1964.

51. Interview granted to AFP by members of the mission on November 6, reports of G. Georges-Picot and F. Crouy-Chanel in *Politique étrangère*, no. 4/5, 1964.

which serves as the base for the manufacture of plastic materials, at a price of 15 million francs. Then in April 1964 a delegation of French shipbuilding technicians announced that the Chinese planned to order in France a steamship and one or more freighters of 15,000–16,000 tons. At the end of the same month, a delegation of the French syndicate of mining equipment builders made its way to China to look into possible future proposals.

The possibilities for the expansion of trade between France and China were examined on April 22, 1964, during a one-day seminar at the Collège Social et Economique. Some 60 industrialists and technicians participated in the seminar. The director of international relations of the Conseil National du Patronat Français, Claude Evain, who had taken part in the Georges-Picot mission, predicted that Chinese orders, in France as elsewhere, would concentrate on chemical-industry installations and means of transportation, for the Chinese were primarily interested in complete sets of equipment of very modern types. Import of Saharan oil, of which there had been talk in January, would no longer be considered by China because of the discovery of an immense oil field in the southwestern part of Manchuria.

Evain also insisted on the difficulties to be overcome on the French side: irregularity of exports and imports (thus the Germans, who were better placed from 1953 to 1958, have had no success in maintaining a regular flow of business) and problems of trade balance and credit. Since 1957, France has had an excess of exports. China's purchases from France have amounted to almost four times her sales to France—a situation which up to now has apparently caused the Chinese no discomfort. But with the increase in French sales, it will clearly be necessary either to increase purchases in China, which will not proceed without difficulties, or to grant her credits. Some thought is also being given to granting credits to African countries in the franc zone and thus to enable them to make purchases in China. Finally, there is competition, especially from the Japanese. At the 1963 Canton fair there were 300 Japanese exhibitors as against 30 French.

This representative of the Patronat Français concluded (in January 1964): We must not, of course, ignore the Chinese market, but neither must we forget that the possibilities of developing trade with the Common Market countries and the United States are much larger. From 1950 to 1962, Europe increased its exports to the United States by 262 per cent; from 1962 to 1970, a further increase of 85 per cent is foreseen.

The visits made to the U.S.S.R. by Giscard d'Estaing in January 1964 and by 18 businessmen representing the powerful Schneider group in April have shown that, while trying to exploit the possibilities offered by China, French exporters-importers have no thought of abandoning the Soviet market to their competitors. The visit of the Minister of Finance ended in the decision to conclude the first five-year trade agreement, which took effect as of January 1, 1965.

If we bear these facts in mind, the sum of the transactions discussed by the Chinese with the members of the French mission, according to François de Crouy-Chanel, who took part in the Georges-Picot mission as delegate of the Syndicat des Etudes pour l'Extrême-Orient, could represent industrial exports of U.S. $200 million a year. Realistically, a flow of U.S. $100 million a year can be foreseen once technical contracts have been signed.[52]

CULTURAL AND DOMESTIC POLITICAL CONSIDERATIONS

The certainly modest but not altogether negligible influence that men of culture, writers, and scientific researchers exercise on policy has worked in favor of resuming contacts with China. In this respect, the action of a personality like Etiemble is significant. Reporting on his trip to China, Etiemble emphasized that "official recognition . . . could not be long delayed without prejudicing our chances irreparably." [53]

All French visitors heard from their Chinese hosts highly flattering comments on French literature and art. Thus, the Vice Minister

---

52. The development of Franco-Chinese trade during 1959–63 was (in millions of francs):

	1959	1960	1961	1962	1963
French exports	190	260	170	210	287
French imports	8	11	78	84	102

The excess of French exports in 1963, equaling 185 million francs, was settled by the Peking government in convertible currency. The major portion of 1963 French sales consisted of wheat, valued at 200 million francs. The French specialized services estimate that in 1964 French deliveries of wheat could have decreased about 50 per cent but that at the same time there should have been an expansion of the volume of total Chinese purchases, especially in the areas of iron and steel, installations, and equipment.

53. *Le Monde*, January 25, 1958.

of Culture, Ch'ien Chun-jui, assured Edgar Faure that translations of Balzac, De Maupassant, Flaubert, and Stendhal were much read in China. "These writings," he said, "give much comfort and stimulation to our workers." [54]

There was also the matter of recovering an outlet to whose loss the sinologues and the missionaries, who had been involved in the teaching of French overseas, were unwilling to resign themselves. Their unwillingness was all the greater as they gained the impression that the desire of People's China for cultural independence of the U.S.S.R. and the Anglo-Saxon countries would favor the resumption of Franco-Chinese relations. One can discern on this point still another curious convergence between Chinese nationalism and a certain French cultural nationalism, both in conflict with mongrelized international culture—the *"sabir international."* [55]

As for the repercussions of the Franco-Chinese rapprochement on French domestic politics, they manifested themselves primarily in a certain embarrassment of the Left, which De Gaulle probably viewed with a look of sly pleasure. For if conservative opinion, through the mouths of André François-Poncet and later Paul Reynaud,[56] expressed its reservations about a policy that would range the United States against France, the French Left, at least its anti-Atlantic wing, could hardly protest in good faith against a manifestation of the very independence it had increasingly demanded. What one representative of the democratic center, Abelin, described as "an adventurous and fragile policy" [57] appeared to a part of the Left as the realization, without its help and against its purposes, of a point in its own program.

It was primarily from the European point of view that one could most convincingly criticize Gaullist diplomacy. Thus Maurice Duverger, while defending De Gaulle's initiatives against "the misunderstanding of the United States," criticized his policy for its "failure to adapt the means to the end. . . . Whether it concerns equality vis-à-vis the United States, aid to the Third World, or even the *force de frappe*, General de Gaulle's policy requires, in order to succeed, that it should not remain a French policy, but that it should become a European policy. But the more likely result of its nationalistic as-

---

54. Edgar Faure, cited, p. 146.
55. Roger Lévy, "La Plus grande Chine," cited, p. 1107; Etiemble, *Parlez-vous franglais?* (Paris: Gallimard, 1964).
56. *Le Figaro*, January 12 and March 28/29, 1964.
57. Speech to the National Assembly, quoted by *Le Monde*, May 2, 1964.

pects and even more of its style is to turn the other countries of Europe away from it." [58]

These objections serve also as a summary of those of the moderate Left and of the Socialists. They, with Gaston Defferre and Guy Mollet, while critical of De Gaulle, also assert their desire to conduct a "policy of national independence" (as Defferre described it in Washington) and to transform the Atlantic alliance in such a way that the United States would treat its allies as equal partners.[59] Integral Atlantism is surely not in fashion in France. Most of its former partisans have fallen back on "European" positions.

It is, however, the Communists who seem to have been most troubled—as much by the recognition of China as by De Gaulle's success among the countries of the Third World. At the first signs of praise from Peking for the patriotism of the French chief of state —praise that coincided with attacks against the French Communist party—*l'Humanité* reacted with humor: "Truly a strange champion of independence, this De Gaulle who proclaimed in his last [July 1963] press conference that for him the American alliance was a basic premise and the Atlantic pact an elementary necessity: by virtue of which the airports of eastern France, especially Toul, Chambley, Chaumont, and Brienne, are nowadays at the disposal of American aircraft for Operation 'Big Lift.' " [60]

The embarrassment of the Communists was even more visible after recognition. Yves Moreau felt obliged to put the militants on guard against the error of "taking De Gaulle for a champion of decolonization and independence. A dangerous error in France itself, as well as beyond our frontiers! It is the policy of monopoly capital, of big banking, that Gaullist power is pursuing." [61] At a meeting of the Central Committee, at the end of March 1964, Raymond Guyot bitterly accused Peking of "not knowing the deeper reasons for the Gaullist foreign policy. . . . The declarations of Mao Tse-tung concerning the atomic bomb would serve," according to Guyot, "as an echo of Gaullist pretensions." [62]

In fact, the anti-Americanism and anti-Atlantism, which the French Communist party strove so hard to inculcate in its clientele,

58. *Le Monde*, March 22, 1964.
59. Statement by Guy Mollet at Rome at the end of his talks with the Italian Socialists, same, May 1, 1964.
60. *L'Humanité*, October 23, 1963.
61. Same, March 16, 1964.
62. AFP dispatch, March 29, 1964.

have turned upon their authors at the present time, when Moscow seems closer to Washington than to Paris and when the "opportunism" of the French Communists is denounced by Peking. It appears, in effect, that the reestablishment of ties with China, regarded as defiance of the United States, has raised De Gaulle's popularity among the social strata which traditionally vote Communist.

The Soviet press is less anti-Gaullist than the French Communist press. "The U.S.S.R. in no way seeks to suppress France's aspirations to grandeur," declared Alexei Adzhubei, the son-in-law of Khrushchev and then editor of *Izvestia*, while on his way to Paris in early April 1964.[63] It seems, in effect, as if the Franco-Chinese rapprochement has resulted, after a first phase of wavering, in a certain *revalorisation* of France in Soviet eyes. As early as the end of February, Podgorny, member of the Presidium, secretary of the Central Committee of the Soviet party, and at the time head of a parliamentary delegation to France, stated to newspapermen: "If at present some obstruction has arisen between the two countries, I am convinced that in the future friendship between France and the U.S.S.R. will be strengthened." [64] Also noted was the unusually warm welcome which Brezhnev, then Soviet chief of state, accorded the new French ambassador, Philippe Baudet. Brezhnev stated that "the U.S.S.R. attributes great significance to continuation and strengthening of its ties of friendship and collaboration with France, a great power which plays an important role in international affairs." [65]

Such a sudden improvement of relations, which also had economic repercussions, seemed a bit disconcerting to anyone who remembered what the Moscow press had written in the month of August 1963.[66] This development can doubtless be explained by the fact that Moscow feels obliged to take account of the position France gained in the Third World through its demonstration of independence of the United States. But other factors contributed: Soviet fear of seeing the rapprochement with the United States, begun under President Kennedy, bog down; Soviet interest in the Gaullist idea of neutralization for South Vietnam; convergences of Soviet and French positions on Laos and to some degree on Cyprus; etc. In any case,

---

63. Same, April 7, 1964.
64. *Le Monde*, February 26, 1964.
65. AFP Moscow dispatch, March 21, 1964.
66. See *Le Monde* editorial, "Rapprochement franco-soviétique?," March 1, 1964.

the establishment of diplomatic relations with China seems not to have diminished the U.S.S.R.'s regard for France.

CONCLUSION

In the year and a half since January 27, 1964, political contacts between France and China have hardly gone beyond the limits of a sympathy which expresses itself in gestures, favorable commentaries, and acts of politeness but not in cooperation or concrete consultations. France and China both affirm their independence, reject the Soviet-American duopoly, defy the test ban treaty, and pursue popularity in the Third World. They encourage and congratulate each other, but the friendship they bear one another seems of a philosophical and sentimental rather than a practical kind. The greatest profit drawn by the two countries from these curious relations, in which there is more form than content, resides in the feeling that the two protagonists have of practicing *politique de grandeur*, of no longer being alone in the world.

Indeed, it is on the level of propaganda that China and France do the most for each other. Each enjoys a good press in the other's capital. The optimism of Edgar Faure seems to have prevailed in government circles. Prime Minister Pompidou has explained, if not justified, China's erratic actions, "which have not always been appreciated," by the fact "that she is not recognized by all and does not feel in her place." [67] The first Chinese atomic detonation aroused lively applause in Paris. "The little Chinese bomb exploded," declared Pompidou, "and instantly China's position in the world was modified. Instantly she got eight columns in one of the newspapers, instantly there was no longer any question of her entry into the United Nations, of her participation in this or that conference, and everyone writes that the moment is near when the United States will not be able to deny her recognition." [68] Thus the "simple little nuclear explosion, as yet primitive, in a Central Asian desert," confirmed in the eyes of the Prime Minister of France the justice of a philosophy which accords to ambition and to displays of power a sharp preference over diplomatic subtleties and moral considerations.

On their side, the Chinese quoted with gratification De Gaulle's declaration in favor of a "European Europe"—that is to say, one

---

67. See his statement in Bombay, quoted by *Le Monde*, February 12, 1965.
68. See same, November 5, 1964.

free of American tutelage. A sentence such as "the determination of world affairs by a few powers does not satisfy the new situation" contained everything Peking wanted, and the Chinese equally relished the conclusions drawn by Alain Peyrefitte from Pompidou's discussions in New Delhi and Karachi: "The three countries . . . consider that bloc politics is obsolete, the return to greater national independence . . . is a factor for *détente* and for peace." [69] The Chinese have missed no chances to flatter French "neo-nationalism." They have shown satisfaction at the development of differences between Paris and Bonn, as well as at the refusal of France to be represented at the 1965 SEATO meeting in London. Of De Gaulle's proposals for a conference of the Big Five (Washington, Moscow, London, Peking, and Paris) to bring the United Nations back to the spirit of the 1945 Charter and for reform of the international monetary system, the *People's Daily* wrote: "De Gaulle has set for the other West European countries an example of daring to defy U.S. domination." [70]

China has expressed a favorable predisposition toward the role which France could eventually play in settling the problem of Vietnam. "We hope," Ch'en Yi said, "that China and France, together with all countries who uphold the Geneva agreements, will contribute in a positive way to the re-establishment and stabilization of peace in Indochina"—this in contrast to the United States, which "stubbornly places a blind faith in armed force." [71] Speaking to French journalists in March, 1965, Chou En-lai added to the eulogy: "France has learned the lesson of colonial wars. She knows that they cannot be won. That is why whenever I meet French friends I ask them why do you not make your American allies profit by your experience." [72] Theoretically the door remained open to mediation by France, mediation which could take place during a new Geneva conference such as De Gaulle had suggested in July 1964. But in practice this mediation, like that proposed by the Commonwealth a year later, was excluded by the intransigent attitude of Peking toward every attempt at a peaceful solution which was not based on the prior withdrawal of American

---

69. Same, February 18, 1965.

70. See De Gaulle's press conference of February 4, 1965, for his proposals and *People's Daily*, February 15, 1965 (reprinted in *Peking Review*, no. 8, February 19, 1965) for Chinese comment on them. It is interesting to note that the French newspaper most frequently quoted in Peking is the official Gaullist organ, *La Nation*.

71. Remarks at a National Day reception given by the French embassy in Peking, as quoted by *Le Monde*, July 15, 1964.

72. *Le Nouvel Observateur*, March 25, 1965.

troops from South Vietnam. De Gaulle apparently does not think that Peking and Hanoi are interested in negotiating. Like most French experts, he is wholly skeptical about the future of anti-Communist and pro-American governments in Saigon, and he feels that the prospect of war with the United States does not frighten the Chinese.

On the question of Vietnam, the French position has come even closer to that of the U.S.S.R. Gromyko, during his visit to Paris in April 1965, obtained some understanding for his idea of conducting negotiations on Vietnam under cover of a conference on Cambodia, but this initiative was blocked by the Chinese and by the objections of the Cambodians. The only possibility left to the Soviet Union was to strengthen its position in North Vietnam by increasing its economic and military assistance. The Gaullist designs expressed by the enigmatic slogan, "from the Atlantic to the Urals," perplex the Soviets. Of course the withdrawal of Americans from Europe and the opening of the West to the East intrigues them, but they are far from resigning themselves to the idea of the inevitable loss of their Asiatic territories for China's gain—a condition set by De Gaulle for the integration of Russia with the Europe of the future.

Chinese penetration in Africa, up to the present, has aroused no official reaction in France. But Paris has done nothing to discourage the diplomatic offensive undertaken at the beginning of 1965 by the Ivory Coast, Niger, Upper Volta, and Dahomey against what Félix Houphouët-Boigny called "the siege of Africa by Chinese communism." [73] The President of the Ivory Coast asserted that in Nanking Africans were being taught "to assassinate those whose eyes are open to the Chinese danger in order to replace them by servile men who would open the doors of Africa to China." Indeed, the leaders of the Francophone countries closest to France had been strongly impressed by the bloody incidents in Niger in October–November 1964, which according to President Hamani Diori, must have been "organized, financed and directed" by Communist China. [74] They discussed this problem with De Gaulle. His reaction is not known, but it can be supposed that he listened to their grievances with understanding. China's penetration in Mali and in Congo (Brazzaville) is not to the taste of the French government.

---

73. Speech quoted by *Le Monde*, January 26, 1965.
74. "The arms used by the rebels had been bought with Chinese money deposited in banks in Brussels, Geneva and Accra." *Le Monde*, February 4, 1965.

Apparently these problems disturbed the good climate between France and China as little as the support given by Peking (through its embassy in Berne) to the small "Marxist-Leninist groups" whose mission is to infiltrate the Communist party of France, which is faithful to Moscow. (The Chinese embassy in Paris, however, would scrupulously avoid everything which might be interpreted as intervention in French politics.) But France's concerns in Africa explain, perhaps as much as its uncertainty about Peking's aims in Vietnam, the lack of haste to invite Chou En-lai to visit France, even though he has made it known that such an invitation would be examined "with all the attention it would deserve." [75]

On the cultural level Franco-Chinese relations have made, according to Chaffard, "a good start." Some 100 Chinese students have arrived in Paris, the exchange of professors was carried out to the satisfaction of both sides, more and more French tourists took the road to China. Abel Gance made his way to Peking to help the Chinese produce a fine film based on the epic Long March, the Peking Opera was applauded in Paris, the pianist Samson François was applauded in Peking, etc. (These good relations, however, do not go as far as the publication of the novels of André Malraux in Chinese translation.)

Finally, in the economic field the outstanding event was the agreement signed in June 1965 with the Société Berliet of Lyons for the purchase of 1,000 trucks. Another agreement provides for the delivery by France over a four-year period of 9,300 tons of nickel from New Caledonia with a total value of 100 million francs. China has also ordered from the Chantiers de l'Atlantique some passenger and cargo vessels, and she seems to want to continue her purchases of wheat. The Chinese pavilion at the Paris Fair, with an area of 3,280 square meters, was the biggest in the Fair, as big as that of the Soviet Union. Some 1,500,000 people visited the pavilion and left in the Golden Book presented to visitors inscriptions such as: "China stands for peace, the United States stands for fascism;" and "The pavilion of the Chinese comrades proves that only true Marxist-Leninists can make their country powerful and their people happy." [76] France on its side will hold in Peking from November 22 to December 4, 1965, a large exhibition of mechanical, electrical, and electronic equipment.

---

75. Georges Chaffard, "Un An apres l'etáblissement des relations diplomatiques," Le Monde, January 28, 1965.

76. Quoted by NCNA, June 1, 1965, from dispatches of its correspondents.

It is certain that the Chinese are receptive to French imports, but their spokesmen believe that French prices are high and conditions of payment often less favorable than those offered by other countries. Restrictive rules concerning the import of Chinese products, which date from 1961, are still being applied by France. Also, as might have been expected, the Chinese exert a certain pressure toward the signing of a commercial agreement and the granting of long-term credits. "In business," they declare, "political reasons are not enough."

Rightly or wrongly, French opinion is convinced that the Franco-Chinese rapprochement has raised the prestige of De Gaulle's France in the underdeveloped countries. This aspect of the problem was analyzed in an interesting manner by Jean Daniel on his return from a trip to the United States, Mexico, and Cuba. Professor Vedel had remarked that the Gaullist reaction to American power was an "underdeveloped reaction." "That is very true," wrote Jean Daniel, "and is perhaps the explanation of its radiation in the Third World." [77] The facts are clear: a cascade of invitations to Latin America; plaudits from Ben Bella, Fidel Castro, and Tito. [78] While De Gaulle enjoys no special popularity at the Sorbonne, the students from Mexico, though noticeably more leftist than those of Paris, gave him a reception. Peking makes no effort to conceal its satisfaction at seeing the countries of Latin America cease to be a private preserve of the United States.

Of course, this intrusion into the Third World, which France promises to help "to develop itself without committing itself to one or the other of the two hegemonies which tend to divide the universe between themselves," [79] caused some irritation in the United States. Even the Yugoslav press, otherwise well-disposed, remarked, concerning one of De Gaulle's allusions to "Latin unity" while he was in Mexico, that the plans of the French chief of state "perhaps exceed the bounds of realism."

Granting these points, could we not interpret the repercussions of De Gaulle's policy not only in terms of rivalry but also in terms of "complementarity"? Jean Daniel implies this position, as does Professor Duverger. Pointing to the difficulties of U.S. policy in Latin America, Duverger arrived at the conclusion "that it is to the

---

77. *Le Monde*, February 5, 1964.
78. See statement by Fidel Castro in same, March 6, 1964; Alec Bebler's comment in the Belgrade *Revue de la politique mondiale*, February 27, 1964.
79. Radio broadcast of De Gaulle address, April 17, 1964.

benefit of the West as a whole that other nations should incarnate, in the eyes of the Latin American peoples, independence and decolonization. In assuming this role, France renders a service to her allies and to the United States, too." Once again, I raise the question but do not attempt to settle it.

No one could deny that behind the *politique de grandeur* there lie ambitions and feelings of rivalry, such as a desire to be repaid for Yalta and other humiliations. We have seen that to be moved by ambition even corresponds to the political philosophy of the person who in actuality devises French policy. Gaullism corresponds to, expresses, and exaggerates a nationalist drive in France. It can, then, be expected that in the immediate future Franco-American polemics will be carried further and that the chill between France and the United States will persist, if only because of France's continuing opposition to bipartite or tripartite nuclear agreements and of the position the French delegates have already taken and will continue to take in favor of admitting Communist China to various international organs and conferences, especially the United Nations.[80]

But in the longer run, can one not suppose that the United States will approach the opinion of Walter Lippmann? He has written: "We, alas, are not free to take advantage of them [the opportunities opened in Asia by the Russo-Chinese conflict]. We must leave the initiative to friendly nations like France and Great Britain, which have not tied themselves up in knots." [81] Powerful forces are at work under the surface in France, and they operate in favor of the strengthening of the alliance—on a new basis. Is it not all a question of proportion?

These, in any case, are problems about which Couve de Murville, in an interview granted to the Associated Press on April 20, 1964, rightly commented that they "should be discussed with much prudence and certainly not in public." We find ourselves, in effect, in the paradoxical situation where good understanding between the allies would require that the harmonization of the interests and views of the partners be denied to the attention of the great press, where it would be mingled with much subjective feeling, and be entrusted to the supposedly frigid rationality of experts and diplomats.

---

80. Edgar Faure confirmed at Kiev, April 1, 1964, that France would vote for the admission of China to the United Nations.

81. *New York Herald Tribune*, April 9, 1964.

Chapter 3

THE FEDERAL REPUBLIC OF GERMANY AND CHINA

Problems of Trade and Diplomacy

BY

HEINRICH BECHTOLDT

The resumption of Sino-German relations after World War II—or more precisely, after the Communist revolution of 1949—was an undertaking completely different from the resumption of relations after World War I. During World War II, in contrast with World War I, relations between Germany and China were by no means completely severed. All contacts with Nationalist China dropped off because of the German Reich's policy of alliance with Japan, but German interests were pursued in the portions of China under Japanese control and later in the areas under the puppet regimes of Manchuria and North China. Indeed, it was even possible to maintain these interests to some extent in 1945. With the establishment of the People's Republic of China, however, the total liquidation of German interests began. The interruption in relations from 1914 to 1918, in comparison, seems like a relatively minor episode. Except for a brief period at the turn of the century, China had always been a commercial problem for Germany, but now it has also become a political problem.

77

HISTORICAL BACKGROUND

Germany did not participate in the overseas undertakings of the European powers which followed the age of discovery. At the end of the 18th century, Austria and Prussia did create a number of overseas companies, but the Napoleonic era put an end to them. Germany first joined the circle of nations interested in China—i.e., in trade with China—in the wake of the Opium War. One year after the Nanking Treaty of 1842, which allowed the British to open five treaty ports in China, the Chinese granted to all Western peoples the same rights in these five ports as the English had, and by 1847 Prussia already had its own consul in Canton. German firms also took part in the China trade which was quickly developing at midcentury. The most important of these firms still exist and still maintain a strong interest in East Asia trade. Favorable conditions were accorded German firms as a result of the treaty between Great Britain and the German Customs Union in 1865—only five years after the Franco-British treaty, which was of decisive significance for ushering in the free-trade era. The number of German firms active in China rose from seven in 1855 to 296 in 1913, and at this juncture the German share in Chinese foreign trade reached 19 per cent of the imports and 28 per cent of the exports.

Compared with Germany's commercial successes, her political and military presence in China constituted no more than a brief episode, although the German war vessels dispatched to the Far East in the 1860s and 1870s also appeared in Chinese ports. Only in 1897 did Berlin determine to establish its own China stronghold, divorced from other foreign settlements and serving the needs of the German navy. It considered the islands of Taiwan and Hainan in this connection. Finally, it occupied Kiaochow Bay and the provincial capital of Tsingtao, but it maintained this position for less than 17 years. By November 1914, Tsingtao lay under Japanese domination, and in December 1914 the German war vessels were destroyed by the English at the Falkland Islands after a naval victory at Coronel.

China did not sign the Versailles peace treaty, but it had ended the state of war with Germany on September 15, 1919. This act provided the basis for the resumption of Sino-German trade. In 1920 there were only nine German firms in China, but by 1927 the number had risen to 307. Germany never fully regained its earlier peak share in Chinese foreign trade—that is, it never again occupied second place behind England and before America and France. Nevertheless, it still ranked fourth behind America, Japan, and England, and in 1937 the German share of Chinese exports reached 15.3 per cent. The end of World War II once more ruined the German position. German property was disposed of, and beginning in 1945, German citizens were transported out of China. Because there was no diplomatic or consular protection, the so-called German Community, the center of which was the German Community in Shanghai, went into action, and in 1949 the Nationalist government provided it with a letter of safe-conduct. It thus appeared that the German Community might have been successful in protecting most German interests. In the end, however, the Community itself had to take on the task of liquidating all German positions and connections.

The exodus of those Germans who had not been transported out of China in 1945 or soon thereafter began in 1950. The steamship "Dundalk Bay" was chartered in Germany to pick them up. It did not have its full complement of passengers when it arrived in Hamburg because many of the Germans in China nurtured the illusion that they would be able to stay on. This illusion added to the subsequent difficulty of repatriating them. By 1954 the repatriation effort had been largely concluded, and on March 25, 1955, Peking declared the German Community in Shanghai officially dissolved. The funeral urns of deceased China-Germans—which the German Community in Shanghai had taken under its protection as the German church was being confiscated—were once more without a home. They were transferred to Germany and laid to rest in a solemn ceremony in Hamburg during a day of public mourning in 1955.

The formal liquidation of the German Community in Shanghai and the transfer of the funeral urns symbolized the end of hundreds of years of Sino-German relations in which the two world wars represented only a passing interval. This period was characterized, on one hand, by the decline of China, and, on the other, by the development of world-wide free trade. Individual and commercial German interests had survived World War II and the civil war in China, but the developments of 1949 and thereafter required a new beginning in Sino-German relations.

POLITICAL RELATIONS

The attitude of the Federal Republic of Germany toward the People's Republic of China stems largely from political considerations. It reflects the extent to which the Chinese foster the Pankow-Moscow policy of a divided Germany, and it is colored by the Hall-

stein Doctrine of 1955. It is further influenced by the China policies
of Germany's allies. Here U.S. policy is preeminent, for in Germany
the United States is regarded as the mainstay of the defense of
Europe. Germany's economic interests, which involve both exports
and imports, are subordinated to political considerations. German
economic circles can expect no greater government effort to expand
trade than political expediency permits. On the other hand, they
hope that Bonn will exploit existing opportunities as much as possible
since Germany's friends (especially the countries of Western Europe)
have begun to do so—although Washington completely refuses to
trade with China.

Moscow-Peking tension first became evident in 1958, and it has
grown more acute each year since. It has focused increasing attention on relations between the Federal Republic of Germany and the
People's Republic of China after a period characterized chiefly by
negativeness. Other factors have sharpened this attention. They
include the indications of a loosening of what has been called the
Pankow-Peking Axis,[1] and the possibility of differences between Moscow and Peking on German policy in general and on Berlin in particular—a possibility for which a precedent exists. The establishment
of full diplomatic relations between Paris and Peking has also had
a significant impact. This statement does not mean that the Federal Republic of Germany wishes to imitate France's action.[2] On
the other hand, German economic circles have undoubtedly been
aroused, and they will not lag a third time behind those of Britain or
France.

All evaluations of the attitude of the Federal Republic of Germany toward the People's Republic of China must be made in light
of post-1949 experiences. If one considers all the problems involved,
the Federal Republic actually has more room for maneuver than other
governments have. During World War II, the German Reich maintained relations with the anti-Chiang Kai-shek regime in Nanking.
After 1945, relations could not be resumed with the Kuomintang on
the Chinese end, and no official diplomatic relations exist as yet with
Taiwan.

The Federal Republic of Germany and the People's Republic of
China were both established in 1949. Up to that time, no postwar

---

1. See Hemen Ray, "Die ideologische Achse Peking-Pankow," *Aussenpolitik*,
v. 11, 1960, p. 819 ff.

2. See Chancellor Erhard's interview in the Italian journal *Le Ore*, February
13, 1964, and his statements during his trip to the United States in June 1964.

German authorities had had the sovereign power to conduct foreign policy or foreign economic activities. Foreign countries had been represented mainly through military missions accredited to the Allied Control Commission. Trade contacts had developed through the JEIA (Joint Export-Import Agency).

At the end of World War II, the Nanking embassy in Berlin had put itself at the disposal of Nationalist China and had transformed itself into a military mission. The two consulates general in Hamburg and Stuttgart had also transferred their loyalties to Chiang Kaishek. In 1949, however, the last commander of the Chinese military mission in Berlin went over to Mao Tse-tung, and his action paved the way for diplomatic relations between Peking and Pankow. The two consulates general in West Germany remained faithful to Chiang Kai-shek. But early in June 1950, before the outbreak of the Korean War, the Chinese officials vacated their offices and residences, and the city authorities received letters announcing that "this office is temporarily closed." [3] Subsequently, the Nationalist Chinese announced that these agencies had been closed in the interests of economy and that the personnel had departed for the United States.

At this juncture, the Federal Republic of Germany would certainly have been grateful if the Chinese consular agencies had remained open, and the contacts probably would soon have blossomed into official diplomatic relations when the Federal Republic gradually began to establish relations with the rest of the world in 1950. Taiwan, however, showed no interest in establishing relations with the Federal Republic. The Allies also brought no pressure to bear on the new German government—probably because they were not interested in a German presence in the Far East or considered it superfluous. In light of the fact that America pressured Japan during 1951–52—in connection with the preparation and subsequent signature of the San Francisco peace treaty—to conclude a separate peace treaty with Taiwan and to establish diplomatic relations with the Nationalists, it is astonishing that John Foster Dulles did not insist on the establishment of official diplomatic relations between Bonn and Taiwan—even at a later date. Although there could be no doubt whatsoever that both the German Federal Republic and Nationalist China were in the same anti-Communist camp, no concrete steps have ever been taken to establish relations between the two governments.

---

3. Information derived from the municipal archives of Hamburg and Stuttgart.

Two developments had a psychologically inhibiting effect. First, of the many ships under Western flags which were still calling at Chinese Communist ports in 1951, only one, the "Mai Rickmers," was captured by the Nationalist Chinese (on April 26, 1951). The German shipping company, R. C. Rickmers, had specialized in the East Asia routes for many decades, and it had sent the "Mai Rickmers" to the Far East as the first ship flying a German flag in those waters since the end of the war. The ship carried cargo for Tientsin and was captured by a Nationalist Chinese gunboat in the Amoy Straits. It was ordered to Keelung, where the cargo destined for Tientsin was unloaded. The vessel was then released. Taiwan has only undertaken such action against a German vessel.[4]

There was also resentment in Germany because the Taiwan government made up its mind relatively late in the day to put a formal end to the state of war. The first move in this direction actually came from Peking. A Communist decree dated April 7, 1955, declared that the war with "Germany," which had begun on December 8, 1941 (with the extension of World War II to East Asia), was officially terminated. On April 11, 1955, the Foreign Minister in Taipei announced "that the puppet government established in Peking by the Soviet Union was not authorized to declare an end to the state of war with Germany." In late May, Chiang Kai-shek proposed to his parliament that the state of war with Germany be ended officially. Although Bonn did not regard a formal declaration ending the state of war as an absolute prerequisite to the establishment of official diplomatic relations with foreign countries, Taipei had up to then rejected the registration of German trademarks on the grounds that a state of war still existed between China and Germany. On October 21, 1955, Taipei announced in due form that the state of war "with the Federal Republic of Germany" had ended. The possibility of establishing diplomatic relations was also envisaged.[5]

Diplomatic relations between Bonn and Taipei, however, were never established. It was not that Chiang Kai-shek's struggle against the Communists and his attitude toward Peking failed to evoke sympathy in Germany. But there had been and were great differences on the Chinese question—first among the Allies of World War

---

4. Ostasiatischer Verein, *Die Entwicklung Ostasiens bis 1951* (Hamburg-Bremen: Author, 1952).

5. Ostasiatischer Verein, *Bericht über das Jahr 1955* (Hamburg: Author, 1956).

II and then among the occupying powers after 1949. In addition, for many years German interest in the issue was too slight to impart any urgency to a decision. Subsequently, the desire to establish diplomatic relations has often been expressed by the Nationalist Chinese at German diplomatic agencies abroad and in invitations to German politicians to visit Taiwan. German reticence has been prompted by Peking's importance—in terms of its relations with the Soviet-controlled zone and, consequently, in terms of Soviet policy on Germany—both now and in the future. Every stiffening of Communist China's position further complicates the central problem of reunification. The Allies and the Federal Republic of Germany have shown an understanding of the problem, and the Nationalist Chinese also have not closed their eyes to it.

At no time has the absence of official diplomatic relations with the Taiwan government reflected an intention of establishing formal and official relations with Peking. The Federal Republic of Germany has in fact pursued a policy of non-recognition vis-à-vis Peking, not merely because this policy is in keeping with the Hallstein Doctrine—which would preclude diplomatic relations with Peking even if there were no government on Taiwan, since Peking had quickly established diplomatic relations with Pankow—but also because until the end of 1962 Ulbricht intensively cultivated trade with the People's Republic of China and maintained his ideological affinity with Mao Tse-tung. Ulbricht did not take a forceful public stand against Peking and in favor of Moscow until the time of the Socialist Unity party (SED) congress in East Berlin in January 1963.

SINO-GERMAN TRADE

The Federal Republic's fundamental political attitude has not prevented and does not now prevent German industrial and trade circles from being interested in export and import trade with the most populous country in the world. This interest existed at the end of the war (that is, even before the final phase of the Chinese civil war), and it persisted after the establishment of the People's Republic in China. There is a long tradition of Sino-German trade, and for decades a number of firms in German ports have specialized in trading with China. Germany has always sought to take advantage of every opportunity and has always demanded the same latitude accorded to other trading nations or unilaterally claimed by other trading nations.

Postwar Sino-German trade developed in three distinct phases. All the problems which arose and continue to arise during these three phases stem from Germany's consideration of the friendly powers upon whose cooperation the Federal Republic depends for its ultimate safety. This fact clearly indicates where the limits to German initiative lie at present and where they must continue to lie. In addition, it must be stressed that the interests of individual business firms must not be confused with those of the German economy as a whole. All responsible people and organizations in Germany well realize that China is not a free and open market and that the volume of China trade in both directions cannot depend exclusively on supply and demand. Yet it is understandable that China trade should arouse constant interest in a country such as Germany, which exports intensively and is so accustomed to imports. The change in Sino-Russian relations has ended the rigid one-sidedness of Peking's economic orientation, and this situation can only enhance the allure of trade.

First phase. Commodity trade between the Federal Republic of Germany and the People's Republic of China began shortly after both were established, even though trading was largely indirect. In 1950, imports totaled DM61.7 million (of which only DM2.7 million were direct), while exports were DM47.8 million (all indirect).[6] In 1951, imports were DM204.9 million (there are no available figures on direct and indirect trade), and exports were DM16.85 million. (See Table 3-1.) Of the German exports to China in 1950, all but DM4.7 worth were exported during the second half of the year. The fact that exports dwindled to DM16.85 million in 1951, however, demonstrates how the war in Korea, which broke out on June 25, 1950, hampered the commencement of postwar China trade. In 1952, imports dwindled to DM73.9 million, and exports to DM11.7 million. These amounts no longer included any direct trade.[7]

In the winter of 1950–51, the United States included the People's Republic of China in the wartime "trading with the enemy"

6. "Indirect" trade in this and later discussion refers to trade conducted through third countries. It has always been a bone of contention between German and Chinese representatives. The Germans have regarded all goods produced in China as "imports from China," but the Chinese have refused to recognize anything but "direct" imports from China as part of Sino-German trade.

7. The presentation of the developments in Sino-German trade is guided by the author's own observations and research, and it is further substantiated by the annual reports, beginning with 1952, of the East Asia Association in Hamburg (see Ostasiatischer Verein, *Jahresbericht*).

TABLE 3-1

Trade between the Federal Republic of Germany and
the People's Republic of China

(in millions of German marks except where otherwise indicated)

	German Imports			German Exports			Balance	
	TOTAL (1)	DIRECT (2)	(3)	TOTAL (4)	DIRECT (5)	(6)	TOTAL (7) Col. 4 minus Col. 1	DIRECT (8) Col. 5 minus Col. 2
		Amt.	%		Amt.	%		
1950	61.7 ᵃ	2.7	4.4	47.8	—	—	−13.9	—
1951	204.9 ᵃ	ᵇ	—	16.85	—	—	−188.1	—
1952	73.9 ᵃ	ᵇ	—	11.7	—	—	−62.2	—
1953	141.1 ᶜ	12.2	8.7	105.0	79.0	75.2	−36.1	+66.8
1954	157.3 ᵃ	4.3	2.7	90.2	43.4	48.1	−67.1	+39.1
1955	192.7 ᶜ	21.8	11.3	109.9	20.1	18.3	−82.8	−1.7
1956	222.9 ᵃ	40.2	18.0	155.8	57.5	36.9	−67.1	+17.3
1957	172.0	42.2	24.5	199.7	173.0	86.6	+27.7	+130.8
1958	245.5	101.2	41.2	681.9	593.8	87.1	+436.4	+492.6
1959	277.8	99.7	35.9	540.7	469.1	86.8	+242.9	+369.4
1960	291.3	119.4	41.0	400.8	337.8	84.3	+109.5	+218.4
1961	159.4	78.2	49.0	123.3	56.3	45.7	−36.1	−21.9
1962	156.4	78.7	50.3	124.5	32.0	25.7	−21.9	−46.2
1963	162.5	86.5	53.2	61.4	22.0	35.8	−101.1	−64.5

(a) Excludes supplies of Chinese products through the Inter-Zonal Agreement.
(b) Not separately reported.
(c) Includes supplies of Chinese products through the Inter-Zonal Agreement.
These were reported as follows: 1953, DM0.15 million; 1954, DM5.76
million; and 1955, DM4.3 million.

SOURCE: Information furnished by the Ostasiatischer Verein, Hamburg.

act. Step by step the Federal Republic of Germany followed the
American policy line. On May 30, 1951, it became mandatory for
German firms to obtain a permit for all commodity exports to China,[8]
and on August 22, 1951, the Bank of German Länder instructed all
the central banks of the Länder (the German states) that no more
orders for payments to China were to be executed. This move was
in accordance with the embargo which had been applied by Washington beginning in the winter of 1950–51 and which had been generalized by the United Nations on May 18, 1951. Not even the deliveries

8. Federal Republic of Germany, Bundesministerium für Wirtschaft, Runderlass Aussenwirtschaft, no. 9, May 30, 1951.

for which Chinese advance payments had already been made were allowed to go through. Peking gave no consideration to the peculiar position of the infant Federal Republic—especially the fact that other West European countries exercised greater freedom of action, at least in executing agreements already concluded. The seizure of the "Mai Rickmers" further checked German initiative.

About a year after hostilities began, the Korean War came to a military standstill, but it was not until the summer of 1952 that the Federal Republic began to discuss revoking the block imposed on payments, an action which would permit execution of the German export agreements that had been negotiated before the U.N. embargo. The block was not revoked until January 23, 1953.[9] By this time, several German firms were seeking to establish contacts with the Chinese through other channels. The International Economic Conference in Moscow in 1952 offered an opportunity to do so. The Chinese delegation wanted to meet with a single German organization for negotiations, so the German firms present at the conference united and presented themselves to the delegation under the name of OSTAG (East, Inc.). A skeleton agreement was drawn up for commodity trade amounting to a total of DM150 million both ways. But the Federal government declined to issue any authorization to OSTAG on the ground that it intended to monopolize West German trade with China. A more important reason, however, was that a firm in the East Zone—the China Export Corporation, Ltd.—wished to be the middleman for OSTAG.

Already in the spring of 1952, the East Asia Association (Ostasiatischer Verein) in Hamburg, which consisted of the German firms interested in trade with Asia, had proposed the establishment of a "China Committee of the German Economy" (China-Ausschuss der Deutschen Wirtschaft) to the Federal government, but the latter had rejected the proposal. Federal Economics Minister Erhard suggested, though, that an "East Committee of the German Economy" (Ostausschuss der Deutschen Wirtschaft) be founded as an organ of the Federal Association of German Industries. This organization would also concern itself with all matters relating to trade with China, for these matters could not be handled at the governmental level. The East Committee of the Germany Economy was established in October 1952. Its founders and members included the Federal Association of German Industries, the German Industry and Trade

---

9. Same, no. 2, January 23, 1953.

Conference (an organization which represented the German chambers of industry and commerce), the General Association for German Wholesale and Foreign Trade (especially its Import Committee), the Working Committee of the German Export Associations, the Federal Association of Private Banking Business, and several other interested organizations. The Federal Association of German Industries administers the East Committee. In December 1952, the East Committee established a "China Working Party" (Arbeitskreis China) with the German industrialist H. Hufnagel as its chairman. The Association of German Machinebuilding Industries and the East Asia Association provide office services for exports and imports respectively. Since the China Working Party of the East Committee of the German Economy was founded, it has handled all contacts between the Federal Republic and the People's Republic of China. (The East Committee, through two other working parties, also handled economic relations with the Soviet Union and the "people's democracies" of Eastern Europe until such time as other organs for that purpose could be established, for the Federal government was unable or unwilling to deal directly with such matters.) These developments laid the organizational base for the second phase of the China trade.

Second phase. The second phase of Sino-German trade was also beset by substantial difficulties. Although the military high point of the Korean War had already been passed in mid-1952, an initial expansion of the embargo list for China was drawn up in September 1952 within the Coordinating Committee (COCOM) in Paris, where a special China Committee (CHINCOM) had been established, and in March 1953 there was a "China Special List." In the summer of 1953 a total embargo on iron and steel was decreed. Toward the end of the Korean War, the China list was almost twice as long as the prohibited list for the Soviet Union and Eastern Europe. The embargo, however, reached its maximum after the conclusion of the armistice in Korea.

The question of payments placed other obstacles in the path of Sino-German trade. Under a Federal government edict, payments for exchanges of goods with non-treaty countries had in principle to be effected in freely convertible currency.[10] Because the dollar was still blocked, only free Swiss francs could be involved. However, the Bank of German Länder made it possible to effect payments with China in sterling even before the payments block was officially re-

---

10. Same, no. 6, September 28, 1951.

voked. Because China was not a "Transferable Account Area," though, each sterling transaction between Germany and China had to be authorized by the Bank of England. This situation constituted a severe dependency.

Lastly, a survey of the difficulties encountered during the new phase of China trade after 1953 must also include the barriers against direct shipping between Germany and China. These barriers meant that German firms were dependent on the ships of other countries. While this situation prevailed, the British government issued a "Control of Trade by Sea Order (China and North Korea) 1953" together with a "list of prohibited cargoes" which British ships could no longer transport to China, and ships navigating under other flags could put into British ports only if they abided by these regulations. The "list of prohibited cargoes" prohibited exports which were permitted on the CHINCOM list, and it was more general than the CHINCOM list—or at least it could be interpreted in broader terms. In effect, non-British exports to China—and particularly German exports to China—were strangled. As a result, German trade organizations exerted ever greater pressure on the Federal government to end the shipping ban. But this goal was not achieved until 1955. On May 27, 1955, the "Hessenstein" undertook a trial run to Shanghai. With the "Hannover"'s call at Shanghai on August 29, 1955, China was included in the homeward-bound itinerary of the German East Asia service, but Chinese ports were not included in the outward-bound service until 1956 and thereafter.

The East German government's attempts to force its way into the trade relations between the Federal Republic and the People's Republic of China were again quickly blocked. The China Export Corporation, Ltd. (CEC) in East Berlin had asserted that it was the German representative of the China National Import and Export Corporation (CNIEC). As the "representative for Germany," the CEC claimed the right to be included in all transactions between German firms and China. In the spring of 1953 the Chinese had agreements countersigned by the CEC. On the basis of a ruling by the Federal government's Trade Policy Committee, though, the Federal Economics Ministry forbade the Central Export Control Bureau to issue export permits if the trade agreements were signed or countersigned by an East German office. From there on CNIEC took matters into its own hands, and when the East German government again offered its services as a middleman for the China trade in December 1953, the Federal government rejected the offer because no one wanted China trade to be merged with inter-zonal trade. After this rejection, neither Pankow nor Peking again tried to pit East Germany against the Federal Republic in the economic domain. Peking had always been interested in direct trade and never really wanted to recognize indirect transactions as Sino-German commodity trade, for such a move would prevent the People's Republic from enhancing its own purchasing power through direct exports to West Germany.

Direct contacts with the Chinese dated back to the summer of 1952. On August 7, 1952, R. Heyn, then the chairman of the East Asia Association, met with the chairman of CNIEC, Lu Hsu-chang, in East Berlin. CNIEC was one of the various trading companies which Peking defined as autonomous economic enterprises under the jurisdiction of the Ministry of Foreign Trade, and it had official representation in East Berlin. (After its dissolution, Peking's representative introduced himself from 1956 on as a representative of the "China Committee for the Promotion of International Trade" without offering any further explanations.) The purpose of the first talk was to pave the way for the interview the Chinese wanted with a representative of the Federal Economics Ministry. This quasi-official meeting took place on October 13, 1952, between the then director of the West-East Division of the Federal Economics Ministry, Dr. Kroll, and the director of the Chinese Trade Delegation in East Berlin, Shi Chih-ang.

In February 1954, the Federal government specifically told CNIEC that the China Working Party of the East Committee was the sole legitimate German representative in negotiations for trade with China. At the same time, the China Working Party submitted its first proposals for commodity exchanges amounting to an annual total of DM200 million in both directions. There were other personal contacts on June 4–6, 1954, during the Geneva Conference. All these negotiations were difficult, for the Chinese demanded extremely one-sided advantages in the terms for deliveries, payments, and arbitration. For this reason the Federal government on November 4, 1954, laid down binding minimum terms.[11] Arrangements for payment by irrevocable letter of credit had to be made, and the endorsing bank must not be located in the Soviet Zone. Furthermore, the place of arbitration must not be located either in the Soviet

---

11. Federal Republic of Germany, *Bundesanzeiger*, November 9, 1954, and Berlin (West Berlin), *Amtsblatt für Berlin*, November 27, 1954.

Zone or in any of the states named in the so-called states list (Länder-liste). In other words, the Federal Republic sought conditions of delivery and payment identical to those which the Chinese demanded for their own sales, and it rejected the attempt to force an acceptance of exclusively Eastern arbitration. Faced with this firm German attitude, the Chinese by the end of 1954 appeared ready to accept identical terms in both directions. Therefore, the first draft of an agreement was submitted to the Chinese on January 24, 1955. This draft agreement was designed to establish the volume of commodity trade and the terms of delivery, payment, and arbitration.

Since the end of 1954 the Chinese had been buying progressively less and less in Germany. At the end of 1955 and the beginning of 1956 this trend was reversed, and direct Chinese imports from the Federal Republic almost tripled in 1956. Yet the decline and subsequent increase were not related to the market situation as such. They were governed instead by considerations of politics and economic planning. Planning requirements, for example, determined the decline in Chinese imports. It was typical, moreover, for the Chinese to begin importing directly from Germany before a settlement on terms and conditions for trade, a settlement which the Germans often considered a prerequisite to transactions, had been reached. In the transactions of 1956, the Chinese accepted the conditions the Germans stipulated—an irrevocable letter of credit and no Eastern arbitration. (This fact demonstrates that tough terms do not obstruct China trade if Peking needs it and that easy terms cannot promote trade if Peking is otherwise disposed.) The Federal Economics Ministry, however, made an exceptional concession on February 16, 1956, when it agreed to Eastern arbitration for certain goods, but this concession did not lead to increased orders.

Despite the expansion of the China trade without an agreement or something akin to an agreement, the China Working Party within the East Committee of the German Economy continued to work toward a formal agreement. An important motive for this effort was Peking's periodic conclusion of trade agreements with the East German government. By 1955, the Eastern Zone occupied second place (immediately behind the Soviet Union) as a trading partner of the P.R.C. with a trade volume of 736.2 million rubles. (In 1955, 82 per cent of Chinese foreign trade was concentrated within the Eastern bloc. The stiff terms set by CHINCOM still obstructed trade with the West.)

In 1956, a few countries began to operate independently without unanimous decisions by CHINCOM—that is, without American approval. For the first time, Chinese delegations visited Germany. A visit to the Hanover Fair in May 1956 was followed by an official reception at the Federal Economics Ministry in Bonn. But the first trade agreement did not materialize until September 27, 1957. It was signed in Peking by Wolff von Amerongen, chairman of the East Committee of the German Economy, and by Nan Han-ch'en, chairman of the China Committee for the Promotion of International Trade.[12]

The agreement was satisfactory with respect to payments (invoicing would as much as possible be in German marks—a provision which was supposed to promote direct trade), inspection of merchandise (inspection was to be conducted before shipment and might be conducted after shipment as well), and a *force majeure* clause (which was intended to protect against claims resulting from the embargo). But it was unsatisfactory in that Zurich could not be named as the sole place of arbitration. The Chinese Deputy Minister of Foreign Trade, Lu Hsu-chang, however, let it be known that neither of the parties to the agreement would be obliged to accept arbitration in any country where it was not diplomatically represented. After the conclusion of the agreement, letters formulating a Berlin clause, which was regarded as a component part of the agreement, were also exchanged. (In 1957 a Berlin clause may not have seemed so significant, but for the current situation it represents an important precedent.) Under the agreement, the volume of commodity trade in both directions was to be increased to DM230 million. The agreement was valid for one year, and no renewal or revision clauses were included. The Chinese did not voice any desire for credits.

The development of China trade at this time was greatly encouraged by two factors. The British government had withdrawn its adherence to the China List of the Eastern embargo by virtue of a statement in the British House of Commons on May 30, 1957, and many countries were handling China in accordance with the COCOM list applicable to the Soviet Union and Eastern Europe. In practice, CHINCOM ceased to exist, although the United States continued to observe a total embargo on trade with China.

---

12. Published as Runderlass Aussenwirtschaft, no. 61/57 in *Bundesanzeiger*, cited, no. 207, October 26, 1957. The Chinese version of the agreement was published in facsimile in *Übersee-Rundschau* (Hamburg), Sonderausgabe, 1958.

In 1957, direct German exports to China increased to DM173 million, or triple the 1956 volume of DM57.5 million. But the leap to DM681.9 million in German exports to China in 1958 (of which DM593.8 million were direct) did not result solely from the trade agreement of September 27, 1957, which after all was only valid until the fall of 1958. It came about mainly because of the interruption in Sino-Japanese trade after the so-called flag incident at Nagasaki [13] and because of exceptionally heavy one-time purchases by the China National Metals Import Corporation. The 1958 export volume has not been equaled since. Exports in 1959 (DM540.7 million) and in 1960 (DM400.8 million), of course, were still significant and far beyond the trade volume envisaged in the 1957 agreement, but even in these two years, a downward trend was already discernible. This fact again proves that China trade is a spasmodic affair determined by requirements within the People's Republic rather than by external supply.

The 1957 trade agreement had to be renewed or renegotiated in the fall of 1958, for it did not include an automatic extension clause.[14] On several occasions in 1958, the East Committee of the German Economy invited the China Committee for the Promotion of International Trade to send a delegation to Germany, since this time the negotiations would have to be conducted in the Federal Republic. But the Chinese failed to reply to these invitations, and in 1958 they began to complain that the volume of direct commodity trade was inadequate. (The following figures show the proportion of direct imports to total German imports from China: 1957, 24.5 per cent; 1958, 41.2 per cent; 1959, 35.8 per cent.) No new trade agreement has been negotiated since. But business in both directions developed along the lines of the pattern set in 1957, and German firms have on occasion agreed to arbitration proceedings in the East. Practically speaking, there have been no critical incidents.

Shortly after the signing of the 1957 agreement, the Chinese let it be known that instead of another agreement or similar quasi-contractual arrangements between the East Committee of the German Economy and the CCPIT, they wanted official agreements at the governmental level. There was no readiness for such agreements on

---

13. First passed on verbally to the author on May 10, 1958, in a conversation with Ch'en Yi, the Chinese Foreign Minister, in Peking.
14. See article nine of the agreement of September 27, 1957 (cited in note 12).

the German side. The Chinese desire for an exchange of trade missions was rejected with the remark that the interrupted talks with German trade circles—that is, with the East Committee, which enjoyed full powers of representation—would first have to be resumed.

Although export figures were high in 1959 and 1960, the level of orders dropped considerably. The end of the 1958 boom could now be foreseen. This trend was typical of what was happening to Chinese trade elsewhere. Soviet credits had reached their peak in 1955 and had not been sizable in 1956 and 1957.[15] Furthermore, Chinese agriculture had suffered a catastrophic decline as a result of the establishment of the people's communes in 1958 and the poor crops from 1959 on. By 1960, Peking had fallen 288 million new rubles behind in deliveries to the Soviet Union, and Moscow had to defer payment of the major portion of these debts until 1964 and 1965.[16] Chinese efforts to find Western trading partners likewise fell through, for no credits could be expected from that direction. In 1963, German exports to the People's Republic dwindled to DM61.4 million—not even one-tenth of the trading volume of 1958 (DM681.9 million)—while the figures for direct deliveries looked even more disastrous. Of DM61.4 million of German exports in 1963, only DM22 million were direct.

Thus ended the second phase in the development of China trade. In contrast with the first phase, which was interrupted by the Korean War, the second phase produced a respectably high level of trade, but it also demonstrated that the growth of China trade could not be expressed by a mathematical constant.

Third phase. There was a new beginning in 1963—a third phase of development for the Federal Republic of Germany. It became apparent in 1963 that Moscow-Peking tensions had been greatly heightened by Chinese frustration at finding themselves subject to Khrushchev's economic pressure and then being left in the lurch when they refused to yield on political and ideological questions. One of the results of these tensions has been the decline in Sino-Russian trade and in trade between the People's Republic of China

---

15. See Heinrich Bechtoldt, *Indien oder China—die Alternative in Asien* (Stuttgart: Deutsche Verlags-Anstalt, 1961/62, and Munich, 1964), especially the chapter "Russian Technology and the Halt of Credits for China."

16. See text of New China News Agency (NCNA) communique on Sino-Soviet trade talks ending on April 7, 1961, in *Survey of the China Mainland Press*, no. 2476, pp. 37–39. The substance of the communique is in *Peking Review*, April 14, 1961, pp. 6–7.

and the "people's democracies" of Eastern Europe. (In earlier times, trade with the latter had been largely carried on by way of Moscow.) Certainly, the Chinese do not want to discontinue their trade relations with the Soviet Union and Eastern Europe altogether, but they have made it abundantly clear that after their debts to Moscow have been settled [17] and their agriculture has been restored,[18] they have no desire to increase trade again to a level which would enable Moscow to use it as a tool for exerting economic pressure.

This situation induced several West European countries to try to revive their own trade relations with China. As far as Great Britain was concerned, this move was a purely commercial matter, for the problem of diplomatic relations had been settled (albeit incompletely) in 1950. In France, the commercial aspect was an element of the political initiative which on January 27, 1964, led to mutual recognition and an agreement to exchange ambassadors. In Germany, both export and import business circles were stirred. Before 1963 ended, representatives of the business firms Demag and Mannesmann visited Peking, and upon their return home they reported keen Chinese interest in a new attempt to develop trade between the Federal Republic and the People's Republic. During the past two years, the Federal Republic has concluded new trade agreements (as well as agreements for the exchange of trade missions) with Warsaw, Bucharest, Budapest, and Sofia, while discussions on the same subject have taken place in Prague. It was only logical that a similar attitude toward Peking should follow. Thus, the Federal government and the German economy—including both industry and trade (that is, both import and export interests)—share a renewed concern with the Chinese problem.

SUMMARY AND CONCLUSIONS

In the beginning, I noted that the attitude of the Federal Republic toward the People's Republic is determined, first and foremost, by political considerations. This fact was demonstrated once again in

17. See "Press Communique of the Fourth Session of the Second National People's Congress," NCNA Bulletin, no. 120318, December 3, 1963. The text of the communique is also in *Peking Review*, December 6, 1963, pp. 6–9.

18. See Edgar Snow's report on an interview with Chou En-lai in Conakry, Guinea, on January 23, 1964. The complete text is in *Die Zeit*, no. 6, February 7, 1964. See also the letter of February 29, 1964, of the seven letters exchanged between the Central Committees of the Soviet and Chinese parties, NCNA Bulletin, no. 050819, May 9, 1964.

the spring of 1964. A basic re-examination of the Federal Republic's attitude toward the P.R.C. by all interested parties had begun, but the Federal government put the subject aside in an attempt to be as accommodating as possible. The decision was made on June 12, 1964, during the Federal Chancellor's talks with President Johnson when Erhard visited Washington.[19]

The basic elements of the German attitude toward Peking can be defined as follows:

1. The diplomatic recognition of the People's Republic of China and an exchange of ambassadors (similar to France's action) is not under consideration, if only because Peking maintains full diplomatic relations with the East German regime. There is no expectation that Peking's relationships with Pankow will change in the foreseeable future;[20] consequently, Bonn has no reason to shift the German position. Furthermore, the Federal Republic gives priority to maintaining its solidarity with the United States, which continues to view non-recognition of Peking as a cornerstone of its policy in Southeast Asia, in the Pacific, and in the world as a whole. The indirect state of war between Washington and Peking over Southeast Asia precludes any change in this policy.[21]

2. A new political element has been injected into the situation by the tension between Moscow and Peking. This tension might change the Chinese attitude toward the Soviet Zone in Germany. It is entirely possible that sooner or later Peking might seek to disrupt Soviet policy in Europe—especially Soviet policy in Germany—just as it sought to disrupt Soviet policy in Asia in attacking India. Since Walter Ulbricht has abandoned his earlier sympathy for Chinese ideology—indeed, he was forced to give it up—there is no compelling reason why Mao Tse-tung should, for example, reject a Berlin clause if a new trade agreement is signed—no matter what form it might take and at what level it might be concluded. Berlin has occasionally been covered in some provisions of the agreements between China and the "people's democracies" of Eastern Europe. In the treaty of friendship between the Soviet Union and the Soviet Zone of Germany, West Berlin was characterized as an "independent po-

19. See the joint communique of June 12, 1964, in *The New York Times*, June 13, 1964.

20. See the statement of the Chinese Minister of Foreign Affairs, Ch'en Yi, made in Peking to Western journalists, *Frankfurter Allgemeine Zeitung*, May 5, 1964.

21. See the communique cited in note 19.

litical entity," but it was not specifically called an independent economic entity.[22]

3. German industrial and foreign-trade circles are just as interested in the expansion of trade with China as their colleagues in other countries of Western Europe, and they speak of the enormous Chinese market potential. But they realize that this theoretically enormous market is not open to extensive supply from abroad. Experience has taught that Chinese imports do not depend upon foreign aspirations or offers. As far as both categories of goods and countries of supply are concerned, these imports depend upon Peking's economic plan and upon its currency reserves. The last are a limiting factor as long as they are too small to cover the deficits left by domestic production. No order from China is a guarantee of stable and continuing business. Each order might turn out to be a one-time transaction even if China has a large and urgent long-term need to import a given product—for example, artificial fertilizers. Nevertheless, German economic circles consider that an agreement, or something akin to an agreement, to regulate trade with China would be useful, for China might then be more inclined to include German supplies and purchasers in its foreign trade provisions.

4. Germans are clearly aware of the difficulties which the Chinese face in paying for imports. Trade with China is bilateral and probably will remain so for a long time to come. Therefore, accounts can only be settled by free reserves, counter deliveries, or credits. For the Chinese, free currency reserves are scarce and will remain scarce. German currency can serve as reserves only to the extent that the quality and appearance of Chinese goods makes them marketable in Germany. Long-term credits from Germany are completely out of the question. In dealing with all the Eastern states, the Federal government has adhered to the arrangements agreed upon within NATO and set forth in the Bern agreement. Recently, longer-term German credits have been extended to East European countries, in line with English and French precedents, but are not to be extended to China. In addition, the Federal government decided in June 1964 that it would not issue trade credit guarantees for exports to China. In any case, people in Germany feel that China trade—even for Western Europe as a whole—can hardly reach such proportions as to expand China's potentials or even to strengthen its military potential.

---

22. See article six of the treaty of June 12, 1964. The text of the treaty is in *The New York Times,* June 13, 1964, and also in *Soviet News* (published by the Soviet Embassy in London), no. 5000, June 15, 1964, p. 159.

5. A sharp distinction is made in Germany between the interests of individual firms and the interests of the economy as a whole. The interests of individual firms are legitimate, but they are not necessarily consistent in every instance with general economic measures and with Germany's economic policy. In the future, German industrial and commercial enterprises will continue striving to do business with the People's Republic—with or without trade credit guarantees or long-term credit possibilities. The obligations which the national economy of the Federal Republic has undertaken vis-à-vis the West, and the European Economic Community in particular, will restrict trade with the East, including trade with China. The increasing number of market ordinances within the EEC decreases the possibilities for trade, especially in the agricultural sector, with countries outside the EEC or the Atlantic area. Thus China can hardly expect to find growing trade opportunities if it offers only farm products for German capital goods or if it insists on barter trade and linked transactions in farm products.

6. The Federal Republic's political interest in expanding China trade might reach significant levels if a general shift of Chinese trade interests from East to West would encourage Mao Tse-tung to maintain his political and economic positions vis-à-vis the Soviet Union. The West as a whole, and the Federal Republic of Germany in particular, are interested in a continuation of Moscow-Peking tensions. Everyone recognizes, however, that the two powers can hardly be played off against one another by the direct intervention of outside forces, and despite their conflicts and differences, they would rely upon each other in case of war. Nevertheless, Chinese purchasing possibilities in Germany and more generally in Western Europe do represent an alternative to China's earlier one-sided dependence on Eastern Europe. Keeping this alternative open might be described as a political imperative, for in critical moments such an alternative might prevent the Chinese from yielding to the Russians and might thus add to the Soviet Union's troubles by burdening it with two political fronts. Increased trade would not create any immediate political (much less military) dangers for the West beyond those which already exist.

7. During the third phase in the development of China trade, the groups and organizations represented in the East Committee of the German Economy have again spearheaded German activities. The East Committee has commissioned research efforts and will undertake further research in the future. The Federal government has

no intention of establishing diplomatic relations with Peking, and
in the context of the present Far Eastern situation, it has dropped the
idea of "formalizing" trade relations with Peking by a formal trade
agreement or by the exchange of trade missions.[23]   However, even
if there are no trade credit guarantees or long-term credit possibilities, German industry and commerce continue to be interested
not only in further business with China but also in an agreement,
or something akin to an agreement, regulating trade between the
two countries.   In other words, they desire an agreement similar
to the one concluded on September 27, 1957, between the East Committee and the China Committee for the Promotion of International
Trade. The possibility of this kind of agreement remains open. As
in 1957, the Federal government would afford the East Committee
the chance to carry out such an agreement, but it is an open question
whether Peking would now be interested in an agreement below the
governmental level. Statements by the Chinese Foreign Minister
Ch'en Yi [24] seem to indicate that Peking would not be interested in
a non-governmental agreement. Furthermore, it would appear that
nothing is more important to Peking than the question of German
credits.[25]   Chinese demands in this area may have been strengthened
by the fact that the Federal Republic did not reserve application of
the strictest provisions of the Hallstein Doctrine when it set up trade
missions in several East European capitals. The initiative of the
French government, which at one fell swoop went all the way to
exchanging ambassadors, might also have had an effect.

8. The decisive criteria for further developments in German
relations with Peking must include an estimate not only of the commercial aspects but also of the political effects of an expansion of
China trade.   In addition to the activities of individual firms, the
East Committee of the German Economy affords an institutional
level of contact which, although unofficial in character, has been
invested with full authority to act. Washington's policy toward
Peking is a still higher political criterion which the Federal govern-

23. See the statement made by Federal Chancellor Erhard at his press conference in Bonn on June 19, 1964, after he had returned from his talks with
President Johnson in Washington, *Wortprotokoll der Bundespressekonferenz,*
June 19, 1964.
    24. See, for example, the statement cited in note 20.
    25. See the report on the visit of Consul Sikora of the German consulate
general in Hong Kong to the Canton Spring Fair, *Handelsblatt* (Dusseldorf), May
13, 1964.

ment applies to Peking. The wars in Southeast Asia constitute a military confrontation (albeit an indirect one up to now) between the United States and the People's Republic of China, and for the time being this situation precludes a radical change in American policy toward Peking. The emergence of divergences in the China policy of Washington and Bonn is conceivable only if Peking makes changes in its Germany policy which would be of significant use to the Federal Republic in its opposition to Soviet policy on Germany. As far as can be seen, there is no evidence of such changes.

Ever since the East bloc ceased to be "monolithic"—that is, ever since Moscow ceased to exercise authority over all the Communist states and over the political opinions of their leaders—German interest in the development of the People's Republic of China has far transcended matters affecting their bilateral relationships. Naturally, there is interest in the potential effects of the Moscow-Peking dispute on the attitudes of the Soviet Union and its policy in Central Europe, but Germans are also asking whether world peace might be endangered in the foreseeable future by the aggressive nature of Communist ideology as cultivated in Peking.

Basic research in Germany has defined the Sino-Soviet dispute as the deepening of a material and political conflict—the sort of conflict which is the more difficult to overcome the longer the ideological dispute continues. This research has recognized the unity of the Russians and Chinese on goals and their differing assessments of the risks involved in Communist aggressiveness. Moscow has more to lose than Peking in the event of war. In this assessment of the realities of the situation, China is viewed as the more unpredictable of the two Communist powers. Its aggressiveness was demonstrated by its attack on India and by its wrath at the outcome of the Cuban crisis in the fall of 1962. Ever since the war in the Himalayas, German experts—and correspondingly German policies—have assumed that China would undertake aggressive actions whenever it could do so without Soviet aid, but that it would not directly confront the United States, for example, unless it were able to drag the Soviet Union over to its side. Mao Tse-tung probably viewed the Cuban crisis as such an opportunity, and this fact accounts for his disappointment at the quick termination of the affair—that is, at Khrushchev's complaisance.

For the time being, because of geographic and political factors, the United States is the main country occupied with Chinese aggressiveness. Great Britain stands second, because of the Malaysian situation, for example.

With respect to the Asian states, German policy rejects neutralization just as it rejects neutralization for Germany. This position will continue so long as neutrality does not assure that Chinese Communists will respect the agreed-upon status of the concerned states. An example of this problem is India, whose policy of non-alignment actually proved to be a provocation to Peking. Another example is Indochina since the Geneva Conference of 1954. The Communists are constantly pressing against South Vietnam and Laos, and the P.R.C. is in every way the ultimate source of this pressure.

India, South Vietnam, and Laos leave no doubt in our minds about what methods Peking will use in the non-Communist Third World whenever it can. Where its instruments of power are inadequate to support direct intervention, it pursues, paradoxically, a coexistence policy like that of the Soviet Union—even though it is conducting an ideological struggle against this policy. This fact accounts for Peking's and Moscow's efforts to repeat the Bandung Conference of 1955 and the Belgrade Conference of 1961 respectively. Other Chinese projects include efforts to conclude border agreements or treaties of friendship with states immediately adjacent to the target areas of Chinese aggression (arrangements with Burma and Nepal in 1960, arrangements with Pakistan and Afghanistan in 1963, and overall policy toward Cambodia). Peking counts such actions as part of the policy of coexistence, but in reality they exemplify the classical method of isolating the true enemy.

Whenever Peking is unable to intervene through subversion or aggression, it employs foreign and technical aid and thus enters the arena of active East-West competition. These undertakings of the P.R.C. attract particular attention in the Federal Republic of Germany. It is feared that the younger generation of non-Western Communists, in their impatience to come to power quickly, might be inclined to follow Chinese rather than Soviet formulae. And it is also feared that the resentments nurtured by the non-Communist governments of the Third World might prompt them to adopt as a diversionary tactic, or as a way out of their internal problems, the policies toward the West which Peking advocates. In its role as one of the most important Western contributors of foreign aid, the Federal Republic of Germany views China's activities as providing a mathematical exponent to the sum of Soviet efforts in this field.

Moscow and Peking are rivals in everything they undertake in the Third World, and there are cases such as India where the current American and Soviet aid efforts have the same objective—namely, supporting Indian resistance to Chinese expansion. On the other hand, the People's Republic of China has joined the Soviet Union as another Communist power on stage in the Third World, and this fact in itself means an increase in Communist activity. By no means do Soviet and Chinese activities cancel each other out. The multiplication of two minuses does not yield a plus in this case.

A number of years ago, a book by Wilhelm Starlinger created a great sensation in Germany.[26] The book renewed the old idea of the "yellow peril" and declared that the population in the overcrowded areas of China would, as if by natural law, eventually spill over into the underpopulated areas of Siberia. There were also responsible politicians in Germany who foresaw a transformation in Russian policy in Europe because of the Chinese pressure on the Soviet Union. However, the so-called Age of the *Völkerwanderung* has long since passed, and there can be no doubt in anyone's mind that the Soviet Union's military power is far superior to that of China. Furthermore, there is not the smallest shred of evidence indicating that Peking can initiate a "reversal of alliances" on its own. Therefore, Germany can have only minor expectations from the conflict between Moscow and Peking. History shows, moreover, that the limited border and territorial conflicts in Central Asia or North Asia have not always—indeed have never once—resulted in great wars which convulsed the world.

The Soviet Union is economically and militarily strong enough to discount the possibility of large-scale Chinese aggression against the U.S.S.R. Therefore, it has no need to take off political or territorial ballast in other areas (*e.g.*, Middle Europe) because of the conflict with the P.R.C. It is probably a source of great satisfaction to the Soviet Union when other powers—such as the United States in Southeast Asia—block China's expansion or support India against China. In such cases, others are exerting the pressure on Peking which the Soviets might otherwise have to supply. They can thus hold fast to their own positions and seek paths which seem to involve limited

---

26. *Grenzen der Sowjetmacht im Spiegel einer West-Ost Begegnung hinter Palisaden von 1945–1954*, Beihefte zum Jahrbuch der Albertus-Universität Königsberg/Pr., no. 9 (Würzburg: Holzner-Verlag, 1955). See also Starlinger's *Hinter-Russland—China*, v. 1 of *Grenzen der Sowjetmacht II* (Würzburg: Marienburg-Verlag, 1957).

risks. The burden which the conflict with Mao Tse-tung places on them is lightened to some extent by Chinese aggressiveness and by the resistance which that aggressiveness generates on the part of the Western countries and their friends. The Chinese Communist regime, furthermore, is hardly well adapted to increasing its pressure on the Soviet Union by compromising with the West. Lastly, if a Soviet or Chinese war with the West broke out, or at least if Moscow or Peking were endangered, the Sino-Soviet alliance of February 14, 1950, would be revived. This alliance has not been completely discarded by either side, and when the danger of a third world war threatened during the Cuban crisis, Moscow and Peking actually stood side by side.

People in Germany have no illusions about the fact that the People's Republic of China poses a more difficult problem than any of the other Eastern powers. They realize that it seizes every opportunity to sabotage the Soviet policy of relieving tensions in order to force the Soviet Union to adopt the Chinese line. Because no one can foretell how long the Soviet Union will hold fast to a realistic evaluation of the world situation—our thoughts turn here to the Cuban crisis—the formulae and methods of the People's Republic of China must always be considered the potential general line of world communism. This peril is always imminent in space and time for the Federal Republic of Germany.

Chapter 4

CANADA AND CHINA
The Dilemmas of a Middle Power

BY

JOHN W. HOLMES *

Canada, like the United States, has not recognized Communist China, but its attitudes and policies have differed considerably from those of its major ally. Whereas the United States has apparently remained firm in its original conviction, Canadian policy may be seen as a persistent but still frustrated effort to realize intentions of a different order.

GOVERNMENT POLICY: A SUMMARY

The original Canadian intention was, without undue haste and after attention to formalities, to recognize the new authorities in Peking. This act was considered at the Conference of Commonwealth Foreign Ministers in Colombo in January 1950, and it was to have been taken, along with most Commonwealth governments, in accordance with the British tradition of recognizing governments, whether one likes them or not, which successfully exercise their authority—an attitude toward recognition which Canada has preferred to more recent heresies. It was not intended as an act of

---

* The author is deeply indebted to Miss Maureen Appel for research on this subject. Her extensive analysis is contained in an unpublished thesis, *Canadian Attitudes to Communist China*, submitted to the Faculty of Graduate Studies and Research of McGill University and dated August 1964.

approval; Canadians have not been inclined to approve Communist governments anywhere. The new government in Peking did, however, profit at first from Canadian disapproval of the Kuomintang, an attitude reflected in the press of the time and strongly held by Canadian diplomats in China. Although the Chinese Nationalists were allies during the war, there had been little close contact with them. Canadians had been neither personally nor emotionally engaged in the postwar effort to bolster the Kuomintang, and there was none of the feeling of having "lost China" which deeply affected American thinking. The Canadian ambassador remained in Nanking rather than follow the Nationalists, and the mission was maintained there under the Communists until February 1951. The Canadian consulate general remained in Shanghai until the end of 1951. No Canadian diplomatic mission has ever been set up in Taipei, although the Chinese Nationalist embassy has been maintained in Ottawa.

There is little doubt that the Canadian intention to recognize the new government and exchange diplomatic representatives would have been fulfilled if the Korean War had not interrupted the process in June 1950. The government was also moving toward favoring Peking representation in the United Nations. The delay can be attributed to caution induced by the increasingly resolute American position and by some resistance within the country, especially from the Conservative opposition, but primarily to an anxiety to wait and see how the dust settled. Once the Korean War took place, the situation was never the same again. The United States became so deeply committed against Peking that recognition by any of its allies was bound to appear more unfriendly than such a move had seemed when the British, Dutch, and others acted before June 1950.

Official Ottawa did not necessarily abandon its original view of the situation. It recognized that while not only American but also Canadian troops were fighting the Chinese, any gesture of this kind was out of the question. As the war moved into the truce stage, however, the difference in the Canadian attitude toward Asian communism became apparent. Canada resisted any effort to extend the Korean War to China and the view that the fighting must be pursued to unconditional surrender of the Communists—out of a basic conviction that the Peking regime was an enormous fact of Asia we would have to learn to live with. There was never any doubt that the Chinese had to be prevented from imposing their will on their neighbors, although there was an inclination to see Chinese actions as the result of defensive as well as offensive impulses. After the fighting had stopped, Canadian official statements and public opinion again began to reflect dissatisfaction with Canada's anomalous position vis-à-vis the Chinese "government"—even though, as a result of Chinese aggressiveness, the Peking regime was regarded less tolerantly than in 1949–50. Canadians were disposed to negotiate *de facto* with Peking representatives, and they became involved in negotiations which went on in the United Nations over the truce and over such questions as the release of prisoners.[1] At the Korea Conference in Geneva in 1954, Canadians, unlike the Americans, had personal contact with the Communist Chinese. The relatively independent position on Asian matters which they expressed in Geneva probably accounted for their selection by the truce signatory powers, including Peking but not Washington, as the most acceptable Western power to serve on the supervisory commissions set up at that time for the three states of Indochina. It was a role which, imposing objectivity if not neutrality, has conditioned Canadian diplomacy in Asia ever since.

The Chinese, after negotiations in Geneva in 1954, returned the last Canadian prisoner of war and in other ways displayed a more amenable disposition. They finally agreed to an exchange of diplomats with the British, and Ottawa was again ready to consider altering the status quo. On his return from an Asian tour in 1954, Prime Minister St. Laurent had struck what became a familiar theme in Canadian pronouncements—that although it was not yet time to act, it would be unwise to make commitments which would make recognition impossible in due course. In August 1955, Lester Pearson, the Secretary of State for External Affairs, went further by suggesting "that the time is coming, and soon, when we should have another and searching look at the problem." Public opinion was now more divided than it had been before the Korean War, but there was little of the bitterness on the issue so notable on the other side of the border during this period. McCarthyism did not intimidate Canadians but rather stimulated those who wanted an independent China policy.

Whenever it looked as if the government might act, bold steps were discouraged either by Chinese attacks on the offshore islands

---

1. Lester Pearson, for instance, was one of a group of three, along with the President of the U.N. General Assembly, Nasrollah Entezam of Iran, and Sir Benegal Rau of India, delegated to contact the Peking representatives in December 1950.

(and later on Tibet and India) or by the biennial imminence of
an American election. Canadians have not been disposed to take
steps which would warm up the China issue for an American campaign, especially if Canada were to figure as villain. The emphasis
in official pronouncements shifted, depending upon the latest Chinese behavior or upon the private views of the spokesman, between
a stress on the reasons for recognition and a stress on the reasons
against it, but there was little clear-cut change in the Canadian position under the Liberals up to 1957 or the Conservatives from 1957
to 1963.

During this period, Canada did not, in spite of its variant approach, deviate from the United States on the main issues. It maintained diplomatic relations with the Nationalists and almost always
voted with the United States on Chinese representation in the United
Nations.

On intercourse with China, however, Canadian policy has been
different. The danger of losing contact with the Chinese is a theme
more highly stressed by Canadian spokesmen than fear of exposure
to Communist propaganda. Canadians who can get visas have been
free, as far as their own government is concerned, to travel to China,
and a good many, including not only journalists but also leaders of
business and finance, members of Parliament, one Cabinet minister,
and one former Cabinet minister, have taken advantage of the opportunity. In late 1964 a Canadian agricultural delegation of 32 visited
China along with a small medical delegation. These were not composed of "fellow-travelers." So many impeccable capitalists have
made the trip that the traveler does not need to fear for his respectability. On two occasions agreements have been reached for reciprocal admission of journalists. The Toronto *Globe and Mail* for the
second time has a correspondent in Peking, and the Canadian government has declared its willingness to receive the same number of Chinese correspondents as there are Canadian correspondents in China.
A correspondent of the New China News Agency arrived in Canada
in July 1964. In 1964–65 two well-known Canadian journalists were
allowed to visit China. The reports of Mark Gayn of *The Toronto
Daily Star* were widely syndicated in the United States, Europe, and
Japan—as had been those of other Canadian correspondents, who
profited greatly from the inability of American journalists to make
the trip. The Peking Opera has performed in Canada, and Peking
officials have visited Canada to discuss trade and other matters. Can-

ada has been willing to trade with Communist China in nonstrategic
items and has found in recent years a market of major economic and
political importance for its grain. The first important trade agreements, made by the Conservative government, were widely credited
with keeping the Prairie Provinces in the Conservative fold in the
1963 election when the Conservatives were losing power in other parts
of the country. Whether this evaluation is true or not, none of the
major political leaders oppose trade with China at the present time,
and there is little evidence of opposition in the country. It is a recent
factor which has affected Canadian attitudes on the general issues
of China policy.

STRATEGIC CONSIDERATIONS

What differentiates the Canadian perspective on China from
that of the United States is that Canada has been much less directly
involved and therefore less emotionally engaged. This statement
does not mean that Canada's is an irresponsible position. It is clear
from the constant debate in the press and Parliament that Canadians
do on the whole recognize the importance of the Chinese fact in the
world and are deeply concerned to find a rational way of dealing with
it. They have been inclined, however, to doubt whether the Communist government could be overthrown and have persistently questioned the wisdom of isolating China.[2] They have never doubted
on which side they would stand in a military confrontation between
the United States and China. As military allies of the United States,
Canadians take for granted that they would be involved in any U.S.-
China hostilities larger than localized fighting on the periphery.
Nevertheless, the alliance is specifically directed at the Atlantic theater and continental defense, and Canada has no direct alliance obligations in the Far East. Canada is not a member of SEATO. Although it is a Pacific country, it has traditionally looked toward
Europe, and since the last war it has left Pacific Ocean defense to its
all-powerful neighbor. Participation in the Korean War was looked
upon as an obligation to the United Nations. Leaving the Far East

---

2. This danger is constantly stressed by the present Secretary of State for
External Affairs. On May 22, 1964, Mr. Martin expressed the hope that "the
decision of France to establish diplomatic relations with Peking will help to reduce
Communist China's continuing isolation." At the same time, he blamed the
Chinese for deliberately making contacts difficult and imposing conditions on those
prepared to enter into relations with them.

to the United States, as well as to Britain and Australia, reflects not a rejection of interest in that area or a failure of responsibility, but a rational division of functions. It is unwise for any smaller ally to try to cover all fronts in which it recognizes an interest. Because the China problem has not involved Canada in important military decisions, China has not been a subject of intense political feeling. Government and opposition have consistently criticized each other for their positions on China, but it has been a pot and kettle debate. A detached and historical approach to revolutionary events in China has been easier for Ottawa than Washington.

Furthermore, the Chinese Communists have until recently paid little attention to Canada and rarely, therefore, exacerbated specifically Canadian feelings. As is customary in Communist countries, Canada has been identified as an unfortunate victim of U.S. pressure. There was evidence in 1964 and 1965 that Peking may be showing more interest in Canada and seeking to identify it as part of the intermediate zone of countries, like Japan, in which the people are struggling against U.S. domination. A *Red Flag* article in July 1964 presented this point of view and added that Canadians had been inspired by the Cuban example. The obvious interest shown by Canadians from time to time in establishing relations with China had, heretofore, failed to arouse the interest of Peking; nor did Peking bother to offer favors in return for Canadian defection. This new classification, however, may have altered Chinese policy toward Canada. Peking of late has been going out of its way to be more considerate to Canadians. In the summer of 1964, for example, it allowed a Canadian Broadcasting Corporation television crew unusual, although by no means total, freedom to make film in the country.

Concern for the capacity of the countries of South Asia to resist Chinese pressures has been an important reason for Canadian caution in recognizing Peking. It was the decisive argument advanced frequently by Howard Green for not changing Canadian policy during his period as Conservative Secretary of State for External Affairs, 1959–63. Even the Liberal Secretary of State, Paul Martin, in his statement of May 22, 1964, suggesting the need for reconsideration, added that "the effect on the stability of countries in Southeast Asia must be assessed with care." Canada and the United States, however, tended to approach this question from different directions. Whereas in the United States concern for "free Asia" meant—until recently at least—Korea, Taiwan, South Vietnam, Thailand, and the Philippines, for Canada the term "free Asia" conjured up Commonwealth Asia: India, Pakistan, and Ceylon. Washington said it was listening to the voice of "free Asia" when it refused to deal with Peking, but to Canadians "free Asia" was insisting on the unwisdom of American policy toward China. During the 1950s, Canadian policy on Asian questions was considerably influenced by Indian arguments. Commonwealth voices from that part of the world were, however, not entirely in unison. The Australians, whose foreign policy in Asia has been more closely aligned than Canada's to that of the United States, usually encouraged a firm stand against the Chinese, and so did the Malaysians when they found their voice in the late 1950s. The Chinese assault on India naturally affected Canadian public opinion considerably, and military assistance was provided. There was some questioning in Canada as to whether it was proper to sell wheat to a nation assaulting a Commonwealth partner, but as the assault did not alter the Indians' own position on recognition, its effect on Canadian policy on that subject has been indecisive. Ten years of involvement in the realities of Laos and Vietnam have made official Canada mindful of the persistence of Communist pressure in South Asia. Fear of the consequences of the moral victory which China would gain in South Asia, through a collapse of the American front of non-recognition, has been a powerful factor in dissuading Canada from altering its position—even though Canadians may not be convinced of the logic behind nonrecognition as a defense against this pressure.

That an aggressive Communist China threatens Canadian interests is assumed by the vast majority and by the government, but this threat is viewed in terms of long-range shifts in the balance of power rather than in the context of bases and military movements. Canadian governments, both Liberal and Conservative, explicitly refused to accept obligations over Quemoy and Matsu, other than what they might incur as members of the United Nations, and they used what influence they had to persuade the United States to get out of these commitments. As for Taiwan, there was no practical alternative to accepting the American evaluation of the island as essential to American strategy, although its strategic importance is often questioned. From the beginning, there has been little sympathy with the Nationalists' ambitions to reconquer the mainland and strong support for all measures by Washington to leash Chiang Kai-shek. Canada has not been a member of SEATO, because of both geography and the incompatibility of membership with its duties in the Indochina commissions, but it has always recognized the importance and the legitimacy of this association, of which not only its close neighbor but also four of its Commonwealth partners are members. Canada sees itself, on account of its remoteness and its lack of special interests in Asia, as having been assigned a special function in the most critical part of that continent, the Indochinese peninsula. This function is different from, but not incompatible with, the interests of its allies more directly involved—although it has been considered incompatible with active Canadian participation in military operations in Vietnam.

THE "TWO-CHINA" ISSUE

The strategic position of Taiwan and the pretensions of the Nationalists may be viewed with skepticism, but the existence of Taiwan remains the heart of the Canadian dilemma on China policy. There is little feeling of obligation to Chiang Kai-shek, although some voices are raised in defense of the island regime—often the voices of journalists or members of Parliament who have visited Taiwan, or members of the small and not very influential community of Chinese-Canadians. Few Canadians, however, can accept the idea that the unwilling Taiwanese should be handed over to the Communist regime. For most Canadians, this issue is the critical barrier to recognition and acceptance of Peking into the United Nations. This attitude is based not on an obligation to the Nationalists but on the right of self-determination. Canadian concern is for the people of Taiwan rather than the Nationalist government.

In earlier years, the status of Taiwan had not appeared a serious problem, and the position of the Nationalist government had seemed less important because it was not expected to survive. The British recognized the Peking regime without committing themselves on Taiwan, and it was assumed that other countries could do likewise. Later, however, the Chinese, sometimes in statements made to Canadian visitors, gave the strong impression they would reject any offer of recognition that was not accompanied by a formal acceptance of Taiwan as part of China. It has been a difficult sticking-point. Canada would appear ridiculous if it made the bold gesture of breaking with the United States on this issue only to be snubbed by Peking. On the other hand, to declare solemnly that Taiwan belonged to the Communists would be not only an act contrary to Canadian views about what is proper, but also an egregious gesture from a lesser power

with little right to dispose of Asian territory. Some staunch advocates of recognition charge that the government has used this problem
as an excuse for timidity. Even if that charge is sustained, however,
the problem of Taiwan is not solved.

The situation has been considerably affected by the French recognition of Peking early in 1964. In Canada, the French decision was
widely regarded as sensible, although General de Gaulle's disregard
for American feelings was as widely deplored—at least in English-
speaking Canada. The French attempted to establish a position
which Canadians had not contemplated, that of recognizing both
Chinese governments (although the French expected, of course, that
the Nationalists would break with them, as the Nationalists did). It
had always been assumed in Ottawa that recognition of Peking would
be accompanied by a withdrawal of recognition from the Nationalists
as the government of China even though Canada might eventually
recognize an independent government of Taiwan. What Ottawa has
wanted to avoid is a situation in which Peking would require it to
accompany recognition with a declaration on the status of Taiwan.
Canada has always preferred what is generally called a "two-China"
policy but which Mr. Martin calls a "one-China, one-Formosa solution." Even Mr. Green, although opposed to recognition, expressed
the hope "that something along the two-China line can be worked
out." [3] If some reasonable formula could be found for recognizing
both the Peking regime, as the government of mainland China, and
an independent government of Taiwan and seating them both in the
United Nations, there is little doubt that the Canadian government
would accept it and that the Canadian public would overwhelmingly
approve. The formula remains, however, as difficult as ever to establish. In the meantime, it is not inconceivable that Canada would,
after rather than before an American election, recognize the Peking
regime as the government of China and withdraw its recognition from
the Taipei regime as the "government of China" but seek, as the
British have done, to maintain *de facto* relations with the inhabitants
of Taiwan until such time as they can be recognized as an entity in
the world. Peking would have to be willing, however, not to tie the
question of the status of Taiwan, as distinct from the status of the
Nationalist government, to the act of recognition. In the case of
France, the Communists seem not to have demanded a declaration

---

3. Canadian Broadcasting Corporation, on the program *Inquiry*, November
14, 1961.

of this kind, and the precedent has, of course, been carefully studied in Ottawa.

The separate questions of diplomatic recognition and seating in the United Nations have been argued in Canada in parallel and with considerable confusion of issues. A principal advantage seen in the recognition of Peking is that it would enable Canada to deal directly with the Chinese on trade and consular matters and to establish independent sources of information on what is going on in the country.[4] Suspicion of information about China from American sources is prevalent. The British experience, however, convinced Canadians that these diplomatic advantages would be only partially achieved unless Canada, like its Scandinavian friends, was prepared to support the seating of Peking in the United Nations. Later, it was generally acknowledged that the Chinese would not accept recognition from any country that did not extend the logic of recognition to its U.N. policy. To oppose U.S. policy in the United Nations would probably have more distressing consequences in Washington than the act of diplomatic recognition, which would not decisively affect the world position of Peking—unless, of course, action by Canada were followed by similar action by Belgium, Australia, and powers of like stature which keep in close touch with Canada on the issue. At times, it has seemed as if action in the United Nations might be considered first, and at other times action on recognition has seemed the advisable first step. The debate on the logical progression, thus, has continued with no fixed conclusions. The need to face up to both issues at once has undoubtedly reinforced the inclination to procrastinate. There has never been any serious suggestion in Canada that the country should withdraw from the United Nations if Peking is admitted. Canada—as its leadership of the 1955 effort to bring about the admission of all outstanding applicants, Communist and non-Communist, illustrates—has favored a universalist approach to the United Nations, for it feels that it is better to have countries subject to the beneficial influences of the organization than free, as outlaws, to do greater mischief. It was, incidentally, Nationalist China's attempt to veto this 1955 Canadian initiative which hardened Ottawa's attitude toward its claims.

---

4. Among the questions which agitated Canadians in the earlier years, and an issue much involved in the arguments on relations with China, was compensation for the so-called Ming Sung ships provided by Canada to the Nationalist government before 1949 and appropriated by the new regime.

TRADE

The question of trade has been of increasing importance in the Canadian attitude toward China. The fact that the British profited little commercially from recognition of Peking dampened enthusiasm in the earlier years. Later, when there were signs that the Chinese market was opening up, it was noted that countries like West Germany seemed to do as well commercially as those which had established diplomatic relations. This belief has been reinforced by the subsequent Canadian experience of large wheat deals arranged through agents in Hong Kong. The Canadian trade commissioner in Hong Kong not only deals with Communist agents there but also makes periodic expeditions to Peking, Shanghai, and Canton.

Up until 1960, Canada maintained a small trade, which roughly balanced, with Communist China. Canada exported industrial products such as steel, aluminum, copper, nickel, zinc, and magnesium as well as pharmaceuticals and medical equipment, wood pulp, and lumber. It imported a variety of Chinese specialties such as shelled walnuts, furs, and textiles. In 1959, Canadian sales to China amounted to Can.$4,370,000, and Chinese sales to Canada totaled Can.$4,840,000. By 1961, Chinese purchases of industrial products had dropped greatly. In that year, however, as a result of the agricultural crisis, large purchases of food grains were made. Canada's exports to China were valued at Can.$13 million in 1960, Can.$125 million in 1961, Can. $147 million in 1962, Can.$105 million in 1963, and Can.$136 million in 1964. In the last three years, the exports have consisted almost entirely of food grains. The fact that China has engaged in this trade out of desperate necessity is recognized in Ottawa, but cautious doubts about its permanence have been giving way to hope that China's need for Canadian foodstuffs may be permanent—because of the enormity of its population and perhaps also because of its recent inclination to be nice to Canada.

Visions of vast Asian markets have constantly intrigued Canada, a country much more dependent on world trade than the United States is. The sharp difference between American and Canadian views on trading with Communist countries, whether it be with China or Cuba, is based on differing estimates of the tactical value of embargoes, but it is conditioned by the fact that the United States can much more easily afford to sacrifice markets to strategy than Canada can. The American argument that Canada is sacrificing principles for commercial gain is likely to be answered by the Canadian view that it is immoral to withhold necessities of life from peoples whose governments one does not like. Neither view should be regarded as completely cynical. The hope for markets in China has affected the views of the Canadian business community, who might otherwise have been expected to share the conservative views on China policy of their associates across the border. There is, of course, opposition to this trade from such vested interests as the textile industries, but the gravest threat to the trade is the fact that reciprocal imports from China are almost impossible to achieve. In 1963, imports from China amounted to little more than Can.$5 million, although this figure rose to Can.$7.9 million in the first 10 months of 1964. The Chinese have indicated that this imbalance cannot continue. But there is little in China that Canadians want to buy, and the government cannot force them to do so.

The fact that Canadian trade has proved possible without recognition might have removed one of the stronger arguments for taking the diplomatic step. On the other hand, it has strengthened the view, now frequently heard, that it is absurd or even unjustifiable to conduct profitable business with a government the existence of which one officially ignores. A slight complication is that there is some trade with Taiwan which might well be lost entirely if recognition were shifted. Exports to Taiwan in 1963 were under Can.$4 million, and imports nearly Can.$6 million—amounts which are close to figures for trade with mainland China before these were multiplied by the recent grain sales. Present exports to Communist China may prove to be a passing phenomenon, but they have probably been the decisive factor in creating what at last seems to be a solid majority opinion in favor of recognizing the Peking regime.

PUBLIC OPINION

Canadian public concern has been largely over the international implications rather than the domestic aspects of Chinese communism. The latter are judged for the most part in relative rather than absolute terms. The anthill quality of the new China is regarded with antipathy rather than with religious horror. It is assumed that life in Asia is everywhere grim and efforts to do something about it are bound to be harsh. These attitudes are to a considerable extent conditioned by the views of those Canadians who know something about

China. There are in Canada, however, few "old China hands" except missionaries.

Canada did have many missionary ties with China, both Catholic and Protestant, but the views of the ex-missionaries and their churches tend to be divided. For the most part they regard what is happening in sorrow rather than in anger. The United Church of Canada, largest of the Protestant bodies, has consistently urged the need for understanding and tolerance.[5] Not even from Roman Catholics has there been a solid and active front against dealings with Communist China—although the intense abhorrence of Communist countries characteristic of majority Catholic opinion across the border is often reflected among French- and English-speaking Catholics.

The tales of returning Canadian travelers have, of course, varied. Few except the pre-convinced have found a utopian society. In general, the returnees have expressed a typically Canadian skepticism, but whether bank presidents or scientists, they have tended to emphasize that the picture is more complex than usually painted and to argue the need for foreigners to come to terms with reality. Most of them have inveighed about the dangers of isolating China and stressed the extent to which Chinese policies are reactions to American policies and positions. There is a persistent, if not dominant, belief that the Chinese will behave nicely if we start treating them nicely—a belief that has not been strengthened in recent years—but little disposition on the whole to minimize the danger of an aggressive China. Canadians' views on the moral aspects of the question are not, of course, consistent. While Canadians usually reject the argument that recognition implies approval, they frequently cite Chinese misbehavior as one of the reasons for hesitation.

According to a Gallup poll in April 1964, 51 per cent of the public favored recognition, and 33 per cent disapproved. A considerably higher per cent, 63 per cent, favored trade relations.[6] It is significant that of those who declared their political persuasion, 51 per cent of the Conservatives, 56 per cent of the Liberals, and 61 per cent of those adhering to the minor parties, favored recognition. These figures represent a remarkable change from a similar 1959 poll which

5. At each of its biennial General Councils since 1952, the United Church has urged recognition of Peking and its admission into the United Nations. French recognition early in 1964 produced official statements urging Canada to do likewise from the Moderator of the United Church and the Anglican Bishop of Ottawa.

6. Canadian Institute of Public Opinion, April 15, 1964.

revealed 32 per cent of the public favorable to recognition, 44 per cent opposed, and 24 per cent with no opinion.[7]   At the time of the 1959 poll the Canadian Institute of Public Opinion noted a much higher percentage of university graduates among those in favor of recognition than among those opposed. The fact that the former are a more articulate group perhaps accounts for the difference between the politicians' assessment of public opinion and the impression given by editorials and public statements that there has always been a vigorous majority critical of the policy of nonrecognition.

Government policy has reflected Canadian opinion pretty faithfully. It has been an expression of the uncertainties of the Canadian consensus. There is nothing in Canada comparable to the so-called China Lobby in the United States or to the conformism of mass opinion on the subject, even though there are voices firmly raised against dealing with "Chinese Reds." It would be surprising if Canadians were entirely unaffected by the fierce views of American journals, broadcasts, and sermons—although the marked independence of Canadian views on China is perhaps the most notable instance of Canadian resistance to the American mass media. There has been no clear division of opinion along party lines. Strong opposition to dealing with Peking has been voiced from time to time by some leaders of the Conservative party both in and out of office and by some Liberal MPs. It is most strongly expressed by members of the right-wing, minority Social Credit party (now rent by schism), which is influenced by the American Right. Their doubts about trade with China contributed to their 1963 defeat in the Prairie Provinces, which had previously been their stronghold. The moderate left-wing New Democratic Party, which is more influential than the Social Creditors, has, along with trade unions, consistently and vigorously advocated measures to end the isolation of China.

It is difficult to find support in the Canadian press for the American view on relations with China although sympathy for the American dilemma is often vouchsafed. On the other hand, there is less certainty about what Canadian policy ought to be. In 1955, when Mr. Pearson raised the issue of Canadian policy to test public opinion and to inaugurate a debate, the results were, as always, indecisive. Those who spoke up were, for the most part, dissatisfied with the status quo, but there was never that clear consensus which would have encouraged the government to take a bold step. Some major newspapers

7. Same, July 11, 1959.

like the Toronto *Globe and Mail* conducted a vigorous campaign on the subject, but it was directed more against the unwisdom of American policy than in support of positive Canadian action. Political leaders and political organs have never been sure enough of voter opinion to become too categorical on Canadian government policy. It has been safer to make the point by scolding Washington. There has been little substantial difference between the English-language and the French-language press on the subject of China. Even during the Korean War, *L'Action Catholique* of Quebec criticized American obstinacy in refusing to admit the fact of the Chinese regime and expressed a preference for the wisdom of British policy. The influential Montreal daily, *Le Devoir*, has consistently criticized the government for following the policy in which *Le Devoir* believes the United States has trapped itself, and the view of the largest French-language daily, *La Presse* of Montreal, is that "recognition of Communist China . . . is not a question of decreeing that Mao's regime is fine, but simply of recognizing that it exists."

The failure of the press and public opinion to point a clear line on Canadian policy could be attributed to a lack of courage or to an unwillingness to take responsibility. Nevertheless, it reflects a recognition that it is American rather than Canadian policy which matters, a suspicion that an independent Canadian gesture would be futile and perhaps pretentious unless it could conceivably affect the American position or the disposition of the U.N. General Assembly. The dilemma of the Canadian government is that Canada's China policy is inextricably involved with Canada's general relations with the United States. In this respect, Canada is of course not unique; the observation is as true of the China policies of Australia or Germany. To assume that this dilemma results from Canadian fear of a neighbor's wrath, however, is to oversimplify. Something much more important is involved—the obligations of a lesser to a major ally, obligations for which there is no ready-made formula. More than any other issue of foreign policy, relations with China have become, in the public eye, the criterion of Canada's independence in *international* affairs. It would be wrong to imply that a majority of those who press the government to recognize the Peking regime act from anti-American impulses. Nevertheless, an anxiety that Canada should not allow itself to be dominated by its large neighbor and ally is a considerable element in the argument for recognition of Peking.

DILEMMAS OF CANADIAN POLICY

It is widely assumed, both by Canadians and foreigners, that Canada's policy on China has been ambivalent because the United States has in some way or other forced Canada to follow American policy on the matter—or perhaps hypnotized Canada into obedience. The U.S. government has never failed to express to the Canadian government its anxiety that Canada should not step out of line. This view has been expressed vigorously and, on occasions, at the highest level, but there is no evidence that normal diplomatic pressure has been accompanied by anything which could legitimately be called threat or blackmail. An issue which has exacerbated Canadian opinion from time to time, and has led to charges of blackmail, is the belief that Canadian subsidiaries have been denied profitable orders from China by U.S. parent companies acting in accordance with U.S. legislation. In fact, however, the U.S. government, in deference to the strength of Canadian feeling, agreed to grant exemptions in these cases. If there is a barrier to such commerce, it seems more likely to result from the disinclination of industries to risk blacklisting by American businessmen or from the personal views and loyalties of American managers with regard to trade with China. It does, of course, take strong will to defy the United States on an issue on which it feels deeply, for Americans protest in full voice. Canadians must constantly be preoccupied with the necessity of having a Congress well-disposed to them since numerous economic issues affecting Canada come before that body. It is not a question of Congress' imposing penalties but merely of its not being disposed to a generous view of Canadian interests if Canadian action irritates it. In the absence of a strong consensus for establishing relations with Peking, the caution of the Canadian government has been fortified by a feeling that it would be rash to anger Congress in order to pursue a matter of principle not directly involving Canadian national interests. This set of interrelationships, if one likes, is a form of economic sanction or blackmail, but it is one which it would be hard to eliminate from international relations in an interdependent world.

Canadian policy has indeed been determined by U.S. policy—not, however, by U.S. pressure but by the fact of U.S. policy. It is this same fact of U.S. policy, though, which has largely determined relations between China and the rest of the world. (I do not mean to suggest that American intransigence rather than Chinese aggres-

siveness has isolated China but that the way in which the United
States chose to view Communist China, whether wise or unwise, has
determined the framework in which relations with China are conducted.)   For Canada and for other lesser allies of the United States,
there is a special need to take U.S. policy into consideration.   They
all recognize their dependence on the power of the United States as
a matter of fact if not of choice.   In a world of cold war, prestige is
a significant element of power.   Rightly or wrongly, the United States
has staked a good deal of its prestige, especially in Asia, on keeping
the Peking government outside normal diplomatic channels, and its
power and influence would be seriously affected by the desertion of its
allies on this issue.   Because the maintenance of U.S. power is a
Canadian national interest rather than the obligation of a "satellite,"
Canadian governments have had to think seriously before embarking
on a step which would affect American prestige.   This consideration
remains strong even if the Canadian government is convinced that
U.S. policy is wrong.   In such situations, the Canadian government
has been free to express its dissent by private representation and
public declaration in the hope of influencing Washington's policy.
While Canadian officials have undoubtedly sought in diplomatic
contacts to temper the rigidity of American views on China, it is
unlikely, in view of the indecision of the Canadian government, that
they have ever bluntly urged the United States to reverse its policy.
If the United States rejects its views, Canada is still faced with making the best of U.S. policy as it is.

    There are, of course, no absolute considerations in determining
the foreign policy of any state.   No country can be expected to support its ally if it is convinced that the ally's policy is disastrous and
must be countered.   The necessity to support the Americans, right or
wrong, must contend constantly with Canada's independent assessment of the forces in the world and with its inclination and obligation
to act in world diplomacy as an independent middle power.   The
commitment to the ally is only one, although an important one,
among many factors.   As a middle power, Canada has an important
obligation in Asia—its role as a member of the truce supervisory
commissions in Indochina.   Furthermore, its position in the Commonwealth and its reputation in the United Nations have enabled
Canada to contribute modestly in the endeavor to find, by compromise or negotiation, solutions for grave confrontations.   It is not a
role that can be played by a country which never exercises its inde-

pendence. It has required, in particular, some detachment from the China policy of the United States, for despite the strong views of the smaller countries on China's periphery, disapproval of U.S. China policy is regarded by the more influential nonaligned powers as the touchstone of good sense in relations with non-European peoples. After the meeting of Commonwealth Prime Ministers in July 1964, Prime Minister Pearson reported to the House of Commons that some of those present had strongly held that the policy of the Western countries toward China was "sterile and fruitless." [8] This view was, in fact, close to unanimous. In the midst of these various pressures, Canada's policy toward China is forged.

There have been, since the Liberals returned to power in 1963, more indications of a change in Canadian policy than there have been in a decade. Spokesmen of the government have indicated their belief in the need to look seriously at the question of relations with China. While avoiding positive declarations, they have expressed frequent doubts about the wisdom of the present position. The Secretary of State for External Affairs, Paul Martin, although he did not suggest "that it would be appropriate to rush into some new formal relationships at this time," did say "that the increasing ostracism of Communist China from the world community may be self-defeating and a potential threat to international stability." "It is not too soon," he added, "for the West to begin to formulate realistic and far-sighted policies toward this Asian giant." [9] He has repeated this theme on numerous other occasions. The Leader of the Opposition, John Diefenbaker, said early in 1964: "You cannot forever deny the existence of a nation of so many millions of people if the UN is to be the institution representative of all nations. The time has come when fullest consideration should be given to this question [the China seat in the United Nations], keeping in mind the preservation of the existence and integrity of the Taiwan government." [10] The Prime Minister was considered to have taken his boldest position to date when, in an address to the Atlantic Treaty Association in Ottawa on September 14, 1964, he went out of his way to say of Communist China: "If we exposed them more to the views of the rest of the world, we might some day expect a more realistic policy from them. The present isolation of China encourages recurring crises." Public

---

8. House of Commons, July 17, 1964.
9. Same, November 1963.
10. *Montreal Star*, January 28, 1964.

opinion increasingly favors a change of policy, and the press is virtually united in unhappiness with the status quo. At a time when relations between the French- and English-speaking communities are delicate, this issue is not likely to divide the country.

Nevertheless, the causes of the persistent dilemma seem no nearer solution. Mr. Diefenbaker's stipulations about Taiwan, which accord with the views expressed by most Canadian spokesmen, seem to rule out any immediately foreseeable formula to which Canada could agree in the United Nations. The Prime Minister, Mr. Pearson, although he frequently talks along the same lines as Mr. Martin, said in July 1964 "that there are many governments, including our own, that could not accept the extension of Communist rule from mainland China to Formosa [Taiwan] without the approval and consent of the people of that island, and until that difficulty in some form was removed it was not going to be easy to recognize the right of a government in Peking to be the government of China in the United Nations and extend its authority over the island of Formosa [Taiwan]." [11]

Moreover, the growing importance of Japanese-Canadian relations means that Canada has to consider the views of Japan as well as the United States in formulating its policy toward China. Mr. Martin acknowledged this fact in the autumn of 1964 on his return from the annual meeting of the Canada-Japan Ministerial Committee in Tokyo, where views on China had been exchanged. The influence of the Japanese government is not likely to encourage Canada to act boldly. It is evident that Japanese caution is a real factor in Canadian policy making, for it serves the purpose of justifying Canadian procrastination on grounds other than American pressure.

In 1965, a new crisis intervened once again to arrest the trend toward adjustment of Canada's formal relations with China. The Canadian government—partly because of its long commitment by membership on the International Control Commission to uphold the Geneva agreements of 1954, which the United States refused to sign —has not been in very close step with the United States over Vietnam. Nevertheless, Canada has given moral support to the United States in its dilemma—although with a more insistent emphasis on the need to negotiate. The intensification of the crisis in Vietnam has forced Canada into a more publicly aligned position which has no doubt been noted in Peking. The anxiety to explore the basis for a

---

11. House of Commons, July 17, 1964.

settlement has made Canadians realize more acutely the frustration of not being able to communicate directly with the Chinese in Peking —as they can with the North Vietnamese by reason of the Control Commission's access to Hanoi.   As Frederick Nossal, former Peking correspondent of the *Toronto Globe and Mail*, wrote in that paper on May 29, 1965: "An offer of recognition by Ottawa would open a new channel of communications to Peking.   China's diplomatic isolation . . . is a serious handicap to peace talks."   Nevertheless, a time when U.S. forces are being increasingly engaged against Communists supported by the Chinese is hardly propitious for Canada to take a major step to alter its relations.   To risk American irritation is one thing; to make what Americans would inevitably look upon as a friendly gesture toward those who are abetting the killing of American soldiers requires a degree of boldness and confidence which has not characterized Canadian policy toward China.   On the other hand, if China were to accept some kind of Geneva-type settlement for Vietnam, an occasion for recognizing Peking might arise which Canada would be happy to seize.

General de Gaulle may have proved that, although one cannot get away with recognizing two Chinese governments, one can recognize Peking without having to accompany it by a formal acknowledgment of Peking's claims to Taiwan.   France has set an example many Canadians would like to follow.   The government, however, is not disposed to do so unless it can minimize the ill effects such a step would have on the United States.   The causes for indecision remain, despite the more forward dispositions and the more positive views of the public.   In these circumstances, the government might prefer to wait for a solution to unfold in the United Nations—perhaps with the view that it could play some part in the unfolding.

Chapter 5

JAPAN AND CHINA

Domestic and Foreign Influences on

Japan's Policy

BY

SHIGEHARU MATSUMOTO

Japan's China policy is not only vitally important for the Japanese; it is also being watched by many nations deeply interested in Asian international relations because of the effect Sino-Japanese relations can be expected to have in that area.

Japan currently has normal commercial relations with Taiwan and normal diplomatic relations with the Nationalist government, seated in Taipei, which asserts that it represents the Republic of China. At the same time, Japan has trade relations with a continental China effectively ruled by the Communist government, seated in Peking, which asserts that it represents the People's Republic of China but which Japan does not formally recognize. The pattern of Japan's relations with China thus differs from those of other free world nations like Canada, the United Kingdom, and France, which also differ among themselves. Like each of these other nations, Japan has a China policy based on national interest, the lessons of past experience, and its other existing international commitments. Furthermore, the sense of a prospective historical mission which Japan is destined to perform in world affairs bears directly on China policy.

SOME BASIC TRENDS

What, then, are the sources of the government's present China policy? Neither legalism, nor idealism, nor sheer economic interest provides the full answer. A great variety of factors have contributed to current China policy. These include the nation-wide aspiration for independence from foreign occupation, the popular demand for political stability, America's Asia policy as it actually affects Japan, and, last but not least, the strong and persistent anti-war sentiment of the Japanese public. An adequate analysis requires consideration of Japan's history since the disastrous defeat in the Pacific war, a history of some 20 years which is not yet well known abroad. Information about startling events in Japan contained in occasional headlines tends to distort the true picture. Japanese sentiments, aspirations, and demands have not been well explained, but Japan's China policy cannot be understood without reference to them.

Aspiration to regain national independence. For nearly seven years after the end of the war, the Japanese waited for a peace treaty which would put an end to foreign occupation. This desire was at last consummated in the signing of the "San Francisco Peace Treaty" of 1951, which restored Japan's normal diplomatic relations with 48 nations[1] and liberated her from restrictions on her trade. Economic recovery and subsequent development began from this point. The treaty also enabled Japan to pursue her course of democratization, consonant with indigenous conditions, on her own responsibility. Thus the treaty largely satisfied the aspiration for independence as then conceived by most of the public. However, it left Japan legally in a state of war with Soviet Russia and China. China was then already torn apart by the prolonged civil war which had given birth to two mutually hostile governments.

The peace treaty was closely followed by the U.S.-Japan Security Treaty, which Washington had in fact made a *sine qua non* for a peace treaty. Hence ratification of the security treaty was vehemently opposed by the political opposition, which was supported by nearly one third of the effective popular votes. Nevertheless, the conservative Liberal party and its government led by Premier Yoshida

---

1. India, Burma, and Yugoslavia declined to attend the San Francisco Peace Conference but made separate treaties with Japan later. No representative of China, Nationalist or Communist, was invited. The Soviet Union, Czechoslovakia, and Poland attended the conference but refused to sign the treaty.

succeeded in obtaining ratification by using its overwhelming majority in the Diet.   The aspiration for independence then came to be closely associated with two other national sentiments—the desire for national security and the desire for autonomy in diplomacy, especially in dealing with Soviet Russia and Communist China.   The ruling party, supported by a majority of the people, prized security over autonomy.   The latter, it was believed, would later be taken care of with the growth of national strength.   The opposition, whose strength lay in an incessant appeal to the popular anti-war sentiment, reasoned that as long as Japan remained in a state of war with Moscow and Peking, the security treaty would aggravate tensions in the Far East. It went so far as to claim that the treaty would involve Japan against her will in another major war in the Far East through the use of Japanese bases and the deployment overseas of American forces stationed in Japan, eventualities which Japan would be helpless to avoid.

Economic development. When the peace treaty came into effect on April 28, 1952, Japan's trade was opened to almost every corner of the world, and her economy received a tremendous impetus.   The United States waived reparations, and the Occupation authorities were farsighted enough to prohibit the wholesale purchase of Japanese stocks by foreign investors.   Already during the Occupation period, American know-how was encouraged in Japanese plants, though on a purely commercial basis.   Without the many kinds of economic, legal, and technological assistance the Americans have given, it would be unthinkable that Japan's economy would have become what it is now.

At present, Japan ranks third in the world in steel production and first in shipbuilding.   Production of consumers' goods has reached unprecedented levels and standards of quality.   Economic growth has been achieved so far without a large amount of trade with China. But Japanese business has come to compete with American business in foreign markets and from now on has to look around for further markets, including mainland China.

The Constitution. While Japan's economic strength is now widely publicized abroad, the new Constitution of 1946 and the depth of popular enthusiasm for it are less well known.   The Constitution was drafted, discussed in the Diet, and promulgated under the Occupation.   Two features permeate the entire document—the idea of peace and the idea of democracy.   Both are heartily accepted by the

Japanese people, who have never forgotten the nightmare of military dictatorship and of subsequent war in Asia and in the western Pacific.

The new Constitution insures parliamentary democracy and provides almost all possible guarantees of fundamental civil rights. The idea of popular sovereignty has been firmly established, and the Emperor is defined as the symbol of the unity of the nation. The freedom of speech enjoyed by the Japanese is almost unprecedented in the modern world. The idea of a welfare state runs through all the relevant articles. In short, under the new Constitution the Japanese are resolved that they will never tolerate dictatorship— Communist, Fascist, or any other. Japan has become almost immune to any possible "communization."

The new Constitution is popularly called a "Peace Constitution." Its Preamble forcefully expresses the national aspiration for peace in all its wording. Japanese anti-war sentiment was endorsed by Article 9, which is generally called "the anti-war clause" and which reads:

> Aspiring sincerely to an international peace based on justice and order, the Japanese people forever renounce war as a sovereign right of the nation and the threat or use of force as means of settling international disputes.
>
> In order to accomplish the aim of the preceding paragraph, land, sea, and air forces, as well as other war potential, will never be maintained. The right of belligerency of the state will not be recognized.

The inclusion of Article 9 was doubtless due partly to the Occupation policy of disarming Japan completely. In the initial days of the Occupation, General MacArthur once had in mind denying Japan even the right of self-defense. But a small group of conservative politicians, led by Hitoshi Ashida, chairman of the Diet Committee on the Constitution, succeeded in having the original draft amended to allow for the legitimacy of the right of self-defense. The amendment (which lay in inserting in the first paragraph the words "Aspiring sincerely to an international peace based on justice" and in the second paragraph the words "In order to accomplish the aim of the preceding paragraph") did not impair the spirit of the article. Legally speaking, the inherent right of self-defense of any sovereign nation can be easily read into the article as amended. However, the impression of the people definitely is that their anti-war sentiment has obtained legal endorsement.

Aspiration for peace. The singular strength and durability of

Japan's anti-war sentiment and aspiration for peace are perhaps beyond the surmise of other nations. The origin of these sentiments was not only defeat by Allied forces in 1945 but Japan's horrible experiences in 14 years of war with the Chinese people. The Japanese directly or indirectly caused the death of some 10 million Chinese, with whom they had a traditional kinship and cultural affinity. The atomic bombings of Hiroshima and Nagasaki also gave every individual Japanese a passionate dread of future nuclear wars. Any military action or policy which tends to increase international tension, therefore, arouses Japanese suspicion and hatred.

Japanese pacifism is not mere sentiment. It is a product of conscience and moral humanism and not a parochial Japanese reaction. It can be and has been exploited for political ends, but even so, it has been a real factor in Japan's domestic and foreign politics.

In the spring of 1951, John Foster Dulles, as a special envoy of President Truman, suggested to Premier Yoshida a security treaty between the two countries and strongly demanded the immediate rearming of Japan.[2] Yoshida agreed to the security treaty only on the condition that no attempt be made to rearm Japan at that time. He had primarily in mind the need for Japan's economic recovery, and he was not unconcerned with the possible adverse reactions of Australia, the Philippines, etc. But he was also sensitive to the strong anti-war sentiment then prevailing in Japan. Therefore, he rejected Dulles's demand as premature. Yoshida's firm stand made him a national hero. In 1952, both the Right-Wing and the Left-Wing Socialist parties voted against ratification of the security treaty on the ground that Japan should not ally herself with either side in the cold war but should adopt a nonalignment policy for the sake of her security.

The United States conducted hydrogen bomb tests at Eniwetok in November 1952 and at Bikini in March 1954. The Bikini test inflicted damage on the crew of the Japanese fishing boat "Fukuryû-Maru No. 5" and aroused a new wave of sentiment in Japan. The Diet was forced to pass a unanimous resolution on the banning of atomic and hydrogen bombs for any nation. Since then, successive conservative governments have always filed strong protests against all nuclear tests, whether carried out in the Pacific, in Siberia, or in the Sahara Desert. Conservative governments in Japan have consistently made cooperation with the United States the keynote of their foreign

2. Dulles's speech to the Japan-America Society, Tokyo, February 2, 1951.

policy, but they have had to and will have to file a protest against all U.S. nuclear tests. Any conservative government would be doomed to fall sooner or later if it nonchalantly disregarded popular anti-war sentiment.

The political upheaval of May–June 1960, which cannot be understood except as an explosion of anti-war sentiment, is an extreme example of this point. The upheaval took place in connection with ratification of the revised U.S.-Japan Security Treaty. There were mass demonstrations with 5 million people participating and a series of bloody clashes with the police. Diet and government functions were temporarily paralyzed, President Eisenhower's proposed visit to Tokyo was canceled, and the Kishi Cabinet eventually fell. Hayato Ikeda, who succeeded Kishi as Prime Minister, learned the lesson of this political unrest and took a very cautious attitude in handling the question of the Nautilus-type submarines calling at Yokosuka Naval Base in 1963. Ikeda's attitude was meant to appease the anti-war sentiment of the Japanese, although he stated in the Diet that the calling of a U.S. nuclear submarine at Yokosuka would legally be in accord with the revised security treaty. Washington has, on the whole, shown patience on this issue.

The origin, nature, and potential vehemence of anti-war sentiment have a direct and indirect bearing upon the attitude of the Japanese people toward the Chinese and therefore upon the China policy which has been formulated and executed by successive conservative governments over the last 15 years. The Japanese people have been firmly determined not to fight the Chinese again unless directly attacked, and most knowledgeable Japanese are sincerely desirous of putting an end to the state of war with mainland China as soon as it is feasible.

OFFICIAL POLICY, YOSHIDA TO ISHIBASHI

In response to popular determination and desire, the Diet passed a unanimous resolution on the promotion of Japan-China trade as the first step toward better relations with China as early as June 1953, while Yoshida was still Prime Minister and even before the formal truce was signed in the Korean War. This resolution was later unanimously reconfirmed by a similar Diet resolution in March 1956 during the Hatoyama administration. The executive branch of the government, however, has had to be more cautious than the legislative branch, for how and when to implement these resolutions have depended not only upon internal but also upon external factors. There have been several internal factors favoring the promotion of China trade—the popular demand for improved relations with Peking, the plight of small business deprived of imports from China, the drive of Japan's growing economy to secure future possibilities in the continental market, the need of appeasing the opposition, etc. The most important external factor has been the attitude of Peking toward Japan. The government, however, has also had to consider the reactions of Taiwan and the United States.

Since the restoration of sovereignty in 1952, there have been six successive conservative Prime Ministers: Shigeru Yoshida (to 1954), Ichirô Hatoyama (1954–56), Tanzan Ishibashi (1956–57), Nobusuke Kishi (1957–60), Hayato Ikeda (1960–64), and Eisaku Satô (1964 to date). All have regarded cooperation with America as the keystone of Japanese foreign policy. Every one of them has also been gravely concerned with China policy in general and the problem of trade with the mainland in particular.

It was Shigeru Yoshida who made the biggest contribution to the establishment of today's friendly relations with the United States. During the Occupation period, he represented defeated Japan and consistently upheld the pride of the Japanese people in his dealings with MacArthur. It was he who signed the San Francisco peace treaty and the security treaty in response to the people's wish to end the Occupation. It was his conviction that a stable and growing economy was the prerequisite to the rebirth of Japan and that, regrettable as the situation might be, the defense of the nation would have to be entrusted to the United States for the time being. He believed that Japan's rearmament for self-defense should await the growth of its economic strength and a decline in the distrust felt by Australia and other foreign nations. Yoshida's thought was that on the two major questions of national interest, the economy and national defense, the interests of the United States and Japan would have much in common in the foreseeable future. He did not personally trust the Soviet Union and was himself strongly opposed to communism. At the same time, however, he held the qualities of the Chinese in respect, and he did not forget for a moment the future importance of the mainland Chinese market and of normal relations as a foundation for trade. These ideas were partly a product of Yoshida's 11 years of diplomatic service in China in his younger days but were also due partly to his clear awareness of the Japanese people's desire for a peaceful trade relationship with continental China.

Before U.S. ratification of the two treaties signed at San Francisco in 1951, Dulles informed Yoshida that there would be difficulties with the U.S. Senate unless the Japanese government would immediately make clear that Japan would not recognize the Peking government but would conclude an early peace treaty with Taiwan. Although Yoshida was convinced that Japan's best course was to make an independent decision on the problem of China after some time had elapsed (a course envisaged in the original understanding between Dulles and Anthony Eden at the time of the peace treaty), he had a good sense of proportion and of timing. He finally decided, though reluctantly, to send a letter [3] to Washington—which satisfied the U.S. Senate. His major consideration was to end the Occupation. Naturally his decision was supported by the Japanese public. At the same time, however, Yoshida had the courage and foresight to state unmistakably in his letter that "the Japanese Government desires ultimately to have a full measure of political peace and commercial intercourse with China which is Japan's close neighbor." Yoshida's letter laid the cornerstone of the China policy which succeeding Prime Ministers followed, with adjustments required by changes in domestic factors and in international relations.

Following Yoshida's letter, the 1952 peace treaty was signed with the Republic of China. This treaty has since governed Japan's relations with Taiwan. In an accompanying exchange of notes, however, both parties recorded their understanding that the treaty applies only to "the territories which are now or which may hereafter be under the control of the Government" in Taipei. For practical purposes, therefore, the treaty does not apply to the mainland, which is now under the control of Peking. Though the state of war between Japan and the Republic of China was terminated, in the opinion of some experts it still legally exists between Japan and the P.R.C.

Thanks to the peace treaty, trade has been going on between Japan and Taiwan. Japan exports largely capital goods ($137,891,000 worth in 1964), and she imports agricultural products such as bananas, sugar, rice, etc. ($140,905,000 worth in 1964). Trade with Taiwan in 1962, when it was normal, accounted for 2.4 per cent of Japan's total

---

3. Letter from Prime Minister Yoshida to Ambassador Dulles, December 24, 1951.

exports and 1.1 per cent of Japan's total imports. Japan provided 36.1 per cent of Taiwan's total imports and took 25.5 per cent of Taiwan's total exports. It is obvious from these figures that this trade means a great deal more to Taiwan than to Japan.

The Japanese government, supported by the Liberal-Democratic party (LDP), continuously pursues a policy of preserving friendly relations with Taiwan. It also wants to maintain the Taiwan Strait as a free passage for Japanese trading vessels. But it dissociates itself from the Kuomintang idea of a "return to the mainland" by the use of arms, for it is well aware that the Japanese people entertain strong anti-war sentiments and do not want any further involvement in a Chinese civil war. The more problematical part of Japan's current China policy, however, lies in dealing with Peking.

Hatoyama, who succeeded Yoshida as Prime Minister toward the end of 1954, obtained overwhelming popular support for early normalization of Japan's relationship with Soviet Russia and with the People's Republic of China. Stalin had been dead for some time, and on October 12, 1954, Moscow and Peking issued a joint declaration expressing "their readiness to take steps to normalize their relations with Japan." After prolonged and difficult negotiations, especially in regard to the southern Kurile islands, Hatoyama, accompanied by Ichirô Kôno, went to Moscow in the fall of 1956 and signed the Joint Declaration of Peace between Japan and the Soviet Union, which cleared the way for Japan's admittance to the United Nations. He also forcefully encouraged the reopening of trade relations with mainland China. The first official trade mission from Peking was allowed to visit Japan in the spring of 1955, and for the first time some of the larger Japanese trading companies and manufacturers participated in negotiations with the Chinese. The negotiations led to the opening of the China Fair in Tokyo and Osaka in 1955 and the Japan Fair in China in 1956. China trade was subsequently conspicuously increased.

Hatoyama sent a strong delegation headed by Tatsunosuke Takasaki, then a Cabinet minister, to the Bandung Conference (1955). There for the first time Takasaki and some other top Japanese officials conversed with Chou En-lai, head of the Chinese delegation. Acting upon an informal request of the U.S. government, and in the interest of Japan, the Japanese delegation also helped to moderate the conflicting views of the participating nations and to draft the "Ten Principles" relating to world peace and cooperation.

Because of Hatoyama's serious illness, Ishibashi succeeded him toward the end of 1956, both as president of the LDP and as head of the government. Like Yoshida and Hatoyama, Ishibashi had resisted the militarists before and during the Pacific war. Both Hatoyama and Ishibashi had enough self-confidence to take the responsibility for fresh initiatives in foreign policy. With cordial relations with the United States almost a *fait accompli*, their major concern was with Soviet Russia and China, and they acted according to their convictions without explicit blessing from Washington. After some two months as Prime Minister, however, Ishibashi was suddenly taken ill, and in February 1957, he was replaced by Kishi, who had been his Foreign Minister.

KISHI'S CHINA POLICY

The new Prime Minister had the reputation of being one of the cleverest politicians of the time. He had made a brilliant record as Minister of Industry and Commerce before and during the war. He shortly declared in the Diet the "three basic principles for Japan's diplomacy": (1) the principle of centering Japan's diplomacy upon the United Nations, (2) the principle of continued cooperation with the United States, and (3) the principle of putting a new emphasis on Japan's responsibility as a member of the Asian nations. The first principle expressed the national aspiration for peace and Japan's determination to devote herself to the cause of the United Nations. It also implied that Japan would act only within the bounds of the United Nations Charter even when the United States requested her to act according to her commitments under the U.S.-Japan Security Treaty. Kishi's emphasis on the second principle—to continue close cooperation with America—was explicitly made partly because of his personal history. He had countersigned Japan's Declaration of War of 1941, and he had been detained as a war criminal in Sugamo prison for three and a half years upon the verdict of the International Military Tribunal. Therefore, he was afraid that Washington might still regard him as *persona non grata*. His fear turned out to be unfounded. He received a cordial welcome in Washington half a year after he became Prime Minister. The third point was partly intended to prepare the ground for a series of negotiations on reparations with several Asian countries and partly to facilitate Japan's trade with these areas as well as with continental China. On the whole,

Kishi's three principles served to implement, with needed adjustments to the newer situation, the policy expressed in Yoshida's letter referred to above. They seemed to cover all the problems of Japan's future diplomacy and all the possibilities within Japan's capability at that time.

All went well with Kishi's declaration of policy for some time. Before going to Washington, he made a trip to six Southeast Asian countries, including Taiwan. Kishi's emphasis on Asian diplomacy was popular in Japan. On Chinese affairs he in practice adopted a policy of dealing respectively with Taipei and with Peking. This policy invited the severest criticism from Peking, which was then extremely sensitive to the idea of "two Chinas." Naturally, Peking reacted most adversely to Kishi's talk with Chiang Kai-shek, during which Kishi concurred in most of Taiwan's basic policies. Nevertheless, Peking did not for a while take any drastic action regarding Japan-China trade, which it also desired.

Upon his return from America, Kishi appointed as his Foreign Minister Aiichirô Fujiyama, a leading businessman of good repute, to whom he gave almost free rein. At just this time, the so-called CHINCOM list was abandoned. Fujiyama saw an opportunity and sent a delegation of parliamentarians and business leaders to Peking to boost China trade if Peking proved accommodating. Peking, however, insisted on the right to hoist Chinese flags at the Chinese commercial attaché's office to be established in Tokyo. Fujiyama refused to acknowledge this right officially because it might imply recognition of the P.R.C., and he insisted on deleting the clause from the joint memorandum which the Japanese delegation had signed in Peking.

At that time, both economies—mainland China's and Japan's —were in a phase of rapid growth. Japan was interested in trade, and China was particularly interested in it because she had begun sensing a colder Soviet attitude toward her. A new joint memorandum was finally worked out on March 5, 1958, and Fujiyama was almost ready to validate it, thanks to a compromise on the question of flags. He made it known, however, that Japan had no political intent whatsoever. At the same time, Fujiyama tried to persuade Taipei, by dispatching a personal message from Kishi to Chiang Kai-shek, to acquiesce in Tokyo's current deal with Peking. But Taipei instantly lodged a strong protest. Also, U.S. Under Secretary of Commerce Walter Williams suggested a more cautious approach to the Japanese government. Peking, having learned of the Japanese government's firm attitude, threatened to suspend the negotiations. An apparent deadlock ensued.

In the meantime, internecine strife had presumably been going on in Peking between a group of experts on Japan in the Chinese government and Communist party on the one side and a larger and stronger militant revolutionary wing of the leadership on the other side. The militants evidently won. Peking started a series of anti-Kishi propaganda moves. It claimed that Kishi was responsible for disrupting Japan-China trade arrangements, and it cited Kishi's visit to Taipei and his personal message to the Generalissimo as actions absolutely hostile to Peking.

In the middle of this precarious situation—that is, in early May —a young Japanese dragged down and tore to pieces a tiny Chinese flag which had been hoisted on the roof of an establishment in Nagasaki, where a modest exhibition of Chinese postage stamps was taking place. Exaggerating this incident out of all proportion, Foreign Minister Ch'en Yi attacked Kishi as if he were the archenemy of the Chinese people, unilaterally abrogated the trade agreement memorandum already signed, and ordered all other trade arrangements made along the lines of the memorandum to be canceled at once.

The whole story of the events resulting in the complete suspension of trade has not yet been told. It seems to the Japanese that at that time Peking's approach to negotiations on trade was much too political, perhaps for internal reasons. A top P.R.C. official frankly admitted, five years later, that Peking's views of the Japanese situation at that time were really not correct. The sudden unilateral abrogation of business commitments was such a shock to some Japanese industrialists that they have not yet recovered and would prefer to await a more opportune time to resume trade talks. On the other hand, Taiwan seems to have overplayed the game of making protests to Japan. On the Japanese side, there was not adequate unity within the government and the conservative party. Although Fujiyama stood amazingly firm in protecting Japan's overall interests, and in resisting protests and warnings from outside, he could not single-handedly sway the tide.

IKEDA'S CHINA POLICY

The tumult gradually subsided, and in time common sense and calm, practical thinking were restored on the same stage with a new setting.   After Kishi's forced resignation in July 1960, Ikeda took the helm of government.   In the general election of November 1960, the majority of the voters wanted political stability more than anything else, and the LDP scored another victory.

The secret of conservative power for nearly 20 years has been to give priority sometimes to a specific national objective and to moderate other popular sentiments, but at other times to give vent to one of the predominant popular sentiments in order to pull the teeth from the opposition's argument and forestall public resentment.   The opposition is apt to appeal to one or two idealistic national sentiments in defiance of some of the more sober national aspirations.   It is sometimes able to stage effective demonstrations of protest, but it has never won a general election.   Conservative leaders are convinced that political stability and domestic tranquillity are "categorical imperatives" for Japan.   Without these, Japan could not develop economically, maintain and develop democracy, and honor her international commitments.   From now on, however, the conservative leaders cannot guarantee political stability unless they meet more effectively the popular demand for autonomy in the conduct of foreign affairs and make positive attempts to normalize relations with Peking. There have already been unmistakable signs showing whither the wind blows.   The political upheaval of June 1960, mentioned above, was one of the most important.

Ikeda, like Hatoyama, tried to take serious account of these national sentiments.   He adopted a "low posture" vis-à-vis the opposition in the Diet—that is, an attitude of paying due respect to the minority.   He spoke more frankly than his predecessors, though never as bluntly as he should have, to his high-echelon American friends about Japan's "unique position in Asia."   In a series of public pronouncements, he assured the Japanese people of more autonomy in the future handling of Japan's diplomacy.

In concrete terms, Ikeda began openly favoring the reopening and gradual expansion of China trade.   In the summer of 1962, Ikeda's government decided to allow Japanese trade with Peking, which had virtually ceased after 1958, to be reopened.   On the one hand, there had been sure signs of Peking's eagerness to resume trade primarily for its own sake rather than for external political purposes. On the other hand, there had been an increasing demand by Japanese business for access to the China market.   It was with great caution, however, that the Ikeda administration moved.   Ikeda officially insisted that there would be no inter-governmental dealings directly connected with China trade and that the trade would be conducted only on a so-called "non-governmental level." His guiding principle was "the separation of economic from political affairs"—an old principle applied since 1953. Everyone knows that in these days, and especially vis-à-vis Communist countries, a complete separation is impossible. However, Ikeda's insistence on the principle was useful. Through the postponement of the question of formal recognition until a more appropriate situation develops, cumulative efforts for the gradual improvement of Sino-Japanese relations could be started with trade. The Japanese government also made clear that it was determined to reject any Chinese interference in Japan's politics.

In September 1962, an important conversation took place in Peking between Chou En-lai and Kenzô Matsumura, a veteran conservative politician who has for long been deeply interested in improving Sino-Japanese relations. Matsumura was then visiting Peking in an informal capacity, but with the virtual endorsement of the Prime Minister himself, and was in a good position to sound out Chinese intentions of reopening trade with Japan. He was followed by a large economic delegation led by the late Tatsunosuke Takasaki, formerly the head of the Japanese delegation to the Bandung Conference. Takasaki's knowledge of and interest in Chinese affairs dated back to his prewar service as an executive of the Manchurian Heavy Industry Development Corporation. He was regarded as an experienced business negotiator. After several weeks of negotiation, he reached an agreement with Liao Ch'eng-chih [4] on a long-range, coordinated plan for future trade between Japan and mainland China, now officially called the "L-T Memorandum of Agreement." Trade conducted according to the terms of the memorandum is called "L-T trade." Highlights of the memorandum were: (1) From 1963 through 1967, Japan-China trade would be carried out on an annual scale of about U.S. $180,000,000 on a barter basis; (2) Japan would export steel, chemical fertilizer, agricultural chemicals, and agricultural machinery to China, while China would export coal, iron ore, corn, soy beans and other miscellaneous beans, salt, and tin; (3) Japanese plant exports involving deferred payment would be subject to further consultation; (4) the memorandum and subsequent concrete agreements based upon it would not be rescinded except by mutual agreement.

---

4. Liao Ch'eng-chih occupies a number of party and government positions. He is, among other things, chairman of the Chinese Afro-Asian Solidarity Committee and the China-Japan Friendship Association. When the memorandum was signed on November 9, 1962, neither its text nor the New China News Agency release describing it specified a capacity in which either signer was acting.

A trade arrangement for 1963 was also agreed upon by Liao and Takasaki. In 1963, Kaheita Okazaki, president of All-Nippon Airways Company, led another delegation to Peking and successfully arranged a trade program for 1964 with Liao.

Apart from L-T trade and plant exports, there still exists a China trade of a special kind, called "friendship trade," which was started in 1960. A mutual desire to have it continued was confirmed in 1962 by the Chinese Committee for the Promotion of International Trade and the Japan-China Trade Promotion Association. This so-called "friendship trade" has been a kind of makeshift procedure. After the complete suspension of Japan-China trade in 1958, Peking allowed in China only those Japanese traders whom it regarded as "friendly toward the Peking regime." The Japanese government acquiesced to this state of affairs. Although such trade alone would not satisfy either party in respect to the scope and terms of future trade agreements, it would be maintained even if L-T trade should be troubled by political complications.

L-T trade and "friendship trade" together amounted to U.S. $310,000,000 in 1964. Japan's exports totaled U.S. $152,739,000, and her imports from China, U.S. $157,750,000. (See Table 5-1.) The total amount of trade in 1964 was not much more than 2 per cent of Japan's foreign trade.

In August 1963, the Japanese government issued a license for the export of a vinylon plant in accordance with an agreement between the Kurashiki Rayon Co., Ltd. and the authorities in Peking. The agreement involves an initial payment upon shipment amounting to one-fourth of the entire price and a five-year deferred payment of the balance. Despite repeated protests by Taipei, the Ikeda administration stuck to the policy of sanctioning plant exports because Ikeda at this time wanted a sort of bridgehead for Japan's China trade. Moreover, plant exports mean a large-scale export of Japanese science and technology to China and will deepen the economic ties between the two countries.

In supporting the plan for developing China trade, including plant exports, Ikeda sensed rightly the mood of business circles, a large segment of whom had become increasingly interested in trying to forestall European competition. He was also able to respond to the popular demand for initial steps for improving Japan-China relations. Furthermore, Ikeda, as an astute political strategist, had the courage to decide in favor of plant exports to China without any American blessing. The political aspects of Ikeda's decision were

TABLE 5-1
Japan's Foreign Trade, 1947–64
(amounts in U.S. $1,000)

	Grand Totals		Mainland China				Taiwan				Hong Kong				United States			
	EXPORTS (A)	IMPORTS (B)	EXPORTS Amt.	% of (A)	IMPORTS Amt.	% of (B)	EXPORTS Amt.	% of (A)	IMPORTS Amt.	% of (B)	EXPORTS Amt.	% of (A)	IMPORTS Amt.	% of (B)	EXPORTS Amt.	% of (A)	IMPORTS Amt.	% of (B)
1947	173,568	526,130	10,164	5.9	5,016	1.0	0.9	0.0	2	0.0	1,794	1.0	0	0.0	4,975	2.9	48,975	7.2
1948	258,276	684,220	4,080	1.6	24,828	3.6	0.1	0.0	17	0.0	10,780	4.1	141	0.02	46,925	18.1	104,394	15.3
1949	509,700	904,845	3,144	0.4	21,756	2.4	5,953	1.1	2,471	0.2	26,602	5.2	1,647	0.2	85,378	16.8	491,128	54.3
1950	820,055	974,339	19,632	2.4	39,328	4.1	38,011	4.6	35,816	3.7	53,342	6.5	805	0.08	179,297	21.9	418,233	42.9
1951	1,354,520	1,995,039	5,828	0.4	21,606	1.1	50,600	3.7	53,025	2.7	61,550	4.5	5,833	0.3	184,936	13.7	694,750	34.8
1952	1,272,915	2,028,193	599	0.04	14,903	0.7	60,666	4.8	63,763	3.1	80,700	6.3	6,872	0.3	229,175	18.0	768,239	37.9
1953	1,274,843	2,409,637	4,559	0.35	29,700	1.2	60,966	4.8	64,038	2.7	62,222	4.8	7,777	0.3	226,839	17.8	757,806	31.4
1954	1,629,236	2,399,404	19,097	1.2	40,770	1.7	65,936	4.0	57,088	2.4	77,263	4.7	3,961	0.2	276,742	17.0	846,939	35.3
1955	2,010,600	2,471,430	28,547	1.4	80,778	3.3	63,827	3.2	80,877	3.3	88,061	4.3	6,169	0.2	449,256	22.3	772,278	31.2
1956	2,500,636	3,229,734	67,339	2.7	83,647	2.6	77,858	3.1	45,508	1.4	134,461	5.3	18,680	0.6	543,314	21.7	1,064,483	33.0
1957	2,858,018	4,283,586	60,485	2.1	80,483	1.9	84,275	2.9	67,255	1.6	130,636	4.5	26,725	0.6	596,583	20.9	1,617,931	37.8
1958	2,876,560	3,033,125	50,600	1.8	54,427	1.8	90,038	3.1	75,641	2.5	100,069	3.4	11,638	0.4	680,394	23.7	1,053,872	34.7
1959	3,456,492	3,599,491	3,648	0.1	18,917	0.5	86,847	2.5	71,547	2.0	129,155	3.7	27,072	0.8	1,030,644	29.8	1,112,914	30.9
1960	4,054,537	4,491,132	2,726	0.06	20,729	0.5	102,236	2.5	63,522	1.4	156,013	3.8	22,952	0.5	1,082,881	26.7	1,545,372	34.4
1961	4,235,596	5,810,432	16,639	0.4	30,895	0.5	96,322	2.3	67,747	1.2	153,527	3.6	24,080	0.4	1,050,964	24.8	2,079,372	35.8
1962	4,916,159	5,636,524	38,460	0.8	46,020	0.8	118,576	2.4	61,375	1.1	192,436	3.9	18,936	0.3	1,400,231	28.5	1,808,967	32.1
1963	5,448,296	6,738,501	62,969	1.2	74,567	1.1	107,142	2.0	122,640	1.8	246,352	4.5	28,772	0.4	1,506,911	27.7	2,077,331	30.8
1964	6,673,191	7,937,543	152,739	2.3	157,750	2.0	137,891	2.1	140,905	1.8	292,042	4.4	28,864	0.4	1,841,582	27.6	2,336,041	29.4

SOURCE: Customs Bureau, Japanese Ministry of Finance

twofold: it had the effect of pulling one of the sharper teeth of the opposition, and it supported Ikeda's claim that he was living up to his pledge for "more autonomy in Japan's diplomacy." China trade, even as it is now being practiced, contributes a great deal toward stability in Japanese domestic politics.

Ikeda's freedom to move in this new direction was naturally circumscribed by his sincere consideration for Japan's partnership with the United States. On the one hand, he was straightforward in telling Secretary of State Dean Rusk [5] that Japan, because of her long historical experience, special knowledge and understanding of neighboring countries, and new economic strength, is in a "unique position" to play an important role in Asian relations and that she is determined to help other Asian nations in cooperation with the United States. On the other hand, Ikeda wrote off an immediate formal recognition of the People's Republic of China in his public utterances and remained consistently concerned with the maintenance of friendly relations with Taiwan. Partly to appease opposition factions within his party, he requested former Prime Minister Shigeru Yoshida to pay an informal visit to Taipei in April 1964 and, three months later, sent Foreign Minister Masayoshi Ōhira to make a courtesy call on the leaders of the Nationalist government. Relations with Taipei, which had been unduly strained during the previous year, were restored to normal.

Ikeda's re-election as party president and as Prime Minister for the third time in July 1964 furnished strong ground for believing that Japan was going ahead along this line—with caution but also with determination.

In support of the basic government attitude in favor of China trade, Japanese business in the spring of 1964 sent to America a strong delegation headed by Yoshizane Iwasa, president of Fuji Bank, one of the four big banks in Japan. These representatives held a series of frank, and therefore successful, talks with their American counterparts. The press, without exception, urged the government to proceed with cumulative steps toward normalizing relations with mainland China.

---

5. Ikeda's luncheon talk addressed to Dean Rusk and other members of the American delegation to the U.S.-Japan Conference on Trade and Economic Affairs, January 27, 1964.

SATÔ'S CHINA POLICY

Ikeda's sudden illness brought Eisaku Satô to office in November 1964. Avoiding further factional strife within the LDP, Satô slipped into Ikeda's shoes but retained all the latter's Cabinet members. He was somewhat unprepared as the new Prime Minister, however, and made a number of contradictory statements regarding his China policy. These apparently brought about a temporary stiffening in Peking's attitude. Liao's visit to Tokyo to arrange a trade program for 1965, a visit originally scheduled for November 1964, was postponed for the time being.

Prime Minister Satô's visit to Washington in January 1965, and a series of conversations with President Johnson and Secretary of State Rusk, have left a mixed impression on the Japanese public. Secretary Rusk applauded Satô's visit as the opening of a new era in U.S.-Japan relations. The Japanese public, however, sensed a certain inconsistency: on the one hand Satô strongly pleaded for more autonomy in Japan's foreign policy, particularly vis-à-vis China; but on the other hand he seemed to associate himself with U.S. determination to protect South Korea and Taiwan, as well as Japan, at a time when the Far Eastern situation was rapidly deteriorating.

At this writing, Satô seems to be in hot water and, for the moment, cannot move positively in either direction. But the present writer believes it is safe to say that there will be no drastic reversal in Japan's China policy as long as the domestic considerations already mentioned prevail and the conservative party continues in power in the foreseeable future. There may, however, be a difference in pace as a result of favorable or unfavorable influences, whether domestic or international.

OPPOSITION VIEWS

While Ikeda's China policy was generally approved by the public, it was bitterly criticized by opposition forces, who advocate more speedy improvement of relations with Peking than Ikeda's "gradualism" provided for. Satô's China policy, though not essentially different from that of Ikeda, has invited still stronger criticism.

The Japan Socialist party (JSP), the major political element of the opposition, holds that there is only "one China" and that Taiwan is a Chinese domestic problem. It favors the early seating of Peking in the United Nations and advocates an early peace treaty with Peking as well as an early abrogation of the treaty with the Republic of China. The JSP does not accept the "principle of separation of economic from political affairs" as justification of the government's gradualism. It favors the early conclusion of a trade agreement on the governmental level, an agreement which would accelerate the development of trade and would be a decisive step toward normal diplomatic relations. As for Japan's security, the JSP advocates the conclusion, immediately after or at the same time as a peace treaty, of a Sino-Japanese non-aggression pact in which other nations interested in the security of the Far East would be expected to join later.[6]

The second important element of the opposition is the Japan Democratic Socialist party (DSP). The DSP's position is that the problem of China will only be solved under the governing idea of "one China and one Taiwan." The DSP contends: (1) that Peking, not Taipei, should be regarded as the legitimate government of China; (2) that, as an interim measure, the government in Taipei should be recognized as a temporary government of the area it now controls; (3) that Peking should be seated in the United Nations and Japan should attempt immediately thereafter to normalize relations with Peking; and (4) that the ultimate status of Taiwan should be determined by the will of the Taiwanese and of the mainland Chinese residing on Taiwan, as freely and legitimately expressed under international inspection and control to be carried out by the United Nations.

The proposals of the DSP concerning Taiwan have been bitterly opposed by Peking and also by Taipei. Therefore, they are apparently impractical, at least for the moment. On December 17, 1964, however, *The Independent Evening Post*, a newspaper in Taipei, expressed doubts about sticking to the idea of "one China" as the best guarantee of the future of Taiwan. We are not certain whether the editorial in question was inspired or at least approved by the Taipei government, but it is significant that a paper in Taipei was allowed to print the article. The DSP's emphasis seems to be on making formal recognition of Peking conditional upon its admittance

6. "Socialist Foreign Policy to Face the General Election," *Japan Socialist Review*, November 1, 1963; "Secretary General Narita Expounds Basic Socialist Policies," *Japan Socialist Review*, November 15, 1963.

to the United Nations and on giving the United Nations a role in deciding Taiwan's future status. It seems to have something in common with the plan of the British Labor party.[7]

Brief mention should be made here of the China policy of the Japan Communist party (JCP), the smallest segment of the opposition in terms of representation in the Diet.[8] The JCP advocates immediate abrogation of the peace treaty with Taiwan and immediate restoration of normal relations with Peking. This policy is certainly clear-cut and may sound similar to that of the JSP. However, there is a fundamental difference between the two in their grasp of the problem of China against the background of world affairs and particularly in their tactics in Japan. The differences have become more marked since the conclusion of the partial nuclear test ban treaty of 1963. The majority of the JCP definitely sides with Peking, while the majority of the JSP sides with Moscow.

The JCP has been trying to propagate its view that the underlying causes for delay in the restoration of normal relations with China are America's Far Eastern military policy, which treats Soviet Russia and China as putative enemies, and the related U.S.-Japan Security Treaty, which limits Japan's diplomatic autonomy. From this view follows the tactic of closely associating the party's movement in favor of immediate restoration of Japan-China relations with its movement against the U.S.-Japan security arrangement. This partisan tactic is believed to appeal to the public's anti-war sentiment, aspiration for "complete autonomy in Japan's diplomacy," and desire for early recognition of Peking. If an appeal to these strong sentiments is successful and if the two movements are effectively combined, the JCP holds, a nation-wide popular uprising with the goal of a Communist revolution by force will become possible. As for Taiwan, the JCP argues that the contention of "two Chinas" is a piece of American strategic and political intrigue and that the so-called Taiwanese independence movement, in which the United States is reported to be interested, is nothing but an example of American "neo-colonialism." [9]

The views on China held by leading intellectuals in Japan have

7. Democratic Socialist Party of Japan, *Decision of Central Executive Committee* [in Japanese] (Tokyo: Author, January 28, 1964).

8. In 1964 JCP representation in the Diet consisted of four members in the House of Representatives and three members in the House of Councillors.

9. Central Committee, Japan Communist Party, *The Policies of the Japan Communist Party* [in Japanese] (Tokyo: Author, May 30, 1962), pp. 35–44.

undoubtedly influenced the formation of the views and policies of
political parties, organized labor, and students. The range of views
among the intellectuals is comparable to that of the political parties.
Despite their differences, it seems safe to say that the intellectuals
have two things in common. First, most of them harbor a feeling
of guilt for the millions of Chinese who were killed during the dark
14-year period when Japan waged war against China; therefore, they
cannot but feel a need to atone for Japan's past crimes.[10] The series
of blunders which the Japanese government and militarists made in
China policy, blunders which led to an attempt to root out anti-
Japanese sentiments by military force and eventually culminated in
the long war beginning with the intervention in Manchuria in 1931,
are still fresh in their memory. They feel somewhat frustrated by the
conservative government's inability to end the state of war with the
Chinese people on the continent. Secondly, a large segment of the
intellectuals is sympathetic to the efforts of the Chinese people to
modernize their society regardless of the fact that these efforts are
being made under the Communist regime. Japanese intellectuals
neither ignore nor are indifferent to the implications of the eventual
emergence of a great Communist power on the Asian continent, but,
nonetheless, they look at the current re-awakening of China with
moral sympathy.

Successive conservative governments have had to counteract the
views of the opposition but at the same time have had to take them
into account from the standpoint of political stability and domestic
tranquillity as well as for the sake of their own survival.

CHINA'S OUTLOOK AND INTENTIONS

In the foregoing pages, I have described Japan's current China
policy and analyzed several background factors, including relevant
international commitments and internal forces. The pages that follow deal with Japan's future China policy. Here I will touch upon
some of the underlying assumptions and possibilities and offer some
suggestions.

First, it is generally agreed in Japan that the Peking regime will
remain in control of the mainland in the foreseeable future. The
crisis of 1959–61 is now almost over, and the Chinese economy is

---

10. Soichirô Ôhara, president of the Kurashiki Rayon Co., Ltd., describes this
guilt feeling in graphic fashion in "Plant Export to China," [in Japanese] *Sekai*,
September 1963.

slowly but steadily on the upward swing again. Important concessions were made in economic practice to cope with the hardships of the Chinese people, although in official theory the basic party line was steadfastly upheld. (As a leader, Mao Tse-tung could hardly be called infallible, but he has certainly demonstrated that he is a great theorist on "contradictions," particularly on those "among the people." There have been contradictory emphases in actual practice and contradictions in timing and in strategy—contradictions for which he has always had a ready explanation. In trying to persuade the people, Mao has always been successful in emphasizing national sentiment and patriotism. He could easily cite concrete examples of confrontations with "imperialist" powers.) To be sure, serious problems still lie ahead even though the food shortage appears over. The Japanese are inclined to believe, however, that the leaders in Peking, aided by the unprecedented number of younger activists who now man the local administrative system, will be able to manage their problems and will keep as firm a grip as ever on the Chinese people.

Second, Chinese communism seems now to emphasize nationalism. More attention will be given to the actual conduct of government and less to partisan polemics. The more weight the leaders give to national interest and to practices consonant with it, the more stable their position will be.

The Chinese revolution, which culminated in the seizure of power in 1949, had three aspects: a Communist revolution, a nationalistic revolution, and an economic revolution. Therefore, to regard what is taking place in China as nothing more than a Communist revolution is much too simple. The view that these events can be explained solely in terms of the awakening of China as a modern nation is also inadequate. But it cannot be denied that the secret of Communist power in China lies largely in the success of nationalistic appeals to the people in general and particularly to the younger generation. In the eyes of the Chinese, Chiang Kai-shek failed to free China from its semi-colonial status, but Mao has succeeded. Ironically, the Japanese invasion helped to awaken Chinese national consciousness. A similar role has been played since 1950 by the American effort to contain Chinese Communist influence through a show of military power and an economic embargo. No doubt, the new Chinese nationalism has been strengthened by the virtual rupture in relations between China and Soviet Russia. Mao, in other words, has never failed to take advantage of the hostile postures of Japan, America, and Soviet Russia.

The new Chinese nationalism, it is true, has been fostered by so-called Marxism-Leninism as expounded and adapted to China by Mao and his group. Still, as in other Communist countries, a dualism of nationalism and communism has been increasingly apparent in China since 1949. Mao has handled this dualism most cleverly and applied it to the conduct of both domestic affairs and foreign policy. The Chinese Communist leaders continue to talk loudly about anti-imperialism and world revolution—particularly when they address the developing countries. But when acting as the government of a nation, these same leaders appear to be prudent in dealing with their neighbors and to avoid provoking the United States unnecessarily. There is the appearance of unity in the highest level of leadership, but in practice some elements of the leadership give greater weight to state considerations and institutions in framing and executing policy, while others give greater weight to party considerations and institutions. The various elements cooperate on some issues but adopt contradictory priorities on others. The recent trend seems to be that state priorities dominate party priorities whenever national interest is the preponderant consideration. Peking's demarches vis-à-vis France and Japan from 1962 through 1964 are cases in point. This trend not only strengthens the Peking regime but also furnishes other countries, including Japan, with a feasible basis for negotiations with Peking. Chinese and Japanese national interests, largely on the trade level, may well continue to coincide in the near future.

Of course, the future of Japan's China policy hinges upon Communist China's policy toward Japan. Has there been any sure indication that the P.R.C.'s present cooperative approach is solidly enough based to warrant a cooperative response from Japan, at least so far as trade is concerned? Yes.

One consequence of the Sino-Soviet rift is that leaders in Peking seem to have been convinced of the need for a long-range view of state planning. "National rebirth through self-reliance" has become their watchword for the public, but they realize that self-reliance is not enough. It may take a generation or two for China to become a modernized nation and a great power; hence, Peking's so called "expansionism" will not be hastily executed, unless deeply provoked. There is also a need for cooperation with other countries—except, for obvious reasons, the United States—on both the trade and political levels. Japan, it seems, has definitely been selected as one of the countries to be wooed. Two important and prolonged conferences, at which Mao himself was present, produced, in 1958, a shift in over-all foreign policy and, in the spring of 1962, a friendly policy toward Japan specifically. The political missionary approach to Japan was quietly abandoned.

A more discreet attitude than before has been manifest through-out the trade negotiations with Japanese representatives since 1962. The important political conversation between Chou En-lai and Kenzô Matsumura (noted above) requires a few more words of explanation in this connection. Chou and Matsumura agreed that both sides were determined to collaborate in permanent friendly relations "for many, many years to come" and "despite whatever may happen." They agreed that each side would refrain from interference in the other's domestic affairs and from open criticism of any international commitments made by the other. Although they tacitly agreed that formal diplomatic recognition should be the ultimate goal, both sides definitely decided that gradualism would be the keynote of their collaboration. They would start with trade and later possibly include cultural exchanges. There was no written document, but the at-mosphere of the conversation and the wording of the exchange of views testify to the determination to pursue a mutually friendly policy. Here is an example of oriental diplomacy—a diplomacy which can happen between the Chinese and the Japanese because of cultural affinity, which survives marked differences in ideology.

The trade negotiations which followed the basic political under-standing have gone smoothly, and a plan to station three trade repre-sentatives from each side in Peking and Tokyo was agreed upon early in the summer of 1964. In addition, an exchange of journalists was effected in the fall of 1964.

Peking's policy toward Taiwan does and will stick to the principle of "one China," but there have been signs of elasticity. Contrary to reports that it would resort to arms to "liberate" Taiwan, since 1958 Peking has consistently followed a policy of patient and watchful waiting, for it firmly believes that time is on its side. Top P.R.C. leaders have stated that they expect to bring Taiwan under Chinese sovereignty without having to resort to the use of arms or, in other words, without a head-on collision with U.S. military forces. Occa-sional bombarding of the offshore islands—often exaggerated in newspaper reports—has been more a political measure than a serious military act. In fact, the Chinese on the coast and the islanders exchange consumer goods during the night. Furthermore, Peking's references to Chiang Kai-shek in the official press have definitely softened. The often-talked-about third Nationalist-Communist coalition seems to be remote, although there may have been informal talks aiming at it. Peking is less concerned about the hostility of immigrants to Taiwan from the mainland than about the possible independence of Taiwan through an evolutionary merger between the native Taiwanese and the upper layer of the recent migrants, for the United States seems to put its main hope on such a merger, and tacitly on the Taiwanese themselves, as a basis for a long-range policy for Taiwan.

JAPAN'S FUTURE RELATIONS WITH CHINA

Regarding future relations between Tokyo, Peking, and Taipei, there are several practical possibilities. To realize them, "timing and method" will be crucial.

First, the prospects for gradual expansion of Japan's trade with mainland China are good so long as political and military complications do not arise and cause mutual distrust. Because of a lack of foreign exchange, Peking for some time to come will have to resort to barter. When China's debt to the Soviet Union is paid off, however, its capacity for export will certainly be increased. Furthermore, if it becomes able to export pig iron to Japan instead of crude, unselected Hainan iron ore, its capacity for import from Japan will be enhanced. Its need for clothing seems almost limitless. When vinylon [11] plants imported from Japan are in full operation, the P.R.C. will be able to reduce its cotton-growing area and plant more rice. Chemical fertilizers—notably urea and ammonium sulfate—agricultural chemicals, dredgers, and cargo boats are also badly wanted from Japan.

Plant exports to developing countries involve deferred payments because of foreign exchange shortages. It is now generally conceded that a three- to five-year deferred payment can be effected on a genuinely commercial basis, but deferred payments for seven years or more are subject to criticism because they may imply economic aid of a political nature. As I have already mentioned, Taiwan objected

---

11. Vinylon is a synthetic fiber developed in Japan.

when the Japanese government, in August 1963, permitted the export of a vinylon plant to mainland China. However, in 1965 a second vinylon plant export was arranged without major repercussions.

Needless to say, Japan will scrupulously observe COCOM limitations, as she has in the past, though some European countries have more than once exceeded them in trading with Peking. The COCOM list will probably be gradually relaxed unless there is a great increase in tension between Washington and Peking.

Secondly, Japan will undoubtedly be able to continue to trade with Taiwan and will also be able to make loans. Taiwan places Japan's amity second only to that of the United States. Taiwan realizes that it overplayed its hand in 1963–64 over the vinylon plant export. The Japanese government made an excessively humble reply to Taiwan's protest. A more balanced view of the future relations of the two governments now seems to prevail. A new Nationalist ambassador arrived in Tokyo in July 1964, and after Foreign Minister Ōhira's visit to Taiwan, Taipei resumed official purchases of Japanese goods, which had been banned since 1963.

A not insignificant section of the Japanese people (not to mention the so-called "Taiwan lobby" in Japanese politics) would urge the government not to take abrupt steps vis-à-vis Peking which would unnecessarily undermine cordial relations with Taipei. Many Japanese, however, are convinced that Taiwan's situation will remain unsettled for many years despite its present prosperity. Political stability there is dependent upon internal adjustment and upon American military aid. Therefore, it must be regarded as somewhat precarious, even if the American military aid continues, unless a merger between the Chinese upper layer and the Taiwanese takes place in due course.

In recent years, the Generalissimo has seemed to emphasize "peaceful penetration" of the mainland as opposed to the dangerous idea of armed invasion. This approach offered promise for the future and gave Taipei more ability to maneuver. Should the P.R.C. be seated in the United Nations, the Nationalist government, regarding the issue as a matter of honor, would certainly withdraw, but Taiwan would still be able to exist without a seat in the United Nations, just as West Germany and Switzerland do. Developments in Vietnam, however, which the Generalissimo is certainly watching, may revive his wishful hope to return to the continent.

Thirdly, a series of cumulative steps is possible which would gradually bring about *de facto* recognition of Peking. The exchange of journalists can be gradually expanded; limitations on numbers and scope of activities can be relaxed. Thus, more objective information will be distributed—to the benefit of others as well as China itself. Academic interchange and tourism can be encouraged. Communications and transportation, *e.g.*, air passage between China and Japan, can be established, albeit on a non-regular basis. Further agreements on fisheries are in the interest of both countries. However, anything smacking of propaganda or domestic intervention will have to be prohibited strictly, and there will have to be intelligent but firm control of passports and visas. If steps like these are carried out in good faith by both sides, a formal trade agreement between the two governments, with, of course, an explicit proviso that it does not mean formal recognition, can be considered at some not-distant date.

There are various ways of clearing up the legal state of war. Both the Japanese and the Chinese want to see this goal accomplished as soon as possible. Simultaneous statements, in one form or another, could be issued by both governments. Further, it would not be difficult to institute talks, on the ambassadorial or some other level, in a third country as Peking and Washington have done. For such arrangements, formal recognition would not be required. There are also other possible mechanisms of inter-governmental contact.

Of course, Japan's future China policy is not easy to predict. It depends upon many factors, some of which are beyond Japan's control. The question of the two Vietnams now casts a dark shadow which might make it impossible for Japan, at least for a time, to proceed in her efforts to normalize her relations with the P.R.C. Apart from this consideration, one of the essential factors at the Tokyo end will be the coordinated will of the conservative party and the Japanese government to develop the current China policy further. If other conditions remain the same, there will be a gradual growth of *de facto* relations with or without official sanction. Such a continuation of Japan's present basic China policy, however, requires that Peking refrain from actions which may be regarded as interference in Japan's politics.

Needless to say, the opposition will increasingly press, no doubt with much public support, for formal recognition as soon as possible. But with Japan's relationship with Taiwan as it is, formal recognition by the Satô administration or any other conservative government is almost unthinkable unless Taiwan decides to sever relations with

Tokyo in protest against some further Japanese action vis-à-vis the mainland.

Fourthly, as for the question of China's representation in the United Nations, the government will go along with the United States so long as there is no clear majority of the members in favor of Peking. But if such a majority emerges in the General Assembly, the United States and Japan will face a crucial problem. Japan's efforts at cooperating with the U.S. government in handling the problem as a "substantive matter" may no longer be valid. Japan will have to rethink the whole question in Asian terms, for her attitude will certainly become a burning domestic issue which might easily disturb her social tranquillity. Even then, Peking's attitude will have to be considered. Although since 1949 the Peking government has continued, until recently, to express its official desire to be seated, it is as yet highly doubtful that Peking would make any compromise on the status of Taiwan. For some time, however, there will probably be disagreement among the member nations, and Japan will have time for study and decision—unless the world changes more rapidly than such conjectures as these.

The United States was instrumental in organizing the United Nations and has consistently upheld its ideals. It cannot, therefore, now afford to destroy the organization over the issue of Peking's seating. Such action would run counter to world opinion. Japan's first principle of diplomacy, as former Premier Kishi once aptly declared, is to support and strengthen the United Nations. Idealism and realism will have to go together in an international effort to settle the problem. Prime Minister Satô has officially expressed his desire to have Peking seated as soon as it becomes feasible.[12] The present writer is also among the Japanese favoring an early seating of Peking, but he believes that as a prerequisite, Peking must do considerable thinking in its own interest.

ESTIMATES OF AMERICAN POLICY

It is true that the Chinese revolution was one of the greatest shocks in recent American history. Nevertheless, U.S. Far Eastern policy from the beginning of the cold war until a few years ago sought largely to counteract Soviet policy. After the unexpected outbreak

---

12. Before the Standing Committee for the Budget, House of Councillors, March 6, 1965.

of the Korean War in 1950, however, American policy also sought to contain Peking's power and, later, to protect peripheral countries from so-called Chinese expansionism. An economic embargo of the mainland was instituted in the hope of retarding the growth of Peking's economic, political, and military power. Washington has regarded Japan as a possible bastion for the free world—first against the Soviet Union and later against Communist China as well. The United States intervened in the Korean War primarily to protect the people of South Korea but also with the indirect aim of safeguarding Japan from Soviet and Peking influence.

While the United States has continued its efforts to develop and maintain the strongest nuclear deterrent in the world, it has now come to be more or less on speaking terms with the Soviet Union. At the same time, the rift between Peking and Moscow has become almost irreconcilable. This fact seems to have enabled the U.S. government to take a harder line vis-à-vis China and to resort to a stronger military policy in South and North Vietnam. Peking has become "enemy no. 1" in American public opinion.

There have been, to be sure, indications of a new American approach to the problem of China. In a speech in San Francisco on December 13, 1963, Roger Hilsman, then Assistant Secretary of State for Far Eastern Affairs, declared "an open door to possible changes" in Peking's attitude. This speech was generally regarded as a follow-up to the U.S. global policy enunciated in the late President Kennedy's address at American University on June 10 of the same year. The significance of these developments, however, seems to have been negated, at this writing, by the series of bombings in North Vietnam since February 1965.

The Japanese government realizes the many difficulties confronting current American undertakings in the Vietnamese area. It has provided medical aid to the Vietnamese, and that aid is being enlarged since the conversations between President Johnson and Premier Satô in January 1965. Most Japanese, however, have been inclined to believe that Chinese incitement of, and ideological and military assistance to, the Pathet Lao, the Viet Cong, and North Vietnam have been unduly dramatized, and that until recently the indigenous origin and growth of the Communist forces in Southeast Asia have not been properly evaluated by the American public. The Japanese people are now concerned because the whole local situation is fast reaching an impasse. They are also concerned about the possibility of a racial war. Such a war will certainly not come about immediately, but it may eventually develop if the situation continues to degenerate in such a manner that the sufferings of non-white peoples in these areas increase to a dangerous degree.

Although most Japanese have no doubt about the American intention to preserve the freedom and to help raise the standard of living of these already war-weary peoples, they are convinced that American efforts in these directions call for prolonged planning, extraordinary patience, and unfailing understanding—to an extent far beyond American anticipation. The Japanese believe, as many Americans do, that the basic condition for success in aiding developing countries lies in aligning one's efforts with the rising tide of nationalistic sentiments and aspirations in these countries, although such a task may be extremely difficult in some cases. Aiding an unpopular government in a developing country will indirectly increase the strength of an opposition capable of arousing nationalistic sentiments.

The several preceding paragraphs are inserted here because the problem of Vietnam is related to the problem of China. Thus, the way the United States handles these two problems will seriously affect Japan's stability and her China policy, and it may undermine the good relations between Japan and the United States.

In Japanese eyes, the American attitude toward China seems to say: "If you, the Chinese, change your attitude, we are ready to change." Several Americans have also said: "We cannot make concessions under duress." The Japanese remember that the same words have often been addressed by Chinese leaders to the Americans in the past. Thus, a deadlock still seems to persist. It will not be solved merely by military measures but will require political negotiations.

The partial nuclear test ban treaty of July 1963 had its roots in the recognition of a basic common interest between Moscow and Washington. The Japanese believe that the time is approaching when the Chinese and the American people will also see a basic common interest in averting a major war between their countries. Under duress or without duress, both sides must find a way out of the deadlock. The Japanese have reason to believe that Peking, in its own interest, will not attempt to corner the Americans but will choose to negotiate and that Washington will not try to press the Chinese to the wall. Conservatism in America and elsewhere requires wise adaptation to world changes, and President Johnson's victory over

Senator Goldwater in 1964 was a salutary sign in Japanese eyes. Knowledgeable people in Japan firmly believe that Washington and Peking will have to talk with each other—perhaps in conference with several of the third nations concerned or at the table of the United Nations—for a settlement in Laos, South Vietnam, and North Vietnam.

Despite the fact that there is a war in Vietnam, the hope that the United States will modify its China policy is not necessarily illusory. The United States had modified its China policy in the past. In 1957, it agreed, largely at British insistence, to a relaxation of the CHINCOM list. As the leader of the free world, the United States has to solidify its ties with other NATO nations by accommodating itself, however reluctantly, to their interests. Recently "independence in partnership" or "coalition diplomacy" have been talked about in America. Furthermore, the United States obviously recognizes that there is a need to communicate with Communist China. As for the problem of disarmament, many Americans have realized that Communist China must be invited to take part in international conferences. Washington and Peking still conduct talks on the ambassadorial level in Warsaw. Although there have been no results of consequence so far, they continue to talk because both believe that such a mechanism is and will be useful as a safeguard against catastrophe. In short, America's China policy has been modified in the past and will be modified in the future. Peking is aware of the facts and possibilities despite its official claim that U.S. policy toward China is unchanged or has been stiffened since the fall of 1964. Most knowledgeable people in Japan hope and expect that America's China policy will soon have to be reviewed and revised in the light of global policy related to world peace. In particular, a re-examination will be absolutely necessary in the interest of preserving amity and cooperation between Washington and Tokyo.

THE NATIONAL SECURITY PROBLEM

In planning and executing China policy, the Japanese people and government naturally bear in mind the national security problem and the possible reaction of the United States to Japan's China policy. All the conservative administrations have loyally cooperated with the general American policy toward the Far East—in Japan's interest and, as the Japanese believe, in the interest of America as well.

While economic problems between the two nations, problems resulting largely from policies connected with the defense of the dollar,
can be threshed out through normal contacts, the defense arrangements now existing have given rise to problems of wider scope and
impact needing careful handling—American use of military bases in
Japan, the constitutionality of Japan's defense forces, the behavior of
some American soldiers, the problem of prior consultation on deployment abroad of American forces in Japan, etc.

By and large, the U.S. government has been considerate of
Japanese sentiments.[13] It has gradually reduced the size of the U.S.
forces stationed in Japan and has promptly scrapped unnecessary
bases. The Japanese public, however, has not yet fully understood
U.S.-Japan security arrangements, largely because they smack of a
continuation of the American Occupation of Japan. Anti-war sentiment has inhibited hard thinking on the problem of Japan's defense.
During the Occupation, national security problems were easily put
out of mind. The U.S.-Japan Security Treaty has fostered a sense
of undue and idle reliance on the United States. During the past 15
years, there have been 22 different Cabinet ministers in charge of
national defense. Neither the leaders nor the people seem yet to
have regained the sense of responsibility and the enthusiasm to tackle
more positively the problem of defending their country by assuming
a respectable share of the burden and by assuming the whole burden
if and when the time comes. The Japanese Self-Defense Forces
(JSDF) have now grown into a 175,000-man land force, a 33,000-man
naval force with 130,000 tons of ships, and a 39,000-man air force
with about 1,000 planes. But the general public still looks at the
JSDF coldly, although there are signs of gradual improvement in
their relations and also indications of more realistic attitudes on
defense among the people.

While the nuclear arms race continues, there persists undeniable
doubt concerning the real contribution of the JSDF to national
security. The general public has little knowledge about problems of
defense or about the strategic significance of Okinawa and Taiwan.
Consequently, defense policies have been seriously probed only by
small groups of persons directly concerned. Plans and strategy for
JSDF operations are also completely dependent on those of the
U.S. military. Naturally, a high morale and *esprit de corps* have not
yet been developed in the JSDF.

---

13. See the U.S.-Japan communique issued in Washington, D.C., on January
19, 1960.

The military partnership begun by the U.S.-Japan Security Treaty of 1951 (revised in 1960 for another 10 years) has indeed had much to do with Japan's economic growth. But it has also produced an ominous difference in views among the people on the vital problem of Japan's defense and on American Far Eastern policy. The majority of the Japanese people feel vaguely secure in remaining under the American wing, but a significant segment is deeply concerned that American policy in Vietnam might develop into a major war affecting Japan's stability and security. So far, conservative leaders have failed to explain this problem convincingly enough to narrow the gap in views. Opposition leaders have not yet presented acceptable alternatives. Under the circumstances, whenever Japan contemplates more autonomous diplomatic action which it believes to be even slightly against the wishes of the United States, the government tends to be extremely sensitive to repercussions in the United States which might cause divergence, if not rupture, in the defense partnership. The government's attitude on the furtherance of Japan's own China policy, an effort supported by a large segment of business leaders and by the public in general, is a case in point.

China's nuclear explosion in October 1964 has so far not seriously affected the attitude of the Japanese people on the problem of defense. The JSP had tried to persuade the Peking leaders to give up the idea by suggesting that they explore the practicality of creating a de-nuclearized zone including Japan and the Chinese continent. A few Japanese scholars had made similar appeals,[14] but Peking has not responded to them. Most Japanese, however, feel that the day when China will have operational nuclear weapons will not be soon in coming.

The U.S.-Japan Security Treaty, which is valid up to 1970, has now come under review. Some Japanese believe that neither Soviet nor Chinese aggression against Japan is likely in the foreseeable future—even if there were no security treaty. Contrary to the U.S. government's statements, several knowledgeable Americans tell us that all or most of the U.S. forces now stationed in Japan can be withdrawn in the not distant future. The opposition is prepared to make a strong argument that the treaty be abolished altogether in 1970. Many responsible Japanese, however, feel the need for a continuing arrangement, more specifically defensive than the present one, to serve deterrent purposes. Such specifically defensive arrangements

14. Yoshikazu Sakamoto, "Sino-Japanese Relations in the Nuclear Age," [in Japanese] *Sekai*, June 1963.

can be more adequately explained to the people and better understood by them. Peking would probably have to acquiesce as long as it wants trade with Japan. In fact, Peking has now stopped quibbling over the revised U.S.-Japan military partnership.

Further moves to improve the existing security arrangement will have to take account of several of the following points:

1. Anti-war sentiment and the aspiration for diplomatic autonomy will have to be weighed properly. Otherwise, political stability will be basically undermined, and any security arrangement might become useless, even from the American point of view.

2. Both a Far Eastern "Locarno" agreement and a plan to create a de-nuclearized zone are desirable and worthy of study as long-range plans, though for the moment impracticable. An international arrangement, involving either bilateral or U.N. guarantees, is necessary for Japan's security. But in any case, more initiative and responsibility in the matter of defense and operational plans are required for Japan.

3. On the one hand, the Japanese people will have to learn that under current circumstances American protection of Japan cannot be divorced from America's overall Asian policy in the near future and that the U.S.-Japan Security Treaty is almost inseparably related to American Korean policy. On the other hand, the American people will have to understand that security and peace in the Far East are prerequisites to the protection of Japan to which the U.S. government has committed itself.

4. Any marked advance or fresh implementation of the American defense line in the Western Pacific area will invite counteraction by the Soviet Union or China—to the detriment of Japan's security. The triangular relations between the United States, the U.S.S.R., and the P.R.C. are subject to change; but there is no development that can now be foreseen which would deprive the U.S.S.R. of an independent effective voice in Far Eastern and Southeast Asian affairs. It might be worthwhile, therefore, for America to explore the possibility of an understanding with the Soviet Union regarding the security of Japan and Korea, and for Japan to study the conditions for stabilizing relations with Communist China. Success in the latter would enhance Japan's prestige and strengthen her ability to contribute toward more secure relations in Asia.

JAPANESE POLITICS AND JAPANESE-AMERICAN RELATIONS

In the 20 years since the war, Japan has become a respectable nation of the world instead of a shameful, vanquished country. Especially since the end of the Occupation in 1952, Japan has grown in economic strength and has established normal international relations with almost all nations, except China. The resurgence of the new Japan arises from her political stability more than anything else. But the political stability which Japan now enjoys is in fact somewhat precarious. It is precarious because many Japanese intellectuals (who exert a strong influence on the opposition parties), organized labor, and university students entertain a deep distrust of the conservative party, the government it supports, and the bureaucracy— despite the fact that the conservative party has won a series of general elections. Much money has been spent in these election campaigns, but no sign of improvement in the situation is yet visible. Moreover, intellectual and opposition criticism of the diplomatic and security policies of successive conservative governments as too soft and all-too-dependent vis-à-vis Washington is not totally groundless. Unquestionably, the attitude of the U.S. government has so far contributed much to Japan's political stability, but Americans should not take that stability for granted. It has been and will be a situation difficult to maintain. It is more easily and often more adversely affected by foreign—especially foreign military—issues than by domestic ones. Apart from the Japanese Communists, however, most of our intellectuals, the opposition parties, organized labor, students, and the general public definitely do not want a *coup d'état* or a violent revolution. They sincerely desire social stability and the gradual growth of Japan's economy and political democracy. Some of the conservative political leaders do realize the necessity of revising the conservative party's unpopular attitudes, but they are in the minority. The crux of the problem, therefore, lies in the quality of Japanese political leadership. So-called top-notch politicians show little enthusiasm for convincing the people of the propriety and value of their policies. They seem to lack the vision to begin coping with the polarizing tendencies latent in the various national sentiments—sentiments which demand "refining" and coordination at the hands of competent leaders. Furthermore, they seem to lack the courage or wisdom with which to persuade Japan's friends among the nations of the world of the rationale of Japanese foreign policy. Hence, they give the impression of merely watching or sounding out the reactions of friendly nations.

Japan, which lies between America and China geographically, is deeply interested in a relaxation in U.S.-China relations, however remote this possibility may be. Because we Japanese are so deeply interested, we might at times be over-optimistic about what is happening. However, the Americans must understand that it is the sincere hope of every Japanese that U.S.-China relations eventually will be improved. Some Japanese leaders have been talking directly to some Peking leaders to try to persuade them that such an improvement presupposes a better understanding of America's policy on their part.

The Japanese people remember that it was China over which Japan and America fought in 1941–45. It is this memory which causes deep anxiety about the important differences between Japanese and American views of the present conditions of mainland China, of the reality of Chinese expansionism, and of China's future direction.

Japan wants to be friendly with the United States for the sake of her own national existence. She also wants, however, to have normal intercourse with Communist China, her neighbor. Japan's existence owes much to peace and security in the Far East. It would be a great mistake, though, for the U.S. government to assume that the conservative government, supported by a parliamentary majority, can do anything it wishes without the consent of Japanese public opinion and to base U.S. actions on that assumption. The Japanese have the right to frame their policies to mean something to themselves first and to others only secondarily.

The fall of the Japanese Empire created a vacuum in Asian power relations. No adequate measures have been taken, even by the United States, to fill the vacuum, and the advent of the new China made it most difficult for the Americans, single-handed, to cope with the situation. The Japanese have gradually come to believe, thanks to their growing economic power and level of technology, that they can and ought to play a role in this situation.

Japan's approach, however, has to be different from that of America because of her nation-wide anti-war sentiments, her new Constitution, her sense of cultural affinity with the Chinese, and her interest in the economic potential of the continent. The Japanese fear that the current American approach tends to isolate and antagonize 700 million Chinese. A closer relationship between Tokyo and

Peking would enable Japan's leaders to talk with their counterparts in Peking on all sorts of problems, including those of Southeast Asia. Can one not hope that Japan might one day be able to act as a bridge between Washington and Peking? In fact, Japan has gradually been building up a position as a moderator. It is the earnest hope of all Japanese that Japan will some day become an effective stabilizing factor in Far Eastern international relations. That day will come sooner if the United States rightly sees the value of Japan's role.

The present writer, an old liberal by credo, strongly opposes having Japan "communized" either by an indigenous subversive force or by Chinese influence or by both. He is convinced that Japan, if she enjoys political stability, will develop into a more democratic nation, remain a good friend of America, and contribute much toward peace in the Far East. If ever there should be a major war between the United States and China, no matter by whom it appeared to be provoked, its impact on Japan's stability would be catastrophic. It might even bring about civil war. As one who has personally spoken to Chinese leaders as bluntly as possible about the importance of knowing and understanding American intentions, this writer feels justified in making a sincere appeal to the United States for reflection and rethinking on the problem of China. The time has come to face "the facts, not the myths." Objective observations, candor, and understanding are now more desirable than ever.

ANNEX

In February 1964, after France's recognition of the P.R.C., a number of questions were raised in the Japanese Diet concerning the state of Japan's China policy and the possible effect on it of the French action. The replies of Prime Minister Ikeda and Foreign Minister Ōhira gave some appearance of inconsistency and left some points obscure. Later a paper was prepared within the Foreign Ministry under the title "Materials for Diet Interpellations on the China Problem." The document can be fully understood only in the context of the February debates. In some quarters it was criticized as evasive, but it provides an unusually concise statement of the problems as seen by the Japanese government at the time and of the declared policy of the government. The document is inserted here by the editor as additional reference material.

The following translation of the Foreign Ministry paper is based on a text printed in *Sankei Sinbun* on March 3, 1964. It is not a full literal translation. Some parenthetical material has been omitted, some portions have been condensed, and some stylistic modifications have been made without intentional sacrifice of substance.—A.M.H.

MATERIALS FOR DIET INTERPELLATIONS ON THE CHINA PROBLEM

I. Basic Policy toward China

Japan's present China policy is based on two premises. First, Japan treats the Chinese Nationalist government on Taiwan as representing China. It concluded a peace treaty with this government and maintains regular relations with it. Second, in view of its historical and geographical connections with mainland China, which has a population of over 600 million, Japan cannot avoid having *de facto* relations of several kinds with mainland China. (In this respect, Japan's position differs basically from that of the United States.)

So long as both the Nationalist government and the Communist regime insist on claiming sovereignty over all of China, it is impossible in practice for Japan to have diplomatic relations with both at the same time. If Japan under present conditions were to establish regular diplomatic relations with the Communist regime, it would mean not only an immediate break in relations with the Nationalist government but a rupture of all relations, particularly economic, with Taiwan itself.

The result would be to endanger the peace and stability of Asia and to impair free world stability. Under present conditions, such a policy would be contrary to Japan's national interests and would not correspond to the desires of the majority of the Japanese people.

The policy which accords with actuality and best secures our national interests is to continue to have *de facto* relations with mainland China, particularly trade relations based on the separation of political and economic affairs, while preserving regular diplomatic relations with the Nationalist government.

Clearly, the situation in which the Nationalist government and the Communist regime insist on conflicting claims to sovereignty over all of China cannot be called normal. But it is not within Japan's capacity independently to normalize the situation. Severance of relations with the Nationalist government and recognition of the Communist regime by Japan would not lead to normalizing the situation; rather, it would cause confusion, and it would not contribute to peace in Asia. In the Japanese view, the only way to deal with the problems involving the Nationalist government and the Communist regime is for the United Nations to take the lead in giving them thorough consideration and producing an equitable proposal for settlement, based on world opinion; this is the approach for which Japan has worked in the United Nations and for which we will continue to work.

II. Communist China's Aggressiveness

For the purposes of Japan's policy, it is meaningless to try to determine in theoretical terms whether Communist China is bellicose or peace-loving. The more urgent business is not to slacken consistent investigation of the intentions and concrete policies of Communist China as a nation toward Asia and Japan.

The Chinese Communist regime, as a Communist regime, aims ultimately at communizing the world; furthermore, it is undeniably true that, in view of facts cited below, not only the Asian countries (including Japan) but all countries in various degrees harbor anxiety concerning the danger of its external expansion (not only by military means, but ideologically, politically, and economically).

1. In the past, large-scale military intervention at the time of the Korean incident, use of force in the Sino-Indian border dispute, use of force in the Taiwan Straits, etc.; in the present, supply of arms to the guerrillas in South Vietnam.

2. Rejection of the priority of peaceful coexistence in the Sino-Soviet controversy; especially, opposition to the partial nuclear test-ban treaty and claiming an independent nuclear arsenal.

3. Refusal to abandon their claim to liberate Taiwan by armed force plus proclaiming the justice of national liberation wars.

Whether Communist China at the present stage will or will not engage in dangerous foreign adventures is a separate question. At present it seems rather to be taking a prudent attitude in external affairs. Thus, it appears improbable that Communist China will take direct military action on the Sino-Indian border, in Korea, or in the Taiwan Straits. Even in the Laos-Vietnam area, it is not to be expected that they will go beyond supply of arms from the rear and other agitational operations to the stage of throwing in their own troops.

We do not believe that Communist China at present has any plan for direct military aggression against Japan. The existence of a danger of military aggression from abroad depends as much on whether Japan is fully prepared to check aggression as on the intentions of others. Only the existence of the U.S.-Japan security system keeps us from feeling any threat of foreign aggression and guarantees our security. Although we have no sense of being menaced by Communist China's military aggression, it is a mistake to think that Japan's security will be guaranteed even under conditions of unarmed neutrality.

Though there is no present danger of direct military aggression against Japan, we still cannot feel completely at ease concerning Communist China. It is common knowledge that Communist China upholds the position that American imperialism is the common enemy of Japan and China. Further, judging by recent statements by Chairman Mao Tse-tung * and by Premier Chou En-lai,**

---

* Mao Tse-tung's statement, "Support the Japanese People's Anti-American Struggle," made to Kazuo Suzuki and others in Peking on January 27, 1964.—Ed.

** Chou En-lai's remarks on U.S. influence on Japan made in an interview with an AFP correspondent in Mogadishu on February 6, 1964.—Ed.

it is clear that Communist China's objective is to destroy the U.S.-Japan security system by alienating Japan from the United States. As for contacts with Communist China, particularly trade, the government will persist in carrying out the principle of separating politics from economics. It is naturally expected that Communist China will try to take advantage of these contacts to foster a pro-Communist Chinese mood among the Japanese people and thus to alienate Japan from the United States and the Republic of China. Needless to say, Japan must take thorough precautions against such an "ideological offensive."

III. The Problems of Representation in the United Nations and Normalization of Diplomatic Relations with Communist China

Japan's basic attitude is as follows:

The problem of China's representation in the United Nations should not be decided as a mere procedural question of whether the Nationalist government or the Communist regime represents China. It is an important problem related to the peace of Asia and to world peace. A formula for solution should be produced, following thorough substantial discussion, which can obtain the approval of world opinion.

It was with this intent that Japan became a sponsor of the resolution designating the problem of Chinese representation as an important question. If the question is thoroughly debated from all angles in the United Nations and if it is shown that the seating of Communist China is necessary and desirable for the preservation of peace in Asia and world peace, it will be natural for Japan to give thought to normalizing diplomatic relations with Communist China. Hitherto Japan has opposed resolutions providing simply that the U.N. seat should be given to Communist China and the Nationalist government be expelled, on the ground that the resolutions do not conform to the aim of maintaining peace in Asia and world peace. Further, the results of the votes on the resolution show that the general trend of world opinion did not support them. It is still too early at present to decide what concrete attitude Japan should take at the next [1964] U.N. General Assembly. We propose to deal with the situation prudently while observing how the majority trend of world opinion develops. France's establishment of diplomatic relations will certainly have an effect on this problem, but one should not hastily conclude that the effect has been decisive. At any rate, Japan does not contemplate changing its basic attitude that the problem will exert an important influence on world peace and that it should be solved in an equitable form, arrived at by thorough, substantive discussions which world opinion will approve.

The question arises whether Japan would proceed to normalize diplomatic relations with Communist China if a resolution to seat her in the United Nations were passed by a bare majority of the U.N. General Assembly. Japan hopes for an equitable solution which will gain the approval of a clear majority of the United Nations. It is the duty of Japan, because of the value it places on the United Nations, to strive to avoid a sharp split of opinions in the United Nations. It is not proper to decide at this point what attitude Japan will take if such a split should nevertheless come about.

Chapter 6

AUSTRALIA AND CHINA
Power Balance and Policy

BY

CORAL BELL

It has become a commonplace to observe that Australian foreign policy is (and must be) dominated by the effort to reconcile the nation's history, which has made it racially, politically, economically, and culturally a transplanted segment of Europe, with the geography which ordains that its closest neighbors should be the Asian powers. Among those Asian neighbors it is inevitably to the most powerful at any particular time that Australian eyes are speculatively turned. Since 1950, the policy of the Australian government has been based on the premise that that power is at present Communist China, and Australian majority opinion, as reflected in election results, has acquiesced in this view, though perhaps with some ambivalence and with some reservations. Attitudes toward China may justly be regarded as the central or catalytic element in Australian diplomatic alignments since 1949. These attitudes have determined the choice, where differences have existed on Asian questions, between what the Prime Minister would call Australia's two "great and powerful friends," America and Britain. They have affected Australia's relationships as between SEATO and the nonaligned powers, and they have qualified attitudes toward a recent enemy, Japan, and a newer and nearer uncertainty, Indonesia.

None of these facts is at all surprising. A foreign policy is essentially a shield; it must naturally be constructed with the direction of the likeliest possible blow in mind. The estimate of the most probable enemy will tend to determine the recognition of the most valuable friend. A dissenting school of opinion in Australia would argue that in this case the contrary has been true: that an ill-considered assumption as to which was the most valuable friend has led to policies which have made or are likely to make an unnecessary enemy. The policy the government has pursued since 1949—nonrecognition of Communist China—is held to have militated against the security interests of Australia. These, it is maintained, lie in the cultivation of friendship with its Asian neighbors.

ATTITUDES PRIOR TO WORLD WAR II

To judge between these views of Australia's policy toward Communist China, one must take account of the factors which affected Australia's relations with an earlier China. One point should be made first, however. Such debate as there has been over policy toward China, though it has involved the four political parties which provide the two alternative governments, has nevertheless been confined to a small number of participants. Three groups are involved: first, the policy makers, including the Prime Minister and successive Ministers of External Affairs, other members of the Cabinet, and senior officers of the Department of External Affairs; second, "articulate" opinion, including leaders of the Opposition, backbenchers on both sides, journalists and academics who write or broadcast about foreign policy, and representatives of interests or pressure groups; third, "grass-roots" opinion, which makes itself felt chiefly by its votes in elections, though a sense of the limits within which it will acquiesce in the government's conduct of affairs is probably built into the souls of successful politicians. The debate over China policy has been fairly lively within "articulate" opinion, but election results since 1949 denote either endorsement of the government's policy or indifference to the whole issue at the level of "grass-roots" opinion.

But if this last sector of opinion has shown no sign of being stirred by the contemporary debate, it contributed powerfully to the formative influences on policy. Long before Australia attained formal nationhood, Australians tended to look anxiously up over the unmanned northern ramparts of their continent toward the multitudinous populations of Asia and scan them for any credible threat. For the first 50 years of this century Japan so obviously filled the bill that it seemed unnecessary to look further. But for much of the 19th century China had been the general choice for the role. In this early attitude toward China one can see an interplay (which still exists) between foreign policy attitudes and a central item of Australian domestic policy, demand for an uninhibited control over immigration. An influx of Chinese miners during the Australian gold rushes of the 1850s had made them an object of fears and antipathies, which were reflected in the legislation of the period. The debate on immigration control was renewed in the 1880s. Terms such as "the Chinese invasion" were used to refer both to a mere influx of population and to an imagined military operation. Australian attitudes toward other Asian peoples in many ways represented a sort of extrapolation of these early attitudes toward the Chinese—just as the legislation that excluded Asian immigration generally grew out of that originally directed specifically against the Chinese.

It is true that the Chinese, as against the Japanese later, were regarded largely as an economic and social threat rather than a diplomatic or military one. It is also true that the imperialisms of the European powers other than Britain in the Pacific were from time to time viewed with greater alarm than anything that might come out of Asia. Nevertheless, these 19th century stances represent a first half-articulated demand of Australian foreign policy. A vague sense of China as a distantly alarming force is woven into the original fabric of Australian national attitudes. Even in those embryo days of policy formation, a preoccupation with the possible consequences for Australia of the difference in strategic priorities between itself and its overseas friends is visible, though the only such friend then under consideration was of course Britain. A *Sydney Morning Herald* editorial of 1895, which might equally well have appeared in 1965, reads:

> To the U.K., with its densely populated area and its distance from the East the possibility of being swamped by the population of Oriental countries is a remote one. . . . With the vast area of Australian territory, at present barely fringed with settlements, lying over against teeming populations of Eastern Asia, and in comparative proximity, the case is different. With us it is not a mere matter of sentiment or of racial prejudice but the grave question of whether we shall preserve our existence as an Anglo-Saxon people. . . .[1]

---

1. Quoted in W. Levi, *Australia's Outlook on Asia* (Sydney: Angus and Robertson, 1958), p. 19.

The turn of the century roughly marks a turn in Australian attitudes as between Japan and China. Japan's defeat of Russia in
1904–05 transformed the old image of the Japanese into something
much more formidable and more relevant to Australia's speculations
about its own security. From 1905 until 1950 the shadow of possible
Japanese expansionism occupied Australian attention almost to the
point of excluding attention to China. When China entered her
modern revolutionary period in 1911, Australian attention was preoccupied with the question of whether the Anglo-Japanese alliance
ought to be renewed. The more perverse extravagances of Australian
policy at Versailles, such as the Prime Minister's conflict with President Wilson over the proposed racial equality clause, were inspired by
apprehensions centering almost exclusively upon Japan. The Japanese attack in Manchuria in 1931 might therefore have been expected
to mark the beginning of a new phase of interest and sympathy in
Australia for China, now the victim of expansionist ambitions which
were widely believed likely to stretch out toward Australia. Yet there
was less visible impulse in Australia than in America or even in Britain
to identify its own security interests with China's. The one initiative
of this period that seemed to offer any prospect of action to restrain
Japan was the Stimson note of 1932, for which neither party in Australia showed any enthusiasm. The then Prime Minister, J. V.
Lyons, was anxious to avoid Australian participation in any war, and
the Labor opposition even opposed Australian participation in economic sanctions.

Several factors must be taken into account in considering this
faintheartedness. The Australian government would certainly have
been influenced by the skepticism of the British government as to
whether the Americans could or would do as much about Japan as the
Secretary of State seemed to be indicating. There existed a minority
crosscurrent of sympathy for Japan on the ground that it represented
order and enterprise as against Chinese warlordism and chaos, some
feeling that the Chinese had brought their troubles on themselves by
anti-foreign policies, and a rather ignoble tendency to calculate thankfully that a Japan so involved with China would have no appetite for
Australia. Neither of the main political parties was particularly
oriented toward the League of Nations. The political right, as the
party of the imperial connection, was content to rest on the principle
of the diplomatic unity of the Empire. The political left, by reaction, was nationalist and isolationist. Thus the notion of collective

security carried little if any more weight than the notion of China as an ally in the balance against Japan. The historian of these events noted sardonically at the time that Australia was "apparently inclined to regard the breakdown of the collective system of security as a cheap price for the privilege of being eaten last." [2]

When the Japanese hostilities against China were stepped up in 1937, however, doubts of the effectiveness of the previous lines of policy became widespread. The Prime Minister told the nation in December 1938 that Australia, for the first time in its history, might find itself in a war zone. He had suggested at the Imperial Conference of 1937 the possibility of a Pacific pact to stabilize the situation, but the idea produced no great response. The Labor opposition resisted it on the ground that it would commit Australia to take sides for or against particular groups of powers.[3] The notion of a Pacific pact was attended by a pervasive vagueness. The Prime Minister's own phrases could hardly have been more indefinite: Australia "would greatly welcome a regional understanding and a pact of non-aggression by the countries of the Pacific, conceived in the spirit and principles of the League," and Australia "would be prepared to collaborate to that end with all the peoples of the Pacific region in a spirit of understanding and sympathy." Presumably both Japan and China would have been eligible for membership in such a pact, but it is not clear whether the Australian understanding and sympathy would have been for China as victim, or for Japan and her efforts to better herself by absorbing large chunks of her neighbor. The proposal came to nothing. Japan was recalcitrant, America and Britain reserved, and only Russia enthusiastic.

Even in the late 1930s, it is difficult to discern any sign that either the policy makers in Canberra or the small circle of Australian informed opinion gave much consideration to China as an element in the power balance. In the two most substantial and influential volumes on Australia's foreign relations published during the interwar period,[4] the only sustained consideration of Chinese affairs is one

---

2. A. J. Toynbee, *Survey of International Affairs for 1932* (London: Oxford University Press, 1933), p. 533.

3. See speech by John J. Curtin, *Australian Parliamentary Debates*, v. 18, 1937, p. 856.

4. Ian C. Ross, ed., *Australia and the Far East: Diplomatic and Trade Relations* (Sydney: Angus and Roberston in conjunction with the Australian Institute of International Affairs, 1935) and Walter G. K. Duncan, ed., *Australia's Foreign Policy* (Sydney: Angus and Robertson in conjunction with the Australian Institute of Political Science, 1938).

article on China as a market for Australian products. Scattered references to China in articles on other subjects invariably treat the country as a passive rather than an active element in world policy. It was really still below the threshold of consideration as either potential ally or potential enemy.

AUSTRALIA AND CHINA, 1941–49

It would be reasonable to see Prime Minister Menzies' decision, made early in 1941, to send an Australian minister to China as the first evidence of a reborn belief that China might be of some moment in Australia's future. At the time, Australia had only two legations, Washington and Tokyo, so the decision represented a fairly radical development in the allocation of Australia's scarce diplomatic resources.

During the war Australia and China shared a major strategic concern—supplies for the Pacific and Asian theater of operations—but this common concern did not always give them a similar scale of military priorities. One illustration of the conflict of interests was the dispute between Churchill and Curtin as to whether the Australian division returning from the Middle East in February 1942 should be diverted to Rangoon to try to save enough of Burma to reduce the isolation of China and thus to ensure that something more than the trickle of supplies possible by other routes got through to Chungking. Perhaps there was never any hope of halting the Japanese at the time. At any rate Curtin insisted that the risk involved was "not a reasonable hazard of war," in light of Australia's vulnerability at the time, and he carried his point. That supply route to China went out of operation for most of the hostilities.

The clash in the competing strategic claims of East Asia and Southeast Asia had in fact been shown even before then in the temporary closing of the Burma Road in 1940 under Japanese pressure. Australia was as much concerned in this decision as Britain, and the basic reasoning behind it was that if Japan were resisted on this point, its troops might make an immediate onslaught on Southeast Asia and down toward Australia.

The "Europe first" grand strategy of Roosevelt and Churchill was one that both China and Australia had reason for resisting. Each could argue that its national existence might be entirely submerged before attention was diverted to the theater of operations vital to itself. This fact gave the two countries a theoretical common interest. But in practice the "Europe first" strategy was maintained and the Asian and Pacific theater had to rub along on what could be spared. Australian and Chinese interests thus became less cooperative than competitive for the resources available.

During the immediate postwar years, 1945–49, Australia might logically have been expected to look to China as a useful and congenial ally. It was no longer a remote, unfamiliar, unconsidered place. There was an Australian ambassador in China, and a Chinese ambassador in Canberra. Both countries were represented on the Far Eastern Commission and on the Allied Council for Japan. They had an urgent and vital interest in common: preventing the resurgence of Japan. They jointly differed, in some important respects, from American policy toward Japan. They were both concerned that the Asian and Pacific area should not be overshadowed in world attention by the Atlantic and European area. Both also felt a good deal of reserve about the re-establishment of the European empires in Asia. The Labor party was still in power in Australia in these years, and the theory that the insecurities of the Pacific had been chiefly due to oppressive and resented European empires was still influential.

Despite these common interests, China was not a particularly important factor in Australian foreign policy, nor more than occasionally an ally in the Far Eastern Commission and the Allied Council for Japan. The great policy issues were the course of the American Occupation in Japan and the nature and date of a peace treaty with Japan, especially the amount of military potential she should be allowed in the future. In the early discussion of a peace treaty, beginning about July 1947, the disputes found Russia and the Kuomintang government supporting a veto for the great powers. This position was incompatible with the Australian Foreign Minister's stand against the great-power veto in general. These early discussions of the peace treaty, however, came to nothing. By 1948, the global conflict between America and Russia was well under way. The negotiations which preceded the setting up of NATO were in train, and America had begun to regard Japan as an essential bastion against Russian power in the Far East. Neither Australian nor Chinese opinion had moved so fast as American, for neither was involved to the same degree with the situation in Europe. Thus Australia voted with China and Russia, against an American veto, on the question of continuing certain restrictions after October 1949.

Some preoccupation with the future security of the Pacific area against other dangers than Japan may, however, be seen shortly afterward, in Dr. Evatt's revival in 1949 of the notion of a Pacific pact. The inspiration was clearly the Atlantic pact, which was just being brought into operation in Europe, plus some anxieties lest the heavy American commitment to Europe might prejudice the firmness of its defensive undertakings in the Pacific and Asia generally. There was never much prospect of this proposal coming to anything. Secretary of State Acheson made it clear in May that America was not interested.[5] But even if the auspices had been otherwise good, the situation of China would have posed the same difficulties as it had in 1937. The military collapse of the Nationalist government was widely deemed to be imminent after January 1949. If a Pacific pact including the Nationalist government were to be set up, presumably its first task would be the military support of that government. It was reported in July 1949 that Chiang Kai-shek had persuaded the Philippines and South Korea to join Nationalist China as the founder-members of a pact and was hoping that Australia and India, among others, would adhere. By this time, however, all levels of Australian opinion regarded the Kuomintang with a good deal of disfavor. Stories of inefficiency and corruption were widespread. Many of them reflected the experiences of Australians who had been connected with United Nations Relief and Rehabilitation Administration's relief work in China. The closing of the American base on Manus, where the Chinese Nationalists had bought the movable property while Australia became the administering power and bought what remained, brought other frictions. The view of Mao Tse-tung's party as just "agrarian reformers" had some currency in Australia, as it did in America and Britain, but how much influence it exerted in policy-making circles would be difficult to determine.

THE RECOGNITION QUESTION, 1949–50

American and Indian reserve toward the idea of a Pacific pact would of course have discouraged Australian persistence, but the government at the end of the year was in any case becoming aware of two other interconnected problems: an election and the issue of recognition of a new regime in Peking. The new Chinese government did not formally proclaim itself and ask for recognition until October 1.

---

5. *The New York Times*, May 19, 1949.

There was thus a period of some seven months, from the beginning of the final military collapse on the mainland, for the problem to be mulled over. Within the Commonwealth, it became clear fairly early that India and Pakistan would accord recognition soon after the new government was proclaimed. Bevin's meeting with Acheson in September apparently led the British government to abandon its earlier hopes of keeping Commonwealth and American policy in line and to make a provisional British decision to recognize the Communist regime. By November, when Australian diplomats from the Asian area conferred with a British envoy, Esler Dening, the Australian government had in effect to decide whether to follow the decision of Britain and the major Asian members of the Commonwealth, or the decision of America.

The assembled Australian diplomats from the Asian area are reported to have recommended, unanimously, that Australia should accord recognition. The Minister, however, rejected the recommendation.[6] This decision of Dr. Evatt's represents a sharp deviation from his previous line of policy, one of whose major premises had been the necessity for Australia to cultivate close and cordial relations with its Asian neighbors. He had risked (and incurred) some unpopularity within his party and elsewhere by the zeal with which he had upheld this principle in the case of Indonesia. A choice which not only ended representation with a major Asian power but caused him to part company with the two main Asian members of the Commonwealth must have been genuinely unpalatable to him. There seems no doubt that it was imposed upon him by the pressure of electoral necessity.

From early in 1949, the Labor government in Australia had been under heavy fire from the Opposition for its alleged "softness to communism" in the domestic context. At this time, Communist influence in the trade unions was still substantial, and a prolonged major strike by the Coal Miners Union, under Communist leadership, had made the winter of 1949 an uncomfortable one for a good many electors. As the election approached in December, the government could not fail to be conscious that there was considerable effectiveness in the Opposition's attack. Some aspects of Dr. Evatt's foreign policy could be reproached for implying a rather more charitable interpreta-

6. J. W. Burton, *The Alternative* (Sydney: Morgan Publications, 1954). Dr. Burton was the secretary of the Department of External Affairs at this time and thus in a position to follow the development of policy.

tion of Soviet than of Western purposes. These included a letter he had dispatched, as President of the General Assembly, about the Berlin blockade and his line of policy in the United Nations concerning the Palestine and Greek crises. The U.S. State Department seems to have been irritated by his presidency of the Assembly and to have found him in general an ambiguous figure.[7] As the Prime Minister's biographer delicately notes: "Through the years when Chifley several times acted as Minister for External Affairs, the dominant influences within that Department were not especially sympathetic with American policy, nor perceptive or appreciative of the complexities of the problems which beset those called upon to direct it." [8]

Whatever the personal views of the Prime Minister and the Minister for External Affairs, or the recommendations of their diplomatic advisers, they had to bear in mind the tactical undesirability of providing more ammunition to the Opposition by recognizing the new government in China. Moreover, recognition would have risked increasing dissension among the Prime Minister's own followers, for the Labor party was already beginning to be troubled by the contest between a Catholic right-wing movement dedicated to the overthrow of Communist leadership in the unions, and a wing of the party which felt that this effort was ill-conceived or overzealous. The tensions so generated were later to result in an actual break and the splitting off of a section as a separate party.[9] This split has been the major factor keeping Labor out of office in recent years. In 1949, however, the conflicts within the party were comparatively subdued, and the Prime Minister of the time, J. B. Chifley, was successful in keeping them so. The large Catholic wing of Labor supporters, nevertheless, was inevitably affected by the reports coming out of China of ill treatment of Catholic missionaries by the Communist authorities. The Archbishop of Melbourne, Cardinal Mannix, the most powerful political-clerical figure ever to emerge in Australian history, thundered against recognition through his diocesan journal and by other means. Chifley thus had reasons for a tactful caution. An additional motive, if one were necessary, was the attitude of the Labor Prime Minister of New Zealand, Peter Fraser, who faced an election 10 days earlier than

7. See James V. Forrestal, *The Forrestal Diaries*, ed. by Walter Millis with the collaboration of E. S. Duffield (New York: Viking Press, 1951), pp. 532, 541.
8. Leslie F. Crisp, *Ben Chifley* (London: Longmans, 1961), p. 290.
9. See B. A. Santamaria " 'The Movement' 1941–1960—an Outline" in H. Mayer, ed., *Catholics and the Free Society* (Melbourne: Cheshire, 1961).

that in Australia and was reluctant to have the issue raised unnecessarily before that time.[10]

Even if a firm decision to recognize had been taken in November, Australia would presumably not have extended actual recognition before the British, who acted on January 6, 1950. There was time, thus, for second thoughts after the election by the party taking office. The new Liberal party government, however, was not in a position to accord recognition immediately after an election which had been fought so much on the issue of communism. Prime Minister Menzies, being a firm adherent of the Commonwealth and in general strongly sympathetic with the spirit of British foreign policy, would probably in normal circumstances have been anxious to heal the divergence between Australia and Britain as early as possible. It is reported that External Affairs Minister Spender called for the papers on the question of recognition in order to review the decision about six months after he came into office[11]—that is, in May or early June 1950. At that point, there were also fairly constant rumors, possibly unfounded, that America itself was moving toward recognition. But the outbreak of the war in Korea changed the whole atmosphere, and indirectly the whole general context, of Australian foreign policy.

Even if the election of 1949 and its result were the proximate causes for Australia's following American rather than British policy on recognition, the element of the fortuitous involved ought not be allowed to obscure the solid historical tendency behind the turn of events. This was by no means the first time that Australia had found the scale of priorities and anxieties imposed on it by geography rather more like America's than like Britain's. There is a considerable parallel between the respective positions of the three countries vis-à-vis China after 1950 and those vis-à-vis Japan after 1900. In 1902, Britain, needing an ally in the Pacific, found what seemed to be a useful one in Japan. But Australia, having as America to live in the Pacific and having as America an immigration policy resented in Japan, tended as America to see the Japanese navy as a potential threat rather than a potential auxiliary. The consciousness that Australia's strategic interests largely paralleled those of America and substantially diverged from those of Britain emerged strongly in comment at the time of the American naval visit of 1908.

---

10. Crisp, cited, p. 294.
11. Burton, cited.

After the First World War, the Australian government did come round to the view that the Anglo-Japanese alliance was useful. But as the postwar period turned into the prewar period, the alliance began to incur some of the blame for the rise of Japanese power in the Pacific. There was a renewed emphasis on the dichotomy of strategic interest between Britain and Australia and the complementarity of strategic interest between America and Australia. This feeling was most vehemently expressed just after the early disasters of the Pacific war. The then Prime Minister's message to the Australian electorate on December 28, 1941, made it clear that Australia refused to regard the Pacific struggle as a subordinate segment of the general conflict and that Australia looked for aid to America, "free of any pangs as to her traditional links with the United Kingdom." December 1941 is the great divide in Australian foreign policy, for it is the moment of traumatic emotional impact of what had previously been only an intellectual understanding of the possible meanings of a difference in strategic priorities.

Even if the choice made in 1949 was in part fortuitous, it nevertheless was in keeping with a sense of common strategic interests with America which had been faintly indicated since the beginning of the century, made fairly explicit in 1908, and rather overdramatically proclaimed in 1941.

AUSTRALIAN AND AMERICAN STRATEGIES: NORTHEAST ASIA

Australian policy concerning China may be seen as dominated since 1950 by the American concept of containment of China, and may be most clearly defined by the degree to which it has endorsed or been reserved toward particular trends and strategies within that general concept. The first and crucial decision, American resistance to the extension of Communist power to South Korea, aroused no problems of policy or of party feelings. This episode, though it must be considered part of the strategic containment of China, was generally regarded at the popular level as a vindication of the notion of collective security and an upholding of the prestige of the United Nations. The Opposition's spokesman on foreign affairs, Dr. Evatt, had been a much more determined protagonist of the United Nations than the leaders of the parties now in government. Thus no Opposition dissent in principle from support of the U.N. operation was

likely. Australian airmen in Japan were immediately available to be
sent to Korea. Later, ground forces were dispatched as a part of the
Commonwealth Division.

Initially, then, the Korean War, though hardly popular, was
almost exempt from criticism by the main body of the Opposition
because of the U.N. connection. As to the American action taken
more specifically against China—the neutralization of Taiwan—it is
perhaps fair to say that at the time the long-term problems stemming
from commitment to the alternative government of China were not
much appreciated. There was, therefore, rather less tendency than
in Britain to regard it with doubt. Australia voted for the resolution
which authorized the crossing of the 38th parallel and the later resolution which named China as aggressor. However, during the period
when involvement in a full-scale war with China appeared possible,
between the approach to the Yalu River and the removal of General
MacArthur, discomfort at the apparent implications of his policy
became widespread in Australian press comment. The underlying
issue in the MacArthur controversy was the degree to which strategic
priority should be given to the Asian as against the European side of
the world balance, and Australia's general attitude might seem logically to imply a pro-MacArthur position. But except for some segments of minority opinion, there has not been much support in
Australia, even at moments of crisis, for policies that seemed to carry
the risk of general war with China. Possibly Australian opinion
would not so definitely have described such hostilities as "a wrong
war at the wrong place and against a wrong enemy," as General Omar
Bradley was to do at the MacArthur inquiry and as British comment
has always tended to do; but though Australia's strategic interests
impose the hope that a considerable share of American resources will
be allocated to security in Asia, they also tend to impose a certain
caution when actual war in Asia—at any rate major war—is contemplated.

Moreover, even after China's entry into the war in Korea, and the
subsequent demonstration that Chinese troops were a formidable
military problem, Australian opinion generally, and most of the policy
makers in Canberra, still did not at this point identify the expansion
of China's sphere of power as the major future threat to Australian
security. That place was still accorded to Japan. Therefore, as
America after Korea moved toward allocating a more important role
to Japan in the balance against China, the Australian government

faced some of the most unpalatable and electorally difficult issues that have confronted it in the postwar period. These issues were involved in the preparation of the Japanese peace treaty.

In terms of American policy, it may be said that the main result of the war in Korea was to effect a general shift of the focus of American alarm at the expansion of the sphere of Communist power from Russia to China, as well as to create a belief that the Communist bloc was turning to actual military adventurism. Enhanced attention to Japan's security and her possibilities as an ally was the natural outcome of this reassessment.

No doubt the American and the Australian viewpoints differed not only because of the vastly greater vulnerability of Australia, but also because of the length of time for which each had been concerned with Japan as a danger. The historical conditioning of the period since 1905 could not be expected to vanish overnight, nor for that matter in five years. Japan remained the only Asian power with a substantial record of successes in naval and air warfare over the great Pacific distances. At the popular level there remained then, and perhaps now, a hangover of the 1930s theory that war is usually precipitated by "have-not" powers in search of economic resources or markets. Japan, infinitely more dependent on external trade than China is ever likely to be, fits this stereotype much better than China. Finally, the memories of Changi prison camp and the Burma railway provided a sharp edge to the misgivings of the policy makers. Moreover, even if the government itself had been entirely convinced that the recruitment of Japan to the Western side of the balance represented a net gain, the problem of making any such view palatable to the electorate was one about which neither party could be enthusiastic. Again one may say that Australia's situation vis-à-vis American-Japanese relations after 1950 paralleled that vis-à-vis British-Japanese relations after 1902. In both cases, she had to weigh the usefulness of her ally's ally in the immediate power balance against the uncertainty of its role in the long-term balance.

On the other hand, once the American government had made it clear that it intended to go ahead with a peace treaty with Japan, which would not incorporate the restrictions on the future development of Japanese economic or military strength that Australia had originally thought necessary, the Australian government could do little about it save seek some offsetting security mechanism. Dr. Evatt described as "a deadly delusion" the assumption, on which he said the treaty was founded, that if Japan were permitted to rearm, it would always use its arms in the interests of the Western democracies against Russia and China. Probably this remark represented an approximation of the average Australian view of the question at the time. Even now it would be difficult to maintain that most Australians have become wholly convinced that Japan is a natural ally or a permanently reliable element in the balance against China, though of course as China's strength has grown and its intransigence became more obvious, the sense that the construction of a balance against China is important to Australia has increased sharply in almost all sections of opinion.

What originally reconciled Australia to Japan's role in the Western security system was neither faith in Japan as a useful ally nor alarm at China, but the American security guarantee for Australia and New Zealand embodied in the ANZUS pact. Consideration of ANZUS as a security mechanism specifically against China has perhaps not played much part in popular assessments of the treaty even now, since it seems relevant rather to the Pacific and to the possibility of warfare with a power with some naval pretensions, such as Indonesia or (though less of a preoccupation in recent years) Japan. The ANZUS agreement has often been treated as if it were an embodiment of the notions, mooted in 1937 and again in 1949, of a Pacific pact. But there is not really much in common between those large, vague, cloudy ideas of a stabilizing arrangement in the Pacific on Locarno or Atlantic pact lines, aimed at solving the general security problems of the area and open for adhesion by most powers, and the simple security arrangement, not aimed at solving any security problems except those of Australia and New Zealand and not open for adhesion even by Britain, which ANZUS embodied.

AUSTRALIAN AND AMERICAN STRATEGIES: SOUTHEAST ASIA

Until 1953, American attention to the problem of containing Chinese power was focused on the Northwest Pacific: Japan, Korea, and Taiwan. From an Australian viewpoint, this focus left a distressing gap between Taiwan and Singapore, which was covered only by the Philippines. For a land power such as China, as against one with a naval and air tradition such as Japan, the only feasible mode of extension southward is via the Indochinese and Malayan peninsulas and the Indonesian or (less probably) Philippine archipelagoes. The preservation of Indochina, Thailand, and especially Malaya and Indonesia against forms of subjugation, subversion, or even conversion that would make them instruments or willing partners of Chinese strength was therefore much more germane to Australian security than, for instance, the preservation of South Korea as a Western foothold. The connection between the Communist insurgents in Malaya and the possible extension of Chinese power southward preoccupied Australia well before America turned its attention to Southeast Asia in 1953–54. American reluctance in the early fifties to undertake commitments to the defense of the mainland territories in Southeast Asia was believed to be the main reason for the U.S. insistence on the exclusion of Britain from the ANZUS Treaty—an exclusion which the Australian government found discomforting, especially as it had to exert considerable effort to persuade New Zealand to agree to it at all.

When America did accept involvement in mainland Southeast Asia it was, of course, in connection with the losing French battle in Vietnam rather than the successful British one in Malaya. This difference between Australia and America in areas of emphasis persists to some degree even now and until about 1964 caused Australian opinion to underestimate the importance for Australian security of developments in Vietnam. Malaya was familiar territory to which Australian troops had been committed in the Second World War. The concept that Australian national interest was directly involved there was much more readily accepted than the notion that Australia has an equal concern with the Indochinese states, although the latter's strategic importance had been demonstrated in the Japanese advance in the Second World War. Besides, censorship prevented the decay of French military power in Indochina from becoming apparent, even to the French, until the military situation in the north was almost past retrieving. As late as March 1954, a brisk official optimism was maintained—even about Dien Bien Phu.

The military debacle of April-May 1954 and the taking of Dien Bien Phu were as notable a shock in Australia as elsewhere. The episode demonstrated how well Mao Tse-tung's theories of guerrilla warfare could be applied outside China where the conditions were suitable; how rapidly a façade of military security could crumble; how speedy the transition from guerrilla campaign to conventional warfare could be; how fast, conceivably, the frontiers of Chinese power could move down to the Gulf of Siam and toward the Malay peninsula. It seemed possible that Ho Chi Minh's writ would shortly run in the whole of Vietnam and make him an almost irresistible influence in Laos and Cambodia. At this time, it is true, a victory for Ho Chi Minh was not universally equated with extension of the area of China's effective power, for it was assumed that Vietnamese nationalism would remain strongly anti-Chinese. On the other hand, there did not seem much basis to believe that Ho would have scope or reason for resisting his powerful friends to the north, especially since he would be dependent on China for the means of reconstructing his country.

Despite Australian interest in the outcome in Vietnam, the first American initiative, Dulles' speech of March 29 calling for "united action" (apparently in the sense of joint military intervention by the Western powers) to save the situation in Indochina, did not meet with any enthusiastic Australian support. External Affairs Minister Casey had reached a view that the prospects for intervention were less than hopeful: ". . . it would not have the backing of the United Nations; it would put us in wrong with world opinion particularly in Asia; it would embroil us with Communist China; it would wreck the Geneva Conference." [12] Moreover, during the crisis period of a month or so after Dulles' speech, when transformation of the war in Vietnam into a general war with China appeared possible, the Australian government again happened to be preoccupied with an election campaign. As in 1949, this complication increased the government's tendency to temporize. In this case, the sitting government, that of Menzies, was returned. It would not be altogether just, however, to ascribe the government's reluctance to be involved to electoral considerations only. The sense that Vietnam was unfavorable ground, morally and politically as well as militarily, on which to make a stand; the fact that the issue of French colonialism was involved; the ambivalence of French policy; Britain's resistance to military action; the denunciation of American proposals by India and Indonesia, with whom Australia was then cultivating good relations; the criticisms of American policy by the Opposition and sections of the press; and the built-in resistance to proposals that would take Australian troops abroad, all played a part.

By the time the election was over, American proposals for military intervention had been transformed into a project for setting up a

---

12. *Australian Parliamentary Debates, House of Representatives*, v. 4, 1954, p. 128.

treaty organization to buttress security in what remained of the area, and the Australian government in general endorsed the American proposals with enthusiasm. Where conflicts between America and Britain remained, Australia appears to have adopted positions nearer in form to the American, but nearer in substance to the British. President Eisenhower had hinted at the prospect of a serious split with Britain. When asked at a press conference whether British membership in the proposed organization was necessary, he replied that the members of the Commonwealth most directly concerned in Southeast Asia were Australia and New Zealand. "A defense system could be created with them and with the Asian countries concerned. It might not be all that would be desired, but it would be something." However, as the immediate fears of a military encounter with China diminished after May and died down almost completely with the partition agreement in July, most of the tension on this point vanished. There remained only the question of how ambitious the proposed treaty organization should be: specifically, how far it should be a boundary fence against the further extension of Chinese or of Communist power. Even before the form of the new treaty was agreed upon at the Manila conference in September, Menzies announced that Australia would accept military commitments abroad as the consequence of the pact and would make increased provision for defense costs.

SEATO undoubtedly commits American strength to preventing the area of the Indochinese peninsula and Thailand, which is the only probable route southward toward Australia for Chinese power, from being conquered militarily. It might, therefore, seem surprising that the organization has not enjoyed a particularly "good press" in Australia.[13] ANZUS, for instance, is far more frequently celebrated as a bastion of Australian security, but ANZUS, though it may protect Australia's own shores (which are unlikely to be approached in the foreseeable future anyway) and her land border with Indonesia in New Guinea (which is more likely to be secured by political success than military treaty), says nothing as to those areas of Southeast Asia whose loss to Chinese hegemony would tip the balance so notably against the West and bring the front line so un-

---

13. For examples of the comparative disfavor with which it has been regarded in scholarly comment, see George Modelski, ed., *SEATO: Six Studies* (Melbourne: Cheshire, 1962) and G. Greenwood and N. Harper, *Australia in World Affairs* (Melbourne: Cheshire, 1957 and 1963).

comfortably close to Australia. The volume of criticism directed at SEATO reflects the fact that it did not entirely meet the prescriptions of any sector of articulate opinion. The liberal left and what may be called the Asia-oriented element in opinion looked askance at it because it alienated the major Asian powers, especially India and Indonesia. Right-wing opinion has disapproved of it because it included Britain and France, who were deemed likely to block effective action by the organization in a crisis. Almost everyone has pointed out that the organization neither creates nor disposes of military strength of its own and that such power as lies behind it is simply American power. These lines of comment should not be taken to mean that Australian opinion generally, or even the critics, would be happy to see the organization dismantled. The demands have been rather to modify it. The Labor party view for most of the period since 1954 has been that the treaty's emphasis on military cooperation is mistaken and that the treaty should be remolded to stress economic, social, and cultural cooperation; but in the renewed Southeast Asian crisis of 1963–65, this argument has been played down, and most Labor parliamentarians would probably now accept the necessity for some form of military alliance in the area. Right-wing and defense-oriented groups such as the Democratic Labor party and the Returned Soldiers League have argued that it should be strengthened by the inclusion of non-Communist Asian states, such as India and Japan, but without considering the difficulties of recruiting these potential allies.

The true weakness of SEATO vis-à-vis China is, no doubt, that it has devised no means of creating in the countries it has endeavored to preserve political institutions strongly enough rooted to grow in the shadow of their northern neighbor. Therefore Western policy in the area necessarily has somewhat the look of being built upon sand. But there are limits to what a diplomatic mechanism can be expected to do. China's shadow has certainly been at least as heavy on the anti-SEATO countries (India and Burma) as on Pakistan and Thailand. In general, the Australian tendency to consider mournfully the indubitable weaknesses of SEATO and to reflect thankfully on the comparative solidity of ANZUS might be held to approximate that of one who contemplates with dismay the cracks in the dam and then congratulates himself that at least he has a fire extinguisher in case the roof should catch alight.

CHINA'S PLACE IN AUSTRALIA'S DEFENSE POLICY

With the development of SEATO and the general movement of events in South Asia, a traditional assumption stemming from the two world wars, that the Middle East was a natural sphere of Australian defense interest and operations, was abandoned. The Prime Minister in 1956 took the decision to station a token Australian force in Malaya. Bluntly interpreted, this move implied an assumption that the sphere of action of Australian troops in any future major war would be Southeast Asia and that the most probable enemy would be China or a lesser South Asian power.

Though assumptions about the terrain in which Australian combat forces would be engaged have influenced training, it would be difficult to maintain that the Australian defense buildup, such as it has been, was in any way geared to the growth of Chinese military strength. Australia undertook something of a rearmament effort in 1950–52, about the time the rest of the Western world was doing so, but this effort slowed down, as that of the NATO area did, when the concept of the "long haul" became operative after 1953. In the late 1950s the percentage of gross national product devoted to defense actually declined, though absolute amounts remained the same. The electorate was not sympathetic to increased defense spending, the causes for alarm were remote, and the low figure (in comparison with other countries) of about 3 per cent could be rationalized by maintaining that Australia ought to continue devoting its resources to national development, which will eventually make for greater strength. This approach was not altogether unreasonable when the long-run problems of living with China were the chief factor in military prediction, for the kind of air and naval strength that China could use directly against the Australian home base seemed to be at least a decade or so off. In any case, the population disparity—15 or so million against 1,000 million by the 1980s—was such as to lead to the conclusion that Australia could add only marginally to her own safety by the strength of her independent arms and must therefore look to a policy of alliances. From the early sixties there was an upturn in Australian defense expenditures, but this development was related less to China than to Indonesia. Indonesia represented a much closer potential source of friction and danger; was endowed with considerable air and naval strength in being (acquired from Russia); and though having 10 times as large a population as

Australia, was at least somewhat less overwhelming in that respect than China.

If by some unforeseeable mischance Australia were forced out of the defensive arrangements with America and Britain on which she now essentially relies against the present and prospective dangers of a situation just off the shores of South Asia, she would presumably have to fall back on a defense concept of the "Fortress Australia" type. Under such a concept, she would look only to protect her own shores against invasion by means of mobile sea and air power, perhaps of a nuclear sort. There is a strand of thought in the Labor party which has in the past favored this kind of armed and neutralist isolationism, but it has almost no support in the other political parties and is at present in abeyance even within the Labor party. For the foreseeable future, defense policy will be framed on the assumption that the Australian national interest requires meeting any apparently expansionist power in South Asia in company with allies and well away from Australia's own shores. In terms of actual forces, this policy clearly means an adequate supply of troops well trained for jungle fighting and the transport aircraft and ground-support aircraft needed to make them effective. How well these requirements were being met by the actual plans projected by the government was still, in 1964, a matter of some debate within the electorate. The 1964 budget called for an increase in defense expenditure, but not an ambitious one, and compulsory selective service for the regular army was reintroduced in November 1964. Professional army opinion was reported to be unfavorable to more extensive call-up schemes. "The policy of the Army is to prepare for limited war on the mobile battle group scale, not on the divisional scale of World War II or Korea." [14] A number of pressures, political and other, were directed against this stand, but all that could be said with certainty was that the speed of the defense buildup would reflect the degree of alarm within the electorate and the demands of Australia's allies.

LATER CONFLICTS INVOLVING CHINA

For about five years after the formulation of SEATO and the 1954 Geneva settlement, tension in Southeast Asia was comparatively eased, and the chief area of friction with China was in the Taiwan Straits. This situation offered some discomfort for Australian policy.

---

14. *The Australian*, August 28, 1964.

The ANZUS treaty may be invoked in the event of attack on the vessels or aircraft of any of its parties. Though the probability that America would actually invoke the treaty was always remote, Australia theoretically appeared liable to be drawn into hostilities over Quemoy and Matsu. The announcement early in the Eisenhower administration of the "deneutralization" of Taiwan, the mutual defense treaty of 1954, the 1955 Congressional resolution empowering the President to use U.S. armed forces as he deemed necessary to protect Taiwan and the Pescadores, and particularly the deliberate ambiguity of Dulles as to whether Quemoy and Matsu were included in the American undertakings were occasions for restiveness in Australian opinion. The Chinese Nationalist government on Taiwan never entirely erased in Australia the impression of decay created during the last years on the mainland. Vague memories of the 1947 massacre on Taiwan and uncertainties as to how far the "mainlanders" are accepted willingly by the Taiwanese, how far they are merely kept in power by a repressive police apparatus, and whether Chiang Kai-shek's successors may not make their own arrangements with the mainland have all tended to produce a degree of reserve concerning the American commitment to the Nationalist regime. In 1958, Menzies expressed the view that Quemoy and Matsu were "not worth a great war," that the Australian government had no commitment to help defend the offshore islands should they be attacked, and that Australia's commitments to mutual defensive action with America under the ANZUS pact excluded military operations in the Taiwan region.[15] The eventual Chinese withdrawal from the 1958 "confrontation" in the Taiwan straits, if one may judge from Russian and Chinese accounts made public in 1963, took place because the Chinese were receiving even less support from their Russian ally than the Americans from their allies. Assuming that the Sino-Soviet schism persists, one may perhaps expect that this is one of the less likely regions of tension for the foreseeable future.

If Taiwan represents, for Australian opinion, one of the most ambiguous areas in respect to the containment of Chinese power, the Indian border region represents the least. No Chinese act did more to alienate such sympathy as previously existed than the hostilities against India at the end of 1962. Those who have been in gen-

---

15. *Sydney Morning Herald*, September 11, 1958. Australia's diplomatic relations with Taiwan are inconsistent at best. It is not represented there, but a Chinese Nationalist ambassador remains in Australia.

eral anxious to improve relations with China have also been, aside from the far left, those who may be called Asia-oriented. They have construed Australia's main foreign policy task as the cultivation of the good will of its Asian neighbors and have maintained that adhesion to the American stand on non-recognition damaged Australia's reputation with such Asian powers as India. This section of opinion characteristically saw in Nehru's conduct of India's foreign relations a farsighted understanding of Asian realities as well as a sort of moral loftiness which offered Australia a foreign policy model preferable to the outmoded and sordid business of power calculations. These judgments once worked in favor of China, but since the hostilities of late 1962 have worked strongly against it. Nehru was the outstanding non-Communist exponent of the charitable view of Chinese purposes and of the view that the relations of military power were of minor importance in Asia. When he nevertheless found himself at war with China; when he discovered that military strength could be, after all, a fairly decisive factor in diplomatic disputes, and that the cultivation of moral influence with other nonaligned powers by no means rallied them usefully to one's side, even as a political force, at a moment of security crisis; when he was heard to say that he had in a sense been living in a world of unreality, the intellectual basis of a whole theory of international politics was cut from beneath the feet of its exponents.

At the popular level India enjoys, as a member of the Commonwealth, the benefit of a general tendency to assume that it is in the right in situations of conflict. Moreover, the Indian border dispute aligns British policy more whole-heartedly with American than any other South Asian issue does. Thus no political or diplomatic tensions or moral qualms have complicated Australian attitudes on this issue. The few defenders of Chinese policy, obliged to maintain that India was at fault, have batted on a very sticky wicket and in an atmosphere of moral disapproval. On the plane of actual government policy, the hostilities were over too soon for much to be done in the way of aid, but some preparatory base has been established in case of future need. The further development of cooperation awaits the evolution of Indian opinion or of events, rather than Australian feeling. Aside from the hesitations that always beset any actual dispatch of troops, it is difficult to see any probable obstacles to the development of mutual defensive arrangements with India.

Next to the dispute with India, Communist China's dispute with

Russia has done the most since 1960 to magnify the image of Chinese ruthlessness. Except among a few specialists, there is not a great deal of understanding in Australia of the finer points of the Sino-Soviet schism. Khrushchev's version of the points at issue, in particular his contention that the Chinese feel that they alone among the great powers would survive nuclear war and that they are therefore entirely unmoved by the risks of international conflict, has held the field almost uncontested at the popular level. Far-left and Communist party opinion adheres at present chiefly to the Russian side of the argument, though a fairly important section has split off into a pro-Chinese party. In the event of a major Pacific crisis (perhaps originating over Vietnam), the pro-Chinese party, which has named itself the Communist party of Australia (Marxist-Leninist), would probably grow at the expense of the pro-Russian party and could perhaps exert enough strength in some key unions to embarrass some potential government measures—for instance, the loading of ships for Vietnam.

The most recent spasm of the Indochina crisis, in 1964–65, has found Australian policy and opinion not visibly more coherent or less baffled by the choice of evils open to the West than it was in 1954. If on the one hand, the military containment of Chinese power or of its ally—the local revolutionary ferment—is abandoned in South Vietnam, the Western foothold in southern Asia becomes perilously constricted to the somewhat encircled Thailand-Malaysia position, and the recreation of China's traditional ascendancy over the whole area looks discomfortingly close. If, on the other hand, the local political base of the Western effort in South Vietnam proves no longer viable, then containment can perhaps only be pursued at military and moral costs which may be unacceptable. In September 1964, the Cabinet was reported to be reassessing Australian policy,[16] but there was no indication in public opinion that it would make any decision other than for a continued endorsement of the American stand. Early in 1965 it took the decision to send as a token of this endorsement a battalion of Australian troops to South Vietnam.

THE RECOGNITION QUESTION, 1965

From the vantage point of early 1965, the prospective dilemmas of Australian policy toward China appear a good deal more formi-

16. *The Australian*, September 1, 1964.

dable than any which have so far been encountered. The 14 years of non-recognition have been a period of postponing the day when the full implications of living with China as a great power in Asia and in the central balance have to be explored. That postponement may have been justified in its results: there is at least one line of interpretation of the changes in the central balance which would provide it with an entirely adequate justification. An alternative line of analysis would maintain that Western policy as a whole (including Australian policy) has made the worst of both worlds. It has been neither placatory enough to give the Chinese government much sense of the possible advantages of diplomatic accommodation nor yet minatory enough really to impede the growth of Chinese power.

The most obvious, but least important, of Australia's dilemmas is posed by the French recognition of the Peking government and the prospect that this example may be followed within a year or two by others and thus erode the voting strength which has so far defeated efforts to seat the representatives of Peking in the United Nations as the government of China. How long, if this erosion proceeds, will the Australian government maintain its present stand on the questions of representation in the United Nations and of recognition?

In answering this question, one must distinguish between the positions of the four political parties and certain influential groups. Since it is unlikely that the issue can be postponed for three years, it is almost certain to arise during the period of office of the present Liberal-Country party coalition. When this government first came to power at the end of 1949, domestic political conditions, reinforced by a desire to avoid embarrassing Australia's chief ally, America, constituted strong enough reasons for non-recognition. By the time the question had come to seem eligible for possible reconsideration, the Korean War was about to break, and any revision of attitude could therefore be postponed. For some years after 1953–54, and especially about the time of the Bandung Conference in 1955, the issue was pressed on the government with some force by sections of articulate opinion. Aside from the considerations that it would complicate relations with America and (if generally followed) enable China to step up its pressures in Southeast Asia through the establishment of consulates, recognition was generally resisted on the ground of China's own intransigence. Since the Peking government insisted that diplomatic relations with itself entailed the breaking of diplomatic relations with the government on Taiwan and the concession that Peking's writ should run there, recognition appeared to demand a morally impossible acquiescence in the prospect of large-scale massacre.

Speaking at the time of the French recognition, Sir Garfield Barwick, then Minister for External Affairs, mentioned only the complication of Taiwan in exposition of Australia's reasons for non-recognition. If some diplomatic convention by which China and Taiwan might be regarded, even temporarily, as separate diplomatic entities could be worked out, the chief formal basis for non-recognition and the moral arguments by which it is justified would no doubt largely disappear. But there has been no indication so far that the Peking government would agree, even as a temporary tactical maneuver, to such a convention. In any case, the real political and diplomatic basis for non-recognition, the desire to avoid embarrassing America, will persist as long as America's own stand on the issue remains unchanged—even though the two political leaders who are at present in charge of Australian policy, Sir Robert Menzies and Mr. Paul Hasluck, may personally sympathize with the British view that, as Churchill said, recognition is extended to secure a convenience and not to confer a compliment.

Mass opinion is too divided or too indifferent to have much impact on the government's decision. A public opinion poll taken about the time of French recognition showed 35 per cent for recognition, 37 per cent against, and 28 per cent undecided. These figures, showing an almost even tripartite division, reflect a slow drift of opinion toward recognition during 1951–58, when "favorable" attitudes rose from 22 to 41 per cent.[17] Curiously enough, the decline in public favor since 1958 has been accompanied by a considerable enhancement of one particular pressure which can command much more solid local backing than the arguments about diplomatic realism and the long-term cultivation of good relations with Asia.

In 1960 the Australian Wheat Board, embarrassed by a record surplus, discovered a most useful market in China, which was then suffering from disastrous grain shortages. The first sale was for cash. Subsequent sales have been on credits spread over a year at rates of interest pitched low enough to enable Australia to compete successfully with Canada. Trade has grown until China is now Australia's fourth customer (after Britain, Japan, and the United

17. *Australian Public Opinion Polls* (Gallup Poll), February 1964.

States). The balance of trade is highly favorable. In 1962–63, Australia sold more than £A64 million worth of goods to China and bought only £A6 million.[18] Total sales over the past three years have been 300 million bushels, worth about £A200 million. The government has not underwritten these credit sales, and the Export Payments Insurance Commission has refused to insure them. Despite some local qualms about China's foreign exchange resources, every payment so far has been met as it has fallen due. Australia's chief import from China is cotton textiles, and 98 per cent of her exports are wheat and wool. Wool sales have so far been less important than wheat, but the wool growers, faced with the competition of synthetic fibres, are looking hopefully to the future China market. The Chairman of the Australian Wool Board was in China on a promotional visit early in 1964, and increased sales as well as Australian training for Chinese technicians in the wool textile industry were foreshadowed.

The domestic political importance of these sales is even greater than might appear from the figures. Both wool and wheat are somewhat vulnerable commodities, and they provide the basis of Australia's export income. The most formidable potential problem is the wheat grower's increasing dependence on the China market. Acreage under wheat has doubled in the last six years, and Communist China bought almost half the record export of 1962–63. Prospects for finding markets elsewhere are poor. Other countries, including France, also have wheat surpluses. Up to now, China's need to import grain has made it unlikely that she would put political conditions on her purchases. But if her home situation improves (as it appears to be doing) and the competition among alternate suppliers continues (as appears probable), China would obviously be in a position to discriminate among them on a political basis. Any such discrimination would be rapidly transmuted into effective political pressure in Canberra. The Country party, which directly represents the interests of farmers and grazers, is an essential element in the government coalition, and its leader, John McEwen, is the Minister for Trade as well as the Deputy Prime Minister. It does not dispose of the argument to point out that the Chinese government has shown no intention of linking its trade policy to the issue of recognition. The fear that it might do so may not be soundly based, but it nevertheless

---

18. I am indebted for these figures, and the trading information in general, to E. J. Donath of the University of Melbourne.

has a political impact, especially among the Country party electorate. In the poll quoted earlier, the main reason given by those favoring recognition of the Peking government was the trading relationship.

Such pressures as the Labor party can exert upon the government would also tend in the direction of recognition. As was said earlier, the Labor party, when confronted with the issue in 1949, deferred action. It was relieved of the necessity to take any by the verdict of the polls. In March 1951, its leader, Chifley, said in Parliament that if his government had been returned to office, it would have supported Communist China's admission to the United Nations "not because we like the Communists or support anything associated with Communism but simply because we are realists. . . . I am not suggesting that we should appease China. But we should not decline to recognize the present Government of China merely because we do not agree with the politics of that country. It would be complete diplomatic foolishness to do that." [19]

Under the leadership of Chifley's successor, Dr. Evatt, a party split occurred in 1954–55. Attitudes toward communism, on the international as well as the domestic level, were a major issue. Since 1955, the Labor party has included in its official platform a plank advocating recognition of Peking. Though the present leadership of the party has departed from the Evatt position on some important foreign policy issues, it is not likely to change on this point, short of some new military adventure on the part of China. One must therefore expect that it will urge recognition on the government and, if the issue is not settled before it comes to office, extend recognition when it does so.

There remains the Democratic Labor party. It is the one party which might oppose recognition with ideological fervor, possibly even after recognition has been accorded by America. The system of preferential voting used in Australia gives this party, despite its small size, a considerable potential influence over the two major parties. But the only party to which it could switch its second preferences, the Labor party, is already committed to recognition.[20] It is therefore

---

19. Crisp, cited, p. 293.

20. The voter numbers *all* the candidates in his electorate in the order of his preference. If no candidate has an absolute majority, the "second preferences" of the candidates with the *least* numbers of votes are distributed to the leading candidates, who are usually Labor and Liberal. Thus by directing its supporters on how to allocate their "second preferences," the Democratic Labor party can, in a number of electorates, secure the election of the Labor or the Liberal candidate. The balance is so close that this factor can determine which party holds office.

unlikely to be able to exert much direct leverage on the policy of the government coalition with respect to the recognition issue.

There would undoubtedly be a marginal political advantage to the Labor party if recognition were undertaken by a Liberal government. The Labor party would be able to say that the government had come round to a policy which the Labor party had been advocating for 10 years. The image of party attitudes on defense and security questions would be somewhat blurred. Those whose votes have been influenced by a conviction that the non-Labor parties are more alive to external threats might reassess their preferences. In a political system as sensitive as that of Australia, such marginal shifts can be important. Other things being equal, the calculation of marginal electoral losses through recognition might offset the influence toward recognition which forces associated with wheat and wool might exert on the governing parties. It is always difficult to say precisely what factors win or lose an election, but in the Australian election of late 1963, a belief that the Labor leadership had an inadequate understanding of the realities of defense and foreign policy seems to have told heavily in favor of the government.

Domestic factors for and against recognition are so evenly balanced that one must assume that the issue will be determined largely by external factors—specifically, the attitude of the American government. If there is a close and long-continued struggle at the U.N. General Assembly over the seating of representatives of Peking, with every vote counting, one would expect Australia to do all it can to avoid embarrassing America. When and if the game is visibly lost, continued non-recognition will seem increasingly pointless, and Australia will lapse into recognition with a resignation about equally touched with apprehension and relief and with the reflection that the change at least ends the awkward postures imposed by the necessity of pursuing trade without diplomatically recognizing the object of one's commercial endeavors.

CALCULATIONS OF THE BALANCE OF POWER

Non-recognition as a diplomatic strategy could hardly have been expected to be permanently viable. Its prospective end is only a small (if symbolic) token of Australia's essential foreign policy problem—how to live securely on the periphery of Chinese power. Whatever advantages one may attribute to non-recognition in terms of the evolution of the central balance, it would be difficult, on the record of the last 15 years, to hold that it had been conspicuously successful in maintaining a reassuring local balance, or series of balances, around that periphery. In fact, it is hard not to see in the present degree of Chinese influence in Burma, Laos, Cambodia, Vietnam, or even Nepal substantial progress toward the restoration of her traditional hegemony in the area. Since this progress was achieved in the teeth of Western opposition and from an initial position of great weakness, it offers a rather chilling forecast of the prospective relationships of power.

Soon enough to concern those now making policy, Communist China will possess an effective nuclear strike power, and its population will be rising toward the one billion mark. Even a minor nuclear strike power will greatly improve her military diplomatic leverage. It will not, of course, make it advantageous for her to *initiate* the use of nuclear weapons, but it will give her a *retaliatory* capability that can be used to counter any Western threat of nuclear strike as a sanction against Chinese *conventional* attack. Even a small stockpile of nuclear weapons and some means of their delivery on nearby Japanese or Indian cities may impose on the West vis-à-vis China the same inhibitions of the nuclear stalemate as are now imposed on it vis-à-vis Russia. Up to 1949, and with less confidence up to 1955, the Western powers could rely in Europe on atomic monopoly or nuclear superiority to offset the Russian advantage in conventional forces. Since that time they have been impelled to look to their own conventional forces because of the counter-deterring growth of Russian nuclear strength. Russian superiority in manpower resources vis-à-vis Western Europe was of course always rather a myth, but it would be a brave man who would maintain that Chinese superiority in manpower resources is a myth. In a situation in which conventional forces can be used without any nuclear inhibition, the problem of the military containment of Chinese power will be a daunting one indeed.

It is not, however, necessarily in Australia's interest, as is sometimes assumed, that the strategic balance should be kept at the nuclear level for the indefinite future. The Australian population is among the most urbanized in the world. We have great open spaces, but we do not live in them. More than 40 per cent of the population lives in the vicinity of just two conurbations, Sydney-Newcastle-Wollongong and Melbourne-Geelong-Ballarat, and much of the rest of it in another half-dozen cities. It is this kind of concentration of people, rather than the size of the land mass, which marks the true index of vulnerability to nuclear warfare, and by this index Australia is as vulnerable even as Western Europe. Australia is to some extent already involved in the central nuclear balance through an American radio communications base at Exmouth Gulf. This involvement will probably grow in importance if, as seems likely, most of the friction points of the future power conflict are round the periphery of China. But once an adversary with a truly effective means of delivery is involved in this area (and it would not necessarily be China), it may become literally a matter of life or death for Australia to keep the struggle non-nuclear.

These problems may seem so distant and intractable as to make it scarcely surprising that Australian policy has tended to avoid contemplating them. Yet since about the end of 1962, the understanding that the part of the world on whose rim Australians live may have just begun to move into its time of troubles has started to impinge on Australian consciousness. The light shed during 1962–65 on the realities of present and prospective power relations in South Asia was almost as bleakly revealing as that of 1941. The military success of the Chinese moves into the Indian frontier provinces, the diplomatic intransigence of Peking, and the obvious inability of Russia to influence its decisions were reminders of the formidable potential behind China's bid to assert its power. The decay and overthrow of the Diem government in Vietnam, the military failure of the successor government, and the instability produced by subsequent *coups d'état* offered a dismaying demonstration that Western material and political backing, even on a large scale, may not be enough to hold the situation. The drift in Laos toward disintegration of the coalition government, *de facto* partition, and *coup d'état* dampened any optimism about the possibilities of neutralization as an alternative to military contest. The attitudes of Prince Sihanouk, a weathercock useful for indicating which way Southeast Asians feel the wind to be blowing, were a further indication of the worsening fortunes of the West in the area.

Besides these tokens of the growth of Chinese strength in Southeast Asia, Australian policy makers had to reckon with a dismaying complication nearer home: the ambiguity of Indonesia's future role in the balance of forces vis à vis China. The most hopeful construction (and the one allegedly sponsored by the American embassy in Djakarta and other American policy makers) is that the Indonesians, with their traditional fear and dislike of the Chinese, will in due course (so long as President Sukarno and his regime are buttressed against a Communist coup, and so long as he is not alienated by resistance to his ambitions to "crush Malaysia") prove a helpful or at least not an actively embarrassing element in the balance against China. The less hopeful view would be that Sukarno's doctrine (that the "new emerging forces" must be backed everywhere against the "old established forces"), with its anti-European racial overtones, is made to order for China, even in its quarrel with Russia and especially in the three-cornered struggle now under way in Africa, Asia, and Latin America. A nationalist Indonesia can, in fact, unconsciously serve China's diplomatic purposes better, in this transition period, than a Communist Indonesia could. For what is the burden of President Sukarno's demands on Malaysia? It is simply that Western (in this case British) power should be removed from the area to leave the way clear for an "Asian solution." Since he is a worthy nationalist, not a dangerous Communist, American opinion may sympathize with this demand. But is not the condition for an uninhibited growth of Chinese power on the Southeast Asian mainland also that Western (in this case mostly American) power should be removed from the area? For the time being, Indonesia and China may be regarded as logical diplomatic fellow travelers. It is not an adequate argument against this thesis to point to potential rivalry over Malaysia. When two major powers are both interested in a minor power, a clash does not necessarily result. Agreement on dismemberment (cf. Poland) or on spheres of influence (cf. Persia, Afghanistan) may be reached. All in all, one might judge that if there were no President Sukarno, Chou En-lai might find it advantageous to invent him.[21]

On this particular issue Australia's interests potentially diverge from those of America. To the framers of American policy, Indo-

---

21. As a parallel to the ambiguity of Indonesia's situation in the present international balance one might cite the ambiguity of Italy's situation in the interwar balance: the Italian-German rivalry over the Balkan peninsula was in fact better developed than the potential Chinese-Indonesian rivalry over the Malaysian peninsula. The "ambiguous" power is necessarily wooed by the leader of the status quo coalition (Britain then, America now) and by the most wholehearted of the revisionist powers (Germany then, China now). In the Italian case, the decision to throw in the national lot with the fortunes of the revisionist powers was taken partly on the basis of the leader's temperament, partly on the basis of diplomatic opportunism. No predictions are offered about the probabilities in the Indonesian case.

nesia must be important primarily from the point of view of its stance vis-à-vis China in the central balance. Neither America itself nor any important American interest is vulnerable to Indonesia. But the same is not true of Australia. It must be preoccupied with Indonesia itself, and not merely with its putative connection with China. If the Sukarno government were succeeded by a right-wing military regime with a strong nationalist bent (an evolution perhaps as likely as a Communist coup) Indonesia's attitude toward China might be transformed. There is not much reason, however, to believe that it would be any less eager to "crush Malaysia," any less unpredictable as a neighbor in New Guinea, or any less formidable an element in the politics of South Asia about the end of this century, when its population will be rising toward the 200 million mark in comparison with Australia's 25 million or so.

ALTERNATIVE FUTURE POLICIES

The present generation of Australian policy makers, reflecting even on the period of their own lifetimes, must be conscious of having to work in a more complex as well as a more dangerous world than ever before, though one a little reminiscent, in theoretical terms at least, of that before the First World War. They have to reckon that Australia's long-term security is likely to be affected not only by the fortunes of its "great and powerful friends" in the central balance, but also certainly by the local balance in the Pacific. Before the First World War, Australian interests in the central balance lay with Britain against Germany. Now they lie with America and Britain in a complex situation where the precise roles of Russia, China, and even France are not fully determined. The local balance then offered only one ambiguous element, Japan. Now it offers two: Indonesia, obviously, and in their hearts most Australians would probably feel Japan also.

Assessments of Australia's long-term interests vis-à-vis China must of course depend on assessments of China's own capabilities and intentions. Some comment would maintain that it ought to depend on whether China is to be viewed chiefly as an Asian great power or chiefly as the embodiment of a revolutionary political doctrine. The author has opted to view it chiefly as an Asian great power, the potential hegemonial power in Asia, and to regard the revolutionary political doctrine simply as an extra weapon in its armory. Such evidence as exists seems to indicate that all but two small sections of Australian opinion (the far-right and the far-left) see it in this light. There is no essential difference between most Australian attitudes toward this one Communist Asian great power and toward the two non-Communist Asian powers which have seemed to mount an equivalent threat, Japan and Indonesia.   Viewing China then simply as the potential hegemonial power in Asia on whose periphery we have to live and bearing in mind that it is a power of notable industry and talent with a long memory, a formidable number of grudges against the West, and a strong imperial tradition, one might say that Australian policy for the next two or three decades might be framed on any one of three basic concepts. Let us call them the assumption of harmony, the assumption of containment, and the assumption of balance.

The assumption of harmony, the notion that there is no likely conflict of interest or that there is even a complementarity of interests between Australia and China, is the premise, articulate or suppressed, behind some of the lines of reasoning which support non-alignment.   Australia's present choice of alignment with America and the West amounts in this view to buying unnecessarily into other people's quarrels. This line of thought does not now, one would estimate, command as much support as it did earlier in the postwar period.   Such support as it does command is more prominent at the level of "articulate" than of "grass-roots" opinion. The author would be inclined to maintain that the whole history of Australian-Chinese relations militates against its having any serious influence on policy in the foreseeable future. That history, briefly, is one of initial suspicion on a social and economic basis (but with some military and political overtones), a period of indifference, a brief and not altogether harmonious period of alliance and diplomatic relations (a total of 8 years out of more than 100), and then again a diplomatic break now maintained for 15 years. To set against this rather bleak record of unconcern, there are the facts that some powerful economic forces in Australia can and do point to a complementarity of economic interests between Australian suppliers of wheat and wool and the vast and hungry China market, that some minor political forces within the country remain dedicated to the proposition that a country run by virtuous Marxist internationalists cannot possibly be a danger to its neighbors (except such of them as have allied themselves with the capitalist camp), and that a few dedicated sinologists point plaintively to the beauty and interest of the civilization they study. These are not much to set against the weight of history and of security preoccupations. Even if the Labor party comes to power and swings to the left in its leadership, no great degree of optimism is likely to creep into the expectations of Australians about their relationship with Communist China.

The second assumption, containment, has been tried, more or less, during the past 15 years. Dare one add, tried and found wanting? Probably it is not much criticized at the "grass-roots" level. There is certainly no electoral evidence of dissatisfaction. So long as America is prepared to operate the policy, Australia is not likely to offer much dissent or abandon its role as one of America's lieutenants. The real difficulty with this policy is its potential future costs. Even the limited costs—in deaths rather than in money—incurred in Korea and in Vietnam have been borne chiefly by America and by the local nationalists. But the supply of local nationalists with the appropriate convictions may give out.

The common phrase that calls local Asian nationalisms "bulwarks" against the flood of Chinese power is overoptimistic. These nationalisms are, no doubt, real and persistent enough. But they ought to be pictured as sandbanks rather than bulwarks. They will accept submersion, disperse, re-form, or change shape. It is part of their strength, but it is no strength to the West. There is said to be an old Thai proverb: "the grass bends, the wind passes over." Prince Sihanouk has apparently decided to make his country's future in China's sphere of power in the spirit of that proverb. Similar decisions by other states in the area would not be altogether surprising. The troubles of Western policy in Vietnam, Laos, and Cambodia have been indicators of the dubious viability of containment as a policy when local conditions are not favorable, even in a phase in which Chinese initiatives have perhaps been restrained by Russian caution and China's own weakness in modern military resources. What will be the costs of containment, for the Western powers, when China will have remedied this weakness and will be able to use conventional or guerrilla forces more boldly? What will be the costs, moreover, if the local nationalists decide, as some have already done, that they must live with China on whatever terms they can secure? One of the great dangers facing the West in the postwar period has always been that of being bogged down in a "Thirty Years' War" in Asia. Such a war is perhaps more possible now than it has ever been. If events should develop in that direction, Australia will no doubt bear its part. Of all the Western powers, it is, after all, the one whose vital interests are most directly involved. But the prospect is hardly encouraging.

There remain the possibilities of the central balance. They may be rather speculative, but where the other vistas are so cheerless, they must seem worth exploring. In this field, Australia itself is, of course, too minor a power to act directly. Its policy makers must nevertheless keep the matter under scrutiny, for Australia will be affected by the action which its more potent friends and allies take —or fail to take. Since 1962, China and Russia have been separate and basically conflicting entities in the central balance, and France has been playing for its own hand. The balance has largely lost the bipolarity of the 1949–62 period and has reverted toward the historically more normal multiple pattern. Australian official opinion has to date shown no enthusiasm for this development as it affects the West. At the SEATO meeting of April 1964, the Minister for External Affairs deprecated the French trial balloon about neutralization of Southeast Asia which has been regarded as the meeting's main outcome. The author believes, however, that as the implications of the changing situation become more apparent, there will be seen to be more room for maneuver than before. To believe that the West need come off the worse for such a change is unreasonably defeatist. This kind of politics may not be an American intellectual or foreign policy tradition, but it is one native to Britain and France. China may perhaps be even less intellectually easy than America in a situation where the lines of conflict are no longer simple.

In a sense, a great power like China gives hostages to fortune merely by becoming an effective member of the central balance. It must *have* some diplomatic assets before the fear of losing them can operate as a restraint on policy. The history of postrevolutionary Soviet foreign policy, as the idea of the Russian national interest reasserted itself and diplomatic connections grew, is suggestive of the possible line of policy change for China. Some of Chou En-lai's diplomacy since French recognition seems to indicate a high priority in Peking for the further reduction of China's earlier isolation, the cultivation of a line of diplomacy which can compete with the Soviet Union's, and a special interest in the European powers as the "second intermediate zone." Such a tendency could conduce toward prudence in South Asia. From a Chinese viewpoint, better the minor devils of British imperialism (as in Malaysia) or French imperialism (as it once was and might be again in Indochina) than the major devil of American imperialism. Conversely, every Chinese advance in independent diplomacy strengthens Russia's potential common interest with America *against* China in the central balance. And the great powers' interests against each other in the central balance must take precedence over peripheral interests, for they involve issues of survival, and not merely of local advantage. Theoretically speaking, over the long term one might expect to look to the central balance as the main restraint on a Chinese reassertion of hegemony in South Asia. If history should prove obliging enough to conform to theory, the wheel will have come full circle for Australia. Its long security in the 19th century was the result of Britain's ascendancy then in the central balance.

Chapter 7

INDIA AND CHINA

Betrayal, Humiliation, Reappraisal

BY

VIDYA PRAKASH DUTT

Indian sentiments and policy toward China have undergone violent fluctuations in the last few years. The emergence of Communist China was welcomed with a great deal of abandon, and most Indians took pride in the glow of friendship with her. Today, the power of this giant, whose hot breath Indians are now feeling, and the ruthless, chauvinistic behavior of her leaders are feared and thoroughly disliked. Whereas the rise of a strong new China signified to most Indians the resurgence of Asia, this very Asian power has chosen to awaken Indians, albeit the hard way, to the realities of the modern world. China has in fact become problem number one for India.

THE POLICY OF FRIENDSHIP

It has to be remembered that the new Chinese regime was established in 1949, when Indian independence was only a couple of years old and when India lacked experience and knowledge of international affairs. Only a handful of people in the country had intimate knowledge of world developments; still fewer were skilled in diplomacy. Inevitably, India had, so to speak, to sense her way along and to make many errors in this process.

When a strong, centralized power was established in China,

many policy problems confronted India. The Government of India was not unaware of these problems. What direction would the revolution in China take, what would be her policy goals, what would be her role in Asia, how would this new power affect the position of Indian frontiers and the security of the country? All these questions engaged the attention of the foreign policy makers. It was decided to seek a friendly China with whom there should be no active hostility, even if there could not be a close camaraderie. It was felt that having China as a friendly neighbor would be in the national interest of India.

What were the hopes and objectives behind the decision to seek contacts with, cultivate, and befriend Communist China? First and foremost, the government thought it would thus insure the friendship of a powerful neighbor and make easier the task of securing our frontiers. The prospect of a prolonged state of hostility, entailing heavy burdens on the people, was viewed with little enthusiasm. It was hoped that China would respond to India's friendship and that a basis for avoiding conflict and misunderstandings would be established. This normalization of relations with a big neighbor was considered a better guarantee of peace on the northern borders than a military buildup and a militant posture. It was thought that the money thus saved might be better spent on economic development to provide inner strength and security to the country.

Other broader interests could also be served through friendship with China. The Chinese revolution could be kept in the mainstream of postwar Asian resurgence and thus be humanized and normalized. Through increasing contacts with the outside world and association with the world community, Chinese policies could perhaps be invested with a sense of responsibility, and the rigors of the cold war could be softened. This end, if attained, would be no mean contribution to the cause of world peace.

Still another consideration which influenced India was the fact that India was already involved in a bitter dispute with one neighboring country, Pakistan. Under such circumstances, inviting the enmity of another neighbor, both big and powerful, was neither good politics nor good economics. In India, Pakistan's military alliance with the West was regarded as primarily aimed at India. Practically all shades of Indian opinion firmly believed that Pakistan had neither the intention nor the desire to fight the Sino-Soviet bloc and that the arms aid would be used chiefly against India. Moreover, India was then taking active measures to expand the frontiers of the "peace area" (comprising nonaligned countries), and in the Indian view, Pakistan's membership in Western military alliances brought the cold war into the Indian sub-continent.

Before recent Sino-Indian hostilities, China too took the view that Pakistan's military agreements with Western countries were a threat not only to China but also to India. Let me cite one example. In March 1959, Pakistan persuaded the United States to sign a bilateral defense agreement which called for collective security against "aggression, direct or indirect." [1]   What struck Indians about this agreement was that it was not confined to resistance to Communist aggression. Pakistan immediately emphasized that the U.S. guarantee was not only against Communist aggression but aggression from any quarter. The *People's Daily*, official organ of the Chinese Communist party, responded with a strong editorial on the subject. As summarized in *Peking Review*, the editorial stated:

> The United States and its followers have also put forward a new idea that 'resistance to any direct or indirect aggression' includes non-Communist aggression. This clearly shows that these new facts were directed not only against the socialist countries but are, *in the first place*, also a threat to such nationally independent neighboring countries as India, Iraq and Afghanistan.[2]

The New China News Agency also circulated a sharp comment against the agreement. It remarked upon the fact that newspapers in Pakistan did not "even attempt to cover up the hostile provisions of the bilateral agreement aimed against India and Afghanistan," and it alleged that the "ruling cliques spare no effort to bring the wolf into the house in an attempt to rely upon American power to maintain their unstable control and to suppress the struggle waged by the people at home." [3]

In accordance with its desire to bring China into the world community and promote the cause of world peace, India advocated admitting the representatives of Communist China to the United Nations. The People's Republic was, first of all, the only govern-

---

1. U.S. Department of State, *Bulletin*, v. 14, no. 1030, March 23, 1959, pp. 416–418. Pakistan's preferred definition of aggression was the same one which it had advocated during the negotiations which preceded the establishment of SEATO five years earlier.

2. *Peking Review*, March 10, 1959.   (Emphasis added.)

3. New China News Agency, Peking, March 6, 1959.

ment which could deliver the goods so far as mainland China was concerned. India's delegate to the United Nations, Benegal N. Rau, made the point this way in September 1950:

> Why did we recognize this new Government of China? For a variety of reasons, the main reason being that, according to the best of our knowledge and information, it is a sound and stable government. . . . As I have mentioned in my draft resolution, and as is well known, the Republic of China is a Member of the United Nations and a permanent member of the Security Council and as such that Republic has a number of obligations laid upon it by the Charter of the United Nations. Who is to fulfil them? A State cannot fulfil obligations except through some government, and obviously only a government exercising effective control over the territory and the people of the Republic of China can fulfil the obligations laid upon the Republic of China. . . . But how can we require the fulfilment of these obligations and yet deny that government its rights under the charter, one of which is the right to be represented in the United Nations? To deny rights and, in the same breath, to insist on obligations is clearly illogical and inconsistent.[4]

Secondly, a solution to the problems of Asia would be facilitated by peaceful negotiations with the new regime—which presupposed China's entry into the councils of the world—and immeasurably hampered by the absence of such negotiations. Prime Minister Nehru said in a speech to the Indian Parliament in September 1954 that it "amazed him how this straightforward question" of recognizing Communist China's credentials had been twisted around and made the cause of infinite trouble. There would be "no settlement in the Far East or South-east Asia," he said, "till this major fact of the People's Government of China is recognized" and it was allowed to come into the United Nations. There was a far greater assurance of security that way than through SEATO, "because if China came into the picture, she would assume certain responsibilities in the United Nations."[5]

Thirdly, support for Peking's representation in the United Nations would strengthen the ties of friendship between India and Communist China, and this friendship would have a salutary effect

4. U.N. General Assembly (5th sess.), *Official Records: Plenary Meetings*, v. 1 (New York: Author, 1951), pp. 9–10.
5. *Statesman* (Delhi), September 30, 1954.

upon the international situation in Asia. As B. N. Rau put it in his speech at the United Nations:

> India has historical and almost immemorial ties of culture and friendship with China. For us, *situated as we are and where we are* [emphasis added], the friendship of China is desirable and natural. We wish to do everything possible to promote the friendly relations that now prevail between us, because we feel that a free and independent China marching with India will be the most effective stabilizing factor in Asia.

The criticism has often been made that while India's decision to support the credentials of Communist China at the United Nations was perfectly legitimate, India eventually became "more royalist than the King" with unfortunate consequences for her relations with many other countries of the world. Moreover, whereas India threw her full support behind China's positions on issues like Taiwan and U.N. membership, there was no corresponding Chinese commitment on some of the issues with which India was most immediately concerned, such as the Kashmir problem. China maintained an equivocal stand on Kashmir. Publicly she called for peaceful resolution of the problem. Privately, however, the Chinese leaders assured India that they understood and appreciated India's standpoint, and in a conversation with R. K. Nehru, the Indian ambassador in Peking, Premier Chou En-lai indicated acceptance of India's position in Kashmir.[6]

At any rate, India developed closer contacts with China. While India took up the cudgels on behalf of China at the world body and other international forums, delegations went to and fro between the two countries. In 1952, a high-powered Government of India cultural delegation went to China. During the next two years a number of delegations were exchanged. Chou En-lai came to India in 1954, and Nehru went to China in 1955. Nehru's efforts to bring Peking closer to Afro-Asian countries at Bandung are well known. In 1956, Indian visitors to China included a parliamentary delegation, an agricultural delegation to take stock of Chinese techniques, and another agricultural delegation to study Chinese cooperatives. Military delegations were also exchanged. In January 1957, Chou En-lai paid a second visit to India to climax the period of Indo-Chinese friendship.

The country generally accepted the lead of the government,

---

6. *Notes and Memoranda and Letters Exchanged between the Governments of India and China, November 1961–July 1962*, White Paper, no. 6 (Delhi: Ministry of External Affairs, 1962), pp. 96–97.

particularly Prime Minister Nehru, in the policy of friendship with China. Sentimentally, Indians were interested in China, but there was no widespread desire or effort to study Chinese developments deeply—to build up an adequate corpus of knowledge about China and to create a body of Chinese specialists. The newspapers, while occasionally critical of some of the dictatorial aspects of the Chinese regime, generally supported the policy of friendship. So, for the most part, did the political parties. The only political party which was consistently "anti-Chinese" and which steadfastly denounced Chinese communism was the Praja Socialist party (PSP), which at that time included the present-day Socialists.

The Socialists were from the beginning acutely suspicious of Communist China, and they shared the worldwide Socialist hatred of communism as the greatest of all evils. They were the most outspoken critics of the Indian government's Tibetan policy and the most vocal champions of Tibetan independence. The Socialists were not the only critics in India of the Sino-Indian agreement on Tibet signed in April 1954, but they were among the most uncompromising. As early as 1951, one of the leaders of the then united Praja Socialist party, Dr. Ram Manohar Lohia, while not objecting to diplomatic relations with China, criticized the government for its attempt to "purchase a shaky friendship" with China and was of the opinion that the Russian "grip over the country [China] is firm." [7] The Socialists wanted to pose a third alternative for the peoples of Asia —the democratic socialist alternative.

Of the two other significant opposition parties in India, the Communist party was inevitably a staunch supporter of China, while the Jan Sangh, a right-wing Hindu party, maintained a critical but ambivalent attitude. One of the unofficial organs of the Jan Sangh, the *Organizer*, for instance, registered unhappiness at Tibet's disappearance, through the Sino-Indian agreement, as a buffer state between China and India, but it also expressed "nothing but pity for those who would want us to quarrel—and even go to war—with China, over the issue of Tibet." [8] A curious fact is that neither the PSP weekly *Janata* nor the *Organizer* thought it fit to write even a full editorial on the subject after the conclusion of the Sino-Indian agreement on Tibet.

Thus, China for many years was not a major foreign policy issue

---

7. Rammanohar Lohia, *India, China and Northern Frontiers* (Hyderabad: Navahind Prakashan, 1963), p. 139.
8. *Organizer*, May 10, 1954.

in India—just as foreign policy itself was not a significant political issue. In 1959, however, the border dispute with China, following the revelation that the Chinese had built a road in Aksai Chin, pushed foreign policy into the forefront of the political battlefield, and policy toward China became a focal point of controversy within the country. Until then, few people had expressed disquiet over the border problem. Occasionally Peking's maps, showing parts of India as Chinese territory, caused some anxiety, but Peking's explanation that it was only reproducing old maps of the Kuomintang period and had not had time to address itself to this matter, while not fully satisfactory, did not create too much alarm.

In fact, a widely, though not universally, accepted assumption about the Sino-Indian agreement on Tibet was that Peking had accepted the Indian position on the border question. The *Times of India*, for instance, found the silence of the agreement on the border question "an acknowledgment of the validity of the existing boundary line." [9] Its political correspondent, commenting on the agreement, noted that time and again Nehru had reiterated India's contention that the McMahon Line marked our border with China. "Therefore," the correspondent added, "where was the need to raise the border line question all over again? In any case the reference to territorial integrity clearly proves that China respects India's stand with respect to the boundary." [10] The *Statesman*, commenting on the fact that no question relating to the actual boundary had been discussed during the negotiations, said: "On that subject India's attitude has already been made perfectly clear." [11] A political correspondent of the *Amrita Bazar Patrika*, Dr. Shridharani, claimed that Nehru had "the satisfaction of showing that he can be tough too. From the very start he ruled out any discussion of the Indo-China frontier, and in the resulting agreement he succeeded in getting a tacit Chinese approval of the McMahon Line." [12] Thus did India's leading newspapers compound one of the costliest blunders in India's recent diplomatic history—the failure to press China for a categorical statement of its position on border alignment between the two countries at a time when China was not prepared for a showdown with India. Thus, also, did China manage, through verbal quibbling and

9. *Times of India*, May 1, 1954.
10. Same, May 6, 1954.
11. *Statesman*, May 1, 1954.
12. *Amrita Bazar Patrika*, June 7, 1954.

duplicity, to create the impression, without really committing itself legally, that there was no cause for worry about border alignment between the two countries.

THE RIFT

The simple but fatal flaw in India's position was that while India's ends were clear, she had none of the means needed to accomplish them. Only the United States could satisfy China's national goals and quiet its national frustration with regard to Taiwan, the China seat in the United Nations, and big-power status. With India and the United States working at cross purposes in regard to Communist China, however, there was no real possibility for the Indian policy to succeed. The policy foundered, in other words, on the rock of a total lack of understanding between New Delhi and Washington.

On the other hand, after 1957 the United States became a major factor in the rift between India and China. At a time when Communist China adopted a policy of intensifying the struggle against the United States, India moved toward a better understanding with the United States.

A gradual change had come over both U.S. and Indian policies. Prime Minister Nehru realized that the era of rigid polarization in the world was coming to an end; the U.S. government was also moving away from Secretary Dulles' view of neutralism as immoral. The change in U.S. approach was already noticeable in the last year of the Eisenhower administration but became marked after the inauguration of President Kennedy. With Kennedy's assumption of office, there was expectation and hope in India about the outlook of the New Frontiersmen in Washington. Nehru himself, it was reported, told a governors' conference in Delhi in November 1960 that as a result of Kennedy's election he expected the United States to follow a more liberal policy toward the underdeveloped countries in Asia and Africa. Kennedy had promised, he said, to bring about a new outlook in U.S. foreign and domestic policies.

The high personal regard in which the two leaders held each other was further shown during Prime Minister Nehru's visit to the United States and his first meeting with President Kennedy in November 1961. At the official welcoming ceremony at Andrews Air Force Base, Kennedy linked Nehru with Lincoln, Franklin D. Roosevelt, and Gandhi and described him as "a leader whose example caused not just his own country but all the peoples of the world to look up to him." Nehru said that Kennedy carried "perhaps the greatest responsibility in this world" and added: "And so we look up to you and to your country and seek to learn from you." [13]   He said that Kennedy stood for peace.   Later, he called Kennedy an "exhilarating person" who did not exude any gloom.[14]

These mutual personal tributes were, in fact, an expression of the better understanding that was developing between the two countries. It was not that the two countries had now adopted identical points of view in foreign affairs, nor had either of them given up its basic standpoint.   India remained nonaligned, and the United States continued to lead a military and political grouping designed to oppose the spread of communism.   But there was greater appreciation of each other's point of view and less annoyance at the differences existing between them.   The complexity of the modern world and the thaw in the previous hardened attitudes and postures impelled reappraisals in both the countries.   These resulted in greater understanding and an expansion of friendly relations.

Peking fell afoul of the growing friendship between India and the United States.   From 1958 on, New Delhi and Peking headed in opposite directions.   The Chinese had concluded that their national interests were not served by a two-power (Soviet-American) *détente*. The Indians felt that they stood to gain by such a development. Peking's interests lay in heightening the tension; New Delhi believed its interests were better served by a lessening of the tensions.

India's nonalignment veered in the direction of better relations with both the United States and the U.S.S.R., a simultaneous approach toward the leaders of the two blocs.   It did not manifest itself in hostility toward the two blocs or one of the two blocs.   Communist China's relations with both the United States and the U.S.S.R., on the other hand, deteriorated.

To Peking, India's friendship with the United States was evidence of her betrayal to the imperialist camp.   The heart of the matter was that this friendship clashed with Peking's pursuit of its own national goals.   The Chinese leaders wanted to create a militant, anti-U.S. front and became sworn enemies of those who tried to cultivate close friendly relations with the United States and soften the struggle.   India became suspect because it did not go along with these Chinese plans.

13. *The New York Times*, November 7, 1961.
14. *Times of India*, November 10, 1961.

The Chinese also pressed the Soviet Union to heighten the tension and not to flinch from a head-on confrontation with the United States. They were gravely disturbed by Soviet attempts at a rapprochement with the United States designed to eliminate or at least to reduce the chances of a world war. Instead, the Chinese advocated a "tit-for-tat" struggle no matter what the consequences. Apparently the Chinese had come to believe that only a policy of struggle, and not negotiations and accommodation, would help achieve Chinese goals—big-power status, a seat in the Security Council, recovery of Taiwan, etc. But the Soviet Union refused to follow the Chinese policy of brinkmanship. Though Peking left no stone unturned to change the course of Soviet foreign policy, Premier Khrushchev refused to comply with the Chinese demand.

Peking then decided to build up under its leadership a huge anti-white front, at the very least an "anti-imperialist front" of Afro-Asian countries and such Latin American and Communist-bloc nations as were prepared to go along with it, which would function as an independent force in world affairs—independent of, indeed hostile toward, both Washington and Moscow. India did not fit into this picture; in fact, India seemed to stand in the way. The nonaligned world appeared hamstrung, in Peking's eyes, by India's masterly inactivity. The meeting of the nonaligned nations at Belgrade, in September 1961, seemed to provide a fair indication. There a number of Afro-Asian leaders wanted to concentrate attention exclusively on problems of anti-colonialism and anti-imperialism and forget about issues of war and peace which were uppermost in the mind of Prime Minister Nehru. Although they outnumbered him, he refused to budge, and they could not have their way because of his position and status.

A fundamental difference of approach has developed between India and China in recent times. China is acutely dissatisfied with its status in the world; India is more or less content with its own role. While India, in keeping with its size and position, has wanted a say in world affairs, and particularly in the settlement of Asian problems, it has neither acted nor sought recognition as a great power, but Communist China's driving passion has been parity of power with the United States and the Soviet Union. Mao has been consumed by the idea of getting acknowledgment as an equal, in power and position, from the leaders of the superpowers, but Nehru did not try to gate-crash their councils. Consequently, the foreign policies of the two countries have increasingly diverged. Peking considers it in its interest to defy the big powers of the world and to prevent them from reaching agreements until the "Middle Kingdom," with its population of 650 million people, has been given a seat too, and India, not being in the race for the big-power club, hopes and works for a relaxation of tensions and for agreements between the big powers so as to solicit their joint interest in the economic progress of the under-developed world.

Paradoxically, the Soviet Union has also been a major factor in the developing Sino-Indian conflict. The fact that India was developing friendly relations not only with Washington but also with Moscow particularly aroused Communist China's ire. Good relations with one were not at the expense of good relations with the other. Indeed, despite India's friendship with Washington, Moscow took increasing interest in India, and its relations with New Delhi remained unimpaired. If anything, Soviet economic aid to India steadily expanded.

The Indian government leaders concluded that the Soviet Union was no longer intent on fomenting revolution in India and was prepared to work with them on the national and international planes. On many crucial national issues, like Kashmir or Goa, support came from the Soviet Union, and it was felt that, so far as national interests and problems were concerned, the Soviet Union was one of the few countries with which there were no serious irritants. Even with such a friendly country as the United States there was a major irritant—U.S. military aid to Pakistan and support for Pakistan on the Kashmir issue. There were no such difficulties with Russia. Prime Minister Nehru believed that in the present-day context ideology would become less and less relevant. As the dispute with China worsened, he became more and more anxious to prevent it from developing into an ideological cold war struggle, which the Chinese Communists were desperately trying to make it, and to prevent Soviet and Communist-bloc support for Chinese policies and ambitions.

India has also been an important factor in the Sino-Soviet "dialogue." The Chinese Communists have themselves made the amazing confession that their differences with the Soviet Union started on September 9, 1959, when Tass issued a statement quoting "leading Soviet quarters" as expressing "regret" over the border incidents between India and China and calling upon the two countries to settle their dispute "in the spirit of friendship." The statement emphasized Soviet cooperation with India in "developing successfully the ideals of peaceful coexistence." The Chinese leaders put the same construction on this statement of neutrality as the Indian leaders: that this neutrality was weighted in favor of India. Peking duly charged that here was the first time that a "socialist" country had not taken the side of a brother "socialist" country in a dispute with a capitalist country.

Though the Chinese have not admitted it, perhaps the date of Sino-Soviet differences and contrasting attitudes over India should be put at July 19, 1958. At that time, Premier Khrushchev proposed a five-power summit to deal with the Middle Eastern crisis and insisted that Prime Minister Nehru should be asked to participate. To the Chinese it was an infuriating thought that the Soviet leader should quietly reconcile himself to keeping China out and, instead, propose bringing India into the big-power club. A study of the record of Indo-Soviet relations after the death of Stalin indicates that the Chinese were probably reacting from more than suspicion. In 1955 Khrushchev, along with Marshal Bulganin, visited India and contrived to bring about a turning point in relations between the two countries. First, he set the pattern of Soviet assistance in Indian economic development, assistance which steadily increased to considerable proportions. Secondly, he came out in full and complete support of the Indian position in Kashmir vis-à-vis Pakistan. This move was a better tonic for Indo-Soviet relations than even Soviet economic aid. (The Chinese, as I have already noted, never made an open and unequivocal commitment to the Indian position in Kashmir.) Then the Soviet leader made considerable efforts to get bigpower status conferred on India. Finally, even as the India-China dispute worsened, the Soviets made cautious commitments of military supplies to India (helicopters, transport planes, and MIG fighters). The scale was modest but sufficient to reveal what the Soviets felt about the India-China dispute.

There was more to the situation than meets the eye. The fact of the matter seems to be—and Peking might have come to that conclusion—that the Soviets had begun by wooing India as a neutral to counterbalance the United States but ended up by wooing India as a counterweight to China. Only India could play that role in Asia, and the Soviets were more aware than anyone else of the direction which China was taking. The Russians knew by then that India was intensely, though not aggressively, nationalistic and, therefore, would not join the Western bloc (unless it was literally compelled to do so). There were no unresolved issues between the two countries to embitter their mutual relations, nor was there any question of rivalry or competition for power. By staking a share in the Indian economic program and by engaging in diversified contacts, the Soviets could influence Indian development toward a relatively "progressive" direction. A friendly, nonaligned, progressive, peaceful India was preferable to a dangerously militant Communist China which was intent on challenging the Soviet position within the bloc and grabbing the leadership of Asia and Africa in the pursuit of its own national goals.

For this reason, it is not hard to see why it became one of the functions of Chinese foreign policy to discredit Nehru and destroy India's nonalignment—to "prove" that Indian neutralism was a "myth" and that India was really hand in glove with "American imperialism." In this way, the Chinese could whittle down support within the international Communist movement for the Soviet policy of friendship with India and even force Moscow to give up this policy.

It has not generally been appreciated abroad just how widely divergent Indian and Chinese foreign policies had become, how far apart they had traveled since 1957. It was not merely a question of a difference here or a difference there but of almost completely opposite courses. The two countries were now pursuing different objectives and had fundamentally different conceptions of their goals and interests. The Tibetan revolt and the border dispute accentuated Indo-Chinese differences and heightened the tension between the two countries, but even without them a clash of opinions and wills would have been inevitable.

Apart from a political confrontation, perhaps there was also an element of economic competition involved. India and China were the two biggest countries of Asia. Their influence was widespread. The developments within the two countries were being watched with close attention all over the world. The two countries had adopted different methods to solve the formidable problems attendant on ending their age-old poverty and economic and social stagnation. China had resorted to total planning in the framework of total control over the political machinery, whereas India had adopted a mixed economy within the context of a parliamentary democracy. The outcome of these efforts, it was believed not only by many people in these two countries but elsewhere, would have a profound impact on developments on the Asian continent. Whether this belief was an oversimplification of the problems facing the Asian countries is another matter. What is significant and relevant here is that it was the general belief in both China and India. Consequently, it became an important goal of the Chinese leaders to prove the superiority of their own system and, at the same time, to attempt to discredit the Indian path. During 1957–58, when this writer was in Peking, the Chinese anxiety to debunk the Indian experiment was forcefully brought home to him.

REPERCUSSIONS OF THE BORDER DISPUTE

The border dispute which came to light in 1959 shook the nation and changed the whole complexion of Indian political life. Foreign policy became an acute issue, and the question of policy toward China polarized opinion within the country. The non-Communist opposition gathered strength and, despite its numerical inferiority, became an effectively vocal critic of the government's China policy. All these parties—the Praja Socialist party, the Jan Sangh, the newly formed Swatantra party, and the split-away Socialist party—bitterly criticized the government for the withering away of Tibetan autonomy and argued that India could have played a far more effective role on behalf of Tibet and thus kept the Chinese menace away from Indian frontiers. (The PSP and the Socialist party were left of center so far as domestic policies were concerned, but they were considerably to the right of the Congress party in foreign policy. The Jan Sangh and the Swatantra party were right-wing parties in both internal and external affairs. The Jan Sangh, as we have noted, was a communal organization appealing to the religious sentiments of the dominant Hindu community; the Swatantra party stood for untrammeled private enterprise at home and alignment with the Western bloc abroad.) The main theme of the opposition was that there must be no negotiations with the Chinese until aggression was completely vacated and that the government must seek to meet the Chinese challenge both politically and militarily. Prime Minister Nehru, on the other hand, pleaded for a dual approach—gradually building up India's military strength and leaving the door open for a rapprochement with China.

Broadly speaking, the Chinese pressure on India began a process of erosion of the left. Both within the country and within the ruling Congress party, the so-called left was demonstrably weakened. The Indian Communist party was greatly embarrassed, and its position came under persistent attack from other parties. Although the party finally responded to the nationalistic fervor aroused by the aggressive Chinese postures, it was on the defensive, and its strength dwindled in the wake of Chinese aggression. Within the Congress party, what are generally known as the left spokesmen—as, for instance, Krishna Menon—found their position increasingly compromised and weakened.

At the same time, the voice of the opposition parties was listened to with greater attention, and the conservative forces, whether outside the Congress or within, became a more formidable force in the country's political life. As a result, Prime Minister Nehru lost considerable initiative in dealing with China and had constantly to look back over his shoulder to watch the opposition's reaction. The slightest indication of any move to negotiate with the Chinese produced angry protests from the opposition parties and large sections of the press.

Events just before the Chinese attack provide a telling illustration. In June and July 1962, the Government of India inched its way toward renewed negotiations with China. On July 26, an Indian note to the Chinese government called upon the Chinese authorities to desist from crossing their own 1956 line and proposed talks to reduce the tension on the border. The publication of the note led to a violent denunciation of the government's "policy of appeasement." Typical of these comments was that by the editor of the *Hindustan Times*. He described the move as the "road to dishonor" and appealed to public opinion to exert itself and prevent the government from bringing about this national humiliation.[15] Similar opinions were vigorously expressed by the opposition members in the subsequent debate in Parliament. The result was that the government declared tamely that it did not intend to enter into formal discussions on the border question without the prior vacation of aggression and that it was merely proposing talks to reduce the tension on the border.

At the same time, neither the government nor its critics had any precise idea of the strength and combat readiness of the Chinese forces on the border. Naturally, the government had somewhat better knowledge of Chinese power and was really being pushed into heroic postures by its critics. Yet it is doubtful if even the government fully appreciated the military realities on the Himalayan peaks. The government believed that there might be some border skirmishes but that China, faced with a stiff, determined stand by India, would

15. *Hindustan Times*, July 18 and August 9, 1962.

yield ground. A full-scale war was not regarded as a serious possibility, nor was India prepared for it. The subsequent Chinese attack demonstrated how faulty our military intelligence was and still more vividly how wrong the government's political assumptions were.

The opposition had even a less clear idea of the risks facing the Indian soldiers and the unequal nature of the fight—at least for the time being. It urged the government to adopt a policy of military confrontation without a proper assessment of the actual situation and the possible consequences. For instance, the *Hindustan Times* editor, while scoffing at government claims in regard to border preparations, nevertheless believed: "For the first time since Chinese aggression in Ladakh began, we were on the point of reaching the stage where the Chinese military threat could be contained with a relatively minor effort on our part." [16]

The real crisis in India's foreign policy started with the massive Chinese attack on India during September–November 1962. It shocked and shook the nation as nothing else had done before. India could not be the same again. Shock, humiliation, and frustrated anger characterized the response of the people. Although the actual fighting was largely confined to elevations of nearly 12,000–16,000 feet, the political consequences of the reverses suffered by India in the remote peaks of the Himalayas have baffled many observers. How could the fighting in those inaccessible, largely unpopulated, mountainous border areas lead to such grave political repercussions within India?

First, the fighting was neither so remote nor so insignificant to the Indians as it appeared from a distance. The North Eastern Frontier areas seemed pretty close to the heartland of the country, and as the Chinese armies moved swiftly toward the outskirts of the plains of Assam, the danger of foreign invasion appeared both real and imminent. It was the first such threat posed to India's very existence as an independent country since the attainment of freedom in 1947. The memories of foreign rule and the struggle for independence were still fresh in the minds of most people. The general feeling which this situation engendered was that the country was in grave peril and that the choice was between enslavement or fighting with all it had to preserve its freedom.

The other aspect of the Indian reaction was that Chinese victories in the Himalayan battle grounds delivered a shattering blow to

---

16. Same, August 9, 1962.

India's pride and self-respect and exposed her military weakness. India had projected a certain image of herself, and perhaps she had also come to believe in her own relative importance in the world. While the world knew that she did not possess a powerful military machine, it nonetheless believed she was a strong, stable, independent country. Though not formally belonging to the category of big powers, she was regarded as a country which counted in world affairs. She had tremendous influence in the Afro-Asian community, and her voice carried a great deal of weight within its councils. This fact was a tribute partly to the size, strength, system, stability, and economic progress of the country and partly to the stature and eminence of its leader, Jawaharlal Nehru.

The Chinese attack questioned India's strength, disturbed its stability, and threatened its independence. It was also calculated to blur India's image, cut her international size, and destroy her influence in the world. A nation whose military weakness had been revealed in so brutal but effective a manner could not continue to enjoy the same prestige as she had before. Instinctively and perhaps spontaneously, India reacted bitterly to this humiliation, with a half-conscious awareness that what she had lost was not merely some mountain passes, soldiers, and equipment but her entire international position. The Chinese had aroused Indian nationalism, the nationalism of an injured and battered country, to a degree which no amount of friction with Western powers had succeeded in creating.

The Indian reaction was all the sharper because it was almost that of a jilted lover. India had gone out of her way to befriend China. In season and out, we had defended and spoken for Chinese rights. In courting China we had risked the displeasure of the West. As Indians saw it, China had been guilty of bad faith and treacherous conduct. Love turned into hate is always more violent than normal, long-standing enmity. Small wonder, therefore, that the Chinese attack provoked such explosive reactions in India.

The fundamentals of India's foreign policy were now open to question. The first reaction of the Soviet Union (in the form of a *Pravda* article written at the height of the Caribbean crisis), which more or less asked India to accept Chinese terms, cast further doubt on the policies which had hitherto been followed. The Prime Minister himself said that India had been "living in an artificial atmosphere of our own creation." The prevailing mood was best reflected by the editor of the *Indian Express*, who wrote:

War teaches a country many valuable lessons. One of the useful lessons which Chinese aggression has highlighted is to demonstrate to the Indian people who their real friends and foes are. ... To pretend that our policy of non-alignment has not received a jolt by recent events and developments is to continue to live in what the Prime Minister rightly labelled as an "artificial atmosphere of our own creation". . . . Let the Prime Minister, therefore, give a lead to the country by implementing his own advice that the massive invasion of India by China should make us realise that we were getting out of touch with reality in the modern world.[17]

Another telling comment came from a columnist of the *Indian Express*, D. R. Mankekar:

At this stage, it is pointless to blame any particular person or pass the buck. Indeed, who can cast the first stone? For the opposition parties must accept their share of the blame in as much as it was they who had goaded the Government into premature action on the northern frontier when it was a fairly well known fact that we were militarily not yet prepared for fruitful action on that border. . . .
    Yet another, a Dullesian, truth brought home to us is that in this world sharply divided between the Communist and non-Communist blocs, there is no room for neutrals—not when the chips are down. . . .
    With the enemy now fighting right inside our territory, there is no time to lose. We must make up the deficiency in our weapons here and now, and from whatever source possible. When the threat to our freedom is right on our soil it is dangerous quibbling to insist that we shall not incur any country's obligation by accepting military aid and that we would go it alone however difficult the task of repulsing the aggression might be.[18]

Subsequent developments have induced second thoughts on the subject, and advocacy of alignment is no longer so insistent. The increasing bitterness of the Sino-Soviet dispute and Moscow's open denunciation of the Chinese attack on India knocked the bottom out of the proposition that there could be no neutrality in this sharply divided world.
    Moreover, there was another body of opinion which regarded the

17. *Indian Express*, November 1, 1962.
18. Same.

Chinese attack as primarily an effort to secure the Aksai Chin road in
Ladakh and, therefore, advocated cautious and limited responses.
For instance, in the view of the editor of the influential *Times of
India*, Chinese military pressure was designed to "compel New Delhi
to accept a negotiated settlement in Ladakh." The North East
Frontier invasion, in his view, was "one step in the softening up
process leading up to the offer of a settlement after a withdrawal in
NEFA, the price of which will be a compromise in Ladakh. This
still remains the only supreme objective of the entire Chinese
strategy." [19]

The Chinese attack resulted in a complete loss of initiative by
India. Developments were so sudden and so overwhelming that the
government, as well as opinion abroad, was almost completely paralyzed. It merely responded to the situations created first by the
Chinese attack and then by China's unilateral cease-fire and withdrawal. There was acute disappointment in India that the Afro-
Asian countries had failed to rally immediately to the support of
India as one of the major nonaligned countries of the world. They
too seemed to have been overwhelmed by the sudden developments
on the Himalayan peaks. But finally some of them seized the initiative and took steps to bring the two sides back to the conference table.
Six of them—Ceylon, the UAR, Ghana, Burma, Indonesia, and Cambodia—met in Colombo and devised certain proposals to facilitate
direct talks between India and China. India had earlier insisted that
the Chinese must vacate their aggression before talks could begin,
and she was initially a little suspicious of the efforts of the six powers.
But she had reason to be eminently satisfied with the results of these
efforts, for the Colombo proposals in effect provided for the restoration of the positions before the Chinese began their massive attack
on September 8. Moreover, these proposals, which India now accepted *in toto*, enabled India to recover some ground diplomatically
and to regain not only her balance but also some of her confidence
and prestige. China, on the other hand, after having made a great
display of welcoming Afro-Asian initiatives and so on, had to reject
the proposals. In the process, she lost some of the initiative she had
gained from her surprise attack.

The Chinese attack has posed new policy questions for India.
How should India meet this threat, this challenge on the northern
frontiers? Should the answer be sought in political, economic, or

---

19. N. J. Nanporia, *The Sino-Indian Dispute* (Bombay: Times of India,
1963), pp. 19–20.

military terms or perhaps in a combination of all of them? What role should India play in Asia? How is India to build up her military strength to acquire the military muscle needed to resist any future Chinese attack and to generate confidence among her own neighbors about her capacity to repel aggression? Can massive military aid from the United States be combined with continued benevolent neutrality on the part of the Soviet Union? Will it be possible to maintain long-term coexistence between the greatly increased Western presence in India and the sensitive, and now fully aroused, Indian nationalism? There are also difficult and painful questions of another sort. Can India afford this vastly increased military effort without fatally undermining economic progress and the stability of the Indian democratic system? How much military assistance is needed from abroad, and can India feasibly obtain this assistance? Interwoven with all these issues are India's other problems, chief of which is the dispute with Pakistan.

Vocal opinion in India has become sharply divided over many of these issues. A section of the people, the Swatantra party, and eminent personalities like Acharya J. B. Kripalani believe that India should abandon nonalignment, enter into a full military alliance with the United States, and fight communism all over Asia. The Praja Socialist party, the Jan Sangh, and the Socialist party do not go that far, but they are equally opposed to any concession to China for the settlement of the border conflict. On the other hand, the dominant view in the Congress party at present regards the Chinese action as essentially the product of aggressive and arrogant nationalism, which must be fought by both military and diplomatic means, but without getting involved in the cold war and without forcing the Soviet Union to line up on the side of China. Up to his death, Prime Minister Nehru continued to advocate the dual approach of building up military strength on the border and leaving open the possibility of a settlement with China, and his successor seems no less committed to that approach. Still another section of opinion looks for the mainsprings of Chinese actions in a peculiar combination of aggressive nationalism and Chinese communism, but it would agree on the need for retaining Soviet neutrality and for employing both military and diplomatic methods in the struggle against Peking. Jaya Prakash Narain, for instance, endorsed the policy of nonalignment, expressed satisfaction with the Soviet stand on the India-China conflict, and counseled patience to those who had criticized that stand.

The Chinese invasion of India had certain political repercussions

222   POLICIES TOWARD CHINA

in India. Perhaps the chief impact was to weaken the authority of Prime Minister Nehru in foreign policy. Hitherto, the Prime Minister's word on foreign affairs had had a ring of finality about it, and only a few critical voices could be heard in opposition. The failure of his China policy and the reverses suffered by the Indian troops during the fighting on the northeast frontier somewhat weakened Nehru's position, and his stewardship of the country's foreign policy was no longer unchallenged. To some extent, the government was hamstrung because of this failure, and it was noticeably reluctant to take bold initiatives. No one can say with certainty how much the concentration of responsibility for the direction of foreign policy was a function of Nehru's unique personality and of the special place he occupied in Indian politics. Now that Lal Bahadur Shastri has become Prime Minister, there may be some changes in the procedures by which decisions in this area are arrived at. The nature of the problems to be dealt with, however, is dictated by the logic of the situation. It would appear that the problems are important enough to demand the attention of the highest level of government.

The erosion of the left which began with the border dispute has increased as a result of the Chinese attack. The Indian Communist party has been gravely weakened and is now split up. The left in the Congress has also been in disarray. Although the Praja Socialist party and the Socialist party have consistently championed a policy of steadfast confrontation with China, it is doubtful if they can claim any substantial accretion of strength because of the Chinese attack. In general, in fact, the Chinese managed to reduce the left, at least temporarily, to an inconsequential minority. In light of India's poverty and economic problems, however, the left may not remain permanently down and out but may rapidly pick up strength again.

THE PROBLEM: WHAT NEXT?

One of the main problems before the country is the lack of clear, coherent, and consistent thinking about the nature of the threat which India faces and the kind of response which is required to meet it. Are we fighting China as an aggressive national power or as a Communist state? Is the threat primarily military or political? Is the confrontation total or partial? Are we aiming at, and should we aim at, a parity of military power with China or only the military strength which would render another attack extremely expensive for the Chinese? What is our role in Asia? Are we to fight the Chinese everywhere in the world or to limit the conflict to securing an honorable and satisfactory settlement regarding the border? As long as there is no clear thinking on these issues, there is little hope of a purposeful and energetic foreign policy for India in the new situation.

There is, of course, general agreement in the country that India must be well prepared to defend itself and not be caught napping again, and a vigorous program to strengthen the armed forces is under way so that resistance would be far more resolute and organized should the Chinese attack again. But there is much difference of opinion about policy alternatives with respect to the China problem and the general role of India in the world today. One course of action would be for India to withdraw into her shell and refuse to get involved in the problems of the world. She could thus concentrate exclusively on her own problems. This line of action, however, is not one which India is likely to pursue. The very fact that India sought military assistance from the United States, the United Kingdom, the U.S.S.R., and other countries to meet the threat of renewed Chinese aggression ruled out a policy of isolation. Other questions like India's association and relationship with the two blocs, and her place and role in Asia, remain the source of much debate and dispute, though. In discussions of the practical policies which India ought to adopt, there is not only a lively difference of opinion but also considerable confusion over the implications of possible policies. Alignment or nonalignment is often discussed in a vacuum without reference to the situation obtaining in the world today. The advocates of alignment (and in the present context they mean alignment with the West) ignore the fact that the United States is hardly eager for India's alignment. Soon after the Chinese attack, the U.S. ambassador in India, John Kenneth Galbraith, indicated as much in a press conference. Similarly the advocates of nonalignment often talk in terms which were valid a few years ago but are hardly relevant now.

After the Chinese invasion, a former commander-in-chief, General Cariappa, summed up the four courses open to India. Course one, according to him, was to "pursue our present effort to persuade China to vacate our land and then discuss in a friendly way the problem in hand." But, as he himself said, in her present mood China would not prove accommodating. He might have added that India in her present mood would not agree to such a course. Course two was to seek military aid from a friendly power (the West and chiefly

the United States) to provide the "tools" India needed to defend
herself against China. This course, in the retired general's view,
called for a reorientation of the policy of nonalignment, and he
pleaded for an immediate appeal for such aid and wanted public
opinion to assert itself on this issue. The third course, according to
General Cariappa, was to appeal to other Asian and African countries
to persuade China to vacate her aggression and then to enter into
friendly negotiations with India. These countries would impress
upon China the need for the solidarity of all Asian and African countries to provide for everlasting world peace. The last course was to
seek Soviet assistance. In the general's view, the Soviet Union was
"the one and only great power who can persuade China to call a halt
to her aggression, vacate our land immediately, and then to discuss
with us her frontier problems." He himself did not believe in the
"often reported alleged estrangement between the U.S.S.R. and
China" but thought that India could "go flat out to appeal to Russia
to step in and help." Thus, Russian sincerity could also be put to
the test.[20]

While one can formulate these four courses of action in slightly
different terms, they have generally been regarded as the policy alternatives which the country should weigh and decide upon. In other
words, should a "solution" to the problem be sought through alignment with the West, through closer relations with the Soviet Union,
or through the agency of the Afro-Asian countries? Implicit in these
alternatives are other questions. Should the challenge be met
through entirely peaceful diplomacy? Should there be an essentially
military solution to the problem? Or is a combination of defensive
arms buildup and diplomatic activity called for?

Although these broadly stated alternatives are generally debated,
there is often confusion regarding their implications. For instance,
General Cariappa himself advocated a simultaneous adoption of all
four of them. In his own words, we should "appeal to Russia as
detailed in course IV, and to the Asian and African countries as in
course III" and at the same time "plan immediately for the implementation of course II" and "continue our peaceful efforts as in
course I." [21] In fact, the general was advocating virtual alignment
with the West and effective and decisive assistance from the Soviet
Union at the same time. How alignment with the West as well as

20. Article in the *Organizer*, Dewali, 1962, pp. 15–16.
21. Same.

with the Soviet Union could be simultaneously effected has not been made clear. Apart from the General, many others have tended to believe, without any apparent evidence, that Moscow would look with equanimity upon India's alignment with the West and would continue to side with India in the dispute with China.

While the alternatives have been theoretically stated, there is little chance of India departing basically from the policy of nonalignment. In a manner of speaking, this policy is too deep-rooted by now to be discarded lightly. The ruling Congress party and the entire country, in fact, accepted it for nearly 15 years. Nehru's successors, who were associated with him in the government, have functioned within its framework for all these years and have to some extent been conditioned by this approach. It has enabled India to play an independent role in international affairs and to preserve her identity in a sharply divided world. There is no mounting pressure or movement in India for scuttling this approach. What has usually been demanded is that in the context of the changing international situation and in the light of the confrontation with China, this policy be applied more flexibly so that India's interests are advanced and India acquires speedily the capability to meet a fresh Chinese attack.

India is too big, and too proud, to submerge itself totally in a foreign-dominated alliance. Indeed, India's refusal to accept Chinese supremacy in Asia has been partly responsible for the Chinese anxiety to expose India's military weakness and, thereby, her inability to function as a major power in Asia.

There is also widespread feeling in the country that India should not magnify the already difficult task which it faces in relation to China by forcing the Soviet Union to the side of Peking through alignment with the West. Soviet willingness to provide economic and limited military assistance is valuable both in reducing the threat from across the Himalayas and in enabling India to play a balancing role against the Chinese drive for hegemony in Asia. While it is not necessary for India to be continually afraid of Soviet reactions to every foreign policy move she makes, it is obvious that continued, but perhaps more flexible, adherence to nonalignment will serve Indian interests by insuring the maintenance of friendly relations with the Soviet Union and of Soviet interest in the stability and security of India.

The world situation, too, has changed beyond measure. There is a thaw in the cold war; old animosities no longer sway people to the same extent. Ideological rigidity on both sides has mellowed into a more sober appraisal of the realities of the world. As a result, the concept of alignment has undergone a transformation and old allegiances are no longer either that strong or that enduring. At a time when the world is moving away from bipolarity, Indian movement toward alignment is not generally considered a realistic course of action. Resilience and flexibility of approach seem more appropriate to the needs of such a situation.

There is, however, almost unanimous agreement among Indians that the Chinese threat to India's territorial integrity must be adequately met and that all necessary measures toward such an end must be taken. Indian nationalism has been deeply hurt, and few people in India would want appeasement of China. The determination to resist Chinese aggression cannot be questioned. From this standpoint, the policy of nonalignment and friendship with both the United States and the Soviet Union is seen as consistent with India's vital national interests.

Within this large framework, India would favor efforts to curb the aggressiveness of Peking. It is highly doubtful, though, that India would like to, or even has the resources to, become the leader of an anti-Chinese alliance in Asia. Government leaders are more likely to view the Indian role as strengthening the nationalist forces in Asia and playing an effective part in the deliberations of the Afro-Asian community. In the latter case, India would adopt a twin approach—support for the freedom and integrity of Asian and African nations against threats from any quarter and exposure of China's aggressive and chauvinistic aims and ambitions.

INDIA, CHINA, AND THE UNITED STATES

India's relations with China and India's policies in Asia cannot be divorced from U.S. relations with India and policies toward Asia. The U.S. government's initial handling of the crisis on the Himalayan frontiers showed great political skill and diplomatic dexterity and left a deep impression in India. The traumatic experience of the Chinese invasion brought India closer to the United States, but it also raised many delicate problems and issues. While India has turned toward the United States for military assistance to achieve an adequate level of preparedness against renewed Chinese aggression, the policy makers of the two countries still must agree on the exact ways and means to obtain that level of preparedness. Indian impatience to achieve self-reliance in defensive equipment and modern weapons (for defense against Communist China) as quickly as possible has yet to be reconciled with American expert opinion on its feasibility. There is as yet no similarity of approach on the question of priorities, and the military and political assumptions of the two countries differ.

The United States is more concerned about India's role in Asia than about the recovery of her lost areas in Ladakh. In fact, the United States would probably not underwrite any Indian effort to recover her territory through military action, nor is it prepared to grant massive military assistance to put Indian military potential on a level with that of the Chinese. U.S. authorities favor a limited buildup for mountain warfare to contain further Chinese aggression. Moreover, U.S. expert opinion is inclined to dismiss the chances of another Chinese attack in the near future. The U.S. government, though, is vitally interested in India's future role in Asia. It would like to see India adopt a more positive attitude toward U.S. moves against Peking and join the United States in efforts to contain Communist China. It wants India to play a central role in the anti-Communist struggle in Southeast Asia.

India, on the other hand, is far more concerned about her territorial integrity and her ability to face China on her frontiers. Her role in Asia and anti-Chinese moves in Southeast Asia are of secondary importance. Another Chinese attack may be unlikely, but no Indian government could risk proceeding with defense preparations on that assumption. The government's first job is to bring about a certain balance of military power on the northeastern and northwestern frontiers and to put India in a position to rebuff renewed Chinese aggression.

As far as India's role in Asia and developments in Southeast Asia are concerned, there is no doubt that her weight will be thrown on the side of the nationalist forces in Asia and that she will support steps to strengthen the independence and territorial integrity of every Asian country. But it is improbable that Indian leaders are thinking of spearheading a general anti-Chinese crusade, and it is even less likely that they will get involved militarily in Southeast Asia. Instead, they will continue to favor political solutions to the problems there. Such solutions would aim not only at checking Chinese expansion but also at reducing foreign interference and the area's involvement in the cold war.

The problem of "conceptual identity" between the two countries is equally important. U.S. opinion regards the Indian subcontinent as a single unit for defense purposes; therefore, it holds that an India-Pakistan agreement is a *sine qua non* for massive military aid to the area. India, theoretically conceding the benefits of an understanding between India and Pakistan, does not consider such an agreement as a practical proposition in the immediate future.

Indeed, the specter of Pakistan haunts U.S.-Indian relations. Both India and Pakistan continue to be deeply suspicious of each other's intentions. The border agreement between Pakistan and Communist China and their open wooing of each other have hardened opinion in India and confirmed earlier suspicions that Pakistan had never intended to fight communism as such. Even Indian opinion friendly to Pakistan has been pointing out that Pakistan, professing to be staunchly anti-Communist, gave away territory to Peking, while India, accused of being soft on communism, chose to fight rather than surrender territory. In any case, India would not reconcile itself to fight for the "desolate extremity" of Ladakh and at the same time give away the heart of Kashmir. The maximum which India could offer, a redrawing of the line of division to give Pakistan more territory in a divided Kashmir, is not the minimum which Pakistan would, or perhaps could, accept.

Although such a situation need not impede limited American military assistance to India, it could obviously be a major irritant in U.S.-Indian relations. Already there is considerable resentment in India over what has appeared to be U.S. pressure to make concessions to Pakistan on the Kashmir issue. While the Indian leaders are prepared to try to develop friendly relations with Pakistan, and recently some moves have been made toward that end, it would be deluding ourselves to believe that New Delhi is envisaging any basic change in the status of Kashmir. The Kashmir issue and U.S. sympathy for Pakistan on this issue (and the earlier military buildup of Pakistan) troubled U.S.-Indian relations in the past and could do so again.

I do not mean to suggest that U.S.-Indian relations are necessarily going to encounter rough weather. I only want to avoid the disillusionment of unwarranted expectations. Close, cordial relations between India and the United States now exist, and with the loosening of existing bloc ties and the changing international situation, there is no reason why relations should not remain warm and friendly. Undoubtedly, cooperation between the two at all levels will not diminish but will continue to grow. The need for intimate, friendly relations is well understood in both countries.

Chapter 8

PAKISTAN AND CHINA

The Scope and Limits of Convergent Policies

BY

KHALID B. SAYEED

Pakistan, long regarded as a faithful ally of the United States, has recently been showing skepticism toward this alliance and an increasing cordiality toward Communist China. Pakistan's recent gestures of friendship toward China seem to be a somersault in the eyes of some Western observers. But to anyone familiar with the history of the Indian subcontinent, this change provides no puzzle. The ruling passion in Pakistan's foreign policy, a passion which has influenced its behavior toward all other countries, has always been fear of India.

The partition of India in 1947 took place on the principle that Muslims in the northwestern and eastern parts of India wanted to establish a separate state. India opposed partition from the outset and, in the eyes of Pakistan, has tried to flout its very logic by occupying the larger portion of Kashmir. Even after India's defeat in the border clash with China, Nehru declared that Indo-Pakistani "confederation remains our ultimate end." [1] *Dawn*, on the other hand, observed: "If the main concern of the Christian West is the contain-

---

1. *The Round Table*, no. 210, March 1963, p. 182.

ment of Chinese Communism, the main concern of Muslim Pakistan is the containment of militarist and militant Hinduism." [2]

India's hostility toward Pakistan perhaps reflects a feeling of guilt that the minority community had to seek separation because it suspected the Hindu majority's good faith. Memoirs like those of Maulana Azad suggest that partition could have been avoided if some Congress party leaders had not been narrow-minded or shortsighted during certain crucial stages of India's recent political history.[3] On the other hand, the existence of Pakistan makes the task of building a secular India on noncommunal lines exceptionally difficult. Some Indians have gone so far as to say that "just as the United States has come to view the aims of the Soviet leadership as the greatest threat to its security, so India looks on Pakistan as the main threat to its security." [4]

The fact remains, however, that India is four times as large as Pakistan in area and more than four times in population. India's industrial base is probably 10 times that of Pakistan. The martial races of West Punjab and the former North-West Frontier province constituted some of the best fighting divisions of the former Indian army, yet Pakistan emerged after partition as a much weaker military power than India. India refused to transfer the military assets which were allotted to Pakistan when the subcontinent was divided. Out of the 40 ordnance depots which contained reserves of all types of stores, equipment, ammunition, and vehicles, only five small retail depots were situated in Pakistan territory. All the 17 ordnance factories which the British had established were located in Indian areas. Before India's border clash with China, Pakistan's armed forces never exceeded a third of India's armed forces, although Pakistan was receiving U.S. aid.

According to Pakistanis, it was because of Indian intimidation that Pakistan had to obtain military assistance from the United States. When India massed troops on the West Pakistan border in March 1950, "Pakistan was practically defenceless. It was necessary for our Prime Minister to go to India and to arrive at a settlement and stave off this impending invasion." [5] In July 1951, India again concentrated

2. *Dawn* (Karachi), April 26, 1963.
3. Maulana Abul Kalam Azad, *India Wins Freedom* (Calcutta: Orient Longmans, 1959).
4. Phillips Talbot and S. L. Poplai, *India and America* (New York: Harper and Brothers for the Council on Foreign Relations, 1958), p. 68.
5. H. S. Suhrawardy, *Statement on Foreign Relations and Defence* [February 22, 1957] (Karachi: Government of Pakistan, n.d.), p. 10.

troops on Pakistan's borders. According to a recent report, it was in August 1951 that General Ayub Khan, the commander-in-chief of the Pakistan army, started thinking of a military alliance with the United States.[6] Pakistan was successful in obtaining U.S. military aid largely through his initiative and efforts.[7]

In the event of a military conflict, East Pakistan would be a relatively easy target. American aid to India has only accentuated Pakistan's fear. A well-equipped Indian army meant for China in the North East Frontier Agency would be "so positioned as to be able to wheel round swiftly to attack East Pakistan." [8] West Pakistan, where the bulk of the army is concentrated, could withstand an Indian attack for some time.

Ever since Pakistan signed the Mutual Defense Assistance Agreement with the United States in May 1954, and joined the Southeast Asia Treaty Organization (SEATO) in September 1954, and the Baghdad Pact (now the Central Treaty Organization—CENTO) in February 1955, Pakistan's political leaders have justified these military alliances as purely of a defensive nature. They all have pleaded that neutralism in such a context is a luxury which Pakistan can ill afford.[9]

PAKISTAN AND SEATO

It was obvious that Pakistani leaders had to defend Pakistan's military alliances with the West on the grounds of Indian hostility and superior military power. But how could the United States agree to give military assistance when it was clear that Pakistan's main concern was the alleged Indian threat and not the defense of Southeast Asia against Communist expansion? Like many other alliances, the Pakistan-U.S. military alliance was based on give-and-take. Pakistani leaders were prepared to pay the price of unpopularity among the Afro-Asian nations because of their fear of Indian intentions. During the April 28–May 2, 1954 conference of the Colombo powers

6. Major-General Fazal Muqeem Khan, *The Story of the Pakistan Army* (Karachi: Oxford University Press, 1963), p. 154.

7. Mohammed Ahmed, *My Chief* (Lahore: Longmans Green, 1960), pp. 73–76.

8. Mohammed Ayub Khan, "The Pakistan-American Alliance: Stresses and Strains," *Foreign Affairs*, January 1964, p. 204.

9. See H. S. Suhrawardy, *Prime Minister's Statement on Foreign Policy* [December 9, 1956] (Karachi: Government of Pakistan, n.d.), pp. 6–7, and *Statement on Foreign Relations and Defence*, cited, pp. 10–11; Malik Firoz Khan Noon, *Pakistan's Foreign Policy* [March 6, 1958] (Karachi: Government of Pakistan, n.d.), pp. 3–4; Malik Firoz Khan Noon, *Democratic Ideals and Foreign Policy of Pakistan* [August 21, 1958], (Karachi: Government of Pakistan, n.d.), p. 8.

in Ceylon, Prime Minister Muhammad Ali Bogra declared that international communism threatened both South and Southeast Asia.[10] By May 1954, Pakistan had firmly aligned itself with the United States, but it was not clear what concrete role Pakistan could play in the defense of Southeast Asia.   Pakistan was not included among the nine countries whose cooperation Dulles sought for the purpose of issuing a joint warning to Communist China.   In June 1954, Foreign Minister Zafrullah Khan was in Washington to assure the United States that Pakistan would cooperate fully in creating a Southeast Asia defense organization.   To gain admission into the proposed pact, Pakistan did its best to impress upon the Western powers that the threat of a Communist attack on its territory was not remote and that it was faced with Communist subversion in East Pakistan.   Pakistan also placed additional troops on its border with Burma as a precautionary step against a possible Communist drive through Burma and Thailand.   Thus, the United States was aware that Pakistan's major consideration in joining Western military alliances was its fear of India but was nevertheless satisfied that Pakistan would play its part in Southeast Asia when the occasion arose.

At the time the Baghdad Pact and SEATO came into being, the United States believed that there was a real threat of Communist attack and subversion both in the Middle East and Southeast Asia. In the Middle East there was the possibility of Soviet penetration, and in Southeast Asia the French had suffered a disastrous defeat at Dien Bien Phu.   Thus, the United States must have felt that Pakistan, because of its unique geographical position, could become one end of the northern tier opposing the Soviet Union in the Middle East and could provide protection to Southeast Asia on its western flank. The United States was also influenced by the consideration that: "In its relations with other Moslem states and with other members of the Afro-Asian bloc, Pakistan can be an efficacious advocate of western policies and can exert a moderating influence on the extreme nationalism and anti-western attitudes of some of the members of these groups." [11]

Once its admission into SEATO was assured, Pakistan tried to persuade SEATO members not to confine the definition of aggres-

---

10. K. Sarwar Hasan, *Pakistan and the United Nations* (New York: Manhattan Publishing Company, 1960), p. 69.

11. *Mutual Security Act of 1958*, Hearings before House Committee on Foreign Relations, 85th Cong., 2d sess., April 15–16, 1958 (Washington: GPO, 1958), p. 1753.

sion to Communist aggression but to allow it to cover all aggression
—no matter what the origin.   Such was the burden of Sir Zafrullah's
remarks at the Manila conference in September 1954.   Pakistan succeeded in getting aggression defined in general terms.[12]   The United
States, however, insisted on interpreting the term only as Communist
aggression, and it inserted an "understanding" to that effect into the
text of the treaty.   Australia had similar misgivings.   Foreign Minister R. G. Casey stated categorically to the Australian Parliament on
October 27, 1954, "that the Australian Government would never regard itself as being committed contractually or morally, to military
action against any member of the Commonwealth." [13]

Lately, Pakistan has become increasingly skeptical of its membership in military pacts, but as recently as December 1960, President
Ayub Khan, commenting on the situation in Laos, declared: "If
Pakistan (as SEATO member) is called upon to shoulder its burden
and responsibility we will never hesitate to do it." [14]   Pakistan's support for SEATO in 1960 should be viewed mainly as its reaction to
China's hostility on India's northeast border—hostility which Pakistan regarded at that time as a potential threat to East Pakistan.   We
shall see later how Pakistan's policy both toward China and SEATO
has undergone a remarkable change.

EARLY RELATIONS WITH COMMUNIST CHINA

Pakistan recognized the People's Republic of China (P.R.C.) on
January 5, 1950, six days after India and one day before Britain.   Out
of a general feeling of insecurity, Pakistan tried to combine friendship with the West with a "correct" attitude toward the growing
power of Communist China.   Pakistan did not hesitate to condemn
North Korea's aggression in 1950.   In October, Sir Zafrullah Khan
went so far as to support the U.S. view that there was nothing sac-

---

12. Article 4 of the Southeast Asia Collective Defense Treaty of September
8, 1954, states:
"Each Party recognises that aggression by means of armed attack in the treaty
area against any of the Parties or against any State or territory which the
Parties by unanimous agreement may hereafter designate, would endanger its
own peace and safety, and agrees that it will in that event act to meet the
common danger in accordance with its constitutional processes.   Measures
taken under this paragraph shall be immediately reported to the Security
Council of the United Nations."
13. See Aslam Siddiqi, *Pakistan Seeks Security* (Lahore: Longmans Green,
1960), pp. 139–140.
14. *Dawn*, December 15, 1960.

rosanct about the 38th parallel and that the whole of Korea should be occupied by U.N. forces. But when the General Assembly branded Communist China as an aggressor in Korea and imposed an embargo on the export of certain categories of goods to areas under the control of Communist China and North Korea, Pakistan abstained from the voting. Similarly, Pakistan at first favored U.N. representation for the People's Republic, but it subsequently voted, until 1960, for the Western-sponsored resolutions postponing consideration of the question.

On August 10, 1954, Pakistan announced that it would participate in the Manila conference. Four days later, the Pakistani ambassador in Peking assured his Chinese hosts, including Chou En-lai, that Pakistan would further develop "the happy and harmonious relations now subsisting between the two countries." *Dawn* (whose recent views are much different) deplored the fact that the Prime Ministers of Burma, Ceylon, India, Indonesia, and Pakistan, meeting at Bogor in December 1954, had agreed to invite the P.R.C. to the Bandung Conference. In *Dawn's* view, the failure of the Prime Ministers to refer to the threat of communism was "a confession of complete ideological surrender." [15] At the Bandung Conference, Prime Minister Muhammad Ali Bogra of Pakistan assured Chou En-lai that Pakistan's membership in SEATO did not imply that Pakistan was against China and that Pakistan did not fear any aggression from Communist China.[16]

Why did the P.R.C. accept these assurances? First of all, being shrewd observers of the Asian scene, the Chinese no doubt knew that Pakistan felt insecure about India, and they probably interpreted Pakistan's alignment with the United States as prompted largely by this feeling and not by hostile intentions toward themselves. Secondly, the Chinese were probably aware that Pakistan was not too deeply involved in the defense arrangements contemplated under SEATO. With the exception of the modest role of the Pakistan navy, no Pakistani troops had participated in SEATO military exercises although Pakistan maintained a larger defense establishment than either the Philippines or Thailand. There was no indication that any groundwork had been laid for SEATO military aid to Paki-

---

15. Same, January 2, 1955.
16. See Chou En-lai's statement, *Statesman* (Delhi), April 30, 1955. This statement was confirmed by Muhammad Ali Bogra, *National Assembly of Pakistan Debates*, June 27, 1962, pp. 622–623.

stan. U.S. military aid to Pakistan seemed to be directed against Moscow and not Peking.[17]

Despite the display of mutual friendliness at Bandung, China and Pakistan were conscious of the differences between them. As an ally of the West, Pakistan feared that denunciations of colonialism by the conference might apply exclusively to Western powers and also condemn those Asian countries which had aligned themselves with the West. On April 22, 1955, Iraq, Japan, Lebanon, Liberia, Libya, Pakistan, Iran, the Philippines, the Sudan, and Turkey put forward a resolution condemning colonialism of both varieties, Communist as well as Western. Chou En-lai proposed another draft resolution on colonialism which was worded so as to demonstrate "China's pacifist spirit and her desire for cooperation." In the Chinese draft, countries with colonies in Asia and Africa were requested to liberate them within a specified period. In subcommittee discussions of the draft the Pakistani representative insisted that reference should be made both to colonies and to Communist satellites, while Chou En-lai opposed any reference to Communist satellites. The compromise resolution which emerged said that "colonialism in all its manifestations is an evil which should speedily be brought to an end." [18]

It had been expected that Prime Minister Nehru would emerge as an outstanding leader and mediator at the Bandung Conference. But it looked as if leadership and influence had gravitated toward Chou En-lai. Such a situation occurred not merely because of China's size but also because of the Chinese Foreign Minister's apparent reasonableness and the obvious rivalry and rift between India and Pakistan. When Muhammad Ali Bogra put forward his "Seven Principles of Peace" and included among them a country's right of self-defense, whether exercised singly or collectively (an obvious reference to Pakistan's military alliances), Nehru maintained that Pakistan's purpose was simply to shield the recently concluded SEATO alliance. He took his stand on the "Five Principles" and said that

---

17. "There is no evidence in the shape of military planning, ground, air or naval exercises, or public statements that preparations have been laid for any SEATO military assistance to Pakistan. United States military aid for Pakistan seems oriented against the U.S.S.R. rather than China (except in so far as it is used to strengthen forces deployed against India), and on either count has little relevance to SEATO purposes." George Modelski, ed., *SEATO: Six Studies* (Vancouver: The University of British Columbia, 1962), p. 133.

18. Mohamed Abdel Khalek Hassouna, *The First Asian-African Conference Held at Bandung, Indonesia (April 18–24, 1955)* (Cairo: League of Arab States, 1955), pp. 99–101, 129.

"it was intolerable humiliation for any Asian or African country to degrade itself by becoming the camp follower of any great power." [19] Chou En-lai, who was also committed to the "Five Principles," suggested that there was no need to be inflexible about numbers and that he was prepared to add or subtract. He also revealed that he had been assured that Pakistan did not expect aggression from China. Because of this conciliatory attitude, the Pakistan Prime Minister at the end of the conference said that Chou En-lai had made a good impression, had displayed reasonableness and moderation, and had thus been successful in winning the friendship of all. [20]

DEVELOPMENT OF FRIENDLY RELATIONS

Recently, when the correspondent of the Associated Press of Pakistan drew Chou En-lai's attention to suggestions from abroad that Sino-Pakistani friendship was contradictory to Pakistan's alignment with the United States, Chou En-lai replied: "We do not deny that there is a certain contradiction. It is precisely for this reason that development of the friendly relations between China and Pakistan has been a process of gradual accumulation." [21] Along what lines have these friendly relations developed?

As I suggested earlier, Pakistan sought to strengthen its ties with the United States through bilateral and regional defense agreements and through economic aid arrangements without antagonizing Communist China. On March 25, 1956, Foreign Minister Hamidul Haq Chowdhury said: "Formal diplomatic relations were established in May 1951. Since then, in spite of some basic differences of approach, our relations have steadily grown." [22] Similarly, Prime Minister H. S. Suhrawardy, referring to the exchange of visits between the Chinese and Pakistani Prime Ministers, said:

> We have both agreed that the difference in our political system and even the divergence of views on many problems will not stand in our way to strengthen the ties of friendship between us and with a view to promoting further our cordial and friendly relations, due importance should be given to commercial and

19. Hasan, cited, p. 73.
20. Hassouna, cited, p. 156.
21. *Morning News* (Dacca), April 12, 1963.
22. *Foreign Relations* [March 1956] (Karachi: Government of Pakistan, 1956), p. 51.

cultural relations between the two countries. A Chinese Trade Delegation is expected to visit Pakistan shortly, and I am sure, this will not only lead to a further increase in trade between the two countries but will also forge another link of friendship.[23]

China-Pakistan trade, based largely upon an exchange of Chinese coal for Pakistani cotton, continued to grow. Communist China, during the years 1950–57, purchased some 200,000 tons of cotton from Pakistan, and in 1958 a new coal-for-cotton barter deal was concluded between the two countries.

During 1959–60, serious differences arose between Delhi and Peking over Chinese oppression in Tibet, Chinese incursions beyond the McMahon Line, and Chinese occupation of territory around Aksai Chin in Ladakh. Chinese probings beyond the McMahon Line in the Northeast provided a threat to East Pakistan. Therefore, on September 1, 1959, President Ayub Khan approached Prime Minister Nehru and suggested that the two countries should think about a joint defense policy in the face of the Chinese threat. Nehru is reported to have dismissed the offer and snapped back: "Joint defence against whom?" [24] Presumably, the President of Pakistan, finding Nehru so unreceptive and fearing the development of a border conflict between Pakistan and China, thought that he should approach the Chinese authorities for a peaceful settlement of the border question. He announced his intention to do so at a news conference on October 23, 1959. He added that though the Chinese government had not claimed any Pakistani territory, the Foreign Office had received a Chinese map which showed certain areas of Pakistan as part of China.

It was obvious to the Chinese that no accord was developing between India and Pakistan. The Chinese must also have noted that Pakistan's letter to the Security Council about "the controversy between India and China" over certain areas of Ladakh had not taken sides. It had merely reminded the Security Council that since Ladakh was a part of the State of Jammu and Kashmir, "no positions taken or adjustments made by either of the parties to the present controversy between India and China" would be considered valid or would affect the status of the territory of Jammu and Kashmir, for, according to the resolutions of the Security Council, the final

23. *Statement on Foreign Relations and Defence,* cited, pp. 3–4.
24. *The Round Table,* no. 210, March 1963, p. 182.

disposition of the state should be made in accordance with the will of the people expressed through a free and impartial plebiscite.[25]

On January 16, 1961, the Foreign Minister of Pakistan announced that the P.R.C. had agreed in principle to demarcate its border with Pakistan. More than a year elapsed before the two governments announced, on May 3, 1962, that they had decided to negotiate an agreement on the border between China's Sinkiang province and the contiguous areas of Hunza and Gilgit, the defense of which was under Pakistan's control. (It was on October 12, 1962—that is, at the time that China and India were engaged in a border war—that actual talks began in Peking. The border agreement was signed in March 1963.) Since the Sino-Pakistani border involved areas in dispute between India and Pakistan, it was announced that the contemplated border agreement would be of a provisional nature. Thus, the communique stated:

> The two sides have further agreed that after the settlement of the dispute over Kashmir between Pakistan and India the sovereign authorities concerned shall reopen negotiations with the Chinese Government regarding the boundary of Kashmir so as to sign a formal boundary treaty to replace this provisional agreement.[26]

During the negotiations, India lodged a strong protest and announced that it would not recognize any agreement which involved Kashmir territory occupied by Pakistan. Peking's reply made it clear that any agreement with Pakistan would be provisional until the Kashmir problem had been satisfactorily settled, and then the reply went a step further in favor of Pakistan by calling the Kashmir question a controversial issue. This stand was widely welcomed in Pakistan. It was in striking contrast to the Soviet Union's stand that Kashmir was an integral part of India. The Soviet Union had turned against Pakistan over the matter of Kashmir only after Pakistan had joined the Baghdad Pact. It had gone so far as to veto the Security Council resolution of June 22, 1962, which merely called upon India and Pakistan to settle the Kashmir dispute through bilateral negotiations. Pakistanis felt that China had as much, if not more, reason to turn against Pakistan because of Pakistan's membership in SEATO and its U.N. votes, up to 1960, in favor of postponing consideration of Peking's representation.

25. U.N. Security Council, *Official Records: Supplement for October, November, and December* 1959, S/4242 (New York: Author, 1959), pp. 76–77.
26. *Pakistan News Digest* (Karachi), May 15, 1962.

Pakistan's neighbors—India, Afghanistan, and the Soviet Union —are hostile; its friends—the United States, Britain, and other members of the Commonwealth—are far away. What choice, Pakistanis argue, did they have except to explore areas of understanding with the Chinese Communists? If U.S. military and economic aid was to be extended to India not only for defensive purposes but also for building India up as the leader of Asia against the Chinese, Pakistan could no longer feel sure of American support in the event of Indian aggression. It is from such a perspective that Pakistan looks at its border agreement with China.

Two hundred miles of border, from the trijunction of Pakistan, Afghanistan, and China to the Karakoram Pass, were defined and demarcated (see Figure 8-1). According to Indian claims, Pakistan surrendered 2,050 square miles of Pakistani-held Kashmir. But a careful analysis of the terms of the border agreement shows that both sides made concessions. The area in dispute was about 3,400 square miles. The compromise arrived at left about 2,050 square miles of the disputed area on China's side. Pakistan, however, gave up only claims on maps, whereas China agreed to withdraw its frontier forces and administration from about 750 square miles. Pakistan insists that the territory it conceded to China had neither been under its control nor under the control of its predecessors, the British authorities. Alastair Lamb's book, *The China-India Border*, based on British records, seems to support Pakistan's case.[27] The territory China surrendered in the Oprang Valley lay beyond the main area of access to the Karakoram Mountains and constituted the principal watershed between the Indus and Tarim river basins. China not only surrendered territory in its effective possession but also discarded the watershed principle upon which it had based its claims. Furthermore, the territory Pakistan gained provides good grazing ground for the Hunza people.

---

27. Lamb points out that as long as the Russian threat to Sinkiang and the northern borders of India was a live factor, the British used to claim and control territory which lay beyond the watershed line. But by 1927, when the Chinese position in Sinkiang had become stronger and the Russian threat had receded, the British modified their maps and decided to abandon most claims to a boundary north of the main Karakoram watershed. See *The China-India Border* (London: Oxford University Press, 1964), pp. 105–114. See also *The Times* (London), March 4 and 6, 1963. For an official statement of Pakistan's position, which seems to be in agreement with Lamb's account, see U.N. Security Council, *Verbatim Record of the 1114th Meeting*, General S/PV. 1114. (New York: Author, May 11, 1964), p. 22.

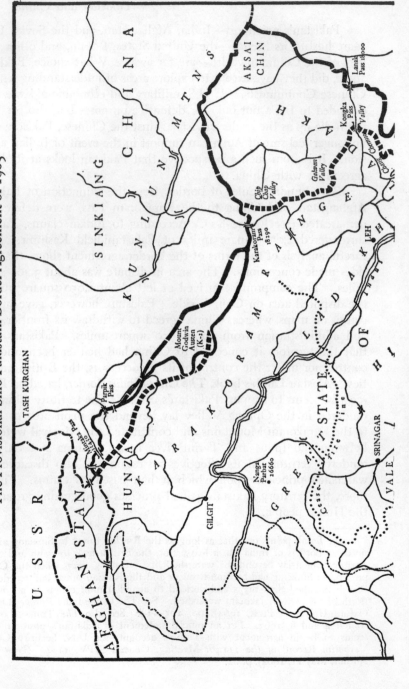

TABLE 8·1

The Provisional Sino-Pakistani Border Agreement of 1963

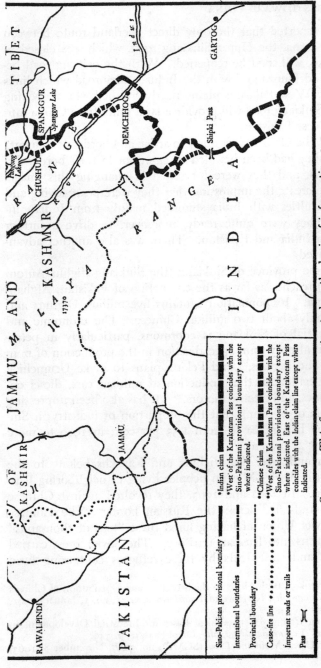

SOURCE: This figure was constructed on the basis of information supplied by the U.S. Department of State. No official Chinese or Pakistani maps were available.

Sino-Pakistan provisional boundary ████████████
International boundaries ■■■■■■■■■■
Provincial boundary ▬▬▬▬▬▬
Cease-fire line ●●●●●●●●●●●
Important roads or trails ▬▬▬▬▬▬
Pass ✕

• Indian claim ████████████
• West of the Karakoram Pass coincides with the Sino-Pakistani provisional boundary except where indicated.

• Chinese claim ■■■■■■■■■
• West of the Karakoram Pass coincides with the Sino-Pakistani provisional boundary except where indicated. East of the Karakoram Pass coincides with the Indian claim line except where indicated.

It is also reported that the only direct overland route between Pakistan and China, the Hunza-Sinkiang road, which was closed in November 1959, will soon be reopened. With the existing road between Gilgit and Hunza and with the Indus Valley road which links Gilgit and the West Pakistan plains nearly finished, the reopening of the Hunza-Sinkiang road will provide a land route from China into the heart of West Pakistan.

Why were the Chinese in a hurry to arrive at a border agreement? In the West, they had been branded an aggressor in their border dispute with India, and they were interested in changing this image. They sought to create the impression that they were peace-loving and that their difficulties with India stemmed mainly from Indian intransigence. They were quite ready, moreover, to drive a further wedge between India and Pakistan. There was also another advantage to be derived.

The Chinese province of Sinkiang (the Sinkiang-Uighur Autonomous Region) reaches as far as the trijunction of Pakistan, Afghanistan, and China. Its population contains five million Uighurs and Kazakhs and only about two million Chinese. The economic and industrial potential of Sinkiang is enormous, particularly in petroleum. There is already some specialization in the production of nonferrous metals and textiles,[28] and Peking plans to make Urumchi a heavy industry center for the production of railroad cars, diesel engines, automobiles, and electric motors.[29] It has also been impressing upon the people of Sinkiang that the proportion of industry in Sinkiang's economy has increased from 1.53 per cent in 1949 to more than 50 per cent at present.[30]

In religion and race, the Uighurs and Kazakhs belong to the same group as the Turkic-Muslim peoples living in neighboring Russian Kazakhstan. In 1962 and 1963, they revolted against Chinese rule, and thousands fled across the Russian border. The Chinese accused the Soviet Union of having lured these "tens of thousands" of Chinese citizens into Russian territory. The Soviet press carried "several letters and statements by these refugees containing lurid

---

28. Ikh Ordiyenko, "Basic Shifts in the Structure and Distribution of China's Industry," *Soviet Geography: Review and Translations*, v. 21, no. 1, January 1961, p. 53.

29. Quei-Sheng Chang, "Geographical Bases for Industrial Development in North-West China," *Economic Geography*, October 1963, p. 349.

30. *Survey of China Mainland Press* (SCMP), no. 3097, November 8, 1963, p. 25.

accounts of the Chinese oppression of non-Chinese nationalities in Sinkiang." [31]   China found it difficult to seal the frontier because of the nature of the terrain.   A revolt in Sinkiang organized by the Muslim tribes with Soviet help would isolate the Chinese position in Tibet.   (A major purpose of Communist China's claim to the Aksai Chin area of Ladakh and its subsequent attack on Indian outposts in Ladakh was to safeguard the road the Chinese had built through Sinkiang and Ladakh into Tibet.)

The Sino-Pakistan border agreement and the subsequent air agreement, which among other things opened the possibility of an air link between Lahore and Kashgar in Sinkiang, were part of a coherent Chinese policy to seek support in the neighboring Muslim countries of Pakistan and Afghanistan.   China signed a border agreement with Afghanistan on November 22, 1963.   These agreements were useful to China in its efforts to cope with unrest among the Turkic-Muslim people of Sinkiang.

Thus, one can see that there must have been considerable Chinese pressure on Pakistan to settle the border problem.   Pakistan could not ignore the danger, if a border agreement were not reached, of a Chinese attack similar to the one on India.   Foreign Minister Z. A. Bhutto revealed such fears in his speech at Dacca on April 8, 1963.

> Surely as a Government it is our responsibility to see that such a situation 'God Forbid' is not repeated for our people in which we are unnecessarily involved in a misunderstanding with a neighbour and a great power.   Surely we would not like to see the tantrums and all the crisis that has been created as a result of misunderstanding over the boundary between People's Republic of China and India.

The fact that Pakistan had, as early as October 1959, requested negotiations on the border question shows Pakistan's anxiety for a settlement.

It is also obvious that Pakistanis had given a good deal of thought to the Sino-Indian conflict and to Pakistan's own relations with China. At the time of the clash itself, Ayub declared that for reasons of terrain and timing it would not result in a full-scale war.   The hot war between India and China would be of a short duration, but the

---

31. Geoffrey Wheeler, "Sinkiang and the Soviet Union," *The China Quarterly*, no. 16, October/December 1963, p. 59.

cold war had long-term prospects. Mian Mumtaz Daultana, a former Chief Minister of West Punjab and for a brief period the Central Defense Minister, assessed the situation in November 1962 in this way:

> The rivalry for Asian domination which both China and India consider to be their "manifest destiny," the ethnic and historical ties of the disputed areas with China, the stringent Chinese ideological emphasis on "conflict" rather than "co-existence" as the operative springs of Communist dialectics, the austerities of the Chinese internal situation, the reckless wooing of India by the West, point to a deeper alienation. My own tentative interpretation is this. The cold war between India and China is likely to be prolonged, the hot war is a very temporary phase, which many circumstances impugn to bring to an early close.[32]

As a result of all these considerations, Pakistan's policy makers decided that it was in Pakistan's interest to forge additional links of understanding with Communist China. Even before the negotiations on the border question were concluded, a trade agreement was signed on January 5, 1963. It provided for reciprocal most-favored-nation treatment in matters of commerce, trade, and shipping. The lists attached to the agreement stated that China would export items like metals, steel products, coal, cement, machinery, chemicals, raw materials, and cereals. Pakistan exports would include jute, jute manufactures, cotton, cotton textiles, leather, sports goods, surgical instruments, chrome ore, and newsprint.[33] China was reported to have become the biggest buyer of Pakistani cotton during 1963–64—302,000 bales out of Pakistan's total export of 539,000 bales. Pakistan's cotton exports had shown signs of decline for some time. The recent Chinese purchases, however, have restored considerable confidence in and stability to Pakistan's cotton market.[34]

Another agreement was reached in the sphere of civil aviation. Pakistan International Airlines had been trying for some time to expand its international services in order to improve its foreign exchange earnings. When it was denied landing rights in Hong Kong for its international service to Tokyo, it approached Chinese aviation authorities in June 1963. By August 1963, a Chinese civil aviation delegation had come to Pakistan to negotiate and sign an agreement

---

32. Cited in *The Round Table*, no. 211, June 1963, p. 289.
33. *Pakistan News Digest* (Karachi), January 15, 1963.
34. *Dawn*, February 25, 1964.

whereby Pakistani planes would be accorded the necessary facilities in Canton and Shanghai. The U.S. State Department's reaction was that the agreement was "an unfortunate breach of the free world solidarity" and that the air link between Pakistan and China would "have an adverse effect on efforts to strengthen the security and solidarity of the sub-continent which the Chinese Communists want to prevent." [35]   The United States also postponed the granting of a loan of $4.3 million for improvements at Dacca airport on the ground that it was unwilling to pay for the improvement of facilities at airports which Chinese Communist airlines might use.   Furthermore, it was suspected in Pakistan that the Americans had pressured the Japanese government not to agree to an amendment in the existing Pakistani-Japanese air accord which would enable the Pakistan airline to operate its flights to Tokyo through China. [36]

The Sino-Indian border conflict, followed by the American decision to give "massive" military aid to India, jolted Pakistan's foreign policy makers and led to what Pakistan's critics have called Sino-Pakistani "flirtation" or "fraternization."   But the agonizing reappraisal of Pakistan's foreign policy had started earlier.   As we shall see later, Pakistan's suspicions and fears of American desertion started taking shape soon after President Kennedy and what *Dawn* called his "Harvard theoreticians" assumed office.   The Foreign Minister, Muhammad Ali Bogra, when attacked by the opposition for his pro-Western policy, declared in June 1962:

> At the time when we entered into these regional pacts and these regional security arrangements there were no ballistic missiles or nuclear weapons. . . .   What was important at that time may not be as important today.   That is why great powers are not giving that much of importance and laying emphasis on these pacts and regional security arrangements.   The whole military thinking has become different. [37]

After the arrival of American and Western military equipment in India, Pakistani authorities showed signs of grave alarm.   Their apprehension and sense of frustration were increased when the Americans refused to put pressure on India by making military aid condi-

---

35. *The Round Table*, no. 213, December 1963, p. 396.
36. *The New York Times*, November 17, 1963.   See also "The Failure of Pakistan-Japan Negotiations on Air Communications," *The Sangbad* (Dacca), November, 14, 1963.
37. *National Assembly of Pakistan Debates*, June 27, 1962, pp. 621–622.

tional on settlement of the Kashmir dispute. Foreign Minister
Bhutto's statement in the National Assembly in July 1963 alarmed
the West about the possibility of a secret understanding between
China and Pakistan. Bhutto said:

> A conflict does not involve Pakistan alone. Attack from India
> on Pakistan today is no longer confined to the security and
> territorial integrity of Pakistan. An attack by India on Pakistan
> involves the territorial integrity and security of the largest State
> in Asia and, therefore, this new element and this new factor that
> has been brought in the situation is a very important factor. I
> would not, at this stage, like to elucidate any further in this
> matter, but suffice it to say that the national interest of another
> State itself is involved in an attack on Pakistan because that State
> and other States have known India's aggressive intentions and
> how India is capable of embarking on aggression against other
> countries. Therefore, a subjugated Pakistan or a defeated Paki-
> stan is not only a question of annihilation for us but also poses
> a serious threat to other countries in Asia and particularly to the
> largest State in Asia. . . .[38]

President Ayub, in an interview with Selig S. Harrison in September 1963, denied that Pakistan had a secret security pact with
China, but as to the possibility of a future Rawalpindi-Peking axis,
he said:

> The answer to that lies with the U.S. authorities. If India
> grows menacingly strong, we shall be in a great predicament and
> shall have to look around for someone to help us. And if we
> are attacked by India, then that means India is on the move
> and wants to expand. We assume that other Asiatic powers,
> especially China, would take notice of that.[39]

In October 1963, Bhutto, confronted with a question about whether
China had assured Pakistan of help if the latter were attacked by
India, said: "There is no assurance, there is no agreement between
China and Pakistan on this matter . . . but there is a strong as-
sumption." [40]

The Chinese extended their support to Pakistan in careful and
calculated stages. Before the border agreement was reached, they
took the position that Kashmir was a disputed area. After the bor-

---

38. *The Round Table*, September 1963, p. 398.
39. *The Washington Post*, September 12, 1963.
40. *Morning News*, October 9, 1963.

der agreement and other understandings, they came out fully in support of Pakistan's stand on Kashmir. The Ayub-Chou joint communique of February 23, 1964, indicated a much greater area of understanding than previous professions of Chinese friendship for Pakistan had.

The President and the Prime Minister agreed that the border dispute between India and China should and can be resolved peacefully through negotiations. They expressed the hope that the Kashmir dispute would be resolved in accordance with the wishes of the people of Kashmir, as pledged to them by India and Pakistan. It would be of no avail to deny the existence of these disputes and to adopt a big-nation chauvinistic attitude of imposing one's will on others. Massive military preparations have never been the answer to international differences. They only create new tensions and bring added burdens to the people. An early settlement of these disputes, they considered, was necessary in the interest of world peace and the well-being of the peoples of Asia.[41]

We have already seen that President Ayub Khan, when he was commander-in-chief of the Pakistan army in 1951, suggested that perhaps the only solution to Pakistan's defense problem was to align itself with a strong and reliable military power like the United States. The average Pakistani might be in the habit of boasting that small Muslim Pakistan could always take on and even trounce big and predominantly Hindu India, but the military view was that since Pakistan could not be defended easily against an Indian attack, protection must be sought through military aid from the United States. To the military authorities, the best way of deterring an Indian attack was to have superior armaments and air power. These were precisely what U.S. military aid provided.

After the American decision to give extensive military aid to India, Pakistan felt insecure once again. Ayub and his military advisers were quite sure that the Chinese had no intention of launching a large-scale military invasion of India. Therefore, the enormous military aid given to India by the West would be used against Pakistan. Even at the time when Indian troops were locked in combat with the Chinese and badly needed reinforcements, most of India's best fighting material stood poised at the Pakistani frontiers. Thus, Pakistan argues that it had to normalize relations with Communist

---

41. *Dawn*, February 24, 1964.

China and befriend it in such a manner that India, having suffered some of its worst military defeats at the hands of the Chinese, would think many times before attacking Pakistan.

Pakistan's policy makers have presumably considered the price which Pakistan may have to pay for China's favorable attitude in the Kashmir dispute. This attitude may cost at least a part of the independence Pakistan has acquired by making clear to Washington that Pakistan cannot be taken for granted and that it has a right as a sovereign state to establish cordial relations with the Chinese. Henceforth, in framing foreign policy, Pakistan's leaders may have to weigh the probable effects of their policy on Peking's declared attitude. "Thus, unless and until the Kashmir dispute is settled, the foreign policy of Western-allied Pakistan may have to take Peking's wishes into consideration to a degree ironically greater than many nonaligned nations." [42]

GROUPS IN PAKISTAN WITH A SIGNIFICANT INTEREST IN CHINA POLICY

As early as 1955, *Izvestia* suggested that Pakistan was not yet completely lost because of its membership in SEATO and CENTO; there were "progressive forces" in Pakistan who were making every effort to extricate the country from its position of dependence and reorient its foreign policy on more independent lines.[43] The Chinese, however, accepted Pakistan's assurances that its membership in SEATO should not be interpreted as a hostile move against the Chinese. Perhaps the Russians felt that it was in their interest to support India not only because it was larger than Pakistan, but because it was not willing to align itself with the United States through a defense pact. The Chinese, on the other hand, were probably aware that India was likely to contest their claim to the leadership of Asia while Pakistan, constantly in conflict with India, would not openly or actively oppose their bid.

The question which arises is: What groups in Pakistan favor a pro-China policy, and what groups support a pro-Western policy? Since all groups agree about the serious danger which India poses, it is difficult for any group to take a public and open pro-Western stand

42. *The Christian Science Monitor*, February 29, 1964.
43. Cited in Werner Levi, "Pakistan, The Soviet Union and China," *Pacific Affairs*, v. 25, no. 3, Fall 1963, p. 216.

in view of American military aid to India after October 1962. Nevertheless, there remains a good deal of room for the advocacy of different policies. The main point of difference is how far the country should go in loosening or reversing its Western ties and how far it should seek to preserve them. Various views are found within the government, among political parties, and in business circles. The variety of views is reflected in the press and in pressures on the government from two directions.

Government. President Ayub Khan, the architect of Pakistan's military alliances with the West, is the responsible head of those groups of army and civil service officers who have become increasingly disenchanted with the West. There has been continuous and steady pressure on him to bring about a radical change in Pakistan's foreign policy, but on several occasions he has taken a stand against such a change. One example of this pressure was the demand of the Basic Democrats, meeting in January 1962 at Larkana (which is Foreign Minister Bhutto's home town), for a reorientation in Pakistan's foreign policy.[44] In Mardan, Ayub said: "If Pakistan did not have friends then she must not lose our half or quarter friends under the present circumstances."[45] In a news conference, he suggested that without "trying to be meddlesome," he was prepared to use his good offices to bring about an understanding between China and the United States. But he recognized the gulf between them.

> As I say, it is a very difficult situation; your people have difficulties, too. After all, they are committed to supporting Chiang Kai-shek, committed to defending Taiwan and so on. It is a political commitment, it is an honorable commitment.[46]

Foreign Minister Bhutto has been closely associated with what has been described as "the normalization of relations with the Soviet Union and Communist China." He has visited both countries. He has consistently argued that the People's Republic of China has the right to occupy the Chinese seat in the United Nations.[47]

Perhaps the most important of the government policy-making groups is the Civil Service of Pakistan. Its members have exercised a decisive influence regardless of who has been in power, the professional politicians or the present leaders. The upper crust and

44. *Morning News*, January 20, 1962.
45. *Dawn*, January 21, 1962.
46. *Pakistan Affairs*, v. 18, no. 4, March 5, 1964.
47. *Dawn*, February 22, 1964.

hard core of these policy makers are men who originally belonged to the Indian Civil Service. At the time of independence, they numbered 94. Several, however, have now reached the age of 60 and have retired. The new regime has also forced a few to retire because of charges of misconduct or inefficiency. Most of these senior civil servants were pro-Western. The younger civil service officers, who are between the ages of 40 and 50, are now exceptionally influential, and they are a different brand. They grew up at a time when the Congress and Muslim League nationalist movements were at their height and exercised a magnetic charm over the students. A large number of them are still loyal to the memory of Jinnah and the Muslim League. These men feel strongly that the United States has made up its mind to support India as the leading power of Asia. They also point out that they have convincing evidence to show that Americans lately have been interfering in the domestic politics of Pakistan. A substantial number of these officers have come to believe that only by cultivating the friendship of Communist China can the future of Pakistan as a separate and independent state be assured. The Pakistan Writers Guild, under the leadership of Secretary-General Qudratullah Shahab, a civil servant, passed a resolution in 1963 describing the Western policy of arming India as against the very existence of Pakistan.[48] A number of young East Pakistan civil servants, between the ages of 30 and 40, are reported to have Socialist sympathies. *Dawn* has charged that certain American embassy officials have labeled some senior Pakistani civil servants as Communists who had influenced Pakistan's decision to reach a border pact with China.[49] Those said to be included in this category are Qudratullah Shahab, now Pakistan's ambassador in Holland and formerly Secretary of Information and Broadcasting, and S. K. Dehlavi, former Secretary of the Ministry of External Affairs, now Pakistan's ambassador in the U.A.R. These charges have been denied by the American embassy officials.

Political parties. In the National Assembly a great majority of the members agree with the government policy of cautious maneuvering to establish cordial relations with China without withdrawing from the military alliance with the United States. Perhaps this viewpoint was most clearly expressed by Qamarul Ahsan.

48. Same, July 30, 1963.
49. Same, March 11 and 12, 1963.

Now, the corner-stone of Pakistan's foreign policy, in my humble opinion, must be a settlement with China on all points. That must be our cardinal aim. That is the safest and wisest course under the present circumstances. Now what about the SEATO and the CENTO? Well sir, they are there. Let them be there. Let us not take any hasty step about them.[50]

Among the dissenters from the majority view is Sardar Bahadur Khan, the former leader of the opposition in the National Assembly. He has argued that unless it is proved that SEATO and CENTO are essential to Pakistan's defense, the country should withdraw from them, for Pakistan has antagonized half the population of the world by being a member of these pacts.[51] Yusuf Khattak, from the Pathan area of West Pakistan, has cited China's amicable border pacts with Burma and Nepal to support his call for a neutral foreign policy.[52] More recently, he has taken a stronger position and advocated Pakistan's withdrawal from pacts like SEATO and CENTO and has pointed out that "the emergence of Chinese leadership in Asia has created many hopes for Pakistan for the first time in 16 years and we may feel secure now from any aggression by India against us."[53] Akhtaruddin Ahmad, a member from East Pakistan who was the deputy head of Pakistan's delegation to China in 1963, has drawn the attention of the Assembly to the fact that East Pakistan may become a base for American-Indian military operations in the North East Frontier Agency in India.

Perhaps the most outspoken group which supports a pro-Chinese foreign policy, including total withdrawal from defense pacts with the West, is the Pakistan National Awami party led by Maulana Bhashani. It draws the bulk of its following from East Pakistan. Bhashani has waged a long and bitter battle to advance his ideas, particularly on foreign policy, ever since he parted company with Suhrawardy's Awami League and formed the National Awami party in 1957. He is known to have strong leftist leanings and is sometimes described as Pakistan's Red Dean of Canterbury. He led a delegation, of both government and opposition members of the National Assembly as well as several industrial and intellectual leaders, to

50. *National Assembly of Pakistan Debates,* November 26, 1962, p. 83.
51. Same, November 24, 1962, p. 46.
52. Same, November 26, 1962, p. 90.
53. *Dawn,* March 28, 1963.

China during September–October 1963. His speeches were widely reported in the Chinese press. Wherever he went, he praised the achievements of the Peking regime and appealed to Afro-Asian governments to convene an Afro-Asian conference. He condemned what he described as U.S. imperialist activities. "The profit-seeking U.S. imperialists, with other imperialist countries, have done their best since the last world war to destroy Afro-Asian solidarity and establish the machinery of oppression." In contrast, Communist China "stands for equality among nations, sympathizes with the oppressed, and helps them to become strong. China has no territorial ambitions at the expense of other countries." [54]

The resolutions passed by the Central Organizing Committee of the Pakistan National Awami party are in the same vein as Bhashani's speeches.

> This meeting of the Central Executive of the National Awami Party fully appreciates the just support extended by the Chinese Government and the people to the Kashmiri people in their just and peaceful struggle for securing the right of self-determination at a time when the big powers of the world are out to support India despite her ruthless suppression of the people of Kashmir.[55]

The party, "while hailing the closer Sino-Pakistan ties," called upon the government to establish closer relations with "all the countries of the world including Socialist countries." It also advocated "an independent and non-aligned foreign policy" and "avoidance of such military pacts as SEATO, CENTO, Pak-U.S. bilateral pacts and such other pacts that may hamper the economic development of the country." [56] It should be pointed out that President Ayub, by his friendly gestures toward Communist China and his strong criticisms of the West for supporting India and letting down Pakistan, has neutralized for the time being the National Awami party's opposition to his regime.

Another critic, Nasrullah Khan, a National Assembly member from West Pakistan and a supporter of the Awami League party of the late H. S. Suhrawardy, perhaps represents the point of view of the majority of Awami League supporters in both sections of the

54. SCMP, no. 3108, November 27, 1963, pp. 19–20. For his other speeches and statements, see SCMP, no. 3099, November 13, 1963, pp. 27–28, and SCMP, no. 3109, November 29, 1963, pp. 46–47.
55. The Dacca Times, March 6, 1964.
56. Same

country, but particularly in East Pakistan. In a National Assembly debate, Nasrullah said that it was not in Pakistan's national interest to establish friendly relations with China when China was obviously pursuing an aggressive type of communism in an attempt to exploit economic conditions in Asia and spread its political influence.[57] It is well known that Suhrawardy consistently advocated a pro-Western foreign policy for Pakistan. *The Dacca Times* has represented this point of view from time to time in a guarded fashion.

> Conceding that India was intransigent in resolving the border dispute with China through negotiation, yet the armed conflict could be avoided, particularly when China was the biggest power. They could seek the mediation of Russia whom India would hardly ignore. . . . We know that China today is trying to prove a good, reasonable neighbour to all the small neighbouring countries, maybe honestly. But at what cost? They are supporting Kings and monarchs in this region. How does this fit in with her ideology? [58]

Business circles. Also vitally interested in seeing that Pakistan does not go too far in cultivating friendship with the Chinese is the small but increasingly influential business and industrialist group. This group owes a good deal of its prosperity to the economic aid which the United States has been giving Pakistan. It has often been characterized as the "American lobby." [59] It is not unduly alarmed by the recent turn of events, and it is confident that under the present leadership Pakistan will not get so entangled with Communist China as to facilitate Communist political infiltration of the country. It believes, as other Pakistanis do, that the United States is endangering the security of Pakistan by strengthening India's military capacity.

In 1963, the Chinese invited a delegation of Pakistani industrialists to visit China. The delegation was led by a well-known East Pakistan lawyer, A. Ahad, and consisted of influential industrialists like Najmuddin Valika, A. K. Khan, and representatives of the Adamjee and Isphahani firms. Ahad described the visit as "a pilgrimage of discoveries" and also remarked that in matters of foreign trade and commerce, China respected the national sovereignty of other countries.[60]

---

57. *National Assembly of Pakistan Debates*, November 28, 1962, p. 171.
58. *The Dacca Times*, September 27, 1963.
59. *Dawn*, March 2 and 12, 1963.
60. *SCMP*, no. 2984, May 22, 1963, p. 35.

Press. Pakistan's newspapers have consistently followed the government line on American military aid to India. In its editorials, however, the *Morning News*, published simultaneously in Dacca and Karachi and controlled by Adamjee, perhaps the largest industrialist in the country, has often been moderate and cautious. While welcoming Chou En-lai's visit to Pakistan and calling for Peking's admission to the United Nations, the *Morning News* said: "Pakistan has no intention of subverting U.S. interest in the region or of wriggling out of her commitments to her allies." It added: "There is no conflict between Pakistan's friendship with her Western allies and the countries of the East." [61]   *Dawn*, on the other hand, claims to represent the nationalist point of view and has often denounced American policy in strong and pungent terms. Its editorials have borne such titles as "Immoral, Illegal"; "Red-Eyed Washington"; "Must Americans Be So Foolish?"; "Not All the Western Arms, Not All the Kennedy Men"; "Uncle, Be Your Age!" One of its editorials offers a clear insight into Pakistan's traditional fears and emotions—especially their religious base:

> For the preservation of our Islamic State and to minimise the risk of Hindu Bharat's aggression against it, we must now turn to China, and this we can do with no risk to our Islamic ideology. In Hindu Bharat Islam is hated because it is Islam and Muslims are periodically butchered in large numbers merely because they are Muslims. In Red China religion as such may be decried, but of all religions only one, namely Islam, is not singled out for denigration and of all communities only one, namely the Muslims, are not singled out for violent persecution.[62]

It is true that the Peking government has been trying to win the goodwill of some of the minorities in China, particularly the Muslims. The Chinese are trying to integrate the Muslims into the body politic of Communist China by indoctrinating them, particularly the younger generation, with the ideas of Marxism-Leninism.[63]   President Ayub's

61. Cited in *The Globe and Mail* (Toronto), February 19, 1964.
62. *Dawn*, April 26, 1963.
63. The Third Chinese Islamic Conference, which took place in Peking in November 1963, set forth the following tasks for the future:
    (1) To urge Islamic circles to study socialism, patriotism and internationalism, concentrating on the fight against imperialism, loving one's country, and keeping the law.
    (2) To assist the government in implementing fully the Party's policy upholding freedom of religious beliefs and promote the self-reform movement among Islamic circles.

regime is also trying to modernize Islam, but it is obvious that there is a vast difference between his approach and that of the Chinese Communists.

PAKISTANI REACTIONS TO U.S. POLICY
TOWARD COMMUNIST CHINA

Pakistan is primarily interested in three aspects of American policy toward Communist China: (1) American efforts to develop the defense and political potential of India as the leader of Asia against Communist China; (2) American attempts to dissuade Pakistan from forging closer links with Communist China; (3) the general American policy throughout South and Southeast Asia, whose aim is to contain Chinese communism within mainland China and ultimately to weaken its power both inside and outside the mainland.

The key to Pakistani fears, emotions, and prejudices is Pakistan's growing concern that the United States has made up its mind to build India up as the bastion of democracy in Asia. Even before President Kennedy came to power, he had urged the United States to give unqualified support to India. Chester Bowles, in Pakistani eyes, was even more lavish in his estimate of India's role. Similarly, the writings of Selig Harrison, who has vigorously opposed U.S. military aid to Pakistan, have disturbed Pakistan's leaders. Harrison has unequivocally stated his point of view as follows:

> India is the great power of South Asia: it is not the business of the U.S. to subsidize Pakistan as a permanent garrison state with a military capability swollen out of all proportion to her size.[64]

Pakistanis also genuinely suspect that American liberals, intellectuals, and New Frontiersmen do not view with sympathy the historical depth and intensity which lie behind Pakistan's Muslim nationalism.

Recent American policy toward India seems to have confirmed Pakistani fears. Pakistanis point out that American naval and nuclear power will be used, if need be, to bolster India's position. They

---

(3) To make a determined effort to strike blows at counter-revolutionary and bad elements operating from among the Islamic circles under the cloak of religion.

(4) To run well the Chinese Islamic Scriptures College and promote academic research work on Islam and study of Islamic teachings, scriptures and historical data. (See *SCMP*, no. 3100, November 14, 1963, p. 14.)

64. "India, Pakistan and the United States," *The New Republic*, August 10, August 24, and September 7, 1959.

argue, however, that China had only limited objectives in the 1962 border clashes and that it is a mere figment of Western imagination to think that China is determined to undertake a large-scale invasion of India. The announcement that the United States intended to send the Seventh Fleet into the Indian Ocean for exercises, therefore, provoked opposition in Pakistan. Pakistanis also ridicule the idea that India can become the leader of Asia, for it is constantly engaged in a bitter conflict with Pakistan and stands humiliated as a result of the 1962 border warfare. Pakistan is also going a step further to weaken India's position by trying to establish close and friendly relations with countries like Nepal, Ceylon, and Burma—all of whom, in Pakistan's view, have not been well disposed toward India.

Pakistan, like other Asian countries, has been concerned about the adverse effects which the European Common Market may have on its trade. Thus, it has been trying to develop trade elsewhere, particularly with China, Japan, and the East European countries. Its Commerce Minister went to Peking in July 1964 for this purpose. After returning from his trip, he announced that Pakistan would accept a $60 million, long-term, interest-free loan China had offered. Pakistan would repay the loan with cotton, jute, and manufactured goods, and it would purchase Chinese machinery, cement, and sugar mills.[65] About the same time, Siddique Dawood, one of Pakistan's wealthiest industrialists, led a Pakistani businessmen's delegation to China. The delegation came back convinced that "China can supply to Pakistan complete power plants, textile machinery, machine tools, rolling stocks, trucks and railway carriages." It is also reported that the Chinese were interested in buying more cotton yarn, "but they did not show any interest to import cotton cloth from Pakistan." [66]

It is difficult at this stage to say whether Pakistan and China will develop strong trade relations with each other, but a pattern of trade is emerging. Pakistan is likely to export manufactured consumer goods and raw materials to China and import materials like coal, cement, and perhaps heavy industrial products and machine tools. It is also clear that Pakistan cannot expect much generosity from China either in the form of aid or loans.

I have already discussed in some detail Pakistani views on how far Pakistan should go in establishing friendly relations with Communist China. The government holds that there is nothing incon-

65. *The New York Times*, August 1, 1964.
66. *Dawn*, July 24, 1964.

sistent in Pakistan's membership in Western defense pacts and in its attempts to normalize its relations with the Peking regime. *Dawn*, however, argues that Pakistan should "discard our faithless Christian allies and forge the closest possible ties with the People's Republic of China." This view does not as yet enjoy universal support in Pakistan. Nevertheless, most Pakistanis would agree that to succumb to Western pressure and abandon the present attempts to befriend Communist China while the West continues to pour arms into India would not only be the height of folly but to "act like their bondslave." [67]

A key to Pakistan's current geopolitical thinking lies in Foreign Minister Bhutto's statement of December 10, 1962. Bhutto rejected the thesis that China would direct its expansion toward India and Pakistan. He dismissed the Sino-Indian conflict as "a question of two giants of Asia feeling their pride hurt." Sino-Pakistani conflict was not probable because Pakistan had no power pretensions which would make it a rival of China and because the Chinese could not easily commit any aggression against Pakistan in view of the limited and relatively inaccessible terrain which constitutes their border. Bhutto's thesis was: "given geography and the power realities of the nuclear age, the military threat to us, if there is one, would come more from the Soviet Union than from China." [68] This position is based on the traditional military view, inherited from the British, that the invasion of the subcontinent has invariably taken place through the passes on Pakistan's northwest frontier. Thus, Pakistan can justify its military and economic relationship with the United States by drawing a distinction between a "safe Peking" and a "menacing Moscow." There are, however, signs that Pakistan is trying to cultivate friendly relations with the Soviet Union as well. One of the major objectives of Ayub's visit to Moscow in April 1965 was to persuade Russian leaders not to support India in its disputes with Pakistan. Russians are likely to be receptive to such attempts, as they are interested in creating a nonaligned South Asia.

Can Pakistan manage to align itself militarily and economically with the United States and still pursue a "neutralist" or "independent" foreign policy likely to embarrass or antagonize Washington? In a revealing statement, Foreign Minister Bhutto has declared: "Some countries are very good experts on being both aligned and

---

67. Same, April 20, 1963.
68. *The Washington Post*, March 10, 1963.

non-aligned. We have yet to learn the art of being both aligned and non-aligned." [69] Pakistan's policy makers are becoming increasingly aware of these dilemmas and have so far shown considerable skill in pursuing what they consider Pakistan's national interests. President Ayub, particularly since the death of Nehru, is becoming conscious of his unique role as a strong ruler of a large South Asian state. Having brought about political stability and impressive economic growth at home, he probably feels that Pakistan can turn its attention to foreign affairs and fill at least part of the vacuum created by India's reduced international stature. In July 1964 he claimed that he had been asked by the United States to approach the Chinese and see if the Chinese could use their influence to arrest the deteriorating situation in Laos. Pakistan passed on the Chinese reply to Washington. Further, "When Mr. Chou En-lai, China's Prime Minister, recently visited Pakistan, half of my talks with Mr. Chou was on relations with the United States." [70] In the same statement, however, Ayub pointed out that if the war is extended to North Vietnam, "it will certainly make China react—I have no doubt in my mind." Speaking in a broadcast interview with the BBC in London, the President said that if there were a confrontation between China and the United States over North Vietnam, Pakistan would not get involved. When reminded of Pakistan's obligations under SEATO, Ayub replied:

> But that was at a time when we had a margin of military power
> to provide and then we were prepared to provide more than our
> share. But now with enlargement of Indian forces and so on
> —India has 3 to 1 and very soon it will have 5 to 1 lead over us
> —it is inconceivable that we can do much. . . . Our capacity has
> been rendered ineffective by the action of our friends.[71]

As the bonds of friendship between Pakistan and China grow, Pakistanis are likely to extend their opposition to the broader and

---

69. See his press conference in Karachi on February 19, 1964. (A typescript report of the press conference was issued by the Press Information Department, Government of Pakistan. The quotation cited may be found on page 14 of that document.)

70. *Morning News* (Dacca), July 14, 1964. The White House has denied that any letters have been exchanged between the President and the Chinese Communist Premier. But Secretary of State Dean Rusk did confirm that the three SEATO countries which maintain diplomatic relations with Peking (United Kingdom, France, and Pakistan) were asked to relay word to the Chinese that the United States intended to stand firm against Communist attacks in Southeast Asia. (See *The Washington Post*, July 26, 1964.)

71. *Morning News*, July 17, 1964.

more general aspects of American policy which are based upon the belief that Communist China's activities are directed against American interests and security. Pakistanis have started to ask why the United States is so implacably opposed to Communist China when it seems willing to come to terms with Communist Russia. It is precisely here that the Chinese doctrine of "Asia for Asians," [72] Mao Tse-tung's championing of the rights of American Negroes, and the subtle hints to Africans and Asians visiting Communist China that they cannot expect equal treatment from white Russian Communists acquire dangerous overtones. *Dawn's* comment is again suggestive:

> And why do the Western Powers persist in dragging Pakistan into their designs to make Asians fight Asians and turn the Yangtse and the Ganges into rivers of Asian blood? [73]

Obviously, Ayub's regime has found in its foreign policy an attractive and useful means of evoking popular support. Ayub has tried to capitalize on the fact that his regime, unlike its predecessors, has given Pakistan political stability and economic development. But these achievements and his attempts to increase the representative character of his regime through a system of Basic Democracies have not won for his government as much popular support as his attempts to pursue an independent foreign policy. This kind of foreign policy, involving increased cordiality with Socialist and Communist regimes, has long been demanded by intellectuals throughout Pakistan, and particularly in East Pakistan.

Have there been any marked changes in the foreign policies of the United States, Pakistan, India, and China? The United States continues to regard Communist China as a threat both to its interests in Asia and to the existence of peaceful and democratic governments in the new nations of Asia. Its military and economic support to India and its annoyance with Pakistan are consistent with this attitude. The United States, from time to time, has indicated that its level of tolerance toward Pakistan's growing relations with China would be breached if Pakistan went "very far" and signed a non-aggression pact or military understanding with China. Pakistan still regards India as its major adversary, and the shifts in Pakistani policy

---

72. Marshal Ch'en Yi, Communist China's Foreign Minister, expounded this doctrine in a recent speech in Pakistan. See *Morning News*, February 24, 1964.

73. *Dawn*, April 20, 1963.

may be interpreted as tactical changes in pursuit of the same objectives. Indian policy, on the other hand, has undergone a significant change. India's two objectives had been nonalignment, coupled with a role as a mediator in world affairs, and containment of Pakistan. Now the Chinese military offensive has rendered the goal of nonalignment somewhat unrealistic and has brought home the fact that India has a more formidable foe than Pakistan, namely Communist China. The basic feature of Chinese foreign policy since the establishment of the Communist regime has been implacable hostility toward the United States, and it had been felt that the Chinese would follow orthodox Communist doctrine and wage ceaseless subversive and revolutionary wars throughout Asia. Now one detects a certain change in Chinese methods. They have been found capable of pursuing their objectives by violent means, in Southeast Asia and on the Indian border, and also by skillful diplomacy in which a combination of a subtle display of strength, trade, border pacts, cultural contacts, etc., is employed.

Chinese attempts to forge close links with Pakistan appear to be directed ultimately at driving a wedge between Pakistan and the United States. When Pakistan warmly reciprocates Chinese gestures of good will, it is bound to create suspicion and resentment in the United States. For example, the joint communiqué signed by Ayub during his visit to China in March 1965 extolled Afro-Asian solidarity and alleged, without mentioning the United States by name, that that country, by introducing nuclear weapons into the Indian Ocean, had posed a threat to the independence of countries bordering that ocean and undermined Asian-African solidarity.[74]

The U.S. reaction has to be seen in the context of its increasing confrontation with Communist China in Vietnam. In testimony before the House Appropriations Sub-Committee on Foreign Operations, Assistant Secretary of State Phillips Talbot stated that the United States was "deeply concerned by the extent of the warming up of relations Pakistanis had with Communist China at a time when the aggressive intentions of Communist China have been increasingly clear." [75] Pakistan seems not unaware of American sensitivity. Foreign Minister Bhutto, a consistent advocate of friendship with China,

---

74. For the text of the joint communiqué, in which Pakistan also opposed schemes for creating two Chinas and the Chinese supported Pakistan's demand for a plebiscite in Kashmir, see *Peking Review*, no. 11, March 12, 1965.

75. See *Dawn*, June 25, 1965, for excerpts from this and other testimony before the Sub-Committee.

signed the communiqué issued by the London meeting of the SEATO Council in May 1965, which contained the charge that the aggression against the Republic of Vietnam was organized and directed by the Communist regime in North Vietnam.

As noted throughout this chapter, variations in Pakistan's relations with China are correlated with variations in America's relations with India. It is not, however, a matter of a simple conditioned reflex, nor do terms like "somersault" and "flirtation" explain accurately Pakistan's present cordiality toward the P.R.C. The concern for national security is the hard core of consistency which runs through the shifts and changes which Pakistan's foreign policy has undergone. Pakistan hopes to draw several dividends from its friendly relations with China—a greater sense of national security vis-à-vis India and China, a status of respectability both among the new Afro-Asian states and the big powers, and a greater national consensus at home, which the present government seems to have failed so far to evoke on domestic issues.

Chapter 9

THE MALAY WORLD AND CHINA

Partner or Barrier?

BY

ARNOLD C. BRACKMAN

In the 1960s, for the first time in the modern era, the Malay peoples [1] have actively been exploring the question of some form of regional unity. Their ultimate success or failure in this effort is likely to have a profound impact upon future events in Southeast Asia. The Malay archipelago comprises about half the area of Southeast Asia, embraces more than 1 million square miles, and contains about 140 million people. It is strategically situated between the continents of Asia and Australia and at the confluence of the South China Sea and the Pacific and Indian oceans.[2] In natural weath and manpower, it is one of the richest regions on earth. Over the centuries, the archipelago has been coveted by India and China and fought over by the West and Japan. It is now a primary objective of the Communist enterprise.

---

1. As employed here, the term "Malay peoples" refers to Indonesians, Filipinos, and Malaysian Malays. In the past, the term "Malaysian peoples" has been widely used to denote the peoples of common Malay racial stock. With the emergence of Malaysia as a sovereign state in 1963, the term can now only lead to confusion.

2. In July 1963, Sukarno renamed the Indian Ocean the Indonesian Ocean. In Malaysia, there have been proposals to rename the South China Sea the Malaysia Sea.

UNITY AND CONFLICT IN THE MALAY WORLD

The concept of a unified Malay world is not new. In the 8th century the Buddhist Malay empire of Sriwidjaja, based on Sumatra, sought to establish hegemony over the Malay world. Six centuries later, Java's Hindu empire of Madjapahit attempted to do the same. These and other less illustrious efforts invariably failed. Primitive weaponry, ineffectual organization, insufficient economic strength, and awesome problems of communications were factors. Another factor, probably decisive, is that the Malay peoples comprise as many separate groups, with distinct customs, languages, physical characteristics, and local nationalisms, as exist on the continent of Europe. From the 15th century onward, this collection of Malay peoples was slowly reshaped into three modern states. The Philippines achieved its independence in 1946. Indonesia proclaimed its independence in 1945 and effectively achieved it in 1949. Malaysia, incorporating Sarawak, North Borneo (Sabah),[3] Singapore, and Malaya (the last had become independent in 1957), was formed in 1963. As a result largely of diverse colonial experiences and heritages, the political, economic, and social development of each of these Malay countries differed markedly.

Yet the rebuilding of direct ties within the Malay world was a logical consequence of the decolonization process. A Filipino commentator could write: "The Malay countries—all at once they look so close together we wonder why we never noticed they seem to be just waiting to be wedded." [4] At the first Malay summit, held July 30–August 5, 1963, in Manila, this sentiment was dramatized. Here Malayan Prime Minister Tunku Abdul Rahman, Philippine President Diosdado Macapagal, and Indonesian President Sukarno took the "initial steps" toward a grouping of the three nations—"Maphilindo," an acronym derived from the first syllables of the names of the three countries.

In a *Declaration*, they described the three countries as "new emerging forces in the region" and declared their intention to strengthen economic, social, and cultural cooperation and to combine

---

3. The former British crown colony of North Borneo was renamed Sabah, presumably its pre-British name, with the birth of Malaysia. It should not be confused with the Indonesian-based rebel movement called the Unitary State of North Borneo, which includes Sarawak, Brunei, and Sabah.

4. Quijano de Manila, "The Malay Confederation," *The Philippines Free Press* (Manila), June 22, 1963.

their efforts "in the common struggle against colonialism" and "the eradication of the vestiges thereof." In a *Joint Statement*, they declared that "the peace and security in their region lies primarily in the hands of the Government and the peoples of the countries concerned." Finally, in an *Accord*, they affirmed that the formation of the projected Malaysia federation must first have "the support of the peoples of the Borneo territories" as ascertained by the U.N. Secretary-General and that North Borneo's inclusion in Malaysia would be "subject to the final outcome of the Philippine claim to North Borneo." The summit documents provided for the early establishment of consultative machinery, but some six weeks later a crisis developed over the formation of Malaysia. Indonesia's dissatisfaction on this score led to a rapid deterioration of relations with Malaysia and to the initiation of Sukarno's campaign to "crush Malaysia" by any means possible, including military. The depth of Sukarno's feeling was dramatically shown on January 7, 1965, when he ordered the withdrawal of Indonesia from the United Nations in protest against Malaysia's election to a non-permanent seat on the Security Council. Maphilindo is thus far from an accomplished fact. Nevertheless, the concept has not been abandoned as a goal to be achieved in the future. The term is still current in the vocabulary of the Malay peoples. It has largely replaced the term "Pan-Malay," which was used by articulate Malay nationalists in the 1920s and 1930s.

To isolate the intrinsic Pan-Malayan elements in the concept of a Maphilindo, a principal factor has been deliberately omitted. Besides the kinship of "color and mien" and the quest for national identity after centuries of foreign rule, the Malay peoples are also bound by varying degrees of suspicion, if not hostility, toward the Chinese. These attitudes transcend the cold war. Rightly or wrongly, the Malay peoples view themselves as besieged by the Chinese, particularly by the overseas Chinese in their midst. These overseas Chinese exercise an economic influence out of proportion to their numbers. Aversion to the Chinese has been intensified by the emergence of a strong and unified mainland China which manifestly desires to extend its power and influence in Southeast Asia. The distinction between communism and the Chinese is often blurred. Since Peking's appeal to overseas Chinese depends largely upon ethnic identification, Malays frequently view Chinese communism as first of all a virulent form of expansionist Chinese nationalism. But the presence of Communist ideology on the mainland has added to the anxiety of many Malay peoples, especially devout Muslims in Indonesia and Malaysia and Catholic Filipinos.

The Filipinos have the fewest inhibitions about the meaning of Maphilindo.[5] Macapagal hailed the Manila summit agreements as "assuring security" for the Malay world, and Foreign Secretary Salvador P. Lopez later observed that "Communist China is the principal goad pushing [us] towards mutual help, cooperation and unity."[6]

Malaysians, 42 per cent of whom were Chinese at that time, took a dim view of these Filipino interpretations—at least for the record. Malaysian leaders, including those of Chinese ancestry, made little effort to conceal the fact that a basic purpose of Malaysia was to neutralize Communist influence among Chinese in Singapore and, to a lesser degree, in Sarawak. They denied, however, that Maphilindo was primarily anti-Chinese in design. Yet the Chinese community in Malaysia was disquieted by the Manila summitry.

Indonesia is officially silent about the Chinese aspect of Maphilindo. But unofficially the Indonesians are voluble. "For you Filipinos and for the Malayans, the menace is communism," an Indonesian official confided at the summit. "For us, the menace is the Chinese. It does not matter whether red or yellow, but it is the Chinese. So, in the end, the enemy is the same."[7] In private, Sukarno, Vice Premiers Subandrio and Chaerul Saleh, and Defense Minister Nasution speak similarly. But Indonesia collaborates closely with China. The unofficial Djakarta line, thus, may not be devoid of sophistry.

Moscow and Peking have largely appeared uninterested in Maphilindo. They have concentrated their agitprop techniques on Malaysia and exhorted Indonesia to "crush" it. The Indonesian Communist party (PKI), however, was initially outspoken in its opposition to a Malay regional grouping. It apparently feared that association with an anti-Communist Malaysia and an anti-Communist Philippines, combined with the lure of an Indonesian-dominated Maphi-

5. Macapagal told the Manila Overseas Press Club on September 4, 1962: "Philippine policy towards communism is straight-forward and unequivocal. We are inflexibly opposed to communism and all its works, and nobody is left in doubt about it."
6. U.N. General Assembly (18th sess.), *Provisional Verbatim Record, 1233rd, Plenary Meeting* (New York: Author, October 8, 1963), p. 12.
7. Quijano, cited.

lindo, might alter Sukarno's friendly posture toward the Communists at home and abroad.   Thus, D. N. Aidit, the party chairman, contended that there was no basis for a Maphilindo since the policies of the three Malay countries were in conflict.   He did not cite examples, but two are especially clear.   First, after the abortive guerrilla rebellions of 1948, the Communist parties in the Philippines and Malaysia were proscribed.   In Indonesia, where a Communist revolt of the same year was crushed, the government later encouraged the party's revival.   Secondly, Indonesia recognizes Peking; the Philippines, Taipei; and Malaysia, neither.   When Aidit realized that Sukarno sought to develop Maphilindo into an Indonesian sphere of influence, however, he radically altered his position, and the PKI warmly endorsed the concept.

In the West, the emergence of Maphilindo met with approval. Some typical comments were: "a buffer against Red Chinese expansion southward"; "by implication the agreement is aimed at Communist China"; "such a confederation could be a powerful bulwark against further Chinese Communist encroachment in Southeast Asia"; "a possible shield against the nightmare of the area, the southward seepage of the Chinese."

The above reactions to Maphilindo provide a fair measure of the interest of both the Chinese Communists and the United States and its allies in the evolution of a regional Malay union.   Chinese interest grows out of the presence of a large overseas Chinese community within the Malay world; the existence of important Communist movements in the area—particularly the PKI, the largest Communist party outside the Sino-Soviet bloc; Peking's active role in the affairs of the Malayan Communist party (MCP) and the Clandestine Communist organization (CCO) in Borneo, both of which are predominantly Chinese;[8] doctrinaire hostility toward the social systems of the Philippines and Malaysia; and, of course, Peking's quest for the leadership of Asia.   U.S. interest grows out of America's position as the major naval power in the Pacific and the adjoining waters; its network of collective and bilateral defense treaties in the area; and the implications of Communist China's hostility for the whole structure of U.S. security in the Pacific.   The United States' overriding

---

8. The CCO is frequently referred to in Sarawak Communist documents as "O," presumably meaning the Organization.   One of its progenitors is the Sarawak Anti-Fascist League, a Communist-inspired organization.   The name CCO was given to the movement by the Special Branch in the colonial period.

concern is to guarantee the integrity of the Pacific island barrier, of which the Malay archipelago is an integral part.

In examining Maphilindo as a potential barrier to Chinese communism, however, we must first consider the struggle for power within the Malay world which the prospect of a regional grouping has crystallized. The question is: What kind of Maphilindo? Is it to be shaped and influenced by Sukarno's brand of authoritarianism or by the representative systems of the Philippines and Malaysia? Is it to be a barrier against the Chinese inside or those outside the archipelago?

Sukarno enjoyed a political advantage over his Malay compeers at the summit and, accordingly, dominated it. Macapagal and Rahman, as elected officials, had to contend with political opinion, an opposition press, and opposition parties at home. Sukarno had suppressed his opposition and was governing Indonesia by fiat. He wholly controlled the press. He was barring elections and only shortly before the Manila conference had had himself installed as President-for-life.[9] Unlike Macapagal and Rahman, therefore, Sukarno was and is responsible primarily to history.

A power struggle within the archipelago strengthens the muted anti-Sukarno opposition in Indonesia and, at the same time, the Communist undergrounds in Malaysia and the Philippines. On one hand, Sukarno is being actively and openly defied by a fellow Malay, Rahman. Rahman has taunted Sukarno for his vanity, his cult of personality, and his responsibility for the collapse of the Indonesian economy. While Sukarno commands overwhelming support in Indonesia today, these Malaysian broadsides have apparently had some effect inside Indonesia, for the regime has made listening to Radio Malaysia a criminal offense.[10]

On the other hand, Indonesia's campaign against Malaysia encourages left-wing and right-wing extremists in Malaysia and the Philippines. For example, the hard-core Communist guerrillas on the Malay peninsula, about 500 men, have been contained in the Thai-Malayan border area for almost a decade, but Chin Peng, the MCP leader, must now sense new opportunities in Sukarno's campaign against Malaysia—if only because it is championed by the Sino-

---

9. On May 20, 1963, Sukarno announced he would accept the Presidency for life as the People's Congress, which consists of 623 Sukarno appointees, had proposed. No member of the Congress had dissented from the proposal.

10. Presidential Decree, no. 13, November 4, 1963. The penalty is a maximum of one year's imprisonment and confiscation of the radio set.

Soviet bloc and is directed at his principal adversary, Rahman.   Similarly, some 1,000 Sarawak Chinese of Communist sympathies have crossed the border into Indonesia to volunteer for guerrilla training.[11] At first, the Indonesian Army was apparently reluctant to arm them, but evidence suggests that by the spring of 1964 it no longer hesitated.   The Indonesian campaign has also aroused extremist Malaysian Muslims, whose antipathy toward the Chinese is close to paranoia—a major element in Singapore's exit from the federation in mid-1965.   Manila's dispute with Malaysia over North Borneo has led to improved relations with Indonesia and has strengthened the position of a small but vocal group of strident Filipino nationalists—for example, those whose views appear regularly in the *Manila Chronicle*.

For the overseas Chinese, particularly in Malaysia, this developing power struggle within the archipelago has deep implications. The conflict revolves around the unceasing struggle between representative and authoritarian forces.   The overseas Chinese as a community have fared immeasurably better under the representative systems of Malaysia and the Philippines than under Sukarno in Indonesia—despite Sukarno's cultivation of good relations with Peking. One reason is that in a representative system, however frail, a minority can make itself heard.   Another reason is Peking's readiness to sacrifice, at least in the short term, overseas Chinese interests for the sake of long-term objectives.   Despite the repression of Chinese in Indonesia, Djakarta and Peking appear to have "harmonized" their foreign policies in pursuit of dual long-term goals: the expulsion of Western influence from Asia and the Pacific and the division of Southeast Asia into complementary Sino-Indonesian spheres of influence.

An expansionist philosophy is one of the coarser fibers in Sukarno's nationalist ideology.   He has long dreamed of a Pan-Indonesia which would "include not only Malaya and Papua but also the Philippines."[12]   And in recent years he has rekindled memories of the

---

11. The Filipinos raised this point directly with Djakarta and were assured that the Chinese were being carefully screened.   In January 1964, an armed raiding party composed of both Indonesians and Chinese was intercepted in Sarawak waters.   This incident confirmed Indonesian and Chinese collusion in military matters.   Subsequent Indonesian raids against the Malayan peninsula in 1964 and in Borneo in 1965 contained Malayan and Sarawakan Chinese Communist elements.

12. Muhammad Yamin, *Naskah Persiapan Undang-undang Dasar 1945* [Preparing the Draft of the 1945 Constitution], (Djakarta: Jajasan Prapantja, 1959), p. 204.   The late Yamin, a Sukarno confidant, was a prominent exponent of Indonesian expansionism.

empire of Madjapahit, whose influence "extended to all present-day Indonesia, including North Borneo and Malaya." [13] In October 1963, after renaming the Indian Ocean, he alluded to a past when Java's influence extended vaguely from Madagascar to Easter Island.

The Pan-Malay dream has, of course, also been nurtured in the Philippines and Malaysia. At the turn of the century, the Filipino revolutionary heroes Rizal and Mabini envisioned a union comprising Borneo, the East Indies, Malaya, and the Philippines. On the Malay peninsula, sentiment for Pan-Malay unity has in the past attracted support as a defense mechanism against potential Chinese domination. But neither the Philippines nor Malaysia possesses the resources to support great-power ambitions. Indonesia is the critical element. Sukarno's own estimate of the Manila summit is therefore of particular interest. He averred:

Whatever may happen . . . two things become clear:
a. Indonesia is no longer treated like the dummy Togog and allowed just to look on alone at alterations to the status quo in the region around it, especially if those alterations concern its safety;
b. Indonesia is recognized as having the right and primary responsibility to guard security and peace in the region together with its neighboring states, the Philippines and Malaya.[14]

Clearly, the question of whether or not a Malay union is a potential barrier against the Chinese and/or communism requires a look at the China policies of the Malay states.

INDONESIA'S CHINA POLICY TO 1958

In 1949, the Malay and Chinese worlds coincidentally underwent an epochal upheaval: The Communists ascended to power in Peking on October 1; the Indonesians, in Djakarta on December 27.

At the outset, relations were strained. The then monolithic international Communist movement was employing a left strategy, and Indonesia was controlled largely by moderate democratic Socialists. The PKI incited disorders, characterized Indonesia as "semicolonial," and sought to fashion a united front from below. Moscow and Peking railed against Sukarno and Hatta as "lackeys of imperial-

---

13. See a speech at Den Pasar, Bali, Antara, April 22, 1957.
14. Independence Day message, August 17, 1963, in Republic of Indonesia, Department of Information, *Official Statements of the Government of the Republic of Indonesia*, v. 1, no. 6314.

ism." The Communist bloc boycotted the Djakarta ceremonies marking the sovereignty transfer. Nonetheless, sentiment in post-revolutionary Indonesia favored normal relations with the new China. Djakarta therefore announced it would recognize Peking if the Chinese first recognized Indonesia, since the Communist regime had been installed earlier. The Chinese, doubtless motivated by a need to attract overseas Chinese support in Indonesia, concurred. Up to this writing, Indonesia is the only Malay nation which maintains diplomatic relations with Peking.

Recognition, however, did not produce an immediate thaw in relations. The arrival in August 1950 of the first Chinese ambassador, a former resident of Indonesia who had taught school in Sumatra and had been a PKI member, coincided with an intensification of PKI-inspired disorders. Rightly or not, there was widespread belief among Indonesians that some of the overseas Chinese had either voluntarily or involuntarily become a source of PKI funds. In 1951, Djakarta restricted Chinese immigration and barred an increase in the embassy staff. After a series of armed incidents involving Communist elements, the government—fearing a repetition of the 1948 PKI putsch—conducted a security sweep. Communists and fellow travelers, including such prominent Chinese Indonesians as Tan Ling Djie, a leading PKI theoretician, were detained. Panic swept the PKI ranks, and party chairman Alimin, who had spent part of World War II at Yenan, took refuge in the Chinese embassy. On November 10, Sukarno warned the Chinese community that "social controversies can very easily become racial controversy" and that Chinese who "propagate communism" seemed unaware that they would become the "first victims" of an Indonesian social revolution.

In 1953, Sukarno, exploiting an alliance between the PKI and the Nationalist party (PNI), was in ascendancy. Relations between Djakarta and Peking at that time were deeply strained. The shift of power within Indonesia, however, coincided with a shift in the Moscow line. The year before, Stalin had reverted to a right strategy of compromise with the bourgeoisie, and he had called for the formation of a united front from above in bourgeois countries (an explanation, in part, for the PKI-PNI alliance). A thaw in Sino-Indonesian relations was imminent.

Two related (and still current) problems—the dual nationality of local Chinese and their role in the economy—affected the course of the thaw.

Chinese settlements have existed in the Indonesian islands since at least the fifth century. Their role in Indonesian society has been a subject of dispute. In Indonesia's coastal ports, the frugal and industrious Chinese gradually displaced the Indonesian merchant class, who, through their Arab contacts, had introduced Islam into Indonesia. Later, after the Dutch had encouraged the immigration of Chinese (primarily laborers), the Chinese became a distinct economic buffer between the Dutch colonists and the Indonesian masses. They served as tax collectors and money lenders and later as wholesalers, distributors, and retailers. Therefore, anti-Chinese sentiment first "found its sharpest manifestation in Moslem circles." [15] As a consequence, the modern Indonesian nationalist movement contained anti-Chinese overtones from the start. The Islamic Trading Association was founded in 1912 in reaction to burgeoning Chinese control of trade. Its establishment followed the Chinese revolution of 1911 and a concomitant rise in nationalist fervor among the Chinese in the islands. Even now, the average Indonesian continues to associate "every Chinese with money, trade or business" and feels that the Chinese pose "a distinct threat to the economic and political survival of Indonesia." [16]

The Chinese, of course, see themselves differently. They contend that although Chinese have settled in the Malay archipelago for centuries, they have "entertained no political or territorial ambitions," that in the colonial period they exercised "no power in determining economy policy," and that Indonesian poverty is not a result of Chinese middle-class "exploitation" but is "one of the consequences of lack of energy on the part of Indonesians." [17] These overseas Chinese statements are culled from the pre-Communist era, but the views remain essentially unchanged today. Like the Nationalist regime before it, moreover, Peking holds that the Chinese in Indonesia "sweat and toil for the well-being of Indonesia" and "actively contribute to Indonesia's economic development." [18]

The tension between the two communities gave the Indonesian revolution of 1945–49 a special characteristic. In a national revolu-

15. H. A., *A Brief Sketch of Indonesian-Chinese Relations* (Jogjakarta: Indonesian Ministry of Information, circa 1946).

16. A. J. Muaja, *The Chinese Problem in Indonesia* (Djakarta: New Nusantara Publishing, circa 1956), p. 5.

17. Chung Hua Tsung Hui, *Memorandum Outlining Acts of Violence and Inhumanity Perpetrated by Indonesian Bands on Innocent Chinese Before and After the Dutch Police Action Was Enforced on July 21, 1947* (Batavia: Author, September 15, 1947), p. 2.

18. New China News Agency (NCNA), December 14, 1959.

tion—assuredly in an anti-colonial one—the middle and lower classes normally are drawn together. But in Indonesia's "plural society" the reverse occurred. National consciousness set the Indonesian masses further apart from the non-Indonesian ruling (Dutch) and middle (Chinese) classes. During the revolution, the overseas Chinese fared badly—especially in East Sumatra and West and East Java.

But the revolution was led by moderate social democrats. The Republic deplored excesses against the Chinese and afforded them protection wherever and whenever it could. It also sought to speed the assimilation of the Chinese into Indonesian society. As early as 1946, a Sjahrir Cabinet adopted a citizenship act patterned on the "passive system." In effect, it bestowed Indonesian citizenship on Chinese who had been born in the islands before the Japanese invasion and had not renounced the Republic. In 1949, under the terms of the transfer of sovereignty, a similar "passive system" was adopted. This system, however, was opposed by orthodox Muslims and secular ultra-nationalists. They favored an "active system" under which a Chinese in Indonesia would have to renounce his ancestral homeland before acquiring Indonesian citizenship—a step which few Chinese would be inclined to take. Future nationalistic economic legislation thereafter, could not be represented as discriminatory, for it would affect only aliens and not "second-class" citizens.

In 1953, after the fall of the moderate Wilopo government, Sukarno encouraged the formation of a government based largely on an informal PNI-PKI alliance. The Nahdatul Ulama party of orthodox Muslims supported him. Moves to improve relations with Peking and to open the issue of dual nationality were foreshadowed. Peking, now pursuing a right strategy, was responsive.[19] Radio Peking abandoned its tirades against "semi-colonial" Indonesia. Djakarta dispatched as its first ambassador to the Chinese Communist regime Arnold Mononutu, a prominent PNI figure. The first Sino-Indonesian trade agreement was signed, and cultural exchanges were launched.

When the Indonesians that year requested negotiations on the question of dual nationality, the Chinese consented. The negotiations eventually led to an agreement at the Bandung Conference in

---

19. In connection with this joint shift in Sino-Indonesian attitudes, it is perhaps startling that the immediate cause for Wilopo's fall was a PKI-engineered incident in Tandjong Morawa, East Sumatra, involving overseas Chinese Communists.

1955. Indonesia and China initialed a treaty embodying the "active system." Both sides hailed the accord as a model which could be applied throughout Southeast Asia. As it turned out, the Chinese delayed ratification and only signed under Indonesian pressure in 1960. Although the treaty was widely applauded, it contained glaring loopholes. Article 14 permitted either side to annul the treaty in 20 years. Clearly, the issue would be resolved only insofar as both parties desired.

In effect, the question of dual nationality only becomes an "issue" if a sovereign non-Chinese power accepts China's principle of "once a Chinese, always a Chinese." No other Malay country has, and the question therefore has not developed into a political issue in either the Philippines or Malaysia. For example, the Filipinos insist on their sovereign right to judge who is and who is not a citizen of the Philippines in accordance with Filipino law. Many Malaysians of Chinese ethnic origin known to the author, both officials and non-officials, reject any suggestion that either Peking or Taipei exercises a claim to their loyalty on racial grounds. Many Indonesians opposed negotiations on the issue with Peking and contended that the citizenship question was solely an internal Indonesian affair.

The 1955 treaty coincided with sweeping developments in Indonesia. Sukarno, in part by intensifying the national claim to West Irian (West New Guinea), had fortified his domestic power. The Communists, by identifying themselves with Sukarno and by placing themselves in the vanguard of those demanding Irian, emerged from the country's first (and only) general election as the fourth largest party—and as a domestic power factor.

Peking immediately sensed a new wind in Indonesia. Shortly after the elections, Defense Minister P'eng Te-huai drew a parallel between China and Indonesia. He said both are "similarly menaced [by the West]—China's territory of Taiwan has yet to be liberated and Indonesia's West Irian remains to be restored." He concluded that this fact "naturally strengthens the mutual sympathy between the peoples of our two countries." [20] In May, Mao Tse-tung hinted to a group of Indonesian journalists that he would like to visit Indonesia. In August, Mme. Sun Yat-sen arrived in Djakarta to attend

---

20. See his remarks on February 27, 1956, at a banquet for Rear Admiral R. Subijakto, the former chief of staff of the Indonesian navy.

Independence Day ceremonies. And in October Sukarno flew to Peking on his first visit.

The setting was historic: a confrontation between Mao and the most powerful and dynamic figure in the Malay world, Sukarno—a militant Marxist mystic endowed with his own revolutionary ideology, fearful of representative government, ignorant of economics, possessed by a phobia of encirclement, and determined to "go it alone," if necessary, to make Indonesia a world power.   Out of this Sino-Malay confrontation, overshadowed at the time by the twin Hungarian and Suez crises, may have emerged the basis for a working relationship between Djakarta and Peking, for the creation of complementary spheres of influence in Southeast Asia.

Peking described Sukarno's visit as "an event of paramount importance" and held that cooperation between China and Indonesia "conforms completely with *the present and long term interests* of both our peoples." [21]   Sukarno echoed these sentiments at banquets and mass rallies.   "You are struggling to regain Taiwan, we are struggling for West Irian," he declared.   "You are not isolated, we are not isolated.   The victory of the Chinese people is the victory of the Indonesian people and the victory of the Indonesian people is the victory of the Chinese people."

But this was 1956.   Sukarno had not yet acquired undisputed mastery over Indonesia.   The dual citizenship treaty, a tripwire in Sino-Indonesian relations, was not yet ratified.   In any event, the Peking dictatorship impressed Sukarno.   On his return home from a world tour, including visits to the United States, the Soviet Union, and China, he cited the last as a "model" for Indonesia and sounded the call for "a new style democracy," "a national democracy," or, as it was finally designated, "a guided democracy."   These sinistrogyrations at home and in foreign policy produced shock waves within Indonesia in 1957–58.   The non-Javanese "outer islands" revolted.

INDONESIA'S POWER POSITION

There were, of course, other important factors leading to the insurrection—conflicts between military leaders, as well as between their ambitions, in various parts of the country and dissatisfaction in the outer islands over the ineffectiveness of the central government and the diversion of the income of the non-Javanese islands for Java's

---

21. *People's Daily (Jenmin Jihpao)*, September 30, 1956.   (Italics added.)

4

444

benefit. Whatever the motivation of the revolt, the political climate in Indonesia radically altered with its suppression. The opposition was discredited. Sukarno ceased to support the PKI-PNI coalition (the PNI was in disarray and largely devoured) and began to play the Communists against the army, whose influence had burgeoned as it put down the rebellion. With the army and the Communists competing for his favor and endorsing his every move, Sukarno enjoyed increased freedom of action—particularly in foreign affairs. From this point forward, the country's approach to foreign affairs showed more and more the impress of one individual's world views and ambitions. Indonesia gradually emerged as a voice of the extreme left within the nonaligned Afro-Asian bloc.

In the execution of foreign policy, Sukarno increasingly relied on Dr. Subandrio, a former member of the Sjahrir-Amir Socialist party and a former ambassador to London and Moscow. Subandrio is polished, resourceful, and articulate. He is an admirer of authoritarian political systems, and he has shown great skill in playing one faction against another in Sukarno's court. His influence has grown since Sukarno brought him into the Cabinet in 1957. He directed the brilliantly successful campaign to wrest West Irian from the Dutch at gun point (with enthusiastic Soviet and Chinese Communist support and with the help of the United States and the U.N. Secretary-General). In 1963, Sukarno named him First Deputy Premier and charged him with the direction of the "crush Malaysia" campaign. A year later he became Sukarno's principal spokesman in domestic as well as foreign affairs. Speculation has arisen that Sukarno may be grooming him as a successor. Subandrio, however, lacks a strong political base, although he has cultivated PNI ties. The army and the Communists mistrust him. Among other responsibilities, he is a director of the political intelligence apparatus. His philosophy is that "it is natural for us to assume that as long as we are firmly resolved to stand on our own feet and oppose colonialism and imperialism, subversive action will still prevail [and] subversive elements should be rooted out." [22]

Subandrio has played a major role in the formulation and execution of China policy. His first substantive experience in this area was the implementation of the external aspects of Sukarno's dual policy toward the Chinese after the collapse of the PRRI-Permesta (1958) rebellion. Externally, Sukarno moved to collaborate with Peking to

22. Antara, November 19, 1963.

276 POLICIES TOWARD CHINA

exclude Western influence from Asia and from the Pacific and Indian oceans. Internally, he moved to "Indonesianize" the economy and, in the process, to discipline the overseas Chinese community. On the surface, these policies would appear to collide, and they did briefly. But Sukarno foresaw that Peking would draw the unavoidable conclusion: Peking must sacrifice, at least for the present, the interests of the overseas Chinese to advance its main objective in Southeast Asia—the expulsion of the West.

From the Indonesian point of view, China was, and is, militarily impotent. She is a land power devoid of naval strength; therefore, she is at a great disadvantage in dealing with an insular power. If China had possessed a common land frontier with Indonesia, Peking undoubtedly would not have tolerated Indonesia's campaign against her local Chinese—nor would Djakarta have embarked upon it. Because of his insular position, Sukarno can deal with Peking on equal terms. Furthermore, even if the Chinese Communists had possessed a naval capability, Peking would have been deterred from an Indonesian adventure by the presence of the U.S. Seventh Fleet, and Sukarno, like everyone else, knew it. Sukarno and Subandrio have recognized that in the event of a Sino-Indonesian incident, the United States would unhesitatingly support a nonaligned Indonesia as it did nonaligned India.

This assessment raises another apparent contradiction in Indonesia's China policy. In dealing with Peking, Sukarno is dependent upon Western sea power although his long-range objective is the removal of this presence from the seas of the Malay world. There is a school of thought, primarily Western, which holds that Sukarno is confident the West will not abandon Southeast Asia (at least its island belt) and that he is therefore content to make anti-Western noises (as he did on December 20, 1963, when he denounced the U.S. plan to extend the operational zone of the Seventh Fleet into the Indian Ocean) while he deals with Peking under cover of Western firepower.

Another glaring weakness in Sukarno's position relative to the great powers is Indonesia's desperate economic situation. The country does not produce a ton of steel and is unable to feed itself. Sukarno is wholly dependent on Soviet and/or Western arsenals. Moreover, since the introduction of "guided democracy," the economy has steadily declined, and Indonesia's dependence on outside sources for weapons and food has correspondingly increased.

Yet Sukarno believes he is operating in foreign affairs from a position of strength, and this assessment clearly affects *his* evaluation of cooperation with the Chinese Communists. The roots of such a position lie in Indonesia's strategic value and in the weakness of the great powers in Southeast Asia as reflected in their ardent competition for Sukarno's good will through military assistance, economic aid, and diplomatic or propaganda support.

Of particular interest in terms of Indonesia's strategic situation vis-à-vis China are the Sino-Soviet rift and the growth of the PKI. The Soviet Union has helped develop the offensive capabilities of the Indonesian sea and air arms. Moscow has provided Djakarta with considerable naval strength, including a 20,000-ton guided-missile cruiser and a flotilla of W-class, ocean-going submarines. In November 1963, General Nasution visited Moscow, and on December 23, 1963, he reported that the Soviet Union had agreed to supply military equipment to replace that cut off by a British arms embargo. The naval aid program continued in 1964–65 with delivery of additional warships, including destroyers. Although the efficiency of the Indonesian navy is open to serious question, it is not inconceivable that Soviet policy in part has been to provide a potentially Communist Indonesia with the naval strength she would require to act independently of the Chinese and the West. This possibility was reflected in Nasution's 1964 New Year's message to the armed forces. "The security of the [Indonesian] Revolution will not be assured as long as there are neo-colonialist armed forces and bases in Southeast Asia," he said.

SINO-INDONESIAN CONFLICT, 1959–60

Indonesia's strategic calculations were clearly dramatized by Sukarno's anti-Chinese campaign in 1958 in the wake of the abortive PRRI-Permesta rebellion. His first target was the Chinese Nationalist residue in the islands—partly on the theory that in the climate of contemporary world affairs one could hit "the Right-wing Chinese first, the better to strike the Leftists afterwards." [23] Taiwan had in fact invited some form of Indonesian retaliation by openly supporting the PRRI-Permesta rebels. By midyear, the "KMT phase" of the anti-Chinese drive was in full tilt. Nationalist Chinese shops, newspapers, theaters, schools, and social organizations were outlawed. For the record at least, Peking applauded the anti-KMT drive,

---

23. *Far Eastern Economic Review*, September 10, 1959.

though later it would maintain that the "true Overseas Chinese should be equated with the Indonesian peoples." [24]   On December 1, 1958, the PKI organ, *Harian Rakjat*, cautioned the government: "Don't be caught up in a tide of chauvinism."   Taiwan threatened that it "would not sit idly by and abandon its nationals." [25]   But apart from denouncing Sukarno and facilitating the repatriation to Taiwan of Chinese who so desired, Taipei was powerless to act—as Peking would be a year later.

The KMT episode had an intriguing sidebar. As the campaign intensified, the Provisional Taiwan Government in Tokyo [26] sent a mission to Indonesia to draw a distinction between Taiwanese and Chinese on Taiwan and to deny that Taiwanese were implicated in the PRRI-Permesta revolt. The mission's arrival incensed Peking, which scented an "intrigue at creating two Chinas." Djakarta expelled the mission and reaffirmed its "one-China policy."

However, no sooner had the furor over the KMT and Taiwanese subsided than the Indonesians turned on the remaining Chinese aliens who, perforce, were either pro-Peking or non-partisan. The character of this phase of the anti-Chinese campaign is controversial. It is, for example, not clear whether Sukarno desired the severe action that was ultimately taken against some of the Chinese. Some observers feel such action may have resulted from army initiative, possibly because of military hyper-nationalism.

The campaign was launched on May 14, 1959, with the announcement that by the first of the new year, aliens would no longer be permitted to operate retail shops in rural areas. Alien proprietors were advised to liquidate their businesses, to sell their shops to Indonesians, or to relocate their businesses in large cities. The ordinance affected about 300,000 Chinese aliens. Peking treated the announcement lightly. The Chinese Communists were apparently convinced that Indonesia would not jeopardize its relations with China.

In October, Subandrio flew to Peking to forewarn the Chinese of Indonesia's determination. A misunderstanding over a joint communique followed, and in November the storm broke. Chinese were

24. *People's Daily*, December 18, 1959.
25. Chinese News Service, April 8, 1958, quoting Cheng Yen-fen, chairman of the Overseas Chinese Affairs Commission. The statement was made in an April 5 report to the Legislative Yuan in Taipei.
26. The unrecognized "Provisional Government" claims to represent 10 million Taiwanese as distinct from the ruling 2 million Chinese Nationalist refugees from the mainland.

evicted from homes and shops. Goods were confiscated. Some
Chinese were beaten, others jailed. The PKI appealed directly to
Sukarno to ease the campaign "for the sake of our own security."
The PKI, like Peking, argued that "the common enemy of the Indonesian and Chinese peoples is imperialism." But Djakarta's rejoinder
was brusque: "We shall, under all circumstances, maintain friendship
with the People's Republic of China but without sacrificing our
national interests." [27]

A Sino-Indonesian dialogue at the diplomatic level ensued.
Peking repeatedly declared that "there is no conflict between the
fundamental interests of our two countries." [28] Peking also advised
Indonesia's Chinese to adopt local citizenship. Lest the overseas
Chinese believe they were being abandoned by the motherland,
Peking emphasized that the mainland awaited them if they desired to
return "to take part in socialist construction." More than 100,000
accepted and returned aboard vessels provided by Peking. In December, Peking appealed to Djakarta to cease "endless arguments" and
announced that it would ratify the 1955 treaty. Peking hurried to
tidy relations with Sukarno, for Tito was in Djakarta in the course of
an Asian tour to strengthen Afro-Asian ties, a cardinal bargaining
point in Yugoslavia's relations with Moscow. Khrushchev also
planned to visit Indonesia in early 1960.

It is not necessary to attribute to the Indonesian government a
degree of foresight, unity, and effective central planning it does not
possess to observe, in retrospect, that the campaign served a number
of purposes. It redressed the internal balance of power by momen-
tarily isolating the PKI from the Indonesian mainstream. It provided another distraction at home from a worsening economic situation, advanced the long-term campaign to break the hold of aliens on
the economy, restored a semblance of nonalignment to Indonesian
foreign affairs, and served notice that Djakarta would not sacrifice its
national interests for the sake of Sino-Indonesian amity.

The harsh character of the anti-Chinese campaign was not lost
on the Filipinos, some of whom privately admired Indonesian force-
fulness. For that matter, it was not lost on Malays in Malaya or on
the Chinese in Singapore, through which thousands of refugees passed
en route to the mainland. Nor did any of these fail to see that
Peking had bowed. Indonesia, of course, had operated from a posi-

27. Subandrio in a statement in Parliament, November 25, 1959.
28. Ch'en Yi note to Subandrio, December 9, 1959. (Italics added.)

tion of strength—the existence of the U.S. Seventh Fleet, Moscow's silence on the overseas Chinese issue, and a marked decline in Peking's popularity among the nonaligned Afro-Asians. The last grew out of Chinese repression in Tibet, border clashes with India, propaganda attacks on Yugoslavia, and a feud with the United Arab Republic.[29] Whether deliberately or not, Indonesia had exploited Peking's Afro-Asian difficulties.

The first troubled phase in Sino-Indonesian relations under Sukarno ended. The dispute smoldered in the months which followed and flared anew in the summer of 1960 when two overseas Chinese were killed and others wounded by soldiers forcibly evacuating alien pockets in rural West Java. For all intents and purposes, however, the crisis was over.

SINO-INDONESIAN COOPERATION, 1960-65

From 1960 onward, relations between Indonesia and Communist China rapidly improved. The Chinese Communists hailed ratification of the 1955 treaty in January 1960 as opening a "new historical stage" in relations between the two countries. By December of that year, Peking was calling for a "closing of ranks" in the "struggle against imperialism." In 1961, the two entered into a Treaty of Friendship and an Agreement on Cultural Cooperation, which Peking said had "tremendous significance" as evidence that "in the struggle against imperialism and colonialism lay *the fundamental interests* of the government and people of China and Indonesia." [30]   Peking that year further pledged "every kind of assistance" for the drive to "liberate" West Irian. Despite its own massive imports of food grains, Peking has also promised to export rice to Indonesia to help Sukarno meet a growing food crisis. In 1963, Indonesia imported 100,000 tons of rice from Communist China. On February 17, 1964, Antara, the official news agency, quoted Chinese embassy sources to the effect that this figure "would even increase" in the future. There was an exchange of state visits, by Sukarno and Subandrio to Peking and by Liu Shao-ch'i and Ch'en Yi to Djakarta. The PKI has cited these developments as proof of the growing friendship between Indonesia and China in their "joint struggle against imperialism." Roeslan Abdul Gani, a Sukarno aide who held many important posts before

29. See *Indonesian Observer* editorial, October 6, 1959. It ties these developments together with a warning to Peking.

30. Peking, NCNA, April 4, 1961.   (Italics added.)

being eased from stage center by his rival, Subandrio, has termed Sino-Indonesian amity "an historical necessity" and has called the Anglo-American presence in Southeast Asia "the power of an outsider which desires to drive a wedge between Indonesia and China." [31] And Peking, in turn, describes this collaboration as "serving *the vital interests* of the two peoples." [32]

During this period, Chinese relations with Indonesia had acquired still another dimension. As the ideological dispute between Moscow and Peking sharpened, the Communist powers began to compete openly for Sukarno's goodwill and the PKI's support. Thus, when Peking openly backed the West Irian campaign, the Russians came forth with $1.2 billion worth of modern weapons to promote tension, if not war, over Irian. The contest for favor has been extended into the "crush Malaysia" campaign.

Both the Russians and the Chinese desperately need Sukarno's goodwill in their contest for PKI support and in their competition for the backing of the nonaligned Afro-Asian states (for example, on the question of whether Russia should be invited to the second Asian-African Conference). They both realize that according to Aidit's evaluation of the internal situation in Indonesia, the PKI's future success may hinge on retaining Sukarno's goodwill for the remainder of his lifetime. Sukarno, after all, provides the PKI with a free hand to train cadres and expand the party's mass base. Accordingly, the Communist power which enjoys the most intimate relations with Sukarno can in turn expect to influence the PKI leadership.

In this connection, one factor in the Sino-Soviet dispute is the question of whether the Communists should pursue a left or right strategy in the nuclear-missile age. Although Peking professes a left strategy, it, like Moscow, has pursued a right strategy in Indonesia (*i.e.*, collaboration with bourgeois nationalism and formation of a united front from above). Thus, the PKI's pro-Peking stance during 1963–65 stems from issues in the Sino-Soviet dispute other than the PKI's own strategy. Aidit has, however, tended to adopt an increasingly "left" line toward the government by exploiting the rapidly deepening economic crisis. Sukarno's working arrangement with Peking, therefore, may have acquired a new urgency—to maintain a checkrein on a more militant PKI .

With the PKI in the "Peking bloc," the Soviet investment in

---

31. See PIA, April 2, 1962, and Antara, July 2, 1964.
32. *Ta Kung Pao* and *Kwangming Daily*, April 4, 1961. (Italics added.)

Sukarno's Irian adventure may have seemed in jeopardy. But in June 1964, Mikoyan flew to Djakarta with still fresher promises of military aid for the "crush Malaysia" campaign. Thus, the Sino-Soviet dispute has given Sukarno new room for maneuver. He can cite to Moscow the PKI's drift toward Peking as evidence of the need for greater Soviet effort in Indonesia. On the other hand, he can cite to Peking the increase in Russian aid to demonstrate the need for greater Peking (and therefore PKI) support for his regime. The dispute has, however, also provided Peking and Moscow with leverage on Sukarno. For example, the PKI has held that the visits exchanged *between Liu and Aidit* in 1963 "consolidated still more the bridge of Indonesian-Chinese friendship erected by President Sukarno." [33] The implication is that if Sukarno desires to collaborate with Peking in ousting the West from Southeast Asia, he must strengthen relations with the PKI. Moscow, however, can tell Sukarno—as Mikoyan apparently did during his Djakarta visit of June 1964—to stay in line on the Sino-Soviet dispute if he desires uninterrupted Soviet military aid. (The West suspended arms shipments in September 1963 when Sukarno launched his "crush Malaysia" campaign.)

In the Irian and Malaysia campaigns, Sukarno has judiciously juggled Sino-Soviet support to advantage against the West. However, an open Sino-Soviet split would endanger Indonesia's interests. If the abyss continues to widen, as now seems likely, it may become too wide for Sukarno to straddle. While his sentiments probably lie with Peking in the ideological dispute, he is dependent on Moscow for military supplies. His difficulties resemble Castro's. Indeed, Sukarno is so troubled by the prospect of a formal Sino-Soviet split that he has written Khrushchev and Mao and appealed to them to patch up their quarrel in the interests of unity against the "imperialists." Whether he has written to Brezhnev since Khrushchev's fall is not known.

Sukarno's identification with Peking is reflected in his developing concept of the "new emerging forces" (NEFO). The term, which Sukarno first employed in 1961, derives from *his* political division of the world into "anti-colonial, progressive" and "colonial and anti-progressive" forces. The concept has had a left bias from the beginning. The complementary category of "old-established forces" (OLDEFO) includes "the imperialists, the capitalists, the colonial-minded people and others like that"; NEFO embraces "nations who

---

33. Peking, NCNA, October 2, 1963. The importance attributed to these party contacts, as against state contacts, deserves to be noted.

want to be free, nations who want to free themselves from colonialism, the Asian nations, the African nations, the people of Latin America and the peoples of socialist countries." In Sukarno's imagery, "all of them form one extraordinarily huge wave and we are all convinced that one day that wave will wipe out all forces of the 'old established forces.'" Subandrio is more direct. He declares that the aim is to "establish a totally new world order." Sukarno, Subandrio, Nasution, and Aidit repeatedly express the belief that Indonesia is "encircled" by OLDEFO—presumably the Anglo-Americans and their allies. Lately, Sukarno has claimed the leadership of NEFO, which, incidentally, includes both Russia and Communist China.

The NEFO concept has snugly fitted the pattern of Sino-Indonesian cooperation in the 1960s. Since 1961, evidence to suggest that China and Indonesia are working in concert to establish complementary spheres of influence, not only in Southeast Asia but also in the Afro-Asian world, has accumulated. Indonesia served as Peking's spokesman at the Colombo conference on the Sino-Indian border dispute. Indonesia has served as the venue for a series of non-governmental, Communist-oriented, "Afro-Asian" labor, youth, journalist, and writers' conferences which the Chinese and Indonesians have dominated. Sukarno, with Peking's encouragement, has also aspired to the leadership of the nonaligned bloc. His hopes rose after Nehru's death, but among the nonaligned states, Sukarno's position has been compromised by his economic crisis and by the large Communist movement within Indonesia.

Until the end of 1962, one could perhaps minimize the growing relationship between Peking and Djakarta as the by-product of narrow self-interest—for example, reciprocity in support of their respective territorial claims. But the common ground is wider than that. On December 8, less than four months after Indonesia's acquisition of West Irian, the Malay world was shaken by a flash-fire revolt in Brunei, the British protectorate on Borneo which has no contiguous border with Indonesian Borneo (Kalimantan). Sukarno, partly in need of a new diversion, immediately committed Indonesia to support of the rebels. So did Peking and Moscow. Within a month, Subandrio was in Peking, where he and the Chinese Communist leadership publicly declared their determination to "continue to struggle unceasingly side by side with all other progressive forces in the world against imperialism, colonialism and neocolonialism."[34] The stage was now set for a joint Sino-Indonesian policy of "confrontation"

34. Joint communique, January 8, 1962.

with Malaysia. This "jointness" was demonstrated by the participation of the CCO in Indonesian-mounted border raids and by identical propaganda lines on Malaysia.

Any persisting doubts about Sino-Indonesian accord on Borneo were dispelled by Chairman Liu Shao-ch'i during his visit to Djakarta in April 1963. Liu and Sukarno, in a joint communique, pledged that they would "*do everything in their power* to further consolidate and develop unity" and expressed "resolute support for the people of North Kalimantan [North Borneo] in their courageous struggle for the right of self-determination and independence and against falling into the trap of neocolonialism in the guise of Malaysia." [35] Djakarta also reaffirmed its opposition to the "scheme of 'two Chinas' " and its support for Peking's "just struggle to liberate Taiwan."

Liu's visit was followed by an outburst of anti-Chinese rioting. In contrast to 1959–60, however, the riots were denounced by *both* Djakarta and Peking. But Indonesian spokesmen privately confided to Malays, Filipinos, and Americans that the rioting reflected Indonesia's historically ingrained fear of China and the Chinese. Thus, as late as 1964, the United States held that "Sukarno and his followers fear domination by Communist China." [36] The rioting appears to have been generated largely by the unremitting deterioration of the economy. Liu's visit unintentionally focused attention on "the rich Chinese exploiters." The incidents, however, did not interfere with the Sino-Indonesian working accord in Southeast Asia. Later that year, for example, Sukarno received a delegation of the National Front for the Liberation of South Vietnam and expressed the "hope that the struggle of the South Vietnamese people will soon end victorious" and that he would be able to "visit a free Saigon one day." On August 17, 1964, he "strongly condemned" the Tonkin air strike by the United States in response to a North Vietnamese PT-boat at-

35. See footnote 3. (Italics added.)
36. Testimony of Defense Secretary Robert S. McNamara before the House Armed Services Committee, January 27, 1964. Denis Warner, the Australian journalist, is among the few who have suggested Indonesian disingenuousness by observing: "*For American ears*, they [Sukarno's aides] professed grave fear of Communist China." (*The New Republic*, March 16, 1963. Italics added.) After Mikoyan's visit to Djakarta in June 1964 and Subandrio's visit to Moscow a month later, a Subandrio aide cited Chinese-Malay communal rioting in Singapore as evidence that Malaysia would be "lost" to the Chinese Communists. Therefore, he argued, the United States should support Djakarta to prevent her from having "a Chinese neighbor next door." The Malaysia concept, of course, was primarily designed to prevent this eventuality. (See *The New York Times*, July 25, 1964.)

tack on destroyers of the Seventh Fleet. In 1965 Indonesia denounced the U.S. role in Vietnam and endorsed the Viet Cong
program for victory.

FUTURE PROSPECTS

But what about tomorrow? By deed and word, Sukarno behaves
like a man in a hurry. He has ample cause. His revolutionary nationalist ideology is a catch-all of unrelated phrases. He has done
no more toward creating a political organization than toy with the
idea, nor has he prepared for an orderly succession. Doubtless, there
will be a last will and testament and rival claims as to his legitimate successor. The economy, moreover, is in disarray. His aides
scramble around the world to beg and borrow military and economic
aid. He is 65 years old.[37] At least five attempts have been made
on his life, and each year he enlarges his personal security guard.
Obviously, Sukarno must achieve his political objective, establishing
Indonesia as a great power with a recognized sphere of influence,
quickly.

By contrast, Peking displays patience. The Chinese Communists have a developed ideology and a disciplined organization, and
Chairman Mao has prepared for succession. Peking openly calcu-
lates that it may take "20 to 30 years to defeat American imperialism"
—well beyond the lifetime of the present Peking leadership. China's
attainment of genuine big-power status by the 1980s might produce
a revision of the 1955 citizenship treaty, which may be reopened
then. Peking apparently foresees a mutually satisfactory working
arrangement with Indonesia for the immediate future in the drive
to expel Anglo-American influence from Southeast Asia.

This "harmonizing" of Sino-Indonesian relations is reflected in
the joint propaganda theme of "Asia for the Asians." China and
Indonesia know that their combined power can dominate Southeast
Asia. This estimate requires little imagination. Sino-Indonesian
land-sea domination of Southeast Asia would be a foregone conclusion if the West should write off Southeast Asia, including its island
belt. In such circumstances, Malaysia and the Philippines would be
smothered by the ambitions of the present Chinese and Indonesian
leaderships. Whether Djakarta would really expect Peking to re-

---

37. He was born June 6, 1901, under the sign of Gemini—which accounts for
his ability, he says, to espouse conflicting philosophies.

spect its sphere of influence among the islands is, however, open to question. Thus, Sino-Indonesian domination of Southeast Asia would not necessarily preclude a clash of interests between Peking and Djakarta. Tension would likely arise between Peking and Djakarta on the issue of whether the Malay peninsula, Singapore, or the isles of the Sulu Sea (the sea frontier between the Philippines and Borneo) were in the Chinese or Indonesian sphere of influence. Both the Chinese Nationalists (in 1920) and the Chinese Communists (in 1954) have expressed interest in these Malay areas as *terra irredenta*. Peking has included them on a widely circulated map as formerly part of imperial China.[38] If a Sino-Indonesian division of Southeast Asia should ever occur—however unlikely it may seem at present—it would also probably generate serious communal friction between the Chinese and Malay communities in Malaysia and become a source of Sino-Indonesian tension.

Sino-Indonesian collaboration into the 1980s is predicated on the Chinese Communists' retention of the mainland through the next generation and on the continued control of an authoritarian, radical nationalist, left-biased regime in Indonesia. There is no assurance that the latter condition will prevail, for an uneasy balance of power has existed in Indonesia since 1945. Clearly, then, political developments in Indonesia might affect Sino-Indonesian relations.

At the extremes of the spectrum of political possibilities are the evolution of a Communist Indonesia and the restoration of representative government and civil liberties as practiced before 1957. Neither of these extremes can be precluded. On the surface, the position of the Communists today appears exceptionally strong. But the PKI has serious liabilities, foremost of which are its dependence on Sukarno's goodwill and its dependence on the mass support of a distinct ethnic group, the Javanese. Its revolutionary ardor has been eroded by the prolonged application of a right strategy, and a Communist bid for power is likely to revive revolutionary and/or separatist sentiment in the outer islands. A separatist movement could be suppressed only if the Soviet-equipped navy and air force remained loyal. There is no guarantee of their loyalty, although Communist infiltration into the air force is especially advanced. Moreover, there is no assurance that a Communist Indonesia would automatically develop closer ties with Peking. A Communist Indonesia might rely on

---

38. On the 1929 "Humiliation Days," see Victor Purcell, *The Chinese in Southeast Asia* (London: Oxford University Press, 1951). For the map, see *Manual of History* (Peking, 1954), p. 19.

Moscow for military assistance to maintain its independence from the mainland. There is also a possibility that Washington would consider supporting a Communist Indonesia to prevent the island barrier from falling within a Chinese sphere of influence. But a Communist Indonesia is likely to be expansionist in nature and thus draw Washington's opposition.

The likelihood that representative government and civil liberties may be restored "after Sukarno" recedes with each passing year as a new generation of Indonesians matures in an arid climate of empty nationalist slogans. But democratic concepts—the existence of opposition parties, free elections, free speech, a free press, etc.—run deep within the Indonesian nationalist movement, and intellectual discontent with "guided democracy" is high. In the unlikely event that the fortunes of the Indonesian social democrats revive, Indonesia would probably maintain a correct but cool relationship with Peking.

Another possibility is the emergence of an army regime. With respect to China policy, this development could have varied results. Such a regime might display an anti-Communist bias since the PKI is the only other disciplined organization in the country and therefore a logical opposition. In this case, the army might repress the PKI and sever relations with the Sino-Soviet bloc. Certainly, in such an event, it would break with Peking, for the further disciplining of the Chinese community (in the urban areas this time) would rank high on its agenda. The danger would be that the PKI might be driven underground and might be able, by exploiting the worsening economic situation and the lack of democracy, to launch a guerrilla war on Java against the regime. Western assistance to the regime would only aggravate the situation and create the conditions for a Communist "war of liberation" patterned after South Vietnam and supported by Peking.

An ultra-nationalist army regime might, however, turn to both Moscow and Washington for military and economic aid to maintain its independence from Peking. It might also turn to Moscow and Peking for support in establishing hegemony over the archipelago. It would pursue the "crush Malaysia" campaign and would also probably expand in a southeasterly direction, toward Portuguese Timor and Australian-administered East New Guinea. However implausible it may seem, Djakarta has accused the Portuguese of firing on Indonesian fishing boats off Timor.[39] As the Australian commitment to defend Malaysia has deepened, the Djakarta press has warned

---

39. Antara, October 23, 1962.

Canberra that Australia's security depends on Indonesian goodwill, and the Indonesian government has already manufactured its first "incident" along the East-West Irian border.[40]   Both Moscow and Peking, their ideological differences notwithstanding, would share an interest in promoting Indonesian-inspired regional tension, if not war.

During 1963-65, there were indications that Nasution's influence, and thus the army's, was waning. His faltering authority and the precipitous rise of navy and air force influence may limit the chances that an army regime will succeed Sukarno. The present chief of staff of the army, General Yani, lacks Nasution's drive and spirit of independence. He was hand-picked for the job by Sukarno.

The most likely development, then, is the emergence of a "national Communist"—or, if you will, "national socialist"—regime after Sukarno. In many respects, this is the kind of regime which has taken shape under Sukarno's "guided democracy." It is the type of regime which appeals to Sukarno's civilian aides—Subandrio, Chaerul Saleh, Roeslan Abdul Gani, and others. As to its "national socialist" content, lately Djakarta has described "Marxism-Sukarnoism" as the theoretical base of the Indonesian state.[41]

There are still other possibilities. In light of Sukarno's opportunism, a radical shift in Indonesia's China policy during his own lifetime cannot be ruled out. A policy revision would clearly attract support in Manila, lessen tension over Malaysia, and revive Maphilindo under Indonesian influence.

The only conclusion one may draw with confidence is that Djakarta's current China policy is unstable because of the uneasy Sukarno-army-PKI balance of power in contemporary Indonesia. *But for the moment,* Indonesia has established a working arrangement with Peking in pursuit of mutual objectives. The "crush Malaysia" campaign is probably the most dramatic element in this harmonization of foreign policies. There is a body of opinion which holds, though, that such an interpretation may be misleading and that Djakarta and Peking are merely using each other to achieve separate objectives. Few, however, contest the conclusion that Sino-Indonesian relations are likely to undergo reappraisal during the succession struggle which must follow Sukarno's passing from the scene.

---

40. *Indonesian Herald,* April 20, 1964.
41. Roeslan Abdul Gani, March 19, 1964, in an address to the fourth national congress of the Association of Supporters of Indonesian Independence (IPKI), a Nasution-sponsored party.

PHILIPPINE CHINA POLICY

Philippine China policy contrasts sharply with Indonesian policy. For all their "Latin" emotionalism, the Filipinos have been openly and coldly calculating about where their true danger lies. Mainland China has replaced Japan as the source of danger in this era. Relations between the Filipinos and the local Chinese have been exacerbated by the emergence of a Communist China and by a surge of latent nationalist feeling among the Filipinos. The specter of a Chinese "fifth column" has tended to magnify the role of the overseas Chinese in the Philippines.

Anti-Chinese feeling in the Philippines is partly an outgrowth of Spanish cultural prejudices, but it also has an economic basis. As in Indonesia, Chinese clannishness, business acumen, and capacity for hard work have given the Chinese a distinct advantage over their Filipino competitors. Despite their relatively small numbers, the Chinese account for 17.4 per cent of the investment in single ownerships, partnerships, and corporations in the Philippines. The Chinese also account for 75 per cent of the total foreign investment in single proprietorships, 94 per cent in partnerships, and 86 per cent in corporations. About 96 per cent of all alien retail stores—the ubiquitous "sari-sari" shops—are owned by Chinese. This extensive Chinese economic activity continues to generate concern among Filipinos over their right to manage their own economy. In Macapagal's view: "Some of these fears are emotional, imaginary and irrational, while others have a foundation in fact." [42]

Nationalist sentiment has led to attempts to remove alien influences from the economy. Within the past decade, for instance, aliens (meaning Chinese) have been barred from engaging in new retail businesses, prohibited from entering the import trade, and banned from certain professions. Altogether, Congress has enacted more than a hundred bills aimed at restricting the economic role of Chinese aliens. They are, however, given the chance to acquire Philippine citizenship.

The perennial question of the "overstaying Chinese" has plagued Manila's relations with Taipei since 1949, when Chinese immigration to the Philippines was suspended. At that time, 2,700 Chinese

---

42. Both the figures and the quotation come from a Macapagal speech before the Federation of Chinese Chambers of Commerce of the Philippines, Manila, September 18, 1962.

fled to the Philippines with temporary visas. When their visas expired, Taipei declined to accept them and pleaded lack of room. Some of the refugees were suspected of concealing Communist sympathies. The issue has been fought in the Philippine courts and has been under protracted diplomatic negotiation without result. While the issue may seem inconsequential, it makes for lively headlines in Manila and stirs base emotions. Indonesia's treatment of its Chinese aliens has goaded popular Filipino feeling. "If Indonesia can stand up to the might of the People's Republic of China on the issue of noninterference, then the Philippines can, with even greater effect, stand up against Taipei," observed the *Manila Times*. But the Foreign Ministry has been reluctant to do so for fear that only Peking would benefit from tension between Manila and Taipei.

Collaboration with Taiwan is an integral element in Philippine foreign policy for reasons of both internal and external security. Former Under Secretary of Foreign Affairs Manglapus has stated the situation candidly: "The non-recognition of Peking is simply a matter of expediency; as long as we recognize National China, our Chinese have something to look to." [43] Externally, Taiwan looms large in the defense of the Philippines. It is readily visible from the Philippine isle of Y'Ami in the Batanes group. It serves as a buffer between the Philippines and Japan. Occupied by the Chinese Nationalists, who are allied with the United States, it does not constitute the military threat that it once posed under Japan and would pose under Communist control.

The Chinese Nationalists have cultivated Filipinos with the same line of reasoning Peking has used to court Djakarta. "Naturally the legitimate interests of the [Philippine] Chinese is always a matter of concern to the Government of the Republic of China," Chiang Kai-shek has explained. "There is, however, a far greater issue confronting us. As our two countries are threatened [by the Communists] we must unite and cooperate with each other in the common struggle. *Under the circumstances*, there is no difference between us which cannot be settled to the satisfaction of both." [44]

This view is widely accepted in Manila. Accordingly, to strengthen ties with the Chinese Nationalists, the Filipinos have shunned the "two-China" concept. For that matter, neither the "two-China" concept nor the question of recognizing Peking has at-

43. *New York Herald Tribune*, March 31, 1957.
44. *Manila Times* interview, June 9, 1956. (Italics added.)

tracted serious attention. On the contrary, the view within and without Macapagal's Liberal administration is that even if the United States recognized Peking, the Philippines would continue to recognize Taipei. Past Nacionalista and Liberal administrations have assumed the same posture. The Philippine strategic interest in preventing Chinese Communist acquisition of Taiwan, coupled with the basically anti-Communist and anti-Chinese sentiments of the Catholic upper and middle classes which rule the islands, has delimited the country's China policy.

A small but vocal minority of the Recto school is interested in exploiting relations with Peking for leverage against the United States on bases, trade, and other aspects of American-Filipino relations. However, regardless of the outcome of the 1965 presidential election, Philippine policy toward Taipei is unlikely to change. Nor has the lure of mainland trade stimulated widespread support, despite its vigorous promotion by some business interests. In 1959, for example, Jesus Marco Roces, vice mayor of Manila, two associates, and four reporters toured mainland China as private persons. Nothing came of their visit, but it opened "one minute crack in the vigorous anti-Communist policy." Generally, trade with the mainland has been opposed for two reasons. (1) It would result in an unfavorable trade balance for Manila. (2) It would strengthen the Chinese hold on the economy. In 1962, Macapagal provided a third reason: "For those who are attracted by the imagined profits of trade with Communist China, our answer is that there is not a single pound of sugar, copra, coconut oil, iron ore or lumber for which Communist China would or could pay us more than what our present customers now pay." [45]

The overriding factor in Philippine China policy, thus, is security. Taiwan, moreover, is only one of three islands involving Philippine defense and Sino-Philippine relations. The other two are Hainan and Borneo.

Hainan has been occupied by the Chinese Communists since April 1950. However, Communist use of the island as a potential staging area against the Philippines has been neutralized by the U.S. Seventh Fleet. Its withdrawal from the South China Sea would therefore impair the security not only of Taiwan but also of the Philippines. Manila's mutual defense pact with the United States,

45. See his speech before the Manila Overseas Press Club, Manila, September 4, 1962.

and its reliance on the Seventh Fleet as a protective shield for its 7,000 islands, is recognition of this state of affairs.

It is, however, with regard to policy toward Borneo that deep controversy has arisen in Manila. As in the case of Taiwan and Hainan, Borneo's strategic importance to the Philippines is also intimately bound up with the question of China and the Chinese.

In 1962, the prospect of radical alterations on the map of the Malay world—the Irian transfer, the emergence of Malaysia—disturbed nationalist-minded Filipinos, who desired to establish a distinct, independent personality in the region. Articulate Filipinos turned their attention to the south. "Surely, Philippine security is involved in what happens in Southeast Asia," *The Philippines Free Press* commented on February 23, 1963. "Previously however, the destiny of Southeast Asia was being decided by everybody but the Philippines; the Philippines was supposed to have nothing to do with it. It was just an American satellite. . . . The Philippines is [now] giving notice to all whom it may concern that what happens in Southeast Asia is its affair."

There were a number of incentives for this turn southward— projection of an Asian identity, a claim to North Borneo, a demonstration of "independence" by dealing with a neutralist power (Indonesia), and the interest of Manila's business community in Borneo's timberlands. The paramount factor, however, directly involved Philippine China policy. The Macapagal administration genuinely feared that Malaysia would not merely fail to stem the spread of Chinese Communist influence in Singapore but would provide a bridge over which the Chinese could cross into North Borneo, 18 miles south of the Philippine frontier. "In the event, God forbid, that Malaysia succumbs to the potent Communist threat on the Asian mainland, with North Borneo under Malaya, there would be created a situation in which a Communist territory would be immediately at the southern frontier of the Philippines, which would pose a grave and intolerable threat to our country," Macapagal asserted.[46] There was also concern that the Soviet arms buildup in Indonesia might promote Indonesian expansionism on Borneo and possibly in the predominantly Muslim areas of the southern Philippines.[47] A Philippine claim on North Borneo would counter an Indonesian claim to the territory.

---

46. State of the Nation address delivered January 28, 1963, before the Fifth Congress.

47. Captain Carlos J. Albert, *Manila Times*, January 20, 1963.

In this atmosphere, on June 22, 1962, the Philippines laid formal claim to sovereignty over British North Borneo (Sabah). The claim is entangled in a net of 19th-century intrigue.[48] In essence, the Philippine argument is that if the area is to be transferred again, it should be transferred to the Philippines.

Philippine possession of North Borneo would create a contiguous frontier with Indonesia. Whether this situation would improve Philippine security is questionable. Some Filipinos, both within and without the administration, have grown increasingly alarmed over the possibility of a Sino-Indonesian *entente cordiale*—a possibility which Indonesia's training and arming of the CCO in Sarawak demonstrates. Moreover, as the Filipinos concede, there is little, if any, enthusiasm in North Borneo for cession to the Philippines.[49] In settling the dispute, however, Manila has offered to abide by a plebiscite.

The British government could have placated Filipino nationalism by permitting a vote on the claim before Malaysia's formation, but it did not see fit to do so. The Macmillan government rebuffed the Philippine claim in the fall of 1962. Macapagal followed up the claim with a novel—more or less improvised—proposal. He suggested the formation of a "Greater Malayan Confederation comprising, *to begin with*, the Federation of Malaya, the Philippines, Singapore, Sarawak, Brunei and North Borneo."[50] He conspicuously omitted Indonesia but left the door ajar for the future. He was vague on details, but he implied that an overwhelmingly Malay-dominated confederation would resolve the Chinese problem in Singapore and the North Borneo question. It, he said, would prevent the Chinese from coming to power in Malaysia. When Indonesia formally declared its opposition to Malaysia as a "neo-colonial" device and threatened to "crush" Malaysia forcibly, Macapagal went a step further and called for a Malay summit. This gathering in turn produced the Maphilindo formula.

On September 16, 1963, Malaysia came into being as a sovereign power. Manila "deferred" recognition, and Djakarta refused it. Malaysia responded by severing relations with both neighbors. Malaysia found itself isolated within the Malay world. And to its surprise, the Philippines found itself in bed with Indonesia and the Sino-Soviet bloc. To further complicate matters, Djakarta, Peking,

48. For details, see The Philippines, *Philippine Claim to North Borneo*, v. 1 (Manila: Bureau of Printing, 1963).
49. Prominent Filipinos in Manila and Sabahans in Jesselton (T'Api-Api) confirmed this fact during extensive interviews with the author in March–April 1964.
50. Press conference, July 28, 1962. (Italics added.)

and Moscow have endorsed the formation of an independent Unitary State of North Borneo composed of Sarawak, Brunei, and North Borneo. Its formation would preclude Manila's claim.[51]

The Macapagal policy toward North Borneo, Malaysia, and Indonesia has encountered domestic resistance. Leaders of the Liberal and opposition Nacionalista parties have strongly criticized it in the conviction that a stable, democratic, and prosperous Malaysia serves the Philippine national interest. The critics contend that failure to endorse Malaysia plays into the hands of Peking as well as Djarkarta.

Since Malaysia was established, the Filipinos have sought to negotiate recognition of Malaysia in return for Malaysia's recognition of the Philippine claim to North Borneo. Unfortunately, Philippine recognition of Malaysia, unless approved by Djakarta, would unleash a new wave of Communist allegations that Manila acted as an "American puppet." For years, the Filipinos have labored in the Afro-Asian world to dispel such fabrications. Moreover, a Philippine-Malaysian rapprochement would heighten Sukarno's genuine concern, if not phobia, about "imperialist" encirclement. Since each of Indonesia's immediate neighbors has British or American defense ties— including independent Singapore—Indonesia might become increasingly dependent on what may be termed its "tacit" alliance with the Chinese Communists.

Yet, as noted earlier, a dramatic reversal of Indonesian policy, especially following Singapore's separation from Malaysia, is not an improbability.[52] It serves Indonesia's interests to strengthen Malay ties and to work for a revival of the Maphilindo concept. The initiative in the Malay triangle rests with Sukarno. At the same time, the central problem—whether to give priority to collaboration with Peking or to the evolution of Maphilindo—is also his. Whatever he decides, Philippine China policy is unlikely to change.

---

51. At a news conference in Manila on January 10, 1964, Subandrio explained that Indonesia would support the Philippines' North Borneo claim, but only if based on self-determination. This stand permitted Indonesia to continue propaganda, military, and financial support of the Azahari rebel government, although Djakarta has not recognized that government. Later in the year, Sukarno also hinted that he would be amenable to the formation of a greater Malayan confederation comprising an independent Indonesia, Philippines, Malaya, Singapore, Sarawak, and Brunei. Kuala Lumpur has said it would agree if the confederation also embraces an independent Sumatra, Celebes, Java, etc.

52. A second Maphilindo summit meeting was held at Tokyo on June 20, 1964, but it failed to resolve the "Malaysia crisis."

MALAYSIA'S CHINA POLICY

The cornerstone of Kuala Lumpur's policy, before and after the formation of Malaysia, has been non-recognition of either Communist China or Nationalist China. The expulsion of Singapore from the federation has not affected this policy. In effect, Kuala Lumpur has declared itself nonaligned in the Chinese civil war.

The internal reasons for this policy are demographic. In Malaysia, the Chinese constituted the largest minority in a nation of minorities, and in truncated Malaysia, the Chinese still make up more than a third of the total population. Moreover, Malaya became independent at the tail end of a Communist rebellion on the peninsula which was led and supported largely by the local Chinese. Malaysia was formed to stem the rising tide of Communist influence among the Chinese in Singapore. Until Djakarta launched its "confrontation," Kuala Lumpur considered Peking's manipulation and control of the Malayan Communist party as its primary internal concern. Against this backdrop, Malaysia—like Malaya before it—has restricted trade and immigration with mainland China and has deported local Chinese Communists as "undesirable aliens."

In terms of external relations, non-recognition provided for maximum flexibility. At the time Malaya became independent, Kuala Lumpur formally adopted neutralism and shunned membership in SEATO. Nonetheless, its foreign policy has leaned toward the West from the beginning. For example, it maintains defense ties with the West through the Anglo-Malaysian Defense Treaty. These have been tightened since "confrontation," though Malaysia retains the right to terminate the treaty at will. Kuala Lumpur has therefore earned the enmity of Peking and has been assailed for "false neutralism."

Internal aspect. Before Singapore's departure, there were about 4.3 million ethnic Chinese in Malaysia out of a total population of 10.2 million. Independent Singapore has a population of 1.8 million, 200,000 of whom are Malays and the remainder almost exclusively Chinese. The Chinese leadership in the area has been alive to the potentially explosive racial situation which the presence of such large numbers of Chinese creates, and, at the outset of the federation at least, it exhibited a reasonably high order of sophistication in allaying fears of non-Malay domination. It repeatedly appealed to the Chinese community to adjust to the demands of Malay nationalism. As Lee Kuan Yew, the Prime Minister of Singapore and the leader for more than a decade of the ruling People's Action Party (PAP), observed, "We are in the center of a Malaysian people; we cannot escape from our environment." [53]

But neither the Malay nor Chinese leadership in Kuala Lumpur and Singapore proved able to control its respective "ultras"; and within a year of Malaysia's formation, Singapore was scarred by racial riots, which set the stage for Singapore's exit from the federation. Yet in the view of responsible Malay and Chinese leaders, the Malaysian experiment was worth the effort; for, in its failure, it demonstrated the need for close collaboration between the island and peninsula even as independent states.

For years, even before World War II, there had been talk—largely speculative—about merging Malaya, Singapore, and the Borneo territories. The arithmetic was simple: the merger, in contrast with a union of Malaya and Singapore alone, would not put the Chinese in a majority.

Many peninsular Malays and still more non-Malays on Borneo would have preferred to retain the pre-Malaysian status quo. But the continued British presence in Singapore and on Borneo ran against the grain of current "world opinion." In Singapore, the Barisan Sosialis (Socialist Front), an aboveground Communist front, had adroitly exploited Chinese cultural chauvinism to press for an end to British rule. Its sights were set on the evolution of "another Cuba." The PAP also clamored for independence, but it favored merger with independent Malaya as, among other considerations, a device to block a Communist assumption of power. Malaya, however, shunned such a merger, for it would upset the delicate ethnic balance on the peninsula.

On May 27, 1961, nevertheless, Rahman, in response to the deteriorating situation in Singapore, and under pressure from both the British and the PAP, publicly dusted off the old plan and proposed the larger federation. The plan was enthusiastically endorsed by the PAP in Singapore and just as vigorously rejected by the Communists. In Borneo the immediate response was lukewarm.

By this time, the local Communists appeared on the way to their ultimate objective. As the result of a series of defections and by-elections, the PAP had come precariously close to losing control of

53. See his address at Nanyang University, Singapore, on October 30, 1960.

the Singapore Legislature to the Barisan Sosialis. This development coincided with concern in the North Borneo territories over Soviet military assistance to Indonesia and the fear that after Irian Sukarno might direct his attention to the north. Thus, the prospect of "another Cuba" and uncertainty about Indonesia's intentions in Borneo prompted Kuala Lumpur reluctantly to reconsider its position. Clearly, the status quo could no longer be maintained.

A diplomatic effort was made to delay an Irian settlement until after Malaysia's formation, but Irian was "liberated" first—in August 1962. (The actual transfer took place on May 1, 1963, at Hollandia [Kota Baru], West Irian.) Within four months, a revolt flamed in Brunei. It was extinguished after a few days, but during that time, it attracted strong support from Djakarta and the Sino-Soviet bloc.

The Brunei revolt quickened the pace of negotiations leading to Malaysia's establishment and eliminated Brunei from the federation. This fact, however, did not appreciably affect "the Malaysian arithmetic." The non-Chinese continued to outnumber the Chinese.

Until the postwar period, Chinese in Malaya and Singapore were considered Chinese nationals and thus aliens. Subsequently, a policy of assimilation was effectively implemented, at varying speeds, and citizenship qualifications were liberalized to the extent that *jus soli* became the basis of Malaysian citizenship.[54] Aliens could be naturalized, but in the naturalization process, they had to renounce allegiance to other states. Thus, like Manila, Kuala Lumpur rejected the Peking-Taipei concept of dual citizenship.

Within Malaysia, however, there were special citizenship and immigration rules. These were designed to prevent the Communists from towing Singapore into the new federation as a Trojan horse. Under Malaya's relatively stringent citizenship regulations, for example, the more than half of Singapore's citizens who are China-born would have been denied citizenship. This culturally unassimilated half had been the backbone of the left wing in Singapore.

The terms of the merger gave Singapore considerable autonomy in education and labor, two areas where the Communists have made the deepest inroads by exploiting Chinese chauvinism (not communism); but Kuala Lumpur retained the attributes of sovereignty, in

54. For an excellent summary of citizenship regulations, see J. M. Gullick, *Malaya* (New York: Praeger, 1963), Appendix I, pp. 223–229.

cluding control of internal security.   In effect, the Malays dominated
the central government.   The Borneo territories also retained a degree of autonomy and, for example, exercised control over immigration
into their states.   Thus, the potential flood of left-wing Chinese
laborers from Malaysian Singapore to Malaysian Borneo was curbed.

But perhaps more than legal safeguards, the Malaysian experiment required the immeasurable goodwill of all the communities at
various levels of society.   As it developed, the communal challenge
was too great.   Malaysia became an arena for an internal power
struggle along racial lines.   The principal characters in the drama
were the Malay leadership in Kuala Lumpur and the Chinese leadership in Singapore.   Following the 1964 Singapore riots, communal
tensions escalated.   By July 1965, Malay extremists openly called
for Lee Kuan Yew's arrest, and the Singapore Chinese talked about
partition.

On August 7, Rahman and Lee Kuan Yew secretly negotiated
a "separation agreement."   Two days later Singapore proclaimed itself
an independent state.   Rahman, in his speech before the Federal
Parliament on August 9, said he was confronted with two choices:
either repressive measures against Singapore and resultant civil war,
which he found "odious" and "repulsive," or Singapore's separation
from the federation.   Whether Singapore was expelled or seceded
will be debated interminably.   At home, the development shocked
Kuala Lumpur, Singapore, and the Borneo territories.   Abroad, it
stunned Malaysia's friends and foes alike (the Indonesians promptly
claimed it was a victory for their confrontation policy).   The dramatic development reopened the catalog of questions which Malaysia
was designed to resolve.   A "third China" had emerged in the center
of the Malay world.

Despite the alarms generated by its emergence, for the moment
sovereign Singapore is hardly comparable to the independent Singapore aimed at by the Communists in the early 1960s.   The separation agreement provides for close economic and military collaboration
between Malaysia and Singapore, including the retention of the
British bases.   Perhaps, in the long term, the most serious consequence of the Singapore separation will be its effect on the Borneo
territories.   Should Sarawak, with its militant CCO movement, opt
for independence, the Chinese brand of communism will be in a
strong position to establish a foothold on the third largest island in
the world and the only island where the three Malay powers—Indo-

nesia, the Philippines, and Malaysia—have directly clashing interests.

External aspect. Since a sovereign Malaysia emerged, Indonesian and Sino-Soviet opposition to the federation has hardened. Moreover, that opposition has led to a new stage in Sino-Indonesian relations, for Indonesia has armed Chinese Communists from Sarawak and has converted Indonesian Borneo into a sanctuary for raids into Malaysia. At the core of Communist hostility is Peking's denunciation of Malaysia "as a British base against the growing national liberation movement in Southeast Asia." The Chinese and Indonesian Communists also oppose Malaysia because it brought the weight of anti-Communist Malaya to bear in curbing Communist activities in Singapore and Sarawak, where the local Communists may have felt they were on the threshold of power. At the core of Indonesian hostility is Sukarno's view that the Malay world should be an Indonesian sphere of influence and that the Anglo-American powers hinder the realization of this objective. For Sukarno, of course, Malaysia's anti-Communist posture denotes a Western bias and therefore "colonialism." In Rahman's view, however, "China and Indonesia are collaborating to crush Malaysia. They want to shatter the peace of this country." [55]

Like Malaya before it, Malaysia contends that neither Peking nor Taipei can claim to represent China as a whole. On this basis, Kuala Lumpur recognizes neither and thereby seeks to remove the controversial issue from the Chinese community.

Until 1960, Malaya voted, along with the United States and the Philippines, to exclude the China item from the U.N. General Assembly's agenda. (Indonesia and Britain voted to include it.) That year, however, Malaya adopted a "two-China" policy and supported Peking's admission to the United Nations. Nevertheless, it emphasized that "we will not have relations with her." [56] This policy was amplified in 1961 during the U.N.'s first full-dress debate on the China question. Malaya declared itself in favor of Peking's admission but added that Malaya "cannot accept any proposal towards this end which by its terms ignores or chooses to ignore the right of the

55. See his speech of November 7, 1963, before a youth meeting of the Malayan Chinese Association (MCA), a part of the ruling Alliance party to which Rahman's United Malay National Organization (UMNO) also belongs. Sukarno tacitly acknowledged this assessment on November 11, 1963, when he charged at a Hero's Day rally that Malaysia was formed to "encircle" Indonesia *and* China.

56. Rahman's London news conference in June 1960 after the Commonwealth Prime Ministers' Conference.

people of Formosa [Taiwan] to maintain their separate political identity and existence." [57]   In substance, the policy of non-recognition was maintained, but the bar on Peking's entry into the United Nations was made more palatable to the Chinese community in Malaya.

Kuala Lumpur has also sought to temper the loyalty of its Chinese citizens by adopting strong moral positions on several questions involving Peking.   At the United Nations in 1959, Malaya sponsored a resolution condemning Peking's suppression of the Tibetan revolt. In 1962, Kuala Lumpur unhesitatingly supported India in the Sino-Indian border clash.   Rahman's action won the plaudits of Malaysians of Indian ethnic origin and strengthened Indian support for the ruling Alliance (which is composed of the United Malay National Organization, the Malay Chinese Association, and the Malay Indian Congress).   But he has denied that condemnation of Peking is motivated by domestic considerations.   "The last thing I would like to do is see the Malayan people taking side by reason of the fact that they originated from India or China," Rahman said to Kuala Lumpur's House of Representatives in November 1962.   The Chinese Communist thrust in the Himalayas, he contended, should be interpreted as "a threat to democracy and a challenge to our way of life."

Peking's hostility toward Malaysia, however, has caused another shift in Kuala Lumpur's China policy.   On October 16, 1963, a month after the federation's creation, Malaysia reverted to Malaya's former policy.   Malaysia voted against the seating of Peking in the United Nations.   In unusually strong language, the Malaysian delegate held that communism had provided a "raw edge [to] Chinese expansionism" and cited Peking's scorn for "peaceful co-existence," its resistance to the "moderating influence of even its greatest ally," its "unprovoked armed aggression on India," and its "cold-shouldering of the nuclear test ban treaty." [58]   He avoided, however, a direct reference to Peking's hostility toward Malaysia.   Thus, *for the present at least*, Malaysia has discarded the "two-China" concept.[59]   Clearly,

57. U.N. General Assembly (16th sess.), *Official Records: Plenary Meetings* (New York: Author, 1962), 1077th Plenary Meeting, p. 1019.

58. U.N. General Assembly (18th sess.), *Provisional Verbatim Record, 1243rd Plenary Meeting* (New York: Author, October 16, 1963), pp. 75–78.

59. A Foreign Ministry spokesman in Kuala Lumpur said that if France succeeded in recognizing two Chinas, "then Malaysia is likely to review its policy on similar lines."   Of course, France failed to achieve this goal.   Taiwan severed diplomatic relations with Paris in February 1964 after Paris had recognized Peking in January.

there will be no revision in Kuala Lumpur's China policy as long as Peking continues to oppose the new federation. For Malaysia, the major security preoccupation is not China as such, but Indonesia and China's potential influence on an independent Singapore.

As for Singapore, its foreign policy is still in the formative stage at this writing. Lee Kuan Yew has declared a policy of nonalignment. He has said Singapore will recognize any state which recognizes the island's sovereignty, apparently an open bid for Indonesian, Chinese Communist, and Russian recognition. However, Singapore has not followed a reciprocal policy in the case of the Chinese Nationalists. The Taiwan regime was among the first governments to recognize the "third China."

As noted earlier, the Singapore-Malaysia separation agreement provides for close collaboration between the two nations. Article V provides that "each party will undertake not to enter into any treaty or agreement with a foreign country which may be detrimental to the independence and defense of the territory of the other party." In sum, Singapore's foreign policy options are limited. Lest there be a misunderstanding, Rahman declared on August 10 that "Malaysia would be greatly concerned if Singapore, as an independent country, established diplomatic relations with China, Indonesia or any other countries in conflict with Malaysia. . . . If Singapore did this," he said, "we will be definitely taking steps to protect our interests." [60]

However, the prospect is very real that the Singapore left wing, with the active support of Indonesia and the Sino-Soviet blocs, will launch a major campaign of agitation against the British bases and the island's agreement with the peninsula. The signs already point in this direction. Indonesia has held out the lure of a resumption of trade with Singapore in return for the dismantling of the British bases. The Singapore Rubber Packers' Association has called for the sending of rubber missions to Peking and Moscow. Thirty left-wing Singapore trade unions, in a joint statement in Chinese, have demanded a general election and the release of local political detainees (Communists). How long can Lee Kuan Yew resist these pressures? In part, ironic as it may seem, the answer may depend on the success of Singapore's collaboration with Malaysia, particularly in the economic field. Clearly, Singapore cannot afford to live in confrontation with *both* Indonesia (and China) and Malaysia.

---

60. Reuters' Kuala Lumpur dispatch, August 10, 1965.

CHINA AND THE MALAY WORLD

In sum, China and the Chinese appear intricately interwoven into the destiny of the Malay peoples. Neither the Malays nor the overseas Chinese in their midst can escape their environment, short of genocide. Yet each of the Malay nations has evolved an independent policy toward China and the Chinese. These policies reflect differences in internal social structures, colonial traditions, geopolitical situations, and leadership.

Indonesia's China policy is based upon the desire of Sukarno and the men around him for power. This desire reflects a deep-seated inferiority complex and is a legacy of Dutch colonialism. During their colonial rule, the Dutch did little, if anything, to provide for Indonesian independence, a democratic tradition, and an Indonesian administration, so it is perhaps no surprise that irresponsible leadership has been the result. In contrast, Anglo-American colonial policy worked toward these ultimate ends. The Filipinos today have a vested interest in their social order and therefore a keen sense of what serves their security. As a result, they recognize Taipei and retain Western defense commitments against the Chinese Communists. The Malaysians and Singaporeans also have a vested interest in their present form of government—a representative system, despite its shortcomings, which is particularly suited to a plural society. Because almost half the population is of Chinese ethnic background, Malaysia seeks to avoid controversy at home by recognizing neither Peking nor Taipei or by recognizing both simultaneously if the "two Chinas" are prepared to accept this solution. Singapore's policy has yet to evolve. It will turn on internal political developments.

Thus, the prospect for the development of a viable Malay regional grouping, much less a "Chinese barrier," is uncertain. The concept of Pan-Malay unity has acted as a catalyst in the struggle for power within the Malay world. As long as this struggle continues, and it is likely to continue for some time, Maphilindo will remain in suspended animation. Accordingly, the evolution of a common Malay policy toward China and the Chinese is remote. But it is patently clear that the idea of Maphilindo has sown the seeds for Pan-Malay unity. In the long term, the sentiment for unity is likely to wax rather than wane—especially as long as what the Malay peoples consider the threat of a strong and unified China persists. Should Singapore or an independent Sarawak slide toward Peking, Maphilindo is likely to be revived sooner than later.

Chapter 10

BURMA AND CHINA

Policy of a Small Neighbor

BY

JOHN H. BADGLEY

"When lightning strikes the log, the chameleon is also destroyed."

—BURMESE PROVERB

This popular Burmese proverb illustrates the current orientation toward China in an era when political power and demands for economic change are dangerously intertwined. Burma has consistently maintained cordial relations with its giant northern neighbor. As the first Asian state to recognize the Communist regime in 1949, Burma initiated a unique relationship—distinct, that is, from her ties with Pakistan and India, other large neighbors who fail to command the same awe as the People's Republic of China.

The mixture of respect and dread which characterizes the Burmese view of China can be partially explained by a simple power analysis. The specific factor of national security, however, operates in the context of the traditional and ideological environment within which the relationship developed. Culture, race, and ideology are very real factors affecting the orientation of the ordinary Burmese toward China.

THE BURMESE IMAGE OF CHINA

The Confucian political system created an attitude toward the Chinese which appears in the inscriptions and historic literature of Burma and which forms one basis for the popular attitude today. It is a perspective expressed not only in proverbs but in the very word used to denote the Chinese. In Burmese, *tayou:* refers to the people of China, whereas other foreigners are identified as *kala*, with modifiers added to indicate race and nationality. Among rural leaders in Burma today, *tayou:* usually evokes a positive sentiment, but *kala* carries pejorative connotations—as it has traditionally.[1] Respect for the Chinese dates from the Ming dynasty and its concept of a Confucian family of nations. The arrangement worked well, for it left Burma free to pursue its own limited expansion against other neighbors but protected it from the invasion of Chinese armies. The Burman monarchs suffered only one major attack from China, and that by alien Mongols before the Ming period. During the long periods when the Burman monarchy was too weak to control dissident ethnic movements or rebellious provinces, the Chinese remained aloof. Burma's only real obligation under the Confucian system was the decennial tributes, sent as much out of curiosity as out of the demands of membership.

I do not mean to imply that the Burmese were never aware of danger from the east. Burman and Shan alliances were frequently formed to repel Yunnanese warlords. Toward the close of the Ch'ing dynasty, the Chinese government encouraged mass migration to the weak kingdoms in Southeast Asia. Paradoxically, French and British colonization may have prevented a far greater migration than actually occurred. Nevertheless, over centuries of relations under the Confucian system, Burma enjoyed more advantages in political freedom than it incurred disadvantages in political obligations. The memory of this durable tradition is not dead today, and insofar as Peking can identify with it, Peking can expect a favorable response from the ordinary Burmese.

Although the Burma policy developed by the Chinese Communists has not always appeared consistent to the Burmese, the ordinary Burmese has come to expect a basic Chinese tolerance of Bur-

1. Judgments about the opinions of Burmans are based upon a stratified sample of about 100 intermediary leaders in one district in Central Burma. The project was conducted by the author between December 1961 and May 1962. Note that in this chapter Burmese refers to all citizens of Burma, whereas Burman refers to the ethnic majority which inhabits Central Burma.

ma's national interests. This popular image of tolerance developed during the Bandung Conference in 1955 and the subsequent bilateral negotiations on trade, technical assistance, and the boundary settlement. The P.R.C. has emerged in the eyes of many Burmese leaders, particularly those of rural origin, as a responsible regime which has dealt with Burma as an equal and with prudence.

Another aspect of Sino-Burmese relations derives from racial and cultural affinity. The old truism that Burma's traditional structure of government was founded on Hindu cosmology, while the way of life was derived from China is relevant today. Burmans frequently speak of a racial tie with the Chinese and deny a similar relationship with India.[2] The Chinese Communists have exploited popular appreciation for Chinese entertainment and art through tours by performers who have captivated rural Burmese audiences. Admiration for the industry of ordinary Chinese, an admiration based on intimate knowledge of immigrants living in Burmese towns and large villages, has been accentuated by Communist propaganda emphasizing the peasant revolution in China. An alleged heritage of goodwill that existed between Burmans and Chinese before the colonial period is thus made believable by current behavior and attitudes.

Among the political leaders of both countries, the language of revolution has been commonplace for the past 15 years. Although the Burmese have spoken in terms of socialism, whereas the Chinese have been avowed Communists, the articulated goals of both elites have been similar—that is, the development of a modern industrial society built upon a traditional agrarian base. I do not mean to say that the Burmese had, until recently, the same enthusiasm for drastic social engineering as the Chinese. Nevertheless, by emphasizing the heritage of political amity and their common language of revolution, both governments have been able to establish a rapport missing in their relations with most other states.

CHINA AND THE PROBLEM OF NATIONAL SECURITY

Burma's modern leadership is acutely aware of its country's relative weakness as compared to the People's Republic of China. The

---

2. This generalization is dangerous, for Burma's Buddhist tradition and its associated culture are derived from India. Nevertheless, in those areas of life not directly related to Buddhist practices, particularly in worldly values regarding social relations and work, Indian customs are not followed. Burmans are aware of their origins as a migratory group from western China and usually claim a greater racial affinity for the Chinese than for the darker Bengalis and Tamils or more Aryan Sikhs.

comparison is unpleasantly obvious: a population ratio of 1 to 30, a national income ratio of 1 to 25, and an armed forces ratio of 1 to 30. In territory, Burma is smaller than the Chinese provinces of Tibet, Sinkiang, or Inner Mongolia. The leader of Burma's independence movement, Aung San, viewed China as one the five great powers and of equal influence to the others insofar as they affected Burma.[3] In his decade of rule, U Nu usually referred to Burma as very small and weak compared to her northern neighbor.[4] Ne Win, Burma's third top national leader since World War II, has met frequently with leaders of the P.R.C. and has encouraged greater rapport with them than with other heads of state.[5] China's successful use of military and diplomatic pressure in Tibet, Laos, and Vietnam and during the invasion of India seems to have particularly impressed Ne Win.

Ne Win and his predecessors have assumed that the easiest way to prevent Chinese military intervention is to eliminate any cause for it—hence the policy of neutralism in the East-West conflict.[6] National security is certainly a most basic concern for any Burmese government, and China's policy toward Burma is the first among the external factors affecting Burma's security. There is evidence that every Burmese administration has been wary of the P.R.C.'s basic motives, yet no government leader has publicly admitted that the Chinese are a threat. For example, U Nu received offers from Peking "to provide assistance" in eliminating the Kuomintang forces in the Shan states. The Burmese government refused but worked desperately, and with eventual success, to remove the troops before the Communists could use them as a pretext to cross the border. Chinese troops did cross into Burma in 1956, but they were with-

3. "Presidential Address, Supreme Council of the AFPFL," *Burma's Challenge* (Rangoon: mimeographed, 1946), p. 21.

4. See his speech to Parliament on March 8, 1951, "Internal and External Problems," *From Peace to Stability* (Rangoon: Government Printing and Stationery Office, 1951), pp. 198–199. Also see his speech to the Chamber of Deputies on September 27, 1957, *Premier Reports to the People* (Rangoon: Government of the Union of Burma, Ministry of Information, 1957), p. 32.

5. Ne Win has met with a key Chinese leader at least once each year since 1959. In 1963 he was host to Liu Shao-ch'i on an extended tour around Burma and in 1964 to Chou En-lai and Ch'en Yi on two different occasions after their Africa trip. Chou En-lai first visited Burma in 1954, has returned eight times, and has been host to Ne Win four times in Peking.

6. For a careful study of neutralism in Burma, see William C. Johnstone, *Burma's Foreign Policy* (Cambridge: Harvard University Press, 1963), especially pp. 77–115.

drawn as strong press and diplomatic pressures developed in Rangoon. The government refused to acknowledge, however, that the incident was of serious concern.[7]

The border. Until the boundary settlement in 1960, a minor cold war persisted along the border. In 1958 near the town of Muse, Burmese immigration officials showed me boundary markers which Chinese troops had moved across the famous Burma Road two years earlier. The officials described the constant alert maintained for agents who crossed the border with the Kachin refugees migrating from Yunnan. The Burmese, of course, quite likely reciprocated in the spy game to gain intelligence about military movements near the border. The 900-mile boundary with China is, therefore, a key consideration in Burma's security. The problem has been exacerbated by the Kachins and Shans, the ethnic minorities living on both sides of the Sino-Burmese border. These ethnic groups had developed a migratory pattern which ignored the boundary, and they dislike control from either government. Shan and Kachin leaders have accused both Peking and Rangoon of suppression in stabilizing the boundary.

Indigenous Communists. A second aspect of Burma's national security which is related to China is the Communist movement. Two Communist parties in Burma, the (erstwhile Stalinist) White Flag BCP and the (erstwhile Trotskyite) Red Flag CPB, have staged continuous armed insurrection against the government since independence. The dominant party, the White Flags (led by Thakin Than Tun), has been in contact with the Chinese Communist party since 1950 and has sent several hundreds of cadres to Kunming and Peking for training. One faction of the party remained in China for most of this period, broadcast propaganda in Burmese, and developed a deep sympathy for the Chinese Communist system of rule. Some 32 Burmans and Kachins returned to Burma in July and August 1963 to negotiate with the Revolutionary Council for amnesty and legal recognition. Several members of this group had Chinese wives and spoke Chinese among themselves at the conference table.[8]

The Communist issue has been the most explosive in Sino-Burmese relations, and it could well have destroyed any existing

---

7. Same, pp. 191–192.
8. Revolutionary Council of the Union of Burma, *Internal Peace Parley* (Rangoon: Author, November 17, 1963). This record of negotiations was released after the breakdown of the discussions.

amity between the two regimes had the insurgent Communists received significant assistance from China. The threat of the Communist insurgents was compounded by that of the ex-militia and Karen insurgents. The latter groups seriously challenged the authority of the central regime for half a decade after independence. By 1954, when the Kuomintang troops issue was largely settled, however, it was apparent to the Burmese government that the Chinese Communists were not going to provide decisive assistance to the White Flags. This period was a time of gravest danger to Burma's national security. That the Chinese Communists set a limit on their commitment to dissident forces was of great significance to the Burmese leadership.

The precise depth of Chinese involvement during that crucial time remains unknown, for the activities of the Chinese embassy, the Bank of China (which was controlled by Peking [9]), and the number of agents who crossed the border remains unrevealed. We cannot even be certain how much information the Burmese government accumulated about Chinese connections with the insurgents. What is certain is that all but about 15 per cent of the Communist and proto-Communist insurgents surrendered between 1954 and 1958. None of them was reported to be armed with weapons from Communist China, and all were led by indigenous Burmese Communists, most of whom had been students at Rangoon University before or during World War II. We must conclude that the P.R.C.'s contribution to the Burmese Communist movement was financial and psychological, not military or logistical.

The Chinese minority. Burma has only half a million Chinese residents; therefore, the threat they might pose to the regime is far less than in Thailand, Malaysia, or Indonesia, where the numbers are much larger. Migration from China has been illegal since independence; however, as suggested above, thousands of refugees have slipped across the border in the past two decades. As in Thailand, the Chinese, particularly those from Fukien and Kwangtung provinces, tend to be assimilated within two to three generations. A ma-

---

9. Although the evidence is not conclusive, many Burmese believed that Chinese obtaining loans from the Peking-controlled banks in Burma were obliged to send their children to Communist Chinese private schools in Rangoon, Mandalay, or the larger towns. Each town with a Chinese population sufficient to support a private school traditionally developed at least a primary institution. These schools normally reflected the political stance of the dominant government in China; however, their major function was to teach Chinese.

jority of Burma's Chinese live in Rangoon, although every town and large village has Chinese entrepreneurs, pawnbrokers, or restaurant owners.

The Chinese Communists, upon gaining power, encouraged Chinese in Burma to support the White Flag liberation movement actively, but policy since Chou En-lai's visits of 1955 and 1956 has been aimed at accommodation with the existing regime. Chou's conversations in Rangoon with leaders of the local Chinese community gave these leaders their first direct contact with the new regime. Chou urged them to forego their Chinese loyalties and become Burmese citizens. This policy relieved a source of real tension that was emerging as the Burmese government increased pressure on elements of the Chinese community to curtail their commercial activities and indirect political support of the insurgents. Between 1954 and 1958, those Chinese loyal to the Anti-Fascist People's Freedom League (AFPFL), the governing party, were allowed, indeed encouraged, to continue their business activities. The military Caretaker Government introduced the concept of "economic insurgents" in 1958 to identify those Chinese and Indian middlemen who had previously dominated Rangoon commerce, exports, and imports. The Revolutionary Council in 1962 severely repressed Chinese and Indian merchants who had aided the politicians, and today the wealthy Chinese and Indians have either migrated or lost their businesses through nationalization.[10] Notwithstanding these pressures, the P.R.C. has not objected to the harsh Burmese policy toward the Chinese minorities and has even lent its tacit support.[11]

These basic issues which involve China in Burma's national security—the boundary, indigenous Communists, and the Chinese minority—have been handled by the P.R.C. with considerable skill. Although the People's Republic was not at all accommodating until the Bandung Conference, and was even obdurate thereafter in the boundary dispute, the Chinese never exacerbated relations with the Burmese government enough to cause it to propagandize against China among the Burmese people. In short, the Chinese have harvested the goodwill of a traditionally favorable Burmese sentiment by avoiding any direct threat to Burma's national security. How,

10. *Far Eastern Economic Review*, v. 43, no. 13, March 26, 1964, p. 656; *The New York Times*, March 1, 1964.
11. "Premier Chou En-lai Reports on His Visit to 14 Countries," *Peking Review*, v. 7, no. 18, May 1, 1964, p. 10.

then, have the Burmese addressed themselves to the Chinese? What has Burma's China policy been over the past two decades?

BURMA'S CHINA POLICY

Of the factors in Burma's policy toward China, three relate to the substance of direct relations between the two countries. These are trade, economic assistance, and territory. Three others relate to Burma's general ideology and international goals. These are non-alignment in great power conflicts, peaceful settlement of international conflicts, and representation of the P.R.C. in the United Nations. Burmese policy in regard to all these factors has required continual consideration, modification, and adaptation to changing conditions.

Trade. Economic relations with Communist China commenced with a substantial barter trade agreement signed in April 1954. The time was one of economic difficulty. More than 80 per cent of Burma's foreign purchases were paid for by rice exports. When the world rice market declined severely in 1953, Burma was confronted with a major price drop and a foreign exchange shortage, and the government was forced to retrench ambitious plans for industrial development. In 1954 every rice contract was important, particularly in previously untapped markets. The barter agreement with China—which called for the exchange of about 10 per cent of Burma's rice exports, 150,000 tons, for Chinese-produced consumer goods —seemed a partial solution, for it opened a new market. The contract was filled over the next two years, but the Burmese declined opportunities to expand trade with China on the ground that many Chinese goods were inferior and not marketable.[12] During 1958-61, exports dropped to an insignificant level. A new trade protocol signed after the boundary settlement was based on a sterling credit sale. Consequently, China paid cash for 10 per cent of the rice Burma exported in 1962. As before, China resold the rice to third parties—primarily Ceylon and Indonesia, from whom the Chinese purchased rubber. The three-way exchange is continuing although no new protocol has been signed.

---

12. Commerce Department, Rangoon University, *Survey of Businessmen's Reaction to Imported Goods from Barter Countries* (Rangoon: Author, 1956). This study was a group project based upon interviews with Rangoon businessmen after a year of barter trade. In paper, textiles, and hardware, the Chinese were competitive with older British and Indian firms; other goods were inferior.

Burma has not found the China trade essential, but the market is sufficiently important to encourage continued ties. As for China, Burmese rice is a negligible addition to the millions of tons of cereals imported from Western countries. The People's Republic has not opposed Burma's policy of selling to available customers, and as the Chinese themselves have shifted their trade to Western states, Burma's trade policy toward the P.R.C. has tended to lose its earlier ideological flavor. Meanwhile, Burma has developed a stable trade pattern with Indonesia, India, Pakistan, Malaysia, and Ceylon, all of whom are customers as important as China in terms of rice sales. Note the variance between exports and imports in Table 10-1.

TABLE 10-1

Direction of the Foreign Trade of Burma, 1959–61

(in millions of U.S. dollars)

	IMPORTS			EXPORTS		
	1959	1960	1961	1959	1960	1961
TOTAL	222.8	260.2	215.5	218.7	223.4	263.7
United States	9.9	9.8	8.2	1.9	.7	1.1
United Kingdom	42.8	37.5	33.9	19.9	20.5	23.9
Japan	50.5	58.5	45.6	8.3	11.3	8.8
India	29.7	20.3	13.1	35.6	34.1	18.9
Malaya and Singapore	5.5	3.6	3.3	21.2	13.7	18.3
Mainland China	16.4	24.9	20.6	.4	6.6	37.7
Ceylon	.3	.9	2.1	25.0	25.4	22.0
U.S.S.R.	3.9	2.8	4.5	.9	4.0	—
Czechoslovakia	3.9	3.6	2.3	1.3	.5	3.1
Pakistan	7.0	12.6	12.1	19.9	18.1	16.9
Indonesia	1.0	3.2	1.0	37.4	42.8	31.5
West Germany	9.8	12.9	9.4	5.5	7.2	3.9
Netherlands	6.5	9.9	6.1	4.2	2.0	2.3
All other countries	35.6	59.7	53.3	37.2	36.5	75.3

SOURCES: Government of Burma, Central Statistical and Economics Department, *Bulletin of Export Trade* and *Bulletin of Import Trade*, 1959, 1960, and 1961.

Economic assistance. Burma accepted Chinese technical assistance in 1954 as part of the barter for rice. The American aid program had been curtailed, on Burma's initiative, in March of the previous year because of the Kuomintang problem in the Shan States. In the spring of 1954, Chinese technical assistance bartered for rice seemed a partial solution to Burma's shortage of foreign exchange for planned capital expenditures. The P.R.C. agreed to construct a large cotton textile factory in Rangoon. Chinese technicians were careful not to propagandize among Burmese or other Communist bloc technicians, and Chinese aid was professionally administered. However, neither the last AFPFL government in 1957 nor the Caretaker military regime renewed the P.R.C.'s aid program, for Burma's foreign exchange position had been stabilized. Also, there is no evidence that the Chinese offered to renew their aid between 1957 and 1960. U Nu's statement in 1948 that "foreign aid could enslave Burma" seemed to have become a tenet of foreign policy which applied to China as well as to the West.[13]

After the renewed amity in the 1960 discussions between Ne Win and Chou En-lai, Burma accepted an $84 million loan offered by Chou En-lai in January 1961. These funds were to be drawn between 1961 and 1967 and repaid from 1971 to 1980. It was the largest loan contract any Burmese government had accepted and included hydroelectric plants and bridges in the Shan states; textile and plywood factories in Central Burma; paper, tire, and sugar plants in the Tenasserim; and expansion of the steel plant initially developed by West Germany. Ne Win's decision to accept a large loan from the P.R.C. was part of a broad policy urged by Brigadier Aung Gyi, Ne Win's second-in-command at that time—a policy of searching for vast new sources of foreign capital to expand the development program. One year after signing the China agreement, Burma concluded a final $200 million reparations agreement with Japan. (An initial $200 million grant made in 1954 was nearly depleted.) A year before, a $31 million road and land reclamation program had been agreed upon with the United States. Finally, the World Bank granted new credit for transportation and harbor improvements.

Chinese technical assistance since 1961 is impressive on paper, but actual deliveries have been small. It marks a third stage in Burma's foreign aid policy. During 1950–53, the United States and Commonwealth countries provided all the foreign aid entering the country. In the second stage, Communist bloc barter aid was accepted along with technical assistance from U.N. agencies, Commonwealth countries, and the Colombo Plan. American aid was once more accepted in 1956. Since 1962, however, all private Western

---

13. See U Nu's speech of June 13, 1948, "The Nature of Leftist Unity," *Towards Peace and Democracy* (Rangoon: Government of the Union of Burma, Ministry of Information, 1948), p. 133.

assistance has been canceled. The new Chinese program got under way early in 1962. With the implementation of this program, the Burma government could make the dubious claim that it had used loans and economic assistance from every conceivable source. During the second phase of Burma's aid policy, Communist and Western aid had been roughly balanced. In the current third phase, the Chinese loan and Japanese reparations commitments far exceed any other programs. Since 1954, however, Japan has contributed, through reparations, more than a third of the total aid delivered to Burma, and Communist China has delivered only a nominal amount. Japan's future commitments exceed China's by a three to one ratio. See Table 10-2 for total aid figures. (One crore [10 million kyats] at the official exchange rate equals about $2 million.)

The decision to accept Chinese Communist assistance was partially an ideological one based on the premise that government-to-government aid was desirable whereas all private aid should be avoided. Burma's previous experience with other foreign aid had not been pleasant. American public and private aid was clouded on both sides by cold war politics and administrative delays.[14] Japanese firms used the reparations agreement to gain unusual profits from inexperienced Burmese purchasers, both in business and government.[15] The largest single aid project in Burma, the Balu Chaung hydroelectric project, cost far in excess of its original estimate, for Japanese contractors operated on a 15–20 per cent cost-plus margin. Reparations payments flowed back to Japan as profits, and Burma received low value for the ostensibly large commitment of capital. By comparison, the efficient handling of China's first small industrial program, purchased out of rice barter during 1955–58, helped foster Ne Win's willingness to accept China's largest loan to any non-Communist power. However, Burma has since equivocated on the projects. This fact suggests that the Revolutionary Council is as wary of China's foreign aid as U Nu was of Western aid back in 1948.

Boundary. Both the trade and aid agreements with China were facets of the larger rapprochement reached through negotiations by the first Ne Win regime of 1958–60 and the last U Nu government of 1960–62. The boundary agreement was founded upon a mutual

14. Probably the most thorough study of a new state's development program and the relationship of U.S. aid to that program is Louis Walinsky's massive *Economic Development in Burma 1951–60* (New York: Twentieth Century Fund, 1962). For Walinsky's assessment of American aid, see pp. 515–534.

15. Same, p. 514.

TABLE 10-2

Aid Commitments and Deliveries to Burma
through September 30, 1960

	COMMITMENTS		DELIVERIES	
	K Crores	As % of Total	K Crores	As % of Total
TOTAL	239.6	100	125.1	100
Japan	119.0 ᵃ	49.7	47.3	37.8
Reparations	95.2	39.7	47.3	37.8
Economic cooperation	23.8	9.3	—	—
United States	63.2	26.3	37.3	29.8
T.C.A. program	9.3 ᵇ	3.9	9.3	7.4
P.L. 480 (Title I)	19.4 ᶜ	8.0	19.1	15.3
Development loan	12.0	5.0	4.3	3.4
P.L. 480(104d)	2.4	1.0	2.4	1.9
Police loan	4.8	2.0	.9	.7
Sale of military goods	1.0 ᵈ	.4	1.0 ᵉ	.8
Special assistance grant	14.3 ᶠ	6.0	.3	.2
India	20.0	8.3	20.0	16.0
U.S.S.R.	21.0 ᵍ	8.8	5.8	4.6
I.B.R.D.	9.3	3.9	7.6	6.1
I.M.F.	7.1	3.0	7.1	5.7

(a) Distributed equally over 10 years beginning Japanese fiscal year 1955–56. Commitments through September 1960 only would be K 52.8 crores.

(b) This program was initiated in September 1950 and terminated in June 1953. Deliveries are here taken as commitments.

(c) Includes shipping cost. In addition, nearly K 1 crore was separately supplied to voluntary-aid societies in Burma.

(d) This sale was for local currency, hence qualifies as aid.

(e) It was anticipated that the real value of surplus military goods to be delivered, because of their bargain prices, would be far in excess of actual purchase cost to Burma.

(f) Excludes grant of K 2.9 crores in local currency as not additive of real resources.

(g) This was the roughly estimated total cost of the six "gift" projects originally agreed upon. Burma subsequently deferred, then canceled, three of the projects.

NOTE: The U.S. programs omit a loan of $17 million in local currency and a $1 million exchange of rice for technicians, which are not aid within our definition. As of January 1964, new commitments not covered by this table were Japan, K 95.0 crores, and P.R.C., K 39.9 crores.

SOURCE: Louis Walinsky, *Economic Development in Burma 1950–60* (New York: Twentieth Century Fund, 1962), p. 511.

desire to settle an ancient problem exacerbated by a concern for national security. The P.R.C. wanted a secure buffer on her south-western flank, and Burma obviously wanted further assurance of China's peaceful intentions. Before the coming of the British, neither Burmans nor Chinese were particularly concerned about a definite border, for the minority Kachins, Shans, and Yunnanese were buffer peoples between the two powers. In the 19th and early 20th centuries, British worry over French imperialism in Indochina caused the Indian Office to demarcate the McMahon Line wherever possible. Some revisions along the northern boundary were made in 1941 through a controversial Sino-British agreement, the Inslein Line. Independent Burma inherited this border. The interpretation on British and Burmese maps, however, differed greatly from Nationalist and Communist Chinese maps. The latter maps showed most of the Kachin state in Yunnan and Sikang. (See Figure 10-1.)

Burma sought to negotiate a settlement roughly along the old McMahon and Inslein lines. In the final agreement, Burma lost three small Kachin villages and 180 square miles of territory near Wa state,[16] but it gained a neck of crucial land crossed by the Burma Road, the Namwan Tract, which had been previously leased from the Chinese. A joint Burmese-Chinese commission completed the physical survey in 1961. Both U Nu and Ne Win publicly approved the settlement as reflecting the Five Principles of Peaceful Coexistence and the resolutions of the Bandung Conference. In terms of national security, the agreement was exceedingly important, for henceforth China could not use the excuse of an undemarcated border as a reason for annexing Burmese territory. In light of the great military disparity between the two powers, Burma (like Nepal, Pakistan, and Afghanistan in 1961 and 1962) profited from a Chinese policy which sought secure boundaries.

The 1960 border settlement marked a change in the position which China had maintained over the previous decade, for the terms were essentially those proposed by U Nu in 1956 but tabled by Chou En-lai in the discussions at that time.[17] By late 1959, the P.R.C. had

16. The three village tracts, Hpimaw, Gawlum, and Kanfang were vigorously defended by Kachin leaders as an integral part of the Kachin community in Burma. U Nu was sufficiently persuaded by this opposition to delay negotiations; however, in 1956 he offered a settlement which was substantially accepted by the Chinese in 1960.

17. Miss Daphne Whittam, former associate editor of the Rangoon *Nation*, presents an authoritative discussion of Burma's policy on the boundary issue in

FIGURE 10-1
The Sino-Burmese Border Settlement of 1960

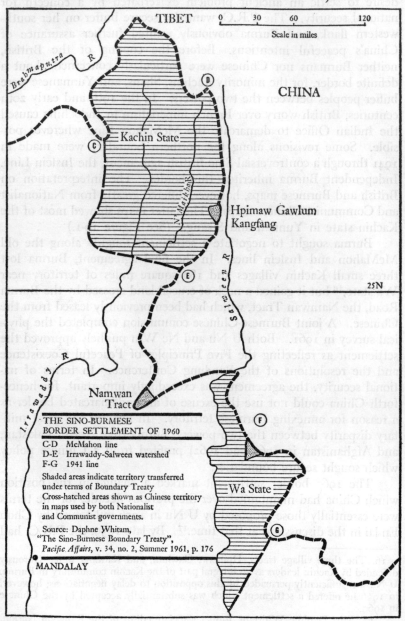

TIBET

0   30   60   120

Scale in miles

Brahmaputra R.

CHINA

Kachin State

Hpimaw Gawlum
Kangfang

N. Maikha R.

Salween R.

25N

Irrawaddy R.

Namwan
Tract

THE SINO-BURMESE
BORDER SETTLEMENT OF 1960

C-D   McMahon line
D-E   Irrawaddy-Salween watershed
F-G   1941 line

Shaded areas indicate territory transferred
under terms of Boundary Treaty

Cross-hatched areas shown as Chinese territory
in maps used by both Nationalist
and Communist governments.

Source: Daphne Whitam,
"The Sino-Burmese Boundary Treaty",
Pacific Affairs, v. 34, no. 2, Summer 1961, p. 176

Wa State

MANDALAY

concluded that the issue was worth resolving, even on Burma's terms, and in January 1960 Ne Win traveled to Peking to initial the treaty. Burma's policy of patience was rewarded.

Ideology and international goals. The first U Nu regime developed the outlook that undergirds Burma's China policy. Nonalignment, peaceful resolution of international conflict, representation of Communist China and all other legitimate governments in the United Nations—these were tenets of U Nu's own political philosophy. All four governments (U Nu, 1948–58; Ne Win, 1958–60; U Nu, 1960–62; Ne Win, 1962–present) have retained these ideological commitments although the first Ne Win government briefly deviated from an otherwise consistent pattern.

Ne Win, upon forming his Caretaker Government in October 1958, stated:

> My Government does not entertain any notion to introduce any changes whatsoever in the foreign policy being pursued. I wish to announce that my Government intends to continue in the practice of strict neutrality free from any entanglements.[18]

Nevertheless, the following year Burma sent its first, and only, observers to SEATO exercises at the behest of Colonels Maung Maung and Tun Sein, leaders of an avowedly anti-Communist faction in the Caretaker Government. This brief flirtation with a military role had little support within the country, particularly since Ne Win's efforts to settle the China border dispute were rewarded several months later.

Every Burmese government has assumed that to become involved in international politics is to risk the loss of national integrity and a division of the country. The line of reasoning has been that Burma is so weak from internal dissension that any strong foreign power is a potential threat to unity.

China, as one of the world powers in the eyes of Burmese leaders, has therefore been discouraged from involvement in domestic issues.

"The Sino-Burmese Boundary Treaty," *Pacific Affairs*, v. 34, no. 2, September 1961, pp. 174–183. In a longer mimeographed paper, "The Border Dispute Between Burma and China," Miss Whittam summarizes a 15-stage policy outlined by U Nu in a speech to the Chamber of Deputies, April 28, 1960. A crucial "package deal" was proposed in 1956 after long negotiations in Peking between U Nu, Kachin, and Chinese leaders. This multifaceted proposal was modified in 1960 but was the basis for the agreement.

18. Speech to Chamber of Deputies, October 31, 1958. See William C. Johnstone, ed., *A Chronology of Burma's International Relations 1945–58* (Rangoon University, 1959), p. 95.

We have seen that both U Nu and Ne Win were eager to stabilize the situation on the border to avoid giving the Chinese a reason for penetrating Burma militarily. The situation is much the same in the realm of politics. Burma's domestic Communists, who have maintained relations with the Chinese Communist party, have not enjoyed legal status since independence. China's efforts to aid these insurgents financially through the Chinese banks in Burma and to propagate Communist doctrine in private Chinese schools have been curtailed by the Revolutionary Council's policy of nationalization. This policy has placed control of foreign and private financial and educational institutions in the hands of Burmese.

In foreign affairs, however, Burmese governments have been tolerant of the same Chinese political and military activities elsewhere which they have repressed in Burma. No Burmese administration has directly opposed the P.R.C.'s use of propaganda or subversion in other countries. Once the Chinese chose to fight in Korea, Burma began to hedge its initial support for U.N. policy. The Burmese delegate abstained from voting on the resolution which condemned the People's Republic as an aggressor in Korea. Similarly, the P.R.C.'s material support for the Viet Cong and the Pathet Lao has not been officially noted by the Burmese. The methods used by Peking in the 1959 invasion of Tibet were considered regrettable by the Ne Win regime, but the matter was called an internal affair. This policy of isolation from the difficulties facing Burma's neighbors has been accentuated since the 1962 coup, but it is not a change of policy from that followed by U Nu. It is founded upon the assumption that Burma, as a power, is insignificant in the play of politics in Southeast Asia.

A complementary assumption, again made by both the U Nu and Ne Win regimes, is that Burmese leaders can play a moral role on the international scene even though Burma should not attempt to assume a military role. Senior Burmese educators and civil servants have been encouraged to seek leadership positions in non-military regional and international organizations. U Thant is the most prominent of these men. Others have gained high posts in the International Labor Organization, the Economic Commission for Asia and the Far East, the International Monetary Fund, the International Bank for Reconstruction and Development, the Food and Agriculture Organization, organizations devoted to solving non-military problems. In pursuit of this same moral role on the international scene, U Nu attempted to serve as an intermediary between Mao and Eisenhower in 1955 and 1956 during his visits to China and the United States. He seriously proposed to both leaders that Burma be the bridge between the United States and the People's Republic. His failure to achieve this goal was, according to close friends, a bitter disappointment.

Naive though such a commitment may seem to some among the great powers, the Burmese policy of attempting to resolve all international problems by non-military means is deeply rooted—a policy unchanged after four different governments in Rangoon. Recent evidence of the Revolutionary Council's effort to apply the principle of nonviolence to the international scene may be found in Burma's policy on the Sino-Indian conflict and the arms control negotiations. After the 1962 crisis on the Indian border, Ne Win actively supported the Colombo proposal. In February 1964, he acted as an intermediary between Chou and Nehru in the continuing negotiations which followed the presentations of the proposal in New Delhi and Peking. Burma's Foreign Minister, U Thi Han, has played an active role in the arms control negotiations at Geneva. U Thi Han has had the full support of the Revolutionary Council in the crucial test ban agreement, which he helped design. In this instance, Burma opposed the P.R.C., which did not sign the test ban agreement.

A third ideological commitment of all of Burma's governments has been the desire to have all peoples officially represented in the U.N. General Assembly. Thus, Burma has supported most independence movements and been active on the Trusteeship Council. In pursuit of this same goal, Burma has consistently advocated the seating of the P.R.C. in the United Nations and has encouraged the mainland regime's participation in specialized U.N. organizations. In regard to the status of the Republic of China (Nationalist), Burma is among those nations which have acceded to the P.R.C.'s principle that there is only one China and that Taiwan belongs under mainland sovereignty.

The Chinese Communists have rewarded the Burmese for their solicitude by referring to them as *paukphaw* or kinfolk. In propaganda to new African states, the People's Republic cites its relationship with Burma as a model relationship between disparate powers.[19] The Burmese have been appreciative but have remained unyielding

19. Robert A. Scalapino, "Sino-Soviet Competition in Africa," *Foreign Affairs*, v. 42, no. 4, July 1964, p. 643; also *Peking Review*, v. 7, no. 1, January 3, 1964, p. 40.

in regard to domestic Communists and the internal distribution of Chinese propaganda. Early in 1964, all foreign propaganda was banned, and foreign cultural centers were placed under government control through a registration act. For the first time since independence, distribution of Chinese Communist literature within Burma has been declared illegal. This act represents one of the most clear-cut distinctions which the Burmese government has made between its domestic and foreign policies. On the international scene, particularly in the United Nations, Burma is among mainland China's foremost advocates; yet within Burma, the Chinese are finding themselves in the same position as the Western states—their advice unwanted and their very presence, in any but a diplomatic role, cause for suspicion. Although Ne Win has been most hospitable to the P.R.C.'s top leaders, the Chinese ambassador in Rangoon reportedly has had no greater contact with the government than have Western diplomats since mid-1963.

VARIANTS OF LEADERSHIP AND THEIR IMPACT ON CHINA POLICY

Burma's policy toward Communist China has been consistent with the several governments' conceptions of national interest. By and large, that policy has not changed since 1950 on basic issues relating to security, nonalignment, nonviolent settlement of disputes, and inclusion of all legitimate governments in the United Nations. Burma, more than other non-Communist states, has been sensitive to the P.R.C.'s aims in international affairs and has consistently respected the mainland regime's right to recognition as a great power.

On certain specific issues, however, the Burmese have been extremely malleable, and their actions have seemed to result from no policy at all. I suggest that in these instances (e.g., Korea, Tibet, Hungary, Vietnam, and now Laos as well as the whole area of foreign aid) the attitudes of U Nu, Ne Win, and the group of advisers who have had the ear of either man were unusually important. It becomes imperative, therefore, to examine in greater detail the types of leadership that Burma has had since independence to point up the variables in Burma's China policy as well as the parameters which we have just analyzed.

The attitudes of Burmese leaders in the past have often been defined in cold war ideological terms. Leader X has been considered pro-Communist or leader Y anti-Communist. Such labels are misleading. The significant commitment in Burma is to a national ideology unfamiliar to those in the West tutored largely by the cold war. In addition, at least four other factors need to be isolated and their influence weighed before the leader's position can be defined: the leader's vision of his *personal role*, his awareness of his character as perceived by other national leaders; the leader's *sense of necessity*, his perception of the policy toward China which is essential to satisfy both his domestic support and the Chinese leadership; the leader's *sensitivity to national power*, his sophistication with regard to roleplaying in international politics, particularly modern small powergreat power relations; and the leader's *sense of history*, the relative importance he assigns to the classic relationship between Burma and China. In these four respects there have been qualitative differences between U Nu and Ne Win and even between the two governments that each man headed.

Personal role. The greatest divergence between the Burmese leaders appears in their conceptions of what role they should play in international politics. U Nu actively sought the role of international mediator. He seriously pressed China and the United States to seek reconciliation. Before attending the Bandung Conference, he asserted that one of his purposes in going was to convince Chou En-lai of the value of settling the East-West conflict by reason. During his 1955 tour of the United States, he repeatedly spoke out against "America's abnormal fear of communism" and assured his audiences that the Peking leaders were sincere, responsible representatives of their country.[20] After forming closer ties with Israel than had any other Asian state, U Nu attempted to persuade President Nasser to accept mediation of the Arab-Israeli conflict.[21] Nasser did not accept the offer. U Nu completed his world tour after formal visits to Israel, Yugoslavia, Britain, and Japan; then he traveled to the Soviet Union and the Scandinavian states in the fall of 1955. He met with Laotian leaders in 1955 and successfully arranged a renewal of the talks between the Pathet Lao and the government. A year later he toured for nearly a month in Communist China. Throughout his travels, the Burmese Premier frequently returned to the theme of his own willingness to engage in international conciliation.[22] During

20. Speech to the National Press Club, *Washington Post*, July 2, 1955; interview, *U.S. News and World Report*, August 5, 1955.
21. Johnstone, *Burma's Foreign Policy*, cited, p. 144.
22. Richard Butwell, *U Nu of Burma* (Stanford University Press, 1963), pp. 190–91.

these last years of the AFPFL government, U Nu clearly perceived himself as an international statesman.

U Nu's optimism of this period was not characteristic of Ne Win during either of his regimes or even of U Nu himself during his last government. Nu, probably influenced by cold war difficulties in his own country as well as the tension between the U.S.S.R. and United States, entered the 1961 Belgrade conference of nonaligned states with less certainty that nuclear war could be avoided.[23] In his last appearance as a statesman of international stature, Nu, with Nehru and Madame Bandaranaike, served primarily as a pleader for peace amid the sharply anti-Western conference delegates. Ne Win's political interests and relations with other national leaders have remained much narrower than Nu's. His only appearance on the international scene was during the Sino-Indian border conflict. His interest in this issue remains. For example, he made a hasty trip to Delhi for a conversation with Nehru before his (Ne Win's) first February 1964 meetings with Chou En-lai and Ch'en Yi. His one planned world tour was canceled in 1963, and his only trips to Europe or the United States have been of an unofficial nature or for medical purposes. It is obvious that Ne Win does not think of himself as a prominent spokesman for Asia as U Nu did. Consequently, his China policy has been founded on specific issues, and he has avoided the role of interpreter of China to the West.

Sense of necessity. U Nu and Ne Win have also displayed sharply different senses of necessity. For Ne Win, Burma's internal unity has been an obsession. He has modified foreign policy to fit the needs of a radical restructuring of both the economy and the constitutional relationships between the Burman majority and the minorities. The Revolutionary Council has dealt more harshly with all disaffected minority leaders, including those in the Chinese community, than either the Caretaker regime or U Nu's two governments. The security-minded Ne Win has been determined to close off avenues of support for insurgent minority groups operating across the ill-defined Pakistan and Thai borders. The Sino-Burmese boundary agreement was only the most newsworthy of three agreements that Burma has signed during the second Ne Win administration. Pakistan and Thailand have also accepted boundary treaties aimed at a final demarcation of Burma's borders. Only the Indian and Laotian borders are not as yet firmly defined.

23. Same, p. 239.

The priority given to the solution of Burma's civil strife causes Ne Win's second administration to pursue a somewhat different course in relations with the P.R.C. than the previous administrations did. As we have seen, both Nu regimes and the first Ne Win government allowed the Chinese to pursue political objectives in Burma by propaganda and financial aid to sympathetic leftist parties. That the Revolutionary Council has seriously tried to eliminate these activities may suggest that Ne Win not only views Burmese national unity as of the highest importance but also that he assumes the Chinese Communist leadership will allow him greater nationalistic expression in the Sino-Burmese relationship than previous Burmese regimes had believed possible.

Sensitivity to national power. U Nu's excessive ambition, during his first government, to play a greater role as an international mediator than Burma's power position would allow can be explained partly by the bipolar nature of world politics in the 1950s, when a reasonable voice from a neutral power was encouraged, and partly by Burma's and U Nu's naivete. The world is more polycentric in the 1960s, and the new states of Asia, including Burma, are no longer so inexperienced. These factors contribute to Ne Win's more limited horizons and his change of role. Nevertheless, he is more acutely sensitive to, and perceives more accurately than U Nu, Burma's real power position in relation to China as well as to other great powers. By depending upon skilled diplomats, U Thi Han as Foreign Minister and James Barrington as ambassador to the United Nations, Ne Win has developed a set of very proper relations with not only Burma's neighbors but also the great powers. He has isolated Burma from the cold war to a degree that he was unable to achieve during the Caretaker Government when he allowed a doctrinaire anti-Communist policy to prevail.

Sense of history. The final distinguishing factor, the leader's sense of history, allows us to see Ne Win and U Nu in a more personal dimension than is possible any other way.

Contemporary Burma is saddled with two profound political traditions.[24] One, from British days, accentuates a Western legal norm, and the second, from the monarchial period, is founded upon social relations and a world view fostered by the Buddhist *dhamma-*

---

24. See John H. Badgley, "Burma: The Nexus of Socialism and Two Political Traditions," *Asian Survey*, v. 3, no. 2, February 1963, for an extended treatment of this point.

thats and *nitis* (ethical writings). The Confucian political system was an adjunct to the earlier tradition, and as I have already noted, it is this system of political relations to which Ne Win seems particularly responsive.

U Nu, rather early in his career as a national leader, established close personal ties with Nehru. In part, this relationship was a product of India's immediate response to Nu's plea for aid in 1949 when the insurgents threatened to destroy the government. There is ample evidence that both men shared a philosophic view of politics based on a respect for Western democracy. U Nu met with Nehru 14 times during the first 10 years of his Premiership. At international conferences, they agreed on basic issues, particularly with regard to cold war politics. When the Afro-Asian conference was first proposed by Indonesia's Foreign Minister in 1954, "Initially only Pakistan's Mohammed Ali was enthusiastic; Ceylon's Sir John Kotelawala was willing to go along, but India's Jawaharlal Nehru and Burma's U Nu, while both nodding polite approval of the idea, were skeptical of the feasibility and value of holding such a conference." [25] By the fall of 1954, Nehru and U Nu had come around to full support of the conference. Once involved, both leaders were concerned with the same issues—effective and judicious use of the United Nations, control of Communist expansion in Cambodia and Laos, and expansion of contacts between East and West. U Nu sided with Nehru when Pakistan introduced the Kashmir issue, and he echoed Nehru's final plea for support of the Five Principles of Coexistence. At the Belgrade Conference, seven years later, Nehru and U Nu again played nearly identical roles. U Nu was fundamentally committed to parliamentary democracy, and like Nehru, he could forgive the West for colonialism because he appreciated its system of democratic government. Thus, although U Nu was a religious conservative in his devotion to traditional Buddhism, he was quite prepared to erase the monarchial tradition of politics and build a modern Burma upon the ideals of the legalistic democracy introduced by the British.

Ne Win, to the contrary, has demonstrated little patience with democracy. His sense of history is akin to that of Burma's district leaders who have had far less exposure to the British educational system than did U Nu and the AFPFL elite. Burman rural society, with its pattern of values still surprisingly intact after 60 years of colonialism, provides these men with a world view quite distinct from

---

25. George McT. Kahin, *The Asian-African Conference* (Ithaca, N.Y.: Cornell University Press, 1956), p. 2.

that of the Westernized elite from whom U Nu was drawn. Ne Win, who was dropped from college his first year and became a postal clerk, has gained recognition from rural leaders—obviously because he has rapport with them. He has failed, however, to gain acceptance among the Westernized professionals and politicians who dominated U Nu's first government. During his first administration, Ne Win allowed himself to be advised by university graduates, officers who, naturally, were most sympathetic to the Western tradition in which they had been schooled. With the 1962 coup, Ne Win determined to surround himself with "his kind of people." Ex-insurgents and former field commanders, most of them high school graduates from district towns and not university graduates, have remained his closest advisers.

Ne Win's model of a modern Burma is founded on a golden era of the past when Burmans were unhampered in their domestic politics and foreign relations. The nationalization schemes imposed by the Revolutionary Council are labeled State Socialism; however, this control of Burma's economic life by the state is remarkably similar to the manner of government practiced by Mindon, Burma's last effective monarch.[26] It is this crystallization of the Burman tradition and the rejection of Western democracy which seems to have caused Ne Win and his Revolutionary Council to share a far greater rapport with the Chinese Communists than U Nu and the AFPFL leadership attained. There is most certainly a kind of traditional reality which the mandarins of Peking recognize in the *mingyis* (great kings) of Rangoon, whom they identify as *paukphaws*. These leaders are kindred spirits who share a heritage of guerrilla warfare, xenophobia, and nationalism that is unique in Asia.

The current regimes of China and Burma are committed to the protection of their respective cultures from Westernization. They share a xenophobia which causes the leaders of both regimes to view cultural relations with foreigners as a political issue. The counter-elite that has emerged in Burma, with its roots in the rural community, has yet to distinguish between *modern* and *Western* institutions. Like the Maoists who would sinify Marxism, current Burmese leaders aspire to permeate all knowledge with a Burman elan. For example, the Burmese Buddhist notion of a life cycle causing rebirth has been transferred into philosophy of history.

---

26. Shway Yoe, *The Burman, His Life and Notions* (New York: Norton, 1963), p. 527.

It cannot be that man has only now acquired very high intellectual faculties and developed civilizations. Looking back on the life span of the world and its changes we can say that man has possibly attained, time and again, levels of civilization much higher than those of our times. It is probable that the conditions that had developed and become similar to those available now must have come to ruin on account of a certain catastrophe which must have taken place in the whole world. All arts and sciences, all records, all machineries and nuclear instruments and such must have then come to rack and ruin, and those men who survived must have retrograded into dark ages.[27]

It seems an understatement to say that Burma's Westernized elite is likely to remain sharply constrained by a counter-elite with a profound commitment to Burmanization. Since 1962, the Revolutionary Council has thrown all its weight into the creation of a single-party state. The Burma Socialist Program party, like the Chinese Communist party, has developed a quasi-military corps of cadres that has successfully eroded power from other competitive groups within the society. Indeed, only the influence of the Buddhist *sangha* now prevents the Revolutionary Council from exercising a totalitarian rule. It may well be that this singular commitment to a nationalistic chauvinism is the source of greatest empathy between current Chinese and Burmese leaders.

FUTURE RELATIONS

Looking to the future, we can discern the guidelines of Sino-Burmese relations. Since the 1955 Afro-Asian conference, the P.R.C. has consistently respected Burma's national security interests. With the exception of the 1956 border dispute, there has been no serious conflict over the boundary, the Chinese minority community in Burma, and the Communist parties sympathetic to Peking, even though there have been several varieties of government in Burma. In all probability, Burma's acknowledged national security interests will not be infringed upon as long as the country remains nonaligned.

The Burmese have devised a style of diplomacy through participation in non-military international organizations and conferences which allows Burma to pursue national objectives in foreign policy without offending China. In the future, Burma's active membership

27. See *The Philosophy of the Burma Socialist Programme Party* (Rangoon, 1963).

in most U.N. affiliates may well be encouraged by the Chinese Communists if they in turn are seated in the United Nations. Moreover, as long as Sino-Indian relations remain strained, Burma may remain an essential intermediary between the two giant states. The Burmese political leadership, whether drawn from the Westernized elite or the emerging traditionalist elite, is likely to preserve the buffer status that both U Nu and Ne Win have created for Burma.

China cannot penetrate Burma politically or militarily without seriously affecting Burma's four remaining neighbors or other states. India, Pakistan, and Thailand have shown their concern for Burma's position by signing friendship or boundary treaties, and they will remain basically committed to maintaining Burma's nonaligned position regardless of other aspects of their foreign relations. The Burmese, in turn, have demonstrated a capacity to deal effectively with the Chinese Communists; therefore, Burma's other neighbors are not likely to press her to modify what begins to appear to be a stable relationship.

In the event of a major conflagration between the United States and Communist China in Southeast Asia, the Burmese would have to reexamine their nonaligned status. Threat of another coup from the alienated Westernized elite in Rangoon, from within the military, or from the insurgent Communists would then become possible. In that event, the source of the new coup would determine the modifications in foreign policy which would ensue. A completely new relationship with China or the United States, however, would be most unlikely. The reasons are readily apparent if we briefly review Burma's policy regarding the Sino-American relationship.

Both U Nu and Ne Win have worked assiduously to maintain a delicate balance in relations with the United States and China. While favoring the admittance of Communist China to the United Nations and searching for a friendly and stable relationship, Burma has also carried on diplomatic and trade relations with the P.R.C.'s acknowledged enemies in Asia. The Republics of Korea and Vietnam, the Philippines, Thailand, and Malaya have all enjoyed proper, if not always close, relations with Burma. Burma has accepted significant amounts of aid from the United States, has armed her military with American weapons, and has, until recently, allowed U.S. propaganda to flow freely into the country to compete with the Chinese Communists. Conversely, the Burmese have not supported SEATO or the U.S. position against seating the P.R.C. in the United

Nations. Nor has any Burmese government endorsed American policy toward Taiwan. Rather, U Nu and Ne Win have advocated the submission of the Nationalist regime to Peking. By these measures, Burmese foreign policy has achieved its fundamental objective of nonalignment.

The Burmese have a saying that the grass is always trampled between two fighting buffaloes. As long as Peking and Washington view each other as primary antagonists in world politics, any Burmese government is likely to regard military confrontation between the two as a threat to Burma's existence. However, as the Chinese expand their trade and political relations around the world and thus increase their alternatives for diplomatic action, the Burmese likewise may perceive positive U.S. action in Asia as less of a threat to the peace. In the crucial area of military policy, the relative restraint displayed by Chinese forces since the invasion of India and by U.S. forces since 1961 in Thailand, Vietnam, and Laos seems to have persuaded all but the radical leftist leaders in Burma that both governments intend to "preserve the peace" in Asia.

The key factor in the Burmese perception of Sino-American relations is the concern for intentions. During Ne Win's second regime, Peking has been more convincing to the Burmese than Washington in claiming to favor Burma's nationalist aspirations. The reverse was true under the earlier governments, when the Westernized elite was dominant. It seems certain that both the P.R.C. and the United States must tolerate diverse kinds of regimes in Southeast Asia as each new state struggles to mesh its own peculiar culture with the crushing demands of modernization. Given this tolerance, any nationalist Burmese leadership is likely to accept the presence of American naval forces in Southeast Asian waters as a counterbalance to Chinese land forces on the Burma border. The trick is to keep the two powers from openly clashing, and here all Burmese governments have agreed that cohesion in Burma is essential to prevent the country from being drawn into a maelstrom like that devouring Vietnam and Laos. Burma's first three governments gave China and the United States "equal time," so to speak, as a device to balance the two against each other. Ne Win has changed the method by canceling all foreign propaganda, but his goal is the same as U Nu's was. From Burma's vantage point, there must be no winner in the competition between China and the United States, for if there is, the chameleon will surely be destroyed with the log.

Chapter 11

CAMBODIA AND CHINA

Neutralism, "Neutrality," and National Security *

BY

MICHAEL LEIFER

Cambodia is probably the example *par excellence* of a non-Communist country whose foreign policy is attuned closely to that of the People's Republic of China. Its apparent acceptance of the Chinese line should be differentiated, for example, from the policy of Gaullist France, which, from the seclusion of the European continent, seeks to thwart the United States in Southeast Asia. Cambodia's foreign policy, which has also, at times, caused considerable anxiety in Washington, operates from no less realistic a base than that which has become associated with *grandeur*. But in Cambodia's case, a deep concern with survival provides the dynamism, and a keen awareness of geopolitical realities, the rationale.

Situated at the south of the Indochinese peninsula with a coastline on the Gulf of Siam, Cambodia is a small country. Only slightly larger in area than England and Wales combined and with a population of less than six million, this Buddhist kingdom (without a king [1]),

---

* This chapter incorporates material which has appeared previously in *The World Today* (a monthly journal published by the Royal Institute of International Affairs, London), January 1964, and in *International Journal*, Spring 1962.

1. While the institution of monarchy still prevails within Cambodia, there is, in fact, no reigning sovereign. The present head of state, Prince Norodom

stands dwarfed in the shadow of the neighboring P.R.C. Cambodia's immediate neighbors are Laos to the north and Thailand and South Vietnam to the west and east. Conflict with the peoples of the two latter countries goes back many centuries, and it has been reactivated in a cold war context since Cambodia achieved independence from French colonial rule.

FROM GENEVA TO BANDUNG

Cambodia, alone of the successor states of French Indochina, emerged territorially unscathed from the 1954 Geneva Conference. Vietnam was divided at the 17th parallel, while in Laos the insurgent Pathet Lao obtained a substantial foothold in the form of regroupment areas in two northern provinces. The insurgents in Cambodia, the Khmer Issaraks, including those bands associated with the Communist Viet Minh, failed to gain either territorial advantage or *locus standi* at Geneva, and the political settlement of July 1954 meant that Cambodia would not share a border with a Communist country. Consequently, with no insurgent strongholds on its soil, and with no bordering sanctuary from which insurgents would be likely to operate, Cambodia was not faced with an immediate and pressing security problem.

In the latter part of 1954, the Cambodian government began to veer toward what her head of state has preferred to describe as a foreign policy of "neutrality." At first, it did not appear in practice to be any distinctive variant of nonalignment. But within the last three or four years, a growing preoccupation with Communist China and with the deteriorating security situation in Laos and particularly in South Vietnam has produced a shift from what might have been

---

Sihanouk, was crowned king in 1941 but abdicated in favor of his father, the late Norodom Suramarit, in March 1955. This unusual procedure was made possible by the French, who introduced a selective method of succession to the throne which did not necessarily take direct descent into account. They were thus able to arrange the coronation of princes who seemed least likely to interfere in affairs of state. The death of King Monivong Sisowath in 1941 led the French to pass over his son. They chose instead the former's grandson by a daughter married to a prince of the alternative senior branch of the royal family.

King Norodom Suramarit, who succeeded his son in 1955, reigned only five years and died in April 1960. Norodom Sihanouk, who had reassumed the title of Prince and who was then Prime Minister, again became head of state. He did not move to nominate a new king, and the institution of monarchy was held to continue through the person of the Queen Mother, Kossamak Nearireat.

considered a policy of orthodox neutralism to a policy of much closer accommodation to the regime in Peking.

In November 1954, the late Prime Minister Nehru of India visited the then King Norodom Sihanouk in Cambodia, and favorable references to a neutralist posture were heard in Phnom Penh soon after. Sihanouk reciprocated the visit just before the Afro-Asian conference at Bandung, and in a joint communique issued from New Delhi in March 1955, the Cambodian leader expressed his appreciation of India's general approach to world problems.[2] The meetings with Nehru were a significant stage in the Prince's intellectual and political development. He was to declare at a later date: "Since he [Nehru] expounded a few principles in international relations which were bearing fruit in lessening international tension I have been following them."[3] But it was not only the magic appeal of the Five Principles of Coexistence or the personality of the Indian leader which influenced Sihanouk. In 1954, according to American sources, Cambodia had asked for U.S. military and economic aid.[4] In 1955, Prince Sihanouk no longer appeared to regard Western military assistance as an immediate necessity. Since the Geneva settlement and the partition of Vietnam, the Communist Viet Minh threat to Cambodia appeared to have receded. But the dynamic presence of the powerful People's Republic of China could not be ignored, and although Cambodia had been promised the protection of the Southeast Asia Treaty Organization (SEATO), there appeared to be little point in accepting this doubtful offer until Chinese hostility had actually been demonstrated. Indeed, to shelter under such protection in a noncrisis situation might well have provoked the very hostility which Cambodia was concerned to avoid.

Prince Sihanouk went to the Bandung Conference in April 1955 disposed toward a policy of nonalignment. In his public statements there, however, he made evident his anxiety about the intentions of the Communist countries present. He declared that Cambodia was

---

2. See *Second Progress Report of the International Commission for Supervision and Control in Cambodia for the Period January 1 to March 31, 1955,* Command Paper 9534 (London: HMSO, 1955), Appendix I, p. 39.

3. *The Hindustan Times* (New Delhi), April 3, 1956.

4. In 1956, in a letter to the Cambodian Foreign Minister, Secretary Dulles asscrted: "It was Cambodia who officially requested military aid on May 20, 1954, and military and economic aid on September 1, 1954." Department of State, *American Foreign Policy: Current Documents 1956* (Washington: GPO, 1959), p. 790.

independent and neutral and, having adopted this position, had "the dangerous privilege of standing the test and application of the Pancha Shila. . . . It will be the task of the more powerful nations to set the example, to give proofs and guarantees to smaller nations." [5] This expression of concern was directed toward the Chinese and North Vietnamese delegations. Later during the conference, Sihanouk stated boldly that the practicability of coexistence would depend on the Communists. It would be up to them to reassure the rest of the world of their peaceful intentions. Chou En-lai, the Chinese Premier and head of his government's delegation, took note of these apprehensive utterances. He invited Sihanouk to lunch and assured him that China would adhere faithfully to the Five Principles of Coexistence in its relations with Cambodia. Chou's private and later public assurances [6] appeared to satisfy the Cambodian leader, and Sihanouk's subsequent behavior would suggest that the meeting at Bandung marked a turning point. He indicated as much during a speech to the Philippine Congress in February 1956. On that occasion Sihanouk pointed out: "So long as the feelings of the government of Communist China . . . are not belied by some sign of change, I cannot, as the present leader of a people which has indicated to me its desire to be neutral, a small people of only five million inhabitants, under no circumstances can [sic] rebuff the friendship of the leader of a people of six hundred million." [7] He further asserted that to join SEATO would provide the Communists with an excuse to intervene. His rationale appeared to be that as long as the Chinese were prepared to be conciliatory, there was little point in being even associated with a military organization directed specifically against China.

Prince Sihanouk's appraisal of the situation was compatible with the extent of the American desire, at that time, for commitment in Southeast Asia. After his return from the Manila conference which established SEATO, Secretary of State Dulles wrote that ". . . the responsibilities of the United States are so vast and far flung that we believe we would serve best not by earmarking forces for particular areas of the Far East but by the deterrent of mobile striking power plus strategically placed reserves." [8] The United States was prepared, however, to equip and help train Cambodia's small army, and Sihan-

---

5. Quoted in George McT. Kahin, *The Asian-African Conference of April 1955* (Ithaca, N.Y.: Cornell University Press, 1956), p. 13.
6. Same, pp. 15, 16.
7. *The Manila Bulletin*, February 4, 1956.
8. *Department of State Bulletin*, v. 31, no. 805, November 29, 1954, p. 822.

ouk was apparently willing to accept a moderate form of assistance which would not incur the antipathy of China. At Bandung, the Chinese Premier had expressed his concern at the prospect of a Cambodian military involvement with the United States, and he had received firm assurances that such an involvement was not intended.[9]

In May 1955, the Cambodian government signed a military aid agreement with the United States despite the public protests which had occurred during Secretary Dulles' visit to Phnom Penh the preceding February. In signing this agreement, the Cambodian government made clear that it had not entered into a military alliance and that the United States had not acquired bases within Cambodia. It informed the International Control Commission to this effect and noted further that Cambodia would scrupulously respect the terms of the Geneva agreement.[10] Although the aid agreement was criticized in the Chinese press as a gross violation of the Geneva accords, Cambodia was not treated harshly or depicted as a willing partner. She was pictured much more as an innocent child duped by the evil machinations of the imperialist power.[11] Meanwhile, two months after the signing of the aid agreement, Sihanouk claimed that Chou En-lai had informed him, during their meeting in Bandung, that "China recognized Cambodia's right to organise her internal defence and get foreign military instructors." [12] This evidence suggests that Peking was not much alarmed by the military-aid agreement (certainly no threat to China) and had received satisfactory assurances that military assistance from the United States would not mean the military presence of the United States within Cambodia.

ECONOMIC AND POLITICAL RELATIONS

From this time, Cambodia, situated precariously close to China, would seek security in friendly relations with the Communist power rather than risk arousing hostility by establishing too close a Western

9. In an interview reported in *Le Monde*, June 13, 1956, Sihanouk said: "During the Bandung Conference, Mr. Chou En-lai asked me during a long discussion what was this military agreement which bound us to the U.S.A. I was able to show him that we had not signed any pact of this kind and it was not Cambodia which had asked for protection of SEATO."

10. See *Third Interim Report of the International Commission for Supervision and Control in Cambodia for the Period April 1 to July 28, 1955*, Command Paper 9579 (London: HMSO, 1955), pp. 5–9.

11. See *People's Daily (Jenmin Jihpao)* editorial of June 24, 1955, *Survey of China Mainland Press* (SCMP), June 25/27, 1955, p. 39.

12. *The Hindu* (Madras), July 13, 1955.

connection. But in receiving American arms and economic assistance, it demonstrated that there existed an alternate road if Cambodia were pushed too hard—particularly by her nearer neighbor North Vietnam, which had directed insurgency throughout Indochina. According to one writer, Prince Sihanouk was informed during his first visit to Communist China in 1956 that if he had any trouble with the Viet Minh, he had only to appeal to Peking to have it stopped.[13] At this time, the Diem regime was in the process of consolidating its position, and the United States had not begun to suffer the reverses in both Laos and South Vietnam which later convinced the Cambodian leader that, for his country, this alternate road was a *cul-de-sac*. But even before then, geographic propinquity and Cambodia's innate physical weakness suggested that there was little future in being associated with ventures which were likely to antagonize the Chinese and which also had no relevancy to the security needs of the moment. As an informed American observer pointed out: "A hostile attitude towards Communist China was a luxury their statesmen would have felt unable to afford even had they wished it." [14]

Early in 1956 Prince Sihanouk made his first visit to Peking; this was followed by further visits in 1958, 1960, 1963, and 1964. In return, Cambodia welcomed Premier Chou En-lai in 1956 and in 1960 and President Liu Shao-ch'i and Foreign Minister Ch'en Yi in 1963. At the time of his initial visit, Prince Sihanouk's hosts could only have been encouraged by the Cambodian leader's public rejection of SEATO's gratuitous offer of protection. In June, their satisfaction at Sihanouk's posture was demonstrated by a grant of equipment, construction material, and merchandise equivalent in value to £8 million.[15] This grant was the first donation of economic assistance to a non-Communist country by the P.R.C.

While the major portion of economic aid received by Cambodia has come from the United States (*i.e.*, up to the end of 1963 when Cambodia requested the termination of U.S. aid), the P.R.C. has provided continuous, if moderate, assistance. Trade and payments

13. See Martin Herz, A *Short History of Cambodia* (New York: Praeger, 1958), p. 127.

14. Richard P. Stebbins, *The United States in World Affairs 1956* (New York: Harper and Brothers for the Council on Foreign Relations, 1957), p. 136.

15. See "Joint Communique Issued by the Governments of China and Cambodia on the Question of Economic Aid to Cambodia, June 22, 1956," in G. V. Ambekar and V. D. Divekar, eds., *Documents on China's Relations with South and South East Asia: 1949–1962* (Bombay: Allied Publishers Private Ltd., 1964), pp. 314–315.

agreements signed in Peking in April 1956 [16] provided for an annual exchange of goods, while the later aid agreement included the establishment of small industrial plants to produce textiles, cement, paper, and plywood. These factories are now in operation. Their working record has not been promising, but their immediate impact cannot be assessed solely in economic terms.[17]

Economic association with China produced, initially, some disturbing internal effects for Cambodia. The entry of Chinese technical missions had political repercussions. These missions served as a point of contact between the Peking government and Cambodia's overseas Chinese community of about a quarter million. The P.R.C. sought to place pro-Peking teachers and textbooks in the Chinese schools and managed to levy a charge on the overseas community to help finance aid projects in Cambodia. After a time, the Cambodian government was forced to ban political activity in the Chinese schools and censored Chinese films coming into the country. Of late, it is believed that Chinese missions behave with a far greater sense of propriety. Indeed, as far back as Sihanouk's second visit to Peking in August 1958, Chou En-lai advised Chinese residing in Cambodia to refrain from all political activities in their host country.[18] China has since provided an additional £4 million (approximately) grant for the expansion of industrial plants and has also come to play an increasing role in the economy. This growing role stems in part from China's willingness to accept Cambodian products which are difficult to export or even to sell at home—such as the output of the Chinese-sponsored factories. Since November 1963, when the Cambodian government decided to nationalize the banks and all export-import businesses, Chinese planning experts have been advising on the operation of state-controlled commercial institutions.

In November 1963, the Cambodian government also requested the United States to end its military and economic assistance programs. So far, Prince Sihanouk has not replaced the American military training mission with a Chinese equivalent but has increased the number of French military advisers. Chinese military aid has been limited and includes only light vehicles and automatic weapons,[19]

---

16. Same, p. 314.

17. See P. H. M. Jones, "Cambodia's New Factories," *Far Eastern Economic Review*, May 9, 1963.

18. "Joint Statement by the Prime Ministers of Cambodia and China issued in Peking August 24, 1958," Ambekar and Divekar, cited, pp. 32–33.

19. See *The New York Times*, December 21, 1963, and March 11, 1964; *New York Herald Tribune*, May 15, 1964.

although an offer of heavier equipment was made in December 1964. However, it would appear that Cambodia is receiving much more in the way of military equipment from the Soviet Union than from China.[20]   Meanwhile, it appears that France, not China, is to provide the bulk of Cambodia's military needs.   In January 1964, Pierre Messmer, the French Minister of Armed Forces, visited Cambodia and made a substantial offer including aircraft and tanks.   In June, Prince Sihanouk paid a visit to Paris, and there it was announced that France would provide Cambodia with credits of f.160 million.[21] This development suggests that Prince Sihanouk, while he values his country's connection with China, also feels the need to preserve some freedom of maneuver as well as to avoid, if possible, any significant Chinese military presence on Cambodian soil.   At the same time, of course, he must have a realistic notion of China's presently limited ability to fill the former place of the United States in the Cambodian economy.   He is also well aware of the rapprochement between Paris and Peking.

Although China has been the largest Communist donor of economic assistance to Cambodia, its offerings have been slight compared with the total volume of American aid.   But since Cambodia's rejection of American assistance, economic ties with China must be evaluated more on their intrinsic merits than solely in political terms, for they have ceased to be a bargaining factor in the cold war.   Still, compared with France's new role and the increasing trade contacts with East European countries, Cambodia's economic association with China should not be overvalued as a contribution to Cambodia's material development.

The P.R.C. appears to have been a model of rectitude in its attitude toward left-wing opposition groups within Cambodia.   Such forces as do exist have not received encouragement from Peking.   No Cambodian Communist party or liberation movement has received even tacit recognition.   Cambodia, unlike its neighbor Laos, has not had a tradition of warring principalities to constantly menace national unity, while a tradition of popular reverence toward the throne has been a powerful cementing factor.   National unity, however, cannot be taken for granted.   Before Prince Sihanouk consolidated his personal position by his dramatic efforts to obtain independence from the French, political activity within Cambodia had taken on a fac-

20. *New York Herald Tribune* (Paris), March 7/8, 1964.
21. *Le Monde*, July 7, 1964.

tional aspect. In March 1955, Prince Sihanouk sought to overcome this dissension and to entrench his own position by launching a mass movement known as Sangkum Reastr Niyum (Popular Socialist Community). This movement proved a successful enterprise. It has won every single seat in the three elections held since independence.[22] Opposition to Sihanouk exists primarily within Sangkum among a leftist-intellectual group, which the Cambodian leader has sought to accommodate rather than to alienate.

The only party to retain a separate identity outside the popular ruling movement has been the Pracheachon (People's Party), although it can now be regarded as virtually defunct. Its membership was drawn largely from ex-Issaraks and from the Vietnamese community in Cambodia. It had the reputation of being both pro-Communist and subservient to the dictates of the North Vietnamese regime. Prince Sihanouk permitted it to exist in a state of open proscription, at least until quite recently. He found it convenient to let the party stand as a target of popular abuse as an anti-national body. But by 1962, the Pracheachon had become so debilitated that it did not think it politic to enter any candidates in the June elections. This decision was not surprising, for five months before the elections, the leader of the Pracheachon, Non Suon (a former member of the Viet Minh), and 13 of his associates were arrested on charges of conspiring with agents of a foreign power to overthrow the regime. It was revealed that captured documents included orders from Communists abroad.[23] A month before polling day, all 14 were sentenced to death, but they got reprieves after the election.

Prince Sihanouk has fulminated continuously about plots directed against his government from Thai and South Vietnamese soil. He has been no less outspoken, at times, about alleged subversive activities directed from Hanoi. For example, in February 1960, in the presence of the Chinese ambassador—as well as other Communist ambassadors—Sihanouk declared that he had abundant proof, including Viet Minh documents, that the Pracheachon was "working indefatigably for the communist world and especially to bring Cambodia under the heel of North Vietnam." [24] And as recently as February 1965 he warned Cambodia's Communists that he would throw them

---

22. See Michael Leifer, "The Cambodian Elections," *Asian Survey*, September 1962.
23. See *Réalités Cambodgiennes* (Phnom Penh), January 19 and 26, 1962.
24. *Cambodian Commentary* (Phnom Penh), March 1960, p. 7.

out of the country unless they stopped campaigning against the government. At no time, however, has he made any complaint about Communist China. On the contrary, he has consistently remarked on the correctness of the Peking regime's relationship with Cambodia.[25] Indeed, there is reason to believe that Sihanouk sees Cambodia's association with China—which seems to fit in with Chou En-lai's design for a zone of peace to China's south—as an obstacle to Communist Vietnamese ambitions, which, since 1930, have been directed toward the whole of Indochina.[26] He evidently has some expectation that China will continue to tolerate an independent, albeit conciliatory, Cambodia within its sphere of interest and will, consequently, have an interest of its own in seeking to thwart any expansionist design emanating from Hanoi.

Sihanouk values Chinese diplomatic support in Cambodia's conflict with Thailand and South Vietnam.[27] His initial visit to Peking in 1956 resulted in a rapid and sustained deterioration of relations with these countries. The governments of Thailand and South Vietnam regarded Cambodia's association with China as a process which could culminate only in a Communist intrusion interposed between them. Cambodia, itself, was seen in the role of a Trojan horse. Its *de jure* recognition of China in July 1958 and the signing of the Sino-Cambodian Treaty of Friendship and Mutual Non-Aggression in December 1960 confirmed these feelings. Cambodia, for her part, has cause for apprehension that, in their anti-Communist zeal, the Bangkok and Saigon governments might reassert traditional territorial claims. A special difficulty has arisen out of the war in South Vietnam. The Saigon government has periodically accused Cambodia of sheltering the Communist Viet Cong, while security forces in hot pursuit have, from time to time, intruded into Cambodian territory with tragic results for the civilian population. For example, there was an incident in March 1964, when the village of Chantrea suffered a South Vietnamese ground and air attack which left 17 dead and

25. For example, see his article "How We See China," *Neak Cheat Niyum* [The Nationalist] (Phnom Penh), September 10, 1963.

26. There is evidence for this assertion in an article Sihanouk wrote for *Réalités Cambodgiennes*, July 14, 1961. In it he pointed out: "Puisque nous étions coincés entre deux pays seatistes, le Bloc Socialiste non seulement nous soutint diplomatiquement, mais encore pria (je le suppose) le Vietminh de suspendre (sans doute très provisoirement) ses activités aux côtés du Pracheachon." See also *Neak Cheat Niyum*, April 15, 1962.

27. For a fuller consideration of this conflict, see Michael Leifer, "Cambodia and Her Neighbours," *Pacific Affairs*, Winter 1961/62.

13 injured.[28]   These intrusions continued throughout 1964 and into 1965.   Diplomatic ties with Thailand were broken in October 1961, and those with South Vietnam in August 1963.   In her tempestuous relations with these two countries, Cambodia has been able to count on constant Chinese expressions of support.   These serve as a deterrent to any consideration which might otherwise be given in Bangkok or Saigon to large-scale action against their mutual neighbor.[29]

Hostility between Cambodia and her immediate neighbors has also involved the United States, with whom Thailand and South Vietnam are allied.   Prince Sihanouk has constantly asserted that the United States has it in its power to control its allies' actions.   Indeed, it was reported in 1961 that "United States ambassador William C. Trimble has found it impossible to convince Sihanouk that Washington is unable to influence Thailand and South Vietnam towards a more conciliatory tone in their relations with Cambodia."[30]   In November 1963 Cambodia, in justifying its request that America should terminate all economic and military assistance, alleged that the U.S. Central Intelligence Agency was supporting the rebel Khmer Serai (Free Cambodia) movement.   While it is known that a Khmer Serai clandestine radio station had been irritating Sihanouk, one should not discount the possibility that the downfall of the Diem regime in Saigon caused him to break the American connection.[30a]   The decision was prompted, perhaps, by fear of yet another inspired coup—this time in Cambodia.   The prospect of an imminent Western collapse in South Vietnam may also have convinced the Cambodian leader of the expediency of an even closer move toward China and her allies.   Indeed, for a while in early 1964, there was talk of establishing diplomatic relations with North Vietnam and the National Front for the Liberation of South Vietnam (NFLSV).   In September–October 1964 during his visit to Peking, Sihanouk held discussions with the North Vietnamese government and the National Liberation Front to try to arrive at a form of mutual (i.e., territorial) recognition.   He

---

28. *The Times* (London), March 24, 1964.

29. A good example of Chinese diplomatic support was the *Statement by the Government of the People's Republic of China Supporting the Fight of the Royal Government of Cambodia for the Safeguard of the Country's Independence and Sovereignty Against Foreign Intervention and Aggression*, Press Release, Royal Cambodian Embassy (London), November 21, 1963.

30. *The New York Times*, November 19, 1961.

30a. Cambodia broke off diplomatic relations with the United States in May 1965 following the publication of an article in *Newsweek* which was considered defamatory to the Queen mother.

hoped that Peking would guarantee the mutual recognition as a step toward obtaining a neutral South Vietnam, but Peking, though friendly, refused to make a formal commitment. Discussions with the Vietnamese were continued at an Indochinese Peoples' Conference held in Phnom Penh in March 1965. In these discussions Sihanouk again sought, without success, an agreement to maintain the non-Communist character of South Vietnam. Such an agreement would serve him as a way to avoid having a border in common with a regime dominated by Hanoi.

"NEUTRALITY" IN PRACTICE

In practicing his policy of "neutrality," Prince Sihanouk has sought, understandably, to combine personal with patriotic motives. He has tried to achieve some international distinction as a mediator. And, insofar as this role has coincided with Chinese interests, he has received backing from the People's Republic. He achieved some success with his proposal for a conference to determine ways to restore peace to Laos, and he had the honor of making the opening address when the conference convened in Geneva in May 1961. On his return to Phnom Penh from Geneva, he declared:

> Our nation is rightly proud of this role and of a prestige which we have not tasted since the 14th Century and this in defence of peace and justice for a brother country. With this prestige and role, we have certainly surpassed ourselves. For the first time in our history we were called upon to assume responsibilities and accomplish a job of world importance and on an equal footing with the greatest and the smallest.[31]

Although Sihanouk's colorful behavior looms large in his international public image, he does not appear to have placed personal interests before those of his country. It is well known that he can feel extraordinary enmity. For example, he announced a public holiday when the Thai Prime Minister, Sarit Thanarat, died. He also enjoys receiving great deference and being received in pomp. Although his behavior has been described as mercurial, imperious, quixotic, and, of course, enigmatic, nevertheless he has, so far, kept a realistic order of priorities in governing the foreign relations of his country. He is made of much sterner stuff than, say, Bao Dai, and

---

31. *Cambodian News* (Canberra), July 1961, pp. 5–6.

he is not likely to retire to the south of France at the first sign of trouble.

There is little that a country of the size and international significance of Cambodia can offer, in any positive sense, to reciprocate China's posture of goodwill. Cambodia has, however, advocated the seating of Communist China in the United Nations and has denounced as unjustifiable the American policy of seeking to contain China. In September 1962, Cambodia recognized China's ally (in the Sino-Soviet dispute) Albania, and at the General Assembly in October 1963, Cambodia and Albania co-sponsored the resolution to seat mainland China. At the end of 1964, the Cambodian National Congress condemned Brazil for sentencing nine Chinese nationals on charges of spying.

Prince Sihanouk has, above all, scrupulously avoided any association which might lead to friction with Peking. Late in 1959, he received an invitation from the then Malayan Prime Minister, Tunku Abdul Rahman, to discuss the formation of a Southeast Asian Friendship and Economic Treaty. The Philippines and Thailand—both members of SEATO—were among those countries which received similar invitations. Prince Sihanouk rejected the idea out of hand. He explained that to join in forming an organization known to be favored by two members of SEATO and sponsored by the anti-Communist government of Malaya would seem to be "temerarious." The official line was: "Our government believes that to create what might become a shadow SEATO would be quite disastrous." [32]

Cambodia's freedom of diplomatic maneuver is clearly not unrestricted. Indeed, the necessity to assess China's reactions seems to be the governing factor in Cambodian foreign policy initiatives and responses. This factor has become increasingly important since the Sino-Indian war broke out and since China's quarrel with the Soviet Union reached the public stage. Even before these events, however, Cambodia's attitude toward China had begun to crystallize under the influence of events in Laos during 1960 and 1961. Prince Sihanouk became convinced then that the United States—the backbone of SEATO—would not be able to maintain its position in Southeast Asia. For him, the defeat of the right-wing faction in Laos had signed SEATO's death warrant.[33] In July 1961, he commented that with the acceptance of neutrality, Laos would move

---

32. *Cambodian Commentary*, January 1960, p. 4.
33. See same, October/December 1961, p. 67.

slowly but surely along the road to "communization." When the agreement to neutralize Laos (in which the United States participated) was announced in June 1962, it was reported that nothing had happened in Laos to make the Prince alter his opinion.[34]

The Sino-Indian war, toward the end of 1962, saw Cambodia extend the practice of "neutrality" beyond the confines of the cold war to the nearer, more violent conflict. Cambodian diplomacy at the time may best be described as discreet, and local press comment displayed no obvious bias toward either side. During a visit to Djakarta, however, Prince Sihanouk informed a correspondent of the New China News Agency that, in his opinion, the P.R.C. could not be criticized for refusing to accept frontiers demarcated by foreigners. He stated that Cambodia greatly appreciated the Chinese decision to cease fire. There can be little doubt that Sihanouk was equally impressed by the Chinese military humiliation of India.

The invitation from the Prime Minister of Ceylon, Mrs. Bandaranaike, to attend the Colombo conference of December 1962 was a mixed blessing for the Cambodian head of state. On the one hand, it accorded him the international distinction which he feels is his due; on the other, it presented a grave dilemma. Participation in a conference of neutrals to consider the Sino-Indian conflict might have meant involvement in collective arbitration of a kind likely to be distinctly offensive to China. This risk certainly outweighed any personal gain Sihanouk might have achieved at a conference at which neither of the actual belligerents was to be represented. About the time of the Colombo meeting, the government weekly *Réalités Cambodgiennes* pointed out: "Good relations with China are the keystone of our foreign policy." Prince Sihanouk's posture at Colombo reflected this feeling.

When the conference convened, Prince Sihanouk carefully linked his country's position with that of Burma, which shares Cambodia's concern about China. He wisely refused to associate himself with any positive set of proposals for resolving the conflict, and he sought, none too successfully, to divert the conference in the direction of conciliation. Adamantly opposed to arbitration, he suggested that the aim of the conference should be to devise some means of inducing China and India to meet as friends. This cautious posture met with approval in China and appeared to cause no great consternation in India, where Cambodian sensitivities seem to be understood.

---

34. *Réalités Cambodgiennes*, June 15, 1962.

While visiting India in February 1963, Prince Sihanouk displayed publicly some sympathy for Cambodia's spiritual homeland. In the Cambodian government press, India was referred to as a sister nation. More significantly, however, the press stressed that "friendship with China is for us as oxygen is to a diver." From New Delhi, the Cambodian leader journeyed to Peking, where it became apparent that political necessity took precedence over cultural affinity. There, Prince Sihanouk received warm praise for his endeavors at Colombo. At a banquet, Chairman Liu Shao-ch'i described Cambodia's friendship as most precious.

During a reciprocal visit by Chairman Liu to Cambodia in May 1963, Prince Sihanouk returned to a theme he had stressed while in China. He remarked on the total absence of chauvinism in Communist China's relations with all other countries, big and small. This gratuitous gesture was gratefully received. The *People's Daily* commented: "This sincere remark of Prince Sihanouk's encourages very much the Chinese government and people."

Further evidence of Cambodia's desire to conciliate China was the announcement in April 1963 that Phnom Penh would not be the site for the Third Southeast Asian Peninsula Games. This decision arose out of differences between the Cambodian Amateur Athletic Federation and the International Amateur Athletic Federation over the hotly disputed Asian Games held in Djakarta. The Cambodian Federation refused to join in condemning Indonesia for excluding Nationalist China and Israel. The Cambodian government enjoys normal diplomatic relations with Israel, so one unavoidably concludes that Cambodia's declared reluctance to become involved in the politics of international sports was, in this case, a product of its unwillingness to condemn the exclusion of Nationalist China— an act which would hardly have endeared it to the government in Peking. The Cambodian AAF has since withdrawn from the IAAF. It also sent a team to participate in the Games of the New Emerging Forces, held in Djakarta in November 1963. Meanwhile, Cambodia's "just action" was applauded by the Chinese Physical Culture and Sports Commission and by the All-China Athletic Federation.

The Sino-Soviet split, in particular, has forced Cambodia to reconsider her diplomatic position. As to the dispute within the Communist camp itself, the Cambodian government, which receives aid from both sides (and even from Yugoslavia), has declared its neutrality. However, issues could well arise upon which it might prove impossible to maintain such an intermediate stand. The successful conclusion, in July 1963, of Soviet, U.S., and British negotiations on a partial nuclear test ban treaty presented such a situation. The almost universal adherence to the treaty, on both sides of the cold war, gave the Cambodian government no chance to adopt a non-aligned position—particularly since Communist China, echoed by Albania, North Vietnam, and North Korea, publicly denounced the accord as a "huge deceit" and "a capitulation before the American imperialists." Cambodia was forced to choose, and it decided, in view of the value of its relationship with China, to adopt the latter's stand. Phnom Penh not only refused to adhere to the treaty but denounced it as a "bargain of dupes and a demagogic act" in the same vein as the Chinese. Prince Sihanouk also echoed China's counterproposal for a world conference, to be attended by heads of government, on general disarmament.[35]

The significance that Prince Sihanouk attaches to his country's association with the P.R.C. is only too apparent in his justification of Cambodia's position on the test ban treaty. He pointed out: "All being considered, we prefer after all to be isolated *with* China rather than *against* China, who is the only country to be ready to fight at our side for our survival if this were directly threatened." [36] When the first Chinese nuclear detonation took place in October 1964, Prince Sihanouk and Foreign Minister Huot Sambath sent notes of congratulations. The atmosphere in Phnom Penh, however, was one of restrained enthusiasm. Nevertheless, Cambodia continued to support the P.R.C.'s nuclear policy. In June 1965 at a meeting of the U.N. Disarmament Commission, Cambodia voted against an Indian resolution deploring the Chinese nuclear tests, which had been carried out in spite of the resolutions adopted by the General Assembly.

Sihanouk's action on the test ban treaty and Chinese bomb tests is logical in light of his assessment of China's power in Asia. The rationale of his position was presented by the official English-language publication *Cambodian Commentary* in September 1963. It asserted that "all Asian leaders are certainly aware that the interlude in their history marked by European intervention in Asian affairs is drawing to a close and the time is fast approaching when

35. Norodom Sihanouk, "The Moscow Treaty and Us," *Neak Cheat Niyum*, September 1, 1963.
36. Same.

they will be faced with that recurrent factor: a resurgent China with which they will have to come to terms as best they may." The Cambodian government gives every indication that it is determined to face up to this view of the situation rather than to be forced to acknowledge it under less favorable circumstances.

A good example of Cambodian sensitivity to a Chinese diplomatic position concerns the proposed international conference to safeguard Cambodia's neutrality and territorial integrity. Such a conference had been advocated with strong Chinese backing from August 1962. A fundamental difficulty to convening it had been the opposition of the United States, Thailand, and South Vietnam. However, in March 1965 following the meeting of the Indochinese People's Conference and new initiatives by the British government, it seemed that a conference would be held. Up to March 17, the P.R.C. continued to approve publicly of the project. But by the end of April the Chinese changed their position because of the likelihood that a conference on Cambodia would be used for negotiations on the question of Vietnam, at a time when the Chinese were adamantly opposed to having them. At this juncture, Cambodia introduced the precondition that South Vietnam should not be represented by the government in Saigon. This move was immediately followed by a Chinese statement which insisted that only the NFLSV represent South Vietnam in any conference on Cambodia.[36a] Because of Cambodia's sense of priorities, the proposed conference had to take second place to Chinese policy on the Vietnam issue.

CHINA AND CAMBODIA'S SECURITY

There can be little doubt, as I have already suggested, that Prince Sihanouk greatly values his country's present relationship with the People's Republic of China. He appears reconciled to Chinese dominance in Asia, and he apparently believes that accommodation is the only possible policy to adopt toward a country he feels is likely to reassert a traditional role. Above all, in terms of national security, there is no real alternative. Prince Sihanouk has lost confidence in the ability of the United States to act as a countervailing force against Chinese dominance in Southeast Asia. France is certainly not equipped, or willing, to fill this role. So Sihanouk is forced into the

---

36a. *Recent Diplomatic Exchanges concerning the Proposal for an International Conference on the Neutrality and Territorial Integrity of Cambodia* Command Paper 2678 (London: HMSO, June 1965), pp. 15–17.

arms of Peking while hoping that he will not be crushed by them.

Cambodia's present association with China is also aimed at countering any predatory behavior on the part of Thailand and South Vietnam. It would seem, however, that Prince Sihanouk's most immediate fear is not of the local allies of the United States or of Communist China itself. It is of a reunited Vietnam under the control of Hanoi, whose ambitions encompass the whole of Indochina. Sihanouk has written: "Whether he is called Gia Long, Ho Chi Minh or Ngo Dinh Diem, no Annamite (or Vietnamese) will sleep peacefully until he has succeeded in pushing Cambodia towards annihilation, having made it first go through the stages of slavery." [37] The Cambodian head of state has become increasingly alarmed at the prospect of Communist takeover in Southeast Asia—particularly in South Vietnam, and he has little confidence in the ability of the West to effect a military solution.[38] In a press interview in mid-1963, he admitted that Cambodia was on friendly terms with North Vietnam because it was a "strong power." "But we could not be friendly with North Vietnam unless South Vietnam stood between our countries as it does now." [39] The following year he informed reporters: "It would be terrible if Cambodia found itself surrounded by a communist Vietnam and Laos." [40] More recently, in a reference to the very real prospect of being face to face with Vietnamese communism, he declared that "that is the most terrible kind." [41]

Prince Sihanouk is certainly well aware, at this stage, that the security of any one of the political units of Indochina cannot be effectively safeguarded independently of the others. He recognizes that the problem of Laos is bound up with the struggle in South Vietnam and that Cambodia's security is linked with both of these disputed territories. Consequently, besides his constant demand for an international guarantee for Cambodia's territorial integrity, he has offered vocal support for President de Gaulle's vague proposals for the neutralization of Indochina—proposals which have found favor in Peking. This support, however, is not unqualified but relates closely to Cambodia's security needs. In December 1963, Sihanouk claimed that De Gaulle wanted both North and South Vietnam to

---

37. *Cambodian News*, January 1963, p. 4.
38. See his article, "South Vietnam's Fate Appears Sealed," same, November 1963.
39. *New York Herald Tribune* (Paris), June 1/2, 1963.
40. Same, March 17, 1964.
41. *The New York Times*, March 7, 1965.

be neutral but that, in his own opinion, North Vietnam was already "too red." He wished to advocate a neutral South Vietnam, as well as a neutral Laos.[42] There can be little doubt that the Cambodian leader wishes desperately to avoid sharing a border with the Hanoi regime. One expectation of his continuing association with China and of his support for Chinese diplomatic positions [43] would seem to be that even if China is not prepared to guarantee a neutral South Vietnam, it will exercise a restraining influence on the Communists in North Vietnam. He evidently hopes that China, in reasserting its traditional role in the *Nanyang*, will come to interpose her power between Cambodia and the growing threat from Hanoi. In an address to the Faculty of Law of the University of Paris in 1964, Prince Sihanouk pointed out: "If our region must one day be submerged by communism, we would wish that it be China and not another socialist country which takes control of our country because we know that she understands us and that she will maintain . . . our territorial integrity." But he significantly continued: "It goes without saying that we shall try right up to the end to be the satellites of nobody." [44]

---

42. Radio Phnom Penh, December 2, 1963. (See the BBC's *Summary of World Broadcasts*.)

43. An even more recent demonstration of this support came in August 1964 after the U.S. air strike on North Vietnamese motor torpedo-boat bases. Prince Sihanouk sent a telegram to President Ho Chi Minh strongly condemning U.S. armed aggression against the Democratic Republic of Vietnam and expressing firm support for the (North) Vietnamese people's courageous struggle against aggression. (Agence Khmer de Presse, quoted by New China News Agency, August 10, 1964). He also denounced the U.S. air strikes on North Vietnam in February and March, 1965.

44. *Réalités Cambodgiennes*, July 4, 1964.

Chapter 12

THAILAND AND CHINA

From Avoidance to Hostility

BY

GEORGE MODELSKI

Thailand today has no border with China. Mountainous parts of
Burma and Laos separate the two countries. Parts of North Thailand are about 100 miles from the nearest Chinese border, and areas
in the Northeast some 300 miles. There is no scope for boundary
disputes. Although there is some communication overland, in recent
centuries most of the contact with China has in fact been by sea.
Nevertheless, China has loomed large in Thai thinking on two
accounts: as a center of political, economic, and cultural influence
and as a prolific source of migrants.

THE HERITAGE

Unlike some other countries discussed in the present volume,
Thailand draws upon a rich tradition in its relations with China.
Much of the story deals with the expansion of the "superior" Chinese
and the retreat of the "barbarian" Thais further and further south
in order to maintain their separate existence. The strong Thai kingdom of Nanchao, which maintained itself for several centuries in
Yunnan, ultimately fell under Chinese vassalage about 900 A.D.
Before the Mongols under Kublai Khan put an end to all vestiges
of autonomy by destroying Nanchao in 1253, however, Thai tribes

had begun to move south again and were establishing new polities in the area now known as Thailand. They set up capitals at Sukhothai (which served as the headquarters of a dominant dynasty between 1238 and 1350), Ayutthaya (1350–1767), and finally at Bangkok (from 1767 onward). These kingdoms too found it necessary to formalize their relations with their big neighbor. King Rama Khamheng of Sukhothai reputedly travelled at least once to the Imperial Court. When a new dynasty established itself at Ayutthaya, it was glad to secure from the Ming court at Nanking what amounted to a recognition of its new status. A pattern was soon set for tributary missions at fairly regular intervals—averaging between one and two a decade. The procedure continued under the Bangkok dynasty, and according to Chinese records, the last mission of this kind visited Peking in 1853.

Hand in hand with these international political relationships went a variety of commercial exchanges and cultural influences. But just as important has been the gradual yet continuous infusion of Chinese migrants into the social system. There is evidence of such migration from the 14th century onward—much of it part of the network of trade with the Nanyang maintained from South China, where Canton served as the entry port for Thai tributary missions. Within Thailand, migration was steadily offset by assimilation (as a result of which many members of the Thai elite have Chinese blood). It grew until early in the 20th century ethnic Chinese began to comprise some 10 per cent of the country's population. The proportion has remained fairly stable since. One author estimates that the Chinese in Thailand totaled 2,315,000 in 1955, of which 696,000 were China-born and the rest local-born.[1] This sizable minority carries on much of the commercial and industrial activity in the country, and it constitutes as much as one-half of the population of the capital city. Therefore, it is little wonder that its conduct and intentions remain among the most important preoccupations of Thai governments.

Extensive international and domestic experience has thus impressed upon Thailand the power and influence of China. But it has also helped to build up an appropriate pattern of discourse between the two. This could, until recently, be described, from the

---

1. G. W. Skinner, *Chinese Society in Thailand* (Ithaca, New York: Cornell University Press, 1957), p. 183. Thailand's is, after Malaysia's, the world's largest community of overseas Chinese.

Thai standpoint, as a pattern of keeping a more or less respectful distance, a pattern of careful avoidance.

The tributary system, it is true, amounted to an acknowledgment of the cultural and political superiority of the Celestial Empire by a large number of small "barbarian" states. "Barbarian" rulers sent missions or traveled themselves to the Chinese capital and received in return the imperial seal as a mark of legitimate authority. The system was essentially a network of relationships between unequal yet independent political entities within a hierarchical international system. Thailand not only was a tributary of the emperor but had tributaries of its own. The regular missions provided the framework for diplomacy and trade, the transmission of culture, and the management of international relations.[2] The tribute purveyed by the missions was in itself no gain to the Empire, for it had to consist of local produce (in the case of Thailand, white elephants, rhinoceros horn and camphor oil, etc.). The value of the offering was usually balanced, if not outweighed, by imperial gifts and the cost of entertaining the mission. For this reason, and also because it facilitated the diffusion of Chinese innovations (e.g., the calendar) and of some procedures of government, the tributary system in a sense operated to provide foreign aid and technical assistance.

While the system served as a framework for acknowledging China's superiority, it also kept Chinese political influence to a minimum—partly because on the Chinese side it was basically an isolationist device to limit contacts with outsiders and to keep the contacts well supervised, and partly because it was inefficient as a method of exercising influence. For instance, the official record we have of Sino-Thai relations during the reign of the Ming dynasty[3] shows no evidence of efforts to influence court politics, the selection of new rulers, or the endemic warfare with Burma. Thus, the tributary relationship did not entail Thailand's submission to Chinese domination. It is wrong to regard this relationship as a precedent for a satellite[4] system or a justification for Chinese supremacy in this region today.

---

2. J. K. Fairbank, *Trade and Diplomacy on the China Coast* (Cambridge: Harvard University Press, 1953), Chapter 2, *passim*. The views of the Chinese court about the nature and functions of the tributary system were not necessarily shared by the tributaries. Few records of missions have been preserved in Thailand, and our picture of the operation of the system comes largely from Chinese sources.

3. T. Grimm, "Thailand in the Light of Official Chinese Historiography: A Chapter in the History of the Ming Dynasty," *Journal of the Siam Society*, v. 49, pt. 1, July 1961, pp. 1–20.

4. Royal Institute of International Affairs, *Collective Defense in South East*

The traditional, agrarian international system centered upon the Chinese Empire collapsed when industrial Europe broke in upon it. As soon as Thailand entered into regular contacts with the West (beginning in 1855 with the Bowring Treaty, which freed trade), it quit sending tribute missions to China, for it had now become part of a new international system. In this system, the previously un-challenged ascendancy of the Empire was balanced by the evident weight of the Western nations.

Those who discuss contemporary non-recognition policy should bear in mind that in the past 110 years, Thailand has had official relations with the Chinese mainland for only four years. For almost a century after the Bowring Treaty, the country maintained no formal ties with Peking. At first, the Empire disdained to enter into rela-tions, on a footing of equality, with what it still regarded as a vassal state. Later, Thailand procrastinated on the grounds of internal instability in China. After the Thai constitutional coup of 1932, some delegations were exchanged between the two countries, but the Thais, now increasingly conscious of the power of the Chinese minority in their midst, refused to place this relationship on an official basis. They feared that formal relations would add to their problems in dealing with the local Chinese. During World War II, Thailand fell into Japan's Co-prosperity Sphere in East Asia, and it incurred the hostility of Chungking as a result. (There was some contact with the Japanese-sponsored Wang Ching-wei regime in Nanking, but secret links were also maintained with Chungking.) Only in 1946, as part of the postwar settlement, did Thailand ex-change diplomatic and consular missions with China. The envoys had barely taken up their posts when the power of the Nationalist regime began to wane. After the Nationalist retreat to Taiwan in 1949, the five consulates so recently established in country areas were closed, and the embassy in Bangkok lost influence. Thailand re-fused to recognize the Communist regime, and, once again, the coun-try was insulated from the Chinese mainland.

DOMESTIC VARIANTS

Speaking to a foreign audience in 1958, Prince Wan Waithaya-korn, then Foreign Minister and today still the senior foreign affairs expert, explained his country's position on SEATO and China thus:

Asia (London: Author, 1956), pp. 58–59. A satellite is defined as a state over which the dominant power "accepts no administrative responsibility but over which its authority is in the ultimate resort absolute."

Thailand decided to join in setting up SEATO with full popular support. . . . In addition to the Vietminh invasion of Laos . . . Red China about that time set up a Thai autonomous state in Yunnan . . . which was preparing for a southward expansion. Any Chinese expansion would constitute a very great danger to my country because out of a population of 22 million we have three million Chinese. . . . It is imperative therefore for the Thai government to resist any Chinese Communist expansion into Thailand . . . [and] to be a member of SEATO. But inasmuch as mainland China has 500 million inhabitants it is equally natural that there should be a feeling in Thailand that SEATO should be really defensive and not at all aggressive. That is why I tell the people at home that my policy toward Red China is not only non-aggressive but also non-provocative.[5]

This statement puts in a nutshell the attitude whose historical background we have examined—fear of China's power and intentions combined with an appreciation of its strength. Even those members of the Thai elite who have called for closer ties with the powerful neighbor in the past decade have stressed their solicitude for their country's interest and their awareness of the problems which would arise in such a relationship. For example, Thep Chotinuchit, who traveled to Peking in 1956 and then became the leading spokesman of the Socialist Opposition (1956–58), emphatically denied, on Thai television, the charge that he tried to "lead Thailand to follow in the footsteps of Red China instead of America." He insisted that "he is a Thai and he loves Thailand no less than others and therefore could absolutely not permit Thailand to be placed under Chinese influence." [6]

A highly developed sense of national interest with respect to China is, in other words, part of Thailand's political heritage. Within this tradition, nevertheless, there are at present two or three variants. Analysis of these is somewhat difficult. Free public discussion of foreign affairs has always been rare, and opposition groups have not been permitted to state their views in the open since late 1958. What we can say, therefore, represents mostly an extrapolation of the debates that agitated Thai politics in the stormy transition period of 1955–58.[7]

5. Prince Wan Waithayakorn, SEATO: *Foundation for National Strength* (Bangkok, 1958), pp. 3–4.
6. *Siam Nikorn*, November 29, 1957.
7. See also George Modelski, "Thailand's Support for SEATO" in *SEATO: Six Studies* (Melbourne: Cheshires, 1962), esp. pp. 117ff.

The ruling element in the country at present is the Military Group. This is the organizational form through which a clique of several score military men who planned and executed the 1957 *coup d'état* now govern the country. In September of that year, the Group, led by Marshal Sarit Thanarat, overthrew the government of Marshal Pibul Songram. It still has a fixed membership and holds regular meetings, but little is known about its procedures of discussion. After Marshal Sarit's death (December 1963), the Group continued in being under Sarit's deputy, General Thanom Kittikachorn, who was promptly promoted to Field Marshal.

In contrast to the uncertainties of policy in 1955–58, when Thailand seemed to be heading for a neutralist position, a break with SEATO, and a rapprochement with China, the policies of the Military Group have led unambiguously toward firmer association with the United States and the severance of all links with Communist China. The Group justified its assumption of power by charging that the Pibul government tolerated "clandestine contacts with Communist elements." In a broader sense, the continuation of its rule has since been legitimized in part by the sense of national emergency created by the events in Laos and the dispute with Cambodia and by China's involvement in both situations. Hence the Sarit government did not find it difficult to end all trade with and personal travel to mainland China in January 1959. Both had flourished in the last years of Pibul's rule. To give the Chinese minority a kind of alternate focus of loyalty, links have to some extent been taken up with Taiwan—even to the point of a royal visit in 1963.

But in the main, the Military Group's basic attitude toward China has been that evolved by nationalistic military men who, with slight interruptions and with varying degrees of civilian participation but with considerable continuity of personnel, have ruled the country since 1932. Fear of the powerful neighbor to the north and the affluent minority in Thailand was a mainspring of Pibul's anti-Chinese measures in 1938–40,[8] 1947–49,[9] and 1952–53. It also dictated at each of these points the search for an appropriate external alignment.

The broadly nationalistic approach of the Military Group has been largely supported by the civil bureaucracy, which forms the bulk

---

8. It is of some interest that the foremost spokesman of Pibul's anti-Chinese measures in 1938, Vichitr Vadakarn, served, after 1958, as Sarit's most influential adviser.

9. In November 1947, alarm over growing (Nationalist) Chinese influence, which stemmed from the establishment of diplomatic relations, was used to justify the overthrow of Pridi Panomyong by a military group led by Pibul.

of the Thai (as distinct from the Chinese) middle class. The military elite and the civil bureaucracy are, in any event, linked in a symbiotic relationship, for whatever government holds power must establish rapport with the civilians who, in their various departments, oversee the daily life of the people. Also part of the ruling group in Thailand, interestingly enough, are the Sino-Thai merchants. Many of them participate in business ventures jointly with members of the Thai military and civilian elite. They supply the capital and the know-how, and the Thais the political connections. (The Chinese minority as such does not, however, partake in Thai politics, and no Thai politicians would wish to appeal for its support.) Since they are part of the ruling group, both the civilian and the Sino-Thai merchant elites would support the China policy of the Military Group.

Somewhat outside this presently dominant cluster, though to a large degree in accord with it, are the Democrats. They are the only semi-open political party which dates back to the early postwar years. Their attitudes are most clearly identifiable in the person of their chief spokesman, Khuang Aphaiwong, thrice Prime Minister in 1944–48. In some ways, they are the most sophisticated and cosmopolitan, conservative and even royalist group in Thailand. They have been identified with the status quo at home and with pro-Western policies abroad. To that extent, they stand somewhat apart from the ruling military-civilian clique, which tends to be more purely nationalistic and may on occasion be more radical. In 1955–58, the Democrats took up a well-defined, anti-Communist Chinese stand, and they effectively attacked their opponents for "selling out to the Chinese" at home and abroad. As a result, they incurred voluminous attacks for being "feudalists" and "hangers-on of the Western powers."

At the other end of the political spectrum we must place the left opposition to the Military Group. Broadly speaking, it includes those groups and individuals who would follow the leadership of the Communists and/or of Pridi Panomyong. Such information as is available about the Communist movement in Thailand suggests that a preeminent role within it is played by ethnic Chinese. During World War II, a Chinese Communist party was active in Bangkok side by side with a Thai, and earlier even a Malayan, Communist party.[10] Since about 1950, the few published references have been

_____

10. A brief account of the "national liberation and workers' movement" in Thailand "where the Chinese workers have been and still are playing the most

to the Communist party of Thailand, but the influence of its Chinese members may account for the fact that the party is now ranged on Peking's side in Sino-Soviet controversies and that it is comparatively ineffective within the country. Its strength cannot be compared, for instance, with that of the powerful parties of Vietnam or Indonesia or even with that of the Pathet Lao. If Vietnamese or Laotian analogies applied, the party would operate publicly through a variety of fronts and groups rather than under its own name.

In this respect, it may have found useful the cooperation of Pridi Panomyong, a senior Thai statesman who has lived in China (more recently in Canton) since 1949. Pridi has been a top-ranking politician since 1932, when he was a member of the group which abolished absolute monarchy. In World War II he was Regent of Thailand (and at the same time the head of the pro-Allied underground movement), and in 1944 he engineered the overthrow of Pibul. He himself fell victim to Pibul in 1947.

Throughout his career Pridi has been associated with phases of policy that came as close to being pro-Chinese as is practicable in a Thai context. While Foreign Minister in 1936–38, he presided over an important exchange of visits with China. The establishment of diplomatic relations in 1946 took place under his auspices, and the first ambassador to Nanking was one of his closest collaborators. In 1949 he once again turned to China (instead of, for example, India, of which we might surmise he knew little and thought less).[11] Thereby he decided, in effect, that those who regard themselves as "out" of the regime in power should look toward China as their source of succor and inspiration.

Pridi staged his Peking debut in 1954. A few days after the signing of the Geneva agreements on Indochina he published in the *People's Daily* an article which created a great stir in Thailand. He pointed to the success of the Democratic Republic of Vietnam and emphasized that the "alleged threat to Thailand's independence . . ." from China and Vietnam was "a fabrication of the reactionary government of Thailand." The relations between these three countries, he argued, should be based upon the Five Principles of Coexistence then in vogue in Sino-Indian relations. He then continued:

important part" is given in N. A. Simoniya, *Overseas Chinese in Southeast Asia—A Russian Study*, Data Paper, no. 45, (Ithaca, N.Y.: Cornell University, 1961), pp. 104, 106–108. See also V. Thompson and R. Adloff, *The Left Wing in Southeast Asia* (New York: Sloane, 1950), pp. 51ff.

11. His visa for the United States was canceled at the last moment.

In order that Thailand can peacefully coexist with the other states on the basis of the above-mentioned Five Principles the Thai people must wage struggle against American imperialism which is holding Thailand in its grip and the reactionary government of Thailand which is subservient to American imperialism. Only by doing so will they be able to do away with forces that place obstacles in the way of Thailand's progress towards peace, independence and sovereignty.[12]

Pridi's article was the opening shot, and a statement of aims, of a skillful campaign to regain a position in Thai politics. That campaign, waged from China, lasted until 1958.[13] For a while, the policies he advocated were echoed by a variety of voices up and down the country (including those of Bangkok's journalists and of the famed Hyde Park speakers), and they seemed to be gaining strength. But in the end, Pridi failed. As the situation seemed to be getting out of hand internally and as alarm spread over Cambodia's recognition of Communist China and over the coup which took Iraq out of the Baghdad Pact, Marshal Sarit struck in force in October 1958. The left opposition, still largely a matter of small counter-cliques rather than of popular movements, found itself in jail or was forced underground or into exile.

A lull set in and lasted until 1964. A Thai Exiles Association functioned in Vientiane for a few months in 1960, but the exigencies of the Laotian civil war compelled its members to seek the protection of the Pathet Lao in the Plain of Jars. The tempo of political warfare quickened only after a station using the name "Voice of the People of Thailand" (Siang Prachachon Thai) began transmissions in March 1962, probably from Laos or China. Its messages have from time to time been reported by Chinese news media in a manner implying endorsement. Peking, of course, has its own separate radio service in Thai; this service broadcast two and a half hours a day on up to six frequencies early in 1965.

In October 1964, in one of its rare public statements, the Communist party of Thailand announced its willingness "to cooperate with any groups or individuals that are against the U.S. imperialists and their lackeys" and its readiness "to work hard for the formation of the patriotic democratic united front." A few weeks later the

---

12. Nai Pridi Panomyong, "The Geneva Conference and the Future of Thailand," *People's Daily (Jenmin Jihpao)*, July 29, 1954.

13. For more details, see Modelski, cited, pp. 124–127.

"Voice" broadcast a manifesto of the "Movement for the Independence of Thailand" calling upon all "patriots and democrats" to work together to "expel the American imperialist aggressors from Thailand," to "unseat the traitorous and despotic government of Thanom," and to "struggle for neutrality, peace, democracy and the prosperity of the people." A "Patriotic Front of Thailand" was set up on January 1, 1965, to implement such a program through the efforts of "all Thai people who love peace and democracy irrespective of political or religious affiliation." [14]

None of these reports mentioned names of participants, and in the absence of such information the import of the reports is hard to evaluate. At the very least, they signify a stepping up of Chinese-sponsored pressures upon Thailand. One clue as to the leadership, however, did come to light when, after a period of quiescence lasting for several years, Pridi Panomyong once again surfaced in Canton in early 1965. At that time the New China News Agency reported that he had called upon the North Vietnamese consul to express support "for the Vietnamese people's struggle against the U.S.A." Thus far Pridi has not publicly endorsed the Patriotic Front, but his reappearance suggests that to some extent he still lends his name to China-based opposition activities even if the executive and operational direction of the newly intensified campaign may lie elsewhere—possibly with leaders of the Communist party and with men like Thim Puripat who were active in parliamentary opposition politics in the 1955–58 era and then escaped abroad.

Adjoining Laos and inhabited by Lao-speaking people, the northeastern provinces of Thailand are regarded as particularly susceptible to the activities of this opposition. So is the South, which is inhabited by a Muslim minority and by Chinese, some of whom have links with the Malayan Communists. Reports of arrests in these two areas have increased. News about the recruitment of young people—some just out of high school—for political training in China has also been featured in Bangkok newspapers. Until now, political change in Thailand has resulted from fissures within the elite itself. These have often been influenced by foreign developments, but they

14. The message from the Communist party of Thailand on the occasion of China's National Day was reported by the New China News Agency (NCNA) on October 1, 1964, and may be found in *Current Background*, no. 744, pp. 33–35. The text of the manifesto of the "Movement for the Independence of Thailand" and the report of the foundation of the "Patriotic Front of Thailand" were published in *People's Daily* on December 14, 1964, and February 5, 1965, respectively.

have occurred in the Thai arena. For the first time, some Thais are now actively at work to overturn the system from without with foreign (to a great extent Chinese) help. For internal support, they are appealing to segments of the Thai public (*e.g.*, farmers in the Northeast) so far largely uninvolved in the political struggle.

ISSUES IN SINO-THAI RELATIONS

A basic issue of Sino-Thai relations is, of course, the question of recognition. Since 1950, Thailand has followed a policy of non-recognition of the mainland regime. By contributing an armed contingent to the U.N. force in Korea, Thailand has also been engaged in hostilities with Communist China. In 1955–58 the policy of non-recognition was under active review and was relaxed somewhat. The ban on exports of rubber was lifted, and other exchanges were initiated with official acquiescence. Foreign affairs spokesmen assured critics that the question of recognition would be considered as soon as Communist China was seated in the United Nations. But the debate died down after 1958.

As was shown earlier, Thailand has reasons to continue its non-recognition policy. Recognition would be a means of conciliating Communist China and thus possibly reducing Peking's backing for adversaries like Cambodia or the exile groups in Laos and in China. Such hoped-for benefits would remain uncertain, however, and the possible effects of recognition upon the Chinese minority might outweigh them. A certain degree of tension, moreover, serves to legitimize the "emergency" features of the present government. On balance, non-recognition is still a viable policy that would be abandoned only if outside pressures for a change became overwhelming (as they did in 1945–46).

A major issue awaiting settlement is the status of the Chinese minority. A treaty similar to the Sino-Indonesian Nationality Treaty of 1955 represents one way of attacking the problem, for the mainland government regards ethnic Chinese, regardless of their birthplace, as Chinese nationals unless an agreement to the contrary has been negotiated. The Indonesian treaty permits an individual to choose either state as his homeland. In the post-Bandung period, Thailand was offered a treaty on similar terms, but so far it has been unwilling to discuss the matter. The issue must, therefore, await developments on the question of recognition.[15] Delaying recogni-

---

15. See David A. Wilson, *China, Thailand and the Spirit of Bandung*, RAND P-2607 (Santa Monica: RAND Corporation, July 1962), pp. 55–57.

tion might, in the absence of immigration, speed up assimilation and thus improve the conditions upon which an agreement might finally be reached.

Since the "Great Leap Forward" and the ensuing economic trouble, trade with China has hardly been an issue in Thailand, but it might become so again. Officially, no trade takes place between the two counties. Hong Kong, of course, serves as the entrepôt through which some goods might be exchanged.[16] Nevertheless, the ban on trade has cut links with the mainland which the Chinese trading community would naturally have cultivated. (The purpose of this ban was not simply to stop trade with Communist China. It was designed to prevent Chinese financing of political activities in Thailand.)

An issue which caused much confusion during 1953–54 was the so-called "Free Thai State of Yunnan." In Prince Wan's speech cited above, this "state," "preparing for a southward expansion," still figured as one of the major causes of fear about Chinese intentions toward Thailand. For several years it served as a major argument for those who saw the future of the area in terms of the territorial expansion of China.

The flurry of excitement over the "state" arose from a routine item circulated by the New China News Agency early in 1953. This item announced the formation of a "Thai nationality autonomous area."[17] A number of similar administrative units for minority groups had been created throughout China. The event would hardly have attracted notice except that the Bangkok government, thinking it recognized the hand of Pridi seeking to create a power

16. In 1958, before the ban and at the high point of the Chinese trade offensive, imports from China were estimated at about 5 per cent of total imports; see D. Insor, *Thailand* (New York: Praeger, 1963), p. 138. In 1960, imports from Hong Kong (which might include a quantity of goods of mainland origin) comprised about 6.5 per cent of total imports of that year, and they were valued at about U.S. $30 million. In recent decades, trade with China has not been important to the national economy, for Thailand's most active business partners have been Malaysia, Japan, the United States, and Britain. Trade with Taiwan rose recently, but it is still at a low level. The value of imports from Taiwan was U.S. $3.7 million in 1960 and U.S. $19 million in 1962.

17. NCNA, January 31, 1953, in *Survey of China Mainland Press* (SCMP), no. 505, pp. 22–24. In status equal to a "district," the area comprised 20,000 sq. km. It was then inhabited by some 200,000 people, one half of whom were ethnic Thais. For contemporary comments, see E. F. Stanton, "Spotlight on Thailand," *Foreign Affairs*, v. 30, no. 1, October 1954, pp. 77, 80; W. J. Donovan, "Our Stake in Thailand," *Fortune*, v. 52, no. 1, July 1955, p. 94. For a report on the recent status of the area, see a UPI dispatch from Hong Kong, *Bangkok Post*, May 28, 1963.

base of his own, chose to regard it as a threat to Thailand. The event was frequently quoted, both by Thais and by foreign observers, in discussions of Chinese aims and in justifications of Thailand's alignment with the West. Calling it a matter of "grave concern," Thai spokesmen referred to this "threat" twice before U.N. organs—in June and September 1954.

It seems clear that as far as the government was concerned the matter was shelved after Premier Chou En-lai's assurances to Prince Wan at Bandung. No connection has been established between Pridi and the "state." The issue has not been raised again, and it would hardly be worth mentioning except that it still crops up in discussions of Chinese motives in standard works on Southeast Asia.[18]

While Peking may have been innocent of promoting the "southern expansion of the Thai state," there is little doubt about its support of opposition movements seeking to overthrow the present Thai government. Pridi Panomyong and those working for him and with him have enjoyed Communist Chinese patronage for more than a decade, and we need not suppose he has been China's only iron in the Siamese fire. Chinese agents have been reported among the northern hill tribes. Pathet Lao and North Vietnamese activities directed against Thailand's integrity (inasmuch as the loyalty of the Lao in the Northeast might be affected) must also have Chinese concurrence.[19] Finally, Cambodia could not have become so utterly hostile (regardless of Thailand's intentions toward her) were it not for the Soviet and Chinese support which Prince Sihanouk has repeatedly called his most reliable source of protection. Subversion and political warfare present real issues for anyone who would regulate affairs in this region.

The Chinese Communists are highly sensitive to the state of the Thai-American alliance. There is reason to believe that membership

18. See V. Thompson and R. Adloff, *Minority Problems in Southeast Asia* (Stanford University Press, 1955), pp. 220ff.; J. K. King, *Southeast Asia in Perspective* (New York: Macmillan, 1956), pp. 193–195; Klaus Mehnert, *Asien, Moskau und Wir* (Stuttgart: Deutsche Verlags-Anstalt, 1956), pp. 367–370; A. Vandenbosch and R. Butwell, *Southeast Asia among the World Powers* (Kentucky University Press, 1958), p. 164; C. Wolf, Jr., *Foreign Aid: Theory and Practice in Southern Asia* (Princeton University Press, 1960), p. 206; Oliver E. Clubb, Jr., *The United States and the Sino-Soviet Bloc in Southeast Asia* (Washington: Brookings Institution, 1962), p. 34.

19. Some connections between the Viet Minh and Thailand are discussed in G. Modelski, "The Viet Minh Complex" in C. E. Black and T. P. Thornton, eds., *Communism and Revolution* (Princeton University Press, 1964), pp. 199–200.

in SEATO (as for instance, in the case of Pakistan) would not, by itself, be an obstacle to normal relations with the P.R.C. But very close military cooperation—and in particular the stationing of U.S. forces in Thailand—would. Until a few years ago Thai governments, while benefiting from American military assistance and playing host to foreign combat units during SEATO exercises, have been reluctant to permit the stationing of troops or the establishment of bases in their country. But during the Laotian crisis of 1962 they allowed themselves to be persuaded to the contrary, and since May of that year United States and other forces have been in Thailand —in mid-1965 some 9,000 men in Air Force and engineers' units.

In April 1962 Peking was already warning Bangkok that it was entering upon "a dangerous road," but the landing of Marines the following month brought forth an outburst of exceptional virulence. "Drive the U.S. aggressors out of Southeast Asia" cried the *People's Daily* in a widely circulated editorial. "The Chinese people . . . absolutely cannot tolerate the establishment by U.S. imperialism in areas close to China of any new military bridgeheads spearheaded against this country." Retaliation against "this serious threat to the security of China" was clearly hinted at in the assertion that "there is no doubt that the broad masses of the people of Thailand will not submit to the rule of U.S. occupation forces without any resistance." [20]

Subversion linked to the question of foreign military presence, as well as the status of the Chinese minority, will thus be the substance of Sino-Thai relations in the coming decade.

SUSPICIONS OF DUPLICITY

Thailand has been a member of the "free world" since 1950, and its policies in respect to China have paralleled those of the Western powers from that time onward. Thai governments, however, have been careful not to overextend their commitments. They have not, for example, subscribed to a guarantee of Nationalist China's territorial integrity on Taiwan. The Thais did not favor an extension of the treaty area of SEATO to Taiwan, and in the 1958 crisis over Quemoy they showed little interest in coming to the defense of the offshore islands (which they had no obligation to do). Later on, though, they cooperated with the United States in supporting General

20. *People's Daily*, May 19, 1962, in *Current Background*, no. 688, pp. 46–47.

Phoumi Nosavan in Laos—just as they may have helped arrange supplies for Nationalist irregulars in Burma earlier.

In fact, Thailand has proved itself to be one of the most reliable allies of the United States. There would be little else to say if it were not for the few years of ferment after 1955—years known in Thailand as the "Era of Democracy." This period, as has been mentioned, was the time of stirring neutralism, doubts about SEATO, and rising contact with Communist China. Only a few years before, the police of General Phao Sriyanond had been most keen to prosecute those even remotely linked to Communist causes or to Communist China. Now they closed their eyes to open propagandizing and undisguised movement to and from the mainland. Those who remembered that Thai leaders operated a pro-Allied underground movement during World War II, while they were formally allied to Japan, suspected foul play.

We have seen that one justification of Marshal Sarit's 1957 coup was Pibul's alleged dealing with Communists. In the years since then, no hard evidence has come to light on this point, and what we know on the subject came chiefly from Sarit himself. He stated that the former government (of which he himself had been a member) had encouraged some people to go to China and that he believed it true to say that General Phao had been "involved." [21]

Prince Sihanouk's recent disclosure of a statement made to him by Chairman Mao Tse-tung, at an official audience but on an unspecified date, provides an additional piece of evidence. The Chinese leader reportedly gave the Cambodians a free hand against South Vietnam, but he counseled caution in dealings with Thailand:

If you wish to punish Ngo Dinh Diem you can go there openly and count fully on our help and support. As for the Thais we hope that you will soon reach agreement with them. It is worth dealing tactfully with them for underneath they do not want an alliance with the Americans. Those who visit us here assure us that they have been forced and constrained to submit to this alliance imposed by force and they will try to be rid of it as soon as possible so that they can adopt the same policy of neutrality as Cambodia. [22]

21. *Bangkok Post*, November 25, 1957.
22. This statement is the "substance" of the interview as related by Prince Norodom Sihanouk in "Thailand and Us," *Cambodian News*, v. 3, no. 12, December 1962, p. 5. At the time he wrote the article, the Prince had visited Peking

Mao's remarks must have referred to the visits which occurred in 1956–58, yet we also know that only few of the Thais who went to China at that time had high standing. Among those whose travels attracted attention were a basketball team, a delegation of labor leaders, a group of entertainers, some students, some Buddhist bonzes, and some opposition members of parliament. The most important of the last group was Thep Chotinuchit, a Cabinet member in an earlier Pibul government. After high level talks in Peking, Thep became the leader of the Socialist Opposition, but he was arrested in October 1958 and is still in prison. Thep's opposition to the alliance was hardly a secret, but it is doubtful that he could have acted in Peking as the spokesman of members of the ruling group.

The most direct accusation of treachery and behind-the-scene dealings with Communist China has been made by C. L. Sulzberger. It appeared in a column he wrote after a few days' visit to Thailand shortly after Sarit's coup.[23] In a piece of writing unusual for its sharpness and directness (Phao was described as "a superlative crook" and Sarit as "a relatively clean scoundrel"), Sulzburger hinted that Sarit might be engaged in treacherous contacts:

> Diplomats . . . have no evidence he is dealing with China. (For some time they had none on Pibul.)

These suspicions rested upon the following analysis:

> Since . . . [Sarit's coup] SEATO has discovered there was treachery in its midst. . . . Gen. Phao Sriyanond, boss of the police and a sort of local Beria, has been dealing with Communist China. Some say this was merely to enlarge his personal fortune. Nobody knows the whole story. The blatant fact is that one of Thailand's key officials was in some kind of negotiations with SEATO's announced enemy. It can only be assumed that Pibul, the dictator, was *au courant*. Meanwhile, newspapers backed by Pibul, by Phao and by Sarit were merrily attacking the West.

The column attracted attention, particularly in Thailand, and some kind of reply was called for. Thanat Khoman, the ambassador

three times—in February 1956, August 1958, and December 1960. He saw Mao Tse-tung on each of these occasions. Circumstantial evidence points to August 1958 as the likely date of Mao's statement.

23. "Thoughts in the Jungles of Asia," *The New York Times*, November 6, 1957.

to Washington (and the present Foreign Minister), made a dignified reply to what he called an "irresponsible" attempt at "character assassination":

> The Thai people believe in the merits of gratitude which in our view enhances the dignity and stature of those who practice it. We are grateful and loyal to those who have been good and kind to us. At the same time we do not easily forget those who abuse us.[24]

Nobody, of course, knows the whole story. But if we recall the large number of individuals from NATO and other countries who have visited Peking or Moscow, we might tend to minimize the whole incident. Nevertheless, we have here a diplomatic situation in which all parties—the Thais themselves, their allies, and their adversaries (both the Chinese and the Cambodians)—believe that the Thais incline to a certain "smartness" and tend to "cave in" or change sides easily under pressure.

All states, and small states in particular, do so; but according to persistent "expert" opinion, fortified by rumors and by witticisms that flourish on the cocktail-party circuit, Thailand is more prone to it than others.[25] We could have here an instance of the self-fulfilling prophesy.

Dispassionately viewed, the evidence for this alleged tendency is weak. Such confusion as did arise in the years we have discussed resulted from the progressive decline of the Pibul regime and the struggle for power that ensued between his lieutenants. External allegiances became issues in it. But once this struggle was over, debate ceased, and the opposition collapsed. Since 1958, Thailand has been a strong ally, and suspicions have remained unfounded. Indeed, such suspicions may recently have caused it to be especially circumspect. On occasions of disgruntlement with certain Western policies (for instance, in September 1962, after the United States had shipped arms to Cambodia), there has been talk of trade and other contacts with the Soviet Union, but practical links with that country are still tenuous. Differences over Vietnam, Laos, and Indonesia militate against closer political understanding. Thailand's ties with the Soviet Union, in fact, are weaker than those of most other Asian, Middle Eastern, and West European states. The Cuban crisis of October

---

24. Letters to the Editor, same, November 30, 1957.

25. We may recall that in 1949 Stewart Alsop described the cave-in policy thus: Thailand, who "worked with Japanese to save fuss, may do it with the Communists too." (*New York Herald Tribune*, July 24, 1949).

1962 saw Thailand promptly ranged behind the United States. Developments in the Sino-Soviet dispute may make desirable a strengthening of links with the Soviet Union, but so far there have been few signs of a move in that direction.

Thailand may yet change its policies as other states have done before. (Its behavior in the Second World War, it should be noted, was akin to that of such small European powers as Denmark, Belgium, Rumania, and Bulgaria.) Its diplomacy, after all, has to keep adjusted to changes in the trends of world politics and must be alive to the possibility that the great powers on which it is relying may weaken in their support, but there is nothing in its record that justifies crass suspicion.

SOURCES OF NEW POLICIES

The sources of new policies lie in two directions: domestic and international. At home, periods of transition between regimes have, in the past, proved unsettling. Marshal Sarit's untimely death was followed by a smooth transfer of authority to his deputy, and the new government has pledged to continue the established policies. According to the official declaration, the government will "carefully observe all treaty obligations" and "will promote friendly relations with other nations through peace based on justice, truth, freedom of the Thai nation, welfare of the people and security of the country." [26] But it may be too early to say that the regime has been stabilized. If a struggle for power develops within the Military Group, China policies might become an issue.

Our examination of Thailand's heritage has brought out the strength and the persistence of the pattern of careful avoidance. Until recently this type of behavior was characteristic of both sides. China largely ignored Thailand, and Thailand avoided gratuitous offence or needless provocation. The pattern is now changing into one of overt and undisguised hostility, however, as a consequence of the spiraling war in Vietnam. Thailand's involvement in the war has been limited but nevertheless significant—because of the difficulties with Laos and Cambodia and because of the presence of U.S. Air Force units on Thai territory. Chinese warnings of "terrible consequences" of "complicity in the U.S. war in Vietnam" [27] have not remained empty words. Peking's blatant sponsorship of the

---

26. *Bangkok World*, December 20, 1963.
27. Commentator in *People's Daily*, April 28, 1965, in SCMP, no. 3448, p. 46.

"Patriotic Front" in a manner which makes it an organization parallel to the Pathet Lao and the National Front for the Liberation of South Vietnam (NFLSV) shows that the recipe for national liberation wars now being tested in Laos and South Vietnam is about to be tried in Thailand.

In past years the alternative alignments open to Thailand were basically three: American-Western, Chinese-Communist, and Indian-neutralist. The first of these proved the most persuasive. The Chinese alignment had, with the qualifications noted earlier, some support, but this support was never strong enough to sway policies. The neutralist line proved least convincing, even at the time of dissatisfaction over Western policies in Laos. Some Thai leaders, such as General Prapart Charusathien, advocated an "independent" foreign policy, a "Thaist" foreign policy, as a way of expressing their wish for more freedom of action on the world stage. Yet they did not propose "neutralism" or favor the rejection of treaty links with the United States or SEATO. Their basic concerns for maintaining national security and for avoiding a confrontation with Communist China were satisfied through the existing arrangements.

In the past Peking sought to further its aims in Thailand in the same way in which it went about seeking the cooperation of, say, the Pakistani, Cambodian, or Burmese governments—with the hope of achieving changes in Thai foreign policy as the result of political evolution in Bangkok. Chairman Mao Tse-tung's statement quoted above illustrates this policy rather well. But some time ago, possibly following developments in Vietnam and the Laotian crises of 1961–62 but also in response to aspirations to promote the world-wide "revolutionary struggle of the oppressed peoples against U.S. imperialism," this policy must have been reviewed, and the decision taken to prepare the ground for a "national liberation war" in Thailand, too.

A landmark of the new policy was the *Manifesto of the Thailand Independence Movement*, issued in November 1964. It was prompted evidently by the deteriorating situation in Vietnam and, as it explicitly stated, by China's first nuclear explosion. "Our struggle," read the *Manifesto*, "is by no means an isolated one. This is especially evident in the light of China's recent atomic experiments which has already created for us a more favorable situation in the international arena." [28] The Movement, which originally repre-

---

28. "Manifesto of the Thailand Independence Movement," *People's Daily*, December 14, 1964.

sented the Left Opposition, joined with the Communist party of Thailand in the "Patriotic Front" for what must be an attempt to mount an armed struggle in the Thai countryside—first of all, no doubt, in the North, the Northeast, and probably also the South. In April–May 1965 Lt. Col. Phayom Chulanond, described as a representative abroad of the Patriotic Front and known to be an old-time supporter of Pridi, was feted in Peking, where reportedly he established contacts with representatives of the NFLSV in China. He also travelled to Ghana to attend a conference of the Afro-Asian People's Solidarity Organization. Following his appearance, the Patriotic Front gained its first international success by being admitted to membership in that organization (to which the NFLSV already belonged).

The year past has witnessed a dramatic and unprecedented change in Thailand's relations with China. China has now set the stage for yet another guerrilla conflict. Unless the war in Vietnam is settled soon on the basis of a negotiated settlement, the flames of that war could ultimately engulf Thailand.

Chapter 13

YUGOSLAVIA AND CHINA
The Wreck of a Dream

BY

JOHN C. CAMPBELL

Yugoslavia is a small Balkan country of less than 20 million people. At first glance, Yugoslav attitudes toward mainland China, huge in area, population, and potential power, might seem of no great consequence. The undeniable importance they have rests not on any relationship of size or of power, not on the bilateral dealings of these two states with one another, but on the different and changing situations in their relations with the Soviet Union. It stems primarily from the peculiar position of the Yugoslav state, under Communist leadership, as a heretical and "revisionist" element outside what has been called the Communist camp and from the emergence of Communist China, for reasons strangely parallel, as a more serious challenge to Communist unity but at the same time a bitter enemy of Yugoslavia. The special significance of Yugoslavia's position derives also from its ambitious efforts to play a world role as a neutralist state, a leader of the nonaligned of Asia, Africa, and, more recently, Latin America.

Yugoslavia's leaders, from the time of the Communist conquest of China, were interested in the Chinese "road to socialism"—not so much because they expected to learn from it or were fascinated by doctrinal questions in themselves as because those questions reflected relationships of power and leadership in the Communist world upon which the existence and success of Yugoslavia's own brand of socialism might well depend. This interest has been almost entirely confined to the Tito regime. Indeed, the people of Yugoslavia have had hardly any attitude at all toward China except indifference based on ignorance or vague hostility based on racial differences. China is so far away, its civilization is so alien, contacts with it have been so scanty, that the world of the average Yugoslav citizen does not encompass it. He is much more concerned with how socialism as practised by the Tito regime will affect him, for good or for ill; with the friendships and enmities of the local Yugoslav and Balkan scene, most of which are deeply rooted in history and thus in the popular consciousness; with the looming presence of Russia in the East and the attractions of the West; and with the continued independence of his country. China has come into this picture only on the outer edges: as ally or enemy of Moscow and as proclaimed protector of an annoying, generally despised neighbor, Albania.

For the Communist leaders of Yugoslavia, however, the concern with China is broad and deep. From the standpoint of public posture and Marxist interpretation of history, they regard the coming to power of the Chinese Communists as a liberating socialist revolution against feudalism, capitalism, and imperialism. They have continued to back the Peking regime's right to take over Taiwan and to represent China at the United Nations. From the standpoint of political realism, however, they look at China, above all, in its relationship to Yugoslav independence. They are alarmed by Chinese pronouncements and policies which appear to threaten that independence in one way or another. And also, for the simple reason that they are Communists, they have had to pay attention to the shaping of communism in China and to the developments in policy and in doctrine which have made them, the Yugoslav leaders, a prime target of Peking's propaganda offensive against "traitors to Marxism-Leninism."

In its early stages, before the Soviets and Chinese openly directed their fire at each other, the great revisionism controversy within the Communist world centered on the Chinese view of Yugoslavia and the Yugoslav view of China, although in many of the Chinese polemics Tito and Yugoslavia have served as euphemisms for Khrushchev and the Soviet Union. Both views may be distorted, but they happen to be based solidly on concepts of national interest and on interpretations of Marx and Lenin to suit those respective concepts. In the Yugoslav case, as in the Chinese, it is necessary to search them out amid the mass of ideological verbiage with which the two parties and propaganda machines have inundated each other.

THE GREAT HOPE: CHINA AS AN ALLY

Mao Tse-tung and his cohorts completed their takeover of the Chinese mainland in the autumn of 1949. It was at this time that the Soviet-Yugoslav dispute was revealing itself in all its bitter antagonism, beyond all hope of compromise—at least so long as Stalin and Tito headed their respective governments and parties. The Soviet Union had just denounced its mutual assistance treaty with Yugoslavia, and the satellite states of Eastern Europe were following suit. In November the Cominform, holding its second meeting to deal with the Yugoslav affair, called upon the Yugoslav workers and peasants to throw out the Titoist clique of spies and murderers and return their country to democracy and socialism.

To Tito and his colleagues, China had all the earmarks of a natural ally, one with which they would feel more comfortable than with the Western powers. Mao had won his own civil war without the help of the Soviet army. He had had his differences with Stalin in the past and might have more in the future. After all, China was a potential great power with national interests of its own. Was it not likely that those interests would clash with Russia's and with Stalin's concept of Communist orthodoxy just as Yugoslavia's had? Did not Mao have a common interest with Tito in avoiding Soviet domination? Such, at any rate, was the hope of the Yugoslav leaders. They were not beyond dreaming of a Communist world in which there would be three recognized centers of independent Marxist thought and practice—Moscow, Peking, and Belgrade.

Unfortunately for Tito, this love affair was rather one-sided. Even before they won control of all the mainland, the Chinese Communists made clear where they stood in the Soviet-Yugoslav dispute. They stood with Stalin and the Cominform. They denounced Tito as a Fascist and compared him to Chiang Kai-shek.[1] While it was

1. H. Arthur Steiner, "Mainsprings of Chinese Communist Foreign Policy," *American Journal of International Law*, January 1950, pp. 86–87. Liu Shao-ch'i's *Internationalism and Nationalism* (English edition, Peking, 1951), written in 1948, accepted uncritically Stalin's policy toward Yugoslavia, though it vigorously defended the complete independence of nations (see Allen S. Whiting, "Contradictions in the Moscow-Peking Axis," in John H. Hallowell, ed., *The Soviet Satellite Nations: A Study of the New Imperialism* [Gainesville, Fla.: Kallman Publishing Co., 1958], p. 147).

true that they were not subordinating themselves to Stalin's dictation, about the last thing they wanted at the time they were consolidating their newly won power and establishing their new institutions was a dispute with the Soviet Union. That relationship was uncertain enough—Mao Tse-tung was soon to visit Moscow for crucial negotiations on its terms in mutual obligations and support—without China's giving signs of sympathy with Tito. When Yugoslavia, on October 5, 1949, proposed the establishment of normal diplomatic relations, Peking did not deign to reply.

Though disappointed at Peking's rebuffs to their friendly advances, Tito and his colleagues stuck to their conviction that Communist China's appearance on the world stage would validate their view of the future socialist world as a commonwealth of independent states. It was China as the maker of its own policies, whatever those policies might be, that intrigued Belgrade. Indeed, ignorance of what was actually taking place in China was the most notable thing about the Yugoslav attitude. There were no Yugoslav diplomats in China, no party ties, no journalists to give first-hand reports. Yugoslavia had no corps of Far East experts either in party ranks or in institutions of learning and research. The Yugoslav press, in 1949 and 1950, was filled with laudatory articles about the great Chinese revolution, its heroic leaders, and the building of a great new socialist power. With a naiveté recalling their earlier devotion to the Soviet Union, Yugoslavia's Communists glorified the new China which had defeated the reactionaries and the imperialists and presumably would defeat Stalinism. They supported the seating of Communist China in the United Nations because, among other reasons, to deny it would only serve Stalin's hegemonistic policy of isolating China and preventing it from playing an independent role in world affairs.[2]

Years passed, and there was no change in China's attitude toward Yugoslavia. Then Stalin died, and there were signs of change in Soviet policy. Khrushchev went to Belgrade in 1955 to blame the past on Stalin and heal the rift with Tito. The preceding December, Communist China had established diplomatic relations with Yugoslavia when this action would no longer be taken as an anti-Soviet move. The Chinese initiative was, of course, in tune with the current Bandung phase of Chinese foreign policy, during which Peking

---

2. Edward Kardelj, statement to a representative of National Broadcasting Company, *Borba*, November 25, 1950. Also see Kardelj's *Problemi Na'še Socijalističke Izgradnje*, v. 2 (Belgrade: Kultura, 1954), p. 316.

was ahead of Moscow in preaching peaceful coexistence.[3] The important point is that the new cordiality in Yugoslav-Chinese relations had nothing to do with any common front against the Soviets.

CHINA AND YUGOSLAVIA IN EASTERN EUROPE, 1955–57

When Vladimir Popović, Yugoslavia's first ambassador to Communist China, arrived in Peking in June 1955, he got a hearty welcome. Yugoslavia, by this time no longer the pariah of the Communist world or the "lackey of the imperialists" though still outside the bloc, had just been formally accepted by Moscow itself as a proper socialist state entitled to follow its own Marxist-Leninist road. China's acceptance of a tie with Yugoslavia illustrated its increasing desire to play a role of its own in the affairs of the socialist camp—in Europe as well as in Asia. The Chinese leaders chose to act at a time when they were not sure what they wanted to accomplish, when Eastern Europe was in a state of flux, when Soviet policy was marked by great confusion and uncertainty (partly because of the continuing struggle for power within the leadership group), and when the Soviet-Yugoslav conflict, despite the agreement supposedly reached in Belgrade, was by no means resolved.

While there has been a flood of recent revelations flowing from charges and countercharges in the Soviet-Chinese quarrel, no full and accurate account of China's role in Eastern Europe can yet be written. There is evidence that the Chinese in 1956 encouraged and supported the idea of greater autonomy for the satellite states, especially Poland.[4] In doing so, they were following the Yugoslav line in some degree, although they did not condone Yugoslavia's neutralism or its acceptance of Western aid. They showed no animus against Yugo-

---

3. In the context of the current open Soviet-Chinese dispute, the Chinese say that in 1954 it was Khrushchev who proposed to them that they improve relations with Yugoslavia "for the purpose of winning it back to the path of socialism;" China did so, although "we did not entertain very much hope for the Tito clique even then." See "Is Yugoslavia a Socialist Country?" *People's Daily* (*Jenmin Jihpao*), September 26, 1963.

4. The Chinese have since asserted that the Soviet leaders made the "grave error" of great-power chauvinism "by moving up troops in an attempt to subdue the Polish comrades by armed force" ("The Origin and Development of the Differences between the Leadership of the CPSU and Ourselves," *People's Daily*, September 6, 1963). Earlier statements of Chinese support for the Polish position came mainly from Polish sources (see Flora Lewis, *A Case History of Hope: The Story of Poland's Peaceful Revolution* [New York: Doubleday, 1958], pp. 182–184, 218).

slavia at this stage once Khrushchev had declared, at the 20th Soviet Party Congress in February, that that country was entitled to find its own road to socialism. The authoritative *People's Daily*, in a long analysis of the Stalin era based on discussions of China's top leaders, pointed to Stalin's handling of Yugoslavia as one of his major errors.[5]

After the Hungarian revolt of 1956, however, Chinese attitudes toward Yugoslavia showed signs of turning sour. Peking's declaration of policy issued in December emphasized its overriding concern with the solidarity of the bloc and the struggle against Western imperialism. Although the references to local diversity and the need for avoiding "great-power chauvinism" must have been pleasing to the Yugoslavs, there was no doubt of China's opposition to the ideas of separatism which Yugoslavia's policies had done so much to encourage in Poland and Hungary. Tito's attacks on "Stalinism," on socialist countries, and on many of the Communist parties, said the Chinese, could only lead to a split in the movement. "Clearly, the Yugoslav comrades are going too far." [6]

The main purpose of Chou En-lai's Europeon tour in early 1957 was to help reestablish the unity of the bloc "under the leadership of the Soviet Union." This line was definitely not Tito's, and Belgrade was not among the capitals which Chou visited. It was some time, however, before Yugoslav-Chinese relations felt the drop in the political temperature. The Chinese seemed to share Khrushchev's hope that Yugoslavia could be brought into closer alignment with the "camp," and they publicly wished the Yugoslavs well in building socialism. The Yugoslav ambassador in Peking had friendly contacts with Chinese officials, including leaders of the Communist party, with whom he could have frank discussions. Numerous delegations exchanged visits between the two countries. The Chinese, however, were not automatically following the Soviet line. They did not rejoice over Khrushchev's ousting of Molotov in mid-1957, one of the reasons for which was the latter's unreconstructed view on reconciliation with Yugoslavia.

Nothing in the direct relations of the two countries could explain the rather sudden hostile turn in China's attitude toward Yugoslavia

---

5. "On the Historical Experience of the Dictatorship of the Proletariat," *People's Daily*, April 5, 1956. See Whiting, cited, pp. 145–146, and Donald S. Zagoria, *The Sino-Soviet Conflict 1956–1961* (Princeton University Press, 1962), p. 55.

6. "More on the Historical Experience of the Dictatorship of the Proletariat," *People's Daily*, December 29, 1956.

in late 1957. The cause, in the Yugoslav view, lay in China's internal affairs, which were marked at this stage by purge and terror and by the need for foreign revisionist devils to blame.[7] Probably it lay also in the broader context of the evolution of the Communist bloc. Both the Soviet Union and China were desperately searching for the right kind of glue to hold the bloc together at a time when each was alarmed by the implications of the recent events in Eastern Europe, uncertain of its course in domestic policy, and suspicious of the prospective role of the other. Their policies were beginning to diverge on major questions of strategy even at this early date. To the Chinese, Yugoslavia more and more represented a hostile and dangerous force, although the Yugoslav regime was making every effort to keep relations on a normal and friendly basis. The Chinese leaders were approaching a critical period, involving great risks, in both internal and foreign policy. Their greatest needs were for discipline and sacrifice at home and for support from Communist brethren abroad. Tito's Yugoslavia, with its relaxed and pragmatic search for new forms of socialism and its disruptive influence on the bloc, could have no place in this scheme of things.

It is interesting that at this very time—the months preceding the Moscow meeting of November 1957—the Soviet leadership was trying to patch up relations with Tito, which were strained because of the Hungarian crisis and the Imre Nagy affair. The Chinese, on the other hand, seemed more and more concerned about revisionism. At it turned out, Tito decided not to go to the Moscow conference at all, for he knew that neither the Soviet nor the Chinese leaders were prepared to meet his terms and that Yugoslavia could not meet theirs. At Moscow the Chinese apparently were much tougher on the subject of "revisionist Yugoslavia" than the Soviets were,[8] and the violence of their attacks on Tito in the spring of 1958 gave the world an early glimpse—though it did not realize the full significance of that glimpse—of Soviet-Chinese differences made manifest in differing attitudes toward Yugoslavia.

For the Yugoslavs, the turn in Chinese policy put an end to many illusions. With the Moscow Declaration, especially its strong condemnation of revisionism and its insistence on the unity of the socialist camp "headed by the Soviet Union" (points strongly pressed

---

7. Such was Tito's view given in an authoritative speech some years later. See *Peti Plenum Centralnog Komiteta Saveza Komunista Jugoslavije* (Belgrade: Komunist, 1963), pp. 25–27.

8. Zagoria, cited, pp. 148–151.

by Mao Tse-tung himself), the die was cast. The subsequent program of the Yugoslav League of Communists, adopted in April 1958, merely elaborated their own road to socialism and confirmed, in the eyes of the Chinese, their incorrigible revisionism. In May, the Chinese came forth with a violent attack which, among other things, called the Cominform resolution of 1948 "basically correct." [9] In June, Ambassador Popović left China on the instructions of his government. Not a single Chinese official saw him off at the Peking airport.

From this point on, the Yugoslavs began to see in China much that they had been unable or unwilling to see before. Journalists and scholars began to publish first-hand reports in the press. For the first time, the Yugoslav people had the chance to read descriptions of what the building of socialism in China actually meant in human terms: the breakup of family ties; the senseless drive for production goals which could not possibly be met; the exploitation of man by man on a scale never approached in any society, capitalist or socialist; the cheapness of human life, the only resource of which China has a plentiful supply; the depth of the regime's fierce pride and of its hatred of outsiders. This period was, of course, the frenzied one of the Great Leap Forward.

Makso Šnuderl, a respected professor at the University of Ljubljana who had visited China, wrote a series of candid articles. In them, he drew a frightening picture of a totally disciplined anthill society in which the people, driven unceasingly to fulfill the regime's impossible economic goals, lived on backbreaking labor and canned slogans, if they could be said to be living at all.[10] The publication of such articles as these showed that the Yugoslav leaders were no longer going to maintain the myths about China they themselves had fostered.[11] Information on what was actually happening in China had

9. "Modern Revisionism Must Be Repudiated," *People's Daily*, May 5, 1958.
10. "From a Journey through China," *East Europe*, January 1959, pp. 31–39. The original articles appeared in *Slovenski Porocevalec* (Ljubljana), August 14–19, 1958.
11. It is interesting that the most serious scholarly study of China written during this same period contains only relatively mild criticism of the Chinese leadership. It attributed the mistakes of the Great Leap Forward and even the anti-Yugoslav campaign largely to Chinese isolation from the rest of the socialist world, ignorance of economic laws, and overemphasis on the role of manpower. See Sonja Dapčević-Orešćanin and Puniša A. Pavlović, *Narodna Republika Kina* (Belgrade: Kultura, 1960), especially pp. 228–239. Mrs. Dapčević-Orešćanin's later work, *Sovjetsko-kineski Spor i Razvoj Socijalizma* (Belgrade: Institut za Medunarodni Politiku i Privredu, 1963), deals directly with the Soviet-Chinese dispute along the lines of the established Yugoslav views.

been available in the West, but the Yugoslavs regarded all such stories with suspicion. Although their officials were in friendly contact with Americans and their scholars had available to them a large body of American research and writing on China, American influence on Yugoslav thinking and policies seems to have been negligible.

YUGOSLAVIA AND THE THIRD WORLD

To understand the depth of the Chinese-Yugoslav antagonism, it is necessary to go beyond the realm of ideology to the more practical aspects of foreign policy. Yugoslavia, from the early 1950s onward, had been developing a calculated and well-advertised policy of positive neutralism. Its initial content was merely dissociation from military blocs of East and West. But Tito was not content with that. He saw Yugoslavia as a partner or leader of states with an interest in avoiding domination by, or alignment with, any of the great powers. In 1954, he made his first visits to Egypt and to India. In the following years he revisited those countries, and he also went to Burma, Indonesia, Ceylon, and a number of African states. He played host to a succession of visiting heads of state and other dignitaries from Asia and Africa. With Nehru and Nasser, he sought to form a sort of high directorate of the nonaligned. Begun during the period of hostility toward the Soviet Union, this policy was pressed without letup even after Yugoslavia started to move toward reconciliation with Moscow. While disclaiming any desire to form a bloc, Tito was certainly interested in being a leader of the new international political force which the emerging Third World was coming to represent.

The Chinese Communists, who had taken a conciliatory line toward neutral states at the Bandung Conference in 1955, were not so concerned about the growth of neutralism; in fact, they applauded it as a means of breaking down the positions and interests of the Western powers. Their line was Afro-Asian solidarity against imperialism and colonialism. But Yugoslavia did not fit into that picture. Tito's attempt to inject his country into Asia as a self-proclaimed Marxist state denouncing great-power blocs and asserting its solidarity with countries like India, Burma, and Indonesia annoyed and occasionally infuriated Mao and his colleagues. What business had Yugoslavia—a state which was neither Asian nor, in their eyes, properly socialist—in mixing into the affairs of a part of the world where China had vital interests in ways which could only be deleterious to those interests? China, not Yugoslavia, was to be the leader and model of these nations' struggle for independence and their march to socialism. What influence could Yugoslavia have on them and on their Communist parties other than to turn them against China?

The spectacular climax of Tito's efforts to assert Yugoslav leadership among the nonaligned countries, and indeed in the councils of the world, was the "summit" conference held in Belgrade in 1961. It did not accomplish very much, but behind the speeches and the show there had been a good deal of solid work by the Yugoslavs. Their parliamentary and labor union delegations and their trade missions turned up in country after country in Asia, the Arab world, and Africa. And most of the visits were returned. The constant Yugoslav themes were the common struggle for peace and coexistence, repudiation of blocs, identity of views on international problems, and cooperation in the United Nations. Yugoslavia extended loans and embarked on modest technical aid programs in some of those countries, and there is no question that Yugoslav ideas went along with the diplomats, trade experts, and technicians. Whatever the communiques said—and they never mentioned China—the Chinese Communists had their own interpretation of what was going on. According to a Yugoslav source, a Chinese "Handbook of Current Events," published in 1958, called the Yugoslav policy of active coexistence "nothing other than an anti-Soviet and anti-Communist policy, whose prime objective consists in sabotaging peace and the solidarity of the progressive forces throughout the world" and in inducing "the governments and political parties of certain Afro-Asian countries to embark on the pro-imperialist, pro-American, anti-Soviet and anti-Communist road." [12]

SOCIALISM AND WAR

By 1959, the Yugoslav Communists were prepared to bury their hopes for good relations with China for some time to come. They decided to place before the world a detailed statement of their own ideological position and to indict Communist China, by name, as their enemy and the enemy of all peace-loving nations. The task

12. Statement of an official spokesman of the State Secretariat for Foreign Affairs, *Review of International Affairs* (Belgrade), February 1, 1959, p. 29.

fell to Edvard Kardelj, who wrote with an authority second only to that of Tito himself.

Kardelj's tract, *Socialism and War*,[13] was both a defense against China's "campaign of political attack" and a counteroffensive to show up Chinese policies as provocative of war and as directed against "the entire front of the international policy of present-day socialism." Thus the Yugoslav Communists, at a time that they were being denounced as revisionists by Moscow as well as by Peking, took upon themselves the task of speaking for "present-day socialism" against the Chinese.

The Chinese attempt to force their policies on others, said Kardelj, had nothing to do with Marxism. Their claim to be the only true interpreters of Marx and Lenin was but a specious claim to a monopoly of truth—a relic of the Stalin age, which had passed away for good. Their ultra-radicalism was but sectarianism expressed in pseudo-revolutionary phraseology, and it bore no resemblance to scientific socialism. What they were trying to do, in Asia and Africa as in Yugoslavia and elsewhere, was to force on other nations policies which resulted from specific Chinese conditions and state interests and had no validity for those nations. They were out of harmony with the aims of socialism. They represented a drive for Chinese hegemony in the socialist world.

Kardelj then set out, quoting copiously from Lenin and adducing the "objective conditions" of today under which the progress of socialism in the world must be pursued, to disprove the Chinese arguments on the inevitability of war with the capitalist states, the necessity of armed revolution, just and unjust wars, aid to revolutionary forces rather than to bourgeois regimes in the colonial world, and the expansion of the area of socialism by force. The Chinese positions on these matters, he pointed out, resembled those of Stalin or of Trotsky, while the Yugoslav positions were firmly grounded in the ideas of Lenin. It is worth noting that they were also consistent with some of those recently expressed by N. S. Khrushchev.

Kardelj does not always do justice to Chinese positions; it has been pointed out that his book tells us more about communism in Yugoslavia than in China.[14] The salient fact is that he seemed to be reading China out of the Communist bloc and his country back in

---

13. Edvard Kardelj, *Socialism and War* (Belgrade: Jugoslavija, 1960).
14. Book review by John W. Lewis, *Journal of Asian Studies*, May 1964, pp. 468–469.

at a time when Moscow was still hurling charges of revisionism at Tito. What he advocated was not only a Yugoslav policy, he said. "This policy, one might say, is even the official policy of the socialist camp." [15] In attacking Yugoslavia, he argued, the Chinese were attacking all other Communist parties and the elementary interests of the peoples of all socialist countries. It was China, not Yugoslavia and apparently not the Soviet Union either, whose course was full of deviations and distortions in the development of socialism.

The socialist world of our time, according to Kardelj, was confronted with "a fateful historical dilemma." It could choose China's way, which, whether the Chinese leaders admitted or desired it, led inevitably to "resolving" the world's contradictions between socialism and capitalism by war; or it could choose Yugoslavia's way, that of progressive internal development of each country within a system of peaceful coexistence, "the only way which corresponds to the spirit and the direct interests of socialism and present-day civilization." [16]

YUGOSLAVIA AND THE SOVIET-CHINESE DISPUTE

The arguments of *Socialism and War* bear a striking resemblance to two other polemics which have shaken the Communist world. The first is the Yugoslav defense and counterattack against the denunciations and pressures which previously came from Moscow: "The current Chinese anti-Yugoslav campaign," as Kardelj said, "has taken over the thoroughly discredited legacy of the Stalin campaign of 1948 and subsequent years." [17] The second is the later Soviet condemnation of the dogmatism and adventurous policies of Peking. These comparisons, while not parallel in every detail, are valid enough to bring out the inadequacy of dealing with Chinese-Yugoslav relations as a bilateral affair. It is necessary to keep an eye at all times on the third party concerned, the Soviet Union—especially in the past few years when the Communist world has been rent by the Soviet-Chinese dispute. Where do Yugoslav attitudes and policies fit into that picture?

Soviet-Chinese differences, though already deep by the late 1950s, first began to come into the open in 1960. At the congress of the Rumanian Workers' party in June, Khrushchev openly clashed with the Chinese representative. At the meeting of 81 Communist

15. *Socialism and War*, cited, p. 112.
16. Same, pp. 147–149.
17. Same, p. 207.

parties in Moscow that autumn, the debates were sharp, and the compromise wording of the ensuing declaration, reached only after painful negotiation, merely papered over the continuing differences. Yugoslavia, so far as anyone could tell from the text, could take no comfort from these events, for it was again condemned as the revisionist archenemy of the international Communist movement. Yet the fury of the continuing Chinese denunciation of the Yugoslavs was not matched in the Soviet Union.

It was in that year, 1960, that Hoxha and Shehu, the top Albanian Communist leaders, made their choice for China and successfully weathered an attempt to unseat them which was apparently backed by the Soviets, although the public blame for it was gratuitously bestowed upon Yugoslavia, Greece, and the American Sixth Fleet.[18] Soviet criticism thereafter was directed more and more toward Albania, while the Chinese redoubled their fire on Belgrade. Thus began the game of insult by proxy. The Soviets and the Chinese heaped upon the Albanians and Yugoslavs, respectively, the abuse they really intended for each other, and Tirana and Belgrade replied in kind. If there was one question certain to inflame the Yugoslavs against China, it was that of Albania. The torrent of scurrilous invective coming from its tiny but troublesome neighbor, combined with the obvious threat to Yugoslavia's territorial integrity, could only infuriate the Yugoslavs. Resentment against the Chinese for their support of Hoxha bit even more deeply into their souls than had their bitterness at all the charges of revisionism and treason to Marxism-Leninism. Chou En-lai brought it to a climax by using his visit to Albania in 1964 to shout insults at the Yugoslavs.

Whatever may have been the motives of the Chinese Communists' fierce attacks on Yugoslavia, the Yugoslavs reacted in the obvious ways: they became more embittered than ever against China, and they began to think about closer relations with the Soviet Union.[19] The arguments of Kardelj's book were embellished and repeated

18. William E. Griffith, *Albania and the Sino-Soviet Rift* (Cambridge, Mass.: The M.I.T. Press, 1963), pp. 47–48. Recently the Chinese have explicitly accused the Soviet leadership of having tried in 1960 to "subvert the leadership of a fraternal party and country" [Albania] ("Letter of the Central Committee of the CPC of February 27, 1964 to the Central Committee of the CPSU," Peking Radio, May 8, 1964).

19. Viktor Meier, a keen analyst of Yugoslav policy, argues that the real purpose of Kardelj's tract was to open the way to a rapprochement with Khrushchev. See William E. Griffith, ed., *Communism in Europe: Continuity, Change, and the Sino-Soviet Dispute*, v. 1 (Cambridge, Mass.: M.I.T. Press, 1964), p. 47.

again and again in the press. Yugoslav politicians and journalists took every opportunity to go beyond ideological argument to speak of the inhumanity of the Chinese leadership and of the system they had imposed on their people. What kind of Marxists were these, as Tito had asked as early as 1958, who presumed to hand out lessons in Marxism to others, but Marxism interpreted "in their own inhuman way"? [20] The idea that the Chinese were beyond comprehension and somehow sinister and inhuman reflected a deep sense of being European which the Yugoslav Communists shared with their own non-Communist countrymen. It was a feeling of aversion that had something in it of the old fear of the Turk, difficult to describe and document but nonetheless real.

The theme of "Oriental" despotism callous to human values as well as to true Marxism was a congenial line of argument to the Yugoslavs, one they had followed in their impassioned pronouncements in the struggle against Stalin. They were frankly shocked by China's drive for nuclear weapons and her apparent indifference to what nuclear war would mean. Talk about war as a necessary means of bringing about the triumph of communism for those who might survive was no comfort to a nation of less than 20 million almost certain to be wiped out. Whether or not Mao Tse-tung ever said that China could lose 300 million in such a war and still have 300 million left to inherit the earth and enjoy communism, Tito, as an illustration of the Chinese leadership's cynical indifference to human life and values, made a point of accusing the Chinese leaders of saying it.[21] What about the hundreds of millions of workers and peasants of other nations who would be wiped out along with the capitalists? What about the common treasures of civilization that would be destroyed? [22]

The Yugoslav criticisms of China set the pattern for the Soviet campaign against Peking which came into the open at the 22nd Con-

20. Speech at Labin, June 15, 1958, in Josip Broz Tito, *Govori i Članci*, v. 13 (Belgrade: Naprijed, 1960), p. 311.

21. Tito's first reference to the alleged statement, which he did not attribute specifically to Mao, appeared in his speech at Labin (same, p. 312). Mikhail Suslov, in the Soviet statement of February 14, 1964, refers to a remark by Mao to Nehru, repeated by Mao at the Moscow conference of 1957, that "even if half of mankind was annihilated, the other half would remain . . . and socialism alone would exist" (*Pravda*, April 3, 1964).

22. Speech at the Seventh Congress of the Union of the Youth of Socialist Yugoslavia, *Borba*, January 24, 1963 (English translation, Belgrade: Jugoslavija, 1963), pp. 13–14.

gress of the Soviet Communist party in 1961 and continued *crescendo* thereafter. A comparison of Kardelj's *Socialism and War* with the fundamental Soviet documents on China shows a remarkably similar set of arguments: the need to avoid nuclear war and coexist with the capitalist world at this stage of history, the dangers of adventurism, the possibility of advancing socialism by peaceful competition, the advantages of tactical cooperation with bourgeois regimes in the developing countries, the folly of sterile dogmatism, and the need to follow the true spirit of Marxism-Leninism rather than the distortions of it of which the Chinese Communists were guilty. We need not assume that the Soviet leaders got their ideas from Tito and Kardelj; nor should we attribute to Yugoslavia the role of stalking horse or disguised spokesman for the Soviets. The Soviets had come gradually to regard Chinese policies with the same concern as the Yugoslavs did, and when the time arrived for them to speak directly about and to China, instead of Albania, they found their own interpretations and interests running parallel to those of Yugoslavia whether they liked it or not.

It was only natural, then, that a rapprochement in Yugoslav-Soviet relations should take place. Tito, for various reasons, was ready for it, and Khrushchev, knowing what the Chinese reaction would be, deliberately undertook it. Soviet statements soft-pedaled talk of the evils of revisionism as exemplified by Tito. Khrushchev himself, who in 1958 had called Yugoslavia a Trojan horse of imperialism and in 1960 had joined in condemning Yugoslav revisionism in the 81-party statement issued in Moscow, began to refer to it as a proper socialist state. In May 1962, he issued what amounted to a public invitation to bury the hatchet. In December, when Tito made his triumphal visit to the Soviet Union, Khrushchev in his presence asked the Supreme Soviet the rhetorical question, "If Yugoslavia is not a socialist state, what is it then?" He then said that because the means of production were in public hands and political power was assumed by the workers and peasants, there could be only one answer.[23] During his visit to Yugoslavia in 1963 he reemphasized the point. His statements came at a time when the Chinese were specifically describing Yugoslavia as a state which was restoring

---

23. *Pravda*, December 13, 1962. See also the authoritative statement of the Soviet Communist party which Suslov made on February 14, 1964: ". . . not only is Yugoslavia a socialist state, but the position of socialism is being strengthened" (Same, April 3, 1964).

capitalism, licking the boots of the American imperialists, and trying to destroy the unity of the international Communist movement. The next step for the Chinese was to call Khrushchev himself a renegade, a "splitter," a restorer of capitalism, and a man who was leading the Soviet Union along the Yugoslav path.

On the Yugoslav side, there was an evident desire not to be smothered in this fraternal embrace, but there were also persuasive reasons for satisfaction. Politically and, one might say, sentimentally, Tito could not help feeling pride and gratification at being received in Moscow, whence in the past he had been denounced as traitor, imperialist spy, and running dog of American capitalism, as a great leader in the world socialist movement. But the strongest reasons for the turn in Soviet-Yugoslav relations lay in the dispute in which both Yugoslavia and the Soviet Union were now engaged with Communist China. Each found that its own national interests and its own role as a socialist state were being threatened by China, and their common reaction drew them together. Of course, when Khrushchev, according to the Chinese, became the most infamous "splitter" of all socialist history, Tito's prominence as the world's greatest sinner in this respect was somewhat diminished.

As the Yugoslav Communists see the Soviet-Chinese dispute, it is not strictly a bilateral conflict but a clash between dogmatic and progressive views within the Communist movement, of which they still consider themselves a part. The Soviet Union, which in Stalin's time stood for dogmatism, has now come over to the progressive side as a result of the evolution of its own society and policies. The Yugoslav position in the basic conflict, they say, has been clear for many years, and their identification of China as the proponent of dogmatism came as early as 1957. All these developments do not mean that they are rejoining any Soviet bloc or recognizing Moscow's leadership of international communism. On the contrary, they insist on their independence as a state and as a party.

THE COMMUNIST FUTURE AND CHINA'S PLACE IN IT

Is Yugoslavia's present antagonism toward China likely to be a momentary or a lasting phenomenon? How do the Yugoslav Communists look upon the China of the future? They know well enough that the future will not be barren of surprises, that changes in leadership in any Communist state (including their own) may bring changes of direction.   Yet they remain Marxists in their "scientific" views on the inevitable advance of socialism.   The question is what kind of socialism it will be.   And here the European background of the Yugoslav leaders and the vital factor of their relations with their own people come to bear on their attitudes.

It is only because the Soviet Union and the nations of Eastern Europe have so greatly modified earlier "Stalinist" positions, both in the domestic order and in foreign policy, that Tito and his colleagues have made common cause with them against China.   It is only because Yugoslav Communists have, since 1948, initiated and permitted trends in Yugoslavia itself which (despite the continued dominant role of the party) have paid some heed to the wishes and hopes of the people that they can feel any solid basis for the future of their country and of their movement.   Yugoslavia is in Europe and will have to find its future in Europe, in tolerable relations both with the Soviet Union and its Eastern European neighbors and with the West. Hence the Yugoslav regime's great hopes for an easing of the cold war.   Hence its doctrine that socialism is gradually moving ahead everywhere, on both sides of the line, and there is no need to fight about it.   Hence its desire to make common cause with the emerging nations and to see them develop independently of the great powers and with their own types of socialism.

It is this area of the struggle, the so-called Third World, where the fundamental differences are clearest.   Both Yugoslavs and Chinese appear to have the same basic purpose: to support the liberation of Asian and African peoples from Western imperialism and neo-colonialism and to encourage their progress to socialism.   One might think there is only a difference over method, over how to help the new nations chase the imperialists out and build socialism.   But that appearance is only on the surface.   Actually, each has a policy which grows out of its own national position and its own search for a role on the world stage.   Yugoslavia is unique in being the only European country and only Communist country which has deliberately sought to be a leader of the new legion of the nonaligned, not as an outsider offering protection or currying favor but as one of the group.

This aspect distinguishes the Yugoslav approach from the Chinese, as from the Soviet.   For the Yugoslavs, the ties with India, Egypt, and the other neutralist states are an integral part of a foreign policy which enables them to assert their independence against both East and West in Europe and to speak in world affairs with a voice far louder than their numbers or resources would justify. Tito's trip to Latin America in 1963, limited to four countries which showed promise of greater independence (of the United States) in foreign policy, was an effort to extend the neutralist Third World into the Western Hemisphere and also to foreclose that region to Peking or to Moscow.[24]

While the Yugoslav message is vaguely socialist, its prime emphasis is on cooperation with nationalist movements and national governments. The Yugoslavs accept Nehru's "socialism" or that of Ne Win, Nasser, Ben Bella, or Sekou Touré as legitimate national variants of the general trend toward a socialist world; therefore, they argue, there is no need for a proletarian internationalism which requires alliance with Moscow, much less with Peking. The Chinese have been courting those same movements and governments, but they have also been preaching a militant revolutionary ideology and cultivating left-wing elements. China, as the Yugoslavs see it, is trying to do to those countries what they had resisted from the Western side—align them in a great-power bloc, "with all that goes with it: a rigid 'common platform,' a leading power and its right to determine the norms of behavior of others." [25]

During the period before the open split between Moscow and Peking, Yugoslav forays in Asia and Africa had been in competition with both and were denounced by both. The Yugoslav version of socialism, which was authoritarian but also experimental and nationalistic, was in many ways a more attractive and less dangerous model for developing nations than the Soviet or the Chinese, as the Yugoslavs did not hesitate to point out. "In you," Ben Bella is reported to have said on a visit to Yugoslavia, "we recognize ourselves." [26] In Africa the Yugoslavs took care to establish party ties, as well as governmental relations, with one-party states such as Ghana and Guinea.[27]

Once the Soviet Union and Communist China were in fierce competition in the area, however, the Yugoslav effort and influence tended to become in many ways a supplement, though not an ap-

---

24. The four countries were Brazil, Chile, Bolivia, and Mexico. Cuba, unfortunately (from the Yugoslav standpoint), had moved past neutralism into the Soviet camp.

25. *Komunist* (Belgrade), May 21, 1964.

26. Tanjug dispatch, March 6, 1964.

27. William E. Griffith, "Yugoslavia," in Zbigniew Brzezinski, ed., *Africa and the Communist World* (Stanford University Press, 1963), p. 128.

pendage, of the Soviet, and the theme of peaceful coexistence even overshadowed that of nonalignment. To the Chinese, those endeavors, on the part of a state professing to be socialist, were anathema. If what the Yugoslavs were doing was no longer anti-Soviet, it was anti-Leninist and anti-Chinese. To the Yugoslavs, the Chinese fulminations were but additional proof that the "inhuman" Chinese regime would deny other nations the right to live.

The fierce competition between Yugoslavs and Chinese came into the open with the maneuvering over rival conferences, the "second Belgrade" and the "second Bandung." These would have largely the same membership but with certain pointed exceptions: China would not qualify as one of the nonaligned, nor would Yugoslavia be admissible to a meeting limited to Asian and African states. The Yugoslavs obviously could not prevent the holding of a "second Bandung," but with the help of India, Egypt, and others they saw to it that the "second Belgrade" (at Cairo) would be held first.

To the Chinese Communists, mainly concerned with outdoing their enemies in Washington and in Moscow, the maneuvers of Yugoslavia in themselves were an annoying diversion and a nuisance rather than a dangerous threat. But they regarded Tito, as some in America regard him from the other direction, as a man who could open doors for Khrushchev in many countries. To them, the "renegade Tito" was sabotaging national liberation movements, flaunting the nonaligned label, collaborating with the reactionaries of all countries, and trying to liquidate the socialist camp. And Khrushchev, abandoning Marxism-Leninism, was "wallowing in the mire" with him. Tito was the teacher, and Khrushchev was sliding down the path of revisionism hard on his heels. Worst of all, he was opposing national liberation movements and wars of national liberation on the flimsy pretext that they might spark a world war.[28] The shift in leadership of the Soviet Union has brought no change in that Chinese line.

Whether Yugoslavia has been playing the Soviet Union's game in the Third World, with or without collusion, is a controversial question. It is hard to disagree with the conclusion that Yugoslav policy, whatever the motivation and ultimate ends, was by 1963 "substantially in line with Moscow." [29] There is no doubt, however, that Tito has not been playing Peking's game and that the more he succeeds in achieving solidarity among the nonaligned, the more he will

---

28. "Is Yugoslavia a Socialist Country?", cited.
29. William E. Griffith, "Yugoslavia," cited, pp. 127–128.

contribute to frustrating the policies of the Chinese leaders in the one area of the world which they see as the key to China's emergence as a real world power.

It is no wonder that the Yugoslavs should be incensed over the Chinese Communists' attack on India, their opposition to the nuclear test ban, and their persistent "sabotage" of efforts to reduce tensions or that Tito should refer to their having committed errors of "Himalayan proportions." In present circumstances, with China at one end of the Communist spectrum and Yugoslavia at the other, hostility is bound to suffuse their attitudes on every issue, ideological or political; and the war of words, according to Communist custom, has to include reciprocal charges of treason and Trotskyism, along with more earthy epithets. The racial factor, moreover, is not absent from the thinking of either side. As a commentator on the Yugoslav radio put it, the Chinese are arguing that they are much closer to the Asian and the African countries than is the Soviet Union, which belongs to the white race; consequently, if the colored peoples unite their forces, they will count for much more in the world.[30] Here the Yugoslavs stress their own and the Soviet view that the struggle for peace and socialism is color-blind and that salvation can never be found in race war. Peaceful coexistence, they maintain, is wholly compatible with anticolonialism and the cause of national liberation.

We may assume that the Yugoslav aim in carrying on the polemic with Peking and preaching peace and moderation is not merely to block the Chinese but also to commit the Soviet Union, as far as possible, to actual policies conforming to its own recent propaganda. Concerned though they are with ideology, the Yugoslav leaders remain intensely practical men of affairs. So long as the Soviet-Chinese split hardens the Chinese sector of the socialist camp in its dogmatism and consolidates the Soviet sector in support of policies of separate roads to socialism within and peaceful coexistence without, Yugoslavia will be Moscow's friend and Peking's enemy. Tito, of course, has long been dealing with great powers. He has been aware that with a new turn of the wheel Moscow and Peking might again come together in "proletarian unity" at his expense. That development may seem unlikely, but Tito is naturally alert to all possibilities. Therefore, he and other Yugoslav spokesmen have warned against any restoration of unity by dictation or by compromise. In other words, any compromise at all by the Soviet Union

---

30. Boris Hrzić over Radio Zagreb, December 17, 1963. See also *Komunist*, May 7, 1964.

with the dogmatists in Peking would be a "rotten compromise," betraying "the fundamental principles upon which the contemporary struggle for socialism rests." [31]

It is always possible that the Chinese line might change. Should the Chinese Communists soften or cease their present hostility toward Belgrade, the Yugoslav leadership, whether Tito or his successors, may see good reason to move toward a position where it can maneuver between China and the Soviet Union as it has maneuvered between the Soviet Union and the West. It certainly does not intend to take part in a reestablished Soviet bloc run by Moscow just for the sake of reading China out of the international socialist movement. Nonalignment, for Yugoslavia, is a principle which may have varied application.

Despite all professions of devotion to the international workers' movement, the main concerns of Yugoslavia's Communist leadership are two: (1) to "build socialism" in Yugoslavia in its own way without being bound in theory or in practice to the pattern of any other state; (2) to pursue an independent foreign policy, which will enable Yugoslavia to deal on its own terms with the Soviet Union, China, the Eastern European states, the nonaligned, and the West.

Communist rule in Yugoslavia—as long as it lasts—never again is likely to be so far removed from Yugoslav society as it was before 1948. While the Communist leaders have never even considered submitting to the democratic test of a free election, ever since the break with Stalin they have been conscious of the need to adapt both policies and doctrines to the realities of the local national scene. They will not be dictated to by any outside power. Even as Tito has made his peace with the Kremlin and talked of Yugoslavia's destiny as inseparable from that of the international workers' movement, those changes which set in with the cataclysmic event of 1948 have widened and deepened—changes which include opening of the doors to the non-Communist world, especially to Yugoslavia's western neighbors. Whether or not the destiny is socialist, it is virtually certain to be Yugoslav and European. From that angle of vision Communist China seems quite alien and very far away.

---

31. Tito's speech to the Fifth Plenum of the Central Committee of the League of Communists of Yugoslavia, May 18, 1963 (*Peti Plenum Centralnog Komiteta Saveza Komunista Jugoslavije*, cited, p. 23); Marko Kozman in *Komunist*, December 12, 1963.

Chapter 14

AFRICA AND CHINA

Symbolism and Substance

BY

COLIN LEGUM

African policies toward China, especially toward the People's Republic of China, have developed in response to a challenge. In analyzing the relationships, one should note that the P.R.C. has on the whole taken the initiative. The African response had been determined by the nature of the P.R.C.'s African policy—its broad principles, its visible objectives, and its specific tactics. It has also been conditioned by African attitudes toward large international problems (nonalignment, disarmament, the role of the United Nations, etc.) and the concrete interests of African governments or political movements.

INTRODUCTION: ATTITUDES AND POLICIES

China's impact on African thinking is that of a largely unknown, revolutionary giant. What exactly does China's challenge portend? Africans are still trying to make up their minds. They acknowledge the actual and potential power of China, but they are still unsure where their encounter will lead.

In African comment, the gigantic size of China is always stressed. Mamadou Gologo, Mali's Secretary of State for Information and Tourism, has called China "a giant nation with a great destiny." [1]

---

1. *Mali Magazine*, quoted by New China News Agency (NCNA), February 26, 1964. This reference may be found in the BBC's *Summary of World Broad-*

The Emperor of Ethiopia has said, "The P.R.C. is today the most populous nation in this globe and the vast potential which its people and its material resources represent, make it certainly one of the most powerful." [2]   In a private conversation with the author, the President of an African state which is exceptionally well disposed to the P.R.C. has mused: "If Mao Tse-tung told all the Chinese to pee at the same time over Africa we would all be drowned."

In respects other than size, African attitudes toward the Chinese are diffuse and contradictory. A cross section of opinions collected during Chou En-lai's African visit shows the variety of the foci of attention:

"They're cultivated people—not rough like the Russians."

"They do things for us because they want to—not because it's good for diplomacy."

"You feel you're sharing the fate of the people. Yes, but don't you want to share a *wealthy* fate?"

"They just talk, talk, talk, talk—nothing but politics."

"Anyway, we don't think much of their girls: they look like men—particularly in those new uniforms."

"We just don't know anything about them. At least we know how to handle the British: we know how to ask them to help, and how to get rid of them!"

"Being yellow doesn't help them much, as far as we're concerned. They're not black, let's face it. Let's *face* it!"

"We want Socialism, but we don't want Chou to tell us what kind of Socialism." [3]

African policies reflect these diverse and tentative attitudes. Though it is impossible to speak of an "African policy" toward China, there are four points of fairly general agreement. First, the "two-China" policy has little validity in the minds of most African leaders despite the fact that until March 1964 more African states recognized Nationalist China than Communist China. Second, the exclusion of the P.R.C. from the United Nations is seen as a serious weakness in international relations. Third, the P.R.C. is widely recognized not only as one of the world's four great powers but as the most revolutionary world power. Fourth, China is felt to share with Africa the experience of colonialism.

casts for the Far East.   All radio broadcasts cited in this chapter may be found in this summary or the summary for the Middle East.

2. NCNA, February 1, 1964.

3. From notes supplied by Anthony Sampson of *The Observer* (London).

These four points peg the area within which Africa and China are conducting a mutual exploration. It is usual to date the beginning of this exploration from the Bandung Conference in 1955. Only five African delegations attended that meeting—Egypt, Ethiopia, Ghana (then still the Gold Coast), Tunisia, and Morocco. Nevertheless, Chou En-lai's impact on the conference first stimulated in Africa a serious awareness of China. Before then, only a relatively few sophisticated African leaders had showed interest in China's struggles against foreign domination or in its Communist revolution. Even at the historic Pan-African Conference in Manchester in 1945, which passed a resolution greeting "the peoples of India, Indonesia and Viet-Minh under President Ho Chi Minh," [4] there was no mention of the Chinese liberation struggle.

As a direct consequence of Bandung, Egypt became the first African country to recognize the Peking regime in 1956. It was another two years before Morocco and the Sudan followed suit. Up to late 1963, only seven more states had established diplomatic relations with Peking (Guinea, 1959; Mali, Somalia, and Ghana, 1960, Tanganyika, 1961; Uganda and Algeria, 1962).

Because Communist China was introduced into Africa as a protégé of the Russians, the Africans' initial impression of the Chinese was that they were an Asian variant of the Soviet bloc. As such, they were firmly classified as belonging to one of the cold war camps. But by 1959, African leaders had become aware of a rivalry between Peking and Moscow. They did not yet observe clear-cut doctrinal differences but only differences on tactics—especially when it came to open support for liberation movements engaged in violent struggles, such as the Union des Populations du Cameroun (UPC). The Africans quickly sensed, however, that the People's Republic wanted to be seen not as an appendage to Russia but as a power in its own right.

A Uganda nationalist leader who visited China in 1958 gained the following impression of Chinese national pride as a factor in attitudes toward both Russia and the United States:

> When I was taken round China I was never told that the technicians engaged in the various enterprises were Russians; I had to pry it out of them. I was flown thousands of miles especially to see a factory which had 75 percent of its machinery made by Chinese. In external affairs their desire was to be seen

4. George Padmore, *Pan-Africanism or Communism?* (London: Dobson, 1956).

as separate from and equal to the Russians; hence their insistence on making separate contacts with Africans, and in giving support to African leaders and movements of their own choice.

An English-speaking Chinaman was in a state of high dudgeon when I asked him if he was educated in the United States, as I later discovered he was. Normally, Africans and Asians are proud of being able to admit that they were educated in America; but not so the Chinese.[5]

The clearest indication the Africans had of the keen Chinese-Russian competitiveness was through the Afro-Asian People's Solidarity Organization (AAPSO), which had been set up in Cairo at the beginning of 1958. Although the initiative for AAPSO had come from the Russians, the Chinese used it as the principal vehicle to establish their first real contacts—especially with black Africa, to which they had only limited access up to 1963. But even these contacts were circumscribed because the majority of African countries had refused to become too closely associated with AAPSO. Although its conferences were well attended, it was run almost entirely by Russia, China, Egypt, and Guinea. The rest of the secretariat was manned principally by representatives of exile groups based in Cairo, notably Dr. Roland-Felix Moumie's Union des Populations du Cameroun. African governments felt that since AAPSO included the Russians and the Chinese, it offended against the canons of nonalignment. This feeling made them cautious. Further, there was deep resentment over the manner in which AAPSO had been created.[6]

The P.R.C.'s AAPSO contacts in Cairo were largely unrepresentative of the African governments. They were young militants —the UPC fighters from Cameroun, young Kenyans who had worked with Mau Mau, left-wing Ugandans and Nigerians, refugees from South Africa and South West Africa, Congolese rebels who went abroad after Lumumba's murder, members of the Angola and Mozambique liberation fronts, and the vigorous young opponents of the now extinct Central African Federation. After 1959, when the P.R.C. established an embassy in Conakry, the same pattern was repeated there. Thus at a time when Russia was building relations with African governments, the P.R.C. dealt (until 1963) primarily

5. Abu Mayanja, former secretary-general of the Uganda National Congress and later Minister of Education in the Kabaka's government of Buganda, in a personal communication to the author.
6. Colin Legum, *Bandung, Cairo, Accra* (London: Africa Bureau, 1958).

on the unofficial level with radical opposition elements. Although these two levels of relationship reflect the different attitudes of Russia and the P.R.C., the P.R.C. had little chance to behave differently during the first five or six years of its presence on the African continent.

African governments were often suspicious and displeased with the P.R.C.'s support for dissident elements, while the latter looked upon the P.R.C. as a more reliable revolutionary friend than the Russians. The Russians took pains to offset this advantage of the Chinese, who did not need to care so much about offending established African governments and could openly espouse the cause of the dissident radicals. The Russians' tactics called for greater subtlety, but they were often more successful than the Chinese.

THE "TWO CHINAS"

When Africans speak about "the Chinese," they usually mean the People's Republic of China. They tend to regard Taiwan as the exile base of Marshal Chiang Kai-shek, who lost the mainland to the revolution and will never regain it. Those who recognized Taiwan did so either because of grievances against the Peking regime—as in the case of Cameroun, Rwanda, and the Congo (Leopoldville)—or, in most cases, out of deference to the wishes of France or the United States. Only a few, like Malagasy, genuinely chose Taiwan on its political merits. The response of several French-speaking African states to General de Gaulle's recognition of Peking shows how slender had been their faith in the "two-China" idea. French recognition may yet turn out to be the decisive factor in finally swinging African opinion, which was already inclined that way, toward accepting a single legitimate government for all the Chinese. Chou En-lai's visit to Africa, which slightly preceded French recognition, also helped to shift opinion.

At the time of Chou En-lai's trip, 18 African states recognized Nationalist China, one (Senegal) claimed to recognize both Chinas but maintained relations only with the Nationalists, 12 recognized Communist China, and 4 recognized neither.[7] After French recog-

7. *Cameroun, Central African Republic, Chad, Congo (Brazzaville)*, Congo (Leopoldville), *Dahomey, Gabon, Ivory Coast*, Liberia, Libya, *Malagasy, Mauritania, Niger*, Rwanda, Sierra Leone, Togo, *Upper Volta*, and South Africa recognized Nationalist China. *Senegal* accorded recognition to both. Algeria, Ghana, Guinea, Kenya Mali, Morocco, Somalia, Sudan, Tanganyika, Uganda, the U.A.R.,

394   POLICIES TOWARD CHINA

nition of Peking, four members of the Francophone Union of African and Malagasy States (UAM) broke their ties with Taiwan and now recognize only the P.R.C.; these are Congo (Brazzaville)—which had opened negotiations with the P.R.C. before De Gaulle's decision—Central African Republic, Senegal, and Dahomey. Only two UAM members, Cameroun and Malagasy, have announced that France's action will not affect their position, but the former has lately begun to reconsider after a Chinese delegation paid a goodwill visit. Two non-UAM states previously neutral—Burundi and Tunisia—have switched to recognition of Peking, but Burundi broke off diplomatic relations about a year after granting recognition. Zambia, upon attaining statehood, promptly recognized the P.R.C., but Malawi took no action. As of March 1965, 18 African countries recognized Peking (Tanganyika and Zanzibar having merged to form Tanzania), 15 recognized Taiwan, and 3 recognized neither China.

Africa has up to now been divided on the question of the P.R.C.'s admission to the United Nations. In 1959, the P.R.C. could count on five African votes at the United Nations, and Taiwan on two. In 1961, both had nine African votes. But as a result of its diplomatic offensive in Africa (especially among the UAM members), Taiwan was able to rally 17 votes against 14 in the 1962 General Assembly. The only direct political advantage the Africans got from the competition between the two Chinas was the admission of Mauritania to the United Nations in a package deal. The Soviet Union withheld its veto over Mauritania, and the West withheld its veto over Outer Mongolia. A Nationalist Chinese veto of Outer Mongolia was fought off by a UAM threat to support the seating of Peking in the United Nations.

Nationalist China's diplomatic assault on Africa started in late 1959 on the advice of Yang Hsi-k'un, now Director for West Asiatic and African Affairs of the Ministry of Foreign Affairs. He correctly foresaw the importance of the new African states in the United Nations. As a result of fact-finding missions, Taiwan decided to offer the African states a program of technical and agricultural cooperation as a *quid pro quo* for their goodwill.[8]

and Zanzibar recognized Peking. Burundi, Ethiopia, Nigeria, and Tunisia recognized neither. (Italicized names in the foregoing lists are those of members of the UAM as it was constituted in 1963.) For further details, see Appendix A of this volume and George T. Yu, "Chinese Rivalry in Africa," *Race*, v. 5, no. 4, April 1964.

8. For surveys of Nationalist China's role in Africa, see Professor David N.

Nationalist China's operations, though comparatively small, have been outstandingly successful—certainly as successful as anything Communist China has done in Africa. Its experts grew rice and other crops in Liberia, introduced dry rice methods into Libya, and helped Malagasy develop techniques of deep-sea fishing. Its African Agricultural Technicians' Seminar in Taiwan proved highly popular. As late as February 1964—after the swing-over to the P.R.C. had begun to gather force—Dr. H. K. Banda's Nyasaland (now Malawi) government decided to send four agricultural officers to the seminar. Although he invited both Peking and Taiwan to his country's independence ceremony in July 1964, the People's Republic refused the invitation.

The predominant feeling of Africans is that they are being put over the barrel on the "two-China" issue as on the "two-Korea" and the "two-Germany" issues. Except for those governments with direct grievances against the P.R.C., the Africans' strongest wish is to escape this dilemma. There is another overriding feeling: that the United Nations is weaker because of the absence of the P.R.C. Only a few African governments, however, have openly favored China's claims over Taiwan itself—notably Ghana, Mali, Algeria, and the United Arab Republic.

COMMUNIST CHINA'S AFRICAN POLICY

The P.R.C.'s African policy operates on two levels, the diplomatic and the ideological.

On the diplomatic level, the P.R.C.'s basic formula is the five principles drawn up by Chou En-lai with Nehru and U Nu in 1954: mutual respect for sovereignty and territorial integrity; nonaggression; noninterference in each other's internal affairs; equality and mutual benefit; and peaceful coexistence. Chou En-lai, during his 1963–64 journey through Africa, reaffirmed these principles, and other Chinese statements at the time amplified their operative meaning. Four points were emphasized: First, China, having won her revolutionary victory earlier than the African states, recognizes her duty "to support those which win later." Mutual benefit is entailed, for any weakening of imperialism benefits China. The value of African policies

Rowe, "Cooperation between the Republic of China and African Countries," *International Bulletin of the African Institute* (Pretoria), August 1963, and Leon M. S. Slawecki, "The Two Chinas in Africa," *Foreign Affairs*, v. 41, no. 2, January 1963.

of "peace, neutrality and non-alignment" is also recognized. Second, the Chinese strongly recommend unity at a number of levels to the Africans—unity of the people in a given country as an essential for successful struggle against imperialism; unity of the African states, through the removal of artificial barriers and in the form they themselves choose; and unity of the African peoples with those of Asia and Latin America in "a common struggle." Third, the Chinese stress self-reliance as the key measure to end economic backwardness and poverty. It may be supplemented, however, by such economic assistance as does not violate the principle of equality of all countries, big and small. China opposes "aggression and intervention in other countries either by force or in the name of providing economic assistance." Fourth, on frontier disputes, Chou En-lai said: "We would like not to interfere or favor any side. Since Africans are brothers, they should solve their difficulties peacefully." [9]

The above themes, broadly speaking, constituted the message Chou En-lai took around Africa with him on his first visit. He was careful, however, to say little in public about the P.R.C.'s ideological challenge—except on the few occasions when he attacked the United States and stressed the need for "revolutionary struggle." In his address to FLN cadres in Algiers, he saluted the independence of Algeria as "a great event in the African national liberation movement of our era . . . a brilliant example of daring to wage an armed struggle and daring to seize victory." [10]   Again, at the end of his visit, he said in Somalia:

> An excellent revolutionary situation exists in Africa . . . the African peoples are demanding complete destruction of the colonial rule through elimination of the colonial forces. . . . The people of many African countries that have won independence are pushing the revolution forward, with the aim of carrying through the national-democratic revolution and building up their countries. [11]

This last sentence reveals that the P.R.C.'s interest in Africa extends beyond the liberation struggle against "the remnants of colonialism" to the phase of post-independence "construction."

---

9. See Chou En-lai's interview with Felix Greene, NCNA, February 5, 1964; *People's Daily (Jenmin Jihpao)* editorial, February 6, 1964; NCNA, February 6, 1964; and Radio Mogadishu, February 4, 1964.

10. NCNA, December 27, 1963.

11. NCNA, February 5, 1964.

P.R.C. representatives carry forward the Chinese ideological challenge in conversation, through their official propaganda, and through their "front" organizations. This challenge rests on the five principles expounded in the arguments against Khrushchev's revisionism. They were recently summed up for African audiences in the following authoritative way: [12] (1) To realize the transition to socialism, the proletariat must wage armed struggle, smash the old state machine, and establish the dictatorship of the proletariat. (2) The peasants are the most dependable allies of the proletariat; the need is for a broad united front based on the worker-peasant alliance. (3) U.S. imperialism is the archenemy of people's revolution in all countries. (4) The revolution of the oppressed nations is an indispensable ally of the proletarian revolution. (5) A successful revolution requires a revolutionary proletarian party faithful to the revolutionary theory and style of Marxism-Leninism.

The practical advice which accompanied the theoretical statement was that "to promote revolution, one must study hard the selected works of Mao Tse-tung,". . . especially his teaching that "the seizure of power by armed force, the settlement of the issue by war, is the central task and the highest form of revolution." The three examples of successful revolutionary struggles which are invariably linked in appeals to African audiences are China, Algeria, and Cuba.

In effect, the Chinese tell Africans that political independence is not real independence; real independence can only come through armed struggle, which the P.R.C. is able and willing to guide. International unity also can come only through struggle. Real liberation cannot be achieved with aid from the United States but only through self-help supplemented by aid from the right kind of friends. The Chinese have an experience of struggle in common with all oppressed peoples, and the underprivileged peoples of the world—who are mostly non-white—have a common cause to defend against the developed nations. The P.R.C. will contribute the weight of its 650 million people to unite the "1,700,000,000 people of Asia and Africa . . . [into] a powerful contingent against imperialism and old and new colonialism, and in defence of world peace. . . . In the face of [their] threat we Asian and African peoples should work more closely together, help each other, and march forward shoulder to shoulder." [13]

---

12. See article printed in *Red Flag* (*Hung Ch'i*) and *People's Daily* and quoted by NCNA, March 30, 1964.

13. Chou En-lai statement quoted by NCNA, January 23, 1964.

The emphasis on "common experience" is reinforced by constant reference to historical links between China and Africa.

> Despite the long distance that separates China from Africa, the friendly contacts and cultural interflow between the Chinese and African peoples date back to ancient times. According to historical records China had trade relations with Egypt as early as the second century. . . . The friendly contacts were not broken off until after the 16th century as western colonialists forced their way into Africa and China.[14]

The Communists have resuscitated the work written by the Chinese scholar Chao Ju-shih in 1225, *A Record of Foreign Nations*. It includes descriptions of Egypt, the Horn of Africa, Zanzibar, and Madagascar. The Communists are careful not to mention that after the Chinese fleet visited East Africa during the Ming dynasty, the commanders of the fleet reported that the countries visited had become subjects of the Emperor and that "the barbarians from beyond the seas have come to audience." [15] Nor do they mention that the fleet brought back black slaves who became known in China as "devil slaves."

Where no historical links can be established, as with West Africa, the emphasis is altered: "Although China and Ghana are thousands of miles apart and separated by great oceans, a common historical destiny has long linked our two peoples closely. In the course of protracted struggles against imperialism and colonialism our two peoples have always sympathized with and supported each other." [16]

CHINESE LESSONS FOR AFRICA

On the diplomatic level, the People's Republic offers at the least a formula for cooperation and mutual sympathy, if not for partnership. On the ideological level, it offers an articulate, and fairly elaborate, theory of international relations. On the action level, it offers itself as a model and encourages Africans to learn from Chinese

14. *People's Daily*, December 14, 1963.
15. W. A. C. Adie, *Chinese Policy Towards Africa*, in Sven Hamrell and Carl G. Witstrand, eds., *The Soviet Bloc* (Uppsala: The Scandinavian Institute of African Studies, 1964).
16. Liu Shao-ch'i, chairman of the P.R.C. on the arrival of Ghana's President Nkrumah at Peking Airport. See *Survey of China Mainland Press* (SCMP), no. 2561, August 18, 1961, p. 36.

experience. This experience, the Chinese maintain, holds four lessons: (1) A poor, developing country can construct a socialist society through self-reliance and by accepting only genuinely distinterested aid. (2) American aid cannot be disinterested, and Russian aid must be carefully scrutinized. (3) A revolutionary struggle is necessary before colonialism and poverty can be eliminated. (4) The poor nations of the world (mainly nonwhite) have a common interest and a duty to cooperate in achieving their own salvation; this salvation cannot come from the rich, powerful (by implication, white) nations.

These lessons are offered to a continent in a complex state of social and political flux. The extent to which Africans are persuaded by the Chinese example depends on their social roles in their own countries, their own convictions and ambitions, and their experience of China. Chinese teachings have strongly influenced African attitudes—but in various directions, some positive and some negative.

China as a model. So far, no African government has been willing to follow Chinese socialist methods, although African leaders have praised the example set by Chinese construction.[17] Many Africans, indeed, return from China with admiration for its achievements and for aspects of its policy.

The Africans are keenly interested in how the Chinese have been industrializing their agricultural society. For this accomplishment there is much praise. The former Prime Minister of Somalia, Shermarke, for example, was deeply impressed by "the great strides made by the Chinese people in the socio-economic field." Sijaona, Tanganyika's Minister for National Culture and Youth, was "highly impressed with Chinese achievements over the past 14 years; the Chinese economy has changed a great deal from agricultural to industrial development." But though most visitors are taken to Chinese communes and praise them, few find them relevant to Africa's needs. Two differences are noted: the overcrowding in China (which neces-

---

17. "Ghana could learn much from China to help Ghanaians in their plans for the development of the country," said President Nkrumah, *Ghana Newsletter* (London), February 7, 1964. "A most profitable lesson for the colonial peoples," said Ferhat Abbas, ex-President of the Algerian Provisional Government, *Peking Review*, October 11, 1960. "From there we derived lessons of particular value to our country at the time of our liberation, and we still firmly and with vision will derive lessons also for the building of our country," said ex-President Ben Bella, Radio Algiers, September 1, 1963.

For a discussion of the possibility of China's becoming an example to other countries, see Roderick MacFarquhar, "The Chinese Model and the Underdeveloped World," *International Affairs* (London), July 1963.

sitates national ownership and collectivization of land) and the African's desire to own his own piece of land. Chief Adam Sapi Mkwawa, Speaker of the Tanzania National Assembly, for instance, cited the "acute shortage of land" in China as the reason for the communes, and he pointed out that this problem was not a factor in the Tanganyika region of Tanzania. Senator Hilo of Kenya stated that government confiscation of land would never work in Kenya, for "the paramount aim of Africans is to own their own land." [18]

On one point most African visitors to China are agreed: what the Communists are doing "is right for the Chinese." But it would be wrong to deduce that they feel they have nothing to learn from the Chinese. There is an astonishingly wide measure of agreement about the aspects of Communist China which most impress Africans. These are the attitude toward hard work, the self-reliance, the discipline, and the enthusiastic "mobilization of the masses." Significantly, these are the elements which many African leaders feel are most lacking in their own societies.

The need for disinterested foreign aid. Government leaders of Algeria, Ghana, Guinea, Mali, and Somalia have all endorsed the view that Chinese aid is disinterested, but not one of them has taken the second step of renouncing Russian or Western aid. A common reaction on this point is that the Chinese are elevating their own experiences with the Russians and the Americans to the status of general doctrine. The Chinese view is strongly supported, however, by many radical opposition leaders in African countries.

The need for a revolutionary struggle. In the Chinese textbook, only Mali and Guinea qualify as countries which have carried through their internal revolution. Algeria has not properly tackled the task of socialist reconstruction. And while Ghana, along with Algeria, displays the correct revolutionary attitude toward colonialism, President Nkrumah's regime has not yet created a successful internal revolution. Ghana rejects this view. For example, James Mercer, Ghana's former ambassador to Peking, has stated: "In many ways there is a striking similarity between what is taking place in China today and the pace of Socialist reconstruction in Ghana under the leadership of Osagyefo." [19] Since nearly all African governments are

---

18. Radio Mogadishu, February 2, 1964; Radio Dar Es Salaam, October 24, 1963; Tanganyika Information Services, Dar Es Salaam, November 1, 1963; Reuters, Mombasa, September 11, 1963.
19. *The Ghanaian Times,* May 4, 1963.

excluded from the Chinese definition of "the correct revolutionary struggle," their attitudes toward the P.R.C., therefore, are understandably suspicious. By the same token, the attitudes of the militant, radical opposition groups—even those which do not fully subscribe to the doctrines of Peking—are sympathetic.[20]

The need for the poor nations to combine against the rich. The Chinese expound this doctrine on three levels. First, by promoting the idea of the "haves" versus the "have-nots," they suggest that the

---

20. An interesting and valuable insight into the attitude of radicals is provided by this personal communication (dated December 9, 1963) to the author from Dr. Chike Obi, a distinguished Nigerian mathematician and leader of the small Dynamic party (which is identified with the pro-government front in Nigeria):

I was deeply impressed by the Chinese—700 million people mobilised under one government and consciously and willingly working very hard to catch up with the technologically advanced countries with the aims to attain and maintain the best of standards of living for themselves and to wipe out forever the stains of the economic and spiritual exploitation of their country by the imperialists of Europe and Japan. The Chinese and the other Far Eastern peoples who have tasted the bitterness of imperialist occupation and who have broken with the West are not *backward* in exactly the same sense as the peoples of the newly independent African countries (with the possible exception of Guinea and Ghana) are backward. The first group of peoples already do manufacture technological goods of all descriptions and have carried out scientific research completely beyond the imagination and dreams of the present rulers of the second group of peoples. In the first group of peoples I see in successful practice what I was led to arrive at by pure theory as the only method by which Nigeria etc., could be properly governed at least for the first 15 years or so of political independence.

During one of my several conversations in Peking with the Chinese and other peoples from Africa, Asia, South America, Central America and Oceania I bluntly confessed that the look and sound of the term 'Marxism-Leninism-Stalinism' are too clumsy for my scientific mind; that, by training, I can understand a certain contribution to knowledge by Marx, for example, being called Marxism; that I can understand a real fundamental extension of Marxism by Lenin, for example, being called Leninism; that I can understand a real fundamental extension of Leninism by Stalin, for example, being called Stalinism; that I cannot understand anything being called by the clumsy title Marxism-Leninism-Stalinism; that I am in truth tired of men who think that new calendars should be inaugurated or new eras should be deemed to start on their accession to power; that it will be interesting to know what would be the name of say, Quantum Mechanics if, beginning with Newton, the names of all those who contributed to what led to Quantum Mechanics are visibly and audibly incorporated in the name!

I love the life in China as I saw it: no worries about money, no worries about private property, no worries about insurance, none of those worries which Nigerians suffer from individually. I am collectivistic by nature and I love the collectivistic organisation of the China. I will organise Nigeria in the same manner whenever I have the power to do so. At the rate this country is going she will lead the world in about 20 years at most.

correct political division is not east v. west, but north v. south. With
the simple proposition of "rich v. poor," several African leaders, like
Tanzania's President Julius Nyerere and Guinea's President Sékou
Touré, feel considerable sympathy; but they react strongly against the
idea of joining an organized international front. It is among young
Marxist African leaders that this idea finds its greatest attraction.[21]

At the second level, this doctrine lapses into racism. Africans,
including African Marxists, tend to react sharply against the attempt
to divide the world on the basis of color. The vehemence of Chinese
feelings about the white races astonishes Africans. The leader of the
Kenya delegation which went to Peking in 1963, John Kali (later Kenya's ambassador to the P.R.C.), spoke on his return of the bitterness
which China's leaders display toward all white men. "They resent
their superiority and want the support of Africans—and the South
Americans—in what they foresee will be an eventual showdown with
the white races." Further, the Chinese spoke of differences between
the Soviet leaders and the Russian people as if they were racial.
"Always they would refer contemptuously to the 'Ukrainian group'
when they spoke of Khrushchev and the men in the Kremlin. They
regarded them as European Russians, imposing themselves on the bulk
of the Russian people—Asiatics," he observed.[22]

It is on the third level—where stress is placed on the common
struggle and the common historical experience under imperialism—
that the Chinese strike a real chord with many diverse groups of
Africans. Zanzibar's President Karume [23] has asserted: "The history
of China and Zanzibar had been identical for about the last 20 years.
The people of China have suffered, and we did." The *Sudan Daily*
(a government paper) described Sudan's welcome to Chou En-lai as

21. The All African Students Conference, a left-wing body in London, formulated its ideas on this question in 1963. These were set forth in an article by
Anthony B. Mabona in *The Ghanaian Times*, May 4, 1963. His conclusions
were:

What is needed is an organised revolution of the poor wherever they
be and whether they be individuals or nations. What is the position of
Africa in this world revolution of the poor? These disinherited of the earth
are mostly concentrated in countries like China, India, and the rest of Asia,
Africa and Latin America. The revolution of the poor then must naturally
find its epicentre of demographic forces represented by China and India and
the rest of freedom-loving Asia. But I suggest that Africa is the continent
that can give a voice to this revolution.

22. Foreign News Service, *The Observer* (London), September 17, 1963.

23. Karume is Vice-President of Tanzania but constitutionally operates in the
style of President of Zanzibar.

an expression of "common experience, mutual aspirations and shared goals." According to Somalia's President Osman, "We have both suffered from the evils of imperialism and colonialism and we both share a common lot." Abdullah Abd as-Samad, leader of the 1964 Algerian jurists' delegation to Peking, also spoke of mutual understanding having arisen through "similar sufferings" and through the waging of "similar struggles against the common enemy—foreign imperialism." [24]

HOW AFRICANS USE CHINA

To think of Africa as a passive, permeable mass upon which China's huge revolutionary forces can exert their will is to misjudge the entire character of the engagement. China's particular national and revolutionary interests find African outlets only where African governments or political leaders see opportunities to use Chinese offers of aid to further their own ends.

When a government, or a government-in-exile, requires a powerful international ally to promote a particular objective. Algeria is the outstanding example of such a situation. In 1958 the Algerian Provisional Government (GPRA) was going through a difficult period. It turned to Peking for aid to compel the reluctant Soviet Union to grant full recognition and to increase its active economic and military support and, secondly, to increase international pressure on France and the West to open negotiations. The then President of the GPRA, Ferhat Abbas, led a mission to Peking in 1960. That mission produced the Sino-Algerian agreement of October 5, 1960, as well as a feeling of close friendship between the two countries. Again, after Col. Boumedienne's coup against Ben Bella in June 1965, the new president welcomed Communist China's immediate recognition because it was vital to the consolidation of his regime that it should be recognized by as many Afro-Asian nations as possible. Despite the fact that Boumedienne's regime was less firmly oriented toward the P.R.C. than Ben Bella's was, the Chinese offered immediate recognition because of their interest in trying to ensure that the pending Afro-Asian conference in Algiers would be held on schedule.

The Algerian tactics were copied by the Somalia government in

24. Radio Zanzibar, February 3, 1964; NCNA, January 24, 1964; Radio Mogadishu, February 4, 1964; Radio Peking, March 10, 1964.

1963 and by Holden Roberto's Provisional Government for Angola (GRAE) in 1964. (The second case will be treated later in conjunction with a discussion of the activities of Roberto's rebel movement, the Union of the Peoples of Angola.)

Until 1962, Somalia's relations with the Chinese were formal and somewhat suspicious. But the deterioration of Somalia's relations with its immediate neighbors as a result of its desire to build a Greater Somalia led to a reshaping of its foreign policy. The Somalis recognized they could not expect much real support from the West, for the Western powers were strongly committed to the support of Ethiopia and Kenya. The Russians, too, appeared lukewarm—mainly because they did not want to weaken their ties with Kenya and her allies in East and Central Africa. It was only when the then Premier, Shermarke, announced his intention to go to Peking to seek aid that the Russians cast caution to the wind and offered to train an expanded Somali army of 20,000 men. Although close Sino-Somali relations were established, the Russians outbid the Chinese in aid promised ($60 million as against $24 million) and actually provided. Having achieved its immediate aims, Somali policy underwent another change after the middle of 1964 when the "pro-Chinese" elements (including Shermarke) were dropped by the President and a new government was elected.

Guinea offers a different example of how the P.R.C. can be useful. Guinea's relations with Peking were close after the Chinese promptly came to Guinea's assistance at the time of independence in 1958, but its ties with Russia were stronger until 1961. As a result of the Solod affair,[25] relations with Russia deteriorated seriously, and Guinea was forced to turn increasingly to the West for aid. Anxious not to damage its image as a devotedly nonaligned state, Guinea strengthened its ties with the Chinese while it maintained more or less formal relations with the Russians.

The short-lived Republic of Zanzibar is the most recent example of a country which turned to the Chinese for economic and political support when its relations with the West underwent radical changes —in this case after the 1964 revolution. The Chinese response was prompt, especially in the provision of arms but the Russians and their

---

25. In December 1961, Daniel Solod, U.S.S.R. ambassador in Conakry, was expelled by the Guinean government on charges of "subversive activities" within the country. These charges arose from the Soviet embassy's contacts with a group of teachers and students who had criticized the official leadership for not adopting more radical policies.

allies (particularly the East Germans) were equally prompt and more effective. Although the Chinese tried to maximize their influence through sympathizers like Mohammed Abdul Rahman (Babu), whose role will be discussed presently, they were rapidly outmaneuvered by the Russians and East Germans and have played a secondary role on the island since the revolution.

When rebel movements turn to China for aid. African rebel leaders engaged in a struggle against a colonial power, or against a government like South Africa's, tend to look with equal favor on Moscow and Peking, but those engaged in fighting an established African government regard the Chinese as more likely to assist them than the Russians. The experience of rebel movements like the Union des Populations du Cameroun, the Rwanda exile movement called The Cockroach, and Pierre Mulele's Jeunesse and the Gbenye-Soumialot national-liberation group of 1964 in the Congo (Leopold-ville) has implanted in African minds the image of Communist China as an uncompromising revolutionary power which is uninhibited by considerations of peaceful coexistence.

The P.R.C.'s first venture into direct and open support for a revolutionary movement in Africa was in Cameroun. In 1959 the Chinese members of the AAPSO secretariat established close relations with Dr. Roland-Felix Moumie [26] and his lieutenants, Ernest Oundie, Kingue Abel, and Osende Afana. Their Union des Populations du Cameroun began its armed struggle in 1959. At first, it relied on Ghana, Guinea, and the U.A.R. for support; later, on the Russians as well. Moumie, a sophisticated Marxist, grew disillusioned with the Russians in 1960, when they not only recognized the new Cameroun Republic as an independent state but sent their Deputy Foreign Minister to the independence celebrations, where Cameroun President Ahidjo seized the occasion to protest against Russian support for the UPC. Subsequently, Moumie complained that Khrushchev had himself urged the UPC to end the guerrilla struggle in favor of constitutional methods.[27] Moumie refused; he turned instead to Peking. The P.R.C. still supports the UPC struggle—both materially and propagandistically, although it sent a goodwill mission to Ahidjo toward the end of 1964. The UPC leaders have unequivo-

26. Moumie was poisoned, allegedly by the French "Red Hand," in Geneva on November 3, 1960.

27. See F. Scatten, *Afrika Schwarz oder Rot* (Hanover: Verlag für Literatur und Zeitgeschehen, 1963).

cally backed Peking against Moscow,[28] despite a fracas in August 1962 when 30 UPC-sponsored Camerounian students were expelled from China after accusing the Chinese of racial discrimination.

P.R.C. policy has estranged the Cameroun government. President Ahidjo has repeatedly accused the People's Republic of "supporting terrorism" in Cameroun and has cited "proof" that Cameroun terrorists are in Communist China. When De Gaulle decided to recognize the P.R.C., President Ahidjo declared:

> France through its most authoritative voice . . . has given the reasons why it decided to recognize China. The Cameroun, through my voice, has given reasons why it has not recognized People's China. On several occasions I have said, and I recently repeated it, that if we do not recognize People's China, it is not because it is Communist. It is because we have observed that it interferes in our internal affairs. I have said that if we have proof that China will no longer interfere in our internal affairs, we will not find it inconvenient to recognize Communist China and vote for its admission to the UN.[29]

Referring to Chou En-lai's statement that "revolution is not for export," he added: "If the Peking Government acts in accordance with what Chou En-lai has said, we shall recognize it at once."

Although the UPC continues to be a thorn in the flesh of Cameroun's government, its capacity for offensive military action has decreased in recent years. The undoubted discontent in Cameroun is due less to UPC activity than to the estrangement of non-UPC political forces as a result of the methods adopted by the Ahidjo government in establishing a single-party state.

The first group of Chinese-trained guerrillas to operate on African soil appeared in the Congo (Leopoldville) early in 1964. Lumumba's mantle had been cast by both Moscow and Peking on Antoine Gizenga, but he was for a long time imprisoned. Pierre Mulele emerged as the new fighting leader. He was a former Minister of Education in Lumumba's government who had escaped to Cairo after Lumumba's fall; from there he was sent to China to undergo

---

28. The UPC supported Mao Tse-tung's appeal of January 12, 1964, for a broad united front against U.S. imperialism and in defense of "world peace." (See a dispatch datelined Accra, NCNA, February 19, 1964.) Osende Afana, UPC representative in Conakry, hailed Premier Chou En-lai's visit to Africa as an event which would "bind the common struggle" against imperialism and colonialism. (See NCNA, January 16, 1964.)

29. Radio Yaounde, February 8, 1964.

training. The Congo government claimed in August 1964 that he had been killed, but he is now definitely known to be still alive.

According to a document released by the Congo government in January 1964, the decision to seek Peking's aid was explained to the exile Congo National Liberation Committee in the following terms:

> We have done everything to get our Russian comrades to help us, but they have never comprehended our difficulties. That is the reason Comrade Mulele left for China. China gave him a course to enter a military school. After having pursued the course, the Chinese friends gave him some material (arms and munitions and certain materials to make plastic bombs). We do not wish to offend our Russian friends, but we judge it best to address ourselves to China. It is because we do not have confidence in the Russians; China has aided Mulele.[30]

Pierre Mulele began his operations in Kwilu province in January 1964. A month later, the Congo Planning Minister, Cleophas Kamitatu, officially accused the Chinese of training the Congolese rebels and supplying them with arms. Mulele's Jeunesse launched its rebellion armed only with spears and bows and arrows. Later its forces are said to have captured modern weapons. The rebellion differed from anything previously seen in Africa. Mulele concentrated the leadership in the hands of the youth of Kwilu province and based himself on the peasants. The Eight Orders given to his supporters show the influence of Mao Tse-tung's teachings.[31]

---

30. See *The African Mail* (Lusaka), January 10, 1964. The document was found on Soviet diplomats returning from a Brazzaville rendezvous with the Congo National Liberation Committee. It was signed by B. L. Lukungu and purports to be a report given at a "restricted meeting" to hear "an explanation from Comrade Yumbu," the head of the pro-Chinese wing of the Party of African Solidarity.

31. For the details set forth in this paragraph, see *The African Mail* (Lusaka), January 10, 1964; *Daily Telegraph* (London), February 13, 1964; Geoffrey Taylor in *The Guardian* (Manchester), February 2, 1964; "Is the Congo on the Threshold of Revolution?", *La Gauche*, February 17, 1964. The Eight Orders which party members were supposed to follow were:
1. Respect all men, even bad ones.
2. Buy the goods of the villagers in all honesty and without thieving.
3. Return borrowed things in good time and without trouble.
4. Pay for things which you have broken, and in good spirit.
5. Do not harm or hurt others.
6. Do not destroy or trample on other people's land.
7. Respect women and do not amuse yourselves with them as you would like to.
8. Do not make your prisoners of war suffer. Do not confiscate and take from them their personal possessions such as rings, money, watches, or indeed anything else.

Since the beginning of the insurrection in Kwilu, the P.R.C. has given it unqualified support.[32] The Chinese press paid particular attention to the fact that Mulele's forces followed the Eight Orders. It quoted with approval a *New York Herald Tribune* report of February 14, 1964, that the danger of the Congolese guerrilla operation "is that it . . . is a definite pilot scheme to adapt revolution to local conditions." A Peking radio program, "Greeting Africa," reported the Kwilu uprising as "a continuation of the Congolese people's fight for independence. . . . Armed U.S. intervention subverted the Congolese people's independence, but it could not bring them to their knees. . . . The Congolese people are giving the patriotic anti-U.S. armed struggle their wholehearted support."

Mulele's rebellion was crushed but not finally broken within a few months. It was soon followed by a much more widespread rebellion initiated by Gaston Soumialot from Burundi and Christophe Gbenye from Congo (Brazzaville). Both these wings of the Congo rebellion received direct and open support from the Chinese in terms of propaganda, financial aid, and arms. It was only after the fall of Premier Adoula and the return of Moise Tshombe in July 1964 that the Russians gave open support to the rebels and provided them with massive arms shipments. But by then the Chinese had firmly established themselves as the open champions of the rebel cause.

Of the two liberation movements in Angola, the Movement of the Angolan Peoples for Liberation (MPLA) has tended to look toward the more radical Pan-African leaders and the Communists, and the Union of the Peoples of Angola (UPA)—the dominant party in the Angola government-in-exile (GRAE)—has appealed more strongly to the less radical African states and to the West. The UPA leader, Holden Roberto, has been a frequent visitor to the United States. His closest ties were with Premier Cyrille Adoula's government in the Congo (Leopoldville), a government which Peking frequently denounced as a U.S. puppet. In 1963 the Organization of African Unity (OAU) recognized the Angolan National Liberation Front (FNLA), which is dominated by Roberto's UPA, as the only legitimate liberation movement. But in December 1963—during Kenya's independence celebrations—Roberto met Ch'en Yi in

32. The discussion in this paragraph is drawn from the following sources in particular: NCNA, January 26 and February 17, 1964; Radio Peking, March 15, 1964. Also of special interest is the article "Lumumba's Successors are Fighting," which was published by *Nodongja Sinmun* (the North Korean paper) on February 6, 1964, and reported by NCNA the same day.

Nairobi. A few weeks later he declared that a radical change in Front policy was imperative. He had abandoned hope of getting effective support from the "hypocritical" Western countries, whom he accused of helping "our enemies." In contrast, "the communists assured me that we can have whatever we need in arms and money." In the beginning of January 1964, Roberto formally announced the GRAE's decision to accept help from the Chinese and from "other Communist" countries.[33]

There are two apparent reasons for Roberto's decision to seek aid from Peking rather than from Moscow. First, the Russians had in the past supported his rivals, the MPLA, and the Chinese were quick to seize the initiative after the OAU had conferred legitimacy on the FNLA. Secondly, his policies had to take account of his relations with the Adoula government. Bad as the Congo's relations with Peking were, relations with Moscow were even worse at the time Roberto started negotiations with the Chinese. But within days of the Congo government's announcement that it would allow Chinese aid to reach the UPA through the Congo,[34] Mulele's Chinese-backed insurrection broke out, and a further deterioration in Sino-Congo relations ensued.

Since January 1964, the attitude of Angolan leaders toward the West and China has undergone considerable change. Jonas Savimbi, at that time still secretary-general of UPA, stated that "the Chinese people were brothers of the Angolan people and were firmly supporting their struggle." [35] Another FNLA leader, Viriato da Cruz, declared that the Angolans would support all liberation struggles including "Vietnam, North Kalimantan and the C.P.R. [P.R.C.] attempt to recover Taiwan and to oppose the 'two Chinas plot.' " [36]

The change of front in Angola was paralleled by a similar development in Mozambique. Before January 1964, Peking supported the Mozambique National Democratic Union, a rival to the Libera-

---

33. See *The New York Times*, January 4 and January 7, 1964, for discussions of Roberto and the developments noted in this paragraph.

34. Marcel Lengema, Acting Foreign Minister of the Congo, stated: "We recognize Mr. Holden Roberto's government as the de jure government of Angola. The way it leads the fight for independence . . . are entirely within its sovereign rights. However, we posed one condition to recognition: all material assistance must be channeled through the Congolese government." See *The New York Times*, January 8, 1964.

35. See his remarks in Cairo, NCNA, April 7, 1964.

36. See his statement at the Afro-Asian Journalists' Conference in Bandung, NCNA, April 24, 1963.

tion Front of Mozambique (FRELIMO), headed by Dr. Eduardo Mondlane. Until then, Mondlane had been regarded as pro-American and in some quarters even as an "American agent." (He was a graduate of and a professor at Syracuse University until he resigned to throw himself into the Mozambique liberation struggle at the end of 1962. He is married to an American.)   FRELIMO is recognized by the OAU as the "legitimate" movement in the Mozambique struggle. In January, Mondlane accepted an invitation to visit Peking. On his return, he said he had been "very much impressed by the enthusiasm of the Chinese people towards the national liberation movement in Africa and their willingness to support the African people's struggle." (Later he went to Moscow and paid a similar tribute to the Russians.) He described Mao Tse-tung's works as "very stimulating to African liberation movements." In February 1964, the organ of FRELIMO condemned the United States, Britain, and other Western powers for supporting Salazar's regime. It added that such support "cannot but signify the coincidence of interests, an imperialist alliance against the popular will." [37]

There is little doubt that the correct explanation of why both Mondlane and Roberto turned to Communist China for support is that they had grown disillusioned with Western policies, they were embarrassed by the pro-Western labels fixed on them, and they needed to show greater results to survive as leaders.[38] They hoped that by turning to Peking they would jolt the West into changing its policies toward Portugal.

In Portuguese Guinea, where four separate liberation groups vie for leadership, the dominant movement is the African Independence Party of Guinea and Cape Verde Islands. Its activities are extensively reported by NCNA and Radio Peking. The attitude of its leader, Amilcar Cabral, toward Peking is shown by his statement on the occasion of Chou En-lai's visit to Conakry:

> The Chinese delegation will surely be accorded the warmest welcome. . . . This welcome will express the active solidarity of the African people with the Chinese people in their struggle. . . . The Chinese people . . . have consistently shown their firm solidarity with the African peoples in their struggle for national liberation and consolidation of their independence.[39]

---

37. *Mozambican Revolution*, February 1964.   Quoted by NCNA, March 21, 1964.

38. See Harry Heintzen, "Angola, Mozambique Leaders Turn to China," *New York Herald Tribune*, January 18, 1964.

39. NCNA, January 16, 1964.

Until quite recently, none of the liberation movements in the Republic of South Africa had adopted a sympathetic attitude toward the Chinese. The two African nationalist movements are the Pan-Africanist Congress (PAC) and the African National Congress (ANC). The ANC is allied with other congresses—notably the Indian National Congress and the Congress of Democrats, both of which are dominated by Moscow-oriented Communists. Although the ANC dominates the Congress alliance and adopts its own policy independent of Communist wishes, it remains neutral, for tactical reasons, in the conflict between the two Communist centers. Moreover, the Chinese attempt to introduce a racist element into the African struggle runs strongly counter to the ANC's firm belief in nonracialism. Nevertheless, certain African leaders feel the example of China's revolutionary struggle is as relevant to South Africa's liberation movement as to Algeria's or Cuba's.[40] Although the PAC refuses to cooperate with the Communists as a matter of policy, there is some recent evidence to suggest that it is divided internally on the question of accepting help from the Chinese. One section within the PAC strongly favors doing so and has sent delegates to Peking to develop better relations, but it is still uncertain how far the PAC will commit itself toward Peking.

There has also been some evidence of interest by dissident groups which support neither the ANC or PAC. Ten colored leaders—members of a National Liberation Front—were convicted in Capetown in April 1964 for membership in the Yui Chi Chan Club, which was alleged to have been based on the teachings of Mao Tse-tung. In 1963 a few South African Communists tried to establish a Peking wing of the Communist party. Their attempt was made through a monthly magazine, *Assagai* [sic], published in London. After a single attack by *The African Communist*, the London-based organ of the Moscow-oriented South African Communist party, it ceased publication. The Chinese effort also seems to be directed at the South African Confederation of Trade Unions (SACTU), within which there is a certain measure of Communist influence. A SACTU delegation went to China in 1961. *Drum* magazine (Johannesburg) reported that efforts were made in Peking in June 1963 to launch a movement in support of armed revolutionary struggle. Perhaps the main point

---

40. Robert Resha, ANC representative in Algiers, has said: "If we are not engaged in a bloody revolution, we cannot overthrow the government. This is the lesson we take into consideration, the lesson of China, of Cuba and of Algeria." Radio Algiers, June 20, 1963.

of the talks between John Marks (erroneously described by the Chinese as chairman of the national executive of the ANC) and Liu Ch'ang-sheng (who, according to *Drum*, has been chosen to mastermind Peking's "campaign to win Africa") was that the British protectorates in southern Africa would be the bases for revolutionaries. Almost immediately, invitations to visit China were sent to African politicians in Basutoland, Swaziland, and Bechuanaland.[41]

The three protectorates first became strongly aware of the P.R.C.'s African efforts after the middle of 1963 when a group of political leaders was invited to Peking. But to date, significant attitudes have emerged only in Basutoland. The Basutoland Congress party (BCP) started to receive financial support from Peking early in 1964. The BCP has its own reasons for seeking aid from Peking. When South African Communists tried to infiltrate its ranks in 1958–59, the fiercely nationalistic BCP expelled them and adopted an uncompromisingly hostile attitude toward them and toward Moscow. It also lent its support to the Pan-Africanist Congress exile organization in Basutoland. Its own orientation was toward Ghana, from which it received assistance. But this aid was apparently insufficient to enable the BCP to fight the crucial pre-independence elections which were scheduled for the end of 1964. With this need in mind, the BCP leader, Ntsu Mokhehle, sent his brother and the party's secretary-general to Peking in July 1964. Their mission appears to have paid off handsomely. If the experience of the pro-Moscow Communists is anything to go by, however, it seems unlikely that Mokhehle's strongly controlled BCP will orient itself toward Peking. The Chinese will probably find that the BCP has used them rather than the other way round.

When individual African leaders seek Chinese support. The Chinese do not restrict their offer of support to revolutionary movements or revolutionary leaders. These the Chinese seek out and help whenever they arise. As a short-term, tactical ploy, though, Peking has chosen individual African leaders whom it establishes as its favorites in particular countries. These privileged leaders are lavishly invested with funds, equipment (usually printing presses), and opportunities to extend patronage (the control of scholarships for students to be sent to China and the control of offers of trips to China). Peking's choice in Uganda was Joseph Kiwanuka, a gadfly in the

---

41. For documentation of the discussion in this paragraph, see *The Times* (London), April 16, 1964; *The African Communist* (London), v. 11, no. 3, April/June 1963, p. 250; *Drum*, September 1963.

political nationalist movement. In Zanzibar, the Chinese selected Mohammed Abdul Rahman (Babu), the Minister of Defense and Foreign Affairs in the revolutionary government and now a minister in the Republic of Tanzania. In the Sudan, their choice was A. M. Kheir, formerly a pro-Moscow Communist active in the World Peace Council headquarters in Prague but now employed by Radio Peking. In Kenya, they selected Oginga Odinga, now Vice President of the Republic. In Somalia, they chose the former Minister of Information Haravi. Their favorite in the Congo was Pierre Mulele.

The African leaders selected in this way are by no means all Communists or even Socialists. This statement is certainly true of Kiwanuka and Odinga. The latter has written:

> I was a teacher before I joined politics and it is still in my blood to assist students. It is in this vein and realization of the urgent need of our people to train for independence that I decided to send our students to Socialist countries. This need not imply my preference for socialism. In fact, I have also sent tens of students to study in America and other capitalist countries.[42]

Many African leaders have their own opportunitistic reasons for identifying themselves with Peking. The financial support they receive and the patronage with which they are invested are of great value in building up their own political positions in their parties. The Chinese interest in their investment is to establish political allies who can be useful to them in the short run. They clearly have no illusions about the limited value of these allies and do not regard them as capable of undertaking the "new wave" of revolutionary activities which the Chinese believe will develop all over Africa in the years to come.

In selecting its favorites, the P.R.C. appears to use two criteria: that they should hold some position of prominence in the radical nationalist movements and that they should be outspokenly critical of Western imperialism and especially of the Americans. Wherever possible, the Chinese seek Africans actively engaged in the mass media; their strongest preference is for key figures in ministries of information. They appear to place no restrictions on the way in which the funds and opportunities for patronage are used. Once selected, their man has complete freedom to use the resources to build up his own prestige and power within his movement.

---

42. In a letter to *East Africa and Rhodesia* (London), June 28, 1962.

These "alliances of convenience" have paid dividends in a number of cases. In Kenya, Odinga has loyally defended the Chinese against attacks by some of his ministerial colleagues, and he has worked hard to restore the Kenya government's shaken confidence as a result of Chinese policy in Somalia and Zanzibar. Haravi played an influential part in preparing Somalia's orientation toward China. Zanzibar's Babu was notably active in preparing his countrymen's willingness to accept Chinese support.

Welcoming the P.R.C.'s recognition of Zanzibar's revolutionary government (extended in January 1964), Babu (in his role as Minister for External Affairs and Trade) called it "a blow to all the imperialists headed by the USA." He added: "The victory of the Zanzibar revolution was only a step in the revolution in Africa, Asia and Latin America. The Zanzibar people must send greetings to chairman Mao Tse-tung because they had learned a lot from his works." This line was pursued in a subsequent government communique addressed to the OAU Foreign Ministers' Conference in Lagos on February 24, 1964. The communique asked: "Is imperialism headed by the US to be allowed to continue to rampage the African scene and thereby ruin the continent politically and economically or are the people of Africa to take immediate action against US imperialism and save this continent from becoming a second Latin America?" [43]

On February 19, Babu, in announcing P.R.C. aid of more than $5 million, said:

> Our policy is that we are aligned with neither the East nor the West. . . . There are some countries which offer aid with strings attached. Some want to procure certain advantages before they offer their aid; and others want us to be economically, if not politically, tied to them for their own interests. . . . Some people say that Zanzibar is the Cuba of Africa. This will be not only the Cuba, but also the paradise of Africa.[44]

Chinese trade and aid. Because all African states are interested in expanding trade and in increasing their sources of foreign aid, Peking's offers of assistance are bound to find a ready response from those countries with which it has established friendly relations. Its total impact in this field, however, has been relatively unimportant— even compared with that of the Russians.

Chinese trading tactics are hardheaded. The total volume of

43. The quotations in this paragraph are from NCNA, January 20 and February 28, 1964.
44. Radio Zanzibar, February 19, 1964.

trade with Africa remains small. Chinese exports to Africa grew from U.S. $1 million in 1955 to U.S. $48 million in 1959 and to $55.5 million in 1962. The import figures for 1959–62 were U.S. $216 million. The Chinese incurred a deficit of about U.S. $13 million in their trade with Africa during 1959–62. The African share of China's trade is only 14 per cent of China's trade with developing countries; this figure, in turn, is only 18 per cent of China's total trade.[45]

These figures do not include the P.R.C.'s trade, involving mainly maize and wool, with South Africa. According to official South African figures, Peking bought U.S. $15.75 million worth of maize and wool in 1962, and this figure tripled in 1963.[46] The People's Republic reacts to African pressure to stop this trade by denying its existence. Peking claims to have boycotted South Africa since 1960.[47] Lately, imports from South Africa have been arranged through intermediaries in Hong Kong. Trade has become so promising that the Verwoerd government sent a trade commissioner there in 1963. His office sent booklets explaining the opportunities for trade with South Africa to all the P.R.C.'s state-buying departments in November 1963.

Until early 1965 the P.R.C.'s economic and technical aid programs in Africa were comparatively small. Its first offer of a really substantial kind was made to Tanzania in March 1965; the Chinese indicated willingness to survey and build a railway link from Tanzania to Zambia at a cost which would be somewhere between U.S. $225 million and U.S. $450 million. P.R.C. promises of aid from 1956 to the middle of 1964 totaled roughly U.S. $240 million, of which less than a quarter has been disbursed. Of the total, U.S. $5 million went to the U.A.R. as a gift in 1956 at the time of Suez. A U.S. $21 million aid and interest-free loan was made to Ghana in

---

45. These statistics are taken from a paper produced for Chatham House by the Overseas Development Institute in November 1964.

46. See *Sunday Times* (Johannesburg), November 3, 1963, and *The New York Times*, January 14, 1964.

47. NCNA was authorized to issue the following statement on July 15, 1963:

The Government of the People's Republic of China and the Chinese people always deeply sympathize with, and resolutely support, the South African people's just struggle against apartheid and for independence and freedom. On the basis of this stand, the Chinese Government has, since July 1960, discontinued all its economic and trade ties with the South African colonial authorities. This stand of the Chinese Government was made clear by the China Council for the Promotion of International Trade in its letter of reply of March 28, 1961, to the South African United Front. (Quoted in the *Sudan Daily News*, July 26, 1963.)

1961. A U.S. $25 million, interest-free loan was granted to Guinea in 1960. A U.S. $21 million loan went to Mali in 1961. About U.S. $54 million was promised to Algeria in 1963, and U.S. $21.6 million was promised to Somalia in 1963. Kenya received a gift of U.S. $3 million and a loan of U.S. $18 million in 1964. Tanzania received an interest-free loan of U.S. $45 million and an outright gift of U.S. $3 million in 1964. There is, however, a wide gap between Chinese promises and performance in the aid field. By the end of 1964, only a tiny part of the loans to Guinea, Somalia, and Tanzania, and probably none of the loan to Ghana, had been disbursed. It is unlikely that more than U.S. $45–60 million have actually been used.

The People's Republic has shown considerable skill in the application of its essentially limited funds and technicians. Apart from Taiwan and Israel, it has done more than any other aid-granting country to make a little go a long way. But to do so, it has had to restrict itself to a few carefully chosen countries. To achieve maximum impact, it has carefully timed the announcement of aid. Its only big gift to the U.A.R. was made in the dark days of the Suez crisis; the loan to Guinea was made at a time when Guinea's economy was at rock-bottom; the loan to Algeria was made in the first flush of independence; the aid for Somalia came in 1963 when the Somalis felt themselves most isolated.

Chinese aid has been carefully devised to achieve two results: to impress the peasants with Chinese know-how and to strengthen the radio, communications, and information services of selected countries. This latter program usually includes special training of key personnel in China.

The Chinese have shown great skill and psychological astuteness in the presentation of their aid policy. They stress that aid is of mutual benefit—that is, the Africans are not simply recipients and the Chinese donors. "Aid is always mutual and not unilateral. The Guinean peoples' struggle against imperialism and old and new colonialism, and their persistence in the national-democratic revolution constitutes an extremely great support for the Chinese people." [48] They also stress that their support "is aid between poor friends who share joys and sorrows without the least intention of maltreating the small and weak countries by the big and strong." [49]

---

48. Joint Guinea- P.R.C. communique after Chou En-lai's visit to Conakry. Quoted by NCNA, January 29, 1964.

49. Chou En-lai statement to Radio Mali (Bamako), January 21, 1964.

Wherever Chou En-lai went on his 1963–64 visit, he tried to persuade African leaders to include an eight-point statement on the nature of P.R.C. aid policies in the joint communiques, but although many countries agreed to insert one or two of the points, only in Mali was the whole policy included.

What impression has Chinese aid made on Africans? The strongest impact at grass-roots level has undoubtedly been in Mali. Here, although, as Chou En-lai has said, Chinese aid "now is very limited," the government has paid tribute "to the line and efficiency of Chinese aid." [50] Apart from the P.R.C.'s contribution to Mali's information services (a contribution which has been of considerable mutual benefit), its major commitment has been assistance for Niger Office, a state-owned agricultural scheme. Several Malian statements illustrate the value of the program.[51] Mamadou Diarrah, the mayor of Koulikoro, expressed satisfaction with the "concrete and positive results" obtained by Chinese agricultural experts and admiration for their "brotherly spirit." Chief Bakulu of the Niono farming sector praised the "grey-haired Chinese specialist, Tang Yao-tzu," with whose help Malian agrotechnicians and state farm workers had accomplished "in a little more than a year what the colonialists had told us would take us 25 years—growing sugar cane in our country." Chief Mamadou Phonba of Kolongo stated that with the help of a Chinese expert who came in 1962, rice paddy production had been raised from an average yield of 1 ton and a maximum of 3 tons per hectare to 5.5 tons in one plot and 6.5 tons in another. Speaking of the Chinese technicians, Awa Keita, the general secretary of the women's organization of the Sudanese Union party of Mali, praised the way the Chinese technicians "have perfectly adapted themselves to the geographical, political, social and working conditions of Mali. Their technical competence is coupled with a scrupulous professional conscience and crowned with a keen sense of human understanding."

AFRICAN STATES' RELATIONS WITH THE P.R.C.

Up to now, we have discussed essentially the interaction between the P.R.C.'s approach to Africa and the responses of a number of individuals or groups. These instances might give a distorted pic-

---

50. Sino-Mali Joint Communique, January 21, 1964. See SCMP, no. 3146, p. 30.
51. See particularly NCNA, January 18 and March 25, 1964.

ture of the P.R.C.'s impact. For an overall estimate, it is necessary to add a short, continent-wide but not exhaustive, review of state-to-state relations. I will refer only briefly to the position of the United Arab Republic. Besides the U.A.R., five other countries—Algeria, Cameroun, Somalia, Congo (Leopoldville), and Tanzania—have shown real interest in and sharp reactions to the Chinese role in Africa.

North Africa. The Afro-Arab states have no common policy or common attitude toward the Chinese; their attitudes range from sharply critical (Tunisia, Morocco, and Libya) to suspicious (the U.A.R. and the Sudan) to friendly but anxious (Algeria).

The Chinese Communists were for a long time contemptuous of the role of the Algerian and French Communist parties in Algeria. It has recently described this role as dancing "to the baton of Khrushchev" and accepting "the revisionist line against armed struggle." The Chinese thoroughly approved the seven-year "war of national liberation" waged by the "Algerian people" (as distinct from the Communist party) and showed their approval (as well as their contempt for Soviet policy) by recognizing the Algerian Provisional Government shortly after it was formed in September 1958.[52]

Though the Chinese never actually sent military aid or volunteers, their support for the FLN is still warmly recalled and, as we have seen above, contributed greatly to the development in Algeria of a sense of "common struggle" and to respect for the Chinese model.[53] Ties were strengthened after independence by frequent exchanges of persons and by a Chinese long-term interest-free loan of U.S. $54 million.

On the face of things, Algeria seemed the likeliest of all African states to ally itself with the P.R.C. But although the bonds remain

---

52. See "The Proletarian Revolution and Khrushchev's Revisionism," *Red Flag* and *People's Daily*, March 31, 1964. Also see Edward Behr, *The Algerian Problem* (London: Penguin, 1961), pp. 219–220.

53. Ex-President Ben Bella went to the opening of the 1963 P.R.C. exhibit in Algiers to show that Algeria "does not forget" Chinese support during "our liberation struggle." He stated that "our National Liberation Army proved an effective and a sure instrument rather similar to the Red Army in the great battles fought in China," and he added that Algeria had "derived lessons of particular value to our country" from China. (See Radio Algiers, September 1, 1963.) Muhammad Habib, chairman of the Union Générale des Travailleurs Algériens, has praised the Chinese, "who have never ceased to support us in the struggle for liberation," for providing "sincere and disinterested aid." (See Radio Peking, November 7, 1963.)

close, the relationship is in fact far from easy. Ben Bella had steadily refused to become involved in the Sino-Soviet conflict. As of March 1964, Algeria had no ambassador in Peking.[54] Ben Bella's Algeria had doubts about the P.R.C. role in the Arab world as a result of Chinese dabbling in Iraqi politics and resented the P.R.C.'s "older brother" attitude toward Algerian socialism. There is evidence that a considerable tussle took place between Ben Bella and Chou En-lai over the wording of the joint communique after the latter's 1963 visit. The Algerians insist they are already engaged in socialist reconstruction—a claim which the Chinese regard as premature. Ben Bella's sudden downfall in July 1965 produced a new element of uncertainty about Algeria's internal and international policies.

Despite the friendly tone of the joint communique issued by President Nasser and Chou En-lai on December 21, 1963, President Nasser professes to be "disillusioned" about the Chinese. They were exceptionally nice at Bandung, and then they let him down. The 1956 trade agreement was "a failure"; they "tricked" him in Iraq.[55] Nevertheless, he feels a sense of gratitude for their prompt support at the time of Suez and for their general support against Israel. The U.A.R., moreover, leans toward the Soviet side of the Sino-Soviet dispute.[56] President Nasser took a line strongly hostile to Peking at the second conference of nonaligned states in Cairo in 1964.

The Sudan regards "the government of the P.R.C. as the only republic of the great Chinese people." [57] Ex-President Abboud's welcome to Chou En-lai was fulsome, but the joint communique of January 30, 1964, covered up a good deal more than it revealed. The

54. After the U.S. State Department published a report in April 1964, naming Algeria as one of four African countries moving toward communism, Cherif Guellal, Algerian ambassador in Washington, commented: "The Americans have never given me the impression that they worried about our policies until now. We don't even have an Ambassador in Peking, and we have no intention of getting into the cold war." *Evening Standard* (London), April 8, 1964.

55. For a valuable review of relations between the U.A.R., the Soviet Union, and the P.R.C. in Iraq, see Hasanayn Haykal "Communists in Iraq," *Al Ahram*, March 29, 1963. One of three reasons he gives for writing this article was "not to give China the opportunity to find a justification for its wrong logic in . . . portraying certain events as proof of strong hostility against the East."

56. Muhammad Hasanayn Haykal, Nasser's chief spokesman, says that the Chinese are wrong in arguing "that the Soviet Union should limit its cooperation and should help only those states which hoist the flags of Marxism and Leninism." ("Voice of the Arabs," Radio Cairo, March 29, 1963.)

57. Radio Omdurman, January 28, 1964.

Chinese role in Iraq and Somalia, the Chinese attitude toward Ethiopia, and especially Chinese support for the Sudan's exiled Communist leader, A. M. Kheir, all cast a shadow.

Tunisia and Morocco are both openly critical of the Chinese, and vice versa. Tunisia consistently voted for the P.R.C.'s admission to the United Nations and accorded recognition early in 1964 on the eve of Chou En-lai's visit. President Bourguiba, however, made his policies clear on several occasions during that visit. As he related to a press conference:

> I told him [Chou En-lai] what shocked us is his manner, style
> and conceptions. I said: you come to Africa as the enemy of
> the capitalist states, of the West, of the socialists, of the neutral-
> ists and the non-aligned, of India, of Tito, of Khrushchev, of
> everybody. You have not chosen an easy policy. I'll say that.
> Don't expect to score much in Africa. Others won't tell you
> straight; I will—you won't get far on this continent.[58]

Although Morocco has also consistently supported the P.R.C.'s entry into the United Nations, their relations were strained before Chou En-lai's visit because of Chinese support for the Moroccan opposition parties. Things grew rapidly worse after the visit. King Hassan insisted that Chou En-lai pay tribute to his government in the joint communique.[59] But a month later, Chou En-lai went out of his way to couple Morocco with Ethiopia as two countries which "should throw off outside control."

West Africa. Of the five politically important West African states (excluding the Francophone UAM members, which will be discussed later), Ghana, Guinea, and Mali are well disposed toward the Chinese, and Nigeria and Liberia are strongly opposed. The three who look with some favor on the Chinese are influenced by a common factor—a desire to counterbalance Russian policies.

In Guinea, the promptness with which the P.R.C. provided aid in the bleak months that followed independence in 1958 stands to China's credit. Chinese aid and trade, however, are not large. A

58. Russell Warren Howe, *Jewish Observer and Middle East Review* (London), April 3, 1964.
59. "Premier Chou En-lai praised the successes achieved by His Majesty's Government and the Moroccan people in their efforts to consolidate national independence and develop the national economy and for the evacuation of foreign military bases, as well as their support to the African peoples in their struggle for national independence." (Sino-Moroccan Joint Communique, NCNA, December 31, 1963.)

1960 agreement provided for a 10-year, interest-free U.S. $25 million loan; in 1962 Guinea imported U.S. $645 thousand worth of goods from China and exported U.S. $540 thousand worth to them. (Russia's aid, in comparison, totals about U.S. $35 million.) Guineans, nevertheless, admire the skill with which Chinese aid was given (15,-000 tons of rice at a time of food shortage) and the modest but earnest application of the Chinese technical experts who have been trying to grow tea and who have built Radio Conakry's new radio station. Secondly, there is a feeling that the Guinean and Chinese revolutions were "born in similar historic conditions, based on the same principles, directed toward similar goals, necessarily partake of the same nature, and are under the same banner and in one and the same historic current, determining the nature of universal evolution." [60] Thirdly, the rupture in Soviet-Guinea relations in 1961 opened the way for closer relations with the Chinese. Peking became Sékou Touré's other leg on which to balance his nonalignment as he turned increasingly to the West, and especially the United States, for aid after 1961.

Although Mali is an associate member of the European Economic Community, its relations with Western countries are of the slenderest nature. While its relations with the Russians are friendly, it is, among all the African states, the most forthright admirer of the People's Republic. Its admiration is tempered, however, by its own strong ethnocentricity. China-Mali relations have prospered as a result of extensive interchanges of cultural missions and exhibitions. P.R.C. aid to Mali since independence totals roughly U.S. $21 million, which is just under half Russia's total. The success of Chinese technical assistance to the Niger Office and other rural programs is consolidated by the efforts of the Ministry of Information, which is staffed by some of the most ardent Peking admirers in Mali.

The eclectic Marxism of Ghana's President Nkrumah owes a great deal to Mao Tse-tung. The revolutionary ideas of the Chinese Communist party figure prominently in Nkrumah's tactics.[61] Since his visit to Peking in August 1961, Sino-Ghanaian relations have

---

60. See Sékou Touré's remarks to Chou En-lai during the latter's visit to Guinea in early 1964, NCNA, January 23, 1964.

61. "In the early years of the CPP and frequently since I urged members to follow the advice of the Chinese: 'Go to the people; live among them; learn from them; love them; serve them; plan with them; start with what they know; build on what they have.'" See Kwame Nkrumah, *Africa Must Unite* (New York: Praeger, 1963).

grown steadily stronger. Nevertheless, Dr. Nkrumah's political philosophy of "Consciencism" in essence rejects Maoist theory. It denies the inevitability of the class struggle in Africa, and it predicates conditions for an evolutionary development from traditional communalism to socialism.[62]

Nigeria supports the P.R.C.'s right to U.N. membership but has no diplomatic relations with Peking. Its official attitude wavers between suspicion and hostility. On February 5, 1964, Radio Lagos, which tends to reflect official thinking, commented:

> . . . the recent tour of Mr. Chou En-lai must have opened the eyes of many African states to the real intent and purpose of the Chinese adventure in Africa. . . . Knowing that African nations are now resolved to take concerted action on all international issues, did Mr. Chou intend to use his friendship with a number of African states to influence that organization? . . . in spite of general courtesy shown to the august visitor by African leaders, there is no doubt that Mr. Chou failed . . . to inspire confidence, especially by some of his public utterances. First of all, there has been the open disagreement by African heads of state over China's failure to sign the nuclear test ban treaty. Conceding, however, that China's action was to blackmail the UN into accepting its membership, Mr. Chou should have at least sought to convince Africa of his sincerity of purpose. . . . There is at least one hope; that Mr. Chou's visit to Africa will open his eyes to the realities of present-day international politics. . . . China cannot do without the support of African nations in the UN.

Nigerian official attitudes stem from the government's concern with Chinese intervention in neighboring Cameroun and from the support the P.R.C. has given to the radical opposition inside Nigeria. These official attitudes are strongly opposed by the Nigeria-China Friendship Association, by the Nigerian Youth Congress, and by a number of radical leaders like Dr. Chike Obi of the Dynamic party.

The Horn of Africa. For about two years after mutual recognition, toward the end of 1960, Sino-Somali relations were formal rather than friendly. As late as March 1963, the Chinese embassy —the biggest foreign delegation in the country—complained that the Somali government newspaper refused to print material supplied by the New China News Agency. In the field of technical assistance, the P.R.C.'s only contribution was to help build Radio Mogadishu's

---

62. Kwame Nkrumah, *Consciencism* (New York: Praeger, 1964).

new 60,000-watt transmitter. This collaboration brought about close relations with the then Minister of Information, Ali Mohammad Haravi.

The deterioration of Somalia's relations with Kenya and Ethiopia in 1962 had adverse effects on its relations with the Western countries and with the Soviet Union, all of whom wished to balance their positions between Somalia and her neighbors. Trips to Peking by Haravi and Premier Shermarke followed. The Chinese offered both economic and military aid—which stimulated the Russians to outbid them. Sino-Somali relations thus became close for a time, but at the price of a loss of confidence in the P.R.C. by Somalia's neighbors. By the middle of 1964, however, the Somalis had reverted to their former, more closely nonaligned position.

Ethiopia had supported the P.R.C.'s admission to the United Nations but withheld diplomatic recognition. As a result of the Sino-Somali accord, Ethiopia's attitude became more outspokenly critical. Emperor Haile Selassie's public exchanges of views with Chou En-lai in the course of the latter's visit in February 1964 were quite frank. Their private exchanges were presumably even more so.

East Africa. All the East African states have recognized the People's Republic, but their attitudes differ widely. Tanzania's relations with Peking are cordial; Kenya's attitude is openly critical; and Uganda is neutral. These attitudes have been conditioned by three factors—the Zanzibar revolution, the Congo rebellion, and internal problems.

Zanzibar's successful revolution in January 1964 was widely attributed to the efforts of the Chinese. Chou En-lai termed this attribution "an honour for us, but I must tell you that we had nothing to do with the events in Zanzibar." [63] Nor was he lying so far as the revolution itself was concerned. Its inspiration came in the first place from Karume's Afro-Shirazi Party Youth Wing, a typical nationalist movement. The plotters recruited to their ranks John Okello, the self-styled Field Marshal, because of his supposed experience with the Mau Mau. Although this experience, like most of his braggardly claims, was fabricated, he did successfully emerge for a time as the spokesman of the rebels' cause—a kind of "black messiah" rather than a disciple of a foreign ideology. Babu's Umma party joined the rebel movement only a few weeks before it struck. Within

---

63. Radio Mogadishu, February 4, 1964.

weeks after the successful coup, Okello was "bought out" by the Revolutionary Council. The pressure for his removal came from Babu and his Umma supporters. Okello's success rubbed off on the Chinese for three reasons: Western press reporting, faulty intelligence, and the swift exploitation of the situation by Babu and his group. Babu, though supported by Peking, describes himself as "an anarchist" with no alignments in the international conflicts.[64]

African reactions to the Zanzibar coup and to the possible role of the Chinese in it were varied. The East African mainland governments, while desiring a change of government, deplored the methods used to achieve it, but there were influential figures in all three governments (notably Odinga in Kenya and Kambona in Tanganyika) who were ready to welcome the new revolutionary government. However, the mutinies which the Zanzibar revolution sparked off in Tanganyika, Kenya, and Uganda strengthened feelings against revolutionary methods. Chinese criticism of the three governments' decisions to invite British troops to deal with these mutinies was deeply resented as interference. Elsewhere in Africa, reactions to the events in Zanzibar were confused. The Muslim countries deplored the anti-Arab complexion of the revolution. Within a month of the revolution, however, the Chinese had been outmaneuvered for influence by the Russians and the East Germans.

When Tanganyika became independent in December 1961, it recognized the P.R.C. But the Tanganyikans strongly disliked the racist approach of the Chinese at the AAPSO conference in Moshi, Tanganyika, at the beginning of 1963, and they were nettled by the Chinese attitude toward the Committee of Nine. The Committee of Nine, or the African Liberation Committee, was set up by the Organization of African Unity to coordinate the struggle of the liberation movements in southern Africa. It was presided over by Tanganyika's (now Tanzania's) Foreign Minister, Oscar Kambona. In August 1963, the Indian, South African, and Kenyan members of the AAPSO executive committee proposed that the organization should establish close relations with the committee. The Chinese resisted strongly on the ground that some "reactionaries" had participated in the 1963 Addis Ababa summit conference (where the OAU was established). To emphasize Chinese objections, the NCNA representative in Dar Es Salaam absented himself from the Tanganyika

---

64. Patrick Seale, *The Observer* (London), March 8, 1964.

capital just before the Committee of Nine held its first meeting.[65] Friendly relations were further impeded by Chinese criticism of President Nyerere's request for British troops to help quell his army's mutiny.

There are, however, elements of common interest between the two countries. Tanganyika's Trade Minister, A. Z. N. Swai, has emphasized the value of strengthening economic and trade relations between the two countries.[66] In one important respect, Nyerere shares a common outlook with Peking. He too divides the world between rich and poor countries and not just between capitalist and socialist countries.[67] At the same time, he reacts contemptuously to the Chinese attempts to divide the world between "white and colored nations." When President Nyerere took the initiative to establish the Republic of Tanganyika and Zanzibar (later renamed the Republic of Tanzania) in April 1964, the P.R.C. chairman, Liu Shao-ch'i, sent a message of "sincere congratulations," and then as Russian and East German influence grew, relations between Nyerere and Peking changed remarkably. It was now the Soviet bloc which was the thorn in Tanzania's flesh, while the Chinese were more interested in persuading Nyerere, in particular, of their good intentions. Therefore, when Nyerere was reorganizing the training of his army in August 1964, he balanced Western with Chinese elements in his training program. The Chinese were asked to provide about a dozen weapons' instructors for three months.[68]

This decision upset Nyerere's Western friends and his neighbors, notably Kenya, Malawi, and Zambia. A series of events in Zanzibar early in 1965 worsened Tanzania's relations with the West, especially with the United States and West Germany; and when Tanzania openly assisted the cause of the Congo rebels (because of their strong

---

65. Alastair Matheson, "China Propaganda Efforts in East Africa," *The Observer* (London), Foreign News Service, no. 19535, August 27, 1963.

66. NCNA, November 18, 1963.

67. "Even between socialist countries the class divisions are getting greater. There are now not only rich capitalist countries and poor countries. There are also rich socialist countries and poor socialist countries. Further, I believe that the socialist countries . . . are now committing the same crime as was committed by the capitalists before. On the international level they are beginning to use wealth for capitalist purposes—that is, for the acquisition of power and prestige." (Address to the AAPSO conference at Moshi on February 4, 1963, Tanganyika Information Department, Dar Es Salaam.)

68. See President Nyerere's interview with the author, *The Observer* (London), August 30, 1964.

objections to the return of Tshombe as Prime Minister), its alignment
was openly questioned in many Western capitals. These suspicions
were fed by the announcement in June 1965 that the P.R.C. had
agreed three months earlier to consider building Tanzania's section
of the railway line to link it with Zambia—a project which the West
had steadily refused to support. To some Western observers it had
begun to look as if the Chinese were succeeding in establishing a
bridgehead in East Africa through Tanzania. But the Chinese took
a less sanguine view of the situation. When Nyerere visited China
in March 1965, he told a mass meeting in Peking that just as he
refused to allow the Americans to choose his friends for him, so he
refused the Chinese the right to do so. He also rejected their racist
views of the liberation struggles in southern Africa. But what subsequently displeased the Chinese even more was Nyerere's statement
that, because of his loyalty to Ben Bella, he would boycott the Afro-
Asian conference if it were held in Algiers after the Boumedienne
coup. He was clearly shocked by the ease and speed with which the
Chinese had been willing to sacrifice Ben Bella because of their obsession with holding the conference on schedule.

The Chinese regarded the Mau Mau rebellion in Kenya as a
patriotic national struggle by peasant guerrillas under strict discipline.[69]
When Vice-Premier Ch'en Yi, who represented the P.R.C. at the
Kenya independence celebration in December 1963, called officially
on the then Minister of Home Affairs Odinga, the latter paid tribute
to China's support for Kenya's struggle for independence—support
which, he said, "Prime Minister Kenyatta and I will never forget."
In reply, Ch'en Yi alluded to the "similar sufferings" the two peoples
had undergone in the past and predicted that after independence both
would work for "the common tasks . . . to fight against the imperialist
policies." [70]

But relations have been far from smooth. The Sino-Somali
economic and military aid agreement of August 1963 was signed at a
time when Kenya-Somali relations were severely strained. Kenyatta
at once made strong private protests to Liu Shao-ch'i and received
assurances that the Chinese would in fact limit the military aid they
gave to the Somalis. Nevertheless, relations remained uneasy. There
were still undiplomatic contacts between Chinese diplomats and

69. For a good description of the P.R.C.'s treatment of the Mau Mau rebellion see Kao Liang's dispatch from Nairobi to NCNA, December 6, 1963.
70. NCNA, December 11, 1963.

certain Kenyan leaders; Kenyatta several times attacked such contacts publicly but without mentioning the Chinese by name. Early in 1964, the Kenya government became suspicious of Chinese activities in Zanzibar, and after Peking's attacks on the requests of the Kenya, Uganda, and Tanganyika governments for British military support to deal with the mutinies in their armies, the Kenyatta government restricted the number of Chinese and other Eastern diplomatic missions in Nairobi, limited NCNA representation, and imposed certain travel restrictions. Nevertheless, Kenyatta wants to establish normal relations, and in March 1964 he sent his first ambassador to Peking. But his efforts at persuading the Chinese to adopt a proper diplomatic attitude toward Kenya went unrewarded. The Chinese, in keen rivalry with the Russians, continued to provide large sums of money to individuals within the Kenya government. Matters began to come to a head early in 1965 when a member of parliament was assassinated as a result of what was generally believed to be an internecine struggle between opposing groups within the Kenya left-wing movement. The Kenyatta government took a firm stand first with the Russians by rejecting their shipment of obsolete arms and then with the Chinese by expelling their NCNA correspondent, who acted as the Chinese embassy's go-between in dealing with certain Kenyan politicians. The latter move was followed by demands in Kenya's parliament for a suspension of diplomatic relations with the P.R.C.

Before independence, Uganda's contact with the P.R.C. was limited to a few visits to China by members of the Uganda National Congress. The result of one of these visits was Peking's decision to support Joseph Kiwanuka. "Jolly Joe" is widely popular but politically insignificant. Ugandians spoke of the Chinese as an "easy touch." Chinese propaganda support for the struggle of "the peasants . . . to get back their lands" caused resentment in the ruling circles of Buganda, for the only peasant land movement was against the Kabaka of Buganda.

On becoming independent in 1961, Uganda recognized the P.R.C. Relations since then have been formal at a government level, but there are signs that some of the younger Ugandian nationalists in the ruling party, the Uganda People's Congress (UPC), have come to regard the Chinese as allies.[71] The activities of this group

71. "The imperialists, in the disguise of the Church missionaries, outdid everybody in blindfolding the African people and keeping them ignorant and mis-

were strongly condemned at the UPC national conference in May 1964, when Uganda's Minister of Interior trounced the "Communists." These attacks became more specific in September 1964 when the Minister of State in the Prime Minister's Office, Grace Ibingira, repudiated the views of youth leaders who had been to Peking. He issued a stern warning to foreign embassies in Uganda not to meddle in local politics. "The UPC," he said, "will not be used as a mouthorgan or a puppet of any foreign power," and he added that the party would not accept people who intended to earn a living by working as puppets.[72] Relations between the two countries have, however, continued to develop on a basis of normal friendship, which was formally sealed by the visit of Premier Milton Obote to Peking in July 1965.

Francophone Africa. It is convenient to lump together the French-speaking countries, except Guinea and Mali, regardless of whether they were once French or Belgian colonies. Their attitudes toward Communist China have been conditioned partly by the policies of France and partly by their own experience. In Cameroun, Congo (Leopoldville), and Rwanda, for example, the Chinese have openly supported armed insurrectionary movements.

Reactions to De Gaulle's recognition of the People's Republic in January 1964 were mixed.[73] Senegal at once took the cue from Paris. Its Foreign Minister explained that "one could not ignore the human potential represented by China, a country with socialist leanings and absolute master of its own destiny." Dahomey "joyfully hailed the realistic attitude of France towards People's China." Congo (Brazzaville) recognized the P.R.C. on February 18, 1964 "as the sole legal government representing all the Chinese People." President Houphouët-Boigny of the Ivory Coast (which recognizes neither Peking nor Taiwan) said that the French action was irrelevant to the attitude his country would adopt. Malagasy's President Tsiranana refused to follow De Gaulle "since it would be contrary to

---

informed about the Uganda peoples' Chinese friends. . . . In spite of all these . . . efforts of the imperialists the anti-imperialist fraternity of the world liberation movement pulled the Chinese and African people together . . . Uganda has much to learn from the experience of the Chinese people in the successful socialist revolution. Uganda has expressed full support to the Chinese people in the struggle against US imperialism. . . ." (*The Pilot*, the UPC paper, quoted by NCNA, January 14, 1964.)

72. *Africa Mail* (Lusaka), September 11, 1964.

73. For the views mentioned in this paragraph, see Radio Leopoldville, January 24, 1964; Radio Cotonou, January 24, 1964; NCNA, January 22, 1964; Radio Abidjan, January 23, 1964; Radio Yaounde, February 8, 1964.

Madagascar's [Malagasy's] interests to recognize Peking. . . . the events in Zanzibar, Tanganyika and Somalia are imperative reasons why the Chinese Communist government should not be recognized." A similar view was expressed by Cameroun's President Ahidjo.

The Kingdom of Burundi recognized the P.R.C. in December 1963. "The Voice of the Burundi people is unanimous: we recognize only People's China." [74] But the government of neighboring Rwanda accused the Chinese of giving support to the Tutsi insurrectionary movement. Here is one of the most ironical situations in Africa. The Cockroach movement seeks to restore the rule of the former Mwami of Rwanda; it represents the minority which, until the successful peasant revolt of 1958, had kept the Hutu majority in serf-like obedience to the Tutsi aristocracy. In Rwanda, therefore, Chinese support goes to "king and aristocracy" against a revolutionary peasants' government. This basic situation is not altered by the fact that the Belgian administration sided with the peasant revolution once it sensed that the revolution was bound to succeed.

Francophone Africa's "honeymoon" with Peking produced some curious results. The P.R.C. had succeeded by the latter part of 1964 in establishing close relations with Burundi, so close in fact that there were the familiar stories of the Chinese having gained a "firm foothold in the heart of Africa." Their position enabled them to maintain contact with the Congo rebel leaders operating along Burundi's frontiers. Then, suddenly, the Chinese were told to pack their bags and depart from the Kingdom in January 1965, only a few days after Burundi's Prime Minister had been assassinated. But their relations with the government of Congo (Brazzaville) have continued to progress steadily. On the other hand, there was strong criticism of Chinese policies in Africa by a majority of the fourteen Francophone African states which met in Mauritania in February 1965 to form a new Pan-African grouping, the Organisation Commune Africaine et Malagache (O.C.A.M.).

INTERNATIONAL TESTS OF SINO-AFRICAN RELATIONS

Apart from the question of whether the People's Republic should be seated at the United Nations, there have been several other international issues which provided a test of African attitudes toward Peking.

---

74. Burundi's Vice-Premier Pie Masumbuko, NCNA, January 14, 1964.

Partial nuclear test ban treaty. The P.R.C.'s bitter denunciation of this treaty was pressed vigorously in its African propaganda and through diplomatic channels. Nevertheless, the African states without exception became signatories. The P.R.C.'s attitude united Africa against the P.R.C., and it strengthened the growing feeling that China might be willing to push its revolutionary ideology and its opposition to peaceful coexistence to extreme lengths. Chou En-lai was clearly aware of this fear. On his first African journey, he did his best to ease it. The first Chinese nuclear test produced mixed reactions. The great majority of African states condemned China's entry into the nuclear race; Ghana was among the critics. But Guinea, Mali, Algeria, and Congo (Brazzaville) welcomed it as a contribution to world peace and stability.

The Sino-Indian Conflict of 1962–63. There was surprisingly little public reaction in Africa to this conflict. The Indian diplomat K. P. S. Menon has offered this explanation:

> Many of our Asian and African friends, like ourselves, seemed somewhat slow to recognise the ruthless phenomenon that present-day China is; and their antipathy to Chinese aggression seemed to differ in inverse proportion to their distance from China. Nevertheless, it is a matter for satisfaction that by and large India has had the sympathy of her Afro-Asian friends in the crisis.[75]

The emphasis here is on "sympathy"; what was lacking in most cases was active support for India.[76] All the UAM members sent messages of sympathy, but only Niger condemned "Chinese aggression." Ethiopia was most explicit in its denunciation of "the Chinese aggressors." Malawi's Prime Minister, Dr. H. K. Banda, asked: "How can people preach solidarity when one major power which attended the conference [Bandung] had attacked another power which was also at the conference?" Nigeria's Prime Minister, Sir Abubakar Tafawa Balewa, said the Chinese theory of "might is right"

---

75. *India News* (New Delhi), January 25, 1964.
76. For a general discussion of the subject, see Dr. Mahendra Kumar, "Reactions and Attitudes of African Countries to Chinese Aggression on India," *Africa Quarterly* (New Delhi), January/March 1963. For the specific reactions noted in this paragraph, see Mrs. Laxmi Menon's statement in the Lok Sabha on January 21, 1963, *The Hindustan Times*, January 22, 1963; Nyasaland (Malawi) Information Department Press Release (Zomba), no. 1194/63, December 18, 1963; *The New York Times*, November 12, 1962.

cannot be tenable and that "any country that embraces it would be condemned."

The Nigerian papers came out strongly against China. The influential *West African Pilot* was in favor of "prompt, direct and adequate aid to India" and saw "an opportunity for concerted action to cage the dragon." [77] The *Daily Telegraph* (Lagos) wrote that peace-loving India "has been forced into violence by Communist China," and that China "has embarked on aggression." [78] The Egyptian press also was hostile toward the Chinese. *Al Goumhouriya* had no doubt that China was the aggressor. It suggested (on November 6, 1962) that India should cease supporting the P.R.C.'s admission to the United Nations to "discourage aggression." The Cairo weekly *Rosal Youssef* called on Russia to stop supplying weapons to China.[79]

Ghana's attitude displeased the Indians most. President Nkrumah, although supporting President Nasser's move for conciliation, protested strongly against the British government's decision to give India "every support"—a decision which "gravely distressed and saddened" him. "Whatever the wrongs and rights," peace could best be served "by refraining from any action that may aggravate the unfortunate situation." [80]

There was a broad measure of agreement among African leaders on two points: that a dispute between Afro-Asian nations should not be allowed to become a cold war issue and that the situation called for the good offices of African and Asian leaders to achieve conciliation. Kenya's Prime Minister Kenyatta declared that his party stood by "positive neutrality" and refused to allow the dispute to "lure us into the western or eastern camps." He also called for a settlement through "peaceful negotiations." [81] A statement by the U.A.R. Presidential Council said the armed conflict

> has caused pain in the hearts of the sons of the UAR who are linked with the Indian and Chinese peoples with bonds of friendship and close cooperation. In view of the serious situation . . .

---

77. See an editorial entitled "Chinese Dragon" and quoted by Radio Lagos, October 31, 1962. *The Pilot* speaks for the National Council of Nigerian Citizens and is closely connected with the Governor General, Dr. N. Azikiwe.
78. See an editorial entitled "Yellow Peril," October 23, 1962.
79. Quoted in *The Hindu* (Madras), November 7, 1962.
80. Radio Accra, October 31, 1962.
81. Quoted in *The Hindu* (Madras), November 4, 1962.

the UAR could not stand by as a spectator. The spirit of Bandung and the principles of Afro-Asian solidarity impelled the UAR to take rapid action and carry out a positive role.[82]

President Nasser's initiative led to the December 1962 Colombo meeting, which was attended by the U.A.R., Ghana, Ceylon, Burma, Cambodia and Indonesia. The proposals which emerged from this meeting met with ready approval from India but with only guarded acceptance by the Chinese. On balance, therefore, African attitudes leaned toward India rather than China. This is certainly the view of the Indians.

Second Afro-Asian conference. Before Chou En-lai set out on his first African mission, the Afro-Asian and nonaligned world was deeply divided on whether the next international conference should be a conference of nonaligned countries or a conference of Afro-Asian countries. Communist China strongly favored the second, while the U.A.R. and Yugoslavia favored the first. One of Chou En-lai's objectives was to win support for a second Bandung conference. While Algeria, Ghana, Guinea, Mali, the Sudan, and Somalia all approved another Afro-Asian conference, only Ghana and Mali indicated they preferred that it precede a nonaligned gathering. The result was that all the African countries which had been at the first Belgrade meeting—except Mali—attended a Colombo meeting in March 1964 to plan a second nonaligned conference. In view of the importance the Chinese had attached to the reverse order, the African rejection of their proposals can only be regarded as a rebuff.

The meaning of this rebuff was forcefully demonstrated at the second conference of nonaligned nations held in Cairo in October 1964 when, despite strong efforts by Indonesia to repudiate competitive coexistence and the United Nations, the conference almost unanimously rejected these primarily Chinese doctrinal ideas. The P.R.C. accordingly redoubled its efforts to ensure the success of the Afro-Asian conference at Algiers, and resolutely continued to oppose Russian participation. It failed, in advance of the conference, to persuade the African members to exclude the possibility of Russia's membership. Its own role in trying to prevent postponement of the Algiers meeting—first, by its prompt recognition of Ben Bella's successors and, second, by its pressure on African members to attend the meeting—produced sharp reactions. One African president notably

---

82. Radio Cairo, October 31, 1962.

friendly to the Chinese told the author that he was "shocked by the cynicism of the Chinese." An African foreign minister, likewise friendly to the P.R.C., commented: "The Chinese seem to have become obsessed with the need to hold the meeting as scheduled. I have seldom before encountered such heavy pressurizing tactics as on this occasion." Having staked so much on the meeting, the Chinese suffered a serious diplomatic setback by its postponement. Their role in this matter did the Chinese more damage in the eyes of African leaders disposed to friendship with them than any single action of theirs since they arrived on the African scene.

The Sino-Soviet conflict. Although Chou En-lai was careful during his first visit to African capitals not to raise in public the issues dividing Moscow and Peking, his representatives were nevertheless active in trying to rally African support against "Khrushchev's revisionism." So far no African country and only one African leader of any influence has publicly backed the Chinese view. The exception is the Malian ambassador to Peking.[83] On the other hand, there have been strong criticisms of the P.R.C.—especially over its attitude toward peaceful coexistence. This issue was repeatedly raised with Chou En-lai. Not only did he agree to allow "peaceful coexistence" to appear in several joint communiques, but in his final press conference before leaving Africa he felt it necessary to explain Chinese policy on this question.

Before his arrival in Africa, Chou En-lai had set his highest hopes on the leaders of Algeria, Mali, Ghana, and Guinea (in that order) for support against Moscow. President Ben Bella, however, stated publicly after Chou En-lai's visit to Algiers that "Algeria had no desire to take sides. . . . Algeria would have to balance its policy so that these differences in no way affected her independence." [84]

Nor have the Chinese received the open support from the liberation movements which they might reasonably have expected. After sounding out the opinion of leaders of the "freedom fighters" in Algiers, Patrick Seale concluded: "The African nationalist leaders refuse to take sides in the Sino-Soviet ideological dispute or to get involved in Great Power conflicts. Their marked preference is for aid from inside Africa rather than from any outside power." [85] A prominent

---

83. Quoted by Simon Malley in *Jeune Afrique* (Tunis), September 30, 1964.
84. In an interview with *Jeune Afrique* (Tunis) quoted by *Le Peuple* (Algiers), January 6, 1964.
85. *The Observer* (London), December 22, 1963.

Southern Rhodesian African leader commented: "We are heartily sick of having Chinese and Russian microphones stuck under our noses wherever we go and being invited to say whether we think China or Russia is giving us more effective aid. It is becoming worse than the rivalry between west and east." [86]

African leaders do not accept at face value the claim that the Sino-Russian conflict is purely ideological. A prominent Kenyan politician, sympathetic to the Chinese, has explained Chinese policy in this way:

> When the Chinese talk about ideology, they are really talking about foreign policy. Their foreign policy is based on their view that they are in a state of war with the United States. They see the Americans sitting in Formosa and in Vietnam, and leading the campaign to keep them out of the U.N. They fear that the Americans are trying to encircle and isolate them. As long as Russia was equally hostile to the Americans, there was a perfect basis for alliance between Moscow and Peking. But once Khrushchev began to talk peace to Kennedy, he was immediately seen by the Chinese to have gone over into the enemy's camp. [87]

This sophisticated understanding of Chinese policies is a useful reminder that even those Africans who look with some favor on Peking are not always gullible or incapable of making their own independent judgments of Chinese tactics.

The role of the United Nations. The Chinese tirelessly charge that the United Nations is under "the control and manipulation of the imperialist countries, headed by the U.S." and that these forces "usurp the name of the U.N. for aggression and intervention." [88] They cite the Congo as the prime example when they claim that U.N. intervention results in neocolonialism. At the International Conference on Economic Sanctions against South Africa, held in London in April 1964, the P.R.C. delegation contested the view that the United Nations could do anything effective about South Africa; nevertheless, the conference agreed to press for sanctions through the United Nations.

---

86. In a personal conversation with the author.
87. Same.
88. See *People's Daily* editorial of December 18, 1963, broadcast by NCNA, December 17, 1963, and Chou En-lai's speech at Kindia, Guinea, NCNA, January 24, 1964.

The African states in general reject the P.R.C.'s policies on the United Nations. Some have their doubts about the way events turned out in the Congo, but the majority backed the U.N. operation there to the end. Faced with the problems of "the remnants of colonialism in southern Africa"—the Portuguese territories, Southern Rhodesia, and South Africa—the Organization of African Unity in 1963 agreed to appeal unanimously to the United Nations. Although the OAU is committed to securing increased representation for the African region, its Charter uncritically declares its belief that "the United Nations is an important instrument for the maintenance of peace and security among nations and for the promotion of the economic and social advancement of all peoples."

FUTURE PROSPECTS FOR SINO-AFRICAN RELATIONS

Chou En-lai's visit to 10 African countries at the end of 1963 and in early 1964 had the same exploratory purpose as the 1961 mission led by Liu Ch'ang-sheng, president of the China-African People's Friendship Association, to eight African states.[89] But Chou's visit was not only exploratory. It was designed to seek African support for the Chinese offensive against the Russians; to establish more firmly the Chinese presence in Africa; to consolidate relations—especially with Algeria, Mali, Guinea, Ghana, and Somalia; and to repair relations with countries like the U.A.R. and Ethiopia.

The results of Chou's visit were mixed. Relations with the U.A.R. were clarified but not significantly improved. Relations with Algeria were, if anything, harmed. It is noteworthy that President Ben Bella visited Moscow as soon as Chou left Algiers and returned again four months later. On the latter visit, he was accorded a place of honor in the Moscow May Day parade and obtained more financial and military aid from the Russians. Relations with Guinea, Ghana, Mali, the Sudan, and Somalia were consolidated. However, President Nkrumah published his philosophical work *Consciencism*, which repudiates the inevitability of class struggle and the necessity for a violent revolution, shortly after Chou's visit. Although Tunisia's President Bourguiba used Chou's visit to recognize Peking, he also used the opportunity to warn the Chinese not to expect to gain too much from their policies in Africa. Relations with Morocco and

89. Chou En-lai visited the U.A.R., Algeria, Morocco, Tunisia, Ghana, Guinea, Mali, the Sudan, Ethiopia, and Somalia, while Liu Ch'ang-sheng visited Guinea, Mali, Ghana, Niger, Upper Volta, Senegal, Togo, and Dahomey.

Ethiopia were harmed by Chou's attacks on their governments before he left Africa.

Chou failed to persuade a single African government to indicate any preference for Peking over Moscow. Except for Mali, he also failed to persuade the African states to support the Chinese attempt to bring about an Afro-Asian conference before the proposed conference of nonaligned states. Seen in its proper perspective, Chou En-lai's mission was a propaganda success but a diplomatic failure. His subsequent visit to Africa in mid-1965 to prepare for the Algiers conference ended in a distinct diplomatic defeat.

Such a verdict, however, needs to be qualified, for Chinese strategy in Africa operates at two levels—diplomatic and ideological. At the first level, the Chinese seek little more than to establish areas of friendship, which they define in official communiques as "establishing normal relations." Such relationships enable them to pursue their work on the ideological level. The Chinese are clearly much more interested in the success of their work at the second level. Here they pursue two parallel courses. They encourage and support violent struggles against either the "remnants of colonialism" or against "American imperialist-dominated African governments"—for example, Cameroun, Congo (Leopoldville), Rwanda—and they train cadres for a Maoist type of revolutionary struggle.

Chinese tactics are designed to meet these short-term and long-term objectives. In the short term, they are willing, even eager to work closely with "bourgeois nationalist" governments and to support opportunistic African nationalist leaders. But their ultimate interest lies in developing "a new wave" of African leaders who, they believe, will rise to power in the struggles which will inevitably develop in the next decade in all those newly independent states which have so far avoided "a violent revolution to smash the old state machine and establish the dictatorship of the proletariat." As was pointed out earlier, in the Chinese book only two African states have taken the first steps in a Maoist revolution—Mali and Guinea; Algeria has stopped short of consolidating the victories of its armed struggles. Thus, when Chou En-lai proclaimed at the end of his first African trip that "an excellent revolutionary situation exists in Africa," he was not merely confirming his own view of historical development. He was outlining the future scope of Chinese policy in Africa.

Chapter 15

THE MIDDLE EAST AND CHINA
The Scope and Limits of Convergent Interests

BY

MALCOLM H. KERR

Of all the states in the Middle East, it has been Egypt whose relations with Communist China have had the greatest continuous significance. Egypt is the most populous of these states and the most influential both within the area and within Afro-Asian and nonaligned councils. She has been governed by a revolutionary nationalist and neutralist regime without interruption since 1952. Together with Syria, she was the first Middle Eastern regime to negotiate, starting in 1955, economic and military aid from the Communist world. In May 1956, Egypt became the first Arab state to recognize the Peking government and to establish diplomatic relations with it. Syria, Sudan, and Yemen quickly followed suit, as did Iraq immediately after her revolution of July 1958. Turkey, Iran, Jordan, Lebanon, Kuwait, and Saudi Arabia have still not done so. (Among the North African states, with which we are not concerned here, Morocco, Algeria, and—belatedly, in 1964—Tunisia recognize Peking; Libya does not. Israel extended recognition in 1950 but has no diplomatic representation in Peking.) Because of Egypt's preeminent position within the eastern Arab world and because of the frequency with which regimes in Syria and Iraq have changed, Chinese relations with the latter two countries, as well as with Yemen, have assumed much of their importance in light of Egypt's own involvement there. They have tended, thus, to be a function of direct Chinese-Egyptian relations.

There are four main respects in which China's role is actually or potentially important to the Egyptians. The first of these relates to Egypt's worldwide diplomatic position vis-à-vis the great powers and within neutralist and Afro-Asian circles. Second is the question of trade with China. Third is the direct Chinese political activity within the Middle East, both past and future, in explicit or implicit support of local Communists. Fourth, there is the possible ideological appeal of China as a model of socialist revolution and forced-draft modernization. This chapter will deal with these four subjects in turn.

INTERNATIONAL ALIGNMENTS

Gamal Abdel Nasser met Chou En-lai and established his first contacts with Peking at the Bandung Conference in April 1955. He was flattered by Chou, Nehru, and Sukarno and presented to the world as one of the principal Afro-Asian leaders. For the first time, his attention was directed beyond Egypt's immediate concerns with Israel, the Arab states, Britain, and the United States. Chou is said to have encouraged him to pursue an active interest in Asia and to cultivate relations with China in particular. Chou also counseled the cultivation of relations with the Soviet Union, with whom Nasser had had no serious dealings until then. Indeed, Nasser's purchase of Czech arms in September 1955, arranged through the Soviet Union, is thought to have been suggested to him first by Chou.

Egypt's formal recognition of Peking and the exchange of diplomatic missions did not take place until May 1956. The immediate significance of this step should be sought not in Nasser's new interest in Asia so much as in his involvement with John Foster Dulles over negotiations for American aid for the Aswan High Dam. In recognizing Communist China, as well as in taking other steps unpalatable to Washington, Nasser in effect seems to have sought to convey to Dulles the political terms under which he was prepared to accept financial aid: an independent, neutralist foreign policy. In addition, it is possible that Nasser, concerned with the possibility of a Western-Soviet agreement to halt further arms shipments to the Middle East, saw China as a back-door, alternative source of arms which was beyond the control of the great powers and of the United Nations.[1] Nothing, of course, came of this notion; but it may be noted that during the Suez war, in November 1956, the Chinese outdid the Soviets by offering to send 280,000 volunteers to Egypt to fight against the Anglo-French expeditionary force.

From 1955 to 1958, Egypt went through a critical phase of antagonistic relations with the Western powers. The Suez crisis was followed by the Eisenhower Doctrine and a dangerous confrontation in the summer of 1958. During this time her flirtation with both the Soviet Union and China reached its peak. A significant illustration was the creation of the Afro-Asian People's Solidarity Organization, which had its headquarters in Cairo, in late 1957. The creation of the AAPSO was inspired by the Soviets and the Chinese; the Egyptians got the secretary-generalship of the permanent council of the organization and played host to the first general congress. Like later congresses, it was attended by unofficial delegates from African and Asian countries, many of whom were Communists or fellow travelers. Loud and bitter denunciations of colonialism and the West and endorsements of Communist causes were the order of the day. As time passed, the Egyptians developed reservations about the organization because of the tendency of the two Communist powers to seek to use it for their own purposes, which were not always consonant with those of Egypt.[2]

After the Sino-Soviet dispute broke into the open, AAPSO meetings became scenes of constant disputes and recriminations between the Chinese and Soviet delegations, in which their respective supporters joined. The Egyptians, while seeking to remain friendly to both parties, found themselves increasingly sympathetic to the Soviets and annoyed by the combative attitudes of the Chinese on a host of small, and occasionally large, issues: the wording of communiques, the sponsorship of this or that front organization, the location of various conferences. In 1961, in a fit of pique, the Chinese withdrew

---

1. For speculation to this effect, see Geoffrey Barraclough and Rachael Wall, *Survey of International Affairs, 1955–1956* (Oxford University Press for the Royal Institute of International Affairs, 1960), p. 306.

2. On Egypt's experience with the Communist powers in the AAPSO, see Charles D. Cremeans, *The Arabs and the World* (New York: Praeger for the Council on Foreign Relations, 1963), pp. 252–254, 268–269.

their permanent representative from the council headquarters in Cairo for a period of six months and suspended their financial contributions.   As a leading Egyptian member of the AAPSO secretariat described the position to this writer, the Chinese by 1965 had largely lost the hope of making effective use of the organization and had taken to relying increasingly on their own front organizations and back-door channels of political activity in Africa and Asia.   At the same time, he insisted, Egypt has not become subservient to Soviet purposes in the AAPSO: on the contrary, it is the Soviets who have come to follow the lead of Egypt and the other "progressive" Afro-Asians.   "We regard the Soviets today," he added, "as virtually a nonaligned power like ourselves."   As evidence for this judgment, he singled out common Soviet and Egyptian positions on peaceful coexistence, the partial nuclear test ban treaty, disarmament, and anti-colonialism.

Meanwhile, the attainment of independence by various African countries has somewhat diminished, though not eliminated, Egyptian interest in AAPSO as an avenue of communication, beyond the reach of colonial rulers, with African nationalist movements.   The Egyptians can now in many cases deal with these same nationalists through official diplomatic channels.   The AAPSO does, however, continue to provide a useful vehicle for anti-Israeli propaganda, especially in those African countries which are officially friendly to Israel and whose governments are reluctant to allow the Organization of African Unity to involve itself in this issue.   In this connection, note must be taken of the unstinted moral support which China, inside and outside the AAPSO, has given to the Arab states against Israel.   This support has considerably cushioned the effect in Cairo of the rancor which Chinese delegates have injected into the daily life of the AAPSO.

While eager to avoid overt tension with Peking, the Cairo government has found the Chinese presence a good reason not to place heavy emphasis on Afro-Asian, as distinguished from "neutral" or "nonaligned," groupings.   Egypt's considerable economic and military reliance on the Soviet Union and Nasser's friendship with Nehru and Tito have doubtless strengthened this tendency.   By 1961, at the time of the Belgrade Conference of nonaligned nations, it was clear that Nasser's neutralism overshadowed his sense of Afro-Asian status. The "Islamic circle"—which, as Nasser described it in his 1953 pamphlet, *The Philosophy of the Revolution*, would have included

Pakistan, Indonesia, Albania, and to some extent the Soviet Union and China, but excluded India and Yugoslavia—had given way to a neutralist circle devoid of any special geographical or cultural stamp.

The Belgrade Conference, and subsequently the 1964 Cairo conference of nonaligned states, symbolized this change in concerns. Tito is not an Afro-Asian, and the Chinese are not neutrals. Belgrade and Peking, furthermore, stand at opposite ends of the spectrum in the struggle within the Communist world. It is plain that Nasser finds Tito a more congenial and appropriate diplomatic partner than he finds Mao or Chou. Nevertheless, the "second Bandung," the Algiers Afro-Asian conference of 1965, was regarded in Cairo as an occasion to be made the most of. It presented, however, an awkward problem from which "nonaligned" conferences have been relatively free: the need to take publicly announced positions between Moscow and Peking—in this instance on the question of Soviet participation as an Asian power in the face of Chinese disapproval. There was no doubt, long before the conference was scheduled to convene, that Cairo favored the presence of the Soviets, if only to offset the Chinese. Nasser hinted at this position in his joint communique with Khrushchev in May 1964, which noted the Soviet role in Africa with approval. But as "nonalignment" came to acquire the secondary connotation of formal neutrality between Moscow and Peking, the Egyptians found it embarrassing to become involved in such issues and consequently avoided taking the initiative on behalf of Soviet representation at Algiers. (Ironically, in 1955 it had been the Chinese who pressed, without success, for Soviet participation in the Bandung Conference.) With the postponement of the Algiers conference following Ben Bella's overthrow in June 1965, the Egyptians were spared the need to take sides at all, at least for the time being.

This resistance to Chinese aims was in the air during Chou En-lai's visit to Cairo in January 1964, at the start of his African tour. The day Chou arrived, Nasser was not even present in Egypt: he was in Tunisia, with Bourguiba and Ben Bella, to celebrate the French evacuation of the Bizerte naval base. Soon afterward, he returned to Cairo to greet Chou politely and joined with him in issuing a friendly communique which recorded China's interest in the development of African countries. The reception, however, did not begin to compare with the lavish and tumultuous welcome that the Egyptian government staged for Nikita Khrushchev on his two-week visit four months later. While no direct public evidence was available, it was generally believed that Nasser had quietly rebuffed Chou's quest for endorsement of his own terms for a second Bandung: in particular, the exclusion of the Soviets.

The close relations developed between Nasser and Nehru became especially significant in 1962 after the Chinese attack on the Himalayan frontier. It was Nasser who took the lead in seeking to mediate the conflict on terms acceptable to India through the six-power conference that met in Colombo, Ceylon. (The other participants were Ghana, Indonesia, Cambodia, Burma, and Ceylon.) Aly Sabry, the Egyptian Prime Minister, who headed his country's delegation in Colombo, appears to have been the only one present with Indian interests at heart. As a basis for conciliation between India and China, he proposed the withdrawal of Chinese forces to their previous positions. Such, of course, were the terms that the Indians themselves had demanded.

Articles in the Cairo press, meanwhile, contained frank accounts of the reasons why the other members of the Colombo conference could ill afford to antagonize China (and why, therefore, India had reserved her attitude toward the conference), as if to imply that Cairo alone among the six was in a position to stand up to the Chinese on India's behalf.[3] A leading newspaper commentator analyzed Chinese motives in invading India under the heading: "Does China want to get rid of Nehru or Khrushchev?" He noted, in the first place, that

China has proved to Asian countries that she constitutes the first military force in the area and that it is she that must be reckoned with at all times . . . she has also insulted India and wounded her pride before the whole world. This insult will leave a deep effect in India which is bound to change India's domestic life radically. China's action has made Indian leaders feel that . . . India needs to build weapons factories and purchase arms. . . . This state of affairs will have an adverse effect on India's development plans. The Chinese action has given the rightist elements in India a golden opportunity which they never dreamed of. For it was the western camp that went to India's help. . . . The Chinese action has caused embarrassment to the Soviet Union, being the leader of the communist camp which still includes China. . . . It may have been China's calculation that if Khrushchev would side with China, the latter would have succeeded in forcing Khrushchev to change his policy and turn his back on the non-

---

3. See, for example, the article by Mahfouz al-Ansary in *Al-Goumhouriya*, December 9, 1962.

communist world.   This would mean that he would lose much within the framework of the Communist movement, notably in Asia and Africa.[4]

However, the invasion of India by no means produced an Egyptian repudiation of friendly ties with the Chinese.   Aly Sabry tried in his public statements in Colombo to convey an impression that Egypt was neutral in the dispute.   During the conference itself, Sabry repeatedly stated that the conference should not perform the role of a court and pass judgment.   Rather the conferees, as friends of both parties, should see that the parties meet and settle their differences on mutually acceptable terms.   At the end of the conference, Sabry referred to "a problem arising between two friendly countries" which aroused world concern and threatened the international solidarity outlined at Bandung:

> The conclusions reached by the conference clearly indicate the benefit of exchanging viewpoints and joint discussions of issues which in its turn enhances understanding among non-aligned countries and contributes to the consolidation of Afro-Asian solidarity.   I appeal to the two conflicting parties to be responsive to the call for peace and to this conference so that they can cooperate together, not only in the interest of China and India, *but also for Afro-Asian solidarity and the policy of nonalignment,* as well as for the maintenance of world peace.[5]

Thus Sabry spoke almost as if the Chinese were themselves a nonaligned power and as if solidarity among the nonaligned were essentially the same as Afro-Asian solidarity.

Press editorials in Cairo reminded their readers of the existence of forces conspiring to drive a wedge between the Afro-Asian countries and urged that this situation was all the more reason for India and China to reconcile their differences.   The "main concern" of the Colombo conferees, declared one editorial, was not borders but was "to protect the trend of the nonaligned countries in international society and to prevent India from deviating from the policy of positive neutralism.   This is the main objective in which Cairo has taken keen interest in all its steps toward solving that problem."[6]   Said another commentator:

---

4. Ahmad Baha ad-Din in *Al-Akhbar*, December 8, 1962.
5. *Cairo Press Review*, December 13, 1962.
6. *Akhir Sa'a*, December 12, 1962.

The six Afro-Asian countries in Colombo have managed to approve the resolutions that are capable of establishing peace at the Sino-Indian borders, and of saving Afro-Asian solidarity from falling into the abyss that has been planned by the opportunists, extremists, and imperialists. . . . The success of this conference has frustrated the conspiracies and the rumors planned prior to and during the convocation of the conference. . . . However essential the disputed territory is, it cannot be compared to what destruction and ruin may befall the world once one of the two disputing countries has refused the resolutions and continued her obstinacy. In this case, this country will give the imperialist nations the chance of a lifetime. We do not want to believe that India or China will give imperialism such a chance. On the contrary, we are sure that wisdom will achieve victory in the end, and that solidarity and coexistence will win in spite of the plotting of the imperialists.[7]

This last comment might be put down to the tendency of some Cairo press commentators to pursue a much more fellow-traveling line than the Egyptian government itself endorses. While doing its duty as a loyal friend of India, however, the U.A.R. regime showed its keen desire not to spoil its relations with the Chinese; and the latter reciprocated.[8] One can well imagine how different Egypt's public response would have been to an attack on neutralist India by a member of the Western camp. Egypt's ambivalent interest in the Sino-Indian conflict was symbolized by the fact that two weeks after the Colombo conference an Indian mission arrived in Cairo to negotiate a trade and payments agreement and was followed almost immediately by a Chinese delegation on a similar mission.

More to the point than trade was the fact that Egypt, as well as all the other Afro-Asian states, could not do anything materially to aid the Indians and could not count on the Soviets doing so. Consequently, unless the conflict was mediated successfully, heavy Indian reliance on British and American aid, to the detriment of Indian nonalignment, seemed a real possibility. In such a situation, the security of Egypt's own position of neutrality between the blocs would suffer. Sabry's seeming double-talk about "Afro-Asian solidarity and the policy of nonalignment" thus made good sense from the standpoint of Egyptian interests. The Egyptians could see Chinese aggres-

---

7. Gamil Abdel Shafi' in *Al-Goumhouriya*, December 14, 1962.
8. See, for instance, the appreciative statement issued by Chinese Deputy Foreign Minister Huang Chen after he consulted with Nasser in Cairo. It is reported in *Cairo Press Review*, December 11, 1962.

siveness as an indirect threat to themselves, and yet, ironically, it was precisely for this reason that they took pains not to antagonize Peking.

In summary, however little direct material interest Egypt or any other Arab state may have in the actions of China, the continuing impulse of the Egyptian government to play a leading role in Afro-Asian and neutralist diplomacy requires the maintenance of good relations with China and continuing interest in the Chinese role. This impulse, of course, is largely a matter of prestige on Egypt's part; but it must be remembered that prestige and international image are matters to which the Egyptian government attaches great importance. Indeed, they constitute a cornerstone of present-day Egyptian foreign policy.

TRADE

China's importance as a trading partner for Egypt has been primarily as a market for Egyptian cotton exports. Exports to China had already reached a modest but not inconsequential level by 1955 (see Table 15-1). At the time of Egypt's recognition of Peking in May 1956, a barter agreement according to which Egypt would export 45,000 tons of cotton for Chinese steel was announced. The years 1957 through 1960 saw a considerable spurt in Egyptian exports to China. They reached their peak in 1960 (the same year, incidentally, that Egyptian exports to the Soviet Union reached their peak). In

TABLE 15-1
Egyptian Trade with China and the U.S.S.R., 1955–March 1964
(in millions of Egyptian pounds)

Year	Total Trade		U.S.S.R.		China	
	Im	Ex	Im	Ex	Im	Ex
1955	187.2	146.0	2.3	7.0	0.3	8.5
1956	186.1	142.3	7.9	5.6	3.9	8.4
1957	182.6	171.6	18.6	31.3	7.2	14.7
1958	240.1	166.3	31.7	28.6	8.7	12.1
1959	222.1	160.5	26.8	28.3	8.3	11.8
1960	232.5	197.8	22.9	30.9	6.8	15.5
1961	238.5	161.2	27.7	25.4	6.6	5.1
1962	301.0	158.3	24.6	24.1	7.7	7.7
1963	398.4	226.8	21.3	44.2	8.7	7.1
1964 (Jan.–Mar.)	83.2	73.1	4.3	12.2	1.7	4.3
TOTAL	1,898.4	1,315.6	188.1	237.6	59.9	95.2

SOURCE: National Bank of Egypt, *Economic Bulletin*, v. 17, no. 3, 1964, pp. 357 ff.

TABLE 15-2
Total Egyptian Trade with Selected Countries,
1955–March 1964

(in millions of Egyptian pounds)

Country	Imports	Exports
U.S.A.	404.8	69.4
West Germany	251.5	69.9
United Kingdom	173.5	52.2
Italy	136.5	86.6
Czechoslovakia	69.8	153.4 ª
Japan	51.0	66.1
India	82.9	85.9
U.S.S.R.	188.1	237.6 ª
China	59.9	95.2

(a) Egypt's favorable balance of trade with the Soviet Union and with Czechoslovakia is only nominal. The export figures presumably include Egyptian cotton and other commodities sent to the Soviet Union and Czechoslovakia in payment for military equipment, but the import figures do not include such equipment. No such consideration is known to enter into figures for trade with China. Admittedly, of course, trade statistics of Communist countries are rendered somewhat arbitrary by special considerations of pricing and exchange rates.

SOURCE: See source in Table 15-1.

1961, 1962, and 1963, however, exports dropped sharply—even below the 1955 level. From 1957 through 1963, meanwhile, Chinese exports to Egypt remained almost constant at an average of 7.5 million Egyptian pounds. Total figures for the period from 1957 to March 1964 show a substantially favorable balance of Egyptian trade with China. Exports totaled £E76.7 million as compared with imports of £E57.3 million. In the peak year of 1960, China stood second only to the U.S.S.R. (see Table 15-2) as a market for Egyptian exports. (She was followed by Yugoslavia and India.) By 1962, she had declined to fifth. Even in her best year as an exporter to Egypt, in 1958, she stood no better than ninth among Egypt's suppliers, and in 1962 she stood tenth. Overall, for the years 1957–1963, China supplied only 3 per cent of Egypt's total imports, as compared with 9.7 per cent for the U.S.S.R., and took 6.2 per cent of Egypt's exports, as compared with 17 per cent for the U.S.S.R.[9]

9. The foregoing figures are computed from tables in National Bank of Egypt, Economic Bulletin, v. 17, no. 3, 1964, pp. 357 ff.

In December 1964, the Chinese and Egyptian governments signed an agreement for what purported to be a substantial package of Chinese assistance to Egypt's industrialization program. China would supply industrial equipment worth a reported $80 million over a 10-year period as an interest-free loan, repayable over 10 years beginning in 1972. The list of specified items included complete textile factories, paper mills, sugar refineries, and equipment for various light industries.

At the same time, the Chinese-Egyptian trade and payments agreement was extended for three years, and the Cairo authorities predicted that under its provisions the annual value of trade would reach £E15 million. Egypt would import from China such sophisticated products as electric generators, mining machinery, and telecommunications equipment and in return would export not only the usual cotton and textiles but also shoes, tires, metal furniture, and even typewriters.

Both these agreements may be regarded with some skepticism. They are skeleton arrangements envisaging the future availability and providing the general commercial procedures for purchase of specified goods. The substance of trade and aid remains to be negotiated on a piecemeal basis without advance commitment to purchase all the items listed. Whether individual Egyptian industrial concerns, though state-owned, will see fit to buy Chinese rather than East or West European machinery simply because it is for sale seems doubtful. It also remains to be seen whether Egypt will produce a sufficient volume of, say, tires (already in scarce supply in Cairo) or typewriters to interest the Chinese. Cotton and textiles, Egypt's traditional exports, will presumably be available; yet even in this regard it was interesting to read in the Cairo press in mid-February 1965 that China was buying 18,000 bales of cotton in Mexico and paying in pounds sterling. One suspects that the aid and trade agreements of December 1964 carried at least as much propaganda as commercial significance.

Thus, while China may continue to be a market of moderate importance for Egyptian cotton exports, she is unlikely to become more than a minor source of imports. In neither field is she in a plausible position to compete with the Soviets, the Czechs, or any of the major Western countries for Egypt's trade—unless, of course, diplomatic hostilities should happen to spoil Egyptian commercial relations with individual Western countries.

China's trade with other Middle Eastern countries has been limited. The conservative Syrian government, on the eve of its overturn early in 1963, was negotiating with Peking for a sizable trade and payments agreement. A small volume of barter trade was carried on with Iraq during the period of the Kassem regime (1958–63).

As a potential grantor of economic aid, China's significance, given her own difficulties, is even less. On a spot basis, however, she has been able to make occasional gestures in the Middle East. After the Suez war, she won Egyptian gratitude with a $4.7 million cash grant. In 1958, she undertook the construction of a highway and a sugar refinery in Yemen on an interest-free loan basis.

In sum, China's ability to contribute to economic progress in the Arab countries compares with that of the Soviet Union somewhat as the ability of the Soviets compares with the major Western powers. Her available resources for aid and trade are far less, but enough to make themselves felt on a selective basis.

POLITICAL ACTIVITY

In the Middle East, as elsewhere, Chinese ability to make a direct political impact on the internal scene is related particularly to the degree of local revolutionary activity. Where governmental authority is not firmly established and especially where revolutionary movements led, infiltrated, or influenced by Communists are active, an opportunity for the Chinese to attempt to carry some weight arises. In such situations in the Middle East, as elsewhere, we find an apparent divergence between the Chinese and the Soviets over the degree to which they are willing to associate themselves with rebellious elements and to risk antagonizing the national government.

Two particular situations in which the local Communist party or Communist-infiltrated opposition movement has been of political significance have arisen in the Middle East within recent years: in Syria from 1957 to about 1959 and in Iraq from 1958 to 1963. In each case, the problem has been complicated by the fact that the government itself has been of the self-styled revolutionary, though non-Communist, variety and made much propaganda of its own regarding its progressive character and program. Both the Soviets and the Chinese have had to decide to what extent these "bourgeois nationalist" regimes deserved support and to what extent they should be opposed through the medium of local dissident elements.

In Egypt itself, this problem has arisen only marginally. Although the Egyptian class of intellectuals includes a good many fellow travelers, the Egyptian Communist party itself has been notoriously weak since well before the 1952 revolution and has been in no position to challenge the authority of the regime. Nasser's harsh treatment of Egyptian Communists, until discontinued in 1964, aroused strong disfavor in Moscow and Peking, but there has been no occasion for the Soviets or Chinese to expect any significant results from support for Egyptian Communists. In both Syria and Iraq, however, the position of local Communists has been of sufficient importance to generate an active Soviet and Chinese interest, and this interest has led both Communist powers into conflict with President Nasser and the U.A.R. regime.

It should be recalled that Syria's entry into the U.A.R. in February 1958 followed a period of rising Communist activity in Syria and infiltration of fellow travelers into high governmental and military positions. There is some evidence that the union itself was hastily brought about in large part as an effort to forestall the progress of Communist influence in Syria. No sooner had the union become a fact than Syrian Communists were set upon systematically by the new authorities in Damascus. The secretary-general of the Syrian Communist party, Khalid Bakdash, quickly fled the country and embarked on a protracted tour of Communist-bloc states. Wherever he went, he spread his intense hostility toward the U.A.R. regime. Communist newspapers in the Middle East (notably *Al-Nida* and *Al-Akhbar* of Beirut) carried on a running attack on Nasser as a bourgeois imperialist stooge and fascist dictator throughout the U.A.R. period. The Lebanese Communist leader Farajallah al-Hilu, on a visit to Damascus in June 1959, was arrested by the U.A.R. authorities and remained in jail despite protests and appeals on his behalf from both Moscow and Peking. Early in 1961, when it became known that Hilu had died under torture in a Damascus prison, the reaction of the Beirut Communist papers was virulent, and that in both the Soviet and Chinese press severely critical. Nonetheless, the Soviet Union, despite its displeasure, did not apply any sanctions against the U.A.R. by reducing or canceling its sizable military- and commercial-aid commitments. Its failure to do so reflected its growing differences with China over the proper response to harassments of bourgeois nationalists such as Nasser.

Meanwhile, the Peking regime unleashed its sharpest rebuke to the U.A.R. government in September 1959, on the occasion of the

10th anniversary of the People's Republic of China. The itinerant Bakdash appeared in Peking at the head of the Syrian Communist delegation and was allowed to make a violent speech attacking the U.A.R. regime as "a terroristic dictatorial regime which applies fascist tactics against all democratic national forces," as an obstacle to true Arab liberation, and as a tool of American imperialism. Syria, said Bakdash, was ruled now by "a dictatorial anarchist regime unparalleled in modern history." The Chinese authorities, as if to rub in the affront to Nasser, broadcast Bakdash's speech over Radio Peking in Arabic to the Middle East.

The reaction from Cairo was prompt and vigorous. The U.A.R. chargé d'affaires withdrew from the anniversary ceremonies. Cairo entered a formal protest to the Peking regime and encouraged a boycott of celebrations of the Chinese anniversary held by the Chinese in Cairo and Damascus.[10] At length, the incident blew over. The new U.A.R. ambassador to Peking, whose departure from Cairo had been delayed by the dispute, assumed his post, and normal relations were resumed.

The Iraqi revolution of July 1958, which overthrew the conservative monarchy, led to a much more serious situation. Within a few months, two things in particular became clear. First, the Iraqi Communist party had emerged from many years underground as a strong, militant body and, together with its fellow travelers, had heavily infiltrated the new regime. Arab nationalist supporters of Gamal Abdel Nasser were soon weeded out and persecuted, and a bitter war of words between Cairo and Baghdad broke out. The U.A.R. authorities and press complained about the subversion of Arab nationalist principles in Iraq by the Communists, whom they labeled foreign agents, and about the alleged efforts of the Iraqi Communists, and implicitly of the Soviets and Chinese as well, to subvert the U.A.R. regime in Syria. Nasser staked his prestige in the Arab world heavily on his confrontation with Kassem and with Communist influence in Iraq. As a result, Chinese and/or Russian activities in the latter country became a direct issue of principle between them and him.

Second, it was clear that the Iraqi Communist party was by no means of a single mind about how it should deal with General Kassem himself. Though something of a fellow traveler, Kassem was not

10. For these and other details, see Donald S. Zagoria, *The Sino-Soviet Conflict, 1956–1961* (Princeton University Press, 1962), pp. 261–262.

eager to relinquish his authority, shaky as it was, to them any more than he was willing to play the role that the Pan-Arab nationalists insisted he should—to accept Nasser's leadership and guide Iraq toward unity with the U.A.R. He had, intentionally or not, allowed the Iraqi Communists to gain substantial control over the so-called Popular Resistance militia. He had allowed his own cousin, Col. Fadel Abbas al-Mahdawi, to use the People's Court, over which he presided, as a forum for Communist propaganda and for low-level attacks on Nasser and the Arab nationalists. He tolerated the publication of a newspaper officially sponsored by the Iraqi Communist party, *Sawt al-Jamahir*. But he had not allowed any Communists to join his Cabinet.

Apparently urged on alternatively from Moscow and Peking, rival factions within the Iraqi Communist party disagreed on the degree of vigor with which they should push for membership in the Cabinet and should strive for a total takeover of power in Iraq. Circumstantial evidence suggests that the Moscow-oriented faction preferred to go slow and to work with Kassem as their most effective medium of influence, while the Peking-oriented faction, led by Aziz Sharif, advocated greater militancy and an effort to take over altogether.[11] Members of the party were responsible for acts of extreme violence on a succession of occasions—notably in Mosul, where a Nasserist uprising was repressed in March 1959, and in Kirkuk, where Communists themselves participated in an uprising against the local authorities the following July. The Arab public outside Iraq, and much of it inside the country, became increasingly disenchanted, indeed disgusted, with the bloodthirstiness of the Communists. After the Kirkuk incident, Kassem took a number of steps against them. He disarmed and disbanded the Popular Resistance force, and he extracted a formal apology, published in the Moscow but not the Peking press, from the Communist leaders for their excesses. With the passage of time, a number of Communists were eased out of their positions and, in some cases, arrested. An insignificant splinter faction of the party, loyal neither to Moscow nor Peking, was recognized in 1960 as the official Communist party of Iraq, and the organ of the main branch of the party, *Sawt al-Jamahir*, was closed down. Mahdawi's People's Court eventually lapsed into inactivity, and Mahdawi himself went on an extended trip to China.

Kassem, however, had by no means turned wholeheartedly against

---

11. Same, pp. 258–260.

communism in Iraq. By the time of his overthrow and execution in February 1963, the evidence of continued Communist presence in his regime was substantial. But it was his ties with the Soviet Union rather than those with China which prospered particularly. He had obtained from the Soviets considerable economic and military assistance; he had sent to Moscow, rather than Peking, large number of Iraqi students; and when, immediately after his demise in 1963, the Baathist leaders of the coup against him proceeded to ferret out individual Communists all over Iraq, kill many, and imprison many more, it was especially from Moscow that bitter accusations and protests against the new government came.

The bloody revenge wreaked against the Iraqi Communists by the Baathists was largely a response to the acts of violence previously committed by the Communists themselves. Inasmuch as these appear to have been inspired more strongly from Peking than from Moscow, it is paradoxical that it was the Soviets who took the Baathist coup with the least grace. Their relations with the new Baathist regime, though not broken altogether, were frigid. Soviet aid to Iraq was almost entirely cut off, technicians were withdrawn, and military shipments were halted. This harsh Soviet reaction perhaps resulted from the fact that although Kassem had, as we have indicated, taken some steps away from the Iraqi Communists after 1959, he had not broken with them completely. More particularly, in their tolerance for Kassem's mild reproval of Iraqi communism, the Soviets had gained the desired end—namely, close ties between the two governments which seemed to be turning Iraq progressively into a virtual Soviet satellite. Now this trend had been reversed, and the Soviets had found themselves betrayed. Meanwhile, Egyptian hostility to Kassem had continued unabated to the bitter end, partly because of the closeness of his ties with the Soviets and his continued tolerance of individual Iraqi Communists. Thus the bitterness in Moscow after February 1963 was matched by jubilation in Cairo.

The Chinese, for their part, could take the outcome as a vindication of their own militant recommendations in 1959. Having already lost any hope of gaining control over the Iraqi Communist movement, and through it any significant stake in Kassem's government, they were more restrained than the Soviets in their reaction to the Baathist coup. For a time they went through motions indistinguishable from those of the Soviets. *People's Daily* carried articles condemning "the massive arrests and massacres in Iraq," [12] while various mass organizations sent cables of protest to Baghdad. But although the new Iraqi regime offered the Chinese no particular opening, it presented the possibility of a fresh start. In February 1964, Khrushchev, speaking to the CPSU Central Committee, charged that "the Chinese leaders openly condoned the bestial deaths of the Iraqi comrades; and immediately following the Baathist coup, they began to seek out contacts with the killers. It has become clear that the Chinese representatives in Iraq want to exploit the Iraqi Communist party's loss of a large number of its leaders and form an opportunist group for them there." [13] After Chou's return from Africa, there was even expectation in some quarters for a time that he would return to the Middle East to visit Iraq, where the Baathist regime had meanwhile fallen but where the Communists were as vigorously suppressed as ever, and Syria, where a companion Baath government still ruled. This trip did not materialize; but the Syrian Baathists, while emerging as Nasser's foremost rivals, managed to cultivate unusually warm relations with Peking and were favored, in June 1965, with a brief visit by Chou to Damascus.

In short, while the violent behavior and open hostility to Arab nationalism of the Iraqi Communists in 1958–59 appear to have reflected Chinese more than Soviet inspiration, it was Soviet-Egyptian rather than Chinese-Egyptian relations, on the whole, which were severely strained by the four-and-a-half years of Kassem's rule and the aftermath of his demise.

IDEOLOGICAL APPEAL AND REVOLUTIONARY EXAMPLE

It is on the ideological level that one might expect to find the most logical basis for China to appeal to the Arabs. This statement is so on two counts: first, China's militancy on colonial questions; second, China's status as a rapidly modernizing society.

As to the first of these considerations, it can be pointed out that where the Soviets have developed an increasingly cautious, even conservative, sense of their own vested interests as a great power in the international arena, the Chinese remain strongly committed to revolution and struggle for national liberation around the world. In the Arab countries, it is the Chinese who have unremittingly pressed for

12. *People's Daily*, February 23 and March 15, 1963.
13. As reported by the clandestine, pro-Soviet Communist radio station, "Voice of the Iraqi People," April 13, 1964.

the removal of Western bases and oil companies and of the remaining British colonial outposts in such places as Aden and Oman—to which the Soviets gave only occasional attention until the time of Khrushchev's visit to Cairo in May 1964. During the Algerian war, it was again the Chinese who recognized the Provisional Government of the rebel FLN from the start and supplied it with arms. The Soviets, evidently wanting to maintain connections with Paris and perhaps wanting to keep the Moscow-oriented French Communist party in Algeria, dragged their feet. In the case of Israel, the Arabs' number one enemy, the Soviet Union had lent its diplomatic support to that nation's creation and admission to the United Nations, and full Soviet-Israeli diplomatic relations, though cool, remain intact. China, on the other hand, has not recognized Israel and has an unblemished record of vituperative declarations against her.

In regard to the second consideration, the thought comes readily to mind that China, like so much of the rest of Africa and Asia, is a poor, overpopulated country with a primitive agricultural economy and a record of subjection to imperialist exploitation, but the Soviet Union is by now a relatively mature and modernized industrial power. Unlike the Soviets, the Chinese have begun their industrial revolution largely from scratch. The harnessing of a peasant population, rather than an already existing industrial proletariat, to the revolution is a process with which the Chinese have had considerably more practical and theoretical concern than the Soviets. Mao's adaptations of Marxism have a more obvious relevance than Soviet experience—not only because Mao recognized the role of the peasants and of other non-proletarian groups within the New Democracy but more particularly because his communism is colored with Chinese nationalism and anti-imperialism. Finally, it may be supposed that the inculcation of a sense of discipline and an appreciation for the value of hard work, as well as the effective mobilization of a mass labor force, would appeal to the ambitions of other countries for economic growth.

In practice, however, neither China's anti-imperialist militancy nor her domestic revolutionary example have exerted strong attractions in Egypt or elsewhere in the eastern Arab world. Her anti-imperialist pronouncements on the Middle East, although presumably received gratefully by those of the public who are aware of them, get comparatively little circulation. They are not, for the most part, backed by any visible Chinese capacity to act effectively. The Chinese cannot exert pressures on the Western powers comparable to Soviet missile-rattling during the Suez war, military threats against Turkey at the time of the Syrian crisis in 1957, or vetoes of Security Council resolutions unacceptable to the Arab states. Furthermore, while the Arabs have long memories of past Western misdeeds, their memories of Soviet shortcomings for various historical reasons tend to be remarkably brief—partly because the Soviets have repeatedly come round to more acceptable positions in time. To Arab opinion, it seems clear that the number one rival of the West in the Middle East is not China, however militant she may be, but the Soviet Union. Moreover, the idea that Western defeats in the Middle East stem primarily from the power of Arab nationalism itself is continually propagated by Arab nationalist propaganda, and there is a consistent tendency to play down the role of even the Soviet bloc, let alone that of the Chinese.

To the U.A.R. government itself, China's continual agitation at international gatherings is annoying in any case, for on occasion it undercuts the U.A.R.'s own tactical moderation. Despite its revolutionary pretenses, the U.A.R. is not always averse to cultivating good relations with conservative African, Asian, and Western governments such as, for instance, Ethiopia, Japan, West Germany, and the United States. Its chosen path of "positive neutralism" requires that its own national purposes, radical as they may sometimes be, not be subverted to Soviet or Chinese interests by either of the major Communist powers.

On the domestic level, while the Nasser government justifiably considers that it is engaged in an extensive social revolution and while it has adopted a good deal of Marxist ideology, its outlook and objectives are rather mild if not downright bourgeois by Chinese standards. Arab Socialism in Egypt, together with its counterparts in other Arab countries, is committed to improving the lot of the masses and to industrialization based on state planning and ownership of enterprise, but its practitioners do not see themselves or their immediate body of supporters as declassé, destitute, or proletarian. They are middle-class people with unsatisfied middle-class aspirations and are unprepared to accept certain conspicuous features of the Chinese revolutionary experience: totalitarian regimentation, class violence, the aversion to even a modest level of private property and inheritance, and—last but not least—hard personal sacrifice. The significance of this last point is least widely grasped by Western commentators on Egyptian socialism. It sets the politically conscious middle classes of Egypt and other Arab countries off from the Algerians, who endured more than seven years of revolutionary war to gain sovereignty over a country lying in economic ruin and who consequently have grown used to sacrifice and hardship as a matter of survival. The Egyptian revolution has been bloodless and has so far made material demands only on the wealthy class. Like the Chinese, the Egyptians are enamored of crash development programs; but while the Chinese have pursued these by using their own meager resources and by half-starving their population, Egyptians prefer to pursue them on the assumption that, thanks to the Soviet and American aid that Nasser's positive neutralism has so successfully secured, they do not really cost anything.

Chapter 16

BRAZIL AND CHINA
The Varying Fortunes of Independent Diplomacy

BY

JOSÉ HONÓRIO RODRIGUES

During the three centuries of Brazil's colonial status, relations with China were unquestionably of secondary import, even insignificant. They cannot be said to have had any influence on the shaping of present-day conditions in Brazil. With rare exceptions, such Oriental customs and practices as may have been introduced were all suppressed in the reversion to a European way of life which began with the transfer of the seat of government from Lisbon to Rio de Janeiro in 1808. Chinese coolies were imported from 1854 to 1894, but the experiment was a complete failure. Commercial relations failed to develop, and there was no strengthening of political ties. Both China and Brazil were have-not countries suffering in varying degrees from the aggressive policies of the Western imperialistic powers.

Brazilian policy toward China from 1881, when the first treaty was signed, to 1961 is of little interest. With the coming of the Republic, Brazilian foreign policy, especially from 1913 to 1961, followed a line of consultation and cooperation with the United States in the Hemisphere and in the world. A striking example of this unrestricted collaboration was Brazil's failure, in 1930, to relinquish voluntarily the extra-territorial rights she enjoyed in China

457

458 POLICIES TOWARD CHINA

as a result of the treaty of 1881. She insisted on awaiting the decision of a naval conference in which she did not even participate (but the United States did). In 1949 she transferred her diplomatic representation in China to Tokyo, headquarters of the Supreme Commander for the Allied Powers, and in 1952 to Taipei—in both cases areas under the control of the United States. Thus we followed American policy in the Far East, though we might have been better advised to be prudent and await developments. By the end of 1950, Great Britain, Sweden, Denmark, and Switzerland had recognized the mainland government. The attitude of the Brazilian government committed it to the acceptance of American leadership in the Far East and more particularly in the United Nations.

When President Jânio Quadros took office in 1961, it seemed that the Brazilian government was determined to break away from slavish adherence to American policy. In so doing, it would be reverting to traditional principles of Brazilian foreign policy:

1. The rejection of entangling political and commercial alliances with the great powers. This precept all Brazilian statesmen, from Pedro II to the liberal and conservative leaders, had observed after 1844, when the treaty with Great Britain expired.

2. The unreserved establishment of commercial relations with any foreign nation. This proposition was set forth in 1808, sincerely desired, but never carried into effect.

Neither President Jânio Quadros nor his Minister of Foreign Relations ventured to put these principles into words, but they put them into practice by pursuing a policy of independence and nonalignment. The errors and excesses committed in carrying it out without the necessary discretion and prudence were harshly criticized by the conservative press, always pro-American. Nevertheless, this policy was neither anti-American nor crypto-Communist. It was aimed at placing the interests of the nation above all else.

BRAZILIAN COMMERCIAL MISSION TO THE PEOPLE'S REPUBLIC OF CHINA

In August 1961, Brazil sent a commercial mission to the People's Republic of China (P.R.C.) to study the possibilities of trade. This action indicated that Brazil would not subordinate her economic interests, if they lay in that direction, to the Far Eastern policy of the United States, which had consistently discouraged her allies from trading with China.

The mission was undoubtedly one of the most important ever

sent abroad by Brazil. It was headed by João Goulart, Vice-President of the Republic, President of Congress and of the Senate, and leader of the Brazilian Labor Party (Partido Trabalhista Brasileiro), and it contained representatives of the Foreign Ministry, the Bank of Brazil, and various state and private economic institutions. Though 90 per cent of the total value of Brazilian exports was absorbed by traditional markets (the United States and Europe), Brazil needed to open up new markets. These were necessary not only to reduce the growing deficit in her balance of payments but also to provide an outlet for the products of her growing industrialization.

There had been a prelude to the Goulart mission. In May 1961, Brazil was visited by a similar delegation from the P.R.C. This delegation opened preliminary talks on the possibilities of trade between the two countries.[1] The opinions expressed about feasibility of trade were founded purely on demographic criteria. They did not take into account the indices of per capita income, the similarity in the classes of exportable goods, and, above all, the system of planned foreign trade adopted by the government of the P.R.C. Nevertheless, studies by the Brazilian Foreign Ministry and the Bank of Brazil supported the belief that regular commercial exchange, on a scale which would be modest at first but would tend to increase, was possible.

Actual contacts between the Brazilians and the Chinese delegation led to the following conclusions:

1. Trade would be possible only under bilateral agreement.

2. In the absence of diplomatic relations, payments would have to be settled by adjustment between national banks—a method Brazil had already adopted in trading with the German Democratic Republic.

3. Hitherto, trade between Brazil and mainland China, conducted on a basis of free commercial currency and operating above all on the London money market, had been excessively irregular. While Brazilian exports to China had reached a value of U.S.$7,494 thousand in 1958, they sank drastically, to U.S.$300, the following year. Then they rose to U.S.$485 thousand in 1960.

4. The P.R.C. was going through an austerity phase in which consumption was sternly restricted and foreign currency economized,

1. Brasil, Ministério das Relações Exteriores, *Relatório do Ministério das Relações Exteriores [Ministry of Foreign Relations Report]* (Rio de Janeiro: Imprensa Nacional, 1961), p. 63. The mission visited Pernambuco, São Paulo, and Rio Grande do Sul, where contracts were signed for the purchase of skins and hides.

and it was employing hard money exclusively for imports deemed indispensable to development or necessary to maintain a minimum standard of well-being for the Chinese people.

5. Since the Chinese preferred to trade where they had bilateral agreements, purchases in Brazil would be residual, i.e., designed to meet requirements not met by countries with which China had bilateral arrangements. Thus Sino-Brazilian trade, if pursued without a bilateral agreement, would tend to be unstable or practically to disappear.

On arriving in Peking, the Goulart mission started negotiations. The approach was purely technical and economic. The discussions, that is, were soberly realistic, and the Chinese made no demands for political or ideological collaboration. According to the mission, "political considerations should not be allowed either to further or to jeopardize the negotiations under way." [2]

From an analysis of the chief products which could be exchanged, it was honestly concluded that there were no grounds for anticipating a significant flow of trade between Brazil and the P.R.C. in the near future. Concrete data on coal, which was to be the major Chinese export to Brazil, could not be obtained because of a Chinese lack of interest or reserve. Therefore, the amount of £10 million, which had been the estimate made in the first conversations, would perhaps be far more than enough to set aside each year to cover the two-way trade.

The objective of the mission was to examine the possibilities for opening up commercial relations between Brazil and the P.R.C. This end was achieved by the signing ad referendum of an adjustment agreement between the Bank of Brazil and the People's Bank of China in Peking on August 21, 1961. The system envisaged was an inter-bank adjustment of the usual kind with a mutual credit allowance of £1.5 million.

TRADE BETWEEN BRAZIL AND THE TWO CHINAS

The actual course of Brazil's trade with the P.R.C. and with the Nationalist government on Taiwan has been affected by political

---

2. Luis Villarinho Pedroso, Relatório da missão comercial do Brasil à República Popular da China e países do Oriente [Report of the Brazilian Commercial Mission to the People's Republic of China and Countries of the Far East] (Colombo: Ministério das Relações Exteriores, mimeographed, September 1961), p. 7. My comments in this section are based on this report.

as well as economic considerations. The scope of trade with Taiwan is more or less determined. The future of trade with the P.R.C. remains to be seen.

Trade with Communist China. Brazilian business had already gained a foothold in Asia in 1961. Japan, which accounted for 40 per cent of all Brazil's exports to Asia, was the most important market, and Indonesia was second.[3] The Goulart mission took on the important task of opening up the Chinese market, ascertaining current methods and practices, and coming to terms on the establishment of a regular flow of trade. It was not the first attempt to promote trade, but it was the most significant and important, as much because of the high standing of the envoys—Goulart was the highest-ranking Latin American government official to visit China up to that time—as because the mission brought about direct commercial relations. Before then, no one had been eager to have anything to do with China or any of the Communist countries. During the government of President Juscelino Kubitschek, the idea of extending foreign trade beyond the traditional bounds of commercial activity was unheard of. The initial contacts, thus, were made abroad.

Brazil entered into business transactions with the P.R.C. in an indirect way for the first time in 1956, but considerable difficulties over payment confronted exporters. In 1957, a Chinese commercial delegation discussed the situation with Brazilian authorities in Argentina. In 1958–59, Ambassador Edmundo Barbosa da Silva, director of the Economic and Consular Department of the Ministry of Foreign Relations, headed a commercial mission to the Soviet Union. From there he proceeded to China, where he examined the possibility of regular trade between the two countries. Other visitors, businessmen and industrialists, also looked into possible ways of engaging in direct commerce to replace the operations which had up to then been conducted entirely through intermediaries.[4]

A careful study of the outlook for trade was advisable on all counts. The growing significance of the Peking government and the scope of the potential market at stake demanded a realistic appraisal of present and future possibilities. The adjustment nego-

3. Instituto Brasileiro de Geografia e Estatística, Conselho Nacional de Estatística, "Mercado Asiatico [The Asiatic Market]," *Flagrantes Brasileiros,* no. 18, 1960, p. 54.
4. With regard to these visits, see Pimentel Gomes, *China, uma nova civilização* [China, a New Civilization] (Rio de Janeiro: Conquista, n.d. [1962?]), pp. 217–218.

tiated by João Goulart offered little hope of large-scale trade, but it did establish direct trading on a sound basis. In December 1961, the SUMOC (Superintendência da Moeda e do Crédito, a government department in control of currency and credit) approved the payment adjustment and trade agreement between the Bank of Brazil and the Bank of China.

On November 29, 1962, a delegation from the Bank of China arrived in Brazil to reopen the conversations begun by Goulart. The official talks [5] were devoted at first to discussions of the nature of each country's system of foreign trade, customs regulations, rate of exchange, etc., and of the disadvantages ascribed by the Chinese to the lack of a Brazilian consulate on the mainland of China.

A basis for the discussion of exports and imports was found in the realization that trade between the two countries had not been very active and had been restricted to a narrow range of products. Brazil's major exports from 1955 to 1961 had been cotton and sugar. Yet at times these had not figured in the statistics at all. It was probable, though, that a certain amount of Brazilian cotton imported by Hong Kong had been reshipped to the mainland. The Brazilian authorities recognized that trade could best be fostered if Brazil purchased iron, steel, and non-ferrous metals from China and China purchased cotton, sugar, rice, and hides from Brazil. At that time, however, Brazil had no cotton to export, nor were there any exportable surpluses of sugar or rice.[6]

The Chinese delegation was exceptionally eager to organize a commercial and industrial exhibition in Brazil, a project which had been the subject of an application to the Quadros government and which had been authorized in July 1961. The resignation of President Quadros and the political slant of the exhibition (the Chinese proposed to use material which had already been exhibited in Cuba) convinced the Brazilian authorities that they should postpone it. However, the insistence of the 1962 delegation made it necessary to review the whole question. The exhibition was finally authorized by President João Goulart, who succeeded President Quadros.

---

5. The following is a summary of Brasil, Ministério das Relações Exteriores, Secretaria Geral Adjunta para Assuntos da Europa Oriental e Asia, *Relatório sôbre a missão commercial da República Popular da China* [*Report on the Commercial Mission of the People's Republic of China*] (Brasilia: Author, mimeographed, January 4, 1963).
6. Hides were certainly available, but, though admittedly of good quality, they were alleged to be too thick in comparison with those used by Chinese manufacturers. Paraná corn was also suggested, but nothing came of the offer.

In reality, the visit of the commercial mission from the P.R.C. brought no concrete results in the way of bills of sale or definitive understandings which would lead to an immediate increase in trade. Nevertheless, the Brazilian commission considered the negotiations useful. A market the size of continental China could not fail, *a priori*, to offer great possibilities eventually.

The Chinese were authorized to open a commercial office similar to that of the German Democratic Republic in Brazil, and visas were issued to the representatives of the Council for the Promotion of International Trade, who arrived to set up the office and organize the exhibition to be held in Niteroi, a state capital just across the Bay of Guanabara from Rio de Janeiro. On April 4, 1964, however, the military group that overthrew the Goulart government arrested the nine Chinese who had come to staff the office and prepare the exhibition. They were charged with being intimately connected with Brazilian leftist organizations and subversive activities despite the fact that they were in the country as employees of a commercial office under the control of the Brazilian authorities. Everything indicates that negotiations for promoting trade between Brazil and the P.R.C. are not likely to be resumed in the near future.

Trade with Nationalist China. On August 20, 1943, the Brazilian government signed a treaty of friendship with the Republic of China. A cultural agreement followed in 1946. When Chiang Kaishek withdrew from the mainland to Taiwan in 1949, the Brazilian embassy staff was transferred first to Tokyo and then to the Nationalist capital of Taipei. An official communique [7] affirmed that Brazil maintained diplomatic relations with the government which the Generalissimo had set up on the island. Thus, Brazilian diplomatic representation in Taiwan is deemed to be a continuation of relations with the Republic of China. The treaty of friendship and the cultural agreement were then concluded not with the precursor of two presently existing states but with the only China recognized by the Brazilian government. Hence, they are instruments binding on Brazil and the Chiang Kai-shek regime.

Seeking to offset the tendency of the Brazilian government to draw closer to the P.R.C. from 1961 on, the Nationalist representatives not only followed the development of the conversations and understandings with keen interest but also sought to promote trade between

---

7. See *Arquivo histórico do Itamarati* [*Historical Archives of Itamaraty*], Files 921: (42) (52).

Taiwan and Brazil. Thus, Brazil signed only an inter-bank adjustment agreement for purposes of trade and payments with the P.R.C., but on December 28, 1962, it concluded a thoroughgoing trade agreement with the Republic of China.[8] Payments, according to this agreement, are to be made in U.S. dollars or any other freely convertible currency, and the contracting parties agree to most-favored-nation treatment of products shipped in either direction.

The Nationalist ambassador declared that the agreement paved the way for increased commercial opportunities which could be exploited to mutual advantage. He stated that the Republic of China would succeed in increasing its trade with Brazil despite the existence of restricting factors, such as the cost of transportation. He was, however, encouraged by the fact that in the last two years the Republic of China had purchased $4 million worth of goods (soybeans, cotton, and rice) from Brazil.[9]

RECOGNITION OF THE PEOPLE'S REPUBLIC OF CHINA

Since such great difficulties have stood in the way of establishing trade relations, it is scarcely surprising that the government has never given serious consideration to recognizing the P.R.C. Important support or stimulation for the government policy comes from strong conservative currents in politics, the armed forces, the Catholic Church, and the press. There are, however, sober thinkers in Brazil who have warned the country of the undeniable reality of the Peking government or outspokenly defended the establishment of relations with the P.R.C. or, if it comes to that, the maintenance of relations with both Chinas.

Some, of course, have even charged that the Brazilian government has refused to recognize Peking because of U.S. pressure and that our Ministry of Foreign Relations merely duplicates the U.S. policy of unwavering hostility toward the P.R.C. The conservative viewpoint, however, has stressed national appreciation of the realities. In 1955, the journalist Austregésilo de Athayde described the Chinese Nationalist government of Taiwan as "a sentinel for the State Department and the Pentagon, an instrument of American policy,

---

8. The exchange of instruments of ratification was made on February 21, 1964, and the agreement came into force on March 21, 1964.

9. *Jornal do Commércio* (Rio de Janeiro), December 29, 1962, and *Jornal do Brasil* (Rio de Janeiro), February 22, 1964.

bristling with peculiarities and idiosyncrasies." [10]   Senator Lourival Fontes, a man of wide political experience, far-reaching knowledge, and most enlightened intelligence, said in the Senate in 1955:

> The Republic of China is a mirror, I will not say of our passive submission to external interests, pressures, and influences, but of the errors and absurdities of an irrational and feckless policy. England and India, amongst other nations, have recognized the plain fact of China simply because it is an undeniable verity. Does the People's Republic of China not have the attributes of a *de facto* government, does it not have a large population adhering to this government, a territory over which this government holds sway, the undeniable prerogatives of independence and sovereignty?   Because it is Communist?   But we maintain relations with Poland and Czechoslovakia, which, besides being Communist, have regimes that did not spring from internal revolutions but were imposed upon them from beyond their frontiers by force of arms.   Because it is a dictatorship?   But we maintain relations with all of the sultanates, despotisms and reactionary tyrannies that are scattered over the globe.

After noting the achievements of the Chinese Communist government, he concluded:

> True enough, we can admit that China has adopted a political regime that we detest and disapprove.   But recognition does not imply agreement and does not signify approval, much less liking.   We have no moral or political reasons, and mainly we have no economic reasons, to prevent us from establishing commercial relations with one of the largest populations and one of the markets hungering the most grievously for imports.

To his way of thinking, nations are not bound by feelings of friendship or separated by conflicting ideologies. "Nations are attracted into alliance by interests in common and driven into conflict by competitive interests." [11]

In 1961, a leader of the Brazilian Labor party, Deputy Almino Afonso, urged that Brazil vote in favor of admitting Peking to the United Nations, but, he stated,

> this action would only make sense if official recognition were

---

10. *O panorama mundial da atualidade* [freely, *An Overall View of the World Today*] (Rio de Janeiro: mimeographed lecture, 1955), p. 5.

11. *Discurso aos surdos* [*A Speech for the Deaf*] (Rio de Janeiro: Livraria José Olimpio, 1955), pp. 28–33.

also to be granted to the People's Republic of China. Little respect could be attached to an ambivalent attitude: we vote to admit China to the United Nations, but we do not recognize its government. It would just be ridiculous to persist in this impasse.[12]

These opinions, clearly set forth from 1955 to 1961, failed to make any impression, it would seem, in government circles. The executive was accused of pretending to be unaware of the realities in Asia and Africa and criticized for its respectful allegiance to the foreign policy of the United States, not only in Latin America but in all areas. But the new government of 1961, decidedly arraying itself in a "new look," set out to be independent. It insisted on being treated on equal terms and was quick to take the initiative without prior consultation—rather like De Gaulle. In seeking to develop friendships and trade in new and uncharted realms, it was unorthodox in international politics. It committed an occasional heresy and steered its own unpredictable course. In this atmosphere public opinion favorable to recognition could express itself more freely. However, the great organs of the press were antagonistic. With the backing of other forces, they took an inflexible stand against even the most elementary economic relations and much more so against recognition. They exerted a formidable pressure to block the policy of Jânio Quadros, and subsequently that of João Goulart, in every direction.

To this widespread pressure must be ascribed, at least in part, the imbroglio of the President's resignation and the succession of the Vice-President to the Presidency.[13] The subject of commercial and political relations with the P.R.C. also produced vehement attacks. One journalist serenely proposed that we ought to "keep Communist China in political quarantine." [14] Assis Chateaubriand, ex-senator and owner of one of the largest chains of newspapers and radio and TV broadcasting stations in Brazil, calmly averred that he did not know "who the mental defective was that invented the existence of a promising market for Brazilian textiles in the great archipelago." [15]

---

12. *Ultima Hora* (Rio de Janeiro), February 24, 1961.

13. It is only necessary to read the newspapers from May through August 1961, to see the impassioned rhetoric with which the policy of ex-President Jânio Quadros was criticized.

14. See the article by Teofilo de Andrade, "Uma questão de bom senso [A Question of Common Sense]," in *O Jornal* (Rio de Janeiro), April 15, 1961.

15. "Uma viagem que não é da China [freely, A Trip that Did Not Bring Good Economic Results]," *O Jornal*, August 27, 1961.

The conservative groups were mainly obsessed with the fear of Communist influence. It was necessary, they said, to avoid ideological contact, the contamination emanating from Communist countries with accredited diplomats. On the other hand, a well-known Catholic leader and writer of wide intellectual and spiritual influence, Tristão de Athayde, devoted two articles to a defense of opening up the Orient and putting an end to the traditional pretense of ignoring mainland China.[16] He criticized the nationalization of "isolationist hysteria" on moral grounds.

> We are imperiling 'Christian civilization' by opening the doors to 'Socialist atheism' . . . . Is it not the moment to inquire whether this religious zeal is always aroused by spiritual motives. . . ? It may be that moralism calls upon us to plug the slightest cracks for fear of catching a 'Socialist' cold, but, as the Church teaches us every day, Christian morality bids us open wide our doors and windows to the modern world, and not be scared of 'drafts.' This attitude alone is consonant with the *Ite* [17] of Christ at the dawn of Christianity, and alone compatible with the true apostolic spirit.

In the second article, Tristão de Athayde wrote that "to consider the Island of Formosa [Taiwan] as representing all China . . . is one of the artifices of international politics that, in the course of time, nature itself ends up by putting to rights. Such is the ineluctable teaching of History." He commended French policy, framed without consideration for the reaction of the United States or of Chiang Kai-shek, and affirmed that "if the Formosa [Taiwan] Republic really is capable of keeping alive on its own, it will one day be independent like Ghana or the Congo."

Before the *coup d'état* of April 1, 1964, the Brazilian government was not considering the possibility of recognizing mainland China, but it was getting ready to face the question of U.N. membership. Because of the great adverse pressure the government had experienced when it set up commercial relations with Communist China, the matter had been shelved then.

---

16. Tristão de Athayde (in real life Alceu Amoroso Lima), "Abertura ao Oriente [Opening up the East]" *Jornal do Brasil* (Rio de Janeiro), February 20, 1964, and "Uma ficção histórica [An Historical Fiction]," *Jornal do Brasil*, February 21, 1964.

17. *Ite*, in the Vulgate, was the first word of Christ's injunctions to his disciples after he had arisen from the dead: "*Go ye* therefore and teach all nations . . . to observe all things whatsoever I have commanded you." *Matthew 28, 19–20*. It is also found at the conclusion of the Roman Catholic mass, *Ite, missa est.*

THE ADMISSION OF COMMUNIST CHINA TO THE UNITED NATIONS

The question of China's representation in the United Nations first came to the fore formally at the Fifth Session of the General Assembly in 1950. For 11 years Brazil always voted in favor of resolutions to postpone the discussion of the issue. These were as regularly approved by the General Assembly, following the leadership of the United States.

Ambassador Osvaldo Aranha, who presided at one regular session and one special session of the General Assembly (in 1947), maintained then and repeated in 1958,[18]

> that the western policy is seriously responsible, not only for thrusting China into the arms of Russia, but above all for preventing it from seeking support and encouragement in the democratic world for its own aspirations and achievements. Peoples cannot be denied an opportunity of freely choosing their destiny, their relations and their friends, as has been done and insistently continues to be done in the case of the Chinese government and the Chinese people. Nothing can be constructed in this world without China and its 600 million inhabitants. . . . To my mind, the incorporation of China in the United Nations will usher in a new era for world politics, that may even prove incompatible with the present aspirations of Russia.

This declaration, despite Aranha's personal importance and influence, had no effect on the foreign policy of the Kubitschek government, which came out unhesitatingly in support of Portuguese colonialism and reinforced Brazil's Pan-American orientation. Though a middle-of-the-road politician, Kubitschek was not allowed by the ultra-conservative opposition to diverge from the traditional line in foreign politics—and this line involved unquestioning agreement with the guidelines of American world policy.

On February 22, 1961—less than a month after taking office—President Jânio Quadros, in a note released by the Cabinet of the Presidency of the Republic, issued "instructions to the Minister of Foreign Relations for Brazil at the next meeting of the United Nations to vote in favor of including the proposal relating to the representation of China in the U.N. among the items of the agenda, the

<hr>

18. *O bloco Soviético no panorama mundial. Sua significacão para o Brasil* [*The Soviet Bloc in the World Panorama: Its Significance for Brazil*] (Rio de Janeiro: mimeographed lecture, 1958).

Minister to dispatch the immediate instructions to this effect to our permanent representative." The note, which was made public immediately,[19] announced the decision to modify the Brazilian position but did not go beyond inclusion of the question in the agenda. There was no indication that Brazil would discuss the merits of the question, and not the slightest mention was made of the existence of the Republic of China on Taiwan.[20]

Quadros took this action to show clearly he intended to be independent of American leadership. Nor did he lose his earliest opportunity of proving that intention. The chief of the Brazilian delegation to the 16th Assembly, Minister Afonso Arinos de Melo Franco, at the very start of the meeting, declared that Brazil would favor "discussion of the question of the representation of China, which, despite its undeniable importance, has long been evaded." [21] The 16th General Assembly (1961) allowed the question to be listed on the agenda for the first time. Brazil voted in favor of the resolution (which was passed by a vote of 61 to 34 with 20 abstentions) to consider the representation of China as an important question to which the two-thirds rule had to be applied.

The change in Brazilian policy cannot be called drastic. Increasing world pressure had induced the United States to free its allies from their engagement to block discussion of the seating of Peking, and Brazil could scarcely be more conservative than the United States. There was, therefore, no truth in the statement of Vice-President Goulart, made to the Hong Kong press on his return from Canton as head of the trade mission, that "Brazil will vote in the U.N. in favor of the admission of Communist China." [22] On the contrary, it voted in favor of a procedural motion (the two-thirds rule) and against the Soviet proposal to substitute Communist China for Nationalist China in all the organs of the United Nations.[23]

After the resignation of Jânio Quadros and the establishment of

---

19. All the Brazilian newspapers of February 23, 1961 published it. See *O Jornal* (Rio de Janeiro) on that date.

20. The present author wrote, at the time, an article branding the note as untimely and precipitate. See "A China, as Nações Unidas e o Brasil [China, the United Nations and Brazil]," in *O Jornal* (Rio de Janeiro), February 25, 1961.

21. U.N. General Assembly (16th sess.), *Official Records,* 10th and 11th Plenary Meetings (New York: Author, 1961).

22. *O Globo* (Rio de Janeiro), January 3, 1962, p. 5.

23. Brasil, Ministério das Relações Exteriores, *Atividades da delegação do Brasil à XVI Sessão da Assembléia Geral das Nações Unidas* [Activities of the Delegation of Brazil to the 16th Session of the General Assembly of the United Nations] (Brasilia: Author, mimeographed, January 3, 1962), p. 5.

the Brazilian parliamentary regime in September 1961, it was announced that:

> in relation to China and the structural organization of the Secretariat (Troika), we shall have to support whatever corresponds most closely to reality in contemporary international life, in view of the Government's conviction that no expedient depending on the use of force or inertia can make a lasting contribution to the maintenance of peace.[24]

In October, Foreign Minister San Tiago Dantas, in answering the question of whether "the Brazilian government is going to support the seating of Communist China in the U.N.," told the Brazilian House of Representatives that "the vote that Brazil has announced as being willing to give is not concerned with the actual seating of Communist China in the U.N., but merely with the proposal to examine the question." He added that as the United States had not renewed the counterproposal to postpone discussion, Brazil would not even have the opportunity of casting that vote.[25]

The merits of the question have yet to be examined. In his inaugural speech at the opening of the 17th Assembly (1962), the Brazilian delegate, Minister Afonso Arinos de Melo Franco, failed to allude to the matter, and Brazil again voted against the Soviet motion to recognize the representatives of Peking.[26] At the 18th Assembly (1963), the inaugural speech of Minister Araujo Castro, chief of the Brazilian delegation, contained no mention of the Chinese problem. Inclusion of the question of Chinese representation on the agenda was approved without opposition. Brazil voted against the Albania draft resolution favoring Peking's representation.

In short, from 1950 to 1960 Brazil was opposed to discussing the matter, and from 1961 to 1963 she was in favor of discussing it but continued to vote against the seating of the Peking government as representing "China." Brazil volunteered no statement on the

---

24. Conselho de Ministros, *Programa de Gôverno. Bases. Análise da situação econômica e social do Brasil* [Government Program: Bases, Analysis of the Economic and Social Situation of Brazil] (Brasilia: Imprensa Nacional, 1961), p. 194.

25. Brasil, *Diario do Congresso* [Congressional Record], October 13, 1961, p. 13.

26. Brasil, Ministério das Relações Exteriores, "Sumário das actividades da delegação do Brasil à XVII Sessão da Assembléia Geral [Summary of the Activities of the Delegation of Brazil at the 17th Session of the General Assembly]," *Noticiario* [mimeographed newsletter], January 7, 1963.

subject except in the opening address at the 16th Session (1961). She merely voted, along with all the countries of Latin America (except Cuba from 1959 on) and the majority of the members of the United Nations to defeat the motion. Thus, the straight line of Brazilian policy was only slightly deflected to allow the inclusion of the subject on the agenda. She continued in her inflexible support for the (steadily diminishing) majority against the seating of the P.R.C. Brazil also opposed admission of the P.R.C. to the World Health Organization and the International Conference on Trade and Development.

The position of France and the attitude of the semi-official organ of the Vatican, the *Osservatore Romano*,[27] might well have influenced the Brazilian vote. But the leaders of the *coup d'état* of April 1, 1964, revealed from the very start an evident fear of contact with the socialist nations—even to the point of breaking off existing relations, as advocated in some quarters. The tendency will be to return to the status quo of 1950–60, particularly since the new government is convinced of the influence of Chinese intrigue on Communist movements in Latin America, including Brazil.

THE EXPANSION OF SINO-LATIN AMERICAN RELATIONS IN THE PAST AND IN THE NEAR FUTURE

For some years now there has been an effort on the part of mainland China to extend its trade beyond its traditional sphere of influence and to open up relations in new areas. In 1959, mainland China received visitors—engaged in goodwill missions, cultural missions, and the like—from nearly all the Latin American countries. These contacts attracted attention not because they are unusual in international relations but because they had not previously taken place between Latin America and Communist China.

Generally speaking, Chinese propaganda has been more successful in Latin America than Russian, not only because China is underdeveloped but also because it has a program to overcome this underdevelopment through industrialization and a decreased dependence on the manipulation of prices by the West. Chinese propaganda spreads the notion that the United States and Europe do not want Latin America to industrialize unless they can control the proc-

---

27. See Tristão de Athayde, "Abertura ao Oriente [Opening Up the East]," cited.

ess.[28]   If the tendency of Latin America were to enter into commercial negotiations with any and every people on the grounds that business is business and trade has no ideology, there would clearly be excellent prospects for the development of Sino-Latin American trade.

As far back as 1960, President Juscelino Kubitschek declared that at the moment he was not contemplating commercial relations with Communist China, but he said this situation might change from one moment to the next.[29]   We have seen above how difficult it proved to be to set up those relations, but it must be admitted that commercial agencies of the P.R.C. are being opened for business all over Latin America.   In March 1964, Uruguay, whose sales of wool to China had not been negligible for several years past, announced that it was considering the establishment of commercial relations with Peking—although this action would not imply recognition.   The same month, the Argentine government likewise authorized a commercial agency of the P.R.C. to be set up in Buenos Aires.   The Argentines argued that not only was Argentina already engaged in trade with the Soviet Union but that those who criticized this trade themselves kept up an exchange of commodities via the European markets.   Recently, Argentina sold 750 thousand tons of wheat to mainland China, and transactions involving further sales of cereals were under discussion in accordance with President Arturo Illia's statement of February 1964.   At that time he had said that Argentina was willing to trade with all nations, including Cuba and Communist China.   A similar policy has been pursued by Mexico.   Sales of wheat and cotton have been made to the P.R.C., though diplomatic relations are maintained only with Nationalist China.   Latin America's commercial relations with the P.R.C. have been broadened at the expense of a decline in Latin American trade with traditional markets, but formidable obstacles still remain in the way of political relations.

The different political treatment accorded the Soviet Union and Communist China in Latin America is perhaps due fundamentally to the divergent method of Communist revolution the two preach.

28. Andrew Marshall, "Latin America: A Problem for the West," *The World Today*, April 1960, pp. 163–164.   On the development of the Communist movement in Latin America, see also Rollie E. Poppino, *International Communism in Latin America: A History of the Movement, 1917–1963* (New York: The Free Press of Glencoe, 1964).

29. Interview published in *New York Herald Tribune* and reproduced in *O Globo* (Rio de Janeiro), February 22, 1960.

Deep-seated social and economic problems cause great discontent and agitation among the peoples of Latin America, but the ruling classes insist on retarding a solution to the problems. They defend the status quo or, at most, argue for gradual reform. This situation helps Communist propaganda to make headway despite the restrictions imposed on the legality of the Communist parties in Latin America since World War II. Though in a minority in Latin America, Soviet-line Communists favor a more flexible strategy involving deep infiltration and exploitation of every political opportunity; they deny the possibility of revolution at the present time. The partisans of the Chinese line, who are more aggressive, more intransigent, and more bitterly opposed to the United States, are bent on stirring up revolt. Whatever the grounds for the line of action which the Soviet Union supports—the doctrine of active and competitive peaceful coexistence, the incapacity of the Latin American Communist parties to seize power by violence, or the political and economic risks entailed in another Latin American revolution to which aid would have to be given—the fact is that it is more peaceful than that which the Chinese support.

Besides, in the European tradition, the strength of communism lies in the urban trade unions, but in Asia it is drawn from rural elements. As the Latin American countries are largely agricultural, the Asian tradition tends to flourish more vigorously there. This situation may also help explain the fact that the P.R.C. is not diplomatically represented in Latin America except in Cuba.

In the absence of important commercial relations, China policy as a substantive problem is not of the greatest urgency in Latin America. Brazilian developments, however, illustrate how the China problem is linked to more urgent political issues. The contest for power in Brazil takes place, broadly speaking, between a conservative oligarchy in which the landlord class is dominant and a grouping of liberal forces ranging from the political left wing to modern industrialists. For the former group, the policy issues of highest priority are national security and avoidance of ideological contamination. The latter group emphasizes overcoming underdevelopment, pursuing trade with all countries, and defending the peace.

There is, however, little or no tendency to think of Communist China as a political model. Even the problem of the doctrines and strategies of the nonaligned countries with reference both to the East-West conflict and to China's relationship to this conflict has had only secondary importance. The Chinese may put Latin America in the same category as Asia and Africa because of their common underdevelopment. But in terms of legal and political institutions and of the image political leadership has of itself, Brazil is more European than Asian or African.

The victory in Brazil of the military movement of April 1964, pro-American and militantly hostile to the Communists, brought to an end the possibility of expanding trade between Brazil and China. The following decisions taken by the government reveal a consistency in its China policy: On September 17, 1964, Congress rejected the commercial agreement, in spite of the fact that the balance of payments was in Brazil's favor. Nine Chinese members of the trade mission were put on trial and, on January 5, 1965, condemned to ten years' imprisonment, despite the "total absence of genuine proofs and evidence," to quote their defender Heraclito Sobral Pinto, then President of the Institute of Lawyers.[30] The nine were deported on April 18, 1965, after having spent a year in prison. All these facts show that leading elements at the time attributed the strikes and unrest which disturbed Brazilian politics, especially during 1963, to the adoption of the Chinese line by the Brazilian Communists.[31]

Subsequent events have underlined the ideological direction of Brazil's foreign policy and its complete loyalty to the policies of the Western bloc led by the United States. Thus, current Brazilian policy does not permit the kind of freedom of diplomatic action enjoyed by Great Britain, which is closely tied to the United States but which recognizes the Peking government, and by France, which is highly independent and which also recognizes Peking; nor does there seem to be any interest in resuming commercial activities, which other leading Latin American countries still carry on.

---

30. Letter published in the *Jornal do Brasil* (Rio de Janeiro), July 28, 1964. The Institute of Lawyers is an academic society, whose members are also prominent in the Bar Association. On the suspect nature of the letter attributed to the Chinese, see an article by Antonio Callado, *Jornal do Brasil*, July 12, 1964.

31. Interview with Marshal Odilio Denys, *O Cruzeiro* (Rio de Janeiro), May 23, 1964.

Chapter 17

TYPES OF CHINA POLICY

BY

A. M. HALPERN

There is a considerable variation among non-Communist countries in the components of China policy. The variation depends on distance, the quality of relations with China before and after the Communist takeover, the way a country views its own role in the world, and the structure of internal politics. It can easily be argued that each case is unique. For purposes of discussion, I divide the individual cases into three families—the European, the underdeveloped and/or nonaligned outside South and East Asia, and the Asian.

EUROPE AND THE THIRD WORLD

Despite the differences recorded in the preceding chapters, there is a family resemblance between the China policies of the West European countries (including Canada). They all view China from a distance. They are in various ways concerned with handling China by methods that will best contribute to the attainment of a stable world order. China has no direct impact on their national security. In this regard they tend to evaluate China as a factor in the world power balance or to be interested in the implications of the Sino-Soviet split for the security of Europe. Trade is a prominent interest in their direct dealings with China. On the status of Taiwan, the positions they favor avoid the extremes of designating Taiwan as properly territory of the People's Republic of China or of committing themselves to permanent support of the Nationalist government as

475

the only legitimate representative of China. They show a preference instead for a solution which will take fully into account the desires and interests of the island's population. They refrain from endorsing policies which proceed from the belief that the mainland regime will collapse or which seem to be directed at the long-term isolation of the P.R.C. They may not regard U.S. views on China as impeccable, but they have little disposition to make the China question an issue for sharp confrontation with the United States.

While there are exceptions and qualifications for each national position, the comparative uniformity of the European point of view emerges by contrast with other areas. The summation given above would not be inapplicable to other West European countries than those covered in this volume. In a few cases, there are special interests. Portugal, for example, has some colonial stakes in Asia and Africa on which China impinges.

I have designated Latin America, Africa, the Middle East, and Yugoslavia as a group primarily because the P.R.C. professes to regard the Third World (if one prefers Communist terminology, the "first intermediate zone") as a uniform category. There is no corresponding unity of these areas in terms of their policies toward China. As José H. Rodrigues has demonstrated above, Brazil (and most of Latin America) belong in the European family. In regard to Africa it is only necessary here to underline some observations made by Colin Legum.

While a number of African states recognize Nationalist China and some of them profit by this association, the general trend in the continent is to think of the mainland, not of Taiwan, as the real China and as a large, important factor in world affairs. In direct dealings, on the part of states or of political movements, the initiative has often been taken by the P.R.C. Depending on local situations, the Chinese approach ranges from friendly cooperation with incumbent governments to support—in some cases regarded locally as a serious problem—of subversive and revolutionary movements. African responses have not been naïve but have shown a lively sense of self-interest and a solid disposition to preserve an independent posture on a number of international questions.

On the level of attitudes, there is a notable sympathy for the P.R.C., which in part derives from a kind of selective perception. There is a tendency to see in Communist China a set of virtues which by no coincidence correspond to what Africans regard as their own major failings. In this sense, but not in regard to economic and political procedures, Communist China is felt to be an encouraging example of what a former "colonial dependency" and underdeveloped country is able to achieve through national discipline and full mobilization of all its resources. This sympathy does not extend to a feeling of racial affinity but does extend to identification with the P.R.C. as a companion among the have-not countries.

Africa, it is commonly said, is in a complex state of flux; it is this condition that apparently expresses itself in the variety of African responses to China. One gets the impression that African policies toward China are as yet in the incipient stage. Two key groups in determining the future are Africa's revolutionary-minded leaders and African youth, to whom the P.R.C. is most attentive in the hope that they will carry out the "second wave" of African revolutions in the 1970s, if not in the latter half of the 1960s.

The state of flux in the Middle East is not really comparable to that in Africa. In their direct dealings with China, the Middle Eastern countries are as much guided by self-interest as the Africans. But China is largely a tangential factor. Middle Eastern experience with China has been mixed. There are some points where the interests of the Middle East and China overlap, especially in those Afro-Asian institutions where the United Arab Republic plays a major role. At these points, U.A.R. and Chinese interests sometimes coincide and sometimes do not. Although Nasser obviously finds Tito's views more congenial than Mao's, the U.A.R. rarely has reason to take positions which the Chinese would find provocative. President Nasser did, however, go along with Tito at the second conference of non-aligned states in Cairo in October 1964 in repudiating the main ideological slogans used by the Chinese in making their bid for leadership of the Afro-Asian-Latin American peoples.

Israel occupies an exceptional position in the Middle East. Apparently its decision to recognize the P.R.C. was taken as a routine matter. There exists a certain basis of sympathy for Communist China, insofar as there are Israelis, among then David Ben Gurion, who think of it as a country which has successfully carried out a socialist program largely in a self-reliant way and not as a creature of the Soviet Union. Such people observe in China a spirit congenial to their own *halutziuth*. The position of the Ministry of External Affairs is painfully simple: Israel has all the enemies it needs; it would like more friends. In 1955, David Hacohen, then minister to Burma, visited China, and there was some prospect that relations might develop. Since the Suez incident of 1956, the P.R.C. has classified Israel among the imperialists and has regarded it as of no value except as a cheap sacrifice to the demands of China's Arab policy. There would be little to add if it were not that P.R.C. and Israeli activities conflict in some parts of Africa where Israel has had programs of technical assistance and where the P.R.C. has displayed cold antagonism.

Yugoslavia's cold war with China is fought out largely in relation to intra-bloc controversies but partly in the circles of the nonaligned. In the latter area Yugoslav interest goes back a long way, to a time shortly after Yugoslavia's expulsion from the Cominform. It is an interest that has been cultivated consistently by Yugoslav diplomacy and by Tito personally. His participation included exchanges of views with Nehru as far back as 1954, with Nasser on a number of occasions since the Bandung Conference, and with several leaders of nonaligned Asian countries in the course of his visit to the area in 1959. The clash of Yugoslav and P.R.C. ambitions in relation to the nonaligned countries has grown steadily sharper since 1958. It came to a head at the Cairo conference of October 1964, where Tito led the fight against the P.R.C. with strong support from the U.A.R. and India and with Moscow cheering from the sidelines. The Yugoslav attitude toward Communist China is not typical for nonaligned countries but has some influence among them.

ASIA

The observer of Asian affairs who can recall the structure of pro-Chinese Communist attitudes of 10 or more years ago experiences a distinct feeling of *déjà vu* on reading about current African attitudes. There have been three watersheds in the development of Asian policies toward China. The first was the Korean War, which precipitated both pro-P.R.C. and anti-P.R.C. attitudes. The second was the 1954 Geneva Conference. Relaxation of tension, which followed the termination of hot wars in Asia and the positive results of the Bandung Conference, removed some limits on action for the neutralist countries. Up to then they had only been able to act negatively, in the hope of preventing an increase in tension and in the fear that positive action would work against their aims by tipping the precarious balance of power even slightly. They avoided not only alliances but the appearance of being on too close terms with either side in the cold war. After the Geneva Conference there was no such impediment to the development of relations with the P.R.C., the U.S.S.R., or Western countries. On the other hand, some anti-neutralist countries drew closer to the United States through such mechanisms as SEATO.

The third watershed was the major strategic shift in P.R.C. foreign policy toward the end of 1957. From that point on, Asia as a whole has been more conscious of China as a power, and a dynamic one at that, and less conscious of China as the bearer of a cause to which one had to react, either for or against, from the standpoint of political morality. Preventive-altruistic neutralism of the pre-1954 variety lost its relevance to the facts soon after the 1954 Geneva Conference and the Bandung Conference of the following year and could no longer serve as a unifying force between countries differently situated. The term "neutralist" itself lost popularity. It was replaced for a while by "active and independent" and later by "nonaligned." The foreign policies of neutralist Asian countries became more nationalist and more concrete.

In contrast to the European and African patterns, then, one outstanding feature of the Asian pattern is the prominence of concern for national security. China impinges directly on the interests of almost all Asian countries. The corollary is that China policy is a matter for constant, not just for occasional, attention. Furthermore, Asia has been a more important target of the P.R.C.'s diplomacy, and for longer, than Europe or Africa. Direct contacts with the P.R.C. have been more numerous and more meaningful in Asia than elsewhere. As noted earlier, trade is not as prominent in Asian thinking about China as in European. Finding a place for the P.R.C. in a stable world order is a more salient matter for Asians than for non-Asians, though for some Asians it is a matter of declining priority. To the various operational questions which arise within this pattern there are in Asia a number of different answers.

In those Asian countries which have adopted an anti-Communist stance, China policies have changed little over the years. In many such cases, communism has a concrete and specific identity as something with which battle has been waged. In the Republic of Korea (South Korea), the overriding consideration is dealing with the Communist-governed northern half of the country. The P.R.C., by its geographical situation and its past and present commitments, as well as by the reciprocal North Korean commitment to the P.R.C., is reckoned as the single most important support of communism. There can hardly be any choice but firm opposition to Communist China and alliance with Nationalist China. The deep and universal Korean desire for unification of the country is thereby sacrificed for an indefinite period. Hardly anybody believes that the desired result could be facilitated by an approach to the P.R.C., and not many people seriously believe that the North Korean regime is open to suggestions which would seem reasonable to the South.

Here, then, is the essence of South Korea's China policy. There are some current worries related to it. Any change in the situation of Taiwan is likely to be in a direction South Korea would not like. French recognition of the P.R.C. aroused anxiety, and South Korea immediately asked for and obtained assurances that no change in France's policy on Korea would follow. South Korea's concern about its future relations with the United States and Japan stems in part from its fear of the P.R.C. The American presence is thought of as the most effective safeguard South Korea can have. One motive for establishing a stable formal relation with Japan derives from uncertainty about Japan's future China policy and an apprehension, as yet largely hypothetical, that some future American disengagement might leave Korea sandwiched between a Japan and a China which will have achieved a meeting of minds.

The logic of South Vietnam's situation and views of China, with allowances for geographical differences, is much the same as South Korea's. Vietnam does not appear to have the tradition of national and cultural integrity that Korea does, and the South Vietnamese seem not so fiercely attached to the ideal of reunification with the North. There are manifest war weariness and political instability in South Vietnam which have no real equivalent in South Korea. China policy as such appears to be a remote concern, even though there is a crucial need, in planning for the near future, to take serious account of possible Chinese intervention in the fighting in Vietnam.

Thai, Filipino, Malaysian, and Australian China policies have been discussed above. Thailand, the Philippines, and Australia have made what they believe to be the necessary choices. Malaysia has few interests which can be significantly promoted by relations with China and many which can be promoted by relations with the West. For this reason, fortified by acute awareness of the problems of building a nation out of diverse ethnic elements, Malaysia has preferred to maintain an anti-Communist stance but to keep itself remote from both Chinas.

The other end of the range of choices is illustrated by the China policies of Burma, Cambodia, and Indonesia. All have been discussed above, and the differences in their attitudes and interests have been described. Here we need only note that Burma tends toward an isolationist version of accommodation with the P.R.C., Cambodia toward a version which concedes the P.R.C.'s future hegemony, and Indonesia toward a more activist version that seems to provide a definite place for Indonesian expansionism and for an understanding with the P.R.C. relating to mutually recognized spheres of influence.

THE SPECIAL CASE OF INDIA

In the majority of cases, there is little ground other than arbitrary opinion for judging whether a particular China policy has been a success or a failure, irrespective of its content. In India the overwhelmingly accepted judgment is that the country's original China policy was a disastrous failure. As V. P. Dutt has pointed out, for a number of years India's China policy was directed primarily at the problem of world order, at obtaining for the P.R.C. an assured international standing. This task was not within India's unaided capacity. Further, after 1958 India was slow in realizing that its own world view and China's were diverging in respect to both ideals and foreign political strategies. Nehru's views of China apparently changed in early 1960, when he discovered that the Chinese showed no inclination to discuss border problems in a spirit of reason and respect for each other's documented case. The growth of Chinese hostility during the next two years, as shown by Chinese charges that Nehru was bringing India into dependence on—if not alliance with—the West and especially by criticism of Nehru's role at the 1961 Belgrade Conference, seems not to have attracted serious notice in India. To the general public at least, if not to the government as well, the incidents of October 1962 in the North East Frontier Agency came as a distinct shock.

The Indian reaction to defeat on the NEFA border was so disproportionate to the purely physical dimensions of the incident that it begs to be explained on other grounds. The defeat was felt not as a mere military loss but as a humiliation and a betrayal—two terms that cropped up regularly in Indian discussions of the event. The public mood continues to be dominated by a permanent mistrust of Communist China, and the government is under pressure to conform to this mood. The incident also provoked serious criticism of the former China policy of the government, which many people felt ought to bear a large share of the blame. One argument often made was that the official policy had not been based on concern for India's national interests and that henceforth no policy should be followed which neglected these interests. Some argued that earlier policies in fact had not deserved the name but had consisted only of presuppositions. When the Chinese proved that the government had been wrong in believing that the P.R.C. had an interest of its own in peace and cooperation and that it would respond to reasonable and friendly approaches, they also demonstrated that India's China policy was little more than a vacuum. It was further argued by the critics that the government showed no ability to make a realistic analysis of China's moves before, during, or after the NEFA crisis. Some of this criticism, especially that emanating from the Swatantra party, was so all-embracing and so heated that it leads one to suppose that China policy was used as a surrogate, an issue upon which dissatisfaction with many aspects of policy, including domestic, could be concentrated. The probability that more issues than China policy were involved is all the greater since some prominent but controversial individual figures—V. K. Krishna Menon for one—were identified with vulnerable positions on China.

In the widespread discussion of alternatives that followed the NEFA affair, almost all aspects of India's foreign policy have been brought under review. On the border questions themselves India appears incapable of taking any effective initiative. There does not seem to be any profit in indefinitely maintaining a hostile posture without having the capacity to rectify the situation, but the P.R.C., which does have the initiative, does not seem prepared to make overtures which will satisfy India's belief that she was subjected to aggression. On the military side, a program of development which appears suitable to recognized needs has been planned and is being implemented. This problem was in some ways the easiest to solve, even though at some otherwise undesirable cost to economic development. The more difficult problems have to do with India's conception of her role in the world.

The value and purpose of nonalignment became a major focus of discussion. The extreme opposition view went so far as to urge that relations with the P.R.C. be broken and that the Chinese Nationalist government be recognized; that a reconciliation with Pakistan, starting with admission of the legitimacy of Pakistan's interest in Kashmir, be sought; and that nonalignment be abandoned in favor of alliance with the United States and Britain. This position is not likely to be adopted, nor is it likely that the government will make a definite choice between extreme alternatives which can be stated in intellectually clear-cut terms. That is, it is not to be expected that the Ministry of External Affairs will develop a stated policy either of withdrawing into isolation and concentrating all attention on domestic problems or of leading an all-Asian anti-P.R.C. movement.

Nevertheless, the value of nonalignment to India is certain to be reviewed. It remains of practical importance insofar as it helps India to retain Soviet cooperation and to obtain some degree of Afro-Asian diplomatic support. The efforts of a group of Afro-Asian powers who met at Colombo to try to mediate the Sino-Indian dispute produced results which were gratifying to India though not of much practical effect. On the other hand, in the early spring of 1964, at the Djakarta preparatory meeting for the convocation of a second Afro-Asian conference, India felt that it confronted a coordinated opposition comprising the P.R.C., Indonesia, Pakistan, and on some matters Algeria, while it was uncertain where support could be found for its own desires. India was still on uncertain footing at the Cairo Conference in October 1964. The cancellation of the conference scheduled for Algiers in June 1965 postponed some problems but did not solve them.

A certain part of India's discomfiture in relation to China comes from the realization that India was not as popular with its neighbors as it had thought, and a corresponding part of India's present China policy is an effort to improve its standing with these neighbors. If in the end India loses faith in nonalignment and in Afro-Asian solidarity, the cause is less likely to be the immediate demands of its China policy than a general drift of the nonaligned and Afro-Asian countries toward individualized nationalist positions. Such a drift would attenuate the common interests which were supposed to have been inherent in geography, similar social and political conditions, and a similar relationship to great-power conflicts. The major line of development for the present is apparently to work on the China problem indirectly, by locating India as favorably as possible in relation to both the United States and the Soviet Union. Nonalignment reinterpreted in this way is not easy to distinguish from reliance on a *détente* between the two great powers.

INDIA'S NEIGHBORS

The reflex effect of the Sino-Indian dispute on the China policies of some of India's closest neighbors has been so important that the development of these policies is best reviewed in this connection. While most Asian countries think of themselves as sandwiched between China and the West, Pakistan, Nepal, and to a lesser extent Ceylon think of themselves as sandwiched between China and India.

The impact of the Sino-Indian conflict on Pakistan's China policy has been covered in detail by K. B. Sayeed. Pakistan has worked out a method of dealing with the P.R.C. which produces some concrete advantages for itself and provides increased flexibility. Its relations with its Western friends have not been seriously compromised. Its prospects for agreement with India, though not improved, are not necessarily worse. The prospects for a betterment of relations with the Soviet Union have perhaps been improved. Flexibility, it appears, may have been bought at a slight sacrifice of internal unity.

Nepal's relationship with India is not comparable to Pakistan's, since Nepal is formally an ally of India. With King Mahendra's assumption of responsibility for government in 1960, the influence of the Nepali Congress party headed by B. P. Koirala declined sharply. This party's orientation was democratic socialist on the theoretical level, and its leaders were of an age to have had a close relation to the Indian struggle for independence guided by the Indian Congress party. This influence has been replaced by that of younger men for whom prewar contacts with India were less meaningful and whose main motive is independent nationalism. Their eyes are set on construction and on the diversification of Nepal's physical and political contacts with the outside world. They are much aware of China's presence on their northern border, but they do not regard their country as an important target of Chinese expansionism in its own right. Rather like Burma, Nepal regards its own weakness as the best guarantee of its security.

The basis of Nepal's China policy, then, is to refrain from unnecessary provocation. Like Pakistan and Burma, it has demarcated its border by agreement with China on what it regards as reasonable terms. If this agreement by itself does not safeguard Nepal's security for all time, it at least lessens the danger of unintentional conflict. The Nepalese obtain economic aid from China which fits into an overall pattern of foreign assistance from several sources. The most controversial item of Chinese aid is the Kathmandu-Kodari road connecting Nepal's capital with Tibet. This project was not favored by the Koirala government because of its potential military value to China, and as a north-south road it does not fit easily into the major Nepalese program of improving East-West transportation. The young nationalists who now govern Nepal found it easier to accept. China policy does not seem a probable source of conflict in the clique politics which are prevalent but which are stabilized by common loyalty to the monarch.

On the whole, the Nepalese feel that their China policy has served their purposes. They noted that immediately after the NEFA incident of 1962, raids along their southern border, which were believed to have been carried out by Nepali Congress exiles residing in India, quickly ceased. Plans are under way for joint U.S.-British military assistance, evidently with India's knowledge and assent and with the P.R.C. taking a surprisingly benevolent view. Nepal's demands on India are modest. They concern such things as control of customs and the style of behavior of India's representatives in Nepal. These require only minor adjustments from India and do not touch the geographic foundations of the symbiotic relationship between the two. It may be that Nepal has by now realized almost all the potential advantages of its China policy and that some of the potential disadvantages may become more visible. The disadvantages would derive from the P.R.C.'s increased contacts with the northern border tribes and with the educated class in the capital city.

Ceylon's geographical situation makes for a less direct involvement in Sino-Indian affairs than Nepal's. The elite of the immediate postwar years was a group which had received its education abroad and which had strong bonds with Britain and India. The group that came to power with S.W.R.D. Bandaranaike was a home-grown elite which favored nationalization of foreign enterprises and a generally neutralist foreign policy. Ceylonese neutralism seems to be of a rather bland variety. It contains no intensely felt pan-Asian component. Trade relations with the P.R.C. date from 1950 and in Ceylonese eyes have been at least satisfactory and at times positively advantageous. Chinese economic assistance has been on the generous side.

Ceylon's most conspicuous involvement in Sino-Indian relations consisted of Mme. Sirimavo Bandaranaike's efforts to mediate the border conflict. It has not been clear where Ceylonese public sympathies lay nor why Ceylon's Prime Minister took on such heavy responsibilities. India competes with Ceylon in the tea and other markets but has provided important support in the educational and other fields. It seems that it is India's size, nearness, and traditional cultural dominance that offend some Ceylonese sensibilities and that relations with China help reduce the feeling of dependence on India.

The viability of Ceylon's China policy depends on domestic political factors. Ceylonese politics reflect deep group divisions— some communal, some social, some religious. The possibility of violent conflict seems always close to the surface. Colombo teems with gossip, some of it concerning improprieties in the P.R.C.'s dealings with sympathetic Ceylonese. If inter-group antagonism should break into open conflict, China policy is one of the issues that might serve as a rallying point. In the 1965 election, which brought about Mme. Bandaranaike's replacement as Prime Minister by Dudley Senanayake, the issue of relations with China played a measurable part.

The P.R.C. shows some interest in isolating India. One opportunity which offers itself is to encourage India's immediate neighbors not necessarily to ally themselves with China but to draw closer among themselves for the promotion of their common interests vis-à-vis India. Pakistan also shows an interest in the idea. India is not without resources in this situation, but neither can it afford to be complacent.

THE SPECIAL CASE OF JAPAN

If India is the outstanding example of a China policy which failed, Japan stands out as a country which has not yet formulated a settled China policy. As an industrialized country which has close relations with the United States and is at the same time a considerable power in its own right, Japan shares all the concerns that enter into the European pattern of China policy. As an Asian country it gives China the same constant attention as do other Asians, and it is equally concerned with adjusting to the proximity of Chinese power. Japan is also a complex open society whose postwar politics have been characterized by free and often vigorous controversy. There is a long record of Sino-Japanese relations. The sustained Japanese effort in the modern era to dominate China stands out in memory, but it was at no time the sole characteristic of the relationship.

One result of history is that Japan contains a large number of people who are well informed on Chinese affairs on many levels. There are many Japanese images of China, and there is hardly any facet of Sino-Japanese relations upon which there are not conflicting, even ambivalent, views. The politically relevant images, even if one excludes the fanatical anti-communism of ultra-right societies (which is still capable of being expressed in acts of terrorism) and the special position of the Japan Communist party, still cover a wide range. On one end there is a conservative element which favors the Chinese Nationalists and places little value, or even frowns, on any relationship other than a purely formal one with Communist powers. This element believes that Japan's future lies with the West and that cooperation with the United States is the indispensable basis of a proper foreign policy. On the other end is a progressive element (to use the term they themselves favor) which regards the Chinese Communists as not only an effective government but one which promotes the real interests of the Chinese people. This element believes that peace and stability in Asia can only be achieved by conceding the legitimacy of the P.R.C. and that the American policy of containment is contrary to Japan's interests. There is a good deal of room in the middle, including room for variation.

Pan-Asianism still exists as a trend in Japanese thinking. It cuts across political lines and provides a thin thread of connection between otherwise divergent views. When Kenzô Matsumura went to China in 1962, for the conversations with Chou En-lai which laid the groundwork for a significant resumption of Sino-Japanese trade, he expressed a hope for friendship between the two countries based on reviving the spirit of such prewar figures as Baron Shigenobu Ôkuma, Mitsuru Toyama, and Torazô Miyazaki. All three had been friends of Sun Yat-sen, but in other respects they did not have much in common.

If one were to specify the characteristics of most of the middle range of opinion, the following should be emphasized. The middle elements (as shown also by public opinion surveys) hold that Japan's present relations with China are unsatisfactory. They generally believe that the basic motives of the P.R.C. are nationalist, not ideological, and that such motives provide a basis for Sino-Japanese understanding. For years it was an article of faith in Japan—in a great deal of Asia, for that matter—that China would not indefinitely be subservient to the Soviet Union but would develop an independent position. The Sino-Soviet dispute has been taken, by some conservatives as well as by liberals, as validation of this forecast. There is a widespread conviction that the Chinese and the Japanese have a special kind of understanding of each other. Some statements of this conviction strike the outside observer as sentimental or even mystical, but it is often phrased in terms that mean simply that the two peoples respond more accurately to each other's behavioral cues than either does to anyone else's.

The absence of official relations between the two countries has not precluded an impressive number of nonofficial contacts, some undertaken with the silent blessing of the Japanese government. The experience of these contacts has confirmed belief in a special ease of communication and thus bolstered the view that ideological differences are not a barrier to productive dealings. Nonofficial contacts have not all been completely harmonious. Japanese businessmen find themselves up against shrewd bargainers and take satisfaction in being equally shrewd. In the 1950s the Japanese Socialists seemed able to find much common ground between their policies for their country and Chinese Communist policies for the P.R.C. In the 1960s Socialist contacts with the Chinese have often resulted in open disagreement, and the Japanese Socialist party has been a major target of Chinese vilification. But even in conflict situations the Japanese feel that their relationship with the Chinese is mutually comprehensible. There is more substance to Japan's nonofficial relations with China than there is to the relations with China of many countries which recognize the P.R.C.

Finally, there is the factor of Japan's desire for autonomy in its foreign affairs. Ten years ago this desire was expressed in a negative form, in open and semi-subterranean public resistance to being used as the "spearpoint of America's Far Eastern policy." Recently, in part as a result of economic recovery, there has been a positive public demand for more original and active policies which will conform to Japan's confidence in itself. A certain discomfort is felt over the unfinished business, which now concerns only China, of restoring normal relations with former enemies. For many Japanese, "peaceful coexistence" is the appropriate term for the normal state of affairs they desire.

The Japanese government has never been without effective answers to limited and short-term issues of China policy. As S. Matsumoto has noted above, it established relations with the Nationalist government in 1952 but carefully specified certain conditions. The maintenance of these relations is now treated by the government as an honorable obligation in and of itself. Besides the demands of honor, the government is somewhat influenced by the practical consideration that Japan's other foreign relations require restoration of full belief in Japan's good faith. The future of Taiwan is at present unavoidably a matter of study. Japan is so near this problem that it cannot help having a special interest in it and cannot exclude itself from taking part in future solutions. The problem at present is to foresee which of several developments, ranging from Nationalist-Communist rapprochement to a gradual drift toward Taiwanese autonomy, is the most likely to occur.

In the field of trade, there would hardly be a policy problem if it were not for actions taken by the Chinese, both Nationalists and Communists, and for the importance to Japan of its relations with the United States. Since 1957 the government position has been one of not interfering with trade but not allowing political conditions, especially any that would imply a change in recognition policy, to be imposed. There is steady pressure from some sectors of the business community, either through the several organizations which exist for this purpose and which represent several types of business interest or from the political opposition—organized and unorganized—which sees in China trade not only economic advantages but a step toward political rapprochement. The limited possibilities of developing trade have meant, however, that powerful sectors of the business community have remained at most indifferent to the issue. At those times when the P.R.C. tried to use trade as a means of putting political pressure on the government, it was not difficult for the government to resist. After 1960, and especially after 1962, when the P.R.C. showed that it would withhold political conditions and that it was disposed to bypass the left-of-center opposition in favor of dealing directly with the established holders of power, the Japanese government took what must be its normal position. Japanese governments do not exist for the purpose of placing artificial obstacles in the path of Japanese enterprise. The development of trade through private channels seems, for the present, largely to satisfy the demands of Japanese businessmen. The growing intimacy between the Chinese and Japanese Communist parties does not leave the Japanese government unconcerned, but it has not as yet created urgent problems.

On matters that can be handled pragmatically, the record of Japan's China policy is one of effectiveness, not to say success. In respect to the large, ultimate issues, the record is less clear. Until

1964, there was comparatively little public discussion, and not many open signs of serious government study, of China's future relation to Japan's national security. The Chinese atomic detonations have of course stimulated attention. The problem is not to cope with a threat of aggression in the short run but to estimate the P.R.C.'s role in the Asian balance of power in the long run. Not much consistent analysis has been made, to all appearances, of the implications for China policy of the future growth of both Japanese and Chinese interests and influence in other parts of Asia. Above all, from the opposition standpoint, the government has not squarely met the problem of China's place in the world order. All these matters involve Japan's relations with the United States. From the government point of view, the question is not so much whether there will be "partnership" with the United States as what the respective roles of the partners will be.

The decision-making process in Japan is complex. Major roles are played by the governing party, the business community, and the bureaucracy. Within the bureaucracy, questions of China policy are the responsibility primarily of the Ministry of Foreign Affairs but on occasion involve the Ministry of International Trade and Industry, the Research Office attached to the Prime Minister, and sometimes others as well. In the course of the normal bargaining process, public opinion, the views of the press and the intellectuals, the demands of the political opposition, and the interests of pressure groups all make themselves felt. Japan's China policy is thus not, as some other Asian policies are, the product of a single mind or the application of a single dominant view. The logic of the situation dictates that changes in China policy will take place slowly but that all Japanese interested in China must be extremely sensitive to changes that may occur outside Japan, especially any changes in U.S. policy toward China, which will affect Japan's position.

THE SPECIAL CASE OF THE UNITED STATES

I intend to deal briefly with two questions: How does U.S. policy toward China compare with the policies of other non-Communist countries? What are the implications for U.S. policy of the variety of these other policies?

As for the first question, it seems clear that the American position vis-à-vis China is unique. The United States is the only non-Communist country whose interests are engaged in all those areas where the interests of the P.R.C. are engaged. The principal area of engagement is Asia. In several obvious cases, American and Chinese Communist interests are in direct conflict. One can make two safe assumptions: that the P.R.C. is a permanent feature of the environment and that the essential interest of the United States is in peace and stability in the area. It follows almost automatically that there is virtually no line of separation between U.S. China policy and U.S. Far Eastern policy. It is almost as automatically true that U.S. China policy is perforce a policy of containment. If the United States continues to be interested in peace and stability in Asia, its policies must be designed to counter threats to them, and the only country which at present has the capacity, not to mention the desire, to present such threats is the P.R.C.

Since the Korean War, the military security of Asia has been so problematical that much of the American effort has been concentrated in this field. It has come to appear that America's Far Eastern policy is little more than a policy of military alliances. Yet it is not inherent in a policy of containment either that it should be primarily a military policy or that it should aim at total isolation of the adversary. There have been some contradictions in the American program for establishing an area-wide collective security structure. To the extent that the program is at the mercy of the willingness of others to take part, it has in actuality tended to divide the area and to make it more difficult for the United States to contribute to the security of some parts of it.

As for the second question, a containment policy is a policy of meeting an adversary on the territory of third parties. It necessarily depends upon the cooperation of those parties. It has come to appear that the United States makes military cooperation the test of all forms of cooperation. Its warmest relations, at least, seem to be determined in this way, and it appears that the United States has confused depth of mutual commitment on this matter for breadth of shared interests. Yet when the security of Asian countries which have no form of military agreement with the United States has been threatened, the United States has acted without reference to formal agreements.

There is an asymmetry in U.S. and Chinese Communist relations to Asia from which the P.R.C. derives a tactical advantage. Since the interests and relations of the United States are with all countries in the area, it cannot avoid anomalies in its position whenever two countries find themselves in conflict. The P.R.C., however, having fewer hostages to fortune, is in a better position to shift its weight according to opportunity. For this reason U.S. policy seems to be dominated by the need to cope with successive crises, while the P.R.C. can respond to these without allowing them to deflect it from pursuing a broader course. Further, on some specific issues the United States has a different type of involvement from its friends. The question of Taiwan is an outstanding example. Here it is not alone a matter of honoring agreements nor simple hostility to Chinese communism that binds the United States to the Chinese Nationalists. Rather it is a whole network of obligations and an unavoidable concern for the reflex effects of a change in the U.S. position on area-wide stability. The responsibilities that the United States has assumed or had thrust upon it limit its freedom of action.

Obviously, the U.S. position affects other countries, either to sustain them in the China policies they would adopt of their own accord or to hold them back. Except for the American presence in Asia, it is doubtful that Asian countries which follow an anti-Communist course could hold to it indefinitely. In many other instances, however, friends of the United States think of themselves as deferring to American wishes against their better judgment. Formerly trade with China was affected in this way, and even now (though the Johnson-Satô talk of early 1965 showed a definite change in the U.S. position) there is a belief that the United States exerts undue pressure in this field. At present, the handling of China's representation in the United Nations is the outstanding cause of unhappiness. The problem has many facets, which are treated in individual chapters of this volume. For a large number of countries, it is only the value they place on their relations with the United States that keeps them from taking what they regard as normal and natural steps.

U.S. policy toward China and the Far East thus operates within limits, but it is not wholly without room for flexibility. There are some logically possible objectives which have been shown to be unattainable or are not within the resources of the United States or are in themselves unreasonable. It is not, for example, feasible to isolate the P.R.C., and it is not likely that the communist regime will collapse from within. Some methods once emphasized by the United States are thus no longer productive. Among them are the embargo on trade. Even if it were possible to "destroy" China, it would be senseless to try. But in respect to the form of the American presence in Asia and to the relative emphasis the United States gives to military as against other aspects of its Asian relations, there is room for development. In view of the variety of Asian China policies and the uniqueness of the American position, one can anticipate that in the future the United States will not find it feasible to work for uniform policies or for complete coordination between its own China policies and those of all its friends. It is more probable, since U.S. policy will be designed in terms of U.S. interests, that coordination will be on a differentiated rather than a multilateral basis. While keeping its eye on every sparrow, the United States will not be able to afford the illusion of omnipotence.

What most concerns friendly critics of the United States, however, is that in following a containment policy the United States may be overlooking a more productive approach, that of seeking areas of agreement with the P.R.C. Many of these friends argue that in light of the dimensions of American stakes, it would appear to be more in the U.S. interest than in anybody else's to find a place for China in a stable world order. They recommend that the United States take the important step of recognizing the P.R.C. Recognition is an intrinsically unimportant matter which has fortuitously acquired an unusual value in American calculations. But even the fortuitous is part of history, and the United States may judge it worthwhile, at least for a time, to pay the price of isolation on this aspect of policy in return for the protection of other interests. A case can be made that direct dealings undertaken prematurely are worse than none at all. If in the course of time a basis for compatibility between U.S. and Chinese objectives becomes evident, there would no longer be any reason to avoid direct dealings. What would be required would be that the P.R.C. should no longer threaten to upset the Asian balance. On a matter so important, responsible American policy must be based on evidence, not on hope alone.

APPENDIX A

Diplomatic Relations with China

The existence since 1949 of two governments claiming sovereignty over all of China has produced varied diplomatic responses from the rest of the world. Some countries recognize and maintain official relations with the People's Republic of China. Some recognize the P.R.C. but do not have official relations with it. Some recognize and maintain official relations with the Government of the Republic of China. Some recognize the G.R.C. but have no official relations with it. Some recognize neither government. This appendix summarizes the situation as of March 1, 1965.

Table A-1 lists, in chronological order of recognition, those countries which have recognized the P.R.C. It also includes the date of the establishment of diplomatic relations (if they have been established) and the type of representation (if any) which the P.R.C. maintains in these countries and which these countries maintain in mainland China. Certain historical details concerning the temporary stationing in China of foreign representatives prior to the formal establishment of relations between states have been omitted. Transfers of recognition from the G.R.C. to the P.R.C. have not been specifically noted, and relations with transitory state governments (like Zanzibar) or with provisional governments and other bodies not formally established as governments of states have not been included. Dates of recognition of other countries by the P.R.C. have likewise been omitted.

The absence of a standard mode of recognition and establishment of diplomatic relations creates certain problems in fixing dates precisely. The date given for recognition is that of the publication of the first communication (other than a vague prediction or statement of intent) in which the country said it recognized the People's Republic. The communication in most instances was an official letter or message to the Chinese government but in some cases was

495

a joint communique, a speech or formal statement by an important government figure, etc. The date given for the establishment of diplomatic relations is that of the publication of the first formal indication of an agreement to exchange representatives. According to circumstances, the indication came in a P.R.C. reply to a message from the country concerned, a New China News Agency announcement, a joint communique, etc. Some peculiarities in individual cases are shown in footnotes.

Table A-2 lists, in alphabetical order, those countries which recognize the G.R.C. It also includes the type of representation which the G.R.C. maintains in these countries and which these countries maintain on Taiwan. It does not contain dates of recognition and the establishment of diplomatic relations, for in many cases these antedate October 1, 1949, when the P.R.C. was formed.

Table A-3 lists those countries which recognize neither the P.R.C. nor the G.R.C.

TABLE A-1

Countries Which Recognize the People's Republic of China
(as of March 1, 1965)

Country	Recognition	Diplomatic Relations [a]	P.R.C. Representation in China [b]	Representation in Country [b]
1. U.S.S.R.	Oct. 2, 1949	Oct. 3, 1949	Embassy	Embassy
2. Bulgaria	Oct. 3, 1949	Oct. 4, 1949	"	"
3. Rumania	Oct. 3, 1949	Oct. 5, 1949	"	"
4. Hungary	Oct. 4, 1949	Oct. 6, 1949	"	"
5. Czechoslovakia	Oct. 5, 1949	Oct. 6, 1949	"	"
6. Democratic People's Republic of Korea (North Korea)	Oct. 5, 1949	Oct. 6, 1949	"	"
7. Poland	Oct. 5, 1949	Oct. 7, 1949	"	"
8. Yugoslavia	Oct. 5, 1949	Jan. 10, 1955	"	"
9. Mongolia	Oct. 6, 1949	Oct. 16, 1949	"	"
10. German Democratic Republic (East Germany)	Oct. 27, 1949	Oct. 27, 1949	"	"
11. Albania	Nov. 21, 1949	Nov. 23, 1949	"	"
12. Burma	Dec. 16, 1949	June 8, 1950	"	"
13. India	Dec. 30, 1949	April 1, 1950	"	"
14. Pakistan	Jan. 5, 1950	May 21, 1951	"	"
15. United Kingdom	Jan. 6, 1950	June 17, 1954	Embassy (chargé)[e]	Embassy (chargé)[e]

Table A-1 (continued)

Country	Recognition	Diplomatic Relations [a]	P.R.C. Representation in China [b]	Representation in Country [b]
16. Ceylon	Jan. 7, 1950	Feb. 7, 1957	Embassy	Embassy
17. Norway	Jan. 7, 1950	Oct. 5, 1954	"	"
18. Denmark	Jan. 9, 1950	May 11, 1950	"	"
19. Israel [d]	Jan. 9, 1950	—	—	—
20. Afghanistan	Jan. 12, 1950	Jan. 20, 1955	Embassy	Embassy
21. Finland	Jan. 13, 1950	Oct. 28, 1950	"	"
22. Sweden	Jan. 14, 1950	May 9, 1950	"	"
23. Democratic Republic of Vietnam (North Vietnam)	Jan. 15, 1950	Jan. 18, 1950	"	"
24. Switzerland	Jan. 17, 1950	Sept. 14, 1950	"	"
25. Netherlands	Mar. 27, 1950	Nov. 19, 1954	Legation (chargé) [e]	Legation (chargé) [e]
26. Indonesia	April 13, 1950	June 9, 1950	Embassy	Embassy
27. Nepal	Aug. 1, 1955	Aug. 1, 1955	"	"
28. United Arab Republic	May 16, 1956	May 30, 1956	"	"
29. Syria	July 3, 1956	Aug 10, 1956	"	"
30. Yemen	Aug. 21, 1956	Sept. 24, 1956	—	Legation
31. Cambodia	July 18, 1958	July 23, 1958	Embassy	Embassy
32. Iraq	July 18, 1958	Aug. 25, 1958	"	"
33. Morocco	Oct. 31, 1958	Nov. 1, 1958	"	"
34. Sudan	Nov. 29, 1958	Dec. 1, 1958	—	"
35. Guinea	Oct. 4, 1959	Oct. 4, 1959	Embassy	"
36. Ghana	July 5, 1960	July 5, 1960	"	"
37. Cuba	Sept. 2, 1960	Sept. 28, 1960	"	"
38. Mali	Oct. 14, 1960	Oct. 27, 1960	"	"
39. Somalia	Dec. 14, 1960	Dec. 16, 1960	"	"
40. Senegal [f]	Mar. 14, 1961	—	—	—
41. Tanzania [g]	Dec. 9, 1961	Dec. 9, 1961	—	Embassy
42. Laos	June 28, 1962	June 28, 1962 [h] July 2, 1962 [h] Sept. 7, 1962 [h]	Embassy	"
43. Algeria	July 3, 1962 [i]	July 3, 1962 [i]	"	"
44. Uganda	Oct. 18, 1962	Oct. 18, 1962	—	"
45. Kenya	Dec. 14, 1963 [j]	Dec. 14, 1963	Embassy	"
46. Burundi	Dec. 23, 1963	Dec. 23, 1963	—	—[k]
47. Tunisia	Jan. 10, 1964	Jan. 10, 1964	Embassy	Embassy
48. France	Jan. 27, 1964	Jan. 27, 1964	"	"
49. Congo (Brazzaville)	Feb. 18, 1964	Feb. 22, 1964	"	"
50. Central African Republic	Sept. 27, 1964	Sept. 29, 1964	"	"
51. Zambia	Oct. 25, 1964	Oct. 29, 1964	"	"
52. Dahomey	Nov. 12, 1964	Nov. 12, 1964	"	"

(a) In some cases, the dates given below conflict with the dates given in individual chapters. Because of the ambiguities involved in fixing the precise dates, no attempt has been made to reconcile these conflicts. For the sake of consistency in this table, however, a standard criterion for establishing dates has been adopted. In each instance, the date is that of the first formal indication of an agreement to exchange representatives. This criterion seems to be the one followed in official publications of the People's Republic of China.

(b) Only permanent diplomatic missions and not consulates general are listed here. The indication that an embassy is maintained does not necessarily mean that an ambassador is actually in residence.

(c) The agreement to exchange representatives covered only chargés d'affaires. Ambassadors have never been exchanged.

(d) Israel recognized the People's Republic of China on January 9, 1950, but diplomatic relations between the two countries have never been established.

(e) The agreement to exchange representatives covered only chargés d'affaires. Ministers have never been exchanged.

(f) Senegal recognized the People's Republic of China on March 14, 1961, but it continued to maintain the diplomatic relations it had established earlier with the Government of the Republic of China. As a result, the P.R.C. refused to establish diplomatic relations with Senegal. On September 19, 1964, Senegal announced it was breaking diplomatic relations with the Nationalist regime. So far, however, it has not established relations with the People's Republic.

(g) On April 22, 1964, the independent states of Tanganyika and Zanzibar united to form the Republic of Tanganyika and Zanzibar. The country's name was then changed to Tanzania on October 29. Both Tanganyika and Zanzibar had recognized and established diplomatic relations with the People's Republic of China before they united. The dates given in the table are those for Tanganyika, which was the first of the two to gain independence.

(h) Because of the chaotic conditions and the maneuvering of rival Laotian factions which followed the formation of the coalition government on June 11, 1962, the date of the establishment of relations with the People's Republic of China is open to doubt. On June 28, Quinim Pholsena, the Foreign Minister of the new coalition government, informed the P.R.C. that Laos recognized the P.R.C. and agreed to establish diplomatic relations. On July 2, the coalition government acting as a body announced it planned to establish relations with the P.R.C. Later, however, a G.R.C. ambassador was received by the king of Laos as the result of maneuvers by the right-wing faction. To clarify the situation, Prince Souvanna Phouma, Premier of the coalition government, signed a joint Laos-P.R.C. communique on September 7, 1962, stating that Laos recognized only the P.R.C.

(i) The dates given for recognition and the establishment of diplomatic relations are those which apply to the Republic of Algeria. The Algerian Provisional Government had recognized the People's Republic of China in December 1958 and subsequently established quasi-official relations with it. After the Republic of Algeria became independent, though, the ritual of formal recognition and establishment of diplomatic relations was carried out again.

(j) The message of recognition sent by Jomo Kenyatta a few days earlier is treated here as not having been an official act of the state until validated by the independence ceremonies of December 14, 1963.

(k) After Burundi's Prime Minister was assassinated in early 1965, Burundi announced it was suspending its diplomatic relations with the P.R.C. Subsequently, it severed them completely.

SOURCES: American Consulate General, Hong Kong, *Current Background,* no. 311, February 1, 1955.
Handbook on People's China (Peking: Foreign Languages Press, 1957), pp. 179–180.
New China News Agency releases and broadcasts, the chief source for which is American Consulate General, Hong Kong, *Survey of the China Mainland Press.*
The New York Times
The China News (Taipei)
The China Post (Taipei)

TABLE A-2

Countries Which Recognize the Government of the Republic of China

(as of March 1, 1965)

Country	Representation on Taiwan [a]	G.R.C. Representation in Country [a]
1. Argentina	Embassy	Embassy
2. Australia	—	"
3. Belgium	—	"
4. Bolivia	—	"
5. Brazil	Embassy	"
6. Cameroun	—	"
7. Canada	—	"
8. Chad	—	"
9. Chile	Embassy	"
10. Colombia	"	"
11. Congo (Leopoldville)	—	"
12. Costa Rica	—	"
13. Cyprus	—	"
14. Dominican Republic	Embassy	"
15. Ecuador	"	"
16. El Salvador	"	"
17. Gabon	—	"
18. Greece	Embassy	"
19. Guatemala	"	"
20. Haiti	—	Legation
21. Holy See	Legation	Embassy
22. Honduras	"	Legation
23. Iran	Embassy	Embassy
24. Italy	—	"
25. Ivory Coast	—	"
26. Jamaica	—	"
27. Japan	Embassy	"
28. Jordan	"	"
29. Republic of Korea (South Korea)	"	"
30. Kuwait	—	"
31. Lebanon	Embassy	"
32. Liberia	—	"
33. Libya	—	"
34. Luxembourg	—	Legation
35. Malagasy Republic	Embassy	Embassy
36. Mauritania	—	"
37. Mexico	—	"
38. New Zealand	—	"
39. Nicaragua	Embassy	"
40. Niger	—	"

Table A-2 (continued)

Country	Representation on Taiwan [a]	G.R.C. Representation in Country [a]
41. Panama	Embassy	Embassy
42. Paraguay	”	”
43. Peru	”	”
44. Philippines	”	”
45. Portugal	—	Legation
46. Rwanda	—	Embassy
47. Saudi Arabia	Embassy	”
48. Sierra Leone	—	”
49. Republic of South Africa	—	—
50. Spain	Embassy	Embassy
51. Thailand	”	”
52. Togo	—	”
53. Turkey	Embassy	”
54. United States	”	”
55. Upper Volta	”	”
56. Uruguay	”	”
57. Venezuela	Legation	Legation
58. Republic of Vietnam (South Vietnam)	Embassy	Embassy

(a) Only permanent diplomatic missions and not consulates general are listed. Among the more important consulates general is the Chinese one in Johannesburg, South Africa, for there are no permanent diplomatic missions in either Pretoria, South Africa, or Taipei, Taiwan.

SOURCES: *China Yearbook, 1963–64* and Information Office of the Republic of China's Permanent Mission to the United Nations.

TABLE A-3

Countries Which Recognize neither the People's Republic of China nor the Government of the Republic of China

(as of March 1, 1965)

1. Andorra
2. Austria
3. Bhutan
4. Ethiopia [a]
5. Federal Republic of Germany (West Germany)
6. Iceland
7. Ireland
8. Liechtenstein
9. Malawi
10. Malaysia
11. Malta
12. Monaco
13. Nigeria [b]
14. San Marino
15. Trinidad-Tobago

(a) A joint Ethiopia-P.R.C. communique issued on February 1, 1964, after a visit to Ethiopia by Chou En-lai said agreement was reached "on the taking of measures to strengthen relations" between the two countries, "including the normalization of relations between the two governments in the near future." So far however, Ethiopia has taken no steps to implement this agreement.

(b) As early as June 18, 1961, Nigerian and P.R.C. representatives agreed on the need for establishing diplomatic relations and exchanging ambassadors at an early date, but Nigeria has never formally recognized the P.R.C.

SOURCES: See sources in Tables A-1 and A-2.

Appendix B

The China Question at the United Nations

Table B-1 — U.N. Votes Related to the China Question, 1950-65a

Countries (by area)	1950 seat	1951 aggr	1951b mora	1952 mora	1953b mora	1954 mora	1955 mora	1956 mora	1957 mora	1958 mora	1959 mora	1960 mora	1961 mora in ques	1961 seat	1962 seat	1963 seat	
SOVIET BLOC																	
1. USSRc	x	—		—		—	—	—	—	—	—	—	—	x	x	x	1
2. Ukraine	x	—		—		—	—	—	—	—	—	—	—	x	x	x	2
3. Byelorussia	x	—		—		—	—	—	—	—	—	—	—	x	x	x	3
4. Czechoslovakia	x	—		—		—	—	—	—	—	—	—	—	x	x	x	4
5. Poland	x	—		—		—	—	—	—	—	—	—	—	x	x	x	5
6. Albania								—	—	—	—	—	—	x	x	x	6
7. Bulgaria								—	—	—	—	—	—	x	x	x	7
8. Hungary								—	—	—	—	—	—	x	x	x	8
9. Rumania								—	—	—	—	—	—	x	x	x	9
10. Mongolia													—	x	x	x	10

Key: x = for   — = against   a = abstained   nv = not voting

(a) The General Assembly votes covered by this table are:
  (1) 1950 – a resolution to oust the representatives of the Republic of China and to seat those of the People's Republic of China.
  (2) 1951 – a resolution to condemn the P.R.C. as an "aggressor" in Korea and a resolution to postpone discussion of the representation question (that is, a "moratorium" resolution).
  (3) 1952-60 – moratorium resolutions similar to that of 1951.
  (4) 1961 – a resolution stating that the General Assembly considered the matter of China's representation an "important question" (passage of a resolution on the subject would require the approval of two-thirds of the members present and voting) and a resolution, like that of 1950, to seat the representatives of the P.R.C.
  (5) 1962-63 – resolutions, like that of 1950, to seat the representatives of the P.R.C.

The dates refer to the year in which the vote occurred, not necessarily to the year in which the Assembly session was convened.

(b) The 1951 and 1953 moratorium votes were not roll-call votes, so only totals are available for these two years.

(c) Permanent members of the Security Council.

Table B-1 — U.N. Votes Related to the China Question, 1950-65[a]

Countries (by area)	1950 seat	1951 aggr	1951[b] mora	1952 mora	1953[b] mora	1954 mora	1955 mora	1956 mora	1957 mora	1958 mora	1959 mora	1960 mora	1961 im	1961 ques	1961 seat	1962 seat	1963 seat	
EUROPE																		
11. France[c]	a	x	x	x	x	x	x	x	x	x	x	x	x	—	x	—	—	11
12. United Kingdom[c]	x	x	x	x	x	x	x	x	x	x	x	x	x	a	a	x	a	12
13. Denmark	x	x	x	x	x	x	x	x	x	x	x	x	—	a	a	a	a	13
14. Netherlands	x	x	x	x	x	x	x	x	x	x	x	x	—	a	a	a	a	14
15. Norway	x	x	x	x	x	x	x	x	x	x	x	x	x	x	x	x	x	15
16. Sweden	x	a	x	x	x	x	x	x	x	x	x	x	x	a	a	x	a	16
17. Yugoslavia	x	a	a	a	—	—	—	—	—	—	—	—	—	—	—	—	—	17
18. Finland									x	x	x	x	x	x	x	x	x	18
19. Belgium	—	x	x	x	x	x	x	x	x	x	x	x	x	—	—	—	—	19
20. Greece	—	x	x	x	x	x	x	x	x	a	a	a	x	a	a	a	a	20
21. Iceland	—	x	x	x	x	x	x	x	x	a	x	a	x	—	—	—	—	21
22. Luxembourg	—	x	x	x	x	x	x	x	x	a	a	a	x	a	a	a	a	22
23. Austria									a	a	a	a	x	a	a	a	a	23
24. Ireland									a	a	x	a	x	a	—	a	a	24
25. Italy							x	x	x	x	x	x	x	x	—	—	—	25
26. Spain							x	x	x	x	x	x	x	—	—	—	—	26
27. Portugal							a	a	a	a	a	a	x	a	a	a	a	27
NORTH AMERICA																		
28. United States[c]	—	x	x	x	x	x	x	x	x	x	x	x	x	—	—	x	—	28
29. Canada	a	x	x	x	x	x	x	x	x	x	x	x	x	—	—	—	—	29
LATIN AMERICA																		
30. Cuba	—	x	x	x	x	x	x	x	x	a	x	x	x	—	x	x	x	30
31. Argentina	a	x	x	x	x	x	x	x	x	x	x	x	x	—	—	—	—	31
32. Bolivia	—	x	a	a	x	x	x	x	x	x	x	x	x	—	—	—	—	32
33. Brazil	—	x	x	x	x	x	x	x	x	x	x	x	x	—	—	—	—	33
34. Chile	—	x	x	x	x	x	x	x	x	x	x	x	x	—	—	—	—	34
35. Colombia	—	x	x	x	x	x	x	x	x	x	x	x	x	—	—	—	—	35
36. Costa Rica	—	x	x	x	x	x	x	x	x	x	x	x	x	—	—	a	—	36
37. Dominican Republic	—	x	x	x	x	x	x	x	x	x	x	x	x	a	a	—	—	37
38. Ecuador	a	x	x	a	x	x	x	x	x	x	x	x	x	—	—	—	—	38
39. El Salvador	—	x	a	a	x	x	x	x	x	x	x	x	x	—	—	—	—	39
40. Guatemala	a	x	x	a	x	x	x	x	x	x	x	x	x	—	—	—	—	40
41. Haiti	—	x	x	x	x	x	x	x	x	x	x	x	x	—	—	—	—	41

	42	43	44	45	46	47	48	49	50	51
42. Honduras	−	x	x	x	x	x	x	x	x	−
43. Mexico	−	x	x	x	x	x	x	x	x	−
44. Nicaragua	−	x	x	x	x	x	x	x	x	−
45. Panama	−	x	x	x	x	x	x	x	x	−
46. Paraguay	−	x	x	x	x	x	x	x	x	−
47. Peru	−	x	x	x	x	x	x	x	x	−
48. Uruguay	−	x	x	x	x	x	x	x	x	−
49. Venezuela	−	x	x	x	x	x	x	x	x	−
50. Jamaica										
51. Trinidad and Tobago									a	a
ASIA AND AUSTRALASIA										
52. *Republic of China*[c]	−	x	x	x	x	x	x	x	x	−
53. Australia	−	x	x	x	x	x	x	x	x	−
54. New Zealand	−	x	x	x	x	x	x	x	x	−
55. Philippines	−	x	x	x	x	x	x	x	x	−
56. Thailand	−	x	x	x	x	x	x	x	x	−
57. Japan	−	x	x	x	x	x	x	x	x	−
58. Malaysia[d]	a	a	a	x	x	x	x	x	x	a
59. Afghanistan	x	−	x				a	a	a	x
60. Burma	x	−					a	a	x	x
61. India	x	−					a	a	x	x
62. Pakistan	x	−	a				x	x	x	x
63. Indonesia[e]	x	−	a	a	a	a	x	x	x	x
64. Cambodia		−			a		x	x	x	x
65. Ceylon		−		a			x	x	x	x
66. Laos		−					x	x	x	x
67. Nepal		−	x			a	x	x	x	x

Key: x = for   − = against   a = abstained   nv = not voting

(d) Malaysia was formed in 1963 by the union of Malaya, Singapore, Sarawak, and Sabah (North Borneo), but Malaya had been a member of the United Nations since 1957. The votes listed for 1957–62 are those of Malaya.

(e) In early 1965, Indonesia withdrew from the United Nations because of the election of Malaysia, with which Indonesia is engaged in a "confrontation," to the Security Council.

Table B-1 — U.N. Votes Related to the China Question, 1950-65[a]

Countries (by area)	1950 seat	1951 aggr	1951[b] mora	1952 mora	1953[b] mora	1954 mora	1955 mora	1956 mora	1957 mora	1958 mora	1959 mora	1960 mora	1961 im	1961 ques	1962 seat	1963 seat	seat
MIDDLE EAST AND NORTH AFRICA																	
68. Israel	x	x	a	x	a	a	a	a	a	a	a	a	x	a	a	a	68
69. Iran		x	x	x	x	x	x	x	x	x	x	x	x				69
70. Iraq		x	x	x	x	x	x	x	x					x	x	x	70
71. Turkey	x	x	x	x	x	x	x	x	x	x	x	x	x				71
72. Lebanon	a	a	a	a	x	x	x	x	x	x	x	x	x		a	a	72
73. Saudi Arabia	a	a	a	a	a	a	a	a	x	a	a	a	x	a	a	a	73
74. Syria[f]	a	x	x	a	a		a		a				x	x	x	x	74
75. U.A.R. (Egypt)[f]	a	a	a	a	a		a							x	x	x	75
76. Yemen	a	a		a	a		a			x	x	x		x	x	x	76
77. Jordan						a	x	a		a	a	a					77
78. Libya						a	a	a	x	a	a	a	x				78
79. Tunisia						a	a	a	x	a	a		x			x	79
80. Morocco						x	x	x	a			a		x	x	x	80
81. Cyprus														x	x		81
82. Algeria													a	a	a	x	82
83. Kuwait														a	x	a	83
84. Malta[g]																	84
AFRICA																	
85. Ethiopia		x	x	x	x	x	x	x	a	a	a			x	x	nv	85
86. Liberia		x	x	x	x	x	x	x	x	x	x	x	x				86
87. South Africa		x	x	x	x	x	nv	x	x	x	x	x	x				87
88. Sudan														x	x	x	88
89. Ghana														x	x	x	89
90. Guinea														x	x	x	90
91. Cameroun												a	x		x	x	91
92. Central African Republic												a	x	a			92
93. Chad												a	x	a			93
94. Congo (Brazzaville)												a	x	a			94
95. Congo (Leopoldville)												nv	x	a			95
96. Dahomey												a	x	a			96
97. Gabon												a	nv				97
98. Ivory Coast												a	x	a			98
99. Malagasy												a	x				99

TABLE TOTALS

No.	Country	1950 seat	1951 aggr	1951[b] mora	1952 mora	1953[b] mora	1954 mora	1955 mora	1956 mora	1957 mora	1958 mora	1959 mora	1960 mora	1961 im ques	1961 mora	1962 seat	1963 seat
100.	Mali												—	—	x	x	x
101.	Niger												a	x	a	—	—
102.	Nigeria												a	a	a	a	a
103.	Senegal												—	x	a	x	x
104.	Somalia												a	a	—	a	—
105.	Togo												a	nv	a	a	—
106.	Upper Volta													x	a		—
107.	Mauritania												a	x		—	a
108.	Sierra Leone													a	x	x	a
109.	Tanzania[h]													a	—	x	x
110.	Burundi															x	x
111.	Rwanda															—	—
112.	Uganda														x	x	x
113.	Kenya[g]																
114.	Malawi[g]																
115.	Zambia[g]																
	For	16	44	37	42	44	43	42	47	48	44	44	42	61	37	42	41
	Against	33	7	11	7	10	11	12	24	27	28	29	34	34	48	56	57
	Abstain	10	9	4	11	2	6	6	8	6	9	9	22	7	19	12	12
	Not voting	0	0	8	0	4	0	0	0	1	0	9	1	2	0	0	1
	TOTAL MEMBERSHIP	59	60	60	60	60	60	60	79	82	81	82	99	104	104	110	111

Key: .x = for   — = against   a = abstained   nv = not voting

(f) In 1958, Egypt and Syria formed the United Arab Republic, and Syria gave up her seat in the General Assembly. That union was dissolved in 1961. Syria then returned to the Assembly as an independent country, but Egypt retained the name "United Arab Republic" for itself.

(g) Admitted to the United Nations since the last vote on the China representation question.

(h) The independent states of Tanganyika and Zanzibar united in April 1964, and the new state was renamed Tanzania in October of that year. At the time of union, both Tanganyika and Zanzibar were members of the United Nations, but only Tanganyika had been a member long enough to vote upon resolutions to seat the representatives of the P.R.C. The votes for 1962–63, therefore, are Tanganyika's.

Sources: 1950–61 — United Nations, *Yearbook of the United Nations.* 1962–63 — United Nations, *United Nations Review.*

Communist China's Trade with Non-Communist Countries

Arriving at figures for Communist China's foreign trade poses many problems. The People's Republic itself has reported only aggregate amounts. Figures reported by its trading partners are not always calculated by the same methods, and there are technical difficulties in converting various published figures to a single currency. Professor Alexander Eckstein, in preparing his study of Communist China's economy for the Council on Foreign Relations project on The United States and China in World Affairs, has developed standardized methods for dealing with the statistics. He has generously given permission for the figures he has derived to be used in this volume. While there are still some unsolved problems and while these figures cannot be taken as absolutely accurate, they are the best available. They are reliable indicators at least of the relative magnitude of the P.R.C.'s trade with different countries or areas and of annual variations in trade volume.

The figures show gross amounts of trade and have not been corrected to exclude re-exports. In most cases, the amounts of these are not known. We do know, however, that from 1952 through 1958 about one third of P.R.C. exports to Hong Kong were re-exported and that from 1959 through 1962 the proportion fell to about 15 per cent.

Figures for 1964 have not as yet been analyzed by the same methods and are therefore not included here. Preliminary figures show a total approaching $2 billion (both ways). If present trends continue, the P.R.C.'s trade with the non-Communist world will soon amount to two-thirds of its total foreign trade.

No attempt has been made to reconcile the figures in this appendix with those given in individual chapters.

Communist China's Imports from the Non-Communist World, 1952–63
(in millions of U.S. dollars)

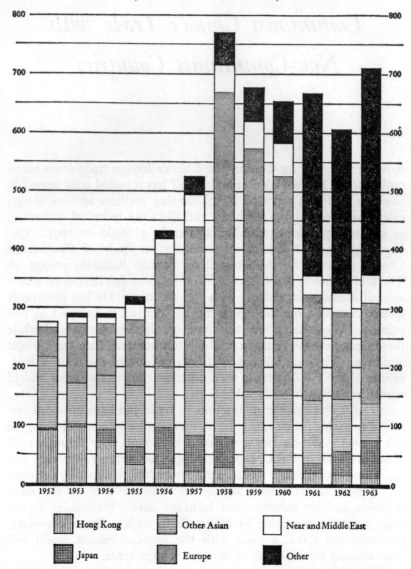

Hong Kong   Other Asian   Near and Middle East

Japan   Europe   Other

Source: Alexander Eckstein, *Communist China's Economic Growth and Foreign Trade: Implications for U.S. Policy* (New York: McGraw-Hill for the Council on Foreign Relations, forthcoming)

Communist China's Exports to
the Non-Communist World, 1952–63
(in millions of U.S. dollars)

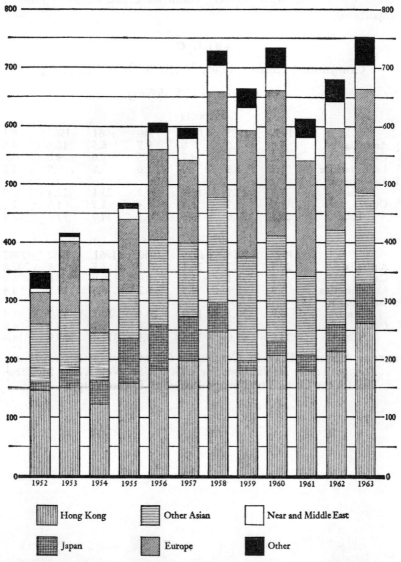

Hong Kong   Other Asian   Near and Middle East

Japan   Europe   Other

Source: Alexander Eckstein, *Communist China's Economic Growth and Foreign Trade: Implications* •
for U.S. Policy (New York: McGraw-Hill for the Council on Foreign Relations, forthcoming)

The following table gives a more detailed breakdown of the P.R.C.'s trade with countries included in the "Others" category in the preceding graphs. The table covers only the years 1957–63, the period when trade with "Other" countries expanded to significant proportions.

TABLE C-1

Communist China's Trade With "Others," 1957–63

(in millions of U.S. dollars)

Exports

	1957	1958	1959	1960	1961	1962	1963
1. Australia	5.4	7.6	7.8	9.7	6.5	10.4	13.6
2. Canada	5.2	5.2	4.7	5.5	3.0	4.0	4.5
3. Latin America	1.3	1.8	.9	.6	.8	.9	1.2
4. Sub-Saharan Africa	7.3	13.7	18.9	19.1	23.1	22.4	21.0
5. Other	1.0	1.3	1.3	1.4	1.5	1.3	2.1
Total	20.2	29.6	33.6	36.3	34.9	39.0	42.4

Imports

	1957	1958	1959	1960	1961	1962	1963
1. Australia	20.5	27.2	30.1	23.5	161.5	97.8	207.8
2. Canada	1.5	8.1	1.8	8.9	120.9	137.0	96.9
3. Latin America	3.9	8.9	4.7	6.2	6.6	27.1	3.4
4. Sub-Saharan Africa	6.8	10.1	15.9	28.4	19.7	15.7	41.4
5. Other	1.7	2.7	7.0	6.5	3.7	3.3	4.9
Total	34.4	57.0	59.5	73.5	312.4	280.9	354.4

SOURCE: Alexander Eckstein, *Communist China's Economic Growth and Foreign Trade: Implications for U.S. Policy* (New York: McGraw-Hill for the Council on Foreign Relations, forthcoming).

Index

COUNCIL ON FOREIGN RELATIONS

PUBLICATIONS

FOREIGN AFFAIRS (quarterly), edited by Hamilton Fish Armstrong.

THE UNITED STATES IN WORLD AFFAIRS (annual). Volumes for 1931, 1932 and 1933, by Walter Lippmann and William O. Scroggs; for 1934–1935, 1936, 1937, 1938, 1939 and 1940, by Whitney H. Shepardson and William O. Scroggs; for 1945–1947, 1947–1948 and 1948–1949, by John C. Campbell; for 1949, 1950, 1951, 1952, 1953 and 1954, by Richard P. Stebbins; for 1955, by Hollis W. Barber; for 1956, 1957, 1958, 1959, 1960, 1961, 1962 and 1963, by Richard P. Stebbins; for 1964, by Jules Davids.

DOCUMENTS ON AMERICAN FOREIGN RELATIONS (annual). Volume for 1952 edited by Clarence W. Baier and Richard P. Stebbins; for 1953 and 1954, edited by Peter V. Curl; for 1955, 1956, 1957, 1958 and 1959, edited by Paul E. Zinner; for 1960, 1961, 1962 and 1963, edited by Richard P. Stebbins; for 1964, by Jules Davids.

POLITICAL HANDBOOK AND ATLAS OF THE WORLD (annual), edited by Walter H. Mallory.

MONETARY REFORM FOR THE WORLD ECONOMY, by Robert V. Roosa (1965).

AFRICAN BATTLELINE: American Policy Choices in Southern Africa, by Waldemar A. Nielsen (1965).

NATO IN TRANSITION: The Future of the Atlantic Alliance, by Timothy W. Stanley (1965).

ALTERNATIVE TO PARTITION: For a Broader Conception of America's Role in Europe, by Zbigniew Brzezinski (1965).

THE TROUBLED PARTNERSHIP: A Re-Appraisal of the Atlantic Alliance, by Henry A. Kissinger (1965).

REMNANTS OF EMPIRE: The United Nations and the End of Colonialism, by David W. Wainhouse (1965).

THE EUROPEAN COMMUNITY AND AMERICAN TRADE: A Study in Atlantic Economics and Policy, by Randall Hinshaw (1964).

THE FOURTH DIMENSION OF FOREIGN POLICY: Educational and Cultural Affairs, by Philip H. Coombs (1964).

AMERICAN AGENCIES INTERESTED IN INTERNATIONAL AFFAIRS (Fifth Edition), compiled by Donald Wasson (1964).

JAPAN AND THE UNITED STATES IN WORLD TRADE, by Warren S. Hunsberger (1964).

FOREIGN AFFAIRS BIBLIOGRAPHY, 1952–1962, by Henry L. Roberts (1964).

THE DOLLAR IN WORLD AFFAIRS: An Essay in International Financial Policy, by Henry G. Aubrey (1964).

ON DEALING WITH THE COMMUNIST WORLD, by George F. Kennan (1964).

FOREIGN AID AND FOREIGN POLICY, by Edward S. Mason (1964).

THE SCIENTIFIC REVOLUTION AND WORLD POLITICS, by Caryl P. Haskins (1964).

AFRICA: A Foreign Affairs Reader, edited by Philip W. Quigg (1964).

THE PHILIPPINES AND THE UNITED STATES: Problems of Partnership, by George E. Taylor (1964).

SOUTHEAST ASIA IN UNITED STATES POLICY, by Russell H. Fifield (1963).

UNESCO: ASSESSMENT AND PROMISE, by George N. Shuster (1963).

THE PEACEFUL ATOM IN FOREIGN POLICY, by Arnold Kramish (1963).

THE ARABS AND THE WORLD: Nasser's Arab Nationalist Policy, by Charles D. Cremeans (1963).

TOWARD AN ATLANTIC COMMUNITY, by Christian A. Herter (1963).

THE SOVIET UNION, 1922–1962: A Foreign Affairs Reader, edited by Philip E. Mosely (1963).

THE POLITICS OF FOREIGN AID: American Experience in Southeast Asia, by John D. Montgomery (1962).

SPEARHEADS OF DEMOCRACY: Labor in the Developing Countries, by George C. Lodge (1962).

LATIN AMERICA: Diplomacy and Reality, by Adolf A. Berle (1962).

THE ORGANIZATION OF AMERICAN STATES AND THE HEMISPHERE CRISIS, by John C. Dreier (1962).

THE UNITED NATIONS: Structure for Peace, by Ernest A. Gross (1962).

THE LONG POLAR WATCH: Canada and the Defense of North America, by Melvin Conant (1962).

ARMS AND POLITICS IN LATIN AMERICA (Revised Edition), by Edwin Lieuwen (1961).

THE FUTURE OF UNDERDEVELOPED COUNTRIES: Political Implications of Economic Development (Revised Edition), by Eugene Staley (1961).

SPAIN AND DEFENSE OF THE WEST: Ally and Liability, by Arthur P. Whitaker (1961).

SOCIAL CHANGE IN LATIN AMERICA TODAY: Its Implications for United States Policy, by Richard N. Adams, John P. Gillin, Allan R. Holmberg, Oscar Lewis, Richard W. Patch, and Charles W. Wagley (1961).

FOREIGN POLICY: THE NEXT PHASE: The 1960s (Revised Edition), by Thomas K. Finletter (1960).

DEFENSE OF THE MIDDLE EAST: Problems of American Policy (Revised Edition), by John C. Campbell (1960).

COMMUNIST CHINA AND ASIA: Challenge to American Policy, by A. Doak Barnett (1960).

FRANCE, TROUBLED ALLY: De Gaulle's Heritage and Prospects, by Edgar S. Furniss, Jr. (1960).

THE SCHUMAN PLAN: A Study in Economic Cooperation, 1950–1959, by William Diebold, Jr. (1959).

SOVIET ECONOMIC AID: The New Aid and Trade Policy in Underdeveloped Countries, by Joseph S. Berliner (1958).

RAW MATERIALS: A Study of American Policy, by Percy W. Bidwell (1958).

NATO AND THE FUTURE OF EUROPE, by Ben T. Moore (1958).

AFRICAN ECONOMIC DEVELOPMENT, by William Hance (1958).

INDIA AND AMERICA: A Study of Their Relations, by Phillips Talbot and S. L. Poplai (1958).

NUCLEAR WEAPONS AND FOREIGN POLICY, by Henry A. Kissinger (1957).

MOSCOW-PEKING AXIS: Strength and Strains, by Howard L. Boorman, Alexander Eckstein, Philip E. Mosely and Benjamin Schwartz (1957).

RUSSIA AND AMERICA: Dangers and Prospects, by Henry L. Roberts (1956).